Dedication

For my mother June Hill, and the memory of my father, Mike Hill.
–Charles Hill

For Gert & Margareta Hult, my parents.
–G. Tomas M. Hult

To my mother, Dorothy McKaig.
–Thomas McKaig

To my father, Wm. George Richardson, CD, OBM
–Wm. Tim G. Richardson

About the Authors

Charles W. L. Hill is the Hughes M. and Katherine Blake Professor of Strategy and International Business at the Foster School of Business, University of Washington. The Foster School has a Center for International Business Education and Research (CIBER), one of only 17 funded by the U.S. Department of Education.

Professor Hill received his PhD from the University of Manchester in the United Kingdom. In addition to the University of Washington, he has served on the faculties of the University of Manchester, Texas A&M University, and Michigan State University.

Professor Hill has published over 50 articles in peer-reviewed academic journals including the *Academy of Management Journal, Academy of Management Review, Strategic Management Journal,* and *Organization Science.* He has also published several textbooks including *International Business* (McGraw-Hill) and *Global Business Today* (McGraw-Hill). His work is among the most widely cited in international business and strategic management.

Professor Hill has taught in the MBA, Executive MBA, Technology Management MBA, Management, and PhD programs at the University of Washington. During his time at the University of Washington, he has received over 25 awards for teaching excellence, including multiple Charles E. Summer Outstanding Teaching Awards, most recently in 2016.

Professor Hill works on a private basis with a number of organizations. His clients have included Microsoft, where he has been teaching in-house executive education courses for two decades. He has also consulted for a variety of other large companies (e.g., AT&T Wireless, Boeing, BF Goodrich, Group Health, Hexcel, Microsoft, Philips Healthcare, Philips Medical Systems, Seattle City Light, Swedish Health Services, Tacoma City Light, Thompson Financial Services, WRQ, and Wizards of the Coast).

Professor Hill has served on the advisory board of several start-up companies. For recreation, Professor Hill enjoys mountaineering, rock climbing, skiing, and competitive sailing.

G. Tomas M. Hult is the John W. Byington Endowed Chair, Professor of Marketing and International Business, and Director of the International Business Center in the Eli Broad College of Business at Michigan State University. The Eli Broad College of Business has a Center for International Business Education and Research (CIBER), one of only 17 funded by the U.S. Department of Education. Professor Hult serves as the CIBER Director, and he is also currently President of the 17-university CIBER coalition.

Professor Hult is an elected Fellow of the Academy of International Business (AIB), one of only about 80 scholars worldwide receiving this honor. He also serves as the Executive Director and Foundation President of AIB. Professor Hult serves on the U.S. District Export Council and holds board member positions of the International Trade Center of Mid-Michigan, Global Business Club of Mid-Michigan, and the Sheth Foundation.

Several studies have ranked Professor Hult as one of the most cited scholars in the world in business and management. He has served as editor of *Journal of the Academy of Marketing Science* and has published more than 60 articles in premier business journals, including *Journal of International Business Studies, Academy of Management Journal, Strategic Management Journal, Journal of Management, Journal of Marketing, Journal of the Academy of Marketing Science, Journal of Retailing, Journal of Operations Management, Decision Sciences,* and *IEEE.*

Professor Hult has also published several books: *International Business* (2017), *Second Shift* (2017), *Global Business Today* (2016), *Global Supply Chain Management* (2014), *Total Global Strategy* (2012), and *Extending the Supply Chain* (2005). He is a regular contributor of articles in the popular press (e.g., *Time, Fortune, World Economic Forum, The Conversation*).

Professor Hult is a well-known keynote speaker on international business, international marketing, global supply chain management, global strategy, and marketing strategy. He teaches in doctoral, master's, and undergraduate programs at Michigan State University, and he is a visiting professor at Leeds University (United Kingdom) and Uppsala University (Sweden).

He also teaches frequently in executive development programs and has developed a large clientele of the world's top multinational corporations (e.g., ABB, Albertsons, Avon, BG, Bechtel, Bosch, BP, Defense Logistics Agency, Domino's, FedEx, Ford, FreshDirect, General Motors, GroceryGateway, HSBC, IBM, Michigan Economic Development Corporation, Masco, NASA, Raytheon, Shell, Siemens, State Farm, Steelcase, Tech Data, and Xerox).

Tomas Hult is a dual citizen of the United States and Sweden, and lives in Okemos, Michigan, with his wife, Laurie, and their children, Daniel and Isabelle. Tennis, golf, and traveling are his favorite recreational activities.

Thomas McKaig has been teaching at the Universities of Guelph and Guelph Humber since 2003 and 2005 respectively, where he has taught both Undergraduate and Executive MBA international business courses. He earned his Diplôme for his thesis on Canada–EEC Trade Relations and Certificat, majoring in International Relations and minoring in European Economics at the Institut d'Etudes Politiques (formerly IHEE) of the Université de Strasbourg. He earned his Honours BA in Political Science from the University of Ottawa.

Thomas McKaig provides advisory services in diverse industries, pinpointing and delivering strategic realignment solutions in areas of business development, operations and management reviews, international trade research, and training. He is Principal in Thomas McKaig International Inc. (TMI), an international development firm (www.tm-int.com). He has worked with clients in the Middle East, Africa, East and West Europe, Central Asia, and North, Central, and South America in the English, French, German, Italian, Spanish, and Russian languages.

He has served as Executive in Residence at the University of Tennessee. In 2017 he was awarded a University of Guelph, Office of the Provost Study and Development Fellowship, "On the Ground Business Information in Latin America". His findings further connect his private sector work in Latin America to classroom learning in his international business courses. In this same year he was the Faculty of Business KeyNote Convocation Speaker for the University of Guelph-Humber's graduating business classes. Previously he was a recipient of its Faculty/Staff Mentoring Award.

He has held executive international marketing and business development positions with the: Royal Canadian Mint for its Gold Maple Leaf Bullion Coin programme; Bullion Management Group; and the World Gold Council.

Brief Contents

Contents

THE *GLOBAL BUSINESS TODAY* APPROACH

Global Business Today is intended for the first international business course at either the undergraduate or the MBA level. Our goal with this fifth Canadian edition is to set new standards for international business textbooks. We have written a book that (1) integrates the Canadian perspective on international business and Canada's place within the international business environment; (2) is comprehensive and up-to-date; (3) goes beyond an uncritical presentation and shallow explanation of the body of knowledge; and (4) focuses on implications for business while making important theories, issues, and practices accessible and interesting to Canadian students.

Over the past five editions, we have worked hard to adhere to these goals. It has not always been easy. An enormous amount has happened over the past decade, both in the real world of economics, politics, and business, and in the academic world of theory and empirical research. Often, we have had to significantly rewrite chapters, delete old examples, bring in new ones, incorporate new theory and evidence into the material, and phase out older theories that are increasingly less relevant to the modern and dynamic world of international business. As noted later, there have been significant changes in this edition—and that will no doubt continue to be the case in the future.

INTEGRATED COVERAGE OF THE CANADIAN PERSPECTIVE

Although this book is geared to the Canadian reader, this does not mean that all examples within are Canadian examples. The authors have written about those realities and examples that best portray chapter topical themes, as well as writing about what the market wants, based upon market research in the academic field. The textbook pays particular attention to small- and medium-sized enterprises, who continue to play a vital role in the Canadian economy, and their push onto the international business scene.

COMPREHENSIVE AND UP-TO-DATE COVERAGE

To be comprehensive, an international business textbook must clearly communicate

- how and why the world's countries differ;
- why a comprehensive review of economics and politics of international trade and investment is necessary in understanding international trade;
- how the functions and form of the global monetary system are tied into global trade;
- how the strategies, objectives, and international structures of international business need to conform to certain guidelines set out by international organizations and other bodies; and
- the special roles of an international business's activities.

This book pays close attention to these issues. Ultimately, a successful business is an informed business. It is our intention to cover, in an in-depth manner, the linkages between success and knowledge on the global business stage. As time moves forward, an increasing number of students will become international managers, and this book will better equip them with knowledge about the strategies, operations, and functions of small and large businesses alike.

The theories behind international trade help students to grasp the scope and execution of international business. Many books convey an adequate task of communicating long-established theories (e.g., the theory of comparative advantage and Vernon's product life-cycle theory), but they ignore important newer works included in *Global Business Today,* such as

- the new trade theory and strategic trade policy;
- the work of Hernando de Soto on the link between property rights and development;
- the work of Nobel prize-winning economist Amartya Sen on economic development;
- Samuel Huntington's influential thesis on the "clash of civilizations";
- the new growth of economic development championed by Paul Romer and Gene Grossman;
- recent empirical work by Jeffrey Sachs and others on the relationship between international trade and economic growth;
- Michael Porter's theory of the competitive advantage of nations;
- Robert Reich's work on national competitive advantage;
- the work of Douglas North and others on national institutional structures and the protection of property rights;
- the market imperfections approach to foreign direct investment that has grown out of Ronald Coase and Oliver Williamson's work on transaction cost economics;
- C.A. Bartlett and S. Ghoshal's research on the transnational corporation;
- the writings of C.K. Prahalad and Gary Hamel on core competencies, global competition, and global strategic alliances; and
- Paul Samuelson's critique of free trade.

In addition to providing cutting-edge theory and examples of the exponentially quickening pace of the international business environment, every effort has been made to ensure that this book is as current as possible when it goes to press. The book includes discussion questions attached to each Management Focus and Country Focus, as well as to the Closing Case. This Canadian edition contains current data from the World Trade Organization, the Organisation for Economic Co-operation and Development (OECD), and the United Nations Commission on Trade and Development (UNCTAD), among others. This book provides readers with a fresh insight into factors influencing Canada and other countries in the world of international trade, Canadian businesses' forays into world markets, and reactions to ongoing economic structural readjustments in 2018 and beyond.

As part of the overall revision process, changes have been made to every chapter in the book. All statistics have been updated to incorporate the most recently available data, which typically refers to 2016. For example, in Chapter 2, the Opening Case looks at how the policies of Russian President Vladimir Putin have shaped the economic, political, and legal systems of that nation and affect the attractiveness of Russia as a destination for international business, while there are two new Country Focus features, as well as a new Management Focus feature discussing allegations that Wal-Mart violated the Foreign Corrupt Practices Act while doing business in Mexico.

New material has been inserted wherever appropriate to reflect recent academic work or important current events. Detailed discussion of the 2008–2009 global financial crisis and its aftermath, including the 2010–2013 sovereign debt crises in the Euro Zone and its implications for international business, have been included in many chapters. Similarly, further discussion of the unrest that continues to sweep across the Middle East following the Arab Spring of 2011 and the ongoing turmoil in Egypt and Syria has been added to the book. And, perhaps most importantly, has been the rise of anti-globalism and protectionism as displayed in the Trump administration and through the Brexit vote.

Here are some examples:

- Chapter 2, "Country Differences in Political Economy," deals with critical forces affecting Canadian businesses working in the global arena.

- Chapter 5, "International Trade Theories," explains various international trade theories while providing practical explanations of their applications within various international companies.

- Chapter 9, "The Foreign Exchange Market," provides insights into how Canadian corporations can receive payment in international transactions. Similarly, foreign exchange risks and various economic theories of exchange rate determination will prove helpful for those individuals and corporations contemplating doing business beyond Canada's borders.

- Chapter 11, "Global Strategy," comprehensively covers leveraging core competencies and formulating global strategies through distributions channels and more.

- Chapter 12, "Entering Foreign Markets," offers insight into reactions in other countries to privatization issues, as described in the Closing Case, "JCB in India."

- Chapter 15, "Global Production, Outsourcing, and Logistics," neatly clarifies the details of global supply management through its opening case, "Apple: The Best Supply Chain in the World?". Significant explanations are provided on strategy, manufacturing and logistics, the strategic roles of foreign factories, and make-or-buy decisions.

- Chapter 16, "Global Human Resource Management," underscores the benefits and disadvantages of human resource management in terms of dealing with expatriate employees. International labour relations complicate the fabric of human resource departments for those companies with foreign operations.

BEYOND UNCRITICAL PRESENTATION AND SHALLOW EXPLANATION

Many issues in international business are complex and thus necessitate considerations of pros and cons. To demonstrate this concept to students, we have adopted a critical approach that presents the arguments for and against economic theories, government policies, business strategies, organizational structures, and so on. This is seen especially in a feature new to this edition, the Debate the Issues box that can be found in every chapter.

Related to this, we have attempted to explain the complexities of the many theories and phenomena unique to international business so the student might fully comprehend the statements of a theory or the reasons a phenomenon is the way it is. These theories and phenomena typically are explained in more depth in *Global Business Today* than they are in other textbooks.

FOCUS ON BUSINESS IMPLICATIONS AND ACCESSIBLE PRESENTATION

The fifth Canadian edition of *Global Business Today* offers many opportunities for students to engage with and apply the material to their lives and their future careers. The features listed below are explained in greater detail in the Learning Features section.

- Each chapter begins with a new or an updated **Opening Case** and concludes with a new or updated **Closing Case** that illustrates the relevance of chapter material for the practice of international business.
- Each chapter also contains two types of focus boxes. Updated **Management Focus** boxes, like the updated cases, illustrate the relevance of the chapter material for the practice of international business. **Country Focus** boxes highlight chapter issues in Canada and other countries.
- **Another Perspective** sidebars, which have been substantially changed and updated in this edition, help students to think critically about adjacent text material.
- **Debate the Issues** sidebars, new in this edition, are ways to practically illustrate the chapter material and get the students engaged.
- Each chapter concludes with an **Implications for Business** section that explains the managerial implications of the chapter material. This feature helps business students to understand the linkage between practice and theory.
- **Sustainability in Practice Cases** help students to understand how businesses are engaging in the solutions to sustainable development challenges.
- **GlobalEdge™ Research Tasks** allow students to practice using real business data.

THE STRUCTURE OF *GLOBAL BUSINESS TODAY,* FIFTH CANADIAN EDITION

Global Business Today, fifth Canadian edition, offers a tight, integrated flow of topics from chapter to chapter.

PART ONE: GLOBALIZATION

Chapter 1 provides an overview of the key issues to be addressed and explains the plan of the book.

PART TWO: COUNTRY DIFFERENCES

Chapters 2, 3, and 4 focus on national differences in political economy and culture and the implications of these differences for ethical decision making. Most international business textbooks place this material later, but we believe it is vital to discuss national differences first. After all, many of the central issues in international trade and investment, the global monetary system, international business strategy and structure, and international business operations arise out of national differences in political economy and culture. To understand these issues, students must first appreciate the differences in countries and cultures.

PART THREE: CROSS-BORDER TRADE AND INVESTMENT

Chapters 5, 6, 7, and 8 investigate the political economy of international trade and investment, fostering understanding of the trade and investment environment in which international business occurs.

PART FOUR: GLOBAL MONEY SYSTEM

Chapters 9 and 10 examine the global monetary system, while detailing the monetary framework in which international business transactions are carried out.

PART FIVE: COMPETING IN A GLOBAL MARKETPLACE

Chapters 11, 12, 13, 14, 15, and 16 move away from the macro environment of the international business realities into the workings of companies within this framework. How do companies adapt their strategies to compete beyond their own borders? How do production and logistics proceed on a global scale? These chapters explain how firms can perform their key functions—manufacturing, marketing, research and development, and human resource management—to compete and succeed in the international business environment.

WHAT'S NEW IN THE FIFTH CANADIAN EDITION?

This fifth Canadian edition not only explains theoretical aspects of international trade but, more importantly, attempts to connect the practical applications involving international trade into a framework of helpful understanding for those exporters, both new and experienced, in this field. Extensive re-writes of content and cases and sidebars have been undertaken. Thought-provoking questions are found at the end of each of the popular Management Focus and Country Focus boxes, as well as for the Closing Case.

CHAPTER-BY-CHAPTER CHANGES

Chapter 1: Globalization. All of the statistics have been updated to the most recent available at the time of this book going to production. A new Opening Case on "The Globalization of Production at Boeing" has been written. The emergence of global institutions is detailed. The Globalization Debate introduces some of the latest antiglobalization ideas found both in the United States and around the world. The innovative spirit of one of Canada's best known corporations shines through in an updated Closing Case, "Tim Hortons—A Canadian Company Looking for New Markets," as this "made-in-Canada" enterprise increases its forays into the American marketplace.

Chapter 2: Country Differences in Political Economy. The discussion of differences in legal systems provides insight into the linkage between corruption and negative economics within a country. Demonstrating this theme is the new Opening Case written about Putin's Russia. A new Country Focus looks at Nigeria, and a new Closing Case, "Ghana: An African Dynamo" depicts the transformation of a socialist system.

Chapter 3: The Cultural Environment. The chapter opens with a new Opening Case on Best Buy and eBay's entry into the Difficult Chinese market. Data throughout has been extensively updated. A new Country Focus "Using IT to Break India's Caste System" is included, as is another new Country Focus on "Islamic Capitalism in Turkey." Various religions and their significance within the world are discussed, and the new Closing Case pertains to Dubai's World Expo in 2020.

Chapter 4: Ethics in International Business. The chapter opens with a new Opening Case about the most corrupt industry sectors based on an OECD study. As well, the chapter has been updated and includes references to recent Canadian events.

Chapter 5: International Trade Theories. Over the past few years, numerous empirical studies have been published that look at the relationship between a country's "openness" to international trade and its economic growth. This work is discussed in this chapter. A new Opening Case looks at the shifting political landscape in attempts to create a new free-trade zone. A new Closing Case, "The Rise of India's Drug Industry," links thematically to international trade theories.

Chapter 6: The Political Economy of International Trade. The contentious bilateral trade issues that have periodically soured Canadian trade relations with the United States over the past couple of decades are dealt with in the context of the World Trade Organization and the North American Free Trade Agreement, as are current U.S. government approaches to NAFTA. There is a new Opening Case, "Sugar Subsidies Drive Candy Makers Abroad," in addition to a new Country Focus, "Are the Chinese Illegally Subsidizing Auto Exports?" and a new Closing Case.

Chapter 7: Foreign Direct Investment. Both up-to-date international foreign direct investment (FDI) flows and FDI figures show the importance of FDI, in its different forms, including mergers and acquisitions, in the economies of Canada and other countries. A new Opening Case on FDI in Nigeria and a new Closing Case on foreign retailers in India neatly *illustrate* the topic of foreign direct investment.

Chapter 8: Regional Economic Integration. The changing views towards regional economic integration are a fairly new phenomena, and are detailed in this chapter. A new Opening Case on "Tomato Wars" within NAFTA shows some of the consequences of regional integration. This theme continues in a new Country Focus on "The Greek Sovereign Debt Crisis." To reflect the importance of the European Union within this chapter, a new Closing Case has been added, "I Want My Greek TV!" Within the text a new section has been added on the Trans-Pacific Partnership, made famous through the 2016 U.S. presidential election cycle.

Chapter 9: The Foreign Exchange Market. The Canadian dollar's recent fall against the U.S. dollar and other currencies is significant for Canadian importers and exporters. Also, economic theories of exchange rate determination are explained because this information is vital to business people conducting business abroad. A new Opening Case, "The Wild Ride of the Brazilian Real," ties in neatly with our chapter's theme, as does the new Closing Case, "The Rise (and Fall) of the Japanese Yen." The Management Focus has been expanded and updated to include hedging across the entire Canadian gold industry.

Chapter 10: The Global Monetary System. One of the more interesting phases of the development and growth of the Canadian economy came during the period in which Canada was under the gold standard from 1854–1914 and 1914–26. Internationally, many policies and institutions have influenced and shaped the value of currencies. The ever-increasing U.S. trade deficit and the fall of the U.S. dollar have wreaked havoc on the international monetary system. The universality of currency problems is depicted in a new Opening Case, "The IMF and Iceland's Economic Recovery." A new Closing Case looks at further currency troubles. A new Management Focus looks at a Canadian company with a new approach to global payments using small amounts of gold as a basis for trade.

Chapter 11: Global Strategy. Multinational corporations have long recognized the importance of leveraging skills, strategic alliances, and competencies in their foreign locations for improved business practices at home and abroad. A new Opening Case, "IKEA's Supply Chain," has been written along with a new Management Focus on creating new yogurt brands in Canada. Both of these detail strategic elements that companies had to implement. A new Closing Case on Ford's international strategy concludes this important chapter.

Chapter 12: Entering Foreign Markets. The ways through which companies enter foreign markets is covered through a look at the pros and cons of greenfield investments and other alternative strategies for entering foreign markets. The new Opening Case, "Market Entry at Starbucks," shows the methods it has taken in different countries around the world. The Canadian-based Management Focus and the Country Focus have been revised. Two new Debate the Issues boxes are included in this chapter, while a new Closing Case, about JCB, describes that company's global reach.

Chapter 13: Exporting, Importing, and Countertrade. The discussion on export assistance to Canadian companies provides a detailed look at the institutional means and mechanisms through which many Canadian companies engage in export, for example, with the assistance of Export Development Canada. A new opening case, "Growing Through Exports," details the role of smaller companies in the exporting and importing world. The three Canadian-based components, the Management Focus, Country Focus, and Closing Case, have been adapted and revised and all further explain exporting, importing, and countertrade.

Chapter 14: Global Marketing, and Research and Development. Global marketing and R&D are what makes or breaks a company. A new Opening Case, "Global Branding of Avengers and Iron Man," shows how branding in the entertainment world can lead to billion-dollar revenues. Several "Another Perspective" boxes have been revised throughout this chapter. Distribution and communication strategies are also discussed within this chapter. The seemingly never-ending American–Canadian softwood lumber issue has also been updated.

Chapter 15: Global Production, Outsourcing, and Logistics. A new Opening Case focuses on Apple, well known for having perhaps the best supply chain in the industry and possibly the world. A new Closing Case on retailer H&M ties the need for a good supply chain with the successful sale of fashion items. A new Country Focus is included on Phillips Electronics in China, while a new Management Focus deals with an issue very dear to the heart of U.S. president Donald Trump: the movement of manufacturing firms back to the United States.

Chapter 16: Global Human Resource Management. Employment legislation can have both positive and negative impacts for foreign businesses operating abroad, and companies must be aware of rules and guidelines so they can act accordingly. A new Canadian Opening Case based on 2017 interviews with Arlene Tober, Consultant in gender issues, titled "Diversity Matters," shows that both globally and within Canada, gender diversity matters to firm performance. The Sustainability in Practice case of Interface has been re-edited, and new "Another Perspective" boxes added throughout.

SUPERIOR LEARNING SOLUTIONS AND SUPPORT

The McGraw-Hill Education team is ready to help instructors assess and integrate any of our products, technology, and services into your course for optimal teaching and learning performance. Whether it's helping your students improve their grades, or putting your entire course online, the McGraw-Hill Education team is here to help you do it. Contact your Learning Solutions Consultant today to learn how to maximize all of McGraw-Hill Education's resources.

For more information, please visit us online: **http://www.mheducation.ca/he/solutions**

Acknowledgements

Numerous people deserve recognition for their assistance in preparing this book.

First and foremost, I would like to thank my mother, Dorothy McKaig, for always being my greatest supporter. Special thanks to my sister Janet McKaig, brother-in-law Geoff Kelly, brother Woody McKaig, and sister-in-law Sara Premi for their always-helpful support and advice.

I would also like to express my sincere appreciation to my Research Director, Jim Helik. He was able to handle my requests for research information and synthesize it to meet my demanding time lines. He exceeded my high expectations in the quality of his input. I would like to offer my gratitude to Sallie L. Storey for her kind assistance through the years. I would like to specially thank Fernando López-Fabregat, current Uruguayan Ambassador to the United Kingdom for providing insights on international business as appearing in Chapter 16. Thank you as well to Arlene Tober for the extensive information she provided both in the Opening Case and throughout Chapter 16. I would like to express my gratitude to Alexander Fry and Rodrigo Ribeiro, Partners with KPMG. Rodrigo and Alexander have been of great personal and professional assistance to me over the past ten years when doing business in Uruguay. Thank you.

I would like to thank Charles W. L. Hill, for creating an excellent textbook and strong base from which this Canadian edition was made possible. As well, I would like to thank Dr. George Bragues, Program Head, Business and Assistant Vice Provost, University of Guelph-Humber, for his continued support and assistance. I would also like to thank Charles Janthur for his international business support.

Market feedback indicated that more expansive coverage of the important role that ethics plays in the international business arena was necessary. We called upon Tim Richardson, who teaches at Seneca College of Applied Arts and Technology and the University of Toronto, Department of Management, www.witiger.com. Tim enthusiastically and ably responded to this request, providing Chapter 4, "Ethics in International Business," rich in Canadian content and current research. We thank him for his invaluable and ongoing contribution to this text.

The team at McGraw-Hill Ryerson was also superb, including Kim Brewster and Alwynn Pinard, Portfolio Manager; Erin Catto, Content Developer; Jessica Barnoski, Supervising Editor; and Margaret Henderson, Copy Editor.

Finally, I extend sincere thanks to the reviewers of the fifth Canadian edition, who provided insightful feedback that helped to shape this book.

Thomas McKaig

Learning Features

Global Business Today, fifth Canadian edition, has a rich selection of learning features that highlight companies' ups and downs in the international business arena, stimulate learning and understanding, and challenge students to respond.

Opening Case

Each chapter begins with an engaging opening case that sets the stage for the chapter. These brief case studies introduce students to critical issues and often challenge their preconceptions. The opening case provides rich, introductory examples from actual countries and organizations.

OPENING CASE

PUTIN'S RUSSIA

The modern Russia state was born in 1991 after the dramatic collapse of the Soviet Union. Early in the post-Soviet era, Russia embraced ambitious policies designed to transform a communist dictatorship with a centrally planned economy into democratic state with a market-based economic system. The policies, however, were imperfectly implemented. Political reform left Russia with a strong presidency that—in hindsight—had the ability to subvert the democratic process. On the economic front, the privatization of many state-owned enterprises was done in such a way as to leave large shareholdings in the hands of the politically connected, many of whom were party officials and factory managers under the old Soviet system. Corruption was also endemic, and organized crime was able to seize control of some newly privatized enterprises. In 1998, the poorly managed Russian economy went through a financial crisis that nearly bought the country to its knees.

Fast-forward to 2017, and Russia still has a long way to go before it resembles a modern democracy with a functioning free market–based economic system. On the positive side, the economy grew at a healthy clip during most of the 2000s and up until 2008, helped in

---

Learning Objectives

Each chapter contains a list of Learning Objectives right after the opening case. These two features tell students what they will know after completing the chapter, and a notation in the chapter indicates where the learning objective is discussed in the text.

 LEARNING OBJECTIVES

By the end of this chapter you should be able to:

1. Define the term *globalization*.
2. Examine the rise of global institutions.
3. Recognize why globalization and innovation are now proceeding at a rapid rate.
4. Illustrate the changing demographics of the global economy.
5. Explain the main arguments in the debate over the impact of globalization on job security, income levels, labour and environmental policies, and national sovereignty.
6. Show how the process of globalization is giving rise to numerous opportunities and challenges that business managers must confront in Canada and beyond.

Debate the Issues

A new feature in this edition is a "Debate the Issues" box in each chapter, outlining different sides to some of the issues raised in each chapter.

DEBATE THE ISSUE

What Will Happen to Manufacturing in the United States?

The United States has the largest and most technologically powerful economy in the world, with a per capita GDP (gross domestic product) of $49,100. Most of the labour force (79.4 percent) is employed in the services sector, with 19.5 percent employed in manufacturing industries, and only 1.1 percent in the agricultural area. China, India, and the European Union have labour forces larger than the United States, which ranks fourth in the world. Data show that the U.S. has become much more of a service economy over the years, as manufacturing jobs have moved to Mexico (which was a frequent refrain of President Donald Trump). Will the U.S. continue to increase its service sector, and does this increase come at the cost of manufacturing and agriculture?

Source: U.S. Central Intelligence Agency, *World Factbook*, www.cia.gov, accessed March 3, 2014.

Another Perspective

With multiple examples per chapter, Another Perspective boxes provide students with an alternate way of thinking about important global issues presented in the text. These not only hone students' critical thinking skills, but also give a deeper understanding of chapter topics.

ANOTHER PERSPECTIVE

UN and International Law

The International Court of Justice (www.icj-cij.org/), located in The Hague (Netherlands), is one of the six major organs of the United Nations. The Court, in existence since 1946, serves as the successor to the Permanent Court of International Justice established by the League of Nations and derives its mandate from one of the statutes forming an integral part of the Charter of the United Nations. The Court has two functions: to render judgements on disputes submitted to it by States and to furnish advisory opinions on questions referred to it by authorized bodies.

Source: International Court of Justice, http://www.icj-cij.org/court.

Country Focus

Country Focus boxes, found in each chapter, provide real-world examples of how different countries grapple with political, economic, social, or cultural issues.

COUNTRY FOCUS

Antiglobalization Protests in France

If someone was only watching North American television during the 2016 U.S. presidential campaign, they might think that calls to "rip up trade agreements" and promote "fair trade, not free trade" are something new, or a feeling only expressed in the United States. However there is a long and global history of actions against globalization.

One night in August 1999, ten men, under the leadership of local sheep farmer and rural activist José Bové, crept into the town of Millau in central France and vandalized a McDonald's restaurant under construction, causing an estimated $150 000 worth of damage. These were no ordinary vandals, however, at least according to their supporters, for the "symbolic dismantling" of the McDonald's outlet had noble aims, or so it was claimed. The attack was initially presented as a protest against unfair American trade policies. The European Union had banned imports of hormone-treated beef from the United States, primarily because of fears that hormone-treated beef might lead to health problems (although EU scientists had concluded there was no evidence of this). After a careful review, the World Trade Organization stated the EU ban was not allowed under trading rules that the EU and United States were party to, and that the EU would have to lift it or face retaliation.

Management Focus

Management Focus boxes, found in each chapter, illustrate the relevance of chapter concepts for the practice of international business.

MANAGEMENT FOCUS

Vizio and the Market for Flat-Panel TVs

Operating sophisticated tooling in environments that must be kept absolutely clean, fabrication centres in South Korea, Taiwan, and Japan produce sheets of glass twice as large as king-size beds to exacting specifications. From there, the glass panels travel to Mexican plants located alongside the U.S. border. There, they are cut to size, combined with electronic components shipped in from Asia and the United States, assembled into finished flat-panel TVs, and loaded onto trucks bound for retail stores in the United States, where consumers spend more than $35 billion a year on flat-panel TVs.

The underlying technology for flat-panel displays was invented in the United States in the late 1960s by RCA. But after RCA and rivals Westinghouse and Xerox opted not to pursue the technology, the Japanese company Sharp made aggressive investments in flat-panel displays. By the early 1990s, Sharp was selling the first flat-panel screens. But as the Japanese economy plunged into a decade-long recession, investment leadership shifted to South Korean companies such as Samsung. Then the 1997 Asian crisis hit Korea hard, and Taiwanese companies seized leadership. Today, Chinese companies are starting to elbow their way into the flat-panel display manufacturing business.

GlobalEDGE/CIBER™ Research Task

Using the text and the GlobalEDGE™ Web site, http://globaledge.msu.edu, students solve realistic international business problems related to each chapter. These exercises expose students to the types of tools and data sources international managers use to make informed business decisions.

Research Task globalEDGE™ globaledge.msu.edu

Use the globalEDGE™ site to complete the following exercises:

1. The "Freedom in the World" survey evaluates the state of political rights and civil liberties around the world. Provide a description of this survey and a ranking, in terms of "freedom," of the leaders and laggards. What factors are considered in this survey when forming the rankings?

2. Market Potential Indicators (MPI) is an indexing study conducted by the Michigan

State University Center for International Business Education and Research (MSU-CIBER) to compare emerging markets on a variety of dimensions. Provide a description of the indicators used in the indexing procedure. Which of the indicators would have greater importance for a company that markets laptop computers? Considering the MPI rankings, which developing countries would you advise this company to enter first?

Critical Thinking and Discussion Questions

These questions are suited for in-class discussion or personal reflection.

Critical Thinking and Discussion Questions

1. Outline why the culture of a country might influence the costs of doing business in that country. Illustrate your answer with examples.

2. Do you think that business practices in an Islamic country are likely to differ from business practices in Canada, and if so, how?

3. What are the implications for an international business of differences in the dominant religions and/or ethical systems of countries in which it is based?

4. Choose two countries that appear to be culturally diverse. Compare the cultures of those countries and then indicate how cultural differences influence (a) the costs of doing business in each country; (b) the likely future economic development of that country; (c) business practices; and (d) business ethics.

Implications for Business

At the end of every chapter, this section spotlights the managerial implications and practical aspects of the chapter material.

IMPLICATIONS FOR BUSINESS

The implications for international business of the material discussed in this chapter fall into two broad categories. First, the political, economic, and legal environment of a country clearly influences the attractiveness of that country as a market and/or investment site. The benefits, costs, and risks associated with doing business in a country are a function of that country's political, economic, and legal systems. Second, the political, economic, and legal systems of a country can raise important ethical issues that have implications for the practice of international business. Here we consider each of these issues.

Key Terms and Learning Objectives Summary

These resources help students review key concepts. The Learning Objectives Summary ties back to the Learning Objectives on the opening pages of each chapter.

Key Terms

foreign direct investment (FDI)

General Agreement on Tariffs and Trade (GATT)

globalization

globalization of markets

globalization of production

international business

International Monetary Fund (IMF)

international trade

Moore's Law

multinational enterprise (MNE)

United Nations

World Bank

World Trade Organization (WTO)

Closing Case

The closing case wraps up the material in the chapter by relating the experience of a company to the practice of international business.

CLOSING CASE

GHANA: AN AFRICAN DYNAMO

The West African nation of Ghana has emerged as one of the fastest-growing countries in sub-Saharan Africa during the last decade. Between 2000 and 2015, Ghana's average annual growth rate in GDP was over 8 percent, making it the fastest-growing economy in Africa. In 2011, this country of 25 million people became Africa's newest middle-income nation. Driving this growth has been strong demand for two of Ghana's major exports—gold and cocoa—as well as the start of oil production in 2010. Indeed, due to recent oil discoveries, Ghana is set to become one of the biggest oil producers in sub-Saharan Africa, a fact that could fuel strong economic expansion for years to come.

Sustainability in Practice

Located at the end of some parts, these vignettes illustrate how businesses are engaging in the solutions to sustainable development challenges.

Sustainability in Practice

ADIDAS GROUP: SUPPLY-CHAIN MANAGEMENT

SITUATION

The Adidas Group is the second largest sportswear manufacturer in the world. Its German holding company, Adidas AG, produces products under the Reebok, Rockport, and Ashworth brands, among others including the flagship Adidas brand.

Existing as a company for almost a hundred years, and with operations all over the world, the company has taken a highly visible and integrated approach to sustainability.

The Complete Course Solution

We listened to educators from around the world, learned about their challenges, and created a whole new way to deliver a course.

Connect2 is a collaborative teaching and learning platform that includes an instructionally designed complete course framework of learning materials that is flexible and open for instructors to easily personalize, add their own content, or integrate with other tools and platforms.

- Save time and resources building and managing a course.
- Gain confidence knowing that each course framework is pedagogically sound.
- Help students master course content.
- Make smarter decisions by using real-time data to guide course design, content changes, and remediation.

MANAGE — Dynamic Curriculum Builder

Quickly and easily launch a complete course framework developed by instructional design experts. Each Connect2 course is a flexible foundation for instructors to build upon by adding their own content or drawing upon the wide repository of additional resources.

- Easily customize Connect2 by personalizing the course scope and sequence.
- Get access to a wide range of McGraw-Hill Education content within one powerful teaching and learning platform.
- Receive expert support and guidance on how best to utilize content to achieve a variety of teaching goals.

MASTER — Student Experience

Improve student performance with instructional alignment and leverage Connect2's carefully curated learning resources. Deliver required reading through Connect2's award-winning adaptive learning system.

- Teach at a higher level in class by helping students retain core concepts.
- Tailor in-class instruction based on student progress and engagement.
- Help focus students on the content they don't know so they can prioritize their study time.

MEASURE — Advanced Analytics

Collect, analyze and act upon class and individual student performance data. Make real-time course updates and teaching decisions backed by data.

- Visually explore class and student performance data.
- Easily identify key relationships between assignments and student performance.
- Maximize in-class time by using data to focus on areas where students need the most help.

Course Map

The flexible and customizable course map provides instructors full control over the pre-designed courses within Connect2. Instructors can easily add, delete, or rearrange content to adjust the course scope and sequence to their personal preferences.

Implementation Guide

Each Connect2 course includes a detailed implementation guide that provides guidance on what the course can do and how best to utilize course content based on individual teaching approaches.

Instructor Resources

A comprehensive collection of instructor resources are available within Connect2. Instructor Support and Seminar Materials provide additional exercises and activities to use for in-class discussion and teamwork.

For more information, please visit www.mheconnect2.com

© David R. Frazier Photolibrary, Inc./Alamy

Chapter 1

Globalization

THE GLOBALIZATION OF PRODUCTION AT BOEING

Executives at the Boeing Corporation, America's largest exporter, like to say that building a large commercial jet aircraft like the 747 or 787 involves bringing together more than a million parts in flying formation. Forty-five years ago, when the early models of Boeing's venerable 737 and 747 jets were rolling off the company's Seattle-area production lines, foreign suppliers accounted for only 5 percent of those parts on average. Boeing was vertically integrated and manufactured many of the major components that went into the planes. The largest parts produced by outside suppliers were the jet engines, where two of the three suppliers were American companies. The lone foreign engine manufacturer was the British company Rolls Royce.

Fast-forward to the modern era, and things look very different. In the case of its latest aircraft, the super efficient 787 Dreamliner, 50 outside suppliers spread around the world account for 65 percent of the value of the aircraft. Italian firm Alenia Aeronautica makes the centre fuselage and horizontal stabilizer. Kawasaki of Japan makes part of the forward fuselage and the fixed trailing edge of the wing. French firm Messier-Dowty makes the aircraft's landing gear. German firm Diehl Luftahrt Elektronik supplies the main cabin lighting. Sweden's Saab Aerostructures makes the access doors. Japanese company Jamco makes parts for the lavatories, flight decks interiors, and galleys. Mitsubishi Heavy Industries of Japan makes the wings. KAA of Korea makes the wing tips. And so on.

Why the change? One reason is that 80 percent of Boeing's customers are foreign airlines, and to sell into those nations, it often helps to be giving business to those nations. In Canada, for example, Boeing directly employs almost 2,000 Canadians. It buys supplies from about 560 firms across Canada.

This trend started in 1974 when Mitsubishi of Japan was given contracts to produce inboard wing flaps for the 747. The Japanese reciprocated by placing big orders for Boeing jets. A second rationale was to disperse component-part production to those suppliers who are the best in the world at their particular activity. Over the years, for example, Mitsubishi has acquired considerable expertise in the manufacture of wings, so it was logical for Boeing to use Mitsubishi to make the wings for the 787. Similarly, the 787 is the first commercial jet aircraft to be made almost entirely out of carbon fibre, so Boeing tapped Japan's Toray industries, a world-class expert in sturdy but light carbon-fibre composites, to supply materials for the fuselage. A third reason for the extensive outsourcing on the 787 was that Boeing wanted to unburden itself of some of the risks and costs associated with developing production facilities for the 787. By outsourcing, it pushed some of those risks and costs onto suppliers, who had to undertake major investments in capacity to ramp up to produce for the 787.

So what did Boeing retain for itself? Engineering design, marketing and sales, and final assembly at its Everett plant north of Seattle, all activities where Boeing maintains it is the best in the world. Of major component parts, Boeing only made the tail fin and wing to body fairing (which attaches the wings to the fuselage of the plane). Everything else was outsourced.

As the 787 moved through development in the 2000s, however, it became clear that Boeing had pushed the outsourcing paradigm too far. Coordinating a globally dispersed production system this extensive turned out to be very challenging. Parts turned up late, some parts didn't "snap together" the way Boeing had envisioned, and several suppliers ran into engineering problems that slowed down the entire production process. As a consequence, the date for delivery of the first jet was pushed back more than four years, and Boeing had to take millions of dollars in penalties for late deliveries. In Canada, Air Canada finally took delivery of its first 787-7 Dreamliner in May 2014 after many delays.

There are now signs that Boeing is rethinking some of its global outsourcing policy. For its next jet, a new version of its popular, wide-bodied 777 jet, the 777X, which will use the same carbon-fibre technology as the 787, Boeing will bring wing production back in-house. Mitsubishi and Kawasaki of Japan produce much of the wing structure for the 787, and for the original version of the 777. However, recently Japan's airlines have been placing large orders with Airbus, breaking with their traditional allegiance to Boeing. This seems to have given Boeing an opening to bring wing production back in-house. Boeing executives also note that Boeing has lost much of its expertise in wing production over the last 20 years due to outsourcing, and bringing it back in-house for new carbon-fibre wings might enable Boeing to regain these important core skills and strengthen the company's competitive position.

Sources: K. Epstein and J. Crown, "Globalization Bites Boeing," *Bloomberg Businessweek*, March 12, 2008; H. Mallick, "Out of Control Outsourcing Ruined Boeing's Beautiful Dreamliner," *The Star*, February 25, 2013; P. Kavilanz, "Dreamliner: Where in the World Its Parts Come From," *CNN Money*, January 18, 2013; S. Dubois, "Boeing's Dreamliner Mess: Simply Inevitable?" *CNN Money*, January 22, 2013; A. Scott and T. Kelly, "Boeing's Loss of a $9.5 Billion Deal Could Bring Jobs Back to the U.S.," *Business Insider*, October 14, 2013; "Air Canada Welcomes First Boeing 787-9 Dreamliner to its Fleet," *Canada Newswire*, July 31, 2015; and *Boeing in Canada*, http://www.boeing.ca/boeing-in-canada/backgrounder.page?8Z0b/Z3iHGrcb5yXR.

Introduction

Over the past several decades, a fundamental shift has been occurring in the world economy. We are moving away from a world in which national economies were relatively self-contained entities, isolated from each other by barriers to cross-border trade and investment; by distance, time zones, and language; and by national differences in government regulation, culture, and business systems. And we are moving toward a world in which barriers to cross-border trade and investment are tumbling; perceived distance is shrinking due to advances in transportation and telecommunications technology; material culture is starting to look similar the world over; and national economies are merging into an interdependent global economic system. The process by which this is occurring is commonly referred to as globalization.

The global dispersal of production of Boeing's 787 Dreamliner, as outlined in the opening case, is one example of this trend towards globalization. More broadly, in this interdependent global economy, a Canadian might drive to work in a car designed in Germany that was assembled in Canada by Ford, from components made in the United Kingdom and Japan, and that were fabricated from Korean steel and Malaysian rubber. She may have filled the car with gasoline at a service centre owned by a Dutch multinational company that changed its name to Shell Canada to obscure its national origins. The gasoline could have been made from oil pumped out of a well in the Hibernia fields off the coast of Newfoundland "and shipped by a shipping line registered in Monaco."[1]

While driving to work, the Canadian might talk to her investment adviser on a Finnish-manufactured, but Texas-assembled Nokia cellphone that is linked through a Nortel PBX system in Toronto. Afterwards, she might turn on her car radio, which was made in Malaysia by a Japanese firm, to hear a popular song composed by an Italian and sung by a group of Quebecois residing in France. The driver might pull into a drive-through Starbucks coffee shop managed by a Korean immigrant and order a "single, tall, nonfat latte" and chocolate-covered biscotti. The coffee beans came from Costa Rica and the chocolate from Peru, while the biscotti was made locally using an old Italian recipe. After the song ends, a news announcer might inform the Canadian listener that financial crisis that started in the U.S. banking sector may trigger a global recession and is sending stock markets down all over the world.

This is the world we live in. It is a world where the volume of goods, services, and investment crossing national borders expanded faster than world output every year during the last two decades of the twentieth century. According to the Bank for International Settlements, foreign-exchange trading in 2014 increased to an average of $5.3 trillion a day. To put this into perspective, this averages out to be $220 billion per hour.[2]

It is a world in which international institutions, such as the World Trade Organization, and gatherings of leaders from the world's most powerful economies have called for even lower barriers to cross-border trade and investment. It is a world where the symbols of material and popular culture are increasingly global: from Coca-Cola and McDonald's to Sony PlayStations, Samsung smartphones, MTV shows, and Disney films. It is a world in which products are made from inputs that come from all over the world. It is a world in which a financial crisis in America can trigger a global economic recession, which is exactly what occurred beginning in 2008.

But not everyone is unanimous in this thinking. It is also a world in which vigorous and vocal groups protest against globalization, which opponents blame for a list of ills, from unemployment in developed nations (especially in manufacturing jobs) to environmental degradation and the Americanization of popular culture. And political leaders are listening. In the recent U.S. presidential election, both Republican and Democratic nominees spoke of renegotiating free trade agreements. The president, Donald Trump, spoke repeatedly about tearing up the North American Free Trade Agreement (NAFTA). Just days after his election, Prime Minister Justin Trudeau said that he was open to looking at this decades-old free trade agreement.

For businesses, despite the current economic slowdown and a rising chorus of voices against free trade, this is in many ways the best of times. Globalization has increased the opportunities for a firm to expand its revenues by selling around the world and reduce its costs by producing in nations where key inputs are cheap. Since the collapse of communism at the end of the 1980s, the pendulum of public policy in nation after nation has swung toward the free-market end of the economic spectrum. Regulatory and administrative barriers to doing business in foreign nations have come down, while those nations have often transformed their economies, privatizing state-owned enterprises, deregulating markets, increasing competition, and welcoming investment by foreign businesses. This has allowed businesses both large and small, from both advanced nations and developing nations, to expand internationally.

The history of Starbucks exemplifies the opportunities that a global economy offers businesses. The original idea for Starbucks came from Italian coffeehouses. After refining the concept in the United States, in 1995 the company started to expand globally. As a result, a company that had only a handful of stores 25 years ago is now one of the world's best-known

The United Nations has the important goal of improving the well-being of people around the world. © *Purestock/Getty Images*

brands with more than 17 000 stores in almost 60 countries. Starbucks has had an impact on consumer behaviour around the world, changing the way people consume coffee and profiting in the process. The company is also changing the way coffee is produced. By committing itself to purchasing only Fair Trade Certified coffee beans, Starbucks is promoting nonexploitive and environmentally sound growing policies in developing nations, and finding that doing good is also good business, because it reinforces the value of the Starbucks brand.

As globalization unfolds, it is transforming industries and creating anxiety among those who believed their jobs were protected from foreign competition. Historically, while many workers in manufacturing industries worried about the impact foreign competition might have on their jobs, workers in service industries felt more secure. Now, this too is changing. Advances in technology, lower transportation costs, and the rise of skilled workers in developing countries imply that many services no longer need to be performed where they are delivered. The same is true of some accounting services. Today, many individual Canadian and U.S. tax returns are compiled in India. Indian accountants, trained in Canadian and U.S. tax rules, perform work for North American accounting firms.[3] They access individual tax returns, perform routine calculations, and save their work so that it can be inspected by a Canadian or U.S. accountant, who then bills clients. As the best-selling author Thomas Friedman has argued, the world is becoming flat.[4] People living in developed nations no longer have the playing field tilted in their favour. Increasingly, enterprising individuals based in India, China, or Brazil have the same opportunities to better themselves as those living in western Europe, Canada, or the United States.

In this book we will take a close look at the issues introduced here and many more. We will explore how changes in regulations governing international trade and investment, when coupled with changes in political systems and technology, have dramatically altered the competitive playing field confronting many businesses. We will discuss the resulting opportunities and threats, and review the strategies that managers can pursue to exploit the opportunities and counter the threats. We will consider whether globalization benefits or harms national economies. We will look at what economic theory has to say about the outsourcing of manufacturing and service jobs to places such as India and China and look at the benefits and costs of outsourcing, not just to business firms and their employees, but also to entire economies. First, though, we need to get a better overview of the nature and process of globalization, and that is the function of this first chapter.

LO1 | What Is Globalization?

As used in this book, **globalization** refers to the shift toward a more integrated and interdependent world economy. Globalization has several different facets, including the globalization of markets, the globalization of production, and the globalization of consumers. The developments in communications technology and a homogenization of economies have resulted in the concept of a worldwide consumer.

The Globalization of Markets

The **globalization of markets** refers to the merging of historically distinct and separate national markets into one huge global marketplace. Falling barriers to cross-border trade have made it easier to sell internationally. It has been argued for some time that the tastes and preferences of consumers in different nations are beginning to converge on some global norm, thereby helping to create a global market.[5] Consumer products such as Citicorp credit cards, Coca-Cola soft drinks, Apple iPods, and McDonald's hamburgers are frequently held up as prototypical examples of this trend. Firms such as Citicorp, Coca-Cola, McDonald's, and Apple are more than just benefactors of this trend; they are also facilitators of it. By offering a standardized product worldwide, they help to create a global market.

There are also many examples closer to home. Eventscape Inc. is a Toronto-based company that builds structures for designers and architects worldwide. Several years ago, Eventscape Inc. was recruited to create a 3-D logo structure for New York's Rockefeller Center. Since then, business has taken off internationally. Projects included framing for a casino stage in Macau, a chandelier for a royal wedding in Abu Dhabi, and most recently a perforated-steel acoustic wall for the Allen Theatre in Cleveland, Ohio (see http://eventscape.com).

Despite the global prevalence of Apple's products and McDonald's hamburgers, the view that national markets are giving way to the global markets should not be pushed too far. As we shall see in later chapters, very significant differences still exist between national markets along many relevant dimensions, including consumer tastes and preferences, distribution channels, culturally embedded value systems, business systems, and legal regulations. These differences frequently require that marketing strategies, product features, and operating practices be customized to best match conditions in a country. For example, automobile companies will promote different car models depending on a range of factors such as local fuel costs, income levels, traffic congestion, and cultural values.

Currently most global markets are not markets for consumer products—where national differences in tastes and preferences are still often important enough to act as a brake on globalization—but are markets for industrial goods and materials that serve a universal need the world over. These include the markets for commodities such as aluminum, oil, and wheat; the markets for industrial products such as microprocessors, DRAMs (computer memory chips), and commercial jet aircraft; the markets for computer software; and the markets for financial assets, from Canadian Treasury bills to eurobonds to futures on the Nikkei index or the Mexican peso.

In many global markets, the same firms frequently confront each other as competitors in nation after nation. Coca-Cola's rivalry with Pepsi is a global one, as are the rivalries between Ford and Toyota, Bombardier and Embraer, Caterpillar and Komatsu, and Sony, Nintendo, and Microsoft in video-game consoles. If one firm moves into a nation that is not currently served by its rivals, those rivals are sure to follow to prevent their competitor from gaining an advantage.[6] As firms follow each other around the world, they bring with them many of the assets that served them well in other national markets—including their products, operating strategies, marketing strategies, and brand names—creating some homogeneity across markets. Thus, greater uniformity replaces diversity. Due to such developments, in an increasing number of industries it is no longer meaningful to talk about "the German market," "the American market," "the Brazilian market," or "the Canadian market"; for many firms there is only the global market.

The Globalization of Production

The **globalization of production** refers to sourcing goods and services from locations around the globe to take advantage of national differences in the cost and quality of factors of production (such as labour, energy, land, and capital). By doing this, companies hope to lower their overall cost structure and/or improve the quality or functionality of their product offering, thereby allowing them to compete more effectively. Consider Bombardier's ongoing global expansion in manufacturing its CS300 series of regional aircraft, with its first sale in November 2016 to Air Baltic, the flag carrier of Latvia.[7]

The global dispersal of productive activities is not limited to giants such as Bombardier. Smaller firms are also tapping into the global marketplace. Matrikon, based in Edmonton, Alberta, was founded in 1988, and was bought by Honeywell International in 2010 in a deal valued at about $145 million (CAD$). Matrikon specializes in performance-monitoring solutions with clients in different industry sectors. Foreign direct investment, along with diversification of its manufacturing, design, and distributor channels, enable Matrikon to build a global competitive advantage for process-improvement software.[8]

As a consequence of the trend exemplified by Bombardier and Matrikon, in many industries it is becoming irrelevant to talk about Canadian products, Japanese products, German products, or Korean products. Given the growth of international outsourcing, manufactured goods are increasingly being described as global products. But as with the globalization of markets, one must be careful not to push the globalization of production too far. As we will see in later chapters, substantial impediments still make it difficult for firms to achieve the optimal dispersion of their productive activities to locations around the globe. These impediments include formal and informal barriers to trade between countries, barriers to foreign direct investment, transportation costs, and issues associated with economic and political risk.

DEBATE THE ISSUE

What Will Happen to Manufacturing in the United States?

The United States has the largest and most technologically powerful economy in the world, with a per capita GDP (gross domestic product) of $49,100. Most of the labour force (79.4 percent) is employed in the services sector, with 19.5 percent employed in manufacturing industries, and only 1.1 percent in the agricultural area. China, India, and the European Union have labour forces larger than the United States, which ranks fourth in the world. Data show that the U.S. has become much more of a service economy over the years, as manufacturing jobs have moved to Mexico (which was a frequent refrain of President Donald Trump). Will the U.S. continue to increase its service sector, and does this increase come at the cost of manufacturing and agriculture?

Source: U.S. Central Intelligence Agency, *World Factbook*, www.cia.gov, accessed March 3, 2014.

ANOTHER PERSPECTIVE

UN and International Law

The International Court of Justice (www.icj-cij.org/), located in The Hague (Netherlands), is one of the six major organs of the United Nations. The Court, in existence since 1946, serves as the successor to the Permanent Court of International Justice established by the League of Nations and derives its mandate from one of the statutes forming an integral part of the Charter of the United Nations. The Court has two functions: to render judgements on disputes submitted to it by States and to furnish advisory opinions on questions referred to it by authorized bodies.

Source: International Court of Justice, http://www.icj-cij.org/court.

Nevertheless, we are travelling down the road toward a future characterized by the increased globalization of markets and production. Modern firms are important actors in this drama, by their very actions fostering increased globalization. These firms, however, are merely responding in an efficient manner to changing conditions in their operating environment—as they should. In the next section, we look at the main drivers of globalization.

LO2   The Emergence of Global Institutions

As markets globalize and an increasing proportion of business activity transcends national borders, institutions need to help manage, regulate, and police the global marketplace and promote the establishment of multinational treaties to govern the global business system. During the past 50 years, a number of important global institutions have been created to help perform these functions. These institutions include the **General Agreement on Tariffs and Trade (GATT)** and its successor, the World Trade Organization (WTO); the International Monetary Fund (IMF) and its sister institution, the World Bank; and the United Nations (UN). All these institutions were created by voluntary agreement between individual nation-states, and their functions are enshrined in international treaties.

The **World Trade Organization** (like the GATT before it) is primarily responsible for policing the world trading system and making sure nation-states adhere to the rules laid down in trade treaties signed by WTO member-states. With the accession of Afghanistan in July 2016, there are 164 countries in the WTO. Currently, the accession process is underway for 21 nations to join WTO.

Over its entire history, and that of the GATT before it, the WTO has promoted lowering barriers to cross-border trade and investment. In doing so, the WTO has been the instrument of its member states, which have sought to create a more open global business system unencumbered by barriers to trade and investment between countries. Without an institution such as the WTO, it is unlikely that globalization would have proceeded as far as it has. However, as we shall see in this chapter and in Chapter 6 when we take a close look at the WTO, critics charge that the WTO is usurping the national sovereignty of individual nation-states.

The **International Monetary Fund** and the **World Bank** were both created in 1944 by 44 nations that met at Bretton Woods, New Hampshire. The task of the IMF was to maintain order in the international monetary system, and that of the World Bank was to promote economic development. In the over 70 years since their creation, both institutions have emerged as significant players in the global economy. The World Bank is the less controversial of the two sister institutions. It has focused on making low interest rate loans to cash-strapped governments in poor nations that wish to undertake significant infrastructure investments (such as building dams or road systems).

The IMF is often seen as the lender of last resort to nation-states whose economies are in turmoil and whose currencies are losing value against those of other nations. Repeatedly during the last decade, for example, the IMF has lent money to the governments of troubled states including Argentina, Indonesia, Mexico, Russia, South Korea, Thailand, and Turkey. More recently, the IMF has taken a very proactive role in helping countries to cope with some of the effects of the 2008–09 global financial crisis.

The IMF loans come with strings attached: in return for loans, the IMF requires nation-states to adopt specific policies aimed at returning their troubled economies to stability and growth. These "strings" have generated the most debate; some critics charge that the IMF's policy recommendations are often inappropriate, while others maintain that, like the WTO, by telling national governments what economic policies they must adopt, the IMF is usurping their sovereignty. We shall look at the debate over the role of the IMF in Chapter 10.

The **United Nations** was established October 24, 1945, by 51 countries committed to preserving peace through international cooperation and collective security. Today nearly every nation in the world belongs to the United Nations; membership now totals 193 countries. When states become members of the United Nations they agree to accept the obligations of the UN Charter, an international treaty that sets out basic principles of international relations. According to the charter, the UN has four purposes: to maintain international peace and security, to develop friendly relations among nations, to cooperate in solving international problems and in promoting respect for human rights, and to be a centre for harmonizing the actions of nations. Although the UN is perhaps best known for its peacekeeping role, one of the UN's central mandates is the promotion of higher standards of living, full employment, and conditions of economic and social progress and development—all issues that are central to the creation of a vibrant global economy. As much as 70 percent of the work of the UN system is devoted to accomplishing this mandate. To do so, the UN works closely with other international institutions such as the World Bank. Guiding the work is the belief that eradicating poverty and improving the well-being of people everywhere are necessary steps in creating conditions for lasting world peace.[9]

LO3 | Drivers of Globalization

Two macro factors seem to underlie the trend toward greater globalization.[10] The first is the decline in barriers to the free flow of goods, services, and capital that has occurred since the end of World War II. The second factor is technological change, particularly the dramatic developments in recent years in communication, information processing, and transportation technologies.

Declining Trade and Investment Barriers

During the 1920s and '30s, many nations erected formidable barriers to international trade and foreign direct investment. **International trade** occurs when a firm exports goods or services to consumers in another country. **Foreign direct investment** occurs when a firm invests resources in business activities outside its home country. Many of the barriers to international trade took the form of high tariffs on imports of manufactured goods. The typical aim of such tariffs was to protect domestic industries from foreign competition. One consequence, however, was "beggar thy neighbour" retaliatory trade policies with countries progressively raising trade barriers against each other. Ultimately, this depressed world demand and contributed to the Great Depression of the 1930s.

Having learned from this experience, after World War II the advanced industrial nations of the West committed themselves to removing barriers to the free flow of goods, services, and capital between nations.[11] This goal was enshrined in the General Agreement on Tariffs and Trade (GATT). Under the umbrella of GATT, eight rounds of negotiations among member states, which then numbered 148, have since worked to lower barriers to the free flow of goods and services. The most recent round of negotiations, known as the Uruguay Round, was completed in December 1993. The

Uruguay Round further reduced trade barriers; extended GATT to cover services as well as manufactured goods; provided enhanced protection for patents, trademarks, and copyrights; and established the World Trade Organization (WTO) to police the international trading system.[12] Average tariff rates for most countries have fallen significantly since 1950 and now stand at about 4 percent.

In late 2001, the WTO launched a new round of talks aimed at further liberalizing the global trade and investment framework. For this meeting, it picked the remote location of Doha in the Persian Gulf state of Qatar. At Doha, the member states of the WTO staked out an agenda. The talks were scheduled to last three years, but even after several historic packages being accepted by 2015, talks are stalled. The Doha agenda includes cutting tariffs on industrial goods, services, and agricultural products; phasing out subsidies to agricultural producers; reducing barriers to cross-border investment; and limiting the use of antidumping laws. If the Doha talks are ever completed, the biggest gain may come from discussion on agricultural products: average agricultural tariff rates are still about 40 percent, and rich nations spend some $300 billion a year in subsidies to support their farm sectors. The world's poorer nations have the most to gain from any reduction in agricultural tariffs and subsidies; such reforms would give them access to the markets of the developed world.[13]

In addition to reducing trade barriers, many countries have also been progressively removing restrictions to foreign direct investment. According to the United Nations, some 90 percent of the 2700 changes made worldwide between 1992 and 2009 in the laws governing foreign direct investment created a more favourable environment for FDI.[14]

Such trends facilitate both the globalization of markets and the globalization of production. Lowering barriers to international trade enables firms to view the world, rather than a single country, as their market. Lowering trade and investment barriers also allows firms to base production at the optimal location for that activity, serving the world market from that location. Thus, a firm might design a product in one country, produce component parts in two other countries, assemble the product in yet another country, and then export the finished product around the world.

Lowering trade barriers has facilitated the globalization of production. According to data from the World Trade Organization, the volume of world trade has grown consistently faster than the volume of world output since 1950.[15] By 2012 the volume of world trade was 32 times larger than it was in 1950, whereas the world economy was 8.9 times larger (these figures are in real terms, which adjust for inflation).

More firms are doing what Boeing does, to a degree, with its aircraft manufacturing: dispersing parts of its production process to different locations around the globe to drive down production costs and increase product quality. The economies of the world's nation-states are becoming more intertwined. As trade expands, nations are becoming increasingly dependent on each other for important goods and services.

It is worth noting the steep drop in world trade that occurred in 2008 and 2009. In 2009, the global economy contracted as the global financial crisis that began with problems in the U.S. subprime mortgage lending market reverberated around the world. The volume of merchandised trade dropped by 12.2 percent in 2009, the largest such decline since World War II. The main reason seems to have been a drop in global consumer demand, although an inability to finance international trade due to tight credit conditions may have also played a role. However, trade did rebound in 2010 with a 14.5 percent growth in volume. By 2012, the long-term trends still seemed firmly in place, the WTO forecast relatively slow growth in trade for a few years as the world grappled with the after-effects of the global financial crisis and the great recession it spawned, as well as the ongoing fiscal problems in many European nations and the

United States. After continued slow growth in 2016, WTO predicts trade recovery in 2017 if the right conditions, that is, policies, are in place.[16]

Evidence also suggests that foreign direct investment is playing an increasing role in the global economy as firms increase their cross-border investments. The average yearly outflow of FDI increased from $26 billion in 1975 to a record $2 trillion in 2007. However, FDI outflows did contract to $1.1 trillion in 2009 and 2010 in the wake of the global financial crisis. In general, over the past 40 years the flow of FDI has accelerated faster than the growth in world trade and world output. For example, between 1992 and 2010, the total flow of FDI from all countries increased around ninefold while world trade by value grew fourfold and world output by around 55 percent.[17] As a result of the strong FDI flow, by 2012 the global stock of FDI was about $23.6 trillion. At least 82 000 parent companies had 810 000 affiliates in foreign markets that collectively employed more than 77 million people abroad and generated value accounting for about 11 percent of global GDP. The foreign affiliates of multinationals had more than $32 trillion in global sales, higher than the value of global exports of goods and services, which stood at close to $20 trillion.[18]

The globalization of markets and production and the resulting growth of world trade, foreign direct investment, and imports all imply that firms are finding their home markets under attack from foreign competitors. This is true in China, where U.S. companies such as Procter & Gamble, Apple and General Motors are expanding their presence. It is also true in Canada, where Japanese and other foreign automobile firms have taken market share away from General Motors and Ford for many decades. And it is true in Europe, where the once-dominant Dutch company Philips has seen its market share in the consumer electronics industry taken by Japan's Panasonic and Sony, and by Korea's Samsung and LG. The growing integration of the world economy into a single, huge marketplace is increasing the intensity of competition in a range of manufacturing and service industries.

Having said all this, declining trade barriers can't be taken for granted. As we shall see in the following chapters, demands for "protection" from foreign competitors are still often heard in countries around the world, including Canada and the United States. Although a return to the restrictive trade policies of the 1920s and '30s is unlikely, it is not clear whether the political majority in the industrialized world favours further reductions in trade barriers. If trade barriers decline no further, at least for the time being, a temporary limit may have been reached in the globalization of both markets and production.

ANOTHER PERSPECTIVE

How Important is the EU Among the Group of Twenty (G20)?

There have been nine G20 Leaders' Summits since they started in 2008. The Group of Twenty includes 19 prominent countries and the European Union. At the "Leaders' Level," following leadership by the United States, United Kingdom, Canada, South Korea, and France from 2008 to 2011, the more recent leadership has included three emerging markets (Mexico in 2012; Russia in 2013; Turkey in 2015) in a four-year span (with Australia the leader in 2014). G20 members represent about 85 percent of global GDP, 80 percent of global trade, and about two-thirds of the world's population. Now, is it really right for the G20 to include 19 countries and all of the EU countries, or should the EU countries be selected individually?

Source: https://www.g20.org/Webs/G20/EN/G20/Participants/participants_node.html

The Role of Technological Change

Lowering trade barriers made globalization of markets and production a theoretical possibility. Technological change has made it a tangible reality. Since the end of World War II, the world has seen major advances in communication, information processing, and transportation technology, including the explosive emergence of the Internet and World Wide Web. Telecommunications is creating a global audience. Transportation is creating a global village. From Buenos Aires to Boston, and from Birmingham to Beijing, people are watching MTV, they're wearing blue jeans, and they're listening to iPods as they commute to work.

The net result of all of this change is a "shrinking globe"—the letter that may have taken two weeks to arrive in a distant location has been replaced by an email message that is received instantaneously, and which encourages a speedy response.

MICROPROCESSORS AND TELECOMMUNICATIONS

Perhaps the single most important innovation has been development of the microprocessor, which enabled the explosive growth of high-power, low-cost computing, vastly increasing the amount of information that can be processed by individuals and firms. The microprocessor also underlies many recent advances in telecommunications technology. Over the past 30 years, global communications have been revolutionized by developments in satellite, optical fibre, and wireless technologies, and now the Internet and the World Wide Web. These technologies rely on the microprocessor to encode, transmit, and decode the vast amount of information that flows along these electronic highways. The cost of microprocessors continues to fall, while their power increases (a phenomenon known as **Moore's Law**, which originally predicted that the number of transistors on a computer chip would double every 24 months).[19] As this happens, the costs of global communications plummet, which lowers the costs of coordinating and controlling a global organization. Thus, between 1930 and 1990, the cost of a three-minute phone call between New York and London fell from $244.65 to $3.32 in inflation-adjusted dollars.[20] By 1998, it had plunged to just 36 cents for consumers, and much lower rates were available for businesses.[21] Indeed, by using the Internet and services such as Skype, the cost of an international phone call has rapidly falling toward zero.

THE INTERNET

The explosive growth of the Internet since 1994 when the first Web browser was introduced is the latest expression of this development. In 1990, fewer than 1 million users were connected to the Internet. By 1995, the figure had risen to 50 million. By 2016 the estimates are at 4 billion people. The WWW has developed into the information backbone of the global economy. In the United States alone, e-commerce retail sales reached nearly $365 billion in 2012, with a forecast growth pointing to nearly $500 billion by

Before the advent of containerization, it could take several days and several hundred longshoremen to unload a ship and reload goods onto trucks and trains. © *Glow Images/SuperStock*

2018 (up from almost nothing in 1998).[22] Viewed globally, the Internet is emerging as an equalizer. It rolls back some of the constraints of location, scale, and time zones.[23] The Internet makes it much easier for buyers and sellers to find each other, wherever they may be located and whatever their size. It allows businesses, both small and large, to expand their global presence at a lower cost than ever before. It enables enterprises to coordinate and control a globally dispersed production system in a way that was not possible 25 years ago.

TRANSPORTATION TECHNOLOGY

In addition to developments in communication technology, several major innovations in transportation technology have occurred since World War II. In economic terms, the most important are probably the development of commercial jet aircraft and superfreighters and the introduction of containerization, which simplifies transshipment from one mode of transport to another. The advent of commercial jet travel, by reducing the time needed to get from one location to another, has effectively shrunk the globe. In terms of travel time, Toronto is now closer to Tokyo than it was to Montreal in the Colonial days.

Containerization has revolutionized the transportation business, significantly lowering the costs of shipping goods over long distances. Before the advent of containerization, moving goods from one mode of transport to another was very labour intensive, lengthy, and costly. It could take days and several hundred longshoremen to unload a ship and reload goods onto trucks and trains. With the advent of widespread containerization in the 1970s and 1980s, the whole process can be executed by a handful of longshoremen in a couple of days. Since 1980, the world's containership fleet has more than quadrupled, reflecting in part the growing volume of international trade and in part the switch to this mode of transportation.[24]

THE GLOBALIZATION OF PRODUCTION

As transportation costs associated with the globalization of production declined, dispersal of production to geographically widespread locations became more economical. As a result of the technological innovations discussed above, the real costs of information processing and communication have fallen dramatically in the past two decades. These developments make it possible for a firm to create and then manage a globally dispersed production system, further facilitating the globalization of production.

A worldwide communications network has become essential for many international businesses. For example, Dell uses the Internet to coordinate and control a globally dispersed production system to such an extent that it holds only three days' worth of inventory at its assembly locations. Dell's Internet-based system records orders for computer equipment as they are submitted by customers via the company's Web site, then immediately transmits the resulting orders for components to various suppliers around the world, which have a real-time look at Dell's order flow and can adjust their production schedules accordingly. Given the low cost of airfreight, Dell can use air transportation to speed up the delivery of critical components to meet unanticipated demand shifts without delaying the shipment of final product to consumers. Dell has also used modern communications technology to outsource its customer service operations to India. When U.S. customers call Dell with a service inquiry, they are routed to Bangalore in India, where English-speaking service personnel handle the call.

ANOTHER PERSPECTIVE

Small Companies Benefit from Globalization, Too

Maddie's Workshop is a kitchen-table start-up that develops original apps for kids, with a child's perspective built into every step from start to finish. The company's first app evolved over the course of almost three years from the initial concept to the marketing of the final product: MaddieDreams. The app, produced for the iPad, offers a unique series of meditations written for children, presented in a child's voice.

Maddie's Workshop began as a mother-daughter hobby, sparked by their interests in technology, yoga, and meditation, and an outlook that one should always be a beginner at something. Together they wrote and recorded the meditations; designed the icons and images; developed the storyboards; taught themselves how to use graphic design, audio, video and other software; learned about coding and building the app; created a Web site, blog, and social media sites; and lastly, took turns encouraging each other to get it done. All this part-time, and before Maddie was 8!

Today, Maddie's Workshop is a thriving, creative small business that is a leader in innovative educational products. Customers from across Canada, England, and Australia have shared their enthusiasm for MaddieDreams and are keenly awaiting future products. MaddieDreams is available on the AppStore/MaddieDreams or through MaddiesWorkshop.com.

Source: Interview with Lisa Orchard, December 2016.

The development of commercial jet aircraft has also helped knit together the worldwide operations of many international businesses. Using jet travel, a North American manager need spend a day at most travelling to her firm's European or Asian operations. This enables her to oversee a globally dispersed production system.

THE GLOBALIZATION OF MARKETS

In addition to the globalization of production, technological innovations have also facilitated the globalization of markets. As noted above, low-cost transportation has made it more economical to ship products around the world, thereby helping to create global markets. Low-cost global communications networks such as the World Wide Web are helping to create electronic global marketplaces. In addition, low-cost jet travel has resulted in the mass movement of people between countries. This has reduced the cultural distance between countries and is bringing about some convergence of consumer tastes and preferences. At the same time, global communication networks and global media are creating a worldwide culture. U.S. television networks such as CNN, MTV, and HBO are now received in many countries, and Hollywood films are shown the world over. In any society, the media are primary conveyors of culture; as global media develop we must expect the evolution of something akin to a global culture. A logical result of this evolution is the emergence of global markets for consumer products. The first signs of this are already apparent. It is now as easy to find a McDonald's restaurant in Tokyo as it is in Toronto, to buy an Apple iPad in Rio as it is in Berlin, or to buy Lululemon yoga apparel in Sydney as it is in Vancouver.

Despite these trends, we must be careful not to over-emphasize their importance. While modern communication and transportation technologies are ushering in the "global village," very significant national differences remain in culture, consumer preferences, and business practices. A firm that ignores differences between countries does so at its peril. We shall stress this point repeatedly throughout this book and elaborate on it in later chapters.

MANAGEMENT FOCUS

Vizio and the Market for Flat-Panel TVs

Operating sophisticated tooling in environments that must be kept absolutely clean, fabrication centres in South Korea, Taiwan, and Japan produce sheets of glass twice as large as king-size beds to exacting specifications. From there, the glass panels travel to Mexican plants located alongside the U.S. border. There, they are cut to size, combined with electronic components shipped in from Asia and the United States, assembled into finished flat-panel TVs, and loaded onto trucks bound for retail stores in the United States, where consumers spend more than $35 billion a year on flat-panel TVs.

The underlying technology for flat-panel displays was invented in the United States in the late 1960s by RCA. But after RCA and rivals Westinghouse and Xerox opted not to pursue the technology, the Japanese company Sharp made aggressive investments in flat-panel displays. By the early 1990s, Sharp was selling the first flat-panel screens. But as the Japanese economy plunged into a decade-long recession, investment leadership shifted to South Korean companies such as Samsung. Then the 1997 Asian crisis hit Korea hard, and Taiwanese companies seized leadership. Today, Chinese companies are starting to elbow their way into the flat-panel display manufacturing business.

As production for flat-panel displays migrates its way around the globe to low-cost locations, there are clear winners and losers. U.S. consumers have benefited from the falling prices of flat-panel TVs and are snapping them up. Efficient manufacturers have taken advantage of globally dispersed supply chains to make and sell low-cost, high-quality, flat-panel TVs. Foremost among these has been the California-based company Vizio, founded by a Taiwanese immigrant. In just eight years, sales of Vizio flat-panel TVs ballooned from nothing to more than $2.5 billion in 2010. By late 2011, the company was the second largest provider to the U.S. market with a 15.4 percent share. Vizio, however, has fewer than 170 employees. These focus on final product design, sales, and customer service. Vizio outsources most of its engineering work, all of its manufacturing, and much of its logistics. For each of its models, Vizio assembles a team of supplier partners strung across the globe. Its 42-inch flat-panel TV, for example, contains a panel from South Korea, electronic components from China, and processors from the United States, and is assembled in Mexico. Vizio's managers continually scour the globe for the cheapest manufacturers of flat-panel displays and electronic components. They sell most of their TVs to large discount retailers such as Costco and Sam's Club. Good order visibility from retailers, coupled with tight management of global logistics, allows Vizio to turn over its inventory every three weeks, twice as fast as many of its competitors, which allows major cost savings in a business where prices are falling continually.

Questions

1. Who benefits when a company such as Vizio outsources its manufacturing and engineering work? Who is negatively affected by this?
2. Are companies with such global webs of linkages only found in the manufacturing sector? Can you give any such examples?

Sources: D. J. Lynch, "Flat Panel TVs Display Effects of Globalization," *USA Today,* May 8, 2007, pp. 1B, 2B; P. Engardio and E. Woyke, "Flat Panels, Thin Margins," *BusinessWeek,* February 26, 2007, p. 50; B. Womack, "Flat TV Seller Vizio Hits $600 Million in Sales, Growing," *Orange County Business Journal,* September 4, 2007, pp. 1, 64; E. Taub, "Vizio's Flat Panel Display Sales Are Anything But Flat," *New York Times Online,* May 12, 2009; and Greg Tarr, "HIS: Samsung Dusts Vizio in Q4 LCD TV Share in the U.S.," *This Week in Consumer Electronics,* April 12, 2012, p. 12.

LO4 The Changing Demographics of the Global Economy

Hand in hand with the trend toward globalization over the past 50 years has been a fairly dramatic change in the demographics of the global economy. As late as the 1960s, four stylized facts described the demographics of the global economy. The first was U.S. dominance in the world economy and world trade picture. The second was U.S. dominance in world foreign direct investment. Related to this, the third fact was the dominance of large, multinational U.S. firms on the international business scene. The fourth was that roughly half the globe—the centrally planned economies of the Communist world—was off-limits to Western international businesses. As will be explained below, all four of these qualities either have changed or are now changing rapidly.

The Changing World Output and World Trade Picture

In the early 1960s, the United States was the world's dominant industrial power by far. In 1960 the United States accounted for 38.3 percent of world output, measured by gross domestic product (GDP). By 2010, the United States accounted for 23.1 percent of world output, still the world's largest industrial power but down significantly in relative size (see Table 1.1). Nor was the United States the only developed nation to see its relative standing slip. The same occurred to Germany, France, and the United Kingdom, all nations that were among the first to industrialize. This change in the U.S. position was not an absolute decline, because the U.S. economy grew significantly between 1960 and 2010 (the economies of Germany, France, and the United Kingdom also grew during this time), even if its share of world exports diminished to 8.7 percent in 2012. Rather, it was a relative decline, reflecting the faster economic growth of several other economies, particularly in Asia. For example, as can be seen from Table 1.1, from 1960 to 2012, China's share of world output increased from a trivial amount to 10.8 percent, making it the world's second largest economy. In 2012 its share of world exports was 11.5 percent. Other countries that markedly increased their share of world output included Japan, Thailand, Malaysia, Taiwan, and South Korea.

TABLE 1.1	**Historical Changing World Output and Trade**		
Country	**Share of World Output, 1960 (%)**	**Share of World Output 2012 (%)**	**Share of World Exports, 2012 (%)**
United States	38.3%	23.1%	8.7%
Germany	8.7	5.1	7.9
France	4.6	3.8	3.2
Italy	3.0	2.9	2.8
United Kingdom	5.3	3.4	2.6
Canada	3.0	2.5	2.5
Japan	3.3	8.5	4.6
China	NA	10.8	11.5

Sources: Output data from World Bank database, February 2014. Trade data from WTO Statistical Database, 2014.

By the end of the 1980s, the U.S. position as the world's leading exporter was threatened. Over the past 40 years, U.S. dominance in export markets has waned as Japan, Germany, and a number of newly industrialized countries such as South Korea and China have taken a larger share of world exports. During the 1960s, the United States routinely accounted for 20 percent of world exports of manufactured goods. But as Table 1.1 shows, the U.S. share of world exports of goods and services had slipped to 8.7 percent by 2012, behind that of China.

As emerging economies such as China, India, and Brazil continue to grow, a further relative decline in the share of world output and world exports accounted for by the United States and other long-established developed nations seems likely. By itself, this is not bad. The relative decline of the United States reflects the growing economic development and industrialization of the world economy, as opposed to any absolute decline in the health of the U.S. economy.

Canada has historically been the top trading partner of the United States, and the United States has been the top trading partner of Canada. Table 1.2 shows that this is still the case when it comes to exports, though Mexico and China have been growing at a faster rate. China is now the number two or number three trading partner to Canada.

Most forecasts now predict a rapid rise in the share of world output accounted for by developing nations such as China, India, Indonesia, Thailand, South Korea, Mexico, and Brazil, and a commensurate decline in the share enjoyed by rich industrialized countries such as Great Britain, Germany, Japan, and the United States. The World Bank, for example, has estimated that if current trends continue, by 2020 the Chinese economy could be larger than that of the United States, while the economy of India will approach that of Germany. The World Bank also estimates that today's developing nations may account for more than 60 percent of world economic activity by 2020, while today's rich nations, which currently account for over 55 percent of world economic activity, may account for only about 38 percent by 2020.[25] Forecasts are not always correct, but these suggest that a shift in the economic geography of the world is now under way, although the magnitude of that shift is still not totally evident. For international businesses, the implications of this changing economic geography are

TABLE 1.2	Canadian Exports To Major Trading Partners	
Agricultural Products	**Year**	**US$ (billion)**
United States	2014	23 705
China	2014	5114
Japan	2014	3791
European Union	2014	2914
Mexico	2014	1895
Non-agricultural Products		
United States	2014	307 643
European Union	2014	29 810
China	2014	15 977
Mexico	2014	7964
Japan	2014	7388

Source: World Trade Organization (WTO), Tariff Profile, Canada, http://stat.wto.org/TariffProfile/WSDBTariffPFView.aspx?Language=E&Country=CA.

clear: many of tomorrow's economic opportunities may be found in the developing nations of the world, and many of tomorrow's most-capable competitors will probably also emerge from these regions.

The Changing Foreign Direct Investment Picture

Reflecting the dominance of the United States in the global economy, U.S. firms accounted for 66.3 percent of worldwide foreign direct investment flows in the 1960s. British firms were second, accounting for 10.5 percent, while Japanese firms were a distant eighth, with only 2 percent. The dominance of U.S. firms was so great that books were written about the economic threat posed to Europe by U.S. corporations.[26] Several European governments, most notably that of France, talked of limiting inward investment by U.S. firms.

However, as the barriers to the free flow of goods, services, and capital fell, and as other countries increased their shares of world output, non-U.S. firms increasingly began to invest across national borders. The motivation for much of this foreign direct investment by non-U.S. firms was the desire to disperse production activities to optimal locations and to build a direct presence in major foreign markets. Thus, beginning in the 1970s, European and Japanese firms began to shift labour-intensive manufacturing operations from their home markets to developing nations where labour costs were lower. In addition, many Japanese firms invested in North America and Europe—often as a hedge against unfavourable currency movements and the possible imposition of trade barriers. For example, Toyota, the Japanese automobile company, rapidly increased its investment in automobile production facilities in the United States and Great Britain during the late 1980s and early 1990s. Toyota executives believed that an increasingly strong Japanese yen would price Japanese automobile exports out of foreign markets; therefore, production in the most important foreign markets, as opposed to exports from Japan, made sense. Toyota also undertook these investments to head off growing political pressures in the United States and Europe to restrict Japanese automobile exports into those markets. However, massive Toyota recalls on a wide cross-section of Toyota vehicles, based on sticking gas pedals and an array of other problems, raised concerns over the manufacturer's longstanding reputation as a quality producer of automobiles.

Table 1.3 illustrates variability of FDI in the recent years due to global economic trends. FDI fell globally in 2008 and 2009, turning positive again in 2010. The year 2011 saw an all time high for global FDI, which has declined since then. Among developing nations, the largest recipient of foreign direct investment has been China, which between 2004 and 2012 received between $60 billion to $100 billion a year in inflows, followed by Brazil, Mexico, and India. As we shall see later in this book, the sustained flow of foreign investment into developing nations is an important stimulus for economic growth in those countries, which bodes well for the future of countries such as China, Mexico, and Brazil—all leading beneficiaries of this trend.

TABLE 1.3	Growth Rates of FDI								
FDI	**2008**	**09**	**10**	**11**	**12**	**13**	**14**	**15**	**2016**
FDI Change	−20.4	−20.4	11.9	17.7	−10.3	4.6	−16.3	11.4	8.4

Source: United Nations Conference on Trade and Development (UNCTAD), *World Investment Report 2015: Reforming International Investment Governance*, http://unctad.org/en/PublicationsLibrary/wir2015_en.pdf, Table 1.1, p. 2.

The Changing Nature of the Multinational Enterprise

A **multinational enterprise (MNE)** is any business that has productive activities in two or more countries. Since the 1960s, there have been two notable trends in the demographics of the multinational enterprise: (1) the rise of non-U.S. multinationals, particularly Japanese multinationals, and (2) the growth of mini-multinationals.

NON-U.S. MULTINATIONALS

In the 1960s, global business activity was dominated by large U.S. multinational corporations. With U.S. firms accounting for about two-thirds of foreign direct investment during the 1960s, one would expect most multinationals to be U.S. enterprises. The second largest source country was the United Kingdom, with 18.8 percent of the largest multinationals. Japan accounted for only 3.5 percent of the world's largest multinationals at the time.[27] The large number of U.S. multinationals reflected U.S. economic dominance in the three decades after World War II, while the large number of British multinationals reflected that country's industrial dominance in the early decades of the twentieth century. The globalization of the world economy together with Japan's rise to the top rank of economic powers has resulted in a relative decline in the dominance of U.S. (and, to a lesser extent, British) firms in the global marketplace. If we look at smaller firms, we see significant growth in the number of multinationals from developing economies.

THE RISE OF MINI-MULTINATIONALS

Another trend in international business has been the growth of medium-sized and small multinationals (mini-multinationals). When people think of international businesses, they tend to think of firms such as General Electric, Volkswagen Group, Sony Corporation, Bombardier, Proctor & Gamble, Samsung, Honda Motor Co. Ltd., ExxonMobil Corporation, and Anheuser Busch Inbev SA—large, complex multinational corporations with operations that span the globe. Although it is certainly true that most international trade and investment is still conducted by large firms, it is also true that many medium-sized and small businesses are becoming increasingly involved in

---

ANOTHER PERSPECTIVE

Free the World

The index published by Canada's Fraser Institute in *Economic Freedom of the World* measures the degree to which the policies and institutions of countries are supportive of economic freedom. The cornerstones of economic freedom are personal choice, voluntary exchange, freedom to compete, and security of privately owned property. Forty-two data points are used to construct a summary index and to measure the degree of economic freedom. According to their 2016 index, Hong Kong retains the highest rating for economic freedom, 9.03 out of 10. The other nations among the top 5 are: Singapore (8.71); New Zealand (8.35); Switzerland (8.25); and Canada (7.98). The world's largest economy, the United States, has suffered one of the largest declines in economic freedom over the past 10 years, pushing it into 16th place. Much of this decline is a result of higher government spending and borrowing and lower scores for the legal structure and property rights components.

Source: The Fraser Institute, Economic Freedom Ranking, http://www.freetheworld.com/2016/economic-freedom-of-the-world-2016.pdf

international trade and investment. For example, consider International Road Dynamics (IRD) of Saskatoon, Saskatchewan. IRD designs automated truck weigh stations, traffic data collection, and toll systems. In the 1990s the company generated 90 percent of its business from the United States. Today, in addition to the United States they sell to Saudi Arabia, Pakistan, India, China, Hong Kong, Indonesia, Korea, Malaysia, Brazil, Colombia, Chile, Ecuador, Honduras, Peru, Uruguay, Mexico and other countries. Although a tiny player, they have made an increasingly larger inroad internationally.[28]

Or consider the case of Iceculture Inc., based in Hensall, Ontario. This innovative private company of 40 employees transforms blocks of ice into works of art. They export to Britain, Europe, South Africa, Iceland, Norway, Japan, United States, and Australia. In all, 27 countries have used Iceculture's ice products. They designed and created the Pontiac Ice Maze for the 2005 Canadian Auto Show. That project utilized 2000 blocks of ice and holds a place in the Guinness Book of World Records as the most original ice design at a high profile venue.[29] The company notes on its Web site (www.iceculture.com/about-us) "Hensall, Ontario, is not exactly the hub of industry in North America, but time after time, customers contact this progressive company based in a small town in the heart of southwestern Ontario."

Finally, look at Carmanah Technologies Inc. of Victoria, B.C., beginning as a manufacturer of solar-powered light-emitting LED lighting fixtures utilizing a patented, proprietary solar-powered technology. The company now operates in three areas: Signals (from airports to marine navigation), Illumination (the products that started the company), and Power (including solar grid connection systems) with clients around the world. In November of 2016, the company expanded by buying a marine operations firm in Estonia. Carmanah is a publicly traded company, with common shares listed on the Toronto Stock Exchange under the symbol CMH.

The Changing World Order

Between 1989 and 1991 a series of remarkable democratic revolutions swept the Communist world. For reasons that are explored in more detail in Chapter 2, in country after country throughout Eastern Europe and eventually in the Soviet Union itself, Communist governments collapsed like the shells of rotten eggs. The Soviet Union is now ancient history, having been replaced by 15 independent republics. Czechoslovakia divided itself into two states, while Yugoslavia dissolved into a bloody civil war among its five successor states. Its new republics are working toward rebuilding peace and prosperity.

Many of the former Communist nations of Europe and Asia seem to share a commitment to democratic politics and free market economics. If this continues, the opportunities for international businesses may be enormous. For nearly half a century these countries were essentially closed to Western international businesses. Now they present a host of export and investment opportunities. Just how this will play out over the next 10 to 20 years is difficult to say. The economies of most of the former Communist states are in very poor condition, and their continued commitment to democracy and free market economics cannot be taken for granted. Disturbing signs of growing unrest and totalitarian tendencies continue to be seen in many Eastern European and central Asian states, including Russia which has shown signs of shifting back to greater state involvement in the economy as well as authoritarian government. Thus, the risks involved in doing business in such countries are very high, but then, so may be the returns.

In addition to these changes, quieter revolutions have been occurring in China, other states in Southeast Asia, and Latin America. The implications for international businesses may be just as profound as the collapse of communism in Eastern Europe. China suppressed its own pro-democracy movement in the bloody Tiananmen Square massacre of 1989. Despite this, China continues to move progressively toward greater free-market reforms. If what is occurring in China continues for two more decades, China may move from third-world to industrial superpower status even more rapidly than Japan did. If China's GDP per capita grows by an average of 6 to 7 percent, which is slower than the 8 to 10 percent growth rate achieved during the past decade, then by 2020 this nation of 1.3 billion people could boast an average income per capita of about $13 000, roughly equivalent to that of Spain's today.

However Figure 1.1 shows that the generally upward path of exports and imports in developing and emerging countries is not a straight line. After several periods where growth was greater than that found in developed countries, and for the world overall, exports have been flat recently, and imports have actually declined. While the general path for developing and emerging countries is positive for the foreseeable future, none of these countries is immune to local and global economic slowdowns.

The potential consequences for international business are enormous. On the one hand, China represents a huge and largely untapped market. Reflecting this, between 1983 and 2013, annual foreign direct investment in China increased from less than $2 billion to $100 billion annually.[30] On the other hand, China's new firms are proving to be very capable competitors, and they could take global market share away from Western and Japanese enterprises (see the Management Focus on China's Hisense). Thus, the changes in China are creating both opportunities and threats for established international businesses.

ANOTHER PERSPECTIVE

Globalization and Complexity

Another way to understand globalization is to think of it as the result of our increasing ability to deal with complexity. Some cultures such as the Chinese, Japanese, and Middle Eastern (see Chapter 3 for high context and high power distance) are inclined to work well with complexity. Will these cultural traits serve as a comparative advantage as globalization proceeds?

As for Latin America, both democracy and free market reforms have been evident there too. For decades, most Latin American countries were ruled by dictators, many of whom seemed to view Western international businesses as instruments of imperialist domination. Accordingly, they restricted direct investment by foreign firms. In addition, the poorly managed economies of Latin America were characterized by low growth, high debt, and hyperinflation—all of which discouraged investment by international businesses. In the past two decades, much of this has changed. Throughout most of Latin America, debt and inflation are down, governments have sold state-owned enterprises to private investors, foreign investment is welcomed, and the region's economies have expanded. Brazil, Mexico, and Chile have led the way. These changes have increased the attractiveness of Latin America, both as a market for exports and as a site for foreign direct investment. At the same time, given the long history of economic mismanagement in Latin America, there is no guarantee that these favourable trends will continue. Indeed, Bolivia, Ecuador, and most notably Venezuela have seen shifts back toward

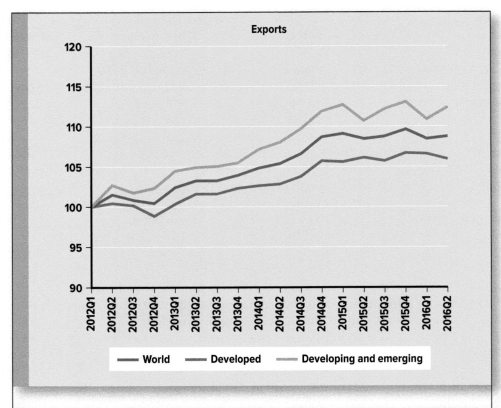

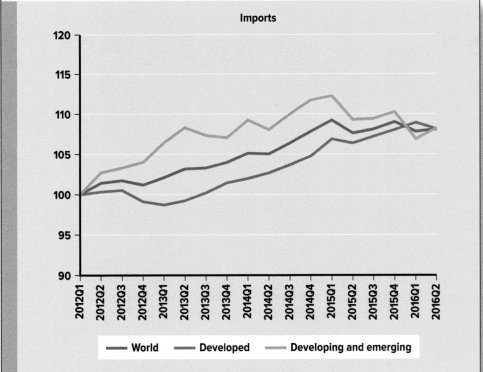

FIGURE 1.1 VOLUME OF MERCHANDISE EXPORTS AND IMPORTS BY LEVEL OF DEVELOPMENT, 2012Q1-2016Q2; SEASONALLY ADJUSTED VOLUME INDICES, 2012Q1=100

Source: © World Trade Organization (WTO) 2017, https://www.wto.org/english/news_e/pres16_e/pr779_e.htm, chart 2

MANAGEMENT FOCUS

China's Hisense—An Emerging Multinational

Hisense is rapidly emerging as one of China's leading multinationals. Like many other Chinese corporations, Hisense traces its origins back to a state-owned manufacturer, in this case Qingdao No. 2 Radio Factory, which was established in 1969 with just 10 employees. In the 1970s, the state-owned factory diversified into the manufacture of TV sets; by the 1980s, it was one of China's leading manufacturers of color TVs, making sets designed by Matsushita under license. In 1992, a 35-year-old engineer named Zhou Houjian was appointed head of the enterprise. In 1994, the shackles of state ownership were relaxed when the Hisense Company Ltd. was established with Zhou as CEO (he is now chairman of the board).

Under Zhou's leadership, Hisense entered a period of rapid growth, product diversification, and global expansion. By 2013, the company had sales of more than $15 billion and had emerged as one of China's premier makers of TV sets, air conditioners, refrigerators, personal computers, and telecommunications equipment. Hisense sold more than 10 million TV sets, 3 million air conditioners, 4 million CDMA wireless phones, 6 million refrigerators, and 1 million personal computers. International sales accounted for more than 15 percent of total revenue. The company had established overseas manufacturing subsidiaries in Algeria, Hungary, Iran, Pakistan, and South Africa and was growing rapidly in developing markets, where it was taking share away from long-established consumer electronics and appliance makers.

Hisense's ambitions are grand. It seeks to become a global enterprise with a world-class consumer brand. Although it is without question a low-cost manufacturer, Hisense believes its core strength is in rapid product innovation. The company believes that the only way to gain leadership in the highly competitive markets in which it competes is to continuously launch advanced, high-quality, and competitively priced products.

To this end, Hisense established its first R&D centre in China in the mid-1990s. This was followed by a South African R&D center in 1997 and a European R&D centre in 2007. The company also has plans for an R&D centre in the United States. By 2008, these R&D centres filed for more than 600 patents.

Hisense's technological prowess is evident in its digital TV business. It introduced set-top boxes in 1999, making it possible to browse the Internet from a TV. In 2002, Hisense introduced its first interactive digital TV set, and in 2005 it developed China's first core digital processing chip for digital TVs, breaking the country's reliance on foreign chip makers for this core technology. In 2006, Hisense launched an innovative line of multimedia TV sets that integrated digital high-definition technology, network technology, and flat-panel displays.

Sources: Harold L. Sirkin, "Someone May Be Gaining on Us," *Barron's*, February 5, 2007, p. 53; "Hisense Plans to Grab More International Sales," *Sino Cast China IT Watch*, November 30, 2006; "Hisense's Wonder Chip," *Financial Times Information Limited—Asian Intelligence Wire*, October 30, 2006; and Hisense's Web site, www.hisense.com.

Questions

1. China, like much of the world, is in the middle of an economic slowdown. What steps can a business take to lessen the impacts of slowdowns/recessions?
2. The electronics business is very competitive. What can Hisense do to remain competitive?

greater state involvement in industry in the past few years, and foreign investment is now less welcome than it was during the 1990s. In these nations, the government has seized control of oil and gas fields from foreign investors and has limited the rights of foreign energy companies to extract oil and gas from their nations. Thus, as in the case of Eastern Europe, substantial opportunities are accompanied by substantial risks.

The Global Economy of the Twenty-First Century

The last quarter century has seen rapid changes in the global economy. Barriers to the free flow of goods, services, and capital have been coming down. The volume of cross-border trade and investment has been growing more rapidly than global output, indicating that national economies are becoming more closely integrated into a single, interdependent, global economic system. As their economies advance, more nations are joining the ranks of the developed world. A generation ago, South Korea and Taiwan were viewed as second-tier developing nations. Now they boast large economies and their firms are major players in many global industries from shipbuilding and steel to electronics and chemicals. The move toward a global economy has been further strengthened by the widespread adoption of liberal economic policies by countries that for two generations or more were firmly opposed to them. Thus, following the normative prescriptions of liberal economic ideology, in country after country we are seeing privatization of state-owned businesses, widespread deregulation, opening markets to more competition, and increased commitment to removing barriers to cross-border trade and investment. This suggests that over the next few decades, countries such as the Czech Republic, Poland, Brazil, China, and South Africa may build powerful market-oriented economies. In short, current trends indicate that the world is moving rapidly toward an economic system that is more favourable for the practice of international business.

On the other hand, it is always hazardous to take established trends and use them to predict the future. The world may be moving toward a more global economic system, but globalization is not inevitable. Countries may pull back from the recent commitment to liberal economic ideology if their experiences do not match their expectations. There are signs, for example, of a retreat from liberal economic ideology in Russia. Russia has experienced considerable economic pain as it tries to shift from a centrally planned economy to a market economy. If Russia's hesitation were to become more permanent and widespread, the liberal vision of a more prosperous global economy based on free market principles might not come to pass as quickly as many hope. Clearly, this would be a tougher world for international businesses to compete in.

Moreover, greater globalization brings with it risks of its own. This was starkly demonstrated in 1997 and 1998 when a financial crisis in Thailand spread first to other East Asian nations and then in 1998 to Russia and Brazil. Ultimately the crisis threatened to plunge the economies of the developed world, including the United States, into a recession. More recently, the 2008-09 recession, which arguably began in the United States with very aggressive mortgage and other lending to those who could not afford it, spread throughout most of the world. We explore the causes and consequences of this and other similar global financial crises in Chapters 9 and 10. For now it is simply worth noting that even from a purely economic perspective, globalization is not all good. The opportunities for doing business in a global economy may be significantly enhanced, but as we saw in 1997–98, the risks associated with global financial contagion are also greater. Still, as explained later in this book, there are ways for firms to exploit the opportunities associated with globalization, while at the same time reducing the risks through appropriate hedging strategies.

LO5 | The Globalization Debate

Is the shift toward a more integrated and interdependent global economy a good thing? Many influential economists, politicians, and business leaders seem to think so. They argue that falling barriers to international trade and investment are the twin engines

Protestors make themselves known at the June 2010 Toronto G20 summit session. In an unprecedented and much-criticized crowd containment strategy by law enforcement officers, over 1000 individuals were locked up for periods of a few hours to a few months. Both law enforcement officers and pockets of protestors who incited the violence by torching cars met in a showdown reminiscent of protests in countries ruled by dictatorships. Was this behaviour necessary and did these protesting initiatives result in any changes? © *simplequiet/iStockphoto.com*

driving the global economy toward greater prosperity. They say increased international trade and cross-border investment will result in lower prices for goods and services. They believe that globalization stimulates economic growth, raises the incomes of consumers, and helps to create jobs in all countries that participate in the global trading system. However, despite the existence of a compelling body of theory and evidence, globalization has its critics.[31] Some of these critics have become increasingly vocal and active, taking to the streets to demonstrate their opposition to globalization, while others have risen to hold political office both in the United States and elsewhere.

Antiglobalization Protests

Street demonstrations against globalization date to 1999, when more than 40 000 protesters blocked the streets of Seattle in an attempt to shut down a World Trade Organization meeting being held in the city. The demonstrators were protesting against a wide range of issues, including job losses in industries under attack from foreign competitors, downward pressure on the wage rates of unskilled workers, environmental degradation, and the cultural imperialism of global media and multinational enterprises, which was seen as being dominated by what some protesters called the "culturally impoverished" interests and values of the United States. All these ills, the demonstrators claimed, could be laid at the feet of globalization. Meanwhile, the World Trade Organization meeting failed to reach agreement, and although the protests outside the meeting halls had little to do with that failure, the impression took hold that the demonstrators had derailed the meetings.

Emboldened by the experience in Seattle, antiglobalization protesters have turned up at almost every major meeting of a global institution. (See the accompanying Country Focus for details.)

COUNTRY FOCUS

Antiglobalization Protests in France

If someone was only watching North American television during the 2016 U.S. presidential campaign, they might think that calls to "rip up trade agreements" and promote "fair trade, not free trade" are something new, or a feeling only expressed in the United States. However there is a long and global history of actions against globalization.

One night in August 1999, ten men, under the leadership of local sheep farmer and rural activist José Bové, crept into the town of Millau in central France and vandalized a McDonald's restaurant under construction, causing an estimated $150 000 worth of damage. These were no ordinary vandals, however, at least according to their supporters, for the "symbolic dismantling" of the McDonald's outlet had noble aims, or so it was claimed. The attack was initially presented as a protest against unfair American trade policies. The European Union had banned imports of hormone-treated beef from the United States, primarily because of fears that hormone-treated beef might lead to health problems (although EU scientists had concluded there was no evidence of this). After a careful review, the World Trade Organization stated the EU ban was not allowed under trading rules that the EU and United States were party to, and that the EU would have to lift it or face retaliation. The EU refused to comply, so the U.S. government imposed a 100-percent tariff on imports of certain EU products, including French staples such as foie gras, mustard, and Roquefort cheese. On farms near Millau, Bové and others raised sheep whose milk was used to make Roquefort. They felt incensed by the American tariff and decided to vent their frustrations on McDonald's.

Bové and his compatriots were arrested and charged. They quickly became a focus of the emerging antiglobalization movement in France that was protesting everything from a loss of national sovereignty and "unfair" trade policies that were trying to force hormone-treated beef on French consumers, to the invasion of French culture by alien American values, so aptly symbolized by McDonald's. Lionel Jospin, France's prime minister, called the cause of José Bové "just." Allowed to remain free pending his trial, Bové travelled to Seattle in December to protest against the World Trade Organization, where he was feted as a hero of the antiglobalization movement. Back in France, Bové's July 2000 trial drew some 40 000 supporters to the small town of Millau, where they camped outside the courthouse and waited for the verdict. Bové was found guilty and sentenced to three months in jail, far less than the maximum possible sentence of five years. His supporters wore T-shirts claiming, "The world is not merchandise, and neither am I."

About the same time, in the Languedoc region of France, California winemaker Robert Mondavi had reached agreement with the mayor and council of the village of Aniane and regional authorities to turn 125 acres of wooded hillside belonging to the village into a vineyard. Mondavi planned to invest $7 million in the project and hoped to produce top quality wine that would sell in Europe and the United States for $60 a bottle. However, local environmentalists objected to the plan, which they claimed would destroy the area's unique ecological heritage. José Bové, basking in sudden fame, offered his support to the opponents, and the protests started. In May 2001, the Socialist mayor who had approved the project was defeated in local elections in which the Mondavi project had become the major issue. He was replaced by a Communist, Manuel Diaz, who denounced the project as a capitalist plot designed to enrich wealthy U.S. shareholders at the cost of his villagers and the environment. Following Diaz's victory, Mondavi announced he would pull out of the project. A spokesman noted, "It's a huge waste, but there are clearly personal and political interests at play here that go way beyond us."

So are the French opposed to foreign investment? The experience of McDonald's and Mondavi seems to suggest so, as does the associated news coverage, but look closer and a different reality seems to emerge. McDonald's has more than 800 restaurants in France and continues to do well there. Between 2005 and 2010, France received $385 billion of foreign direct investment, more than any other European nation with the exception of Britain. French enterprises are also investing across borders at record levels.

COUNTRY FOCUS   *Continued*

In this decade, Canada has experienced these kinds of trade-related protests. On May 18, 2010, three self-proclaimed "anarchists" firebombed a Royal Bank branch in Ottawa's Glebe area. The bank suffered $500 000 worth of damages. Dramatic video of the blast was posted on a Web site. along with a message stating that the bank was targeted because it was a major sponsor of the 2010 Vancouver Olympics, which were being hosted "on stolen indigenous land." The men were members of the activist group, FFFC-Ottawa and they vowed to disrupt the 2010 G20 Summit that was to be held in Toronto's financial district. One week before the summit, they were arrested during raids and faced charges ranging from arson to mischief to careless storage of ammunition.

Questions

1. What does the fact that McDonald's has so many locations in France, which are also some of the most profitable locations around the world, tell you about the feelings of a large proportion of the French population?
2. France has long been one of the most-favoured locations for inward foreign direct investment. Will this change in the future?

Sources: "Behind the Bluster," *The Economist*, May 26, 2001; "The French Farmers' Anti-global Hero," *The Economist*, July 8, 2000; C. Trueheart, "France's Golden Arch Enemy?" *Toronto Star*, July 1, 2000; and J. Henley, "Grapes of Wrath Scare off U.S. Firm," *The Economist*, May 18, 2001, p. 11; Siri Agrell, "Firebomb in Ottawa," *The Globe and Mail*, May 19, 2010; and Sarah Boesveld, "Police arrest three men in Ottawa bank firebombing," *The Globe and Mail*, June 18, 2010.

ANOTHER PERSPECTIVE

Prime Minister Trudeau's View on Globalism

"What we're facing right now—in terms of the rise of populism and divisive and fearful narratives around the world—it's based around the fact that globalisation doesn't seem to be working for the middle class, for ordinary people," said Prime Minister Justin Trudeau in an end-of-year interview with a British newspaper. "And this is something that we identified years ago and built an entire platform and agenda for governing on."

He went on to address the fears of people who may have felt that they have been left behind by the global economic system. "We were able to sign free trade agreement with Europe at a time when people tend to be closing off," he said.

He concluded, "Quite frankly if we can show—as we are working very hard to demonstrate—that you can have engaged global perspectives and growth that works for everyone ... then that diffuses a lot of the uncertainty, the anger, the populism that is surfacing in different pockets of the world."

Source: Ashifa Kassam and Laurence Mathieu-Léger, "Justin Trudeau: 'Globalisation Isn't Working for Ordinary People'," December 15, 2016, *The Guardian*, https://www.theguardian.com/world/2016/dec/15/justin-trudeau-interview-globalisation-climate-change-trump.

While violent protests may give the antiglobalization effort a bad name, the scale of the demonstrations shows that support for the cause goes beyond a core of protesters. Large sections of the population in many countries believe that globalization harms living standards and the environment. Both theory and evidence suggest that many of these fears are exaggerated, but this may not be communicated clearly. Both politicians and business people need to do more to counter these fears.

If the 2016 U.S. presidential election is any indication, many politicians did the exact opposite, by pandering to peoples' fears about job loss and economic decline. Many protests against globalization are tapping into a general sense of loss at the passing of a world in which barriers of time and distance, and vast differences in economic institutions, political institutions, and the level of development of different nations produced a world rich in the diversity of human cultures. The United Kingdom's vote to withdraw from the European Union in 2016, known as "Brexit" (short for British exit) and will be covered in later chapters, is an example of this type of popular protest vote.

Globalization, Jobs, and Income

Some Canadian firms have outsourced jobs to developing countries, provoking fears that this process will have long-term harmful effects on Canada's well-being as a whole. As evidence of this outsourcing trend, Gildan Activewear Inc., a Montreal-based company, closed its operations in Canada, the United States, and Mexico in 2007, resulting in employee layoffs. Following these layoffs, Gildan concentrated its sewing facilities in Honduras, Dominican Republic, and Nicaragua.[32] However, another result of these changes is that the company has grown and now produces Under Armour and New Balance Brands under license. In late 2016 it was financially strong enough to make a bid for the bankrupt American Apparel chain, based in the United States.[33]

This fear is supported by anecdotes. For example, D. L. Bartlett and J. B. Steele, two journalists for the Philadelphia Inquirer who gained notoriety for their attacks on free trade, cite the case of Harwood Industries, a U.S. clothing manufacturer that closed its U.S. operations, where it paid workers $9 per hour, and shifted manufacturing to Honduras, where textile workers received 48 cents per hour.[34] Because of moves such as this, argue Bartlett and Steele, the wage rates of poorer Americans have fallen significantly over the past quarter of a century.

In the past few years, similar fears have arisen with respect to services, which have increasingly been outsourced to nations with lower labour costs. The popular feeling is that when Canadian banks and other large companies outsource service activities to lower-cost foreign suppliers, they are "exporting jobs" to low-wage nations and contributing to higher unemployment and lower living standards in their home nations (in this case, Canada).

Supporters of globalization reply that critics of these trends miss the essential point about free trade—the benefits outweigh the costs.[35] They argue that free trade will result in countries specializing in the production of those goods and services that they can produce most efficiently, while importing goods and services that they cannot produce as efficiently. When a country embraces free trade, there is always some dislocation, but the whole economy is better off as a result. According to this view, it makes little sense for Canada and the United States to produce textiles at home when they can be produced at a lower cost in Honduras or China (which, unlike Honduras, is a major source of North American textile imports). Importing textiles from China leads to lower prices for clothes in Canada and the United States, which enables consumers to spend more of their money on other items. At the same time, the increased income generated in China from textile exports increases income levels in that country, which helps the Chinese to purchase more products produced in North America.

The same argument can be made to support the outsourcing of services to low-wage countries. By outsourcing its customer service call centres to India, Dell can reduce its cost structure, and thereby its prices for PCs. North American consumers benefit from this development. As prices for PCs fall, North Americans can spend more of their money on other goods and services. Moreover, the increase in income levels in India allows Indians to purchase more North American goods and services, which helps create jobs in both Canada and the United States. In this manner, supporters of globalization argue that free trade benefits all countries that adhere to a free trade regime.

If the critics of globalization are correct, three things must be shown. First, the share of national income received by labour, as opposed to the share received by the owners of capital (e.g., stockholders and bondholders), should have declined in advanced nations as a result of downward pressure on wage rates. Second, even though labour's share of the economic pie may have declined, this does not mean lower living standards if the size of the total pie has increased sufficiently to offset the decline in labour's share—in other words, if economic growth and rising living standards in advanced economies have offset declines in labour's share (this is the position argued by supporters of globalization). Third, the decline in labour's share of national income must be due to moving production to low-wage countries, as opposed to improvement in production technology and productivity.

Several studies shed light on these issues.[36] First, the data suggest that over the past two decades, the share of labour in national income has declined. The decline in share is much more pronounced in Europe and Japan (about 10 percentage points) than in the United States and the United Kingdom (where it is 3 to 4 percentage points). However, detailed analysis suggests the share of national income enjoyed by skilled labour has actually increased, suggesting that the fall in labour's share has been due to a fall in the share taken by unskilled labour. A study by the IMF suggested the earnings gap between workers in skilled and unskilled sectors has widened by 25 percent over the past two decades.[37] The average income level of the richest 10 percent of the population in developed economies was nine times that of the poorest 10 percent, according to 2010 data. The ratio in the United States was among the highest, with the top 10 percent earning 14 times as much as the bottom 10 percent.[38] These figures strongly suggest that unskilled labour in developed nations has seen its share of national income decline over the past two decades.

However, this does not mean that the living standards of unskilled workers in developed nations have declined. It is possible that economic growth in developed nations has offset the fall in the share of national income enjoyed by unskilled workers, raising their living standards. Evidence suggests that real labour compensation has expanded in most developed nations since the 1980s, including the United States. Several studies by the Organization for Economic Cooperation and Development (OECD), whose members include the 34 richest economies in the world, conclude that while the gap between the poorest and richest segments of society in OECD countries has widened, in most countries real income levels have increased for all, including the poorest segment. In a study published in 2011, the OECD found that between 1985 and 2008, real household income (adjusted for inflation) increased by 1.7 percent annually among its member-states. The real income level of the poorest 10 percent of the population increased at 1.4 percent on average, while that of the richest 10 percent increased by 2 percent annually (i.e., while everyone got richer, the gap between the most affluent and the poorest sectors of society widened). The differential in growth rates was more extreme in the United States than most other countries. The study found that the real income of the poorest 10 percent of the population grew by just 0.5 percent a year in the United States between 1985 and 2008, while that of the richest 10 percent grew by 1.9 percent annually.[39]

As noted earlier, globalization critics argue that the decline in unskilled wage rates is due to the migration of low-wage manufacturing jobs offshore and a corresponding reduction in demand for unskilled workers. However, supporters of globalization see a more complex picture. They maintain that the weak growth rate in real wage rates for unskilled workers owes far more to a technology-induced shift within advanced economies away from jobs where the only qualification was a willingness to turn up for work every day and toward jobs that require significant education and skills. They point out that many advanced economies report a shortage of highly skilled workers and an excess supply of unskilled workers. Thus, growing income inequality is a result of the wages for skilled workers being bid up by the labour market and the wages for unskilled workers being discounted. In fact, evidence suggests that technological change has had a bigger impact than globalization on the declining share of national income enjoyed by labour.[40] This suggests that a solution to the problem of slow real income growth among the unskilled is to be found not in limiting free trade and globalization, but in increasing society's investment in education to reduce the supply of unskilled workers.[41]

Finally, it is worth noting that the wage gap between developing and developed nations is closing as developing nations experience rapid economic growth. For example, one estimate suggests that wages in China will approach Western levels in two decades.[42] To the extent that this is the case, any migration of unskilled jobs to low-wage countries is a temporary phenomenon representing a structural adjustment on the way to a more tightly integrated global economy.

Globalization, Labour Policies, and the Environment

A second source of concern is that free trade encourages firms from advanced nations to move manufacturing facilities to less developed countries that lack adequate regulations to protect labour and the environment from abuse by the unscrupulous.[43] Globalization critics often argue that adhering to labour and environmental regulations significantly increases the costs of manufacturing enterprises and puts them at a competitive disadvantage in the global marketplace vis-à-vis firms based in developing nations that do not have to comply with such regulations. Firms deal with this cost disadvantage, the theory goes, by moving their production facilities to nations that do not have such burdensome regulations or that fail to enforce the regulations they have.

If this is the case, one might expect free trade to lead to an increase in pollution and result in firms from advanced nations exploiting the labour of less developed nations.[44] This argument was used repeatedly by those who opposed the 1994 formation of the North American Free Trade Agreement (NAFTA) between Canada, Mexico, and the United States. They painted a picture of U.S. manufacturing firms moving to Mexico in droves so that they would be free to pollute the environment, employ child labour, and ignore workplace safety and health issues, all in the name of higher profits.[45]

Supporters of free trade and greater globalization express doubts about this scenario. They argue that tougher environmental regulations and stricter labour standards go hand in hand with economic progress.[46] In general, as countries get richer, they enact tougher environmental and labour regulations.[47] Because free trade enables developing countries to increase their economic growth rates and become richer, this should lead to tougher environmental and labour laws. In this view, the critics of free trade have got it backward—free trade does not lead to more pollution and labour exploitation, it leads to less. By creating wealth and incentives for enterprises to produce technological innovations, the free market system and free trade could make it easier for the world to cope with problems of pollution and population growth. Indeed, while pollution levels are rising in the world's poorer countries, they have been rising modestly or falling in developed nations. In one case, Canada's total greenhouse gas (GHG) emissions in 2015 were 722 megatonnes (Mt) of carbon dioxide equivalent (CO_2 eq.), or 18% (111 Mt CO_2 eq.) above the 1990 emissions of 611 Mt CO_2 eq.[48] However, the total emissions fell 18 percent per unit of GDP in this 25-year time period.[49] Drawn from a study undertaken for the OECD, it appears that the better a country performs economically, the more it does to protect the environment.[50] A number of econometric studies have found consistent evidence of a hump-shaped relationship between income levels and pollution levels.[51] As an economy grows and income levels rise, initially pollution levels also rise. However, past some point, rising income levels lead to demands for greater environmental protection, and pollution levels then fall. A seminal study by Grossman and Krueger found that the turning point generally occurred before per capita income levels reached $8000.[52]

Supporters of free trade also point out that it is possible to tie free trade agreements to the implementation of tougher environmental and labour laws in less developed countries. NAFTA, for example, was passed only after side agreements had been negotiated that committed Mexico to tougher enforcement of environmental protection regulations. Thus, supporters of free trade argue that factories based in Mexico are now cleaner than they would have been without the passage of NAFTA.[53]

They also argue that business firms are not the amoral organizations that critics suggest. While there may be some rotten apples, most business enterprises are staffed by managers who are committed to behave in an ethical manner and would be unlikely to move production offshore just so they could pump more pollution into the atmosphere or exploit labour. Furthermore, the relationship between pollution, labour exploitation, and production costs may not be as suggested by critics. In general, a well-treated labour force is productive, and it is productivity rather than base wage rates that often has the greatest influence on costs. The vision of greedy managers who shift production to low-wage countries to exploit their labour force may be misplaced.

Globalization and National Sovereignty

Another concern voiced by critics of globalization is that today's increasingly interdependent global economy shifts economic power away from national governments and toward supranational organizations such as the World Trade Organization, the European Union, and the United Nations. As perceived by critics, unelected bureaucrats now impose policies on the democratically elected governments of nation-states, thereby undermining the sovereignty of those states and limiting the nation-state's ability to control its own destiny.[54]

The World Trade Organization is a favourite target of those who attack the headlong rush toward a global economy. As noted earlier, the WTO was founded in 1994 to police the world trading system established by the General Agreement on Tariffs and Trade. Many economists and politicians maintain that the power of supranational organizations such as the WTO is limited to that which nation-states collectively agree to grant. They argue that bodies such as the United Nations and the WTO exist to serve the collective interests of member states, not to subvert those interests. Supporters of supranational organizations point out that the power of these bodies rests largely on their ability to persuade member states to follow a certain action. If these bodies fail to serve the collective interests of member states, those states will withdraw their support and the supranational organization will quickly collapse. In this view, real power still resides with individual nation-states, not supranational organizations.

Globalization and the World's Poor

Critics of globalization argue that despite the supposed benefits associated with free trade and investment, over the last hundred years or so the gap between the rich and poor nations of the world has gotten wider. In 1870 the average income per capita in the world's 17 richest nations was 2.4 times that of all other countries. In 1990 the same group was 4.5 times as rich as the rest.[55] While recent history has shown that some of the world's poorer nations are capable of rapid periods of economic growth—witness the transformation that has occurred in some Southeast Asian nations such as South Korea, Thailand, and Malaysia—there appear to be strong forces for stagnation among the world's poorest nations. A quarter of the countries with a GDP per capita of less than $1000 in 1960 had growth rates of less than zero from 1960 to 1995, and a third had growth rates of less than 0.05 percent.[56] Critics argue that if globalization is such a positive development, this divergence between the rich and poor should not have occurred.

Although the reasons for economic stagnation vary, several factors stand out, none of which have anything to do with free trade or globalization. Many of the world's poorest countries have suffered from totalitarian governments, economic policies that destroyed wealth rather than facilitated its creation, scant protection for property rights, and war. Such factors help explain why countries such as Afghanistan, Cuba, Haiti, Iraq, Libya, Nigeria, Sudan, Vietnam, and Zaire have failed to improve the economic lot of their citizens during recent decades. A complicating factor is the rapidly expanding populations in many of these countries. Without a major change in government, population growth may exacerbate their problems. Promoters of free trade argue that the best way for these countries to improve their lot is to lower their barriers to free trade and investment and to implement economic policies based on free market economics.[57]

On the other hand, it is also true that many of the world's poorer nations are also being held back by large debt burdens. Of particular concern are the 40 or so highly indebted poorer countries (HIPCs), which are home to some 700 million people. Among these countries, on average the government debt burden is equivalent to 85 percent of the value of the economy, as measured by gross domestic product, and the annual costs of serving government debt consumes 15 percent of the country's export earnings.[58] Servicing such a heavy debt load leaves the governments of these countries with little left to invest in important public infrastructure projects, such as education, health care, roads, and power. The result: the HIPCs are trapped in a cycle of poverty and debt that inhibits economic development. Free trade alone, some argue, is not sufficient to help these countries bootstrap themselves out of poverty. What is needed is large-scale debt relief for the world's poorest nations to give them the opportunity to restructure their economies and start the long climb toward prosperity. Supporters of debt relief also argue that new democratic governments in poor nations should not be forced to honour debts that were incurred and mismanaged long ago by their corrupt and dictatorial predecessors.

In the late 1990s, a debt relief movement began to gain ground among the political establishment in the world's richer nations.[59] Fuelled by high-profile endorsements ranging from Irish rock star Bono (who has been a tireless and increasingly effective advocate for debt relief), to Pope John Paul II, the Dalai Lama, and influential Harvard economist Jeffry Sachs, the debt relief movement was instrumental in persuading the United States to enact legislation in 2000 that provided $435 million in debt relief for HIPCs. In 2005, the Group of Eight nations (G8) including Canada and the United States, cancelled about $60 billion of debt owed them by the world's poorest countries. Yet around the same time, other countries such as China, India, and Brazil offered loans and credits to these same poor countries. Thus, the net overall effect of these actions is that HIPC debt remains high.

For such a program to have a lasting effect, however, debt relief must be matched by wise investment in public projects that boost economic growth (such as education) and by the adoption of economic policies that facilitate investment and trade. The rich nations of the world can also help by reducing barriers to the importation of products from the world's poorer nations, particularly tariffs on imports of agricultural products and textiles. Debt relief is not new—it has been tried before.[60] Too often in the past, however, the short-term benefits were squandered by corrupt governments who used their newfound financial freedom to make unproductive investments in military infrastructure or grandiose projects that did little to foster long-run economic development. Developed nations, too, contributed to past failures by refusing to open their markets to the products of poor nations. If such a scenario can be avoided this time, the entire world will benefit.

LO6 | Managing in the Global Marketplace

As their organizations increasingly engage in cross-border trade and investment, managers need to recognize that the task of managing an **international business**, one that engages in international trade or investment, differs from that of managing a purely domestic business in many ways. At the most fundamental level, the differences arise from the simple fact that countries are different. Countries differ in their cultures, political systems, economic systems, legal systems, and levels of economic development.

Differences between countries require that an international business vary its practices country by country. Managers within international businesses must develop strategies and policies for dealing with cross-border government interventions.

Cross-border transactions also require that money be converted from the firm's home currency into a foreign currency and vice versa. Since currency exchange rates vary in response to changing economic conditions, an international business must develop policies for dealing with exchange rate movements. A firm following a misguided policy can lose large amounts of money, while a firm that adopts the right policy can increase the profitability of its international transactions.

In this book we examine all these issues in depth, paying close attention to the different strategies and policies that managers pursue to deal with the various challenges created when a firm becomes an international business. Chapters 2 and 3 explore how countries differ from each other with regard to their political, economic, legal, and cultural institutions. Chapter 4 examines the role of ethics in international business. Chapters 5 to 8 look at the international trade and investment environment within which international businesses must operate. Chapters 9 and 10 review the international monetary system. These chapters focus on the nature of the foreign exchange market and the emerging global monetary system. Chapters 11 and 12 explore the strategy of international businesses. Chapters 13 to 16 look at the management of various functional operations within an international business, including production, marketing, and human relations. By the time you complete this book, you should have a good grasp of the issues that managers working within international business have to grapple with on a daily basis, and you should be familiar with the range of strategies and operating policies available to compete more effectively in today's rapidly emerging global economy.

IMPLICATIONS FOR BUSINESS

As we will see throughout this book, the international business arena is becoming an increasingly open environment for goods and services to be bought and sold. For example, Canadian businesses can no longer operate in an insular manner, according to their own rules and regulations. Business managers need to see the world of strengths, weaknesses, opportunities, and threats in a global sense. What once were viable business survival and expansion strategies no longer work. Businesses are now forced to address the broader scope of commercial realities brought forth over the years through the General Agreement on Trade and Tariffs, and evolved through the World Trade Organization. Other synchronous tools of the globalization wave, as cited at the beginning of this chapter, are the United Nations, the World Bank, and others. Foreign direct investment, a crucial strategy in the globalization process, will be discussed in later chapters.

As, noted earlier, the World Trade Organization (WTO) consisted of 164 members. The WTO is the host to new negotiations, under the "Doha Development Agenda" launched in 2001. In some circumstances, WTO rules support maintaining trade barriers, for example, to protect consumers or prevent the spread of disease. Membership requires that ground rules for international commerce, including contracts, be followed, thus binding governments to keep their trade policies within agreed limits.

Starting in 1948, the General Agreement on Tariffs and Trade (GATT) had provided the rules for the system. Over the years, GATT evolved through several rounds of negotiations. The last and largest GATT round was the Uruguay Round, which lasted from 1986 to 1994 and led to the WTO's creation. Whereas GATT had mainly dealt with trade in goods, the WTO and its agreements now cover trade in services, and in traded inventions, creations, and intellectual property.[61]

Membership comes with responsibilities, but also with benefits. Adhering to the World Trade Organization initiatives on a plethora of trade-related issues are paramount to a country's accession to inclusion into the "WTO club." Poorer countries might benefit from easier access to financing through international funding agencies. In South America, commercial and customs unions such as Mercosur and the Andean Pact are opening new doors for South American companies within these intra-markets. The Caribbean nations, through CARICOM, are benefiting through the same less restrictive commercial markets.

Other similar types of initiatives include: ASEAN, the Association of Southeast Nations; AU, the African Union; CAFTA, the Central American Free Trade Agreement; CARICOM, the Caribbean Community; CEMAC, the Communauté Economique et Monétaire de l'Afrique Centrale; EAC, the East African Community; GCC, the Gulf Co-operation Council; JSEPA, the Japan/Singapore Economic Partnership Agreement; MERCOSUR, the Mercado Comun del Sur; and NAFTA, the North American Free Trade Agreement.[62] The European Union is very close to the WTO's concept of how free trade areas should appear.

THE NORTH—SOUTH DIVIDE

The World Trade Organization is aiming for a world free of customs duties and trade barriers. Whether that goal will be attained is still to be determined. The transformations have not been, and will not be, smooth. Many of the world's wealthier nations appear to be pitted against the poor. In this north (wealthy)—south (developing countries) divide, there is continual divergence of views on the benefits of a "WTO world," frequently played out in much publicized WTO antiglobalization protests. Developing countries fear that they do not have the means and know-how to compete against the significantly more efficient industries of wealthy nations. In theory, as developing countries "subscribe" to WTO trade practices, standards of living and social and political stabilities will increase and the economic gap between rich and poor nations will narrow.

THE ROLE OF TECHNOLOGY IN INTERNATIONAL TRADE

Without technology, the degree of globalization as we know it today would be less dominant. According to proponents of global free trade, the sheer volume of the world's business lends to decreased costs, contributing to increased purchasing power and rising standards of living. The Internet has resulted in rapid border clearance of shipments of foods internationally, while reducing costs in communications. After the September 11, 2001, terrorist attacks, technology has become core to the secure growth of international trade, proving that technology can benefit both rich and poor nations.

Key Terms

foreign direct investment (FDI)

General Agreement on Tariffs and Trade (GATT)

globalization

globalization of markets

globalization of production

international business

International Monetary Fund (IMF)

international trade

Moore's Law

multinational enterprise (MNE)

United Nations

World Bank

World Trade Organization (WTO)

LO   Learning Objectives Summary

This chapter sets the scene for the rest of the book. We have seen how the world economy is becoming more global, and we have reviewed the main drivers of globalization and argued that they seem to be thrusting nation-states toward a more tightly integrated global economy. We have looked at how the nature of international business is changing in response to the changing global economy; we have discussed some concerns raised by rapid globalization; and we have reviewed implications of rapid globalization for individual managers. These major points were made in the chapter:

1. Over the past several decades, we have witnessed the globalization of markets and production. The globalization of markets implies that national markets are merging into one huge marketplace. However, it is important not to push this view too far.

2. As markets globalize, institutions need to help manage, regulate, and police the global marketplace, and to promote the establishment of multinational treaties to govern the global business system. During the past 50 years, a number of important global institutions have been created to help perform these functions.

3. Several factors seem to underlie the trend toward globalization: declining trade barriers and changes in communication, information, and transportation technologies.

4. There have been dramatic changes in the demographics of the global economy over the past 50 years. As late as the 1960s, four facts described the demographics of the global economy. The first was U.S. dominance in the world economy and world trade picture. The second was U.S. dominance in world foreign direct investment. The third fact was the dominance of large, multinational U.S. firms on the international business scene. The fourth was that roughly half the globe—the centrally planned economies of the Communist world—was off-limits to Western international businesses. All four of these qualities either have changed or are now changing rapidly.

5. The benefits and costs of the emerging global economy are being hotly debated among business people, economists, and politicians, not just in the United States but around the world. The debate focuses on the impact of globalization on jobs, wages, the environment, working conditions, and national sovereignty.

6. Managers need to recognize that the task of managing an international business differs from that of managing a purely domestic business in many ways. Differences between countries require that an international business vary its practices country by country. Managers within international businesses must develop strategies and policies for dealing with cross-border government interventions.

Critical Thinking and Discussion Questions

1. Describe the shifts in the world economy over the past two decades. What are the implications of these shifts for international businesses based in Great Britain? North America?

2. "The study of international business is fine if you are going to work in a large multinational enterprise, but it has no relevance for individuals who are going to work in small firms." Evaluate this statement.

3. How have changes in technology contributed to the globalization of markets and production? Would the globalization of production and markets have been possible without these technological changes?

4. "Ultimately, the study of international business is no different from the study of domestic business. Thus, there is no point in having a separate course on international business." Evaluate this statement.

5. How might the Internet and the World Wide Web affect international business activity and the globalization of the world economy?

6. If current trends continue, China may be the world's largest economy by 2050. Discuss the possible implications for such a development for:
   a. the world trading system.
   b. the world monetary system.
   c. the business strategy of today's European- and Canadian-based global corporations.

Research Task   globalEDGE™   globaledge.msu.edu

Use the globalEDGE™ site to complete the following exercises:

1. Your company has developed a new product that is expected to achieve high penetration rates in all the countries in which it is introduced, regardless of the average income status of the local populace. Considering the costs of the product launch, the management team has decided to initially introduce the product only in countries that have a sizeable population base. You are required to prepare a preliminary report with the top ten countries of the world in terms of population size. Since growth opportunities are another major concern, the average population growth rates also should be listed for management's consideration.

2. You are working for a company that is considering investing in a foreign country. Management has requested a report regarding the attractiveness of alternative countries based on the potential return of FDI. Accordingly, the ranking of the top 25 countries in terms of FDI attractiveness is a crucial ingredient for your report. A colleague mentioned a potentially useful tool called the "FDI Confidence Index," which is updated periodically. Find this index, and provide additional information regarding how the index is constructed. You may also wish to look at DFAIT's Web site at http://www.international.gc.ca/index.aspx.

CLOSING CASE

TIM HORTONS—A CANADIAN COMPANY LOOKING FOR NEW MARKETS

To many Canadians, there is nothing that defines our country more than stopping off for a coffee (and donut) at a Tim Hortons location. Tim Hortons is a Canadian, and more recently a North American, success story.

Tim Hortons opened its first location in Hamilton, Ontario, in 1964. There were only two items on the menu at that time: coffee and donuts. The chain expanded but, more importantly, as consumers' tastes changed, Tim Horton's adapted its menu. Timbits were added to the menu in 1976, with muffins, cakes, pies, croissants, and cookies all added in the early 1980s. In the 1990s there were bagels, flavoured cappuccino, and later iced cappuccino. Today, there are flavoured teas, soup, fresh sandwiches, croissants, and pastries. The company does not stand still and is launching the Tassimo brand of single serve coffee as well.

However, despite the growth of its menu, Tim Hortons stayed true to its focus of offering good coffee (that must be served within 20 minutes of being brewed, otherwise it is not served) in convenient locations. This "convenience factor" means that most locations are open 24 hours a day (a long-standing tradition), but more recently the company has expanded into drive-thru locations, as well as locations in "nonconventional" locations such as shopping malls, hospitals, and university campuses.

Today there are over 3700 locations across Canada, and the United States. It serves more coffee than any restaurant chain except Starbucks. It is one of the largest publicly-traded, quick-service restaurant chains in Canada, and the fourth largest in North America.

For many years, some analysts have said that the Canadian market is nearly fully saturated with Tim Hortons locations, and the company has proven them to be wrong with continued Canadian growth. Nonetheless, expansion into the United States seems to be a natural next step for the company, and indeed there are currently 550 restaurants in the United States. But the U.S. market has been a difficult fit for Tim Hortons in the past, and the Canadian market has also been tough for U.S. chains to enter.

One example is Krispy Kreme Doughnuts and their failed attempt to break into the Canadian market. This company was founded in 1937 and is headquartered in North Carolina. Krispy Kreme became known for its freshly baked donuts, with each location lighting a sign in its window when a batch of hot, fresh donuts had been produced. Yet for much of its history, the company was only located in the southeastern United States.

That changed in the late 1990s. The company opened its first store in New York City in 1996, and later its first location in California in 1999. This was followed by very fast growth. In April 2000, the company's stock went public on the New York Stock Exchange. And then it all began to fall apart for Krispy Kreme. The company was hit by an accounting scandal that called into question the company's overall profitability during its period of fantastic growth. Numerous vice-presidents were removed from the company and lawsuits from angry shareholders forced the company into a massive restructuring.

The United States has proven to be a tough market for Tim Hortons. Much of the company's U.S. expansion came through its purchase, in 1995, by Wendy's International. Through the late 1990s, as Wendy's struggled with profitability and closed some of its locations, the Tim Hortons unit (and its success in Canada) drove much of Wendy's growth. Wendy's was never able to develop outstanding synergies between its brand and Tim Hortons. In 2005, major company shareholders applied pressure on Wendy's to spin off Tim Hortons back into a separate company. In March 2006 Tim Hortons was partially spun-off from Wendy's and was a completely separate company as of September 2006.

This independence lasted for less than a decade. In December 2014, the company was bought by Burger King, with both restaurants operating under the name Restaurant Brands Inc. This new company became the third-largest fast-food chain on the planet, with 18 000 locations

The deal, valued at $12 billion, has plans to open many more restaurants "at a significantly greater pace" than what Tim Hortons had previously planned, according to a press release issued when the companies merged. http://globalnews.ca/news/1724238/its-official-tim-hortons-burger-king-become-one/

Time will tell whether access to greater synergies and capital will result in greater fortunes for this global company, which is still headquartered in Canada.

Sources: Tim Hortons Web site, http://www.timhortons.com; http://www.cbc.ca/archives/entry/1995-us-burger-giant-buys-tim-hortons-doughnut-chain; Krispy Kreme Web site, www.kripsykreme.com; Yahoo Finance, http://finance.yahoo.com/q?d=t&s=kkd; Dawn Calleja "What Are They Putting in That Coffee?" *Report on Business Magazine*, October 2010; and "Tim Hortons Coffee Now Available in Florida, California, Hawaii, Alaska and More," Tim Hortons Press Release, https://www.timhortons.com/ca/en/corporate/news-release.php?id=7589.

Case Discussion Questions

1. How can a company like Tim Hortons maintain its quality when it is operating in different markets around the globe?

2. Is there anything wrong with a company like Tim Hortons sticking to a marketplace that it knows well?

3. Can a company grow too quickly? What are the problems associated with fast growth?

Sustainability in Practice

ADIDAS GROUP: SUPPLY-CHAIN MANAGEMENT

SITUATION

The Adidas Group is the second largest sportswear manufacturer in the world. Its German holding company, Adidas AG, produces products under the Reebok, Rockport, and Ashworth brands, among others including the flagship Adidas brand.

Existing as a company for almost a hundred years, and with operations all over the world, the company has taken a highly visible and integrated approach to sustainability.

APPROACH TO SUSTAINABILITY

Adidas Group's ambition is to be a sustainable company. As the company states:

> Being a sustainable business is about striking the balance between shareholder expectations and the needs and concerns of our employees, the workers in our supply chain and the environment. We truly believe that acting as a responsible business — one which is fully committed to respecting human rights—will contribute to lasting economic success.
>
> We are continuously working towards becoming a more sustainable company. While we have been in this game for a long time, we will never stop learning and improving our sustainability efforts. For us, it is about being prepared, setting the right pace and having both the drive and stamina to go the distance. It is about being persistent, overcoming setbacks and difficulties and never giving up on the overall goal. Just like a true athlete never would.
>
> We have a long track record in sustainability and are proud of our accomplishments, but we will never rest on our laurels. We constantly strive to improve our sustainable performance while acting upon our leadership role and listening to the expectations of our stakeholders and consumers. One example is our extended Sustainability Strategy 'Sport needs a space', which pushes the limits of our own ambitions further than ever before. A direct outcome of our business strategy 'Creating the New', 'Sport needs a space' translates our overall sustainable efforts into tangible goals that have a direct impact on the world of sport we operate in.
>
> As a global sports company, we believe that through sport we have the power to change lives. This is supported by research we have conducted. It shows that our consumers believe that sport makes us healthy and happy, that it creates value and empowers people. An impressive 92% even say that sport has a positive impact on our society. But for sport to change lives, it needs a space to exist, a field to play on, an ocean to surf or a mountain to climb – and these spaces are increasingly endangered due to man-made issues including human rights violations, pollution, growing energy consumption and waste. Based on our love of sport and responsibility as a globally operating company, we want to be the guardians of these spaces. Thus, we have developed a holistic strategy that seriously tackles the challenges that endanger the spaces of sport and simultaneously our planet and people.
>
> Our Sustainability Strategy 'Sport needs a space' identifies six strategic priorities to address the issues and challenges of the spaces where sport is made (all places where products are created, designed, manufactured and shipped), sold (own retail, wholesale and e-commerce) and played (from the indoor court to the outdoor pitch all over the world).
>
> Following the entire lifecycle of sport, our most holistic Sustainability Strategy to date supports us in creating responsibly across our entire supply chain, with tangible and measurable goals, and ensures that sport remains a source of happiness for all people.

You can read in detail about Adidas' sustainability practices, at: http://www.adidas-group.com.

APPROACH TO SUPPLY CHAIN MANAGEMENT

For any company operating with many different suppliers around the world, bringing sustainability to supply chain management is no easy task. Adidas accomplishes this through stated workplace standards, policies, and guidelines. Its workplace standards, for example are clear and unequivocal. Regarding two highly visible areas, namely forced labour and child labour, the company states, "Business partners must not use forced labour, whether in the form of prison labour, indentured labour, bonded labour or otherwise. No employee may be compelled to work through force or intimidation of any form, or as a means of political coercion or as punishment for holding or expressing political views. Business partners must not employ children who are less than 15 years old, or less than the age for completing compulsory education in the country of manufacture where such age is higher than 15."

These guidelines implement the standards and cover matters from health and safety and employment guidelines through to environmental and worker cooperative guidelines. They are translated into ten languages, and can be found at http://www.adidas-group.com.

The company monitors the activities of suppliers itself as well as through independent parties. The company is a member of the Fair Labor Association (FLA), which makes it subject to external assessments by independent monitors, to participation in a third-party complaint system, and to public reporting. Since the company joined the FLA in 2005, over 300 independent assessments have been conducted at Adidas' suppliers.

Source: adidas Web site, http://www.adidas-group.com/en/; adidas Workplace Standards, http://www.adidas-group.com/media/filer_public/2013/07/31/english_workplace_standards_en.pdf; and adidas Supply Chain Approach, http://www.adidas-group.com/en/sustainability/compliance/supply-chain-approach/.

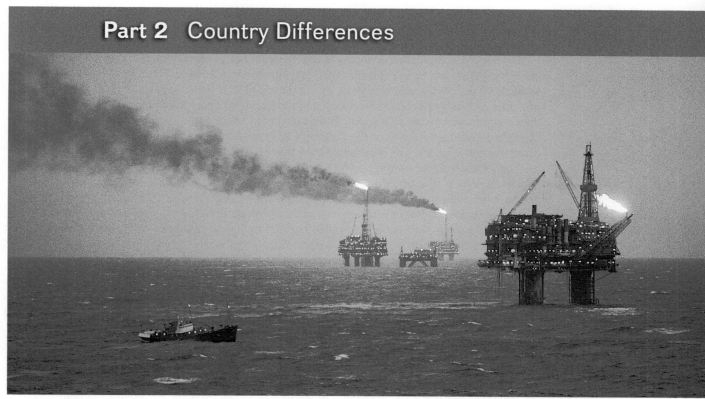

© Michael Saint Maur Sheil/Getty Images

Chapter 2
Country Differences in Political Economy

PUTIN'S RUSSIA

The modern Russia state was born in 1991 after the dramatic collapse of the Soviet Union. Early in the post-Soviet era, Russia embraced ambitious policies designed to transform a communist dictatorship with a centrally planned economy into democratic state with a market-based economic system. The policies, however, were imperfectly implemented. Political reform left Russia with a strong presidency that—in hindsight—had the ability to subvert the democratic process. On the economic front, the privatization of many state-owned enterprises was done in such a way as to leave large shareholdings in the hands of the politically connected, many of whom were party officials and factory managers under the old Soviet system. Corruption was also endemic, and organized crime was able to seize control of some newly privatized enterprises. In 1998, the poorly managed Russian economy went through a financial crisis that nearly bought the country to its knees.

Fast-forward to 2017, and Russia still has a long way to go before it resembles a modern democracy with a functioning free market–based economic system. On the positive side, the economy grew at a healthy clip during most of the 2000s and up until 2008, helped in large part by high prices for oil and gas, Russia's largest exports (oil and gas accounted for 75 percent of all Russian exports). Between 2000 and 2013, Russia's gross domestic product (GDP) per capita more than doubled when measured by purchasing power parity.

On the other hand, the economy is overly dependent upon commodities, particularly oil and gas. When prices fell, Russia's GDP fell with it. From 2014 to 2015, Russia's GDP fell by almost 40 percent in just one year. Its current GDP is at levels last seen in 2010. Much of Russia's oil and gas production remains in the hands of enterprises in which the state still has a significant ownership stake. The government has a controlling ownership position in Gazprom and Rosneft, two of the country's largest oil and gas companies. The government used the rise in oil and gas revenues during the last decade or so to increase public spending through state-led investment projects and increases in wages and pensions for government workers. While this boosted private consumption, there has been a dearth of private investment, and productivity growth remains low. This is particularly true among many state-owned enterprises that collectively still account for about half of the Russian economy.

Russian private enterprises are also hamstrung by bureaucratic red tape and endemic corruption. The World Bank ranks Russia 92nd in the world in terms of the ease of doing business and 88th when it comes to starting a business (for comparison, the United States is ranked 4th and 20th, respectively). The state and state-owned enterprises are famous for pushing work to private enterprises that are owned by political allies, which further subverts market-based processes.

On the political front, Russia is, at best, a highly imperfect pseudo-democracy. Since 1999, Vladimir Putin has exerted increasingly tight control over Russian politics, either as president or as prime minister. Under Putin, potential opponents have been sidelined, civil liberties have been progressively reduced, and the freedom of the press has been diminished. For example, in response to opposition protests in 2011 and 2012, the Russian government passed laws increasing its control over the Internet, dramatically raised fines for participating in "unsanctioned" street protests, and expanded the definition of treason to further limit opposition activities. Vocal opponents of the régime—from business executives who do not tow the state line to protest groups such as the punk rock protest band Pussy Riot—have found themselves jailed on dubious charges. To make matters worse, Putin has recently been tightening his grip on the legal system. In late 2013, Russia's parliament, which is dominated by Putin supporters, gave the president more power to appoint and fire prosecutors, thereby diminishing the independence of the legal system.

Freedom House, which produces an annual ranking tracking freedom in the world, classifies Russia as "not free" and gives it low scores for political and civil liberties. Freedom House notes that in the March 2012 presidential elections, Putin benefited from preferential treatment by state-owned media, numerous abuses of incumbency, and procedural "irregularities" during the vote count. Putin won 63.6 percent of the vote against a field of weak, hand-chosen opponents, led by Communist Party leader Gennadiy Zyuganove, with 17.2 percent of the vote. Under a Putin-inspired 2008 constitutional amendment, the term of the presidency was expanded from four years to six. Putin will be eligible for another six-year term in 2018.

If oil and gas prices return to previous high levels, Putin will probably be able to remain in control of Russia. However, the state has expanded public spending to such an extent over the last decade that should oil and gas prices fall significantly, or stay at their current rates of around $50 a barrel for oil, Russia could very quickly be enveloped in a financial crisis. Russia also faces the twin problems of a falling birthrate and an aging population, which means that demands on the state to fund pensions and health care will increase in the future, further straining government finances.

Sources: "Putin's Russia: Sochi or Bust," *The Economist*, February 1, 2014; "Russia's Economy: The S Word," *The Economist*, November 9, 2013; Freedom House, Freedom in the World 2014: Russia, https://freedomhouse.org/report/freedom-world/2014/russia; K. Hille, "Putin Tightens Grip on Legal System," *Financial Times*, November 27, 2013; and Russia GDP 1989-2017, http://www.tradingeconomics.com/russia/gdp.

> ## LO   LEARNING OBJECTIVES
>
> **By the end of this chapter you should be able to:**
>
> 1. Give examples of how the political systems of countries differ.
> 2. Distinguish how the economic systems of countries differ.
> 3. Explain how the legal systems of countries differ.
> 4. Explain what determines the level of economic development of a nation.
> 5. Summarize the main changes that are currently reshaping the political, economic, and legal systems worldwide.
> 6. Describe how transition economies are moving toward market-based systems.
> 7. Explain the implications of changes in political economies.

Introduction

As noted in Chapter 1, international business is much more complicated than domestic business because countries differ in many ways. Countries have different political, economic, and legal systems. Cultural practices can vary dramatically from country to country, as can the education and skill level of the population, and countries are at different stages of economic development. All these differences can and do have major implications for the practice of international business. They have a profound impact on the benefits, costs, and risks associated with doing business in different countries; the way in which operations in different countries should be managed; and the strategies international firms should pursue in different countries. A main function of this chapter and the next is to develop an awareness of and appreciation for the significance of country differences in political systems, economic systems, legal systems, and national culture. Another function of this chapter and the next is to describe how the political, economic, legal, and cultural systems of many of the world's nation-states are evolving and to draw out the implications of these changes for the practice of international business.

The opening case illustrates some of the issues covered in this chapter. A quarter of a century ago, Russia was a communist state with a centrally planned economy. After the collapse of the Soviet Union in 1991, there were a series of reforms in Russia aimed at creating a sustainable democracy with an economic system based upon free market principles. However, as the case makes clear, under the leadership of Vladimir Putin, Russia has progressively curtailed hard-won democratic freedoms. Moreover, although the economy of Putin's Russia is a long way removed from the central planning of the Soviet era, the state not only continues to account for around 50 percent of economic activity, the government has also extended its direct and indirect control over businesses in strategically important sectors—such as oil and gas—running them, in effect, as an extension of the government. Putin has also extended his control over the legal system, gaining new powers to appoint and dismiss prosecutors. Clearly the economic, political, and legal system that now prevails in Russia is different in many respects from that which we find in many advanced and developing nations around the world. As will become clear in this chapter, such differences have nontrivial implications for international business.

This chapter focuses on how the political, economic, and legal systems of countries differ. Collectively we refer to these systems as constituting the political economy of a country. We use the term **political economy** to stress that the political, economic, and legal systems of a country are not independent of each other. They interact with and influence each other, and in doing so they affect the level of economic well-being in a country. In addition to reviewing these systems we also explore how differences in political economy influence the benefits, costs, and risks associated with doing business in different countries, and how they affect management practice and strategy. In the next chapter, we will look at how differences in culture influence the practice of international business. The political economy and culture of a nation are not independent of each other. As will become apparent in Chapter 3, culture can affect political economy—political, economic, and legal systems in a nation—and the converse can also hold true.

LO1 Political Systems

The economic and legal systems of a country are shaped by its political system.[1] As such, it is important that we understand the nature of different political systems before discussing economic and legal systems. By **political system** we mean the system of government in a nation. Political systems can be assessed according to two related dimensions. The first is the degree to which they emphasize collectivism as opposed to individualism. The second dimension is the degree to which they are democratic or totalitarian. These dimensions are interrelated: systems that emphasize collectivism tend toward totalitarian, while systems that place a high value on individualism tend to be democratic. However, a large grey area exists in the middle. It is possible to have democratic societies that emphasize a mix of collectivism and individualism. Similarly, it is possible to have totalitarian societies that are not collectivist.

Collectivism and Individualism

The term **collectivism** refers to a political system that stresses the primacy of collective goals over individual goals.[2] When collectivism is emphasized, the needs of society as a whole are generally viewed as being more important than individual freedoms. In such circumstances, an individual's right to do something may be restricted on the grounds that it runs counter to "the good of society" or to "the common good." Advocacy of collectivism can be traced to the ancient Greek philosopher Plato (427–347 BC), who in the *Republic* argued that individual rights should be sacrificed for the good of the majority and that property should be owned in common. It should be noted that Plato did not equate collectivism with equality—he believed that society should be stratified into classes, with those best suited to rule (which for Plato, naturally, were philosophers and soldiers) administering society for the benefit of all. In modern times, the collectivist mantle has been picked up by socialists.

SOCIALISM

Modern socialists trace their intellectual roots to Karl Marx (1818–1883), although socialist thought clearly predates Marx (elements of it can be traced back to Plato). Marx argued that the few benefit at the expense of the many in a capitalist society where individual freedoms are not restricted. According to Marx, the pay of workers does not reflect the full value of their labour. To correct this perceived wrong, Marx advocated state ownership of the basic means of production, distribution, and exchange (i.e., businesses). His logic was that if the state owned the means of production, the state could ensure that workers were fully compensated for their labour. Thus, the idea is to manage state-owned enterprise to benefit society as a whole, rather than individual capitalists.[3]

In the early twentieth century, the socialist ideology split into two broad camps. The **communists** believed that socialism could be achieved only through violent revolution and totalitarian dictatorship, while the **social democrats** committed themselves to achieving socialism by democratic means and turned their backs on violent revolution and dictatorship. Both versions of socialism waxed and waned during the twentieth century. The communist version of socialism reached its high point in the late 1970s, when the majority of the world's population lived in communist states. The countries under Communist Party rule at that time included the former Soviet Union; its Eastern European client nations (e.g., Poland, Czechoslovakia, Hungary); China; the Southeast Asian nations of Cambodia, Laos, and Vietnam; various African nations (e.g., Angola, Mozambique); and the Latin American nations of Cuba and Nicaragua. By the mid-1990s, however, communism was in retreat worldwide. The Soviet Union had collapsed and had been replaced by a collection of 15 republics, most of which were at least nominally structured as democracies. Communism was swept out of Eastern Europe by the largely bloodless revolutions of 1989. Apart from China, communism hangs on only in some small states, such as North Korea and Cuba.

Social democracy also seems to have passed a high-water mark, although the ideology may prove to be more enduring than communism. Social democracy has had perhaps its greatest influence in a number of democratic Western nations including Australia, Great Britain, France, Germany, Norway, Spain, and Sweden, where Social Democratic parties have from time to time held political power. Other countries where social democracy has had an important influence include India and Brazil. Consistent with their Marxists roots, many social democratic governments nationalized private companies in certain industries, transforming them into state-owned enterprises to be run for the "public good rather than private profit." Protected from significant competition by their monopoly position and guaranteed government financial support, many state-owned companies became increasingly inefficient. In the end, individuals found themselves paying for the luxury of state ownership through higher prices and higher taxes. Many Social Democratic parties were voted out of office during the 1970s and 1980s.

INDIVIDUALISM

Individualism is the opposite of collectivism. In a political sense, individualism refers to a philosophy that an individual should have freedom in his or her economic and political pursuits. In contrast to collectivism, individualism stresses that the interests of the individual should take precedence over the interests of the state. Like collectivism, individualism can be traced to an ancient Greek philosopher, in this case Plato's disciple Aristotle (384–322 BC). In contrast to Plato, Aristotle argued that individual diversity and private ownership are desirable. In a passage that might have been taken from a speech by contemporary politicians who adhere to a free market ideology, he argued that private property is more highly productive than communal property and will thus stimulate progress. According to Aristotle, communal property receives little care, whereas property that is owned by an individual will receive the greatest care and therefore be most productive.

Individualism was reborn as an influential political philosophy in the Protestant trading nations of England and the Netherlands during the sixteenth century. The philosophy was refined in the work of a number of British philosophers including David Hume (1711–1776), Adam Smith (1723–1790), and John Stuart Mill (1806–1873). The philosophy of individualism exercised a profound influence on those in the American colonies who sought independence from Great Britain. Individualism underlies the ideas expressed in the Declaration of Independence.

ANOTHER PERSPECTIVE

Turkey: Government Determined to Privatize Publicly Funded Theatres

Deputy Prime Minister and Justice and Development Party (AK Party) government spokesperson Bülent Arınç announced recently that the government is determined to privatize and halt funding for state-run theatres. Arınç said although municipalities have been running these theatres and paying the salaries of the players, neither the quality of nor the public interest in the theatres has increased significantly.

"In an area like arts, freedom should be maintained in a better way. Let's say there is an employer on the one side and employees on the other side: It is not possible to establish a healthy relationship between them. You see [theatre artists] revolt against even a simple regulation change," Arınç said.

The deputy prime minister also noted that the Ministry of Finance and the Ministry of Culture and Tourism are working to see under which circumstances the privatization of theatres will increase their quality.

Source: "Arınç: Gov't determined to privatize publicly funded theaters," *World Bulletin*, May 3, 2012, www.worldbulletin. net/?aType=haber&ArticleID=89359.

Individualism is built on two central tenets. The first is an emphasis on the importance of guaranteeing individual freedom and self-expression. As John Stuart Mill put it,

> The sole end for which mankind are warranted, individually or collectively, in interfering with the liberty of action of any of their number is self-protection . . . The only purpose for which power can be rightfully exercised over any member of a civilized community, against his will, is to prevent harm to others. His own good, either physical or moral, is not a sufficient warrant . . . The only part of the conduct of any one, for which he is amenable to society, is that which concerns others. In the part which merely concerns himself, his independence is, of right, absolute. Over himself, over his own body and mind, the individual is sovereign.[4]

The second tenet of individualism is that the welfare of society is best served by letting people pursue their own economic self-interest, as opposed to some collective body (such as government) dictating what is in society's best interest. Or as Adam Smith put it in a famous passage from *The Wealth of Nations,* an individual who intends his own gain is

> led by an invisible hand to promote an end which was no part of his intention. Nor is it always worse for the society that it was no part of it. By pursuing his own interest he frequently promotes that of the society more effectually than when he really intends to promote it. I have never known much good done by those who effect to trade for the public good.[5]

The central message of individualism, therefore, is that individual economic and political freedoms are the ground rules on which a society should be based. This puts individualism in conflict with collectivism. Collectivism asserts the primacy of the collective over the individual, while individualism asserts the opposite. This underlying ideological conflict has shaped much of the recent history of the world. The Cold War, for example, was essentially a war between collectivism, championed by the now-defunct Soviet Union, and individualism, championed by the United States. From the late 1980s until about 2005, the waning of collectivism was matched by the ascendancy of individualism. Democratic ideals and market economics replaced socialism and communism in many states. Since 2005, there have been some signs of a swing back toward left-leaning socialist ideas in several countries, including several Latin America nations such as Venezuela, Bolivia, and Paraguay, along with Russia (see the Country Focus later in this chapter which details what has been occurring in Venezuela). Also, the global financial crisis of 2008–2009 may cause some reevaluation of the trends of the past two decades, and the pendulum might tilt back the other way for a while.

DEBATE THE ISSUE

What About People's Future Rights?

Individualism versus collectivism is a century-old debate topic and an inherently interesting issue. For example, does an individual's life belong to him or her or to the community, society, or country in which he or she resides? Most people have a direct and immediate answer, but it is not a consensus, but rather, it depends upon in which country you reside or to which personal "compass" you subscribe. Everyone has tendencies toward being both individualistic and collectivistic but prefers one way more than the other. So, which of these ideas—individualism or collectivism—do you think is correct, and which cultural belief do you prefer and why?

Source: The Objective Standard Web site, www.theobjectivestandard.com, accessed March 3, 2014.

Democracy and Totalitarianism

Democracy and totalitarianism are at different ends of a political dimension. **Democracy** refers to a political system in which government is by the people, exercised either directly or through elected representatives. **Totalitarianism** is a form of government in which one person or political party exercises absolute control over all spheres of human life and opposing political parties are prohibited. The democratic–totalitarian dimension is not independent of the collectivism–individualism dimension. Democracy and individualism go hand in hand, as do the communist version of collectivism and totalitarianism.

DEMOCRACY

The pure form of democracy, as originally practised by several city-states in ancient Greece, is based on a belief that citizens should be directly involved in decision making. In complex, advanced societies with populations in the tens or hundreds of millions this is impractical. Most modern democratic states practise what is commonly referred to as **representative democracy**. In a representative democracy, citizens periodically elect individuals to represent them. These elected representatives then form a government whose function is to make decisions on behalf of the electorate. A representative democracy rests on the assumption that if elected representatives fail to perform this job adequately, they will be voted down at the next election.

To guarantee that elected representatives can be held accountable for their actions by the electorate, an ideal representative democracy has a number of safeguards that are typically enshrined in constitutional law. These include (1) an individual's right to freedom of expression, opinion, and organization; (2) a free media; (3) regular elections in which all eligible citizens are allowed to vote; (4) universal adult suffrage; (5) limited terms for elected representatives; (6) a fair court system that is independent from the political system; (7) a nonpolitical state bureaucracy; (8) a nonpolitical police force and armed service; and (9) relatively free access to state information.[6]

TOTALITARIANISM

In a totalitarian country, all the constitutional guarantees on which representative democracies are built—such as an individual's right to freedom of expression and organization, a free media, and regular elections—are denied to the citizens. In most totalitarian states, political repression is widespread and those who question the right of the rulers to rule find themselves imprisoned or worse.

Four major forms of totalitarianism exist in the world today. Until recently the most widespread was **communist totalitarianism**. As discussed earlier, communism is a version of collectivism that advocates that socialism can be achieved only through totalitarian dictatorship. Communism, however, is in decline worldwide and many of the old Communist Party dictatorships have collapsed since 1989. The major exceptions to this trend (so far) are China, Vietnam, Laos, North Korea, and Cuba, although all of these states exhibit clear signs that the Communist Party's monopoly on political power is under attack.

A second form of totalitarianism might be labelled **theocratic totalitarianism**. Theocratic totalitarianism is found in states where political power is monopolized by a party, group, or individual that governs according to religious principles. The most common form of theocratic totalitarianism is based on Islam and is exemplified by states such as Iran and Saudi Arabia. These states limit freedom of political and religious expression while the laws of the state are based on Islamic principles.

A third form of totalitarianism might be referred to as **tribal totalitarianism**. Tribal totalitarianism has arisen from time to time in African countries such as Zimbabwe, Tanzania, Uganda, and Kenya. The borders of most African states reflect the administrative boundaries drawn by the old European colonial powers, rather than tribal realities. Consequently, the typical African country contains a number of different tribes. Tribal totalitarianism occurs when a political party that represents the interests of a particular tribe (and not always the majority tribe) monopolizes power. Such one-party states still exist in Africa.

A fourth major form of totalitarianism might be described as **right-wing totalitarianism**. Right-wing totalitarianism generally permits some individual economic freedom but restricts individual political freedom on the grounds that it would lead to the rise of communism. One common feature of most right-wing dictatorships is an overt hostility to socialist or communist ideas. Many right-wing totalitarian governments are backed by the military, and in some cases the government may be made up of military officers. The fascist regimes that ruled Germany and Italy in the 1930s and 1940s were right-wing totalitarian states. Until the early 1980s, right-wing dictatorships, many of which were military dictatorships, were common throughout Latin America. They were also found in several Asian countries, particularly South Korea, Taiwan, Singapore, Indonesia, and the Philippines.

ANOTHER PERSPECTIVE

Is Representative Democracy the Best Way?

Chile is a country in South America that borders the South Pacific Sea. Neighbouring countries include Argentina, Bolivia, and Peru—also representative democracies. Chile has a strategic location relative to sea lanes between the Atlantic and Pacific Oceans, including the Strait of Magellan, the Beagle Channel, and the Drake Passage. Chile has a market-oriented economy in which the prices of goods and services are determined in a free price system. The government system is a republic (and it returned to a democracy in 1990). The chief of state and head of government is the president. Presidential and congressional elections are held periodically, with each election since the post-Pinochet era (which ended in 1988) being viewed as free and fair.

Source: Michigan State University, globalEDGE, http://globalEDGE.msu.edu/countries/chile/government.

LO2 | Economic Systems

It should be clear from the previous section that there is a connection between political ideology and economic systems. In countries where individual goals are given primacy over collective goals, we are more likely to find free market economic systems. In contrast, in countries where collective goals are given pre-eminence, the state may have taken control over many enterprises, while markets in such countries are likely to be restricted rather than free. We can identify three broad types of economic systems—a market economy, a command economy, and a mixed economy.

Market Economy

In a pure **market economy**, all productive activities are privately owned, as opposed to being owned by the state. The goods and services that a country produces, and the quantity in which they are produced, are not planned by anyone. Rather, production is determined by the interaction of supply and demand and signalled to producers through the price system. If demand for a product exceeds supply, prices will rise, signalling producers to produce more. If supply exceeds demand, prices will fall, signalling producers to produce less. In this system consumers are sovereign. The purchasing patterns of consumers, as signalled to producers through the mechanism of the price system, determine what is produced and in what quantity.

For a market to work in this manner there must be no restrictions on supply. A restriction on supply occurs when a market is monopolized by a single firm. In such circumstances, rather than increase output in response to increased demand, a monopolist might restrict output and let prices rise. This allows the monopolist to take a greater profit margin on each unit it sells. Although this is good for the monopolist, it is bad for the consumer, who has to pay higher prices. It also is probably bad for the welfare of society. Since a monopolist has no competitors, it has no incentive to search for ways to lower production costs. Rather, it can simply pass on cost increases to consumers in the form of higher prices. The net result is that the monopolist is likely to become increasingly inefficient, producing high-priced, low-quality goods, while society suffers as a consequence.

Given the dangers inherent in monopoly, the role of government in a market economy is to encourage vigorous competition between private producers. Governments do this by outlawing monopolies and restrictive business practices designed to monopolize a market (antitrust laws serve this function in the United States). Private ownership also encourages vigorous competition and economic efficiency. Private ownership ensures that entrepreneurs have a right to the profits generated by their own efforts. This gives entrepreneurs an incentive to search for better ways of serving consumer needs. That may be through introducing new products, by developing more efficient production processes, by better marketing and after-sale service, or simply through managing their businesses more efficiently than their competitors. In turn, the constant improvement in product and process that results from such an incentive has been argued to have a major positive impact on economic growth and development.[7]

Command Economy

In a pure **command economy**, the goods and services that a country produces, the quantity in which they are produced, and the prices at which they are sold are all planned by the government. Consistent with the collectivist ideology, the objective of a command economy is for government to allocate resources for "the good of society." In addition, in a pure command economy, all businesses are state owned, the rationale being that the government can then direct them to make investments that are in the best interests of the nation as a whole, rather than in the interests of private individuals. Historically, command economies were found in communist countries where collectivist goals were given priority over individual goals. Since the demise of communism in the late 1980s, the number of command economies has fallen dramatically. Some elements of a command economy were also evident in a number of democratic nations led by socialist-inclined governments. France and India both experimented with extensive government planning and state ownership, although government planning has fallen into disfavour in both countries.

While the objective of a command economy is to mobilize economic resources for the public good, the opposite seems to have occurred. In a command economy, state-owned enterprises have little incentive to control costs and be efficient because they cannot go out of business. Also, the abolition of private ownership means there is no incentive for individuals to look for better ways to serve consumer needs; hence, dynamism and innovation are absent from command economies. Instead of growing and becoming more prosperous, such economies tend to be characterized by stagnation.

Mixed Economy

Between market economies and command economies can be found mixed economies. In a **mixed economy**, certain sectors of the economy are left to private ownership and free market mechanisms while other sectors have significant state ownership and government planning. Mixed economies were once very common throughout much of the world, although they are becoming much less so. Not long ago, Great Britain, France, and Sweden were mixed economies, but extensive privatization has reduced state ownership of businesses in all three countries.

In mixed economies governments tend to take into state ownership troubled firms whose continued operation is thought to be vital to national interests. For example, in 2008 the U.S. government took an 80 percent stake in AIG to stop that financial institution from collapsing, the theory being that if AIG did collapse, it would have very serious consequences for the entire financial system. The U.S. government usually prefers market-oriented solutions to economic problems, and in the AIG case, the intention was to sell the institution back to private investors as soon as possible. The United States also took similar action with respect to a number of other troubled private enterprises, including Citigroup and General Motors. In all these cases, the government stake was seen as nothing more than a short-term action designed to stave off economic collapse by injecting capital into troubled enterprises in highly unusually circumstances. As soon as it was able to, the government sold these stakes. In early 2010, for example, the U.S. government sold its stake in Citigroup. The government stake in AIG was sold off in 2012, and by 2014 it had also disposed of its stake in GM.

LO3 | Legal Systems

The **legal system** of a country refers to the rules, or laws, that regulate behaviour, along with the processes by which the laws are enforced and through which redress for grievances is obtained. The legal system of a country is of immense importance to international business. A country's laws regulate business practice, define the manner in which business transactions are to be executed, and set down the rights and obligations of those involved in business transactions. The legal environments of countries differ in significant ways. As we shall see, differences in legal systems can affect the attractiveness of a country as an investment site and/or market.

Like the economic system of a country, the legal system is influenced by the prevailing political system (although it is also strongly influenced by historical tradition). The government of a country defines the legal framework within which firms do business—and often the laws that regulate business reflect the rulers' dominant political ideology. For example, collectivist-inclined totalitarian states tend to enact laws that severely restrict private enterprise, while the laws enacted by governments in democratic states where individualism is the dominant political philosophy tend to favour private enterprise and consumers.

Here we focus on several issues that illustrate how legal systems can vary—and how such variations can affect international business. First, we look at some basic differences in legal systems. Next we look at contract law. Third, we look at the laws governing property rights with particular reference to patents, copyrights, and trademarks. Fourth, we look at laws covering product safety and product liability.

Different Legal Systems

There are three main types of legal systems—or legal traditions—in use around the world: common law, civil law, and theocratic law.

COMMON LAW

The common law system evolved in England over hundreds of years. It is now found in most of Great Britain's former colonies including Canada, outside of Quebec. **Common law** is based on tradition, precedent, and custom. *Tradition* refers to a country's legal history, *precedent* to cases that have come before the courts in the past, and *custom* to the ways in which laws are applied in specific situations. When law courts interpret common law, they do so with regard to these characteristics. This gives a common law system a degree of flexibility that other systems lack. Judges in a common law system have the power to *interpret* the law so that it applies to the unique circumstances of an individual case. In turn, each new interpretation sets a precedent that may be followed in future cases. As new precedents arise, laws may be altered, clarified, or amended to deal with new situations.

CIVIL LAW

A **civil law** system is based on a very detailed set of laws organized into codes. When law courts interpret civil law, they do so with regard to these codes. More than 80 countries, including Germany, France, Japan, Canada (Quebec), and Russia operate with a civil law system. A civil law system tends to be less adversarial than a common law system, since the judges rely upon detailed legal codes rather than tradition, precedent, and custom, which they interpret. Judges under a civil law system have less *flexibility* than those under a common law system. Judges in a common law system have the power to *interpret* the law, while judges in a civil law system have the power only to *apply* the law.

THEOCRATIC LAW

A **theocratic law** system is one in which the law is based on religious teachings. Islamic law is the most widely practised theocratic legal system in the modern world, although usage of both Hindu and Jewish law persisted into the twentieth century. Islamic law is primarily a moral rather than a commercial law and is intended to govern all aspects of life.[8] The foundation for Islamic law is the holy book of Islam, the Koran, along with the Sunna, or decisions and sayings of the Prophet Muhammad, and the writings of Islamic scholars who have derived rules by analogy from the principles established in the Koran and the Sunna. Since the Koran and Sunna are holy documents, this means the basic foundations of Islamic law cannot be changed. However, in practice, Islamic jurists and scholars are constantly debating the application of Islamic law to the modern world. Moreover, many Muslim countries have legal systems that are a blend of Islamic law and a common or civil law system. Further, in the province of Ontario, the use of sharia, or Islamic law, has been instituted for those Muslims wishing to resolve marital agreements and other civil disputes, and to make decisions. Ontario's 1991 Arbitration Act allows religious groups to resolve family disputes within the traditions of their faith. Catholics and Ismaili Muslims use the provisions of the Arbitration Act, and Hassidic Jews have been running their own Beit Din arbitrations based on Jewish law for years. Rulings are to be binding, but must be consistent with Canadian laws and the Charter of Rights.[9]

ANOTHER PERSPECTIVE

No Interest in Islamic Banking? Why?

How can a banking system operate without interest (*riba* in Arabic)? The basic economic idea is that commercial risk should be shared. In the Western approach, interest guarantees the banker a return, so on a collateralized loan, the banker avoids much of the commercial risk that's inherent in business. No matter what happens to the business, the banker gets a return. In contrast, Islam requires that the banker share this commercial risk. If the business venture is successful, the banker shares the profit. If the venture doesn't do well, neither does the banker. The value of community in Islam is stronger than the value of individual profit.

Although Islamic law is primarily concerned with moral behaviour, it has been extended to cover certain commercial activities. An example is the payment or receipt of interest, which is considered usury and outlawed by the Koran. To the devout Muslim, acceptance of interest payments is seen as a very grave sin; the giver and the taker are equally damned. This is not just a matter of theology; in several Islamic states it has also become a matter of law. In 1992, for example, Pakistan's Federal Shariat Court, the highest Islamic law-making body in the country, pronounced interest to be un-Islamic and therefore illegal and demanded that the government amend all financial laws accordingly. In 1999, Pakistan's Supreme Court ruled that Islamic banking methods should be used in the country in the future.[10]

Differences in Contract Law

The difference between common law and civil law system can be illustrated by the approach of each to contract law (remember, most theocratic legal systems also have elements of common or civil law). A **contract** is a document that specifies the conditions under which an exchange is to occur and details the rights and obligations of the parties involved. Many business transactions are regulated by some form of contract. **Contract law** is the body of law that governs contract creation and enforcement. The parties to an agreement normally invoke contract law when one party believes the other has violated either the letter or the spirit of an agreement.

Since common law tends to be relatively ill specified, contracts drafted under a common law framework tend to be very detailed with all contingencies spelled out. In civil law systems, however, contracts tend to be much shorter and less specific because many of the issues typically covered in a common law contract are already covered in a civil code. This implies that it is more expensive to draw up contracts in a common law jurisdiction, and that resolving contract disputes can be a very adversarial process in common law systems. On the other hand, common law systems have the advantage of greater flexibility and allow for judges to interpret a contract dispute in light of the prevailing situation. International businesses need to be sensitive to these differences since approaching a contract dispute in a state with a civil law system as if it had a common law system may backfire (and vice versa).

When contract disputes arise in international trade, there is always the question of which country's laws apply. The phrase "comity of nations" refers to the legal doctrine under which countries recognize and enforce each others' legal decrees. To try to resolve this issue, a number of countries, including Canada, have ratified the **United Nations Convention on Contracts for the International Sale of Goods (CISG)**. CISG establishes a uniform set of rules governing certain aspects of the making and performance of everyday commercial contracts between sellers and buyers who have their places of business in different nations. By adopting CISG, a nation signifies to the other nations that have adopted it that it will treat the convention's rules as part of its law. CISG applies automatically to all contracts for the sale of goods between different firms based in countries that have ratified the convention, unless the parties to the contract explicitly opt out. Since its inception in 1988, it has been ratified by 80 countries.

When firms do not wish to accept the CISG, they often opt for arbitration by a recognized arbitration court to settle contract disputes. The most well known of these courts is the International Court of Arbitration of the International Chamber of Commerce in Paris, which handles more than 500 requests per year from more than 100 countries.[11]

Property Rights

In a legal sense, the term *property* refers to a resource over which an individual or business holds a legal title; that is, a resource that it owns. Resources include land, buildings, equipment, capital, mineral rights, businesses, and intellectual property (such as patents, copyrights, and trademarks). **Property rights** refer to the bundle of legal rights over the use to which a resource is put and over the use made of any income that may be derived from that resource.[12] Countries differ significantly in the extent to which their legal system protects property rights. Although almost all countries have laws on their books that protect property rights, the reality is that in many countries these laws are not well enforced by the authorities and property rights are violated. Property rights can be violated in two ways—through private action and through public action.

PRIVATE ACTION

In this context, **private action** refers to theft, piracy, blackmail, and the like by private individuals or groups. Although theft occurs in all countries, a weak legal system allows for a much higher level of criminal action in some than in others. For example, in Russia in the chaotic period following the collapse of communism, an outdated legal system, coupled with a weak police force and judicial system, offered both domestic and foreign businesses scant protection from blackmail by the "Russian Mafia." Successful business owners in Russia often had to pay "protection money" to the Mafia or face violent retribution, including bombings and assassinations (about 500 contract killings of businessmen occurred per year in the 1990s).[13]

Russia is not alone in having Mafia problems (and the situation in Russia has improved significantly since the 1990s). The Mafia has a long history in the United States (Chicago in the 1930s was similar to Moscow in the 1990s) and in Canada. In Japan, the local version of the Mafia, known as the *yakuza*, runs protection rackets, particularly in the food and entertainment industries.[14] However, there was a big difference between the magnitude of such activity in Russia in the 1990s and its limited impact in Japan and North America. This difference arose because the legal enforcement apparatus, such as the police and court system, was weak in Russia following the collapse of communism. Many other countries from time to time have had problems similar to or even greater than those experienced by Russia.

PUBLIC ACTION AND CORRUPTION

Public action to violate property rights occurs when public officials, such as politicians and government bureaucrats, extort income or resources from property holders. This can be done through a number of legal mechanisms such as levying excessive taxation, requiring expensive licences or permits from property holders, or taking assets into state ownership without compensating the owners. It can also be done by illegal means, or corruption, by demanding bribes from businesses in return for the rights to operate in a country, industry, or location.[15] For example, the government of the late Ferdinand Marcos in the Philippines was famous for demanding bribes from foreign businesses wishing to set up operations in that country.[16] The same was true of government officials in Indonesia under the rule of ex-President Suharto.

Corruption has been well documented in every society, from the banks of the Congo River to the palace of the Dutch royal family, from Japanese politicians to Brazilian bankers, and from Indonesian government officials to the New York City Police Department. No society is immune to corruption. However, there are systematic

TABLE 2.1	Corruption Perceptions Index	
Country	**Rank**	**Score**
Denmark	1	91
Finland	2	90
Sweden	3	89
Canada	9	83
United States	16	76
North Korea	167	8
Somalia	167 (tied)	8

Source: Data taken from 2016 Corruption Perceptions Index. Please see http://www.transparency.org/cpi2015#results-table.

differences in the extent of corruption across countries. In some countries, the rule of law is such that corruption is kept to a minimum. Corruption is seen and treated as illegal, and, when discovered, violators are punished by the full force of the law. Unfortunately, in other countries the rule of law is weak and corruption by bureaucrats and politicians is rife. Corruption is so endemic in some countries that politicians and bureaucrats regard it as a perk of office and openly flout anti-corruption laws. Political corruption is nothing new to Canada and our first Prime Minister, Sir John A. Macdonald introduced Canada to its first major scandal (known as the Pacific Scandal) forcing his eventual resignation in 1873. In 2012, the Ontario government was caught up in the Ornge scandal (the province's air ambulance service) when the province spent over $700 million, with little oversight at a time when the number of patients being transported by the service declined.[17] Table 2.1 presents the Corruption Perception Index (CPI), created by Transparency International. The index presents data concerning the degree of corruption as seen by business people, academics, and risk analysts in different countries. A country's score indicates the perceived level of public sector corruption on a scale from 0 to 100, where 0 means that a country is perceived as highly corrupt, and 100 means that it is perceived as very clean.

Economic evidence suggests that high levels of corruption significantly reduce the economic growth rate in a country.[18] By siphoning off profits, corrupt politicians and bureaucrats reduce the returns to business investment and, hence, reduce the incentive for both domestic and foreign businesses to invest in that country. The lower level of investment that results has a negative impact on economic growth. Thus, we would expect countries with high levels of corruption such as Somalia and North Korea to have a much lower rate of economic growth than might otherwise have been the case. A detailed example of the negative effect that corruption can have on economic progress is given in the accompanying Country Focus, which looks at the impact of corruption on economic growth in Nigeria.

THE AMERICAN FOREIGN CORRUPT PRACTICES ACT AND CANADIAN BILL S-21

In the United States, the **Foreign Corrupt Practices Act** was passed during the 1970s following revelations that U.S. companies had bribed government officials in foreign countries in an attempt to win lucrative contracts. This law makes it a violation of U.S. law to bribe a foreign government official to obtain or maintain business over which that foreign official has authority, and it requires all publicly traded companies (whether or not they are involved in international trade) to keep detailed records to allow someone to determine whether a violation of the act has occurred.

COUNTRY FOCUS

Corruption in Nigeria

When Nigeria gained independence from Great Britain in 1960, there were hopes that the country might emerge as an economic heavyweight in Africa. Not only was Nigeria Africa's most populous country, but it also was blessed with abundant natural resources, particularly oil. Despite this, Nigeria remains one of the poorest countries in the world. According to the 2012 Human Development Index compiled by the United Nations, Nigeria had "low human development." The country ranked 153rd out of the 187 covered. Gross national income per capita was just $2102; almost 40 percent of the adult population was illiterate; and life expectancy at birth was only 52.3 years.

What went wrong? Although there is no simple answer, a number of factors seem to have conspired to damage economic activity in Nigeria. The country is composed of several competing ethnic, tribal, and religious groups, and the conflict among them has limited political stability and led to political strife, including a brutal civil war in the 1970s. With the legitimacy of the government always in question, political leaders often purchased support by legitimizing bribes and by raiding the national treasury to reward allies. Civilian rule after independence was followed by a series of military dictatorships, each of which seemed more corrupt and inept than the last (the country returned to civilian rule in 1999).

During the 1990s, the military dictator Sani Abacha openly and systematically plundered the state treasury for his own personal gain. His most blatant scam was the Petroleum Trust Fund that he set up in the mid-1990s, ostensibly to channel extra revenue from an increase in fuel prices into much-needed infrastructure projects and other investments. The fund was not independently audited, and almost none of the money that passed through it was properly accounted for. It was, in fact, a vehicle for Abacha and his supporters to spend at will a sum that in 1996 was equivalent to some 25 percent of the total federal budget. Abacha, aware of his position as an unpopular and unelected leader, lavished money on personal security and handed out bribes to those whose support he coveted. With examples like this at the very top of the government, it is not surprising that corruption could be found throughout the political and bureaucratic apparatus.

Olusegun Obasanjo was elected President of Nigeria in 2003 on a platform that included a promise to fight corruption. © *Rawpixelimages/ Dreamstime.com*

Has the situation in Nigeria improved since the country returned to civilian rule in 1999? In 2003, Olusegun Obasanjo was elected president on a platform that included a promise to fight corruption. By some accounts, progress has been seen. His anticorruption chief, Nuhu Ribadu, claimed that whereas 70 percent of the country's oil revenues were being stolen or wasted in 2002, by the mid-2000s the figure was "only" 40 percent. But in its most recent survey (2016), Transparency International still ranked Nigeria 136th out of 167, suggesting that the country still has a long way to go.

Questions

1. How can a company operate in a country such as Nigeria and yet still adhere to its own ethical framework?

2. Should a company try to influence a country to become less corrupt? How would it do this?

Sources: "A Tale of Two Giants," *The Economist*, January 15, 2000, p. 5; J. Coolidge and S. Rose Ackerman, "High Level Rent Seeking and Corruption in African Regimes," World Bank policy research working paper no. 1780, June 1997; D. L. Bevan, P. Collier, and J. W. Gunning, *Nigeria and Indonesia: The Political Economy of Poverty, Equity and Growth* (Oxford, UK: Oxford University Press, 1999); "Democracy and Its Discontents," *The Economist*, January 29, 2005, p. 55; A. Field, "Can Reform Save Nigeria?" *Journal of Commerce*, November 21, 2005, p. 1; "A Blacklist to Bolster Democracy," *The Economist*, February 17, 2007, p. 59; J. P. Luna, "Back on Track: Nigeria's Hard Path towards Reform," *Harvard International Review*, 29, no. 3 (2007), p. 7; and Transparency International, Corruption Perceptions Index, 2016.

In May 1997, the Organization for Economic Cooperation and Development (OECD) called for the negotiation of a binding convention by the end of 1997 to address the bribery of foreign public officials, and recommended that member states submit legislative proposals to their national legislatures to criminalize such bribery and seek their enactment by the end of 1998. On June 21, 1997, leaders of the G7 countries (including then Prime Minister Chrétien) issued a statement in Denver endorsing this approach and timetable for the OECD. Negotiations of the Convention on Combating Bribery of Foreign Public Officials in International Business Transactions (the OECD Convention) concluded on November 21, 1997, and Canada signed the Convention in Paris on December 17, 1997. In the Final Communiqué of the G8 Birmingham Summit, dated May 17, 1998, heads of state or government pledged to make every effort to ratify the OECD Convention by the end of 1998.[19]

Out of these initiatives grew Canada's **Bill S-21,** an Act regarding the Corruption of Foreign Public Officials and the Implementation of the Convention on Combating Bribery of Foreign Public Officials in International Business Transactions that was introduced in the Senate on December 1, 1998. The Corruption of Foreign Public Officials Act received Royal Assent on December 10, 1998 (S.C. 1998, c. 34). Canada ratified the OECD Convention on December 17, 1998.

As with the U.S. Foreign Corrupt Practices Act, the Canadian Bill S-21 does have "loophole" provisions to cover for those instances in which a bribe might be solely a perception, due to cultural considerations of gift-giving, in other countries. Paragraph 3(3)(a) of Bill S-21, sets out a lawful exception that an accused could use as a defence, namely, that the payment was lawful in the foreign state or public international organization for which the foreign public official performs duties or functions. If successful, this would be a full defence to the offence in subsection 3(1). Paragraph 3(3)(b) sets out an additional defence. To use this defence, the accused must show that the loan, reward, advantage, or benefit was:

- a reasonable expense,
- incurred in good faith,
- made by or on behalf of the foreign public official, and *directly related* to the promotion, demonstration or explanation of the person's products and services or to the execution or performance of a contract between the person and the foreign state for which the official performs duties or functions.[20]

This defence is virtually identical to a defence in the U.S. Foreign Corrupt Practices Act.

ANOTHER PERSPECTIVE

How Important Are Intellectual Property Rights?

Burundi is a landlocked country in the Great Lake region of Eastern Africa. Neighbouring countries include Rwanda, Tanzania, and the Democratic Republic of the Congo. Burundi is hilly and mountainous, with access to Lac Tanganyika. The government system is a republic, with the chief of state and head of government being the president. Burundi has a traditional economic system in which the allocation of available resources is made on the basis of primitive methods, and many citizens engage in subsistence agriculture. At the same time, Burundi was last of the 131 countries ranked in the 2013 International Property Rights Index (IPRI). The IPRI is conducted by a partnership of 74 international organizations. The IPRI takes into account legal and political environment, physical property rights, and intellectual property rights.

Source: The International Property Rights Index, www.internationalpropertyrightsindex.org.

The Protection of Intellectual Property

Intellectual property refers to property that is the product of intellectual activity, such as computer software, a screenplay, a music score, or the chemical formula for a new drug. Ownership rights over intellectual property are established through patents, copyrights, and trademarks. A **patent** grants the inventor of a new product or process exclusive rights for a defined period to the manufacture, use, or sale of that invention. **Copyrights** are the exclusive legal rights of authors, composers, playwrights, artists, and publishers to publish and disperse their work as they see fit. **Trademarks** are designs and names, often officially registered, by which merchants or manufacturers designate and differentiate their products (e.g., Christian Dior clothes). In the high-technology "knowledge" economy of the twenty-first century, intellectual property has become an increasingly important source of economic value for businesses. Protecting intellectual property has also become increasingly problematic, particularly if it can be rendered in a digital form and then copied and distributed at very low cost via pirated CDs or over the Internet (e.g., computer software and music and video recordings).[21]

The philosophy behind intellectual property laws is to reward the originator of a new invention, book, musical recording, clothes design, restaurant chain, and the like for his or her idea and effort. Such laws are a very important stimulus to innovation and creative work. They provide an incentive for people to search for novel ways of doing things, and they reward creativity. For example, consider innovation in the pharmaceutical industry. A patent will grant the inventor of a new drug a 20-year monopoly in production of that drug. This gives pharmaceutical firms an incentive to undertake the expensive, difficult, and time-consuming basic research required to generate new drugs (it can cost $500 million in R&D and take 12 years to get a new drug on the market). Without the guarantees provided by patents, it is unlikely that companies would commit themselves to extensive basic research.[22]

The protection of intellectual property rights differs greatly from country to country. While many countries have stringent intellectual property regulations on their books, the enforcement of these regulations has often been lax. This has been the case even among some of the 185 countries that are part of the World Intellectual Property Organization and have signed the **Paris Convention for the Protection of Industrial Property**, an important international agreement to protect intellectual property.[23] Weak enforcement encourages the piracy of intellectual property. China and Thailand have recently been among the worst offenders in Asia. Pirated computer software is widely available in China. Similarly, the streets of Bangkok, the capital of Thailand, are lined with stands selling pirated copies of Rolex watches, Levi's blue jeans, DVDs, and computer software.

Piracy in music recordings is rampant. The International Federation of the Phonographic Industry claims that about one-third of all recorded music products sold worldwide are pirated (illegal) copies, suggesting that piracy costs the industry more than $4.5 billion annually.[24] The computer software industry also suffers from lax enforcement of

A security guard stands near a pile of pirated CDs and DVDs before they were destroyed at a ceremony in Beijing on Saturday, February 26, 2005. Thousands of pirated items were destroyed in the event, one of a number of activities, including an antipiracy pop concert later that day, that were staged by China's government to publicize its antipiracy efforts. © ChinaFotoPress/Getty Images

COUNTRY FOCUS

Venezuela under Hugo Chávez, 1999–2013

On March 5, 2013, Hugo Chávez, the president of Venezuela, died after losing a battle against cancer. Chávez had been president of Venezuela since 1999. A former military officer who was once jailed for engineering a failed coup attempt, Chávez was a self-styled democratic socialist who won the presidential election by campaigning against corruption, economic mismanagement, and the "harsh realities" of global capitalism. When he took office in February 1999, Chávez claimed he had inherited the worst economic situation in the country's recent history. He wasn't far off the mark. A collapse in the price of oil, which accounted for 70 percent of the country's exports, left Venezuela with a large budget deficit and forced the economy into a deep recession.

Soon after taking office, Chávez worked to consolidate his hold over the apparatus of government. By 2012, Freedom House, which annually assesses political and civil liberties worldwide, concluded Venezuela was only "partly free" and that freedoms were being progressively curtailed.

On the economic front, things remained rough. The economy shrank in the early 2000s, while unemployment remained persistently high (at 15 to 17 percent) and the poverty rate rose to more than 50 percent of the population. A 2003 study by the World Bank concluded Venezuela was one of the most regulated economies in the world and that state controls over business activities gave public officials ample opportunities to enrich themselves by demanding bribes in return for permission to expand operations or enter new lines of business. Indeed, despite Chávez's anticorruption rhetoric, Transparency International, which ranks the world's nations according to the extent of public corruption, noted that corruption increased under Chávez. In 2012, Transparency International ranked Venezuela 165th out of 174 nations in terms of level of corruption. Consistent with his socialist rhetoric, Chávez progressively took various enterprises into state ownership and required that other enterprises be restructured as "workers' cooperatives" in return for government loans. In addition, the government took over large rural farms and ranches that Chávez claimed were not sufficiently productive and turned them into state-owned cooperatives.

In mid-2000, the world oil market bailed Chávez out of mounting economic difficulties. Oil prices started to surge from the low $20s in 2003, reaching $150 a barrel by mid-2008. Venezuela, the world's fifth-largest producer, reaped a bonanza. On the back of surging oil exports, the economy grew at a robust rate. Chávez used the oil revenues to boost government spending on social programs, many of them modeled after programs in Cuba. In 2006, he announced plans to reduce the stakes held by foreign companies in oil projects in the Orinoco regions and to give the state-run oil company a majority position.

Riding a wave of popularity at home, in December 2006 Chávez won reelection as president. He celebrated his victory by stepping on the revolutionary accelerator. Parliament gave him the power to legislate by decree for 18 months. In late 2010, Chávez yet again persuaded the National Assembly, where his supporters dominated, to once more grant him the power to rule by decree for another 18 months.

Notwithstanding his ability to consolidate political power, on the economic front Venezuela's performance under Chávez was decidedly mixed. His main achievements were to reduce poverty, which fell from 50 percent to 28 percent by 2012, and to bring down unemployment from 14.5 percent at the start of his rule to 7.6 percent in February 2013. State-owned enterprises helped Chávez achieve both these goals.

However, despite strong global demand and massive reserves, oil production in Venezuela fell by a third between 2000 and 2012 as foreign oil companies exited the country. Inflation surged and was running at around 28 percent per annum between 2008 and 2012, one of the highest rates in the world. To compound matters, the budget deficit expanded to 17 percent of GDP in 2012 as the government spent heavily to support its social programs and various subsidies. (Most recently, Venezuela's GDP has been shrinking every quarter since the beginning of 2014).

Questions

1. What do you think will happen if oil prices continue to stay below $100 a barrel?
2. What are the broader implications to the country's economy, and its people, of having such a highly regulated economy for over 15 years?

Source: D. Luhnow and P. Millard, "Chavez Plans to Take More Control of Oil away from Foreign Firms," *The Wall Street Journal*, April 24, 2006, p. A1; R. Gallego, "Chavez's Agenda Takes Shape," *The Wall Street Journal*, December 27, 2005, p. A12; "The Sickly Stench of Corruption: Venezuela," *The Economist*, April 1, 2006, p. 50; "Chavez Squeezes the Oil Firms," *The Economist*, November 12, 2005, p. 61; "Glimpsing the Bottom of the Barrel: Venezuela," *The Economist*, February 3, 2007, p. 51; "The Wind Goes Out of the Revolution—Defeat for Hugo Chavez," *The Economist*, December 8, 2007, pp. 30–32; "Oil Leak," *The Economist*, February 26, 2011, p. 43; "Medieval Policies," *The Economist*, August 8, 2011, p. 38; and "Now for the Reckoning," *The Economist*, May 5, 2013; and Venezuela GDP Annual Growth Rate, http://www.tradingeconomics.com/venezuela/gdp-growth-annual.

intellectual property rights. Estimates suggest that violations of intellectual property rights cost personal computer software firms revenues equal to $59 billion in 2010.[25] According to the Business Software Alliance, a software industry association, in 2012 about 57 percent of the world's personal computer users admit to pirating software. Some of the worst countries were China, Russia and, perhaps surprisingly, the United States (see Map 2.1). Canada did not make this top 20 list.

International businesses have a number of possible responses to violations of their intellectual property. They can lobby their respective governments to push for international agreements to ensure that intellectual property rights are protected and that the law is enforced. Partly as a result of such actions, international laws are being

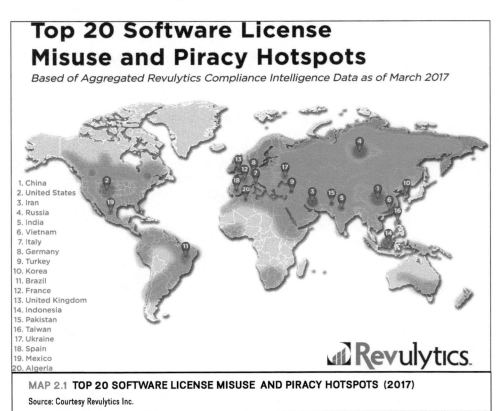

MAP 2.1 TOP 20 SOFTWARE LICENSE MISUSE AND PIRACY HOTSPOTS (2017)

Source: Courtesy Revulytics Inc.

strengthened. As we shall see in Chapter 6, the most recent world trade agreement, signed in 1994, extends the scope of the General Agreement on Tariffs and Trade to cover intellectual property for the first time. Under the new agreement, known as the Trade Related Aspects of Intellectual Property Rights (or TRIPS), as of 1995 a council of the World Trade Organization is overseeing enforcement of much stricter intellectual

MANAGEMENT FOCUS

Did Wal-Mart Violate the Foreign Corrupt Practices Act?

In the early 2000s, Wal-Mart wanted to build a new store in San Juan Teotihuacan, Mexico, barely a mile from ancient pyramids that drew tourists from around the world. The owner of the land was happy to sell to Wal-Mart, but one thing stood in the way of a deal—the city's new zoning laws. These prohibited commercial development in the historic area. Not to be denied, executives at the headquarters of Wal-Mart de Mexico found a way around the problem: They paid a $52,000 bribe to a local official to redraw the zoning area so that the property Wal-Mart wanted to purchase was placed outside the commercial-free zone. Wal-Mart then went ahead and built the store, opening it in late 2004 despite vigorous local opposition.

A former lawyer for Wal-Mart de Mexico subsequently contacted Wal-Mart executives at the company's corporate headquarters in Bentonville, Arkansas. He told them that Wal-Mart de Mexico routinely resorted to bribery, citing the altered zoning map as just one example. Alarmed, executives at Wal-Mart started their own investigation. Faced with growing evidence of corruption in Mexico, top Wal-Mart executives decided to engage in damage control rather than coming clean. Wal-Mart's top lawyer shipped the case files back to Mexico and handed responsibility for the investigation over to the general council of Wal-Mart de Mexico. This was an interesting choice as the very same general council was alleged to have authorized bribes. The general council quickly exonerated fellow Mexican executives, and the internal investigation was closed in 2006.

For several years nothing more happened; then, in April 2012, *The New York Times* published an article detailing bribery by Wal-Mart. The *Times* cited the changed zoning map and several other examples of bribery by Wal-Mart—for example, eight bribes totalling $341,000 enabled Wal-Mart to build a Sam's Club in one of Mexico City's most densely populated neighbourhoods without a construction license, or an environmental permit, or an urban impact assessment, or even a traffic permit. Similarly, thanks to nine bribe payments totalling $765,000, Wal-Mart built a vast refrigerated distribution centre in an environmentally fragile flood basin north of Mexico City, in an area where electricity was so scarce that many smaller developers were turned away.

Wal-Mart responded to *The New York Times* article by ramping up a second internal investigation into bribery that it had initiated in 2011. By mid-2013 there were reportedly more than 300 outside lawyers working on the investigation, and it had cost more than $300 million in fees. In addition, the U.S. Department of Justice and the Securities and Exchange Commission both announced that they had started investigations into Wal-Mart's practices. In November 2012, Wal-Mart reported that its own investigation into violations had extended beyond Mexico to include China and India. Among other things, they were looking into the allegations by the *Times* that top executives at Wal-Mart, including former CEO Lee Scott Jr., had deliberately squashed earlier investigations.

Questions

1. What would you do, as a senior executive, when presented with a case such as this?
2. What would you say to someone who responds that "bribery is just a cost of doing business"?

Sources: David Barstow, "Vast Mexican Bribery Case Hushed Up by Wal-Mart after Top Level Struggle," *The New York Times*, April 21, 2012; Stephanie Clifford and David Barstow, "Wal-Mart Inquiry Reflects Alarm on Corruption," *The New York Times*, November 15, 2012; and Nathan Vardi, "Why Justice Department Could Hit Wal-Mart Hard over Mexican Bribery Allegations," *Forbes*, April 22, 2012.

property regulations. These regulations oblige WTO members to grant and enforce patents lasting at least 20 years and copyrights lasting 50 years. Rich countries had to comply with the rules within a year. Poor countries, in which such protection generally was much weaker, had five years of grace, and the very poorest have 10 years.[26] (For further details of the TRIPS agreement, see Chapter 6.)

In addition to lobbying governments, firms can file lawsuits on their own behalf. Firms may also choose to stay out of countries where intellectual property laws are lax, rather than risk having their ideas stolen by local entrepreneurs. Firms also need to be on the alert to ensure that pirated copies of their products produced in countries with weak intellectual property laws don't turn up in their home market or in third-world countries. American computer software giant Microsoft, for example, discovered that pirated Microsoft software, produced illegally in Thailand, was being sold worldwide as the real thing.

Product Safety and Product Liability

Product safety laws set certain safety standards to which a product must adhere. **Product liability** involves holding a firm and its officers responsible when a product causes injury, death, or damage. Product liability can be much greater if a product does not conform to required safety standards. There are both civil and criminal product liability laws. Civil laws call for payment and monetary damages. Criminal liability laws result in fines or imprisonment. Both civil and criminal liability laws are probably more extensive in the United States than in any other country, although many other Western nations also have comprehensive liability laws. Liability laws are typically least extensive in less developed nations. A boom in product liability suits and awards in the United States resulted in a dramatic increase in the cost of liability insurance. Many business executives argue that the high costs of liability insurance make American businesses less competitive in the global marketplace.

In addition to the competitiveness issue, country differences in product safety and liability laws raise an important ethical issue for firms doing business abroad. When product safety laws are tougher in a firm's home country than in a foreign country and/or when liability laws are more lax, should a firm doing business in that foreign country follow the more relaxed local standards or should it adhere to the standards of its home country? While the ethical thing to do is undoubtedly to adhere to home-country standards, firms have been known to take advantage of lax safety and liability laws to do business in a manner that would not be allowed back home.

LO4 The Determinants of Economic Development

The political, economic, and legal systems of a country can have a profound impact on the level of economic development and hence on the attractiveness of a country as a possible market and/or production location for a firm. Here we look first at how countries differ in their level of development. Then we look at how the political economy affects economic progress.

Differences in Economic Development

Different countries have dramatically different levels of economic development. One common measure of economic development is a country's gross national product per head of population. Prior to 2001, the term GNP (gross national product) was commonly

TABLE 2.2	GNI Per Capita For Select Countries	
Country	**1962**	**2015**
Australia	$1,840	$60,070
Canada	2,340	47,540
Russia	N/A	11,450
Uganda	N/A	700
United States	3,280	55,900

Source: The World Bank Group, GNI per capita, Atlas method (current US$), http://data.worldbank.org/indicator/NY.GNP.PCAP.CD.

used by the World Bank as a yardstick for economic activity of a country; it measures the total value of the goods and services produced annually. Since 2001 the term GNP is increasingly being replaced by the acronym **GNI (gross national income)**. The new measure, GNI, totals the income of all citizens of a country, including the income from factors of production used abroad.

Different countries have different levels of development. Table 2.2 summarizes the GNI per capita of some of the world's wealthiest and poorest countries. The World Bank Atlas method is used. It calculates gross national income per capita in U.S. dollars for certain operational purposes. The World Bank then uses the Atlas conversion factor to reduce the impact of exchange rate fluctuations in the cross-country comparison of national incomes. The Atlas conversion factor for any year is the average of a country's exchange rate (or alternative conversion factor) for that year and its exchange rates for the two preceding years, adjusted for the difference between the rate of inflation in the country.[27]

GNI per capita figures can be misleading because they don't consider differences in the cost of living. For example, although the 2015 GNI per capita of Australia was $60,070, exceeding that of the United States, which was $55,900, the lower cost of living in the United States meant that an American could actually afford more goods and services than an Australian. To account for differences in the cost of living, one can adjust GNI per capita by purchasing power. Referred to as **purchasing power parity (PPP)** adjustment, it allows for a more direct comparison of living standards in different countries. The base for the adjustment is the cost of living in the United States. To consider the PPP adjustment, GNI per capita for a particular country is adjusted up (or down) depending upon whether the cost of living is lower (or higher) than in the United States, For example, in 2015, while the GNI per capita in Australia was $60,070 (Atlas Method), the PPP per capita was $44,570, suggesting that the cost of living was higher in Australia. Table 2.3 gives the GNI per capita measured at PPP in 2015 for a selection of countries.[28] From the table we can also see the extreme poverty in the poorest nations of the world and the significant gap in GNI per capita

TABLE 2.3	GNI Per Capita For Select Countries With PPP	
Country	**1990**	**2015**
Australia	$16,670	$44,570
Canada	19,290	44,010
Russia	8,000	23,770
Uganda	500	1,820
United States	23,730	57,540

Source: The World Bank Group, GNI per capita, PPP (current international $), http://data.worldbank.org/indicator/NY.GNP.PCAP.PP.CD and World Development Indicators database, http://databank.worldbank.org/data/download/GNIPC.pdf.

when compared to the wealthiest developing nations. Note that Canada appears significantly down the list which shows that Canadians are much poorer than they used to be.

To complicate matters, in many countries the "official" figures do not tell the entire story. Large amounts of economic activity may be in the form of unrecorded cash transactions, or barter agreements. People engage in such transactions to avoid paying taxes, and although the share of total economic activity accounted for by such transactions may be small in developed economies such as the United States, in some countries (India being an example), they are reportedly very significant. Known as the *black economy* or *shadow economy*, estimates suggest that in India it may be around 50 percent of GDP. Estimates produced by the European Union suggest that in 2012 the shadow economy accounted for around 10 percent of GDP in the UK and France, but 24 percent in Greece and as much as 32 percent in Bulgaria.[29]

Broader Conceptions of Development: Amartya Sen

The Nobel prize-winning economist Amartya Sen has argued that development should be assessed less by material output measures, such as GNP per capita, and more by the capabilities and opportunities that people enjoy.[30] According to Sen, development should be seen as a process of expanding the real freedoms that people experience. Hence, development requires the removal of major impediments to freedom: poverty as well as tyranny, poor economic opportunities as well as systematic social deprivation, neglect of public facilities as well as the intolerance of repressive states. In Sen's view, development is not just an economic process, but it is a political one too, and to succeed requires the "democratization" of political communities to give citizens a voice in the important decisions made for the community. This perspective leads Sen to emphasize basic health care, especially for children, and basic education, especially for women. Not only are these factors desirable for their instrumental value in helping to achieve higher income levels, but they are also beneficial in their own right. People cannot develop their capabilities if they are chronically ill or woefully ignorant.

Sen's influential thesis has been picked up by the United Nations, which has developed the **Human Development Index (HDI)** to measure the quality of human life in different nations. The HDI is based on three measures: life expectancy at birth (which is a function of health care); educational attainment (which is measured by a combination of the adult literacy rate and enrolment in primary, secondary, and tertiary education); and whether average incomes, based on PPP estimates, are sufficient to meet the basic needs of life in a country (adequate food, shelter, and health care). As such, the HDI comes much closer to Sen's conception of how development should be measured than narrow economic measures such as GNI per capita—although Sen's thesis suggests that political freedoms should also be included in the index, and they are not. The Human Development Index is scaled from 0 to 1. Countries scoring less than 0.5 are classified as having low human development (the quality of life is poor), those scoring from 0.5 to 0.8 are classified as having medium human development, while those countries that score above 0.8 are classified as having high human development.

Amartya Sen, Nobel Prize winner, advocates for assessing the capabilities and opportunities enjoyed by citizens of a country. © PRAKASH SINGH/AFP/Getty Images

ANOTHER PERSPECTIVE

What If We Were a Community of 100 People?

The "Miniature Earth" project was developed by Allysson Lucca in 2001 as a way to better illustrate and create understanding of differences in the world. He thought that reducing the world's population to a community of only 100 people would be a useful and easy-to-understand illustration of various dynamics in the global marketplace. And, this Miniature Earth captures a variety of issues related to the political economy and economic development that are discussed in the chapter of the text. At the basic level, if the earth were a community of 100 people, 61 people would be Asian, 13 African, 12 European, 8 North American, 5 South American, and 1 would be from Oceania. Twenty people own 75 percent of the financial wealth. If you could decide, how would you redistribute wealth among the 100 people: Make some richer or make the wealth among people more even, or let market forces distribute wealth as we have it now?

Source: The Miniature Earth, www.miniature-earth.com

Political Economy and Economic Progress

It is often argued that a country's economic development is a function of its economic and political systems. What then is the nature of the relationship between political economy and economic progress? This question has been the subject of vigorous debate among academics and policy makers for some time. Despite the long debate, this remains a question for which it is not possible to give an unambiguous answer. However, it is possible to untangle the main threads of the academic arguments and make a few broad generalizations as to the nature of the relationship between political economy and economic progress.

INNOVATION AND ENTREPRENEURSHIP ARE THE ENGINES OF GROWTH

Agreement is fairly wide that innovation and entrepreneurial activity are the engines of long-run economic growth.[31] Those who make this argument define **innovation** broadly to include not just new products, but also new processes, new organizations, new management practices, and new strategies. Thus, the Toys "R" Us strategy of establishing large warehouse-style toy stores and then engaging in heavy advertising and price discounting to sell the merchandise can be classified as an innovation because Toys "R" Us was the first company to pursue this strategy. Innovation is also seen as the product of entrepreneurial activity. Often, entrepreneurs first commercialize innovative new products and processes, and entrepreneurial activity provides much of the dynamism in an economy. For example, the economy of the United States has benefited greatly from a high level of entrepreneurial activity, which has resulted in rapid innovation in products and process. Firms such as Google, Facebook, Dell Computer Corp., Microsoft, and Oracle were all founded by entrepreneurial individuals to exploit advances in technology, and all these firms created significant economic value by helping to commercialize innovations in products and processes. Thus, one can conclude that if a country's economy is to sustain long-run economic growth, then the business environment must be conducive to the consistent production of product and process innovations and to entrepreneurial activity.

INNOVATION AND ENTREPRENEURSHIP REQUIRE A MARKET ECONOMY

This leads logically to a further question: What is required for the business environment of a country to be conducive to innovation and entrepreneurial activity? Those who have considered this issue highlight the advantages of a market economy.[32] It has

ANOTHER PERSPECTIVE

Purchasing Power Parity and Big Macs

The Economist, a British weekly magazine worth taking a look at, compares currency valuations across countries by examining the prices of Big Macs sold at McDonald's. The Big Mac index applies the idea of purchasing power parity by assuming that across national-level economies, the Big Mac price should be at parity. By comparing exchange rates using the Big Mac price as a basis, the index describes the over- or undervaluation of the country's currency. This index is published in April and October. You can find the most recent one at www.economist.com.

been argued that the economic freedom associated with a market economy creates greater incentives for innovation and entrepreneurship than either a planned or a mixed economy. In a market economy, any individual who has an innovative idea is free to try to make money out of that idea by starting a business (by engaging in entrepreneurial activity). Similarly, existing businesses are free to improve their operations through innovation. To the extent that they are successful, both individual entrepreneurs and established businesses can reap rewards in the form of high profits. Thus, market economies contain enormous incentives to develop innovations.

In a planned economy, the state owns all means of production. Consequently, entrepreneurial individuals have little economic incentive to develop valuable new innovations, since it is the state, rather than the individual, that captures most of the gains. The lack of economic freedom and incentives for innovation was probably a main factor in the economic stagnation of so many former Communist states and led ultimately to their collapse at the end of the 1980s. Similar stagnation occurred in many mixed economies in those sectors where the state had a monopoly (such as health care and telecommunications in Great Britain). This stagnation provided the impetus for the widespread privatization of state-owned enterprises that we witnessed in many mixed economies during the mid-1980s and is still going on today (privatization refers to the process of selling state-owned enterprises to private investors).

A study of 102 countries over a 20-year period provided evidence of a strong relationship between economic freedom (as provided by a market economy) and economic growth.[33] The study found that the more economic freedom a country had between 1975 and 1995, the more economic growth it achieved and the richer its citizens became. The three countries that had persistently high ratings of economic freedom from 1975 to 1995 (Hong Kong, Switzerland, and Singapore) were also all in the top ten in terms of economic growth rates. In contrast, no country with persistently low economic freedom achieved a respectable growth rate. For the 16 countries for which the index of economic freedom declined the most during the 1975–95 period, gross domestic product fell at an annual rate of 0.6 percent.

INNOVATION AND ENTREPRENEURSHIP REQUIRE STRONG PROPERTY RIGHTS

Strong legal protection of property rights is another requirement for a business environment to be conducive to innovation, entrepreneurial activity, and hence economic growth.[34] Both individuals and businesses must be given the opportunity to profit from innovative ideas. Without strong property rights protection, businesses and individuals run the risk that the profits from their innovative efforts will be expropriated, either by criminal elements or by the state. The state can expropriate the profits from innovation through legal means, such as excessive taxation, or through illegal means, such as demands from state bureaucrats for kickbacks in return for granting an individual or firm a license to do business in a certain area (i.e., corruption). According to the Nobel prize-winning economist Douglass North, throughout history many governments have displayed a tendency to engage in such behaviour. Inadequately enforced property rights reduce the incentives for innovation and entrepreneurial activity—since the profits from such activity are "stolen"—and hence reduce the rate of economic growth.

The influential Peruvian development economist Hernando de Soto has argued that much of the developing world will fail to reap the benefits of capitalism until property rights are better defined and protected.[35] De Soto's arguments are interesting because he says the key problem is not the risk of expropriation, but the chronic inability of property owners to establish legal title to the property they own. As an example of the scale of the problem, he cites the situation in Haiti, where individuals must take 176 steps over 19 years to own land legally. Because most property in poor countries is informally "owned," the absence of legal proof of ownership means that property holders cannot convert their assets into capital, which could then be used to finance business ventures. Banks will not lend money to the poor to start businesses because the poor possess no proof that they own property, such as farmland, that can be used as collateral for a loan. By de Soto's calculations, the total value of real estate held by the poor in third-world and former communist states amounted to more than $9.3 trillion in 2000. If those assets could be converted into capital, the result could be an economic revolution that would allow the poor to bootstrap their way out of poverty.

THE REQUIRED POLITICAL SYSTEM

There is a great deal of debate as to the kind of political system that best achieves a functioning market economy with strong protection for property rights.[36] We in the West tend to associate a representative democracy with a market economic system, strong property rights protection, and economic progress. Building on this, we tend to argue that democracy is good for growth.[37] However, some totalitarian regimes have fostered a market economy and strong property rights protection and have experienced rapid economic growth. Four of the fastest-growing economies of the past 30 years—South Korea, Taiwan, Singapore, and Hong Kong—had one thing in common at the start of their economic growth: undemocratic governments! At the same time, countries with stable democratic governments, such as India, experienced sluggish economic growth for long periods. In 1992, Lee Kuan Yew, Singapore's leader for many years, told an audience, "I do not believe that democracy necessarily leads to development. I believe that a country needs to develop discipline more than democracy. The exuberance of democracy leads to undisciplined and disorderly conduct which is inimical to development."[38] Others have argued that many of the current problems in Eastern Europe and the states of the former Soviet Union arose because democracy arrived before economic reform, making it more difficult for elected governments to introduce the policies that, while painful in the short run, were needed to promote rapid economic growth. China, which maintains a totalitarian government, has moved rapidly toward a market economy.

However, those who argue for the value of a totalitarian regime miss an important point: if dictators made countries rich, then much of Africa, Asia, and Latin America should have been growing rapidly from 1960 to 1990, and this was not the case. Only a certain kind of totalitarian regime is capable of promoting economic growth. It must be a dictatorship that is committed to a free market system and strong protection of

Although Hong Kong switched from a British colony to Chinese sovereignty in 1997, its economy still displays democratic influence. This shopping district street in Hong Kong could be mistaken for a big city street in the United States. What do you think are some of the reasons that places like Hong Kong, Singapore, and Taiwan have flourished, while others in Eastern Europe, the former Soviet Union, and India have not? © *Rodrigo A Torres/Glow Images*

property rights. Also, there is no guarantee that a dictatorship will continue to pursue such progressive policies. Ghana continues to make strides, but dictators are rarely so benevolent. Many are tempted to use the apparatus of the state to further their own private ends, violating property rights and stalling economic growth. Given this, it seems likely that democratic regimes are far more conducive to long-term economic growth than are dictatorships, even benevolent ones. Only in a well-functioning, mature democracy are property rights truly secure.[39] We should not forget Amartya Sen's arguments that we reviewed earlier. Totalitarian states, by limiting human freedom, also suppress human development and therefore are detrimental to progress.

ECONOMIC PROGRESS BEGETS DEMOCRACY

While it is possible to argue that democracy is not a necessary precondition for a free market economy in which property rights are protected, subsequent economic growth often leads to establishment of a democratic regime. Several of the fastest-growing Asian economies adopted more democratic governments during the past two decades, including South Korea and Taiwan. Thus, while democracy may not always be the cause of initial economic progress, it seems to be one consequence of that progress.

A strong belief that economic progress leads to adoption of a democratic regime underlies the fairly permissive attitude that many Western governments have adopted toward human rights violations in China. Although China has a totalitarian government in which human rights are abused, many Western countries have been hesitant to criticize the country too much for fear that this might hamper the country's march

ANOTHER PERSPECTIVE

Mobile Phones Figure in Banking Innovation

For people in underdeveloped countries, banking is next to impossible. But that's changing for people in India, now that Eko, a not-for-profit organization, has partnered with the State Bank of India to create an innovative banking system. In areas where no bank exists, local merchants serve as "human ATMs," accepting payments and deposits and processing withdrawals, using mobile phones and special encryption pads to record transactions. Eko's brainstorm—harnessing the potential of mobile phones—has seen almost immediate success in a country where more than 403 million people have a phone yet 187 million have no bank account. Eko's 350 outlets across India serve about 42 000 customers daily.

Source: "Geithner: India Innovations Add Bank Customers," *Reuters*, April 6, 2010, www.reuters.com.

toward a free market system. The belief is that once China has a free market system, democracy will follow. Whether this optimistic vision comes to pass remains to be seen.

Geography, Education, and Economic Development

While a country's political and economic system is probably the big locomotive driving its rate of economic development, other factors are also important. One that has received attention recently is geography.[40] But the belief that geography can influence economic policy, and hence economic growth rates, goes back to Adam Smith. The influential Harvard University economist Jeffrey Sachs argues that

> throughout history, coastal states, with their long engagements in international trade, have been more supportive of market institutions than landlocked states, which have tended to organize themselves as hierarchical (and often military) societies. Mountainous states, as a result of physical isolation, have often neglected market-based trade. Temperate climes have generally supported higher densities of population and thus a more extensive division of labour than tropical regions.[41]

Sachs's point is that by virtue of favourable geography, certain societies were more likely to engage in trade than others and were thus more likely to be open to and to develop market-based economic systems, which in turn would promote faster economic growth. He also argues that, irrespective of the economic and political institutions a country adopts, adverse geographical conditions, such as the high rate of disease, poor soils, and hostile climate that afflict many tropical countries, can have a negative impact on development. Together with colleagues at Harvard's Institute for International Development, Sachs tested for the impact of geography on a country's economic growth rate between 1965 and 1990. He found that landlocked countries grew more slowly than coastal economies and that being entirely landlocked reduced a country's growth rate by roughly 0.7 percent per year. He also found that tropical countries grew 1.3 percent more slowly each year than countries in the temperate zone.[42]

Education emerges as another important determinant of economic development (a point that Amartya Sen emphasizes). The general assertion is that nations that invest more in education will have higher growth rates because an educated population is a more productive population. Some rather striking anecdotal evidence suggests this is true. In 1960, Pakistanis and South Koreans were on equal footing economically. However, just 30 percent of Pakistani children were enrolled in primary schools, while 94 percent of South Koreans were. By the mid-1980s, South Korea's GNP per person

Democracy in the Arab World: New Realities in an Ancient Land?

Democracy is finally making an appearance in the Ancient Lands of the Middle East, as witnessed by the recent uprisings known as the "The Arab Spring." Wissam Yafi, an expert in technology and international development, believes geo-economic, geo-social, technological, and geo-political forces will lead to inevitable changes in the Arab world. Economic forces will make these governments cut many of the social services offered, putting people out of work, which will lead toward democratic alternatives. Technology is another major binding force connecting populations across the Middle East, which will mean less censorship; something that has been widespread in many parts of the Arab world. People will continue to challenge the status quo as rapid urbanization, population growth, and movements toward self-determination grow. Wissam Yafi has a lot of guesses on what will happen. Do you agree with his forecasts?

Source: P. Salem, W. Yafi, "Inevitable Democracy in the Arab World: New Realities in an Ancient Land," Carnegie Endowment for International Peace, April 18, 2012, carnegieendowment.org/2012/04/18/inevitable-democracy-in-arab-world-new-realities-inancient-land/a7jk.

was three times that of Pakistan's.[43] A survey of 14 statistical studies that looked at the relationship between a country's investment in education and its subsequent growth rates concluded investment in education had a positive and statistically significant impact on a country's rate of economic growth.[44] Similarly, the work by Sachs discussed above suggests that investments in education help explain why some countries in Southeast Asia, such as Indonesia, Malaysia, and Singapore, have been able to overcome the disadvantages associated with their tropical geography and grow far more rapidly than tropical nations in Africa and Latin America.

LO5   States in Transition

The political economy of many of the world's nation-states has changed radically since the late 1980s. Two trends have been evident. First, during the late 1980s and early 1990s, a wave of democratic revolutions swept the world. Totalitarian governments collapsed and were replaced by democratically elected governments that were typically more committed to free market capitalism than their predecessors had been. The change was most dramatic in Eastern Europe, where the collapse of communism brought an end to the Cold War and led to the breakup of the Soviet Union, but similar changes were occurring throughout the world during the same period. Across much of Asia, Latin America, and Africa there was a marked shift toward greater democracy. Second, there has been a strong move away from centrally planned and mixed economies and toward a more free market economic model. We shall look first at the spread of democracy and then turn our attention to the spread of free market economics.

The Spread of Democracy

One notable development of the past 30 years has been the spread of democracy (and, by extension, the decline of totalitarianism). Map 2.2 reports on the extent of totalitarianism in the world as determined by Freedom House. This map charts political freedom in 2016, grouping countries into three broad groupings: free, partly free, and

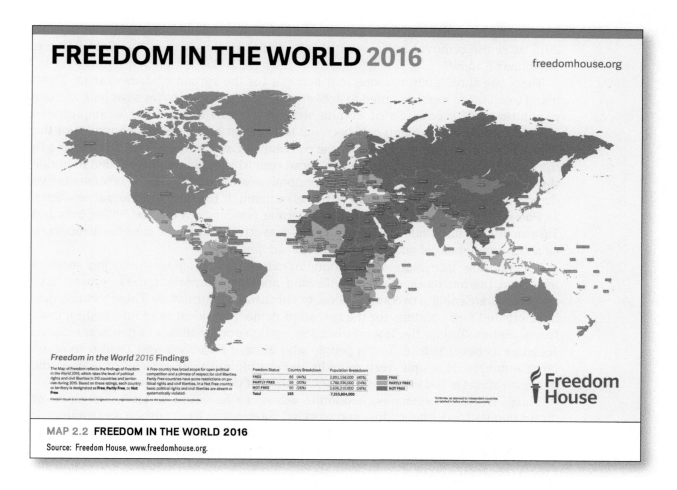

Freedom in the World 2016 Findings

The Map of Freedom reflects the findings of Freedom in the World 2016, which rates the level of political rights and civil liberties in 210 countries and territories during 2015. Based on these ratings, each country or territory is designated as **Free, Partly Free,** or **Not Free.**

A Free country has broad scope for open political competition and a climate of respect for civil liberties. Partly Free countries have some restrictions on political rights and civil liberties. In a Not Free country, basic political rights and civil liberties are absent or systematically violated.

Freedom House is an independent nongovernmental organization that supports the expansion of freedom worldwide.

Freedom Status	Country Breakdown		Population Breakdown	
FREE	86	(44%)	2,891,158,000	(40%)
PARTLY FREE	59	(30%)	1,788,336,000	(24%)
NOT FREE	50	(26%)	2,636,310,000	(36%)
Total	195		7,315,804,000	

FREE
PARTLY FREE
NOT FREE

Territories, as opposed to independent countries, are labeled in italics when rated separately.

Freedom House

MAP 2.2 FREEDOM IN THE WORLD 2016

Source: Freedom House, www.freedomhouse.org.

not free. In "free" countries, citizens enjoy a high degree of political and civil freedoms. "Partly free" countries are characterized by some restrictions on political rights and civil liberties, often in the context of corruption, weak rule of law, ethnic strife, or civil war. In "not free" countries, the political process is tightly controlled and basic freedoms are denied.

Freedom House classified some 40 percent of the world's countries as free in 2016. These countries respect a broad range of political rights. Another 24 percent of the world's countries were classified as partly free, while 36 percent of the countries were classified as not free. The number of democracies in the world has increased from 69 nations in 1987 to 122 in 2012, slightly below the 2006 total of 123. But not all democracies are free, according to Freedom House, because some democracies still restrict certain political and civil liberties. For example, Russia has consistently been rated "not free" since the early 2000s.

Many of the newer democracies are to be found in eastern Europe and Latin America, although there also have been notable gains in Africa during this time, such as in South Africa and more recently Libya. Entrants into the ranks of the world's democracies during the last 25 years include Mexico, which held its first fully free and fair presidential election in 2000 after free and fair parliamentary and state elections in 1997 and 1998; Senegal, where free and fair presidential elections led to a peaceful transfer of power; Ukraine, where popular unrest following widespread ballot fraud in the 2004 presidential election resulted in a second election, the victory of a reform candidate, and a marked improvement in civil liberties (although sadly, the reform candidate also proved to be corrupt); and Libya, which held successful elections in 2012 after the removal by popular revolt of that country's long-standing dictator, Muammar Gaddafi.

There are three main reasons that account for the spread of democracy.[45] First, many totalitarian regimes failed to deliver economic progress to the vast bulk of their populations. The collapse of communism in eastern Europe, for example, was precipitated by the growing gulf between the vibrant and wealthy economies of the West and the stagnant economies of the communist East. In looking for alternatives to the socialist model, the populations of these countries could not have failed to notice that most of the world's strongest economies were governed by representative democracies. Today, the economic success of many of the newer democracies—such as Poland and the Czech Republic in the former communist bloc, the Philippines and Taiwan in Asia, and Chile in Latin America—has strengthened the case for democracy as a key component of successful economic advancement.

Second, new information and communication technologies—including satellite television, fax machines, desktop publishing, and, most important, the Internet—have reduced a state's ability to control access to uncensored information. These technologies have created new conduits for the spread of democratic ideals and information from free societies. Today, the Internet is allowing democratic ideals to penetrate closed societies as never before. Young people who utilized Facebook and Twitter to reach large numbers of people very quickly and coordinate their actions organized the demonstrations in 2011 that led to the overthrow of the Egyptian government.

Third, in many countries, economic advances have led to the emergence of increasingly prosperous middle and working classes that have pushed for democratic reforms. This was certainly a factor in the democratic transformation of South Korea. Entrepreneurs and other business leaders, eager to protect their property rights and ensure the dispassionate enforcement of contracts, are another force pressing for more accountable and open government.

Despite this, it would be naive to conclude that the global spread of democracy will continue unchallenged. Democracy is still rare in large parts of the world. In sub-Saharan Africa in 2013, only 10 countries were considered free, 19 were partly free, and 20 were not free. Among the post-communist countries in eastern and central Europe and the former Soviet Union, only 13 are classified as free (primarily in eastern Europe). And there is only 1 free state among the 18 nations of the Middle East and North Africa—although it remains to be seen how the wave of unrest that spread across the Middle East during 2011–2013 will change this. Moreover, there are disturbing signs that authoritarianism is gaining ground in several countries where political and civil liberties have been progressively limited in recent years, including Russia, Ukraine, Indonesia, and Venezuela. In Egypt, after a brief flirtation with democracy, the military stepped in, removing the government of Mohamed Morsi, after Morsi and his political movement, the Muslim Brotherhood, had exhibited its own authoritarian tendencies. The military-backed government, however, has also acted in an authoritarian manner, effectively reversing much of the progress that had occurred after the revolution of 2011.

The New World Order?

The end of the Cold War and the "new world order" that followed the collapse of communism in Eastern Europe and the former Soviet Union, taken together with the collapse of many authoritarian regimes in Latin America, have given rise to intense speculation about the future shape of global geopolitics. Author Francis Fukuyama has argued that "we may be witnessing . . . the end of history as such: that is, the end point of mankind's ideological evolution and the universalization of Western liberal democracy as the final form of human government."[46] Fukuyama goes on to say that the war of ideas may be at an end and that liberal democracy has triumphed.

Others have questioned Fukuyama's vision of a more harmonious world dominated by a universal civilization characterized by democratic regimes and free market capitalism. In a controversial book, the influential political scientist Samuel Huntington argues that there is no "universal" civilization based on widespread acceptance of Western liberal democratic ideals.[47] Huntington maintains that while many societies may be modernizing—they are adopting the material paraphernalia of the modern world, from automobiles to Coca-Cola and MTV—they are not becoming more Western. On the contrary, Huntington theorizes that modernization in non-Western societies can result in a retreat toward the traditional, such as the resurgence of Islam in many traditionally Muslim societies:

> The Islamic resurgence is both a product of and an effort to come to grips with modernization. Its underlying causes are those generally responsible for indigenization trends in non-Western societies: urbanization, social mobilization, higher levels of literacy and education, intensified communication and media consumption, and expanded interaction with Western and other cultures. These developments undermine traditional village and clan ties and create alienation and an identity crisis. Islamist symbols, commitments, and beliefs meet these psychological needs, and Islamist welfare organizations, the social, cultural and economic needs of Muslims caught in the process of modernization. Muslims feel a need to return to Islamic ideas, practices, and institutions to provide the compass and the motor of modernization.[48]

Thus, the rise of Islamic fundamentalism is portrayed as a response to the alienation produced by modernization.

In contrast to Fukuyama, Huntington sees a world that is split into different civilizations, each of which has its own value systems and ideology. In addition to Western civilization, Huntington predicts the emergence of strong Islamic and Sinic (Chinese) civilizations, as well as civilizations based on Eastern Orthodox Christianity (Russian), Hinduism (Indian), and Japanese, African, Latin American culture and values. Huntington also sees the civilizations as headed for conflict, particularly along the "fault lines" that separate them, such as Bosnia (where Muslims and Orthodox Christians have clashed), Kashmir (where Muslims and Hindus clash), and the Sudan (where a bloody war between Christians and Muslims has persisted for decades). Huntington predicts conflict between the West and Islam and between the West and China. He bases his predictions on an analysis of the different value systems and ideology of these civilizations, which in his view tend to bring them into conflict with each other. While some commentators originally dismissed Huntington's thesis, in the aftermath of the terrorist attacks on the United States on September 11, 2001, Huntington's thesis received new attention.

If Huntington's views are even partly correct—the events of September 11 added weight to his thesis—they have important implications for international business. They suggest many countries may be increasingly difficult places in which to do business, either because they are shot through with violent conflicts or because they are part of a civilization that is in conflict with an enterprise's home country. Huntington's views are speculative and controversial. It is not clear that his predictions will come to pass. More likely is the evolution of a global political system that is positioned somewhere between Fukuyama's universal global civilization based on liberal democratic ideals and Huntington's vision of a fractured world. That would still be a world, however, in which geopolitical forces periodically limit the ability of business enterprises to operate in certain foreign countries.

More Egyptian protests in 2011 were organized through social networking. © *Jonathan Rashad/Getty Images*

The Spread of Market-Based Systems

Paralleling the spread of democracy since the 1980s has been the transformation from centrally planned command economies to market-based economies. More than 30 countries that were in the former Soviet Union or the Eastern European communist bloc are now changing their economic systems. A complete list of such countries would also include Asian states such as China and Vietnam, as well as African countries such as Angola, Ethiopia, and Mozambique.[49] There has been a similar shift away from a mixed economy. Many states in Asia, Latin America, and Western Europe have sold state-owned businesses to private investors (privatization) and deregulated their economies to promote greater competition.

The underlying rationale for economic transformation has been the same the world over. In general, command and mixed economies failed to deliver the kind of sustained economic performance achieved by countries adopting market-based systems, such as the United States, Switzerland, Hong Kong, and Taiwan.

The Heritage Foundation's index of economic freedom is based on ten indicators, such as the extent to which the government intervenes in the economy, trade policy, the degree to which property rights are protected, foreign investment regulations, and taxation rules. A country can score between 1 (least free) and 100 (most free) on each of these indicators. The higher a country's average score across all ten indicators, the more closely its economy represents the pure market model. According to the 2016 index, which is summarized in Map 2.3, the three most-free countries in the world are Hong Kong, Singapore, and New Zealand. Canada comes in at #6, ahead of the United Kingdom at #10 and the United States at #11.

Economic freedom does not necessarily equate with political freedom. For example the top two of the countries in the Heritage Foundation index, Hong Kong and Singapore, cannot be classified as politically free. Hong Kong was reabsorbed into

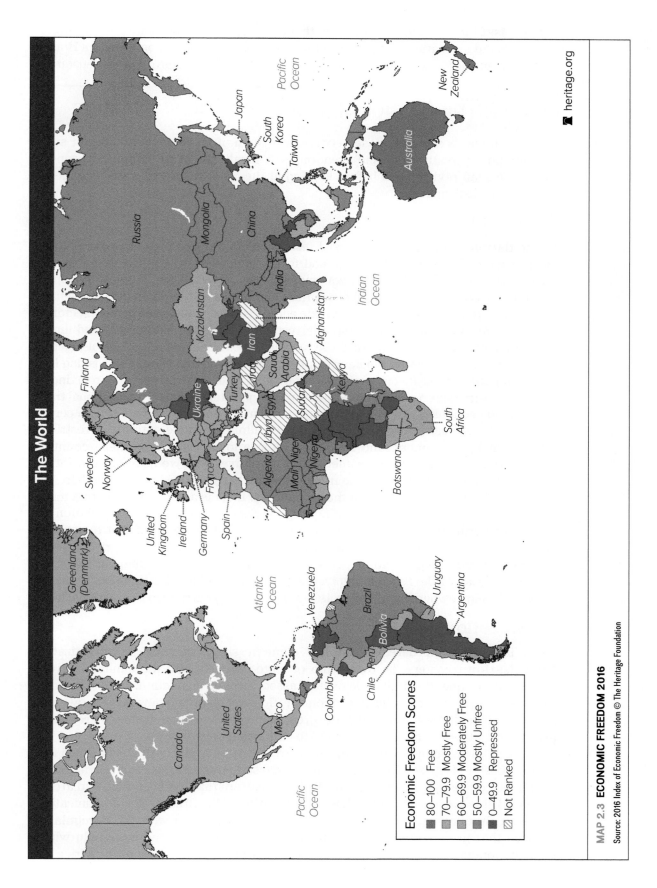

The World

Pacific Ocean

Canada

United States

Greenland (Denmark)

Atlantic Ocean

Mexico

Colombia

Venezuela

Chile

Peru

Bolivia

Brazil

Uruguay

Argentina

Pacific Ocean

Sweden

Norway

Finland

United Kingdom

Ireland

Germany

Spain

France

Russia

Kazakhstan

Mongolia

China

India

Ukraine

Turkey

Iran

Iraq

Saudi Arabia

Afghanistan

Japan

South Korea

Taiwan

Egypt

Libya

Algeria

Mali

Niger

Nigeria

Sudan

Kenya

South Africa

Botswana

Indian Ocean

Australia

New Zealand

Economic Freedom Scores

- 80–100 Free
- 70–79.9 Mostly Free
- 60–69.9 Moderately Free
- 50–59.9 Mostly Unfree
- 0–49.9 Repressed
- Not Ranked

heritage.org

MAP 2.3 ECONOMIC FREEDOM 2016

Source: 2016 Index of Economic Freedom © The Heritage Foundation

communist China in 1997, and the first thing Beijing did was shut down Hong Kong's freely elected legislature. Singapore is ranked as only partly free on Freedom House's index of political freedom due to certain practices, such as widespread press censorship.

LO6   The Nature of Economic Transformation

The shift towards a market-based economic system often entails a number of steps: deregulation, privatization, and creation of a legal system to safeguard property rights. We shall review each before looking at the track record of states engaged in economic transformation.

Deregulation

Deregulation involves removing legal restrictions to the free play of markets, to the establishment of private enterprises, and to the manner in which private enterprises operate. Before the collapse of communism, the governments in most command economies exercised tight control over prices and output, setting both through detailed state planning. They also prohibited private enterprises from operating in most sectors of the economy, severely restricted direct investment by foreign enterprises, and limited international trade. Deregulation in these cases involved removing price controls, thereby allowing prices to be set by the interplay between demand and supply; abolishing laws regulating the establishment and operation of private enterprises; and relaxing or removing restrictions on direct investment by foreign enterprises and international trade.

In mixed economies, the role of the state was more limited, but here too, in certain sectors the state set prices, owned businesses, limited private enterprise, restricted investment by foreigners, and restricted international trade. For these countries deregulation has involved the same kind of initiatives that we have seen in former command economies, although the transformation has been easier because there was always a vibrant private sector in these countries. India is a good example of a mixed economy that is currently deregulating large areas of its economy. Deregulation has involved reforming the industrial licensing system that made it difficult to establish private enterprises and opening areas that were once closed to the private sector (including electricity generation, parts of the oil industry, steelmaking, air transport, and some areas of the telecommunications industry). It has also involved removing limits on foreign ownership of Indian assets and lowering barriers to international trade.

Privatization

Hand in hand with deregulation has come a sharp increase in privatization. **Privatization** transfers the ownership of state property into the hands of private individuals, frequently by the sale of state assets through an auction.[50] Privatization is seen as a way to unlock gains in economic efficiency by giving new private owners a powerful incentive—the reward of greater profits—to search for increases in productivity, to enter new markets, and to exit losing ones.[51]

The privatization movement started in Great Britain in the early 1980s when then Prime Minister Margaret Thatcher started to sell state-owned assets such as the British telephone company, British Telecom (BT). In a pattern that has been repeated around the world, this sale was linked with the deregulation of the British telecommunications industry. By allowing other firms to compete head to head with BT, deregulation ensured that privatization did not simply replace a state-owned monopoly with a private monopoly. Privatization has become a worldwide movement. In Africa, for example, Ghana, Mozambique, and Zambia are leading the way with very ambitious privatization plans. Zambia put more than 145 state-owned companies up for sale, while Mozambique has already sold scores of enterprises, ranging from tea plantations to a chocolate factory. The most dramatic privatization programs, however, have occurred in the economies of the former Soviet Union and its Eastern European satellite states. In the Czech Republic, three-quarters of all state-owned enterprises were privatized between 1989 and 1996. In Russia, where the private sector had been almost completely repressed before 1989, 50 percent of GDP was in private hands by 1995, again much as a result of privatization. And in Poland, the private sector accounted for 59 percent of GDP in 1995, up from 20 percent in 1989.[52] However, Poland also illustrates how far some of these countries still have to travel. Despite an aggressive privatization program, Poland still had 4000 state-owned enterprises that dominate the heavy industry, mining, and transportation sectors.

The ownership structure of newly privatized firms also is important.[53] Many former command economies, for example, lack the legal regulations regarding corporate governance that are found in advanced Western economies. In advanced market economies, boards of directors are appointed by shareholders to make sure managers consider the interests of shareholders when making decisions and try to manage the firm in a manner that is consistent with maximizing the wealth of shareholders. However, some former Communist states lack laws requiring corporations to establish effective boards. Often in such cases, managers with a small ownership stake can gain control over the newly privatized entity and run it for their own benefit while ignoring the interests of other shareholders. Sometimes these managers are the same Communist bureaucrats who ran the enterprise before privatization. Because they have been schooled in the old ways of doing things, they often hesitate to take drastic action to increase the efficiency of the enterprise. Instead, they continue to run the firm as a private fiefdom, seeking to extract whatever economic value they can for their own betterment (in the form of perks that are not reported) while doing little to increase the economic efficiency of the enterprise so that shareholders benefit.

Legal Systems

As noted earlier in this chapter, laws protecting private property rights and providing mechanisms for contract enforcement are required for a well-functioning market economy. Without a legal system that protects property rights, and without the machinery to enforce that system, the incentive to engage in economic activity can be reduced substantially by private and public entities, including organized crime, that expropriate the profits generated by the efforts of private-sector entrepreneurs. As noted earlier, this has become a problem in many former Communist states. When communism collapsed, many of these countries lacked the legal structure required to protect property rights, all property having been held by the state. Although many states have made big strides toward instituting the required system, it will be many more years before the legal system is functioning as smoothly as it does in the West. For example, in most Eastern European nations, the title to urban and agricultural property is often uncertain because of incomplete and inaccurate records, multiple pledges on the same property, and unsettled claims resulting from demands for restitution from owners in the pre-Communist era. Also, while most countries have improved their commercial codes, institutional weaknesses still undermine contract enforcement. Court capacity is often inadequate, and procedures for resolving contract disputes out of court are often inadequate or poorly developed.[54]

LO7 Implications of Changing Political Economy

In practice, the road that must be travelled to reach a market-based economic system has often been rocky.[55] This has been particularly true for the states of Eastern Europe in the post-Communist era. In this region, the move toward greater political and economic freedom has sometimes been accompanied by economic and political chaos.[56] Most Eastern European states began to liberalize their economies in the early 1990s. They dismantled decades of price controls, allowed widespread private ownership of businesses, and permitted much greater competition. Most also planned to sell state-owned enterprises to private investors. However, given the vast number of such enterprises and how inefficient many were, which made them unappealing to private investors, most privatization efforts moved forward slowly. In this new environment, many inefficient state-owned enterprises found that they could not survive without a guaranteed market. The newly democratic governments often continued to support these money-losing enterprises to stave off massive unemployment. The resulting subsidies to state-owned enterprises led to ballooning budget deficits that were typically financed by printing money. Printing money, along with the lack of price controls, often led to hyperinflation.

A study by the World Bank suggests that the post-Communist states that have been most successful at transforming their economies were those that followed an economic policy best described as "shock therapy." In these countries—which include the Czech Republic, Hungary, and Poland—prices and trade were liberated quickly, inflation was held in check by tight monetary policy, and the privatization of state-owned industries was implemented rapidly. Among the 26 economies of Eastern Europe and the former Soviet Union, the World Bank found a strong positive correlation between the imposition of such shock therapy and subsequent economic growth. Speedy reformers suffered smaller falls in output and returned to growth more quickly than those such as Russia and Ukraine that moved more slowly.[57]

Despite variations within the group, in general, the transformation of former command economies has progressed significantly.

Implications

The global changes in political and economic systems discussed above have several implications for international business. The ideological conflict between collectivism and individualism that so defined the twentieth century is less in evidence today. The West won the Cold War, and Western ideology has never been more widespread than it was at the beginning of the millennium. Although command economies still remain and totalitarian dictatorships can still be found around the world, the tide has been running in favour of free markets and democracy.

The implications for business are enormous. For the best part of 50 years, half of the world was off-limits to Western businesses. Now all that is changing. Many of the national markets of Eastern Europe, Latin America, Africa, and Asia may still be undeveloped and impoverished, but they are potentially enormous. With a population of 1.5 billion, the Chinese market alone is potentially bigger than that of the United States, the European Union, and Japan combined! Similarly India, with its 1.3 billion people, is a potentially huge future market. Latin America has another 600 million potential consumers. It is unlikely that China, Russia, Poland, or any of the other states now moving toward a free market system will attain the living standards of the West anytime soon. Nevertheless, the upside potential is so large that companies need to consider making inroads now.

However, just as the potential gains are large, so are the risks. There is no guarantee that democracy will thrive in the newly democratic states of Eastern Europe, particularly if these states have to grapple with severe economic setbacks. Totalitarian dictatorships could return, although they are unlikely to be of the communist variety. Although the bipolar world of the Cold War era has vanished, it may be replaced by a multipolar world dominated by a number of civilizations. In such a world, much of the economic promise inherent in the global shift toward market-based economic systems may evaporate in the face of conflicts between civilizations. While the long-term potential for economic gain from investment in the world's new market economies is large, the risks associated with any such investment are also substantial. It would be foolish to ignore these.

IMPLICATIONS FOR BUSINESS

The implications for international business of the material discussed in this chapter fall into two broad categories. First, the political, economic, and legal environment of a country clearly influences the attractiveness of that country as a market and/or investment site. The benefits, costs, and risks associated with doing business in a country are a function of that country's political, economic, and legal systems. Second, the political, economic, and legal systems of a country can raise important ethical issues that have implications for the practice of international business. Here we consider each of these issues.

ATTRACTIVENESS

The overall attractiveness of a country as a market and/or investment site depends on balancing the likely long-term benefits of doing business in that country against the likely costs and risks. Below we consider the determinants of benefits, costs, and risks.

Benefits

In the most general sense, the long-run monetary benefits of doing business in a country are a function of the size of the market, the present wealth (purchasing power) of consumers in that market, and the likely future wealth of consumers. While some markets are very large when measured by number of consumers (for example China and India), low living standards may imply limited purchasing power and, therefore, a relatively small market when measured in economic terms. While international businesses need to be aware of this distinction, they also need to keep in mind the likely future prospects of a country. In 1960, for example, South Korea was viewed as just another impoverished Third World nation. Currently, it is the world's 11th largest economy measured in terms of GDP. International firms that recognized South Korea's potential in 1960 and began to do business in that country may have reaped greater benefits than those that wrote off South Korea.

By identifying and investing early in a potential future economic star, international firms may build brand loyalty and gain experience in that country's business practices. Such investments will pay substantial dividends if that country achieves sustained high economic growth rates. In contrast, late entrants may find that they lack the brand loyalty and experience necessary to achieve a significant presence in the market. In the language of business strategy, early entrants into potential future economic stars may be able to reap substantial first-mover advantages, while late entrants may fall victim to late-mover disadvantages.[58] (**First-mover advantages** are the advantages that accrue to early entrants into a market. **Late-mover disadvantages** are the handicap that late entrants might suffer.)

A country's economic system and property rights regime are reasonably good predictors of economic prospects. Countries with free market economies in which property rights are well protected tend to achieve greater economic growth rates than command economies and/or economies where property rights are poorly protected. It follows that a country's economic system and property rights regime, when taken together with market size (in terms of population), probably constitute reasonably good indicators of the potential long-run benefits of doing business in a country.

Costs

A number of political, economic, and legal factors determine the costs of doing business in a country. With regard to political factors, the costs of doing business in a country can be increased by a need to pay off the politically powerful to be allowed by the government to do business. The need to pay what are essentially bribes is greater in closed totalitarian states than in open democratic societies where politicians are held accountable by the electorate (although this is not a hard-and-fast distinction). Whether a company should actually pay bribes in return for market access should be determined on the basis of the legal and ethical implications of such action. We discuss this consideration below.

With regard to economic factors, one of the most important variables is the sophistication of a country's economy. It may be more costly to do business in relatively primitive or undeveloped economies because of the lack of infrastructure and supporting businesses. At the extreme, an international firm may have to provide its own infrastructure and supporting business, which obviously raises costs. When McDonald's decided to open its first restaurant in Moscow, it found that to serve food and drink indistinguishable from that served in McDonald's restaurants elsewhere, it had to vertically integrate backward to supply its own needs. The quality of Russian-grown potatoes and meat was too poor. Thus, to protect the quality of its product, McDonald's set up its own dairy farms, cattle ranches, vegetable plots, and food processing plants within Russia. This raised the cost of doing business in Russia, relative to the cost in more sophisticated economies where high-quality inputs could be purchased on the open market.

As for legal factors, it can be more costly to do business in a country where local laws and regulations set strict standards with regard to product safety, safety in the workplace, environmental pollution, and the like (since adhering to such regulations is costly). It can also be more costly to do business in a country like the United States, where the absence of a cap on damage awards has meant spiralling liability insurance rates. It can be more costly to do business in a country that lacks well-established laws for regulating business practice (as is the case in many of the former Communist nations). In the absence of a well-developed body of business contract law, international firms may find no satisfactory way to resolve contract disputes and, consequently, routinely face large losses from contract violations. Similarly, local laws that fail to adequately protect intellectual property can lead to the "theft" of an international business's intellectual property and lost income.

Risks

As with costs, the risks of doing business in a country are determined by a number of political, economic, and legal factors. Political risk has been defined as the likelihood that political forces will cause drastic changes in a country's business environment that adversely affect the profit and other goals of a particular business enterprise.[59] So defined, **political risk** tends to be greater in countries experiencing social unrest and disorder or in countries where the underlying nature of a society increases the likelihood of social unrest. Social unrest typically finds expression in strikes, demonstrations, terrorism, and violent conflict. Such unrest is more likely to be found in countries that contain more than one ethnic nationality, in countries where competing ideologies are battling for political control, in countries where economic mismanagement has created high inflation and falling living standards, or in countries that straddle the "fault lines" between civilizations, such as Bosnia.

Social unrest can result in abrupt changes in government and government policy or, in some cases, in protracted civil strife. Such strife tends to have negative economic implications for the profit goals of business enterprises. For example, in the aftermath of the 1979 Islamic revolution in Iran, the Iranian assets of numerous U.S. companies were seized by the new Iranian government without compensation. Similarly, the violent disintegration of the Yugoslavian federation into warring states, including Bosnia, Croatia, and Serbia, precipitated a collapse in the local economies and in the profitability of investments in those countries.

Although likely never at risk from a violent Yugoslav-type disintegration, the perception of Canada as a unified and politically stable country has, over the past four decades, been intermittently tested in the eyes of the world. The FLQ crisis of the 1960s brought bombings, violence, and political kidnappings to Montreal. Since then, however, the flare-ups have been, for the most part, peaceful. Quebec separatism, still on the Parti Québécois agenda as an achievable reality, has taken a back seat over the past few years to economic concerns.

On the economic front, economic risks arise from economic mismanagement by the government of a country. **Economic risk** can be defined as the likelihood that economic mismanagement will cause drastic changes in a country's business environment that adversely affect the profit and other goals of a particular business enterprise. Economic risks are not independent of political risk. Economic mismanagement may give rise to significant social unrest and hence political risk. Nevertheless, economic risks are worth emphasizing as a separate category because there is not always a one-to-one relationship between economic mismanagement and social unrest. One visible indicator of economic mismanagement tends to be a country's inflation rate. Another tends to be the level of business and government debt in the country.

In Asian states such as Indonesia, Thailand, and South Korea, businesses increased their debt rapidly during the 1990s, often at the bequest of the government, which was encouraging them to invest in industries deemed to be of "strategic importance" to the country. The result was overinvestment, with more industrial (factories) and commercial capacity (office space) being built than could be justified by demand conditions. Many of these investments turned out to be uneconomic. The borrowers failed to generate the profits required to meet their debt payment. In turn, the banks that had lent money to these businesses suddenly found that they had rapid increases in nonperforming loans on their books. Foreign investors, believing that many local companies and banks might go bankrupt, pulled their money out of these countries, selling local stock, bonds, and currency. This action precipitated the 1997–98 financial crisis in Southeast Asia. The crisis included a precipitous decline in the value of Asian stock markets, which in some cases exceeded 70 percent; a similar collapse in the value of many Asian currencies against the U.S. dollar; an implosion of local demand; and a severe economic recession that affected many Asian countries for years. In short, economic risks were rising throughout Southeast Asia during the 1990s. Astute foreign businesses and investors, seeing this situation, limited their exposure in this part of the world. More naive businesses and investors lost everything.

Fast forward to 2008–09, when the worldwide financial crisis described in the first chapter sorely tested the free-market principles of many governments. In the United States, for example, as major financial companies such as Bear Sterns, Lehman Brothers, and AIG Insurance faced bankruptcy, the federal government tried various approaches, ranging from a do-nothing approach, to finding a stronger firm to buy out the company, to cash infusions in the billions of dollars from the government. At the same time, other companies, such as General Motors, came to Washington looking for help and received aid from the government.

This shows that in a crisis, even political administrations committed to free trade, open markets, and laissez-faire capitalism did not hesitate to take a more activist role in both the economy and in the future of specific companies.

The worldwide financial crisis has affected entire countries and not just companies. Countries borrow money to fund their spending and in times of crisis find that their tax base shrinks. Property values decline, affecting municipal revenues, people shop less, affecting sales and value-added tax revenues, and fewer people are employed, affecting revenue from income taxes. Yet different countries felt the crisis in different ways.

Iceland saw the collapse of its three largest banks in 2008. Their combined lending had grown over the years to a combined total that was six times that of the GDP of the entire country. As global assets collapsed, the value of the debts declined, and as this news became known, depositors quickly withdrew their own money, causing a traditional "run on the bank." Greece faced different, but related challenges. The economic slowdown, combined with decades of expansive government spending, led to increasing government deficits. In 2010, the country's deficit was one of the highest in the world, relative to the country's GDP. However, just as importantly, it was determined in 2010 that the country had misrepresented its debt situation to the European Union in order to stay within EU guidelines.

Ireland also faced extreme challenges as the worldwide property market collapsed, beginning in 2007. Government deficits increased, unemployment increased, and businesses failed, which led the country to slip into a major recession in the Fall of 2008. In November of 2010, the European Union and the International Monetary Fund created an €85 billion rescue package for the country.

On the legal front, risks arise when a country's legal system fails to provide adequate safeguards in the case of contract violations or to protect property rights. When legal safeguards are weak, firms are more likely to break contracts and/or steal intellectual property if they perceive it as being in their interests to do so. Thus, **legal risk** might be defined as the likelihood that a trading partner will opportunistically break a contract or expropriate property rights. When legal risks in a country are high, an international business might hesitate entering into a long-term contract or joint-venture agreement with a firm in that country. For example, in the 1970s when the Indian government passed a law requiring all foreign investors to enter into joint ventures with Indian companies, U.S. companies such as IBM and Coca-Cola closed their investments in India. They believed that the Indian legal system did not provide for adequate protection of intellectual property rights, creating the very real danger that their Indian partners might expropriate the intellectual property of the American companies—which for IBM and Coca-Cola amounted to the core of their competitive advantage.

Overall Attractiveness

The overall attractiveness of a country as a potential market and/or investment site for an international business depends on balancing the benefits, costs, and risks associated with doing business in that country. Generally, the costs and risks associated with doing business in a foreign country are typically lower in economically advanced and politically stable democratic nations and greater in less developed and politically unstable nations. The assessment is complicated, however, by the fact that the potential long-run benefits are not dependent only upon a nation's current stage of economic development or political stability. Rather, the benefits depend on likely future economic growth rates. Economic growth appears to be a function of a free market system and a country's capacity for growth (which may be greater in less developed nations). This leads one to conclude that, other things being equal, the benefit–cost–risk trade-off is likely to be most favourable in politically stable developed and developing nations that have free market systems and no dramatic upsurge in either inflation rates or private-sector debt. It is likely to be least favourable in politically unstable developing nations that operate with a mixed or command economy or in developing nations where speculative financial bubbles have led to excess borrowing.

ETHICS AND REGULATIONS

Country differences give rise to some important and contentious ethical issues. Three important issues that have been the focus of much debate in recent years are (1) the ethics of doing business in nations that violate human rights; (2) the ethics of doing business in countries with very lax labour and environmental regulations; and (3) the ethics of corruption.

Ethics and Human Rights

One major ethical dilemma facing firms from democratic nations is whether they should do business in totalitarian countries, such as China, that routinely violate the human rights of their citizens. There are two sides to this issue. Some argue that investing in totalitarian countries provides comfort to dictators and can help prop up repressive regimes that abuse basic human rights. For instance, Human Rights Watch, an organization that promotes the protection of basic human rights around the world, has argued that the progressive trade policies adopted by Western nations toward China have done little to deter human rights abuses.[60] According to Human Rights Watch, the Chinese government stepped up its repression of political dissidents in 1996 after the Clinton administration removed human rights as a factor in determining China's trade status with the United States. Without investment by Western firms and the support of Western governments, many repressive regimes would collapse and be replaced by more democratically inclined governments, critics such as Human Rights Watch argue. Firms that have invested in Chile, China, Iraq, and South Africa have all been the direct targets of such criticisms. The 1994 dismantling of the apartheid system in South Africa has been credited to economic sanctions by Western nations, including a lack of investment by Western firms. This, say those who argue against investment in totalitarian countries, is proof that investment boycotts can work (although decades of U.S.-led investment boycotts against Cuba and Iran, among other countries, have failed to have a similar impact).

In contrast, some argue that Western investment, by raising the level of economic development of a totalitarian country, can help change it from within. They note that economic well-being and political freedoms often go hand in hand. Thus, when arguing against attempts to apply trade sanctions to China in the wake of the violent 1989 government crackdown on pro-democracy demonstrators, the U.S. government claimed that U.S. firms should continue to be allowed to invest in mainland China because greater political freedoms would follow the resulting economic growth.

Since both positions have some merit, it is difficult to arrive at a general statement of what firms should do. Unless mandated by government (as in the case of investment in South Africa) each firm must make its own judgments about the ethical implications of investing in totalitarian states on a case-by-case basis. The more repressive the regime, however, and the less amenable it seems to be to change, the greater the case for not investing.

Ethics and Regulations

A second important ethical issue is whether an international firm should adhere to the same standards of product safety, work safety, and environmental protection that are required in its home country. This is of particular concern to many firms based in Western nations, where product safety, worker safety, and environmental protection laws are among the toughest in the world. Should Western firms investing in less developed countries adhere to tough Western standards, even though local regulations don't require them to do so? This issue has taken on added importance in recent years following revelations that Western enterprises have been using child labour or very poorly paid "sweatshop" labour in developing nations. Companies criticized for using sweatshop labour include the Gap, Disney, Wal-Mart, Loblaw's Joe Fresh, and Nike.[61]

Again there is no easy answer. While the argument for adhering to Western standards might seem strong, on closer examination the issue becomes more complicated. What if adhering to Western standards would make the foreign investment unprofitable, thereby denying the foreign country much-needed jobs? What is the ethical thing to do? To adhere to Western standards and not invest, thereby denying people jobs, or to adhere to local standards and invest, thereby providing jobs and income? As with many ethical dilemmas, there is no easy answer. Each case needs to be assessed on its own merits.

Ethics and Corruption

A final ethical issue concerns bribes and corruption. Should an international business pay bribes to corrupt government officials to gain market access to a foreign country? To most Westerners, bribery seems to be a corrupt and morally repugnant way of doing business, so the answer might initially be no. Some countries have laws on their books that prohibit their citizens from paying bribes to foreign government officials in return for economic favours. As noted earlier, in the United States the Foreign Corrupt Practices Act prohibits U.S. companies from making "corrupt" payments to foreign officials to obtain or retain business, although many other developed nations lack similar laws. Similarly, the Canadian Corruption of Foreign Public Officials Act encompasses the same spirit of checks and balances against corrupt business practices on the international stage. Trade and finance ministers from the member states of the OECD, an association of the world's 20 or so most powerful economies, are working on a convention that would oblige member states to make the bribery of foreign public officials a criminal offence.

However, in many parts of the world, payoffs to government officials are a part of life. One can argue that not investing ignores the fact that such investment can bring substantial benefits to the local populace in terms of income and jobs. From a pragmatic standpoint, the practice of giving bribes, although a little evil, might be the price that must be paid to do a greater good (assuming the investment creates jobs where none existed before and assuming the practice is not illegal). Several economists advocate this reasoning, suggesting that in the context of pervasive and cumbersome regulations in developing countries, corruption may actually improve efficiency and help growth! These economists theorize that in a country where pre-existing political structures distort or limit the workings of the market mechanism, corruption in the form of black-marketeering, smuggling, and side payments to government bureaucrats to "speed up" approval for business investments may actually enhance welfare.[62] Arguments like this persuaded the U.S. Congress to exempt certain "grease payments" from the Foreign Corrupt Practices Act. Similarly, the Corruption of Foreign Public Officials Act allows for exemptions under such circumstances.

However, other economists have argued that corruption reduces the returns on business investment.[63] In a country where corruption is common, the profits from a business activity may be siphoned off by unproductive bureaucrats who demand side payments for granting the enterprise permission to operate. This reduces the incentive that businesses have to invest and may hurt a country's economic growth rate. One economist's study of the connection between corruption and growth in 70 countries found that corruption had a significant negative impact on a country's economic growth rate.[64] Given the debate and the complexity of this issue, one again might conclude that generalization is difficult. Yes, corruption is bad, and yes, it may harm a country's economic development, but yes, there are also cases where side payments to government officials can remove the bureaucratic barriers to investments that create jobs. This pragmatic stance ignores, however, that corruption tends to "corrupt" both the bribe giver and the bribe taker. Corruption feeds on itself, and once an individual has started to agree to demands for side payments, pulling back may be difficult if not impossible. This strengthens the moral case for never engaging in corruption, no matter how compelling the benefits might seem.

Key Terms

Bill S-21	copyrights
civil law	democracy
collectivism	deregulation
command economy	economic risk
common law	first-mover advantages
communist totalitarianism	Foreign Corrupt Practices Act
communists	gross national income (GNI)
contract	Human Development Index (HDI)
contract law	individualism

innovation

late-mover disadvantages

legal risk

legal system

market economy

mixed economy

Paris Convention for the Protection of
Industrial Property

patent

political economy

political risk

political system

private action

privatization

product liability

product safety laws

property rights

public action

purchasing power parity (PPP)

representative democracy

right-wing totalitarianism

social democrats

theocratic law

theocratic totalitarianism

totalitarianism

trademarks

tribal totalitarianism

United Nations Convention on Contracts for
the International Sale of Goods (CISG)

LO Learning Objectives Summary

This chapter has reviewed how the political, economic, and legal systems of different countries vary. The potential benefits, costs, and risks of doing business in a country are a function of its political, economic, and legal systems. These major points were made in the chapter:

1. Political systems can be assessed according to two dimensions: the degree to which they emphasize collectivism as opposed to individualism, and the degree to which they are democratic or totalitarian. Collectivism is an ideology that views the needs of society as being more important than the needs of the individual. Collectivism translates into an advocacy for state intervention in economic activity and, in the case of communism, a totalitarian dictatorship. Individualism is an ideology built on an emphasis of the primacy of individual's freedoms in the political, economic, and cultural realms. Individualism translates into an advocacy for democratic ideals and free market economics. Democracy and totalitarianism are at different ends of the political spectrum. In a representative democracy, citizens periodically elect individuals to represent them and political freedoms are guaranteed by a constitution. In a totalitarian state, political power is monopolized by a party, group, or individual, and basic political freedoms are denied to citizens of the state.

2. There are three broad types of economic systems: a market economy, a command economy, and a mixed economy. In a market economy, prices are free of controls and private ownership is predominant. In a command economy, prices are set by central planners, productive assets are owned by the state, and private ownership is forbidden. A mixed economy has elements of both a market economy and a command economy.

3. Differences in the structure of law between countries can have important implications for the practice of international business. The degree to which property rights are protected can vary dramatically from country to country, as can product safety and product liability legislation and the nature of contract law.

4. Countries differ in their level of development. The rate of economic progress in a country seems to depend on the extent to which that country has a well-functioning market economy in which property rights are protected.

5. Many countries are now in a state of transition. There is a marked shift away from totalitarian governments and command or mixed economic systems and toward democratic political institutions and free market economic systems.

6. The shift to market-based economies needs a number of steps, including deregulation, privatization, and the creation of a legal system protecting property rights.

7. The attractiveness of a country as a market and/or investment site depends on balancing the likely long-run benefits of doing business in that country against the likely costs and risks.

Critical Thinking and Discussion Questions

1. "Free market economies stimulate greater economic growth, whereas state-directed economies stifle growth." Evaluate this statement.

2. "A democratic political system is an essential condition for sustained economic progress." Evaluate this statement.

3. What is the relationship between corruption in a country (for example, bribe taking by government officials) and economic growth? Is corruption always bad?

4. The Nobel Prize-winning economist Amartya Sen argues that the concept of development should be broadened to include more than just economic development. What other factors does Sen think should be included in an assessment of development? How might adoption of Sen's views influence government policy? Do you think Sen is correct that development is about more than just economic development? Explain.

5. During the late 1980s and early 1990s, China was routinely cited by various international organizations such as Amnesty International and Freedom Watch for major human rights violations, including torture, beatings, imprisonment, and executions of political dissidents. Despite this, in the late 1990s, China received record levels of foreign direct investment, mainly from firms based in democratic societies such as the United States, Japan, and Germany. Evaluate this trend from an ethical perspective. If you were the CEO of a firm that had the option of making a potentially very profitable investment in China, what would you do?

6. You are the CEO of a company that has to choose between making a $100-million investment in Russia or the Czech Republic. Both investments promise the same long-run return, so your choice is driven by risk considerations. Assess the various risks of doing business in each of these nations. Which investment would you favour and why?

Research Task globalEDGE™ globaledge.msu.edu

Use the globalEDGE™ site to complete the following exercises:

1. The "Freedom in the World" survey evaluates the state of political rights and civil liberties around the world. Provide a description of this survey and a ranking, in terms of "freedom," of the leaders and laggards. What factors are considered in this survey when forming the rankings?

2. Market Potential Indicators (MPI) is an indexing study conducted by the Michigan State University Center for International Business Education and Research (MSU-CIBER) to compare emerging markets on a variety of dimensions. Provide a description of the indicators used in the indexing procedure. Which of the indicators would have greater importance for a company that markets laptop computers? Considering the MPI rankings, which developing countries would you advise this company to enter first?

CLOSING CASE

GHANA: AN AFRICAN DYNAMO

The West African nation of Ghana has emerged as one of the fastest-growing countries in sub-Saharan Africa during the last decade. Between 2000 and 2015, Ghana's average annual growth rate in GDP was over 8 percent, making it the fastest-growing economy in Africa. In 2011, this country of 25 million people became Africa's newest middle-income nation. Driving this growth has been strong demand for two of Ghana's major exports—gold and cocoa—as well as the start of oil production in 2010. Indeed, due to recent oil discoveries, Ghana is set to become one of the biggest oil producers in sub-Saharan Africa, a fact that could fuel strong economic expansion for years to come.

It wasn't always this way. Originally a British colony, Ghana gained independence in 1957. For the next three decades, the country suffered from a long series of military coups that killed any hope for stable democratic government. Successive governments adopted a socialist ideology, often as a reaction to their colonial past. As a result, large portions of the Ghana economy were dominated by state-owned enterprises. Corruption was rampant and inflation often a problem, while the country's dependence on cash crops for foreign currency earnings made it vulnerable to swings in commodity prices. It seemed like yet another failed state.

In 1981, an air force officer, Jerry Rawlings, led a military coup that deposed the president and put Rawlings in power. Rawlings started a vigorous anticorruption drive that made him very popular among ordinary Ghanaians. Rawlings initially pursued socialist policies and banned political parties, but in the early 1990s, he changed his views. He may well have been influenced by the wave of democratic change and economic liberalization that was then sweeping the formally communist states of eastern Europe. In addition, he was pressured by Western governments and the International Monetary Fund to embrace democratic reforms and economic liberalization policies (the IMF was lending money to Ghana).

Presidential elections were held in 1992. Prior to the elections, the ban on political parties was lifted, restrictions on the press were removed, and all parties were given equal access to the media. Rawlings won the election, which foreign observers declared to be "free and fair." Ghana has had a functioning democratic system since then. Rawlings won again in 1996 and retired in 2001. Beginning in 1992, Rawlings started to liberalize the economy, privatizing state-owned enterprises, instituting market-based reforms, and opening Ghana up to foreign investors. Over the next decade, more than 300 state-owned enterprises were privatized, and the new, largely privately held economy was booming.

Following the discovery of oil in 2007, Ghana's politicians studied oil revenue laws from other countries, including Norway and Trinidad. They put in place laws designed to limit the ability of corrupt officials to siphon off oil revenues from royalties to enrich themselves; something that has been a big problem in oil-rich Nigeria. Some oil revenues are slated to go directly into the national budget, while the rest will be split between a "stabilization fund" to support the budget should oil prices drop and a "heritage fund" to be spent only when the oil starts to run out.

Despite all of its progress over the last two decades, Ghana still has many issues to deal with. Although Ghana ranks better than most African nations, there is still a perception that corruption is a problem, particularly in the police force and the allocation of government contracts. Inflation rose to greater than 13 percent in 2013, and the budget deficit widened to 12 percent of GDP as the ruling political party stepped up public spending in advance of presidential and general elections, which it narrowly won. Despite economic progress, as many as a third of Ghanaians still live on less than $2 a day, and Ghana still needs to upgrade its power, water, and road infrastructure. On the other hand, oil revenue is starting to flow and will increase over time, which—if used wisely—will give Ghana a chance to fix some of its problems and solidify its gains.

Sources: D. Hinshaw, "In an African Dynamo's Expansion, the Perils of Prosperity," *The Wall Street Journal*, December 30, 2011, p. A9; "Dangerously Hopeful," *The Economist*, January 2, 2010, p. 36; "Carats and Sticks," *The Economist*, March 3, 2010, p. 68; "Rawlings: The Legacy," *BBC News*, December 1, 2000, http://news.bbc.co.uk/2/hi/africa/1050310.stm; "Ghana GDP Expands 2.1% in Q4 2012," *Ghana Statistical Service*, April 12, 2013; and "Ghana: Get a Grip," *The Economist*, December 21, 2013.

Case Discussion Questions

1. After gaining independence from Britain, Ghana's economy languished for three decades. Why was this the case? What does the Ghana experience teach you about the connection between economic and political systems and economic growth?

2. What where the main changes that Jerry Rawlings made in the Ghanaian political and economic systems? What were the consequences of these changes? What are the lessons here?

3. What external forces helped to persuade Rawlings to change political and economic practices in Ghana? Do you think he would have made the changes he did without these external forces?

4. If Ghana had discovered large oil reserves in the 1980s instead of the 2000s, do you things might have played out differently? Why?

5. What is the difference between the approach of Nigeria toward oil revenues and that of Ghana (the Nigerian experience is documented in the Country Focus feature in this chapter)? Which approach is in the best long-run interests of the country?

6. What does Ghana need to do to remain on its current track of sustained economic growth?

© Kevinbrine/Dreamstime.com

Chapter 3
The Cultural Environment

OPENING CASE

BEST BUY AND EBAY IN CHINA

The People's Republic of China opened up to foreign investments in the late 1970s. Since that time, numerous companies have tried to establish operations and sell their products to customers in China. Many more companies will try in the years to come—China is expected to have some 190 million people in the middle- and upper-income categories by 2020. This is an increase from only about 17 million people in these income brackets today. China's purchasing power for virtually all products and services has strong potential, and foreign companies will seek these market opportunities. What have we learned culturally that can help Western-based companies in China's marketplace?

Some background on China can serve as a starting point for better understanding the culture in China and what some well-known companies, such as Best Buy and eBay, have done to target the Chinese marketplace. The motivation for many foreign companies to enter China—beyond those that have been there for a few decades for reasons of low-cost production—was the triple growth of the Chinese economy that was seen from

2000 to 2010. China overtook Japan to become the second largest economy in the world behind just the United States and its large population makes for an enormous target market. Investment from foreign companies was the largest driver of China's growth in the decade from 2000 to 2010. However, many companies also increased their exports to China. The United States, for example, saw its companies increase exports to China by 542 percent from 2000 to 2011 (from $16.2 billion to $103.9 billion), while total exports to the rest of the world increased only 80 percent in the same time period.

Interestingly, while foreign investments grew, domestic consumption as a share of the Chinese economy declined from 46 percent in 2000 to 33 percent in 2010. This consumption decline—coupled with slower growth globally and, ultimately, the worldwide economic downturn that started in 2008—raised questions about China's momentum. Right now, around 85 percent of mainstream Chinese consumers are living in the top 100 wealthiest cities. By the year 2020, these advanced and developing cities will have relatively few customers who are lower than the middle- and upper-income brackets. The expectation is that these consumers will be able to afford a range of products and services, such as flat-screen televisions and overseas travel. This begs the question, can the unprecedented Chinese growth really continue, and would it come from increased consumption?

The resounding answer is yes according to research conducted by McKinsey & Company. McKinsey found that, barring another major economic shock similar to what we saw in 2008, China's gross domestic product (GDP) will continue to grow. The growth from 2010 to 2020 is expected to be about 7.9 percent per year, which is still far above the expected growth for the United States (2.8 percent annually), Japan (1.2 percent annually), and Germany (1.7 percent annually)—the three countries in the top four worldwide economies along with China. And, the key is that consumption will now be the driving force behind the growth instead of foreign investment. The consumption forecast opens up opportunities for foreign companies to engage with Chinese consumers who are expected to have more purchasing power and discretionary spending.

But culturally translating market success from one country or even a large number of countries to the Chinese marketplace is not necessarily as straightforward as it may seem. Often, a combination of naïveté, arrogance, and cultural misunderstanding have led many well-known companies to fail in China. Lack of an understanding of issues such as local demands, buying habits, values, and beliefs led to struggles for companies that had been very successful elsewhere in the world. Let's take a brief look at Best Buy and eBay as two examples.

Best Buy, the mega-store mainly focused on consumer electronics, was founded in 1966 as an audio specialty store. Best Buy entered China in 2006 by acquiring a majority interest in China's fourth largest appliance retailer, Jiangsu Five Star Appliance, for $180 million. But culture shock hit Best Buy, according to Shaun Rein, the founder of China Market Research Group. He pointed to a few reasons for this culture shock and lack of success. First, the Chinese will not pay for Best Buy's overly expensive products unless they are a brand like Apple. Second, there is too much piracy in the Chinese market and this reduces demand for electronics products at competitive market prices. Third, like many Europeans, the Chinese do not want to shop at huge mega-stores. So, these three seemingly easy-to-understand cultural issues created difficulties for Best Buy. To solve these issues, Best Buy believed they would have to develop and implement a different business model for the Chinese market than they have used elsewhere. Now, how far should a company go outside of its normal business model to adhere to cultural values and beliefs of a new market? Strategically moving forward, Best Buy opted to close all of its Best Buy–branded stores in China and focus on its wholly-owned, local Jiangsu Five Star chain of stores. But will this new strategic business model be successful with the new makeup of customers in China expected by 2020?

eBay, the popular e-business site focused on consumer-to-consumer purchases, was founded in 1995. The company was one of the true success stories that lived through the dot-com bubble in the 1990s. It is now a multi-billion-dollar business with operations in more than 30 countries. But China's unique culture created problems for eBay in that market. For eBay, contrary to the widespread cultural issues that faced Best Buy, one company in particular (TaoBao) and one feature more specifically (built-in instant messaging) shaped a lot of the problems that eBay ran into in China. Some 200 million shoppers are using TaoBao to buy products, and the company accounts for almost 80 percent of online transaction value in China. Uniquely, TaoBao's built-in instant messaging system has been cited as a main reason for its edge over eBay in China. Basically, customers wanted to be able to identify a seller's online status and communicate with them directly and easily—a function not seamlessly incorporated into eBay's China system. Clearly, built-in instant text messaging is a solvable obstacle in doing business in China. It sounds easy now when we know about it, but may not always be the case when we take into account all the little things that are important in a market. How can a foreign company entering China ensure that it tackles the most important "little" things that end up being huge barriers to success as we approach the year 2020, when China is expected to have significantly increased purchasing power among its middle class?

Sources: B. Carlson, "Why Big American Businesses Fail in China," *GlobalPost*, September 22, 2013; Y. Atsmon, M. Magni, L. Li, and W. Liao, "Meet the 2020 Chinese Consumer," *McKinsey Consumer & Shopper Insights*, March 2012; "Exports to China by State 2000–2011," The US-China Business Council, 2012; and A. Groth, "Best Buy's Overseas Strategy is Failing in Europe and China," *Business Insider*, November 4, 2011.

LO | LEARNING OBJECTIVES

By the end of this chapter you should be able to:

1. Explain what is meant by the culture of a society.
2. Identify the forces that lead to differences in social culture.
3. Identify the business and economic implications of differences in culture.
4. Recognize how differences in social culture influence values in the workplace.
5. Demonstrate an appreciation for the economic and business implications of cultural change.

Introduction

International business is different from domestic business because countries are different. In Chapter 2 we saw how national differences in political, economic, and legal systems influence the benefits, costs, and risks associated with doing business in different countries. In this chapter, we will explore how differences in culture across and within countries can affect international business. Several themes run through this chapter.

The first theme is that business success in a variety of countries requires cross-cultural literacy. By cross-cultural literacy, we mean an understanding of how cultural differences across and within nations can affect the way business is practised. In these days of global communications, rapid transportation, and global markets, when the era of the global village seems just around the corner, it is easy to forget just how different various cultures really are. Underneath the veneer of modernism, deep cultural differences often remain. Westerners in general, and North Americans in particular, are quick to conclude that because people from other parts of the world also wear blue jeans, listen to Western popular music, eat at McDonald's, and drink Coca-Cola they also accept the basic tenets of Western (or even American) culture. But this is not true. Increasingly, the Chinese are embracing the material products of modern society. Anyone who has visited Shanghai, for example, cannot fail to be struck by how modern the city seems, with its skyscrapers, department stores, and freeways. But beneath the veneer of Western modernism, long-standing cultural traditions rooted in a 2000-year-old ideology continue to influence business transactions. In China, *guanxi*, or relationships backed by reciprocal obligations, are central to getting business done. Firms that lack sufficient *guanxi* may find themselves at a disadvantage when doing business in China. In this chapter, we shall argue that it is important for foreign businesses to gain an understanding of the culture, or cultures, that prevail in countries where they do business.

The opening case deals with precisely this point. We focused on two well-known and, by most standards, very successful global companies—Best Buy and eBay—and their venture into China. The failure of both companies in China was due in large part to their inability to come to grips with the cultural differences between China and the United States. Best Buy displayed a remarkable lack of cross-cultural literacy when it did not gauge the price sensitivity of the Chinese consumers, when it did not account for very well-known issues related to piracy in the electronics market, and when it did not understand the type of shopping experience Chinese customers really wanted. Previous success with their established business model directly led to Best Buy's lack of success in the Chinese market. Likewise, but at a more fine-grained level, eBay ran into its own cultural issues in China. eBay failed to recognize the power of the established market leader (TaoBao) and the core feature provided by this market leader—built-in instant messaging. Customers valued, depended on, and saw instant messaging as an integral part of their shopping experience. Generalizing from the examples of Best Buy and eBay, in this chapter we argue that it is important for foreign businesses to gain an understanding of the culture that prevails in those countries where they do business and that success requires a foreign enterprise to adapt to the culture of its host country.[1]

Another theme developed in this chapter is that a relationship may exist between culture and the cost of doing business in a country or region. Different cultures are more or less supportive of the capitalist mode of production and this may affect the costs of doing business. For example, some observers have argued that cultural factors lowered the costs of doing business in Japan and helped to explain Japan's rapid economic assent during the 1960s, '70s, and '80s.[2] By the same token, cultural factors can sometimes raise the costs of doing business. Historically, class divisions were an important aspect of British culture, and for a long time, firms operating in Great Britain found it difficult to achieve cooperation between management and labour. Class divisions led to a high level of industrial disputes in that country during the 1960s and 1970s and raised the costs of doing business in Great Britain relative to the costs in countries such as Switzerland, Norway, Germany, or Japan, where class conflict was historically less prevalent.

The British example, however, brings us to the final theme we will explore in this chapter: culture is not static. It can and does evolve, although the rate at which culture can change is disputed. Important aspects of British culture, and this can be found in Canada, have changed significantly over the past 20 years, and this is reflected in weaker class distinctions and a lower level of industrial disputes. Between 1995 and 2005, the number of days lost per 1000 workers due to strikes in the United Kingdom was, on average, 28 each year, significantly less than in the United States (33 each year), Ireland (81), and Canada (168).

In 2012, 250 000 working days were lost due to strikes in the United Kingdom, and this is the lowest number of working days lost since 2005; in Canada in 2016, 633 900 days were lost.[3] Similarly, there is evidence of cultural change in Japan, with the traditional Japanese emphasis on group identification giving way to greater emphasis on individualism.

Finally, it is important to note that multinational enterprises can themselves be engines of cultural change. In India, for example, McDonald's and other Western fast-food companies may help to change the dining culture of that nation, drawing them away from traditional restaurants and toward fast-food outlets.

We open this chapter with a general discussion of what culture is. Then we focus on how differences in social structure, religion, language, and education influence the culture of a country. We then discuss the process of cultural change. The implications for business practice will be highlighted throughout the chapter and summarized in a section at the end.

LO1 What Is Culture?

Scholars have never been able to agree on a simple definition of culture. In the 1870s the anthropologist Edward Tylor defined culture as "that complex whole which includes knowledge, belief, art, morals, law, custom, and other capabilities acquired by man as a member of society."[4] Since then hundreds of other definitions have been offered. Geert Hofstede, an expert on cross-cultural differences and management, defined culture as "the collective programming of the mind which distinguishes the members of one human group from another. . . . Culture, in this sense, includes systems of values; and values are among the building blocks of culture."[5] Another definition of culture comes from sociologists Zvi Namenwirth and Robert Weber, who see culture as a system of ideas and argue that these ideas constitute a design for living.[6]

Here we follow both Hofstede, and Namenwirth and Weber by viewing culture as a system of values and norms that are shared among a group of people, and that when taken together constitute a design for living. By **values** we mean abstract ideas about what a group believes to be good, right, and desirable. Put differently, values are shared assumptions about how things ought to be.[7] By **norms**, we mean the social rules and guidelines that prescribe appropriate behaviour in particular situations. We shall use the term **society** to refer to a group of people who share a common set of values and norms. While a society may be equivalent to a country, some countries harbour several "societies" (i.e., they support multiple cultures) and some societies embrace more than one country.

Understanding rituals and symbolic behaviours is essential to doing business in foreign countries. © *Bloom Productions/ Getty Images*

Values and Norms

Values form the bedrock of a culture. They provide the context within which a society's norms are established and justified. They may include a society's attitudes toward such concepts as individual freedom, democracy, truth, justice, honesty, loyalty, social obligations, collective responsibility, the role of women, love, sex, marriage, and so on. Values are not just abstract concepts, they are invested with considerable emotional significance. People argue, fight, and even die over values such as freedom. Values also often are reflected in the political and economic systems of a society. As we saw in Chapter 2, democratic free market capitalism is a reflection of a philosophical value system that emphasizes individual freedom.

ANOTHER PERSPECTIVE

Conducting Business Overseas

Culture plays a huge role when conducting business overseas. Everyday issues such as how different cultures view time, relationships between men and women, social observances, hierarchical structure in business, the role of religion in everyday life and so on are all based on cultural values and norms. It is important to observe cultural cues and become as savvy as possible before venturing into the international arena. Here are a couple of good Web sites that deal with intercultural communication, manners, etiquette, and skills needed when going overseas. The Web site www.cyborlink.com deals with etiquette, manners, and culture; and this one from Michigan State University is a comprehensive Web site that offers links to other valuable resources, such as the international business news from BBC: http:// globaledge.msu.edu.

Norms are the social rules that govern people's actions toward one another. Norms can be subdivided further into two major categories: folkways and mores. **Folkways** are the routine conventions of everyday life. Generally, folkways are actions of little moral significance. Rather, folkways are social conventions concerning things such as the appropriate dress code in a particular situation, good social manners, neighbourly behaviour, and the like. While folkways define the way people are expected to behave, violation of folkways is not normally a serious matter. People who violate folkways may be thought of as eccentric or ill-mannered, but they are not usually considered to be evil or bad. In many countries, foreigners may initially be excused for violating folkways.

A good example of folkways concerns attitudes toward time in different countries. People are very time conscious in Canada. Canadians tend to arrive a few minutes early for business appointments. When invited for dinner to someone's home, it is considered polite to arrive on time or just a few minutes late. The concept of time can be very different in other countries. It is not necessarily a breach of etiquette to arrive a little late for a business appointment; it might even be considered more impolite to arrive early. Arriving on time for a dinner engagement can be very bad manners. In Great Britain, for example, when someone says, "Come for dinner at 7:00 P.M.," what he means is "come for dinner at 7:30 to 8:00 P.M." The guest who arrives at 7:00 P.M. is likely to find an unprepared and embarrassed host. Similarly, when an Argentinean says, "Come for dinner any time after 8:00 P.M." what she means is: "don't come at 8:00 P.M.—it's far too early!"

Mores are norms that are seen as central to the functioning of a society and to its social life. They have much greater significance than folkways. Accordingly, violating mores can bring serious retribution. Mores include such factors as indictments against theft, adultery, incest, and cannibalism. In many societies, certain mores have been enacted into law. Thus, all advanced societies have laws against theft, incest, and cannibalism. However, there are also many differences between cultures as to what is perceived as mores. In Canada, for example, drinking alcohol is widely accepted, whereas in Saudi Arabia the consumption of alcohol is viewed as violating important social mores and is punishable by imprisonment (as some Western citizens working in Saudi Arabia have discovered).

Culture, Society, and the Nation-State

We have defined a society as a group of people who share a common set of values and norms; that is, people who are bound together by a common culture. However, there is not a strict one-to-one correspondence between a society and a nation-state. Nation-states are political creations. They may contain a single culture or several cultures. While the French nation can be thought of as the political embodiment of French culture, the nation of Canada has at least three cultures—an Anglo culture, a French-speaking "Quebecois" culture, and a First Nation culture. Similarly, many African nations have important cultural differences between tribal groups, as exhibited in the early 1990s when Rwanda dissolved into a bloody civil war between two tribes, the Tutsis and Hutus. Africa is not alone in this regard. India is composed of many distinct cultural groups. During the Gulf War, the prevailing view presented to Western audiences was that Iraq was a homogenous Arab nation. But the chaos that followed the war revealed several different societies within Iraq, each with its own culture. The Kurds in the north do not view themselves as Arabs and have their own distinct history and traditions. There are two Arab societies: the Shiites in the south and the Sunnis who populate the middle of the country and who rule Iraq (the terms *Shiites* and *Sunnis* refer to different sects within the religion of Islam). Among the southern Sunnis is another distinct society of 500 000 "Marsh Arabs," who live at the confluence of the Tigris and Euphrates rivers, pursuing a way of life that dates back 5000 years.[8]

ANOTHER PERSPECTIVE

Sticky Problems in Culture Research

Conducting research across cultures is difficult. Travelling to and building collaborative relationships in other countries is time-consuming, sometimes difficult, and always full of surprises. But one of the most interesting challenges is how to be certain that the concept on which you are working or about which you want to communicate has a similar meaning across the culture border. This challenge is far more than language translation; it is concept translation, or what researchers call *concept equivalence*. Take the complicated concept of bribery, for example. Does it mean the same thing in Manitoba as it does in an undeveloped, centralized economy such as North Korea? What do you think?

At the other end of the scale we can speak of cultures that embrace several nations. Several scholars argue that we can speak of an Islamic society or culture that is shared by the citizens of many nations in the Middle East, Asia, and Africa. As you will recall from the last chapter, this view of expansive cultures that embrace several nations underpins Samuel Huntington's view of a world that is fragmented into different civilizations including Western, Islamic, and Sinic (Chinese).[9]

To complicate things further, it is also possible to talk about culture at different levels. It is reasonable to talk about "Canadian society" and "Canadian culture," but there are several societies within Canada, each with its own culture. One can talk about Afro-Canadian culture, Acadian culture, Asian-Canadian culture, Hispanic culture, Native-Canadian culture, Irish-Canadian culture, the people of Newfoundland with their unique dialect, and Western culture. Although Canada is a multicultural country with many vibrant and new communities, particularly settling in major centres across Canada, its early founding cultures still carry clout in today's society. English Canadians view their culture as unique and different from that of its counterpart in the United States, although with each passing year, the similarities between Americans and Canadians are growing (as evidenced by a fragmenting health care system, increasing gun use in crime in Canada, evaporating social programs, and rising poverty). The historic and unquestioned notion of Canada as a cultural mosaic seemed apt in the late 1970s when this concept became imbedded into the Canadian psyche. At that time it provided comfort to Canadians to think they were different than the American to the south. However, looking beyond the approach to multiculturalism funded by provincial or federal governments and popular in the late 1900s, most second-generation Canadians integrate into Canadian society in a manner similar to that of the U.S. "melting-pot" scenario. The Americans have their First Nation culture, their Cajan culture, and their Latino culture, so in certain respects one might feel that the United States is more of a cultural mosaic than Canada, where only the First Nations culture and the Quebec culture, entwined in its own unique Quebecois language, customs, cuisine, and joie de vivre, have survived and flourished over the centuries. The point is that the relationship between culture and country is often ambiguous. One cannot always characterize a country as having a single homogenous culture, and even when one can, one must also often recognize that the national culture is a mosaic of subcultures.

LO2   The Determinants of Culture

The values and norms of a culture do not emerge fully formed. They are the evolutionary product of a number of factors, including the prevailing political and economic philosophy, the social structure of a society, and the dominant religion, language, and education (see Figure 3.1). We discussed political and economic philosophy at length in Chapter 2. Such philosophy clearly influences the value systems of a society. For

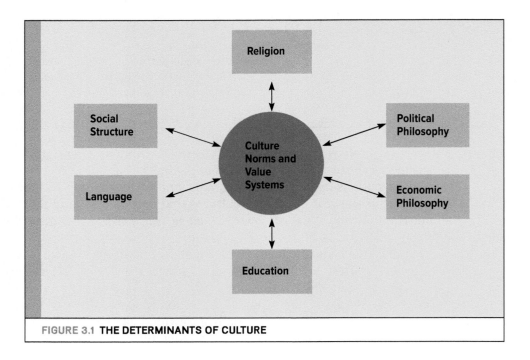

FIGURE 3.1 **THE DETERMINANTS OF CULTURE**

example, the values found in the former Soviet Union toward freedom, justice, and individual achievement were clearly different from the values found in Canada, precisely because each society operated according to a different political and economic philosophy. Below we will discuss the influence of social structure, religion, language, and education. Remember that the chain of causation runs both ways. While factors such as social structure and religion clearly influence the values and norms of a society, the values and norms of a society can influence social structure and religion.

LO3 Social Culture

A society's "social structure" refers to its basic social organization. Although social structure consists of many different aspects, two dimensions are particularly important when explaining differences between cultures. The first is the degree to which the basic unit of social organization is the individual, as opposed to the group. Western societies tend to emphasize the primacy of the individual, while groups tend to figure more largely in many other societies. The second dimension is the degree to which a society is stratified into classes or castes. Some societies are characterized by a relatively high degree of social stratification and relatively low mobility between strata (e.g., Indian), while other societies are characterized by a low degree of social stratification and high mobility between strata (e.g., Canadian).

Individuals and Groups

A **group** is an association of two or more individuals who have a shared sense of identity and who interact with each other in structured ways on the basis of a common set of expectations about each other's behaviour.[10] Human social life is group life. Individuals are involved in families, work groups, social groups, recreational groups, and so on. However, while groups are found in all societies, societies differ according to the degree to which the group is viewed as the primary means of social organization.[11] In some societies, individual attributes and achievements are viewed as being more important than group membership, while in other societies the reverse is true.

THE INDIVIDUAL

In Chapter 2, we discussed individualism as a political philosophy. However, individualism is more than just an abstract political philosophy. In many Western societies, the individual is the basic building block of social organization. This is reflected not just in the political and economic organization of society, but also in the way people perceive themselves and relate to each other in social and business settings. The value systems of many Western societies, for example, emphasize individual achievement. The social standing of individuals is not so much a function of whom they work for, as of their individual performance in whatever work setting they choose.

The emphasis on individual performance in many Western societies has both beneficial and harmful aspects. In Canada and the United States, the emphasis on individual performance finds expression in an admiration of "rugged individualism" and entrepreneurship. One benefit of this is the high level of entrepreneurial activity in the United States, Canada, and other Western societies. New products and new ways of doing business (e.g., personal computers, photocopiers, computer software, biotechnology, supermarkets, and discount retail stores) have repeatedly been created in North America by entrepreneurial individuals. One can argue that the dynamism of the Canadian and U.S. economies owe much to the philosophy of individualism.

Individualism also finds expression in a high degree of managerial mobility between companies, and this is not always good. While moving from company to company may be good for individual managers who are trying to build impressive résumés, it is not necessarily beneficial for the companies they leave behind. The lack of loyalty and commitment to an individual company, and the tendency to move on when a better offer comes along can result in managers who have good general skills but lack the knowledge, experience, and network of interpersonal contacts that come from years of working within the same company. An effective manager draws on company-specific experience, knowledge, and a network of contacts to find solutions to current problems, and companies may suffer if their managers lack these attributes.

One positive aspect of high managerial mobility is that executives are exposed to different ways of doing business. The ability to compare business practices helps Western executives identify how good practices and techniques developed in one firm might be profitably applied to other firms.

The emphasis on individualism may also make it difficult to build teams within an organization to perform collective tasks. If individuals are always competing with each other on the basis of individual performance, it may be difficult for them to cooperate. One study of U.S. competitiveness by the Massachusetts Institute of Technology concluded that U.S. firms are being hurt in the global economy by a failure to achieve cooperation both within a company (e.g., between functions; between management and labour) and between companies (e.g., between a firm and its suppliers). Given the emphasis on individualism in the American value system, this failure is not surprising.[12] The emphasis on individualism in the United States, while helping to create a dynamic entrepreneurial economy, may raise the costs of doing business due to its adverse impact on managerial stability and cooperation.

The high degree to which individualism is appreciated is not as prevalent in Canada as in the United States. For example, in the United States, neither of the two political parties espouse the great degree of government interference in the daily lives of Americans that we tend to see happening to Canadians through high taxes, group social programs, and government-sanctioned (both perceived and real) interference in business.

THE GROUP

In contrast to the Western emphasis on the individual, the group is the primary unit of social organization in many other societies. For example, in Japan, the social status of an individual is determined as much by the standing of the group to which he or she belongs as by his or her individual performance.[13] In traditional Japanese society, the group was the family or village to which an individual belonged. Today the group has frequently come to be associated with the work team or business organization to which an individual belongs. In a now-classic study of Japanese society, Nakane has noted how this expresses itself in everyday life:

> When a Japanese faces the outside (confronts another person) and affixes some position to himself socially he is inclined to give precedence to institution over kind of occupation. Rather than saying, "I am a typesetter" or "I am a filing clerk," he is likely to say, "I am from B Publishing Group" or "I belong to S company."[14]

Nakane goes on to observe that the primacy of the group to which an individual belongs often evolves into a deeply emotional attachment in which identification with the group becomes all important in one's life. One central value of Japanese culture is the

Using IT to Break India's Caste System

Modern India is a country of dramatic contrasts. Its information technology (IT) sector is among the most vibrant in the world with companies such as Tata Consultancy Services, Cognizant Technology Solutions, Infosys, and Wipro emerging as powerful global players. Cognizant is an interesting company in that it was founded as a technology arm of Dun & Bradstreet (USA) in 1994 but is typically considered an Indian IT company because a majority of its employees are based in India. In fact, many IT companies locate or operate in India because of its strong IT knowledge, human capital, and culture.

Traditionally, India has had one of the strongest caste systems in the world. At the core, the caste system has no legality in India, and discrimination against lower castes is illegal. India has also enacted numerous new laws and social initiatives to protect and improve living conditions of lower castes in the country. Historically, however, India's caste system was an impediment to social mobility. But, steadily the stranglehold on people's socioeconomic conditions is becoming a fading memory among the educated, urban middle-class Indians who make up the majority of employees in the high-tech economy. Unfortunately, the same is not true in rural India, where some 70 percent of the nation's population still resides. There, caste remains a pervasive influence.

For example, a young female engineer at Infosys who grew up in a small rural village and is a dalit (sometimes called a "scheduled caste") recounts how she never entered the house of a Brahmin, India's elite priestly caste, even though half of her village were Brahmins. When a dalit was hired to cook at the school in her native village, Brahmins withdrew their children from the school. The engineer herself is the beneficiary of a charitable training scheme that Infosys launched in 2006. Her caste, making up about 16 percent of the country (or around 165 million people), is among the poorest in India, with some 91 percent making less than $100 a month, compared to 65 percent of Brahmins.

To try to correct this historic inequality, politicians have talked for years about extending the employment quota system to private enterprises. The government has told private companies to hire more dalits and members of tribal communities and warned that "strong measures" will be taken if companies do not comply. Private employers are resisting attempts to impose quotas, arguing with some justification that people who are guaranteed a job by a quota system are unlikely to work very hard. At the same time, progressive employers realize they need to do something to correct the inequalities, and unless India taps into the lower castes, it may not be able to find the employees required to staff rapidly-growing, high-technology enterprises. Thus, the Confederation of Indian Industry recently introduced a package of dalit-friendly measures, including scholarships for bright lower-caste children. Building on this, Infosys is leading the way among high-tech enterprises. The company provides special training to low-caste engineering graduates who have failed to get a job in industry after graduation. While the training does not promise employment, so far almost all graduates who completed the seven-month training program have been hired by Infosys and other enterprises. Infosys programs are privatized version of the education offered in India to try to break down India's caste system.

Questions

1. Is it easier for a local company or an international company to break through social and class barriers?

2. Can you think of other similar examples from other countries?

Source: B. Hardzinski, S. Grillot, and M. Addison, "Breaking Down India's Caste System Through Education," *KGOU*, November 29, 2013, http://kgou.org/post/breaking-down-india-s-caste-system-through-education, accessed March 7, 2014. "With Reservations: Business and Caste in India," *The Economist*, October 6, 2007, pp. 81–83; and Eric Bellman, "Reversal of Fortune Isolates India's Brahmins," *The Wall Street Journal*, December 24, 2007, p. 4.

importance attached to group membership. This may have beneficial implications for business firms. Strong identification with the group is argued to create pressures for mutual self-help and collective action. If the worth of an individual is closely linked to the achievements of the group (e.g., firm), as Nakane maintains is the case in Japan, this creates a strong incentive for individual members of the group to work together for the common good. In Japan, a nation known for its strict work ethic, the Japanese language even has a word for dying from overwork—***karoshi***. Some argue that the success of Japanese enterprises in the global economy during the 1970s and 1980s was based partly on their ability to achieve close cooperation between individuals within a company and between companies. This found expression in the widespread diffusion of self-managing work teams within Japanese organizations, the close cooperation between different functions within Japanese companies (e.g., between manufacturing, marketing, and R&D), and the cooperation between a company and its suppliers on issues such as design, quality control, and inventory reduction.[15] In all these cases, cooperation is driven by the need to improve the performance of the group (i.e., the business firm).

The primacy of the value of group identification also discourages managers and workers from moving from company to company. Lifetime employment in a particular company was long the norm in certain sectors of the Japanese economy (estimates suggest that between 20 and 40 percent of all Japanese employees have formal or informal lifetime employment guarantees). Over the years, managers and workers build up knowledge, experience, and a network of interpersonal business contacts. All these things can help managers perform their jobs more effectively and achieve cooperation with others.

However, the primacy of the group is not always beneficial. Just as North American society is characterized by a great deal of dynamism and entrepreneurship, reflecting the primacy of values associated with individualism, some argue that Japanese society is characterized by a corresponding lack of dynamism and entrepreneurship. Although it is not clear how this will play out in the long run, Canada and the United States could continue to create more new industries than Japan and continue to be more successful at pioneering radically new products and new ways of doing business.

Social Stratification

All societies are stratified on a hierarchical basis into social categories—that is, into **social strata**. These strata are typically defined on the basis of characteristics such as family background, occupation, and income. Individuals are born into a particular stratum. They become a member of the social category to which their parents belong. Individuals born into a stratum toward the top of the social hierarchy tend to have better life chances than individuals born into a stratum toward the bottom of the hierarchy. They are likely to have better education, health, standard of living, and work opportunities. Although all societies are stratified to some degree, they differ in two related ways of interest to us here. First, they differ from each other with regard to the degree of mobility between social strata, and second, they differ with regard to the significance attached to social strata in business contexts.

SOCIAL MOBILITY

The term **social mobility** refers to the extent to which individuals can move out of the stratum into which they are born. Social mobility varies significantly among societies. The most rigid system of stratification is a caste system. A **caste system** is a closed system of stratification in which social position is determined by the family into which a person is born, and change in that position is usually not possible during an individual's lifetime. Often a caste position carries with it a specific occupation. Members of one caste might be shoemakers, members of another caste might be butchers, and so on. These occupations are embedded in the caste and passed down through the family to succeeding generations. Although the number of societies with caste systems has diminished rapidly during the twentieth century, one partial example still remains. India has four main castes and several thousand subcastes. Even though the caste system was officially abolished in 1949, two years after India became independent, it is still a powerful force in rural Indian society where occupation and marital opportunities are still partly related to caste.

A **class system** is a less rigid form of social stratification in which social mobility is possible. A class system is a form of open stratification in which the position a person has by birth can be changed through his or her own achievements and/or luck. Individuals born into a class at the bottom of the hierarchy can work their way up, while individuals born into a class at the top of the hierarchy can slip down.

DEBATE THE ISSUE

Is Social Class Determined by Income?

In the text, we said that a class system is a less rigid form of social stratification in which social mobility is possible. It is a form of open stratification in which the position a person has by birth can be changed through his or her own achievements or luck. Social class can broadly be divided into three levels, including upper (or rich), middle, and lower (or poor). These levels appear to be tied to income, but does a high income automatically bring power and prestige? Is it the income that should determine social class, or is it the social class that will determine the income? Or, is income just a small portion of social class status?

Source: D. Francis, "Where Do You Fall in the American Economic Class System?" *US News and World Report*, September 13, 2012.

While many societies have class systems, social mobility within a class system varies from society to society. For example, some sociologists have argued that Britain has a more rigid class structure than certain other Western societies, such as Canada and the United States.[16] Historically, British society was divided into three main classes: the upper class, which was made up of individuals whose families for generations had wealth, prestige, and occasionally power; the middle class, whose members were involved in professional, managerial, and clerical occupations; and the working class, whose members earned their living from manual occupations. The middle class was further subdivided into the upper-middle class, whose members were involved in important managerial occupations and the prestigious professions (e.g., lawyers, accountants, doctors), and the lower-middle class, whose members were involved in clerical work (e.g., bank tellers) and the less prestigious professions (e.g., schoolteachers). Although Canada is steeped in British tradition, to this day there are nonetheless fewer signs of class difference within this country, as Canada has evolved in a more egalitarian light under the shadow of its U.S. neighbour.

Historically, the British class system exhibited significant divergence between the life chances of members of different classes. The upper and upper-middle classes typically sent their children to a select group of private schools, where they would not mix with lower-class children, and where they picked up many of the speech accents and social norms that marked them as being from the higher strata of society. These same private schools also had close ties with the most prestigious universities, such as Oxford and Cambridge. Until recently, Oxford and Cambridge guaranteed to reserve a certain number of places for the graduates of these private schools. Having been to a prestigious university, the offspring of the upper and upper-middle classes then had an excellent chance of being offered a prestigious job in companies, banks, brokerage firms, and law firms run by members of the upper and upper-middle classes.

In contrast, the members of the British working and lower-middle classes typically went to state schools. The majority left at age 16, and those that went on to higher education found it more difficult to get accepted at the best universities. When they did, they found that their lower-class accent and lack of social skills marked them as being from a lower social stratum, which made it more difficult for them to get access to the most prestigious jobs.

As a result of these factors, the class system in Britain perpetuated itself from generation to generation, and mobility was limited. Although upward mobility was possible, it could not normally be achieved in one generation. While an individual from a working-class background may have established an income level that was consistent with membership in the upper-middle class, he or she may not have been accepted as such by others of that class due to accent and background. However, by sending his or her offspring to the "right kind of school," the individual could ensure that his or her children were accepted.

According to many commentators, modern British society is now rapidly leaving this class structure behind and moving toward a classless society. For example, the number of students in lower- to middle-class Islington (part of London, England) having applied and having been accepted into universities has grown substantially recently, indicating that the walls between classes have thinned considerably in modern-day England.

The class system in the United States is less extreme than in Britain and mobility is greater. Like Britain, the United States has its own upper, middle, and working classes. However, class membership is determined principally by individual economic achievements, as opposed to background and schooling. Thus, an individual can, by

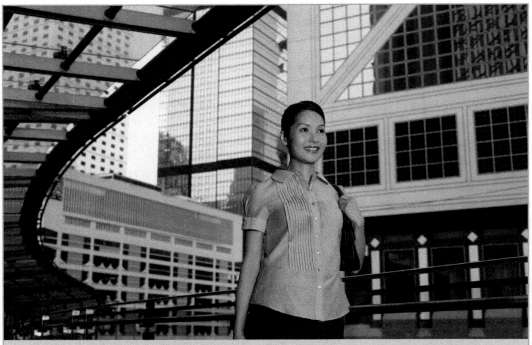

Until the 1970s, social mobility in China was very limited, but now sociologists believe a new class system is emerging in China based less on the rural–urban divide and more on urban occupation. © moodboard/SuperStock

his or her own economic achievement, move smoothly from the working class to the upper class in a lifetime. Successful individuals from humble origins are highly respected in American society.

SIGNIFICANCE

From a business perspective, the stratification of a society is significant if it affects the operation of business organizations. In American society, the high degree of social mobility and the extreme emphasis on individualism limits the impact of class background on business operations. The same is true in Japan, where most of the population perceives itself to be middle class. In a country such as Great Britain, however, the relative lack of class mobility and the differences between classes have resulted in the emergence of class consciousness. **Class consciousness** refers to people perceiving themselves in terms of their class background, which shapes their relationships with members of other classes.

This has been played out in British society in the traditional hostility between upper-middle-class managers and their working-class employees. Mutual antagonism and lack of respect historically made it difficult to achieve cooperation between management and labour in many British companies and resulted in a relatively high level of industrial disputes. However, as noted earlier, the last two decades have seen a dramatic reduction in industrial disputes (the level of industrial disputes in the United Kingdom is now lower than in the United States), which bolsters the arguments of those who claim that the country is moving toward a classless society.

An antagonistic relationship between management and labour, and the resulting lack of cooperation and high level of industrial disruption tends to raise the costs of production in countries characterized by significant class divisions. In turn, this can make it more difficult for companies based in such countries to establish a competitive advantage in the global economy.

Religious and Ethical Systems

Religion may be defined as a system of shared beliefs and rituals that are concerned with the realm of the sacred.[17] **Ethical systems** refer to a set of moral principles, or values, that are used to guide and shape behaviour. Most of the world's ethical systems are the product of religions. Thus, we can talk about Christian ethics and Islamic ethics. However, there is a major exception to the principle that ethical systems are grounded in religion. Confucianism and Confucian ethics influence behaviour and shape culture in parts of Asia, yet it is incorrect to characterize Confucianism as a religion.

The relationship among religion, ethics, and society is subtle and complex. There are thousands of religions in the world today, but in terms of number of adherents, four dominate—Christianity with about 2.5 billion, Islam with about 1.7 billion, Hinduism with about 1.1 billion, and Buddhism with about 500 million. (Map 3.1)

Table 3.1 shows the religious face of Canada. Although many other religions have an important influence in certain parts of the modern world (for example, Judaism) their numbers pale in comparison with these dominant religions (however, as the precursor of both Christianity and Islam, Judaism has an indirect influence that goes beyond its numbers). We review these four religions, along with Confucianism, focusing on their business implications. Some scholars have argued that the most important business implications of religion centre on the extent to which different religions shape attitudes toward work and entrepreneurship and the degree to which the religious ethics affect the costs of doing business in a country.

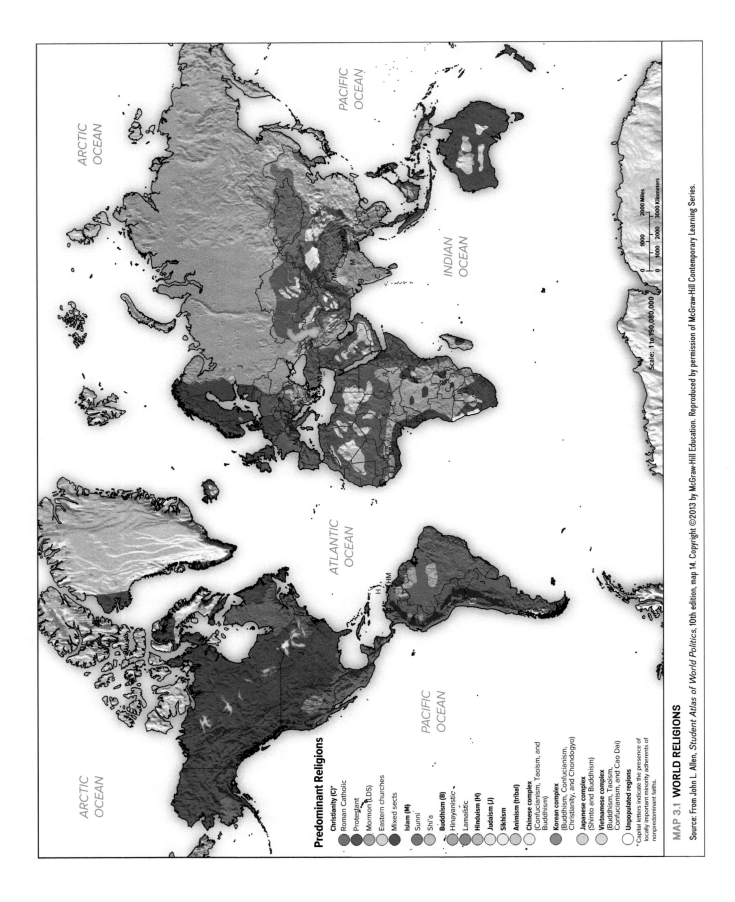

Predominant Religions

Christianity (C)*
- Roman Catholic
- Protestant
- Mormon (LDS)
- Eastern churches
- Mixed sects

Islam (M)
- Sunni
- Shi'a

Buddhism (B)
- Hinayanistic
- Lamaistic

Hinduism (H)

Judaism (J)

Sikhism

Animism (tribal)

Chinese complex
(Confucianism, Taoism, and Buddhism)

Korean complex
(Buddhism, Confucianism, Christianity, and Chondogyo)

Japanese complex
(Shinto and Buddhism)

Vietnamese complex
(Buddhism, Taoism, Confucianism, and Cao Dai)

Unpopulated regions

*Capital letters indicate the presence of locally important minority adherents of nonpredominant faiths.

Scale: 1 to 190,080,000

0   1000   2000 Miles
0 1000 2000 3000 Kilometers

MAP 3.1 WORLD RELIGIONS

Source: From John L. Allen, *Student Atlas of World Politics*, 10th edition, map 14. Copyright ©2013 by McGraw-Hill Education. Reproduced by permission of McGraw-Hill Contemporary Learning Series.

TABLE 3.1	Major Religions In Canada
Religion in Canada	**% of Population**
Christian	67.3%
Muslim	3.2
Hindu	1.5
Sikh	1.4
Buddhist	1.1
Jewish	1.0
No affiliation	23.9

Source: 2011 National Household Survey: Immigration, place of birth, citizenship, ethnic origin, visible minorities, language and religion, Statistics Canada, http://www.statcan.gc.ca/daily-quotidien/130508/dq130508b-eng.htm?HPA.

It is hazardous, and ultimately useless, to make sweeping generalizations about the nature of the relationship between religion and ethical systems on the one hand and business practice on the other. As we shall see, while some scholars argue that there is a relationship between religious and ethical systems and business practice, in a world where nations with Catholic, Protestant, Muslim, Hindu, and Buddhist majorities all show entrepreneurial activity and sustainable economic growth, it is important to view such proposed relationships with skepticism. While the proposed relationships may exist, their impact is probably small compared to the impact of economic policy.

Christianity

Christianity is widely practised around the world. About 20 percent of the world's population identify themselves as Christians. The vast majority of Christians live in Europe and the Americas, although their numbers are growing rapidly in Africa. Christianity grew out of Judaism. Like Judaism, it is a monotheistic religion (monotheism is the belief in one god). A religious division in the eleventh century led to the establishment of two major Christian organizations—the Roman Catholic church and the Orthodox church. Today the Roman Catholic church accounts for more than half of all Christians, most of whom are found in Southern Europe and Latin America. The Orthodox church, while less influential, is still of major importance in several countries (e.g., Greece and Russia). In the sixteenth century, the Reformation led to a further split with Rome; the result was Protestantism. The nonconformist nature of Protestantism has facilitated the emergence of numerous denominations under the Protestant umbrella (e.g., Baptist, Methodist, Calvinist).

ECONOMIC IMPLICATIONS OF CHRISTIANITY: THE PROTESTANT WORK ETHIC

Some sociologists have argued that of the main branches of Christianity—Roman Catholic, Orthodox, and Protestant—the latter has the most important economic implications. In 1904, German sociologist Max Weber made a connection, which has since become famous, between Protestant ethics and "the spirit of capitalism."[18] Weber noted that capitalism emerged in Western Europe. He also noted that in Western Europe,

> Business leaders and owners of capital, as well as the higher grades of skilled labour, and even more the higher technically and commercially trained personnel of modern enterprises, are overwhelmingly Protestant.[19]

According to Weber, there was a relationship between Protestantism and the emergence of modern capitalism. Weber argued that Protestant ethics emphasize the importance of hard work and wealth creation (for the glory of God), and frugality (abstinence from worldly pleasures). According to Weber, this value system was needed to facilitate the development of capitalism. Protestants worked hard and systematically to accumulate wealth. However, their ascetic beliefs suggested that rather than consuming this wealth by indulging in worldly pleasures, they should invest it in the expansion of capitalist enterprises. Thus, the combination of hard work and the accumulation of capital, which could be used to finance investment and expansion, paved the way for the development of capitalism in Western Europe and subsequently in the United States. In contrast, Weber argued that the Catholic promise of salvation in the next world, rather than this world, did not foster the same kind of work ethic.

Protestantism also may have encouraged capitalism's development in another way. By breaking away from the hierarchical domination of religious and social life that characterized the Catholic church for much of its history, Protestantism gave individuals significantly more freedom to develop their own relationship with God. The right to freedom of form of worship was central to the nonconformist nature of early Protestantism. This emphasis on individual religious freedom may have paved the way for the subsequent emphasis on individual economic and political freedoms and the development of individualism as an economic and political philosophy. As we saw in Chapter 2, such a philosophy forms the bedrock on which entrepreneurial free market capitalism is based. Building on this, some scholars claim there is a connection between individualism, as inspired by Protestantism, and the extent of entrepreneurial activity in a nation.[20] Again, one must be careful not to generalize too much from this historical sociological view. While nations with a strong Protestant tradition such as Britain, Germany, and the United States were early leaders in the industrial revolution, in the modern world there is clearly significant and sustained entrepreneurial activity and economic growth in nations with Catholic or Orthodox majorities.

Islam

With around 1.7 billion adherents, Islam is the second largest of the world's major religions. Islam dates back to AD 610, when the Prophet Muhammad began spreading the word, although the Muslim calendar begins in AD 622 when Muhammad, to escape growing opposition, left Mecca for the oasis settlement of Yathrib, later known as Madina. Adherents of Islam are referred to as Muslims. Muslims constitute a majority in more than 35 countries and inhabit a nearly contiguous stretch of land from the northwest coast of Africa, through the Middle East, to China and Malaysia in the Far East.

Islam has roots in both Judaism and Christianity (Islam views Jesus Christ as one of God's prophets). Like Christianity and Judaism, Islam is a monotheistic religion. The central principle of Islam is that there is but the one true omnipotent God. Islam requires unconditional acceptance of the uniqueness, power, and authority of God and the understanding that the objective of life is to fulfill the dictates of his will in the hope of admission to paradise. According to Islam, worldly gain and temporal power are an illusion. Those who pursue riches on Earth may gain them, but those who forgo worldly ambitions to seek the favour of Allah may gain the greater treasure—entry into paradise. Other major principles of Islam include: (1) honouring and respecting parents; (2) respecting the rights of others; (3) being generous but not a squanderer;

(4) avoiding killing except for justifiable causes; (5) not committing adultery; (6) dealing justly and equitably with others; (7) being of pure heart and mind; (8) safeguarding the possessions of orphans; and (9) being humble and unpretentious.[21] There are obvious parallels here with many of the central principles of both Judaism and Christianity.

Islam is an all-embracing way of life governing the totality of a Muslim's being.[22] As God's surrogate in this world, a Muslim is circumscribed by religious principles—by a code of conduct for interpersonal relations—in social and economic activities. Religion is paramount in all areas of life. The Muslim lives in a social structure that is shaped by Islamic values and norms of moral conduct. The ritual nature of everyday life in a Muslim country is striking to a Western visitor. Among other things, orthodox Muslim ritual requires prayer five times a day (it is not unusual for business meetings to be put on hold while the Muslim participants engage in their daily prayer ritual), requires that women should be dressed in a certain manner, and forbids the consumption of either pig meat or alcohol.

ISLAMIC FUNDAMENTALISM

The past two decades have witnessed the growth of a social movement often referred to as "Islamic fundamentalism."[23] In the West, Islamic fundamentalism is associated in the media with militants, terrorists, and violent upheavals, such as the September 11, 2001, attacks on the World Trade Center and Pentagon in the United States, the bloody conflict occurring in Algeria, or the killing of foreign tourists in Egypt. This characterization is very misleading. Just as "Christian fundamentalists" in the West are motivated by sincere and deeply held religious values firmly rooted in their faith, so are "Islamic fundamentalists." The violence that the Western media associates with Islamic fundamentalism is perpetrated by a very small minority of radical "fundamentalists" who have hijacked the religion to further their own political and violent ends (some Christian "fundamentalists" have done exactly the same, including Jim Jones and David Koresh). The vast majority of Muslims point out that Islam teaches peace, justice, and tolerance, not violence and intolerance, and that Islam explicitly repudiates the violence that a radical minority practices.

The rise of fundamentalism has no one cause. In part, it is a response to the social pressures created in traditional Islamic societies by the move toward modernization and by the influence of Western ideas, such as liberal democracy, materialism, equal rights for women, and by Western attitudes toward sex, marriage, and alcohol. In many Muslim countries, modernization has been accompanied by a growing gap between a rich urban minority and an impoverished urban and rural majority. For the impoverished majority, modernization has offered little in the way of tangible economic progress, while threatening the traditional value system. Thus, for a Muslim who cherishes his traditions and feels that his identity is jeopardized by the encroachment of alien Western values, Islamic fundamentalism has become a cultural anchor.

Fundamentalists demand a rigid commitment to traditional religious beliefs and rituals. The result has been a marked increase in the use of symbolic gestures that confirm Islamic values. In areas where fundamentalism is strong, women once again are wearing floor-length, long-sleeved dresses and covering their hair; religious studies have expanded in universities; the publication of religious tracts has increased; and more religious orations are heard in public.[24] Also, the sentiments of some fundamentalist groups are increasingly anti-Western. Rightly or wrongly, Western influence is blamed for a range of social ills, and many fundamentalists' actions are directed against Western governments, cultural symbols, businesses, and even individuals.

In several Muslim countries fundamentalists have gained political power and tried to make Islamic law (as set down in the Koran, the bible of Islam) the law of the land. There are good grounds for this in Islam. Islam makes no distinction between church and state. It is not just a religion; Islam is also the source of law, a guide to statecraft, and an arbiter of social behaviour. Muslims believe that every human endeavour is within the purview of the faith—and this includes political activity—because the only purpose of any activity is to do God's will.[25] (Muslims are not unique in this view; it is also shared by some Christian fundamentalists.) The fundamentalists have been most successful in Iran, where a fundamentalist party has held power since 1979, but they also have had an influence in many other countries, such as Algeria, Afghanistan (where the Taliban established an extreme fundamentalist state), Egypt, Pakistan, the Sudan, and Saudi Arabia.

ECONOMIC IMPLICATIONS OF ISLAM

Some explicit economic principles are set down in the Koran.[26] Many of the economic principles of Islam favour free enterprise. The Koran speaks approvingly of free enterprise and of earning legitimate profit through trade and commerce (the Prophet Muhammad was once a trader). The protection of the right to private property is also embedded within Islam, although Islam asserts that all property is a favour from Allah (God), who created and so owns everything. Those who hold property are regarded as trustees who are entitled to receive profits from it, rather than owners in the Western sense of the word, and they are admonished to use it in a righteous, socially beneficial, and prudent manner. This reflects Islam's concern with social justice. Islam is critical of those who earn profit through the exploitation of others. In the Islamic view of the world, humans are part of a collective in which the wealthy and successful have obligations to help the disadvantaged. Put simply, in Muslim countries, it is fine to earn a profit, so long as that profit is justly earned and not based on the exploitation of others for one's own advantage. It also helps if those making profits undertake charitable acts to help the poor. Furthermore, Islam stresses the importance of living up to contractual obligations, of keeping one's word, and of abstaining from deception.

Given the Islamic proclivity to favour market-based systems, Muslim countries are likely to be receptive to international businesses as long as those businesses behave in a manner that is consistent with Islamic ethics. Businesses that are perceived as making an unjust profit through the exploitation of others, by deception, or by breaking contractual obligations are unlikely to be welcomed in an Islamic country. In addition, in Islamic countries where fundamentalism is on the rise, hostility toward Western-owned businesses is likely to increase.

In the previous chapter, we noted that one economic principle of Islam prohibits the payment or receipt of interest, which is considered usury. This is not just a matter of theology; in several Islamic states, it is also a matter of law. In 1992, for example, Pakistan's Federal Shariat Court, the highest Islamic law-making body in the country, pronounced interest to be un-Islamic and therefore illegal and demanded that the government amend all financial laws accordingly. In 1999, Pakistan's Supreme Court ruled that Islamic banking methods should be used in the country after July 1, 2001.[27]

Islamic Capitalism in Turkey

For years now, Turkey has been lobbying the European Union to allow it to join the free trade bloc as a member-state. If the EU says yes, it will be the first Muslim state in the union. Many critics in the EU worry that Islam and Western-style capitalism do not mix well, and that as a consequence, allowing Turkey into the EU would be a mistake. However, a close look at what is going on in Turkey suggests this view may be misplaced. Consider the area around the city of Kayseri in central Turkey. Many dismiss this poor, largely agricultural region of Turkey as a non-European backwater, far removed from the secular bustle of Istanbul. It is a region where traditional Islamic values hold sway. And yet, it is also a region that has produced so many thriving Muslim enterprises that it is sometimes called the "Anatolian Tiger." Businesses based here include large food manufacturers, textile companies, furniture manufacturers, and engineering enterprises, many of which export a substantial percentage of their production.

Local business leaders attribute the success of companies in the region to an entrepreneurial spirit that they say is part of Islam. They point out that the Prophet Muhammad, who was himself a trader, preached merchant honour and commanded that 90 percent of a Muslim's life be devoted to work in order to put food on the table. Outsider observers have gone further, arguing that what is occurring around Kayseri is an example of Islamic Calvinism, a fusion of traditional Islamic values and the work ethic often associated with Protestantism in general and Calvinism in particular.

Within Kayseri, the influence of Islam is plain to see. Many companies set aside rooms and time for 15-minute prayer breaks. Most of the older businessmen have been to Mecca on the pilgrimage that all Muslims are meant to make at least once in a lifetime. Few of the cafés and restaurants in Kayseri serve alcohol, and most women wear a head scarf.

At the Kayseri sugar factory, one of the most profitable in the region, a senior manager says Islam has played a large part in improving the profitability of the enterprise. For a long time the factory bought most of its sugar beet from a single monopoly supplier, who charged a high price. But because Islam preaches equal opportunity in business, managers at the sugar factory decided the Islamic thing to do was diversify the supply base and encourage small producers to sell beets to them. Today, the factory buys sugar beets from 20 000 small growers. Competition among them has lowered prices and boosted the factory's profitability. The same manager also noted, "If you are not a good Muslim, don't pray five times a day, and don't have a wife who wears a head scarf, it can be difficult to do business here."

However, not everyone agrees that Islam is the driving force behind the region's success. Saffet Arslan, the managing director of Ipek, the largest furniture producer in the region (which exports to more than 30 countries), says another force is at work—globalization! According to Arslan, over the past three decades local Muslims who once eschewed making money in favour of focusing on religion are now making business a priority. They see the Western world, and Western capitalism, as a model, not Islam, and because of globalization and the opportunities associated with it, they want to become successful. At the same time, Arslan is a practising Muslim who has built a mosque in the basement of Ipek's headquarters building so that people can pray while at work.

If there is a weakness in the Islamic model of business that is emerging in places such as Kayseri, some say it can be found in traditional attitudes toward the role of women in the workplace, and the low level of female employment in the region. According to a report by the European Stability Initiative, the same group that holds up the Kayseri region as an example of Islamic Calvinism, the low participation of women in the local workforce is the Achilles' heel of the economy and may stymie the attempts of the region to catch up with the countries of the European Union.

Questions

1. List any other ways that you can think of where religion promotes or hinders modern capitalism.
2. Can adherence to any religion, on a country-wide basis, coexist with modern business practices? Give examples.

Sources: D. Bilefsky, "Turks Knock on Europe's Door with Evidence That Islam and Capitalism Can Coexist," *The New York Times*, August 27, 2006, p. 4; and "European Stability Initiative," Islamic Calvinists, September 19, 2005; archived at www.esiweb.org.

Hinduism

Hinduism has approximately 1.1 billion adherents, most of whom are on the Indian subcontinent. Hinduism began in the Indus Valley in India more than 4000 years ago, making it the world's oldest major religion. Unlike Christianity and Islam, its founding is not linked to a particular person. Nor does it have an officially sanctioned sacred book such as the Bible or the Koran. Hindus believe that a moral force in society requires the acceptance of certain responsibilities, called *dharma*. Hindus believe in reincarnation, or rebirth into a different body after death. Hindus also believe in *karma*, the spiritual progression of each person's soul. A person's karma is affected by the way he or she lives. The moral state of an individual's karma determines the challenges he or she will face in their next life. By perfecting the soul in each new life, Hindus believe that an individual can eventually achieve *nirvana*, a state of complete spiritual perfection that renders reincarnation no longer necessary. Many Hindus believe that the way to achieve nirvana is to lead a severe ascetic lifestyle of material and physical self-denial, devoting life to a spiritual rather than material quest.

ECONOMIC IMPLICATIONS OF HINDUISM

Max Weber, who is famous for expounding on the Protestant work ethic, also argued that the ascetic principles embedded in Hinduism do not encourage the kind of entrepreneurial activity in pursuit of wealth creation that we find in Protestantism.[28] According to Weber, traditional Hindu values emphasize that individuals should be judged not by their material achievements, but by their spiritual achievements. Hindus perceive the pursuit of material well-being as making the attainment of nirvana more difficult. Given the emphasis on an ascetic lifestyle, Weber thought that devout Hindus would be less likely to engage in entrepreneurial activity than devout Protestants.

Mahatma Gandhi, the famous Indian nationalist and spiritual leader, was certainly the embodiment of Hindu asceticism. It has been argued that the values of Hindu asceticism and self-reliance that Gandhi advocated had a negative impact on the economic development of post-independence India.[29] But one must be careful not to read too much into Weber's arguments. Modern India is a very entrepreneurial society, and millions of hardworking entrepreneurs form the economic backbone of India's rapidly growing economy.

Historically, Hinduism also supported India's caste system. The concept of mobility between castes within an individual's lifetime makes no sense to traditional Hindus. Hindus see mobility between castes as something that is achieved through spiritual progression and reincarnation. An individual can be reborn into a higher caste in his next life if he achieves spiritual development in this life. Insofar as the caste system limits individuals' opportunities to adopt positions of responsibility and influence in society, the economic consequences of this religious belief are somewhat negative. For example, within a business organization, the most able individuals may find their route to the organization's higher levels blocked simply because they come from a lower caste. By the same token, individuals may get promoted to higher positions within a firm as much because of their caste background as because of their ability. But the caste system has been abolished in India, and its influence is now fading.

Buddhism

Buddhism was founded in India in the sixth century BC by Siddhartha Gautama, an Indian prince who renounced his wealth to pursue an ascetic lifestyle and spiritual perfection. Siddhartha achieved nirvana but decided to remain on Earth to teach his followers how they too could achieve this state of spiritual enlightenment. Siddhartha became known as the Buddha (which means "the awakened one"). Today Buddhism has 350 million followers, most of whom are found in Central and Southeast Asia, China, Korea, and Japan. According to Buddhism, suffering originates in people's desires for pleasure. Cessation of suffering can be achieved by following a path for transformation. Siddhartha offered the Noble Eightfold Path as a route for transformation. This emphasizes right seeing, thinking, speech, action, living, effort, mindfulness, and meditation. Unlike Hinduism, Buddhism does not support the caste system. Nor does Buddhism advocate the kind of extreme ascetic behaviour that is encouraged by Hinduism. Nevertheless, like Hindus, Buddhists stress the afterlife and spiritual achievement rather than involvement in this world.

ECONOMIC IMPLICATIONS OF BUDDHISM

The emphasis on wealth creation that is embedded in Protestantism is not found in Buddhism. Thus, in Buddhist societies, we do not see the same kind of historical cultural stress on entrepreneurial behaviour that Weber claimed could be found in the Protestant West. But unlike Hinduism, the lack of support for the caste system and extreme ascetic behaviour suggests that a Buddhist society may represent a more fertile ground for entrepreneurial activity than a Hindu culture.

Confucianism

Confucianism was founded in the fifth century BC by K'ung-Fu-tzu, more generally known as Confucius. For more than 2000 years, until the 1949 Communist revolution, Confucianism was the official ethical system of China. Confucianism has almost 400 million followers of the teachings of Confucius, principally in China, Korea, and Japan. Confucianism teaches the importance of attaining personal salvation through right action. Although not a religion, Confucian ideology has become deeply embedded in the culture of these countries over the centuries and through that affects the lives of many millions more. Confucianism is built around a comprehensive ethical code that sets down guidelines for relationships with others. The need for high moral and ethical conduct and loyalty to others are central to Confucianism. Unlike religions, Confucianism is not concerned with the supernatural and has little to say about the concept of a supreme being or an afterlife.

ECONOMIC IMPLICATIONS OF CONFUCIANISM

Some scholars maintain that Confucianism may have economic implications as profound as those Weber argued were to be found in Protestantism, although they are of a different nature.[30] Their basic thesis is that the influence of Confucian ethics on the cultures of China, Japan, South Korea, and Taiwan, by lowering the costs of doing business in those countries, may help explain their economic success. In this regard, three values central to the Confucian system of ethics are of particular interest— loyalty, reciprocal obligations, and honesty.

In Confucian thought, loyalty to one's superiors is regarded as a sacred duty, an absolute obligation. In modern organizations based in Confucian cultures, the loyalty that binds employees to the heads of their organization can reduce the conflict between management and labour that we find in more class-conscious societies. Cooperation between management and labour can be achieved at a lower cost in a culture where the value systems emphasize loyalty.

However, in a Confucian culture, loyalty to one's superiors, such as a worker's loyalty to management, is not blind loyalty. The concept of reciprocal obligations also comes into play. Confucian ethics stress that superiors are obliged to reward the loyalty of their subordinates by bestowing blessings on them. If these "blessings" are not forthcoming, then neither will be the loyalty. In China this Confucian ethic is central to the concept of *guanxi,* which refers to relationship networks supported by reciprocal obligations. Similarly, in Japan this ethic finds expression in the concept of lifetime employment. The employees of a Japanese company are loyal to the leaders of the organization, and in return the leaders bestow on them the "blessing" of lifetime employment. The lack of mobility between companies implied by the lifetime employment system suggests that managers and workers build up knowledge, experience, and a network of interpersonal business contacts over the years. All these can help managers and workers perform their jobs more effectively and cooperate with others in the organization. One result is improved economic performance for the company.

A third concept found in Confucian ethics is the importance attached to honesty. Confucian thinkers emphasize that, although dishonest behaviour may yield short-term benefits for the transgressor, dishonesty does not pay in the long run. The importance attached to honesty has major economic implications. When companies can trust each other not to break contractual obligations, the costs of doing business are lowered. Expensive lawyers are not needed to resolve contract disputes. In a Confucian society, there may be less hesitation to commit substantial resources to cooperative ventures than in a society where honesty is less pervasive. When companies adhere to Confucian ethics, they can trust each other not to violate the terms of cooperative agreements. Thus, the costs of achieving cooperation between companies may be lowered in societies such as Japan relative to societies where trust is less pervasive.

For example, it has been argued that the close ties between the automobile companies and their component parts suppliers in Japan are facilitated by a combination of trust and reciprocal obligations. These close ties allow the auto companies and their suppliers to work together on a range of issues, including inventory reduction, quality control, and design. The competitive advantage of Japanese auto companies such as Toyota may in part be explained by such factors.[31] Similarly, the combination of trust and reciprocal obligations is central to the workings and persistence of *guanxi* networks in China. Someone seeking and receiving help through a *guanxi* network is then obligated to return the favour and faces social sanctions if that obligation is not reciprocated when it is called upon. If the person does not return the favour, his reputation will be tarnished and he will be unable to draw on the resources of the network in the future. It is claimed that these relationship-based networks can be more important in helping to enforce agreements between businesses than the Chinese legal system. Some claim that *guanxi* networks are a substitute for the legal system.[32]

Language

One obvious way in which countries differ is language. By language, we mean both spoken and unspoken means of communication. Language is a defining characteristic of a culture.

Spoken Language

Language does far more than just enable people to communicate with each other. The nature of a language also structures the way we perceive the world. The language of a society can direct the attention of its members to certain features of the world rather than others. The classic illustration of this phenomenon is that whereas the English language has but one word for snow, the language of the Inuit (Eskimos) lacks a general term for it. Instead, because distinguishing different forms of snow is so important in the lives of the Inuit, they have 24 words that describe different types of snow (e.g., powder snow, falling snow, wet snow, drifting snow).[33]

Because language shapes the way people perceive the world, it also helps define culture. In countries with more than one language, one also often finds more than one culture. Canada has an English-speaking culture and a French-speaking culture. The early phases of official bilingualism in Canada were often met with suspicion. Nowadays, Canadian bilingualism is not only acceptable, but also a useful resource. French is a valuable asset to Canadians' international trade and often synchronous diplomatic interests. In the world of diplomacy, French resonates strongly from the Caribbean to Africa and across Europe. While Canadians can make their voices heard at Commonwealth conferences, so too can they be heard at Francophone meetings around the world. Often on the tails of diplomacy, business deals can follow. Belgium is divided into Flemish and French speakers, and tensions between the two groups exist; in Spain, a Basque-speaking minority with its own distinctive culture has been agitating for independence from the Spanish-speaking majority for decades; on the Mediterranean island of Cyprus, the culturally diverse Greek- and Turkish-speaking populations of the island engaged in open conflict in the 1970s, and the island is now partitioned into two parts. While it does not necessarily follow that language differences create differences in culture and, therefore, separatist pressures (e.g., witness the harmony in Switzerland, where four languages are spoken), there seems to be a tendency in this direction.[34]

Chinese, particularly Mandarin, is the "mother tongue" of the largest number of people, followed by Spanish and English (see Another Perspective "Can You Speak the Most Important Languages?"). However, the most widely spoken language in the world is English, followed by Spanish, Russian, and Arabic[35] (i.e., many people speak English as a second language). English is increasingly becoming the language of international business. When a Japanese and a German business person get together to do business, it is almost certain that they will communicate in English. However, while English is widely used, learning the local language yields considerable advantages in business. Most people prefer to converse in their own language, so speaking the local language can build rapport, which may be very important for a business deal. International businesses that do not understand the local language can make major blunders through improper translation. For example, the Sunbeam Corporation used the English words for its "Mist-Stick," a mist-producing hair-curling iron, when it entered the German market, only to discover after an expensive advertising campaign that *mist* means excrement in German. General Motors was troubled by the lack of enthusiasm among Puerto Rican dealers for its new Chevrolet Nova. When literally translated into Spanish, *Nova* means star. However, when spoken it sounded like "no va," which in Spanish means "it doesn't go." General Motors changed the name of the car to Caribe.[36]

Unspoken Language

Unspoken language refers to nonverbal communication. We all communicate with each other by a host of nonverbal cues. The raising of eyebrows, for example, is a sign of recognition in most cultures, while a smile is a sign of joy. Many nonverbal cues, however, are culturally bound. A failure to understand the nonverbal cues of another culture can lead to a failure of communication. For example, making a circle with the

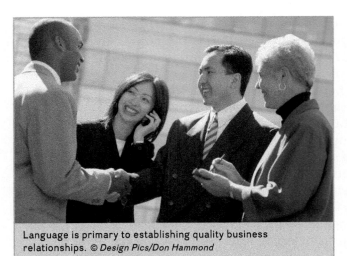

Language is primary to establishing quality business relationships. © *Design Pics/Don Hammond*

thumb and the forefinger is a friendly gesture in Canada, but it is a vulgar sexual invitation in Greece and Turkey. Similarly, while most Canadians and Europeans use the thumbs-up gesture to indicate that "it's all right," in Greece the gesture is obscene.

Another aspect of nonverbal communication is personal space, which is the comfortable amount of distance between people. In Canada, the customary distance apart adopted by parties in a business discussion is 1.5 to 2.5 metres (5 to 8 feet). In Latin America, it is 1 to 1.5 metres (3 to 5 feet). Consequently, many North Americans unconsciously feel that Latin Americans are invading their personal space and can be seen backing away from them during a conversation. In turn, the Latin American may interpret such backing away as aloofness. The result can be a regrettable lack of rapport between two business people from different cultures.

ANOTHER PERSPECTIVE

Can You Speak the Most Important Languages?

Mastering your own native language is critically important to doing business in your own home country. Mastering the language of a foreign country (or subcultures) with which you want to do business is also an added value in any cross-cultural relationship. English leads the way in terms of business languages, but which languages are important after English? Spanish? No, not necessarily. The three languages that are important for business after English are Mandarin Chinese, French, and Arabic. Spanish is fifth, so it is clearly important, but not as useful as English, Mandarin, French, and Arabic because of the number of people who speak these languages. Did you know that you can now learn a new language online? Check out the Language Resources on globalEDGE (globalEDGE.msu.edu/global-resources/language-resources), and learn a new language (including Mandarin, French, Arabic, and Spanish).

Source: S. Kim, "Top 3 Useful Foreign Languages for Business Excludes Spanish," *ABC News*, September 2, 2011, http://abcnews.go.com/blogs/business/2011/09/top-3-useful-foreign-languages-for-business-excludes-spanish, accessed March 8, 2014.

Education

From an international business perspective, one important aspect of education is its role as a determinant of national competitive advantage.[37] The availability of skilled and educated workers seems to be a major determinant of the likely economic success of a country. In analyzing the competitive success of Japan since 1945, for example, Michael Porter notes that after the war, Japan had almost nothing except for a pool of skilled and educated human resources.

> With a long tradition of respect for education that borders on reverence, Japan possessed a large pool of literate, educated, and increasingly skilled human resources … Japan has benefited from a large pool of trained engineers. Japanese universities graduate many more engineers per capita than in the United States … A first-rate primary and secondary education system in Japan operates based on high standards and emphasizes math and

science. Primary and secondary education is highly competitive … Japanese education provides most students all over Japan with a sound education for later education and training. A Japanese high school graduate knows as much about math as most American college graduates.[38]

Porter's point is that Japan's excellent education system was an important factor explaining the country's postwar economic success.

The recent trend to outsource information technology jobs to India, for example, is partly due to the presence of significant numbers of trained engineers in India, which in turn is a result of the Indian education system. It would make little sense to base production facilities that require highly skilled labour in a country where the education system was so poor that a skilled labour pool was not available, no matter how attractive the country might seem on other dimensions. It might make sense to base production operations that require only unskilled labour in such a country.

The general education level of a country is also a good index of the kind of products that might sell in a country and of the type of promotional material that should be used. As a direct example, a country where more than 70 percent of the population is illiterate is unlikely to be a good market for popular books. But perhaps more importantly, promotional material containing written descriptions of mass-marketed products is unlikely to have an effect in a country where almost three-quarters of the population cannot read. It is far better to use pictorial promotions in such circumstances.

LO4 Culture and the Workplace

How a society's culture affects the values found in the workplace is of considerable importance to an international business with operations in different countries. Management process and practices may need to vary according to culturally determined work-related values. For example, if the cultures of the United States and France result in different work-related values, an international business with operations in both countries should vary its management process and practices to account for these differences.

Probably the most famous study of how culture relates to values in the workplace was undertaken by Geert Hofstede.[39] As part of his job as a psychologist working for IBM, Hofstede collected data from 1967 to 1973 on employee attitudes and values for more than 100 000 individuals. This data enabled him to compare dimensions of culture across 40 countries. Hofstede isolated five dimensions that he claimed summarized different cultures—power distance, individualism versus collectivism, uncertainty avoidance, masculinity versus femininity, and long-term versus short-term orientation.

Hofstede's **power distance** dimension focused on how a society deals with the fact that people are unequal in physical and intellectual capabilities. According to Hofstede, high power distance cultures were found in countries that let inequalities grow over time into inequalities of power and wealth. Low power distance cultures were found in societies that tried to play down such inequalities as much as possible.

The **individualism versus collectivism** dimension focused on the relationship between the individual and his or her fellows. In individualistic societies, the ties between individuals were loose and individual achievement and freedom were highly valued. In societies where collectivism was emphasized, the ties between individuals were tight. In such societies, people were born into collectives, such as extended families, and everyone was supposed to look after the interest of his or her collective.

Hofstede's **uncertainty avoidance** dimension measured the extent to which different cultures socialized their members into accepting ambiguous situations and tolerating uncertainty. Members of high uncertainty avoidance cultures placed a premium on job security, career patterns, retirement benefits, and so on. They also had a strong need for rules and regulations; the manager was expected to issue clear instructions, and subordinates' initiatives were tightly controlled. Lower uncertainty avoidance cultures were characterized by a greater readiness to take risks and less emotional resistance to change.

Hofstede's **masculinity versus femininity** dimension looked at the relationship between gender and work roles. In masculine cultures, sex roles were sharply differentiated and traditional "masculine values," such as achievement and the effective exercise of power, determined cultural ideals. In feminine cultures, sex roles were less sharply distinguished, and little differentiation was made between men and women in the same job.

The fifth dimension, **long-term versus short-term orientation,** was found in a later study among students in 23 countries around the world, using a questionnaire designed by Chinese scholars. It deals with virtue regardless of truth. Values associated with long-term orientation are thrift and perseverance; values associated with short-term orientation are respect for tradition, fulfilling social obligations, and protecting one's "face."

Hofstede created an index score for each of four dimensions that ranged from 0 to 100 and scored high for high individualism, high power distance, high uncertainty avoidance, and high masculinity. He averaged the score for all employees from a given country. Table 3.2 summarizes this data for 20 countries. Western nations such

TABLE 3.2	Work-Related Values for 20 Selected Countries			
	Power Distance	Uncertainty Avoidance	Individualism	Masculinity
Argentina	49	86	46	56
Australia	36	51	90	61
Brazil	69	76	38	49
Canada	39	48	80	52
Denmark	18	23	74	16
France	68	86	71	43
Germany (F.R.)	35	65	67	66
Great Britain	35	35	89	66
Indonesia	78	48	14	46
India	77	40	48	56
Israel	13	81	54	47
Japan	54	92	46	95
Mexico	81	82	30	69
Netherlands	38	53	80	14
Panama	95	86	11	44
Spain	57	86	51	42
Sweden	31	29	71	5
Thailand	64	64	20	34
Turkey	66	85	37	45
United States	40	46	91	62

Source: From Geert Hofstede, "The Cultural Relativity of Organizational Practices and Theories," *Journal of International Business Studies,* 14, Fall 1983, pp. 75–89. Reprinted with permission.

as Canada, the United States, and Great Britain score high on the individualism scale and low on the power distance scale. At the other extreme are a group of Latin American and Asian countries that emphasize collectivism over individualism and score high on the power distance scale. Table 3.2 also reveals that Japan's culture has strong uncertainty avoidance and high masculinity. This characterization fits the standard stereotype of Japan as a country that is male dominant and where uncertainty avoidance exhibits itself in the institution of lifetime employment. Sweden and Denmark stand out as countries that have both low uncertainty avoidance and low masculinity (high emphasis on "feminine" values).

Hofstede's results are interesting for what they tell us in a very general way about differences between cultures. Many of Hofstede's findings are consistent with standard Western stereotypes about cultural differences. For example, many people believe Americans are more individualistic and egalitarian (they have a lower power distance) than the Japanese, who in turn are more individualistic and egalitarian than Mexicans. Similarly, many might agree that Latin countries such as Mexico place a higher emphasis on masculine value—they are machismo cultures—than the Nordic countries of Denmark and Sweden.

However, one should be careful about reading too much into Hofstede's research. It has been criticized on a number of points.[40] First, Hofstede assumes there is a one-to-one correspondence between culture and the nation-state, but as we saw earlier, many countries have more than one culture. Hofstede's results do not capture this distinction. Second, the research may have been culturally bound. The research team was composed of Europeans and Americans. The questions they asked of IBM employees and their analysis of the answers may have been shaped by their own cultural biases and concerns. So it is not surprising that Hofstede's results confirm Western stereotypes, since it was Westerners who undertook the research!

Third, Hofstede's informants worked not only within a single industry, the computer industry, but also within one company, IBM. At the time, IBM was renowned for its own strong corporate culture and employee selection procedures, making it possible that the employees' values were different in important respects from the values of the cultures from which those employees came. Also, certain social classes (such as unskilled manual workers) were excluded from Hofstede's sample. A final caution is that Hofstede's work is now beginning to look dated. Cultures do not stand still; they evolve, albeit slowly. What was a reasonable characterization in the 1960s and 1970s may not be so today.

Still, just as it should not be accepted without question, Hofstede's work should not be dismissed entirely either. It represents a starting point for managers trying to figure out how cultures differ and what that might mean for management practices. Also, several other scholars have found strong evidence that differences in culture affect values and practices in the workplace, and Hofstede's basic results have been replicated using more diverse samples of individuals in different settings.[41] Still, managers should use the results with caution, for they are not necessarily accurate.

Hofstede subsequently expanded his original research to include a fifth dimension that he argued captured additional cultural differences not brought out in his earlier work.[42] He referred to this dimension as "Confucian dynamism" (sometimes called *long-term orientation*). According to Hofstede, **Confucian dynamism** captures attitudes toward time, persistence, ordering by status, protection of face, respect for tradition, and reciprocation of gifts and favours, which some say could be attributed to Hofstede's fifth dimension. The label refers to these "values" being derived from

Confucian teachings. As might be expected, East Asian countries such as Japan, Hong Kong, and Thailand scored high on Confucian dynamism, while nations like Canada and the United States scored low. Hofstede and his associates went on to argue that their evidence suggested that nations with higher economic growth rates scored high on Confucian dynamism and low on individualism—the implication being Confucianism is good for growth. However, subsequent studies have shown that this finding does not hold up under more sophisticated statistical analysis.[43] During the past decade, countries with high individualism and low Confucian dynamics such as the United States have attained high growth rates, while some Confucian cultures such as Japan have had stagnant economic growth. In reality, while culture might influence the economic success of a nation, it is just one of many factors, and while its importance should not be ignored, it should not be overstated either. The factors discussed in Chapter 2—economic, political, and legal systems—are probably more important than culture in explaining economic growth rates over time.

ANOTHER PERSPECTIVE

How Strong is Your National Identity?

As we have found out in this chapter, a lot of measures exist to assess cultural values and norms. Self-assessment is one of the best ways to better know yourself, and we encourage you to take a rigorous cultural personality test such as what Hofstede has developed. How strong is your personal national identity? On a scale from 1 to 7, with 1 being "strongly disagree" and 7 being "strongly agree" (and with scores of 2, 3, 4, 5, and 6 being in between those two extremes), rate yourself on these four questions:

1. My country has a strong historical heritage (national heritage).
2. People from my country are proud of their nationality (cultural homogeneity).
3. A true native of my country would never reject their religious beliefs (belief system).
4. It is always best to purchase products made from my home country (consumer ethnocentrism).

   If you scored above 23 in total for the four questions, you have a strong "national identity"; if you scored below 9 you have a weak "national identity." Most people fall in between these two extremes.

Sources: B. Keillor and T. Hult, "A Five-Country Study of National Identity: Implications for International Marketing Research and Practice," *International Marketing Review*, 1999, pp. 65–82; B. Keillor, T. Hult, R. Erffmeyer, and E. Babakus, "NATID: The Development and Application of a National Identity Measure for Use in International Marketing," *Journal of International Marketing*, 4 (1996).

LO5 | Cultural Change

Culture is not a constant; it evolves over time. Changes in value systems can be slow and painful for a society. In the 1960s, for example, American values toward the role of women, love, sex, and marriage changed significantly. Much of the social turmoil of that time reflected these changes.

Change, however, does occur and can often be quite profound. For example, at the beginning of the 1960s, the idea that women might hold senior management positions in major corporations was not widely accepted. Many scoffed at the idea. Today, it is a reality. For example, in 2012 Virginia Rometty became the CEO of IBM and in 2014 Mary T. Barra became the CEO of General Motors. No one in the mainstream of North American society now questions the development or the capability of women in the business world. North American culture has changed (although it is still more difficult for women to gain senior management positions than men).

Similarly, the value systems of many ex-Communist states, such as Russia, are undergoing significant changes as those countries move away from values that emphasize collectivism and toward those that emphasize individualism. While social turmoil is an inevitable outcome of such a shift, the shift will still probably occur.

Others have also broken through the Chinese cultural barrier. For example, Mark Rowswell comes from the Toronto area, but is well known in China under his stage name of "Dashan." He first went to China in 1988, and has built his reputation there as a comedic performer who bases his routines on some of the subtleties of Chinese culture and the Chinese way of life. You can find out more about him at http://www.dashan.com.

Some claim that a major cultural shift is occurring in Japan, with a move toward greater individualism.[44] The model Japanese office worker, or "salaryman," is pictured as being loyal to his boss and the organization to the point of giving up evenings, weekends, and vacations to serve the organization, which is the collective of which he is a member. However, a new generation of office workers does not seem to fit this model. An individual from the new generation is more direct than the traditional Japanese. He acts more like a Westerner, a *gaijian*. He does not live for the company and will move on if he is offered a better job. He is not keen on overtime, especially if he has a date. He has his own plans for his free time, and they may not include drinking or playing golf with the boss.[45]

Several studies have suggested that economic advancement and globalization may be important factors in societal change.[46] For example, evidence shows that economic progress is accompanied by a shift in values away from collectivism and toward individualism.[47] Thus, as Japan has become richer, the cultural emphasis on collectivism has declined and greater individualism is being witnessed. One reason for this shift may be that richer societies exhibit less need for social and material support structures built on collectives, whether the collective is the extended family or the paternalistic company. People are better able to take care of their own needs. As a result, the importance attached to collectivism declines, while greater economic freedoms lead to an increase in opportunities for expressing individualism.

The culture of societies may also change as they become richer because economic progress affects a number of other factors, which in turn influence culture. For example, increased urbanization and improvements in the quality and availability of education are both a function of economic progress, and both can lead to declining emphasis on the traditional values associated with poor rural societies.

As for globalization, some have argued that advances in transportation and communication technologies, the dramatic increase in trade that we have witnessed since World War II, and the rise of global corporations such as Hitachi, Disney, Microsoft, and Levi Strauss, whose products and operations can be found around the globe, are creating the conditions for the merging of cultures.[48] With McDonald's hamburgers in China, Levis in India, Apple products in South Africa, and MTV everywhere helping to foster a ubiquitous youth culture, some argue that the conditions for less cultural variation have been created. But culture is not a one-way street, with the large necessarily dominating the small. For example, major Canadian retailers like Tim Hortons, Lululemon, and Roots have expanded into the United States and other countries.

At the same time, one must not ignore important countertrends, such as the shift toward Islamic fundamentalism in several countries, the separatist movement in Quebec, or the continuing ethnic strains and separatist movements in Russia. In many ways such countertrends are a reaction to the pressures for cultural convergence. In an increasingly modern and materialistic world, some societies are trying to reemphasize

MANAGEMENT FOCUS

Working in China

Trevor Buss juggled his university studies in Toronto with a full-time career that frequently takes him to China. During his many trips to China, he has learned how to be successful while adhering to age-old customs and traditions. Demonstrating some knowledge of the local customs allows for enhanced business contacts, as local business people appreciate the extra effort made to be sensitive to their culture.

When travelling in China, Trevor makes certain that if he is going to a business lunch or dinner in a rural area he has left the remainder of his day open. There are many customs and rituals, particularly in rural areas, where much socializing is expected. Trevor offers some good advice on doing business in China. The hierarchy of seniority, even in small companies, is paramount. Never make anyone lose face. Have a proper title on your business card and ensure that you present yourself in a professional manner.

As he is frequently invited for dinner, customs as basic as seating arrangements can have a bearing on the outcome of business negotiations. For example, the guest of honour is always seated on the right facing toward the door. The host will try to establish the order of command, and seating may change based simply on the title on your business card or how the guest perceives your position in the company.

As for smoking, Trevor has noticed that cigarettes are offered throughout meetings, even for non-smokers. He has found that by the end of some meetings he has 20 or 30 cigarettes lined up in front of his plate. Expectancies are that men smoke, while it is frowned on for women to smoke.

Unlike in Canada, toasting (and drinking) in China is more customary. If not willing to imbibe, it is best to tell the host that one's inability to drink is due to medical reasons.

Foreigners are normally expected to drink two shots of bai jiu, a Chinese rice wine (between 35 and 65 percent alcohol), with each guest. Two drinks are the norm. The drinks go up in counts of two, not one, so if toasting be certain to have two drinks per toast. Through rotating toasts, it is possible to acquaint oneself with everybody at the reception.

As a sign of respect when toasting or drinking, make sure the lip of your glass remains lower than the glass of the person toasting. Trevor has found this quite funny to watch, since the host will often try to get their glass lower than yours. He has even found himself tipping his glass on an angle to try and get the lip of the glass lower. When drinking across the table from somebody it is also customary to tap the table with the glass. *Gan bei* means "bottoms up" and if this is met with silence, then the glass must be emptied. It is customary to demonstrate this by tipping the emptied glass towards the centre of the table to show everyone that it is empty.

When eating, meals are served to the centre of the table. The guest is expected to try most dishes first, though a guest may be excused from this if the host knows that the guest is not too familiar with Chinese customs.

China's impressive economic growth has also brought about rapid changes in (but not limited to) business and social customs. Western business people are well advised to work through a highly qualified and thoroughly fluent translator, well versed with changing business customs.

In summary, here are a few guidelines:

- Travel with some basic knowledge of the host's business. Learn some basic Mandarin, but be prepared for some potential embarrassments. For example, the word used for "colleague" in China is also the slang word for mistress or lover used by Malaysian Mandarin-speaking people.
- Go with an open mind and do not expect business to be done quickly. You need to build a relationship before any business transaction will occur.
- To avoid potential embarrassment, get a good translator/business partner who can help with translation, local customs, and colloquial terms.

MANAGEMENT FOCUS *Continued*

Questions

1. Can a cultural misstep be so important that it could dramatically affect a business deal?
2. Give examples that you have witnessed or hear about when local customs are not fully understood by foreign businesses.
3. Are there cultural differences between Canada and the United States affecting businesses? Give some business examples.

Source: Interview with Trevor Buss, former Ryerson University student, Toronto.

their cultural roots and uniqueness. Cultural change is not therefore unidirectional, with national cultures converging toward some homogenous global entity. Also, while some elements of culture change quite rapidly—particularly the use of material symbols—other elements change only slowly if at all. Thus, just because people the world over wear blue jeans and eat at McDonald's, one should not assume they have also adopted North American values—for more often than not, they have not.

IMPLICATIONS FOR BUSINESS

International business is different from national business because countries and societies are different. In this chapter, we have seen just how different societies can be. Societies differ because their cultures vary. Their cultures vary because of profound differences in social structure, religion, language, education, economic philosophy, and political philosophy. Three important implications for international business flow from these differences. The first is the need to develop cross-cultural literacy. There is a need not only to appreciate that cultural differences exist, but also to appreciate what such differences mean for international business. A second implication looks at the connection between culture and ethics in decision making. A third implication for international business centres on the connection between culture and national competitive advantage. Making the matter even more complex is that new "types" of customers are grouping in ways that do not mirror national borders. For example, some firms may target the "Asian" customer, rather than the Chinese customer or the Korean customer. Still other firms might target "North American seniors," seeing it as one type of demographic, rather than one with Canadian, American, and Mexican distinctions.

ANOTHER PERSPECTIVE

A Hierarchy of Concepts?

Perhaps culture is a deeper-level concept, one upon which the values of the economic, political, and legal systems rest. For example, Canada adopts legislation whose goal is to maintain fairness and a level playing field. These values are consistent with a culture that has a low power distance and values the individual. The high levels of competition in the Canadian economy, both among companies and among individuals, can be seen to support the high levels of individualism that are central to Canadian culture. Contrast the focus on the individual in Canada with the Chinese value of *guanxi*. The Canadian notion of fairness, the level playing field, can be seen as the basis for prohibiting insider trading in Canada. Yet for the Chinese, *guanxi* suggests that the holder of privileged information relevant to the market would have an obligation to share this information with friends. Such an obligation supports networked, close relationships and obligation to the group.

CROSS-CULTURAL LITERACY

One of the biggest dangers confronting a company that goes abroad for the first time is the danger of being ill-informed. International businesses that are ill-informed about the practices of another culture are likely to fail. Doing business in different cultures requires adaptation to conform to the value systems and norms of that culture. Adaptation can embrace all aspects of an international firm's operations in a foreign country. The way deals are negotiated, the appropriate incentive pay systems for salespeople, the structure of the organization, the name of a product, the tenor of relations between management and labour, the manner in which the product is promoted, and so on, are all sensitive to cultural differences. What works in one culture might not work in another.

Benefits

To combat the danger of being ill-informed, international businesses should consider employing local citizens. They must also ensure that home-country executives are cosmopolitan enough to understand how differences in culture affect the practice of international business. Transferring executives overseas at regular intervals to expose them to different cultures will help build a cadre of cosmopolitan executives. An international business must also be constantly on guard against the dangers of **ethnocentric behaviour.** Ethnocentrism is a belief in the superiority of one's own ethnic group or culture. Hand in hand with ethnocentrism goes a disregard or contempt for the culture of other countries. Unfortunately, ethnocentrism is prevalent; many Americans are guilty of it, as are many Canadians, Japanese people, British people, and so on. Ugly as it is, ethnocentrism is a fact of life, one that international businesses must be on continual guard against.

CULTURE AND COMPETITIVE ADVANTAGE

One theme that repeatedly surfaced in this chapter is the relationship between culture and national competitive advantage. Put simply, the value systems and norms of a country influence the costs of doing business. The costs of doing business in a country influence the ability of firms to establish a competitive advantage in the global marketplace. We have seen how attitudes toward cooperation between management and labour, toward work, and toward the payment of interest are influenced by social structure and religion. It can be argued that the class-based conflict between workers and management in class-conscious societies, when it leads to industrial disruption, raises the costs of doing business in that society. Similarly, we have seen how some sociologists have argued that the ascetic "other-worldly" ethics of Hinduism may not be as supportive of capitalism as the ethics embedded in Protestantism and Confucianism. Also, Islamic laws banning interest payments may raise the costs of doing business by constraining a country's banking system.

Japan presents an interesting example of how culture can influence competitive advantage. Some scholars have argued that the culture of modern Japan lowers the costs of doing business relative to the costs in most Western nations. Japan's emphasis on group affiliation, loyalty, reciprocal obligations, honesty, and education all boost the competitiveness of Japanese companies. The emphasis on group affiliation and loyalty encourages individuals to identify strongly with the companies in which they work. This fosters an ethic of hard work and cooperation between management and labour "for the good of the company." Similarly, reciprocal obligations and honesty help build an atmosphere of trust between companies and their suppliers. This encourages them to enter into long-term relationships with each other to work on inventory reduction, quality control, and joint design—all of which have been shown to improve an organization's competitiveness. This level of cooperation has often been lacking in the West, where the relationship between a company and its suppliers tends to be a short-term one structured around competitive bidding, rather than one based on long-term mutual commitments. In addition, the availability of a pool of highly skilled labour, particularly engineers, has helped Japanese enterprises develop cost-reducing process innovations that have boosted their productivity.[49] Thus, cultural factors may help explain the competitive advantage enjoyed by many Japanese businesses in the global marketplace. The rise of Japan as an economic power during the second half of the twentieth century may be attributed in part to the economic consequences of its culture.

It has also been argued that the Japanese culture is less supportive of entrepreneurial activity than, say, American society. In many ways, entrepreneurial activity is a product of an individualistic mindset, not a classic characteristic of the Japanese. This may explain why American enterprises, rather than Japanese corporations, dominate industries where entrepreneurship and innovation are highly valued, such as computer software and biotechnology. Of course, there are obvious and significant exceptions to this generalization. Masayoshi Son recognized the potential of software far faster than any of Japan's corporate giants, set up his company, Softbank, in 1981, and has since built it into Japan's top software distributor. Similarly, dynamic entrepreneurial individuals established major Japanese companies such as Sony and Matsushita. But these examples may be the exceptions that prove the rule, for there has been no surge in entrepreneurial high-technology enterprises in Japan equivalent to what has occurred in Canada and the United States.

For the international business, the connection between culture and competitive advantage is important for two reasons. First, the connection suggests which countries are likely to produce the most viable competitors. For example, one might argue that Canadian enterprises are likely to see continued growth in aggressive, cost-efficient competitors from those Pacific Rim nations where a combination of free market economics, Confucian ideology, group-oriented social structures, and advanced education systems can all be found (e.g., South Korea, Taiwan, Japan, and increasingly China).

Second, the connection between culture and competitive advantage has important implications for the choice of countries in which to locate production facilities and do business. Consider a hypothetical case where a company has to choose between two countries, A and B, for locating a production facility. Both countries are characterized by low labour costs and good access to world markets. Both countries are of roughly the same size (in terms of population) and both are at a similar stage of economic development. In country A, the education system is undeveloped, the society is characterized by a marked stratification between the upper and lower classes, and there are six major linguistic groups. In country B, the education system is well developed, there is a lack of social stratification, group identification is valued by the culture, and there is only one linguistic group. Which country makes the best investment site?

Country B probably does. In country A, conflict between management and labour, and between different language groups, can be expected to lead to social and industrial disruption, thereby raising the costs of doing business.[50] The lack of a good education system can also be expected to hinder successful business.

The same kind of comparison could be made for an international business trying to decide where to push its products, country A or B. Again, country B would be the logical choice because cultural factors suggest that in the long run, country B is the nation most likely to achieve the greatest level of economic growth.

Connections between countries also occur because of flows of capital and similarities of business. For example, there are many close ties between Canada and Latin America in the mining sector. Canada has a long history in resource extraction, and is bringing this experience to copper, gold, and silver mines in Latin America. For their part, Latin American resource companies are finding that Canada is a source of financing, through their listing of company stock on the Toronto Stock Exchange.

But as important as culture is, it is probably far less important than economic, political, and legal systems in explaining differential economic growth between nations. Cultural differences are significant, but their importance in the economic sphere should not be overemphasized. For example, earlier we noted that Max Weber argued that the ascetic principles embedded in Hinduism do not encourage entrepreneurial activity. While this is an interesting academic thesis, recent years have seen an increase in entrepreneurial activity in India, particularly in information technology, where India is rapidly becoming an important global player. The ascetic principles of Hinduism and caste-based social stratification have apparently not held back entrepreneurial activity in this sector!

CULTURE AND BUSINESS ETHICS

Many ethical principles are universally held across cultures. For example, basic moral principles such as "don't kill" or "don't steal" apply everywhere, despite differences in local culture. Similarly, in all cultures it is regarded as unethical to unilaterally and without reason break a business agreement. As Adam Smith pointed out more than 200 years ago, if people cannot trust each other to honour agreements, business activity will not take place, and economic growth will not occur. A certain level of faith that agreements will be honoured—that parties to a transaction will do the ethical thing—is required to encourage economic activity no matter what the culture. In the West, the legal system, particularly the system of contract law, evolved to help assure people that agreements will be honoured, but the legal system is designed to deal only with the exceptions to the general principle (which is embedded in our culture) that one should honour agreements. In nations that lack a similar legal tradition, other institutions have emerged to help assure people that business agreements will be honoured.

As we pointed out earlier, *guanxi* networks may fulfill that role in China. Individuals who break agreements will have their reputation tarnished and will be unable to draw on the *guanxi* network in the future. Whether we are talking about China or the West, however, the basic principle remains the

ANOTHER PERSPECTIVE

Online View of a New Culture

Visit the online versions of some English-language daily newspapers in major foreign cities to get a sense of their cultures and their markets. Look at the ads and business names. Check out the classifieds. A good first link is the *Daily Nation* (Nairobi, Kenya) at http://www.nation.co.ke

same—it is unethical to break business agreements without good reason, and those that do will face sanctions (either legal or cultural).

Although many ethical principles are universal, some are culturally bound.[51] Earlier in the chapter we saw that Japanese have a word for dying from overwork—*karoshi*, which also implies loyalty. Traditionally, it was perceived to be ethical for Japanese workers to die of overwork for the company and unethical for them to have more than one job in one's lifetime. In Canada, it is not unusual for an individual to have many jobs within one's lifetime.

When faced with conflicting ethical principles, international businesses may be confronted with difficult dilemmas. For example, *guanxi* networks are often supported by the idea of reciprocal gift giving. But if a Western company gives a "gift" to a government official, as an attempt to build a relationship that may be useful in the future, that company may subsequently be accused of bribery and supporting corruption. What then is the ethical thing to do?

One response to such a dilemma is to argue that because customs vary from country to country, businesses should adopt the customs (and by extension, ethical practices) of the country in which they are currently doing business. This is the *relativist* or "when in Rome" approach to business ethics. It is also a dangerously flawed approach.[52] It would suggest, for example, that if slavery is practised in a country, it is okay to practise slavery when doing business in that nation. Obviously, this is not the case. Similarly, as several Western businesses have discovered, just because local sweatshops in parts of Asia employ child labour and pay them below subsistence wages, it does not follow that one should adopt the same practices. Ethical values are not like a coat that one puts on in certain seasons and certain places and takes off elsewhere. You cannot leave your ethics behind as you venture around the globe. This suggests that one answer to the question "Whose ethics do you use in international business?" is "Your ethics."[53]

But what should "your ethics" be? The answer is somewhat clearer than it used to be. Organizations such as the United Nations have pushed hard to get countries to ratify agreements that have clear ethical implications. An important example is the Universal Declaration of Human Rights, which has been ratified by almost every country and lays down basic principles that should always be adhered to irrespective of the culture in which one is doing business. For example, Article 23 of this declaration states that:

1. Everyone has the right to work, to free choice of employment, to just and favourable conditions of work, and to protection against unemployment.

2. Everyone, without any discrimination, has the right to equal pay for equal work.

3. Everyone who works has the right to just and favourable remuneration ensuring for himself and his family an existence worthy of human dignity and supplemented, if necessary, by other means of social protection.

4. Everyone has the right to form and to join trade unions for the protection of his interests.

Clearly, the rights to "just and favourable work conditions," "equal pay for equal work," and remuneration that ensures an "existence worthy of human dignity" embodied in Article 23 imply that it is unethical to employ child labour in sweatshop settings and pay less than subsistence wages, even if that happens to be common in some countries. But does that mean one should not employ children or buy from suppliers who employ children, even if that is common in a certain country? Here the ethical thing to do becomes less clear. If the choice for the child is between living on the streets and begging for food or working in an apparel factory for subsistence wages, what should a firm do? Should it continue to sanction the employment of child labour as a lesser evil? Again probably not, but neither should the firm simply wash its hands of the situation. If a firm already has a relationship with a supplier that is employing child labour and that fact is suddenly uncovered, walking away from that relationship because of moral outrage may do more harm than good to the children whose interests the firm wishes to protect. In such circumstances, the ethical thing to do may be to find a way to improve life for the children.

For example, when Levi Strauss found that one of its suppliers employed child labour, it did not terminate the relationship. Instead, it looked into the situation. It discovered that many of the women who worked in the factory brought their children to work with them because there was no local school and because the pittance that the children earned kept the family's income above subsistence level. So Levi Strauss built a school for the children under 14, and it paid the parents the additional money that their children would otherwise have earned. This was a small price for Levi Strauss to pay, but it made a big difference in the lives of the affected children.

Grey areas will always exist that require managers to use their own moral judgment to solve ethical dilemmas, but those judgments should be made with regard to a high ethical code. Consider again the example of giving gifts to support relationships. What is the ethical thing to do? Should one respond to the cultural expectation that a gift should be given, and do so to try to build a relationship that might pay dividends in the future? In nations such as China, where reciprocal gift giving is common and helps to cement *guanxi* relationships, this is a reasonable approach, although it may conflict with Western notions of fair play.[54] For example, consider a situation where two Western companies are competing to win a supply contract from a Chinese firm. Imagine that the firm that wins the contract is not the lowest bidder but is the firm that employed the son of the CEO of the Chinese firm as a consultant to advise it on the negotiations. The losing company might believe that principles of fair play have been violated here, but this is not necessarily so. Rather, the winning firm has simply recognized that relationships matter in China and employed an individual with connections to help it win the contract. By employing the son of the CEO, the firm that won the bid helped someone in the CEO's *guanxiwang,* which increased the probability that this "gift" or gesture would be reciprocated.

The practice becomes obviously problematic, however, when government officials are the recipients of the gifts, either directly or indirectly, for then the gifts can be construed as bribery. There is a dividing line between corruption and legitimate gift giving to support business transactions. It is a line that a manager with a strong moral compass should be able to recognize.

Reflecting on such dilemmas, the ethicist Thomas Donaldson has argued that when thinking through ethical problems in international business, firms should be guided by three principles.[55]

1. Respect for core human values (human rights), which determine the absolute moral threshold for all business activities.

2. Respect for local tradition.

3. The belief that context matters when deciding what is right and what is wrong.

Donaldson's point is that respect of core human values must be the starting point for all ethical decisions. Once those are assured, businesses must also respect local cultural differences, which he defines as traditions and context. Thus, Donaldson argues that "gift giving" is not unethical, even though some Western businesses might feel that it is wrong. Gift giving does not violate core human values and is important in the context of some cultures such as China and Japan. By the same token, Donaldson would condemn as unethical decisions that clearly violate core human values. Employing child labour at less than subsistence wages would fall into that category.

Key Terms

caste system	masculinity versus femininity
class consciousness	mores
class system	norms
Confucian dynamism	power distance
ethical systems	religion
ethnocentric behaviour	social mobility
folkways	social strata
group	society
individualism versus collectivism	uncertainty avoidance
karoshi	values
long-term vs. short-term orientation	

LO   Learning Objectives Summary

We have looked at the nature of social culture and studied some implications for business practice. The following points have been made:

1. Culture is a complex whole that includes knowledge, beliefs, art, morals, law, customs, and other capabilities acquired by people as members of society. Values and norms are the central components of a culture. Values are abstract ideals about what a society believes to be good, right, and desirable. Norms are social rules and guidelines that prescribe appropriate behaviour in particular situations. They are influenced by political and economic philosophy, social structure, religion, language, and education.

2. The social structure of a society refers to its basic social organization. Two main dimensions along which social structures differ are the individual–group dimension and the stratification dimension. In some societies, the individual is the basic building block of social organization. These societies emphasize individual achievements above all else. In other societies, the group is the basic building block of social organization. These societies emphasize group membership and group achievements above all else. All societies are stratified into different classes. Class-conscious societies are characterized by low social mobility and a high degree of stratification. Less class-conscious societies are characterized by high social mobility and a low degree of stratification. Religion may be defined as a system of shared beliefs and rituals that is concerned with the realm of the sacred. Ethical systems refer to a set of moral principles, or values, that are used to guide and shape behaviour. Language is one defining characteristic of a culture. It has both a spoken and an unspoken dimension. In countries with more than one spoken language, we tend to find more than one culture. Formal education is the medium through which individuals learn skills and are socialized into the values and norms of a society. Education plays an important role in the determination of national competitive advantage.

3. Individual and group associations have different implications for business. Class consciousness also affects business to different degrees. In Canada and the United States, where social mobility is high, the impact of class background is limited. The value systems of different religious and ethical systems also have different implications for business practice, such as the Protestant work ethic and Islam's proclivity to favour a market-based system.

4. Geert Hofstede studied how culture relates to values in the workplace. Hofstede isolated four dimensions that he claimed summarized different cultures: power distance, uncertainty avoidance, individualism versus collectivism, and masculinity versus femininity.

5. Culture is not a constant; it evolves over time. Economic progress and globalization seem to be two important engines of cultural change. One danger confronting a company that goes abroad for the first time is to be ill-informed. To develop cross-cultural literacy, international businesses need to employ host-country nationals, build a cadre of cosmopolitan executives, and guard against the dangers of ethnocentric behaviour. The value systems and norms of a country can affect the costs of doing business in that country. Although many ethical principles are universal, some are culturally bounded. What is not ethical in one country might be common in another. Despite this, the "when in Rome" approach to business ethics is dangerous. International businesses need to adhere to a consistent set of ethics derived from a high moral code.

Critical Thinking and Discussion Questions

1. Outline why the culture of a country might influence the costs of doing business in that country. Illustrate your answer with examples.

2. Do you think that business practices in an Islamic country are likely to differ from business practices in Canada, and if so, how?

3. What are the implications for an international business of differences in the dominant religions and/or ethical systems of countries in which it is based?

4. Choose two countries that appear to be culturally diverse. Compare the cultures of those countries and then indicate how cultural differences influence (a) the costs of doing business in each country; (b) the likely future economic development of that country; (c) business practices; and (d) business ethics.

5. "It is unreasonable to expect Western businesses active in developing nations to adhere to the same ethical standards that they use at home." Evaluate this statement.

6. A Western firm is trying to get a licence from the government of a developing nation to set up a factory in that country. The firm knows the factory will bring many benefits to the country. It will provide jobs in an area where unemployment is high and it will produce exports for the country, allowing that nation to earn valuable foreign exchange. So far, the government official with whom the firm is negotiating has been noncommittal, neither rejecting nor approving the request, but simply asking for more and more information. The firm has been told that relationships are important in this country, and that if it hired the daughter of the government official as a consultant, she could use her influence to get the licence application approved, to everyone's betterment. What should the firm do?

Research Task globalEDGE™ globaledge.msu.edu

Use the globalEDGE™ site to complete the following exercises:

1. You are preparing for a business trip to Venezuela where you will need to interact extensively with local professionals. Therefore, you consider collecting information regarding local culture and business habits before your departure through various government travel advisory Web sites. Prepare a short description of the most striking cultural characteristics that may affect business interactions in this country.

2. Asian cultures exhibit significant differences in business etiquette when compared to Western cultures. For example, in Thailand it is considered offensive to show the sole of the shoe or foot to another. Find several additional tips regarding the business etiquette of a specific Asian country of your choice.

CLOSING CASE

WORLD EXPO 2020 IN DUBAI, UAE

The United Arab Emirates (UAE) was established in 1971 and is a country located in the Middle East. The country is often called "the Emirates" or simply "UAE." UAE borders the Gulf of Oman and the Persian Gulf. Neighbouring countries include Oman and Saudi Arabia, and UAE also shares sea borders with Quatar, Iran, and Pakistan. Strategically, UAE is in an important location along the southern approaches to the Strait of Hormuz, a transit point for the world's crude oil. UAE is also in the top 10 countries for the largest oil reserves in the world.

The geography of UAE includes lots of rolling sand dunes of desert and also mountains in the eastern part of the country. The government consists of a federation with specified powers delegated to the UAE federal government and other powers reserved to the member emirates (equivalent to principalities). The chief of state is the president and the head of government is the prime minister. UAE has an open-market economy in which the prices of products and services are set using a free price system.

The foundation for this market economy lies in the collaboration between the seven emirates that are part of the UAE. They include the emirates of Abu Dhabi, Ajman, Dubai, Fujairah, Ras al-Khaimah, Sharjah, and Umm al-Quwain. Each emirate is governed by a hereditary emir, similar to succession planning in countries with royalty (king or queen) as the head of state. These emirs jointly make up the Federal Supreme Council, which serves as the highest legislative and executive body in the UAE. One of the seven emirs is selected as the president of the United Arab Emirates. The capital of the country is Abu Dhabi, Islam is the official religion, and Arabic is the official language. Most people have heard of Abu Dhabi and Dubai because they are the country's centres of commercial and cultural activities. Dubai is UAE's most populous city, with more than 2 million people, and it has emerged as a true global city with an eclectic cultural makeup. It also has a strategic location as a business gateway for the Middle East and Africa for multinational enterprises from all of the world's continents.

Dubai has frequently been rated as one of the best places to live in the Middle East (although it is also one of the most expensive). The emirate of Dubai has been ruled by the Al Maktoum family since 1833; the emirate is considered a constitutional monarchy. In 2013, the Norway-based Global Network for Rights and Development ranked UAE as the 14th country in its annual International Human Rights Indicator report. This was a first among Arab countries, with the next Arab country on the list, Tunisia, at a distant 72nd place. Only about 10 percent of the population in Dubai are Arabs, with the remaining 90 percent being expatriates. Most of the expatriates are from Asia, with India (50 percent) and Pakistan (16 percent) prominently featured. The largest group of Westerners is from the United Kingdom.

With this eclectic cultural background, Dubai's bid to host the World Expo 2020 with a theme of "connecting minds, creating the future" makes sense both logically and strategically. The theme resonates well with issues related to culture. In essence, the theme illustrates and acknowledges differences in culture (as does this chapter), and the theme supports the notion that we strive to emphasize similarities across the globe.

The idea is that today, multinational enterprises have to evaluate their core uniqueness and how they can leverage this strategic uniqueness in the global marketplace. The leveraging of the uniqueness typically requires a focus on similarities across cultures instead of differences. Connecting minds is a great way to illustrate how people, companies, and countries can stress the importance of looking for similarities first and then focus on the similarities that outweigh the differences in creating strategic options.

As with any World Expo, the expectation is that the world will be treated to an important event in the year 2020 in Dubai. The Expo on "connecting minds, creating the future" will span six months, following World Expo 2015 in Milan, Italy, and World Expo 2017 in Astana, Kazakhstan. The expectation is also that countries will showcase who they are and what they can do in the spirit of today's era of "nation branding." Tracing history, the best known first World Expo was held in the Crystal Palace in Hyde Park, London (United Kingdom) in 1851 under the title of "Great Exhibition of the Works of Industry of All Nations." Since 1928, the Bureau International des Expositions (International Exhibitions Bureau) has served as an international sanctioning body for the World Expo. These Expo showcases have generally gone through three eras: the era of industrialization (1851–1938), the era of cultural exchange (1939–1987), and the era of nation branding (1988–present).

The theme for Dubai's World Expo 2020 is a direct connection to its cultural values and beliefs in facilitating connections and pioneering new ideas. The organizers expect 70 percent of the 25 million visitors to originate outside UAE, making it the most globally oriented World Expo in its long history. The idea is that the global community will come together and explore creative and pioneering solutions to three key drivers of global development: sustainability, mobility, and opportunity. As viewed by the World Expo 2020 organizing team, sustainability centers on lasting sources of energy and water. Mobility focuses on smart systems of logistics and transportation. And opportunity refers to new paths to economic development.

Sources: Expo 2020, expo2020dubai.ae/en, accessed March 5, 2014; globalEDGE—United Arab Emirates: Introduction, http://globaledge.msu.edu/countries/united-arab-emirates, accessed March 5, 2014; A. Ahmed, "After Winning Expo, Emirate Fumes at Allies It Says Didn't Back It," *The New York Times*, January 6, 2014; S. Potter, "Expo 2020 Win to Boost Dubai Sukuk on Spending: Islamic Finance," *Bloomberg Businessweek*, November 27, 2013; and "Dubai—It's Bouncing Back," *The Economist*, November 23, 2013.

Case Discussion Questions

1. What forces shaped the culture in the country of UAE and Dubai in particular? How similar or different are these forces from those that shaped the culture of Western nations?

2. What kinds of misunderstanding, if any, are likely to arise between Western-based visitors and people from the UAE during World Expo 2020?

3. If you were in a position to advise a Western company that was considering doing business in UAE for the first time, what would your advice be?

4. Using Dubai as an example, do you believe that cultural similarities among people can outweigh cultural differences that exist in terms of doing business together in the future?

© Image Source/Getty Images

Chapter 4

Ethics in International Business

THE MOST CORRUPT INDUSTRY SECTORS?

You can talk about bribery and corruption based on the inability of local and regional governments to source revenue through taxation—leading to government officials accepting bribes for "processing" services—but over and above that, consider what might be some of the main business sectors that have a significant number of ethical problems based on the way those sectors are structured and how enterprises fundamentally operate.

In a widely circulated 2014 study, the Organization for Economic Co-operation and Development (OECD) investigated hundreds of bribery and corruption situations globally. Many interesting trends and outcomes were revealed by the OECD study and one particular revelation was that approximately two-thirds of all cases involved four business sectors. The sectors identified by the OECD as being most corrupt, were

- Extraction (mining, oil & gas, logging, etc.)
- Construction (building)
- Transportation (highways, bridges, railroads, airports, etc.)
- IT (Information and Telecommunications)

All four of these sectors are areas of business within which Canada has companies that are competitive, innovative, and profitable.

Extraction Many mining projects in Latin America, Africa, Asia, and of course Canada, are operated, or joint ventured by Canadian mining companies. According to National Resources Canada (the federal government ministry dealing with mining, oil, and gas) "Canadian companies account for the dominant share, by far, of the value of all mineral exploration programs planned worldwide by the larger companies." Some of the large projects, such as the Alberta oil sands, are well known worldwide. Other Canadian mining operation locations are not so well known—for example, as reported by globaljournalist.org, "Canada is the largest stakeholder in Africa's mining sector. As of 2011, 155 Canadian companies were operating in 39 countries in Africa."

Construction SNC Lavalin Group based in Montreal, over 100 years old, is the largest construction company in Canada and with a revenue over $9 billion. It is bigger than the second-, third-, and fourth-largest Canadian companies.

Transportation Canada's auto assemblers Ford, G.M., and Chrysler may be subsidiaries of American conglomerates, but the products they produce are exported to many destinations and competitively priced along with the Japanese-Canadian operations of Toyota in Cambridge, Honda in Alliston, and Suzuki in Ingersoll. The auto assemblers' productivity in terms of volume and competitive technology is further enhanced by the fact that world famous Magna auto parts, founded in Canada, produces parts and components in great variety and quantity which fuels the auto industry in Canada. In addition to cars and trucks we also have well-known Bombardier, which has global operations producing planes, trains, and recreational products such as snow machines, ATVs, and personal watercraft.

IT In Canada, IT was dominated by Blackberry in the early years of the new millennium. But we have had telecomm "rockstars" before such as Northern Telecomm, which produced much of the physical and digital infrastructure of the Internet in the 1980s and 1990s from a global network of facilities and factories in many countries. In the later years of the second decade of the new millennium there are a number of emerging IT products and services companies that are showing their competitiveness on a global scale; these include Shopify (which showed a growth rate of 26 000 percent in 2014), Hootsuite (for managing social media), PointClickCare (cloud-based software for Long-Term Care), and PBS (PoweredBySearch.com), one of Canada's fastest growing companies that does SEO search engine optimization and inbound marketing.

Why the extraction industry is vulnerable to corruption Extraction is the most commonly known form of mining. Drilling for oil and gas, and cutting down trees involve huge amounts of real estate as well as transportation routes to get the products to areas where it can be used in various manufacturing processes. Since a number of mining projects involve large companies from first-world nations operating in remote regions of developing nations, there are many situations involving payments to get permission from several levels of government to access the land containing the resources.

Corruption also happens when the people employed in the extraction operation need to buy certain things and there may be a limited supply due to the remoteness of the location.

The processing of extraction resources can also lead to corruption, such as stealing of uncut diamonds, gold in the form of ingots, etc. The stages at which resources are extracted are also vulnerable to corruption when various "players" try to intercept the steps to take out quantities before the price increases at the next stage or before taxes get applied by a particular level of government. An amusing example for Canadians would be the $30 million maple syrup heist in Quebec in the summer of 2012. As widely reported in several national media outlets, police were eventually able to make arrests in December 2012 after investigations in to how the expensive liquid was, literally, siphoned off over the course of a year with allegations that people working in the warehouse colluded with some of those arrested. During the 2016 trial in which some of the accused were found guilty, it was revealed that the perpetrators had re-branded the syrup and made it appear as if it was from New Brunswick—the allegation being that once the syrup is moved into new barrels, there is no way to ascertain the original location of the source, a challenge which is similarly faced by people moving diamonds and gold ingots.

Why the construction industry is vulnerable to corruption

Large-scale construction projects can take place any place on the planet, but the ones that seem to be most vulnerable to corruption are those involving buildings and roadways in highly-congested urban areas where space is restricted and the cost of carrying out the project is usually challenged by a government agency that wants to spend as little as possible of the public's taxpayer dollars—at the same time making sure that the result is safe for using by hundreds of thousands of citizens.

The corruption "opportunities" in construction begin with how the government selects the particular large company (or for giant projects, a consortium of companies) to build the particular project. When you have elected officials and their designates making decisions about large projects involving millions and millions of dollars, it is irresistible for the competing construction companies to offer kickbacks or bribes to the decision makers in order to win the bid. Additionally, after a particular company has won a bid to construct a huge project, they have to make sure that the money they pour in to erecting the building ends up being less than what they bid for, otherwise it will be unprofitable. The profitability challenge can be met two ways: (1) If there is a cost overrun, the company can try political maneuvering to get the government to authorize additional money for the increase in costs. Sometimes this can be blamed on weather challenges or an unexpected increase in costs of materials that comes from a far distance where currency exchange rates fluctuated. (2) The company can cut costs by using cheaper materials (which may affect safety), or they simply use less quantity of particular materials—such as reducing the amount of steel rebars in the concrete walls and floors, a situation which was one of the reasons the clothing factory collapsed in Bangladesh 2013 killing more than a 1000 garment workers and injuring 2500+.

In the summer of 2015 the Bangladesh authorities pressed charges against 40+ people, including the owner of the factory and a number of government officials. Joe Fresh, which is a well-known clothing brand owned by Loblaw Companies, faced criticism from various groups for having used the Rana Plaza factory for producing low-priced garments that were sold in Canada. Accusations against the owners of the building include the accusation that the building had additional stories added, even though it was not structurally strong enough to support the additional weight. CBC's investigative journalism program *Fifth Estate* won an International Emmy for its documentary about the factory collapse and the subsequent exposé about the plight of the garment workers in Bangladesh. Notwithstanding the media scrutiny for its garment production operations, several Canadian media reports noted that, a year after the factory collapse, Loblaw had significantly increased its outsourcing to Bangladesh.

Why the transportation industry is vulnerable to corruption

The transportation industry is very diverse and covers shipbuilding, railroads, cars and trucks, and the places and facilities within which they are manufactured and operated. Shipbuilding used to be down in many regions around the world, including the Maritimes in Canada, but as the decades passed, Japan replaced Europe as a location of production, followed later by Korea, then China. With the advent of advanced technologies and competitive fuel prices, long-distance trucking has had an impact on the freight train business. However, Canada still has a competitive enterprise, Bombardier, which fights to retain its' customer base in the passenger train business, particular subway cars and light rail transit.

Most subway car contracts involve a large municipal government, usually with the involvement of a regional or national government since the costs of the project are usually beyond what the urban area can afford with its limited tax revenues. In the bidding process and selection of railcar companies, municipal politicians deal with immense pressure from lobbyists acting on behalf of the large railcar manufacturers and there are a number of situations in which bribery takes place as well as bid rigging.

As reported in several American newspapers in September 2016, the Chicago Transit Authority (CTA) awarded a $1.3 billion deal (for building subway cars) to a company owned by the Chinese government, despite the allegations that a bid by Canada's Bombardier scored higher in satisfying the required criteria. Bombardier, which had previously sold subway cars to the CTA, accused that the bidding process was "rigged." Bombardier publicly stated their belief that the Chinese firm won the contract because Chicago was desperate for foreign investment. Completing this deal with a Chinese company would encourage foreign investment from China to the city, alleviating serious economic problems the region was facing.

Why the IT industry is vulnerable to corruption
The IT industry includes physical devices—everything from smartphones, tablets, and super computers that run large corporations and government agencies—and the software used on those devices. Both the hardware side and the software side are challenged by fast-paced advances in the technological environment and an intensely competitive environment, which is, in turn, stressed by the tyranny of quarterly earnings results and the expectations of global investors.

Sources: "Scale of international bribery laid bare by new OECD report," OECD 2014, http://www.oecd.org/newsroom/scale-of-international-bribery-laid-bare-by-new-oecd-report.htm; Arlene Drake, "Canadian Global Exploration Activity," Natural Resources Canada, http://www.nrcan.gc.ca/mining-materials/exploration/8296.

LO LEARNING OBJECTIVES

By the end of this chapter you should be able to:

1. Explain the source and nature of ethical issues and dilemmas in an international business.

2. Show how important it is for managers to consider ethical issues when making strategic and operating decisions.

3. Identify the causes of poor ethical decision making in international business organizations.

4. Describe the different approaches to business ethics that can be derived from moral philosophy, and show how these approaches can help managers make international business decisions that do not violate ethical norms.

5. Discuss the steps that managers can take to promote an awareness of ethical issues throughout the organization and to make sure that ethical considerations enter into strategic and operational decisions.

Introduction

The previous two chapters detail how societies differ in terms of their culture and their economic, political, and legal systems. We also mapped out some of these implications for the practice of international business. This chapter focuses on the ethical issues that arise when companies do business in different nations. Many of these ethical issues arise precisely because of differences in culture, economic development, politics, and legal systems. It can also be argued that advances in the technological environment (principally the Internet and social media) allow more people to know more information about ethical issue on a global basis.

Ethics as Affected by Different Environments

The circumstances that affect ethical considerations in the second decade of the new millennium are circumstances caused by continued changes in the:

- political environment (regional, national, and international), and the consequent laws and regulations that are established (discussed in Chapter 2, noting the Canadian law, Bill S-21);
- social-cultural environment, which has been influenced by immigration patterns worldwide and a continued movement of populations from rural to urban areas;
- technological environment (faster Internet access speeds, more mobile devices such as smartphones and tablets to access Web content, social media), which has affected communications regionally and globally and also affected the work environment and productivity;
- economic environment, which sees currency fluctuations and international NGOs like the IMF and World Bank playing a more significant role in national and regional economies. The need for corporations to remain economically competitive also influences corporate objectives and has consequences for consumer priorities;
- competitive environment, which is causing companies to make decisions in a global context and resulting in actions that sometimes negatively affect their employees, customers, and host country governments.

There has always been pressure on companies to behave ethically, While in years past the pressure was somewhat intense, in this new millennium, the mistakes of a corporate executive can have international repercussions. Nowadays, ethical mistakes can easily be posted on YouTube, Twitter, and Facebook, easily becoming a headline story for CNN or a Google news site. The Internet makes it possible for millions of people to know about a company's violation as soon as the information is made public.

The term *ethics* refers to accepted principles of right or wrong that govern the conduct of a person, the members of a profession, or the actions of an organization. **Business ethics** are the accepted principles of right or wrong governing the conduct of business people, and an **ethical strategy** is a strategy or course of action that does not violate these accepted principles.

In our society and others, many ethical principles are codified into law—prohibitions against murder, stealing, and incest, for example—but many others are not—such as the principle that an author should not plagiarize another's work. As long as it does not involve word-for-word copying, plagiarism does not technically violate copyright law, but it surely is unethical. Similarly, the history of science is replete with examples of researchers who claim their idea was "stolen" by an unscrupulous colleague for his own personal gain before the originator had the chance to file for a patent or publish the idea himself. Such behaviour is not illegal, but it is obviously unethical.

This chapter looks at how ethical issues can and should be incorporated into decision making in an international business. We start by looking at the source and nature of ethical issues and dilemmas in an international business. Next, we review the reasons for poor ethical decision making. Then we discuss the different philosophical approaches to business ethics. We close the chapter by reviewing the different processes that managers can adopt to make sure that ethical considerations are incorporated into decision making in an international business firm.

LO1 Ethical Issues in International Business

Many of the ethical issues and dilemmas in international business are rooted in the fact that political systems, law, economic development, and culture vary significantly from culture to culture and nation to nation.

Rules, regulations, laws, and guidelines that may have been created to serve the local citizens are now being influenced by events and circumstances far away from the municipality. Politics at the local and national level are also strongly affected by a worldwide shift in the social-cultural environment. Many groups of identified cultures use technology and economic influence to exert pressure on governments to change rules and regulations, for example to allow gay marriage, to permit sharia law, to change the age of retirement, or to ban smoking in public restaurants. As we shall outline, most of the different environments an international manager must work within are often intertwined.

Ethics in the Changing Political Environment

Consider how politics has an effect on ethics. In the new millennium, the people you elect to run the government in your jurisdiction are also affected by political results in other national and international circumstances. A recent example that Canadians will be familiar with is the global coverage of President Donald Trump's tweets and comments about everything from "fake news" to accusations about his phones being bugged, from changes to immigration regulations to oil pipeline deals and NAFTA.

CORRUPTION

As noted in Chapter 2, corruption has been a problem in almost every society in history, and it continues to be one today. There always have been and always will be corrupt government officials. International businesses can still gain economic advantages by making payments to corrupt officials. But in 1997, the trade and finance ministers from the member states of the Organisation for Economic Co-operation and Development (OECD) followed the U.S. lead and adopted the **Convention on Combating Bribery of Foreign Public Officials in International Business Transactions.**[1]

The convention, which went into force in 1999, obliges member states to make the bribery of foreign public officials a criminal offence. The convention excludes facilitating payments made to expedite routine government action from the convention. To be truly effective, however, the convention must be translated into domestic law by each signatory nation, and that is still in process. To encourage countries to implement of local regulations fitting the convention, the OECD created a Web site in which each country is listed and "progress-to-date" is discussed.[2]

In 2009 one of the tools produced by the OECD backed Anti-Bribery Convention was a lengthy booklet discussing "Tax Deductibility of Bribes to Foreign Public Officials." The booklet stated that each signing country should be creating rules and regulations such that corporations cannot maintain "off-the-record" books or other false document processes to declare bribery amounts as expenses under other categories.[3]

Some economists have argued that corruption reduces the returns on business investment and leads to low economic growth.[4] In a country where corruption is common, unproductive bureaucrats who demand side payments for granting the enterprise permission to operate may siphon off the profits from a business activity. This reduces businesses' incentive to invest and may retard a country's economic growth rate.

PERCEPTIONS OF CORRUPT POLITICIANS IN CANADA

Canada is not immune to its own corruptions. There have been reports on corruption in far-ranging government and businesses in Quebec. One of the reasons that corruption in Quebec is a lightning rod of criticism from the rest of Canada is a fact (widely reported) that Quebec agencies, departments, and ministries receive millions of dollars from the federal government in Ottawa—money that comes from taxpayers across the country. Western provinces such as Alberta and British Columbia raise strong objections that the federal tax that comes out of their populations is going to fund questionable activities in Quebec. Such Western frustration has led to the rise of separatist parties in British Columbia and Alberta that want to cease paying taxes to Ottawa and create an independent political entity in western Canada—a situation which does not bode well for Canadian unity in the second decade of the new millennium.

Maclean's magazine had written critical articles of the sponsorship scandal in Quebec in 2005. In September 2010, *Maclean's* was the target of several national and provincial politicians for launching a cover story that boldly called Quebec "The Most Corrupt Province in Canada." Later, Brian Segal, the president of *Maclean's* parent company, Rogers Publishing, said ". . . we sincerely regret any offence that the cover may have caused . . . ," however the point was made through several articles in the controversial issue that the Quebec "government has lurched from one scandal to the next, from political financing to favouritism in the provincial daycare system to the matter of Charest's own (long undisclosed) $75,000 stipend, paid to him by his own party, to corruption in the construction industry."[5]

Montreal Mayor Gerald Tremblay resigned in 2012 amid allegations of corruption in the Quebec construction industry, but Toronto Mayor Rob Ford is probably the highest profile Canadian mayor ever. Negative international media coverage becomes an issue for international business and ethics, as discussed in the next section. In Ontario in 2013, Toronto residents witnessed local, provincial, national, and international media coverage of the saga of Mayor Ford. Mayor Ford was under investigation for substance abuse as part of a police investigation into Toronto gangs. He subsequently admitted to all incidents but remained in office, although his mayoral powers were greatly restricted by a council vote that transferred much of his authority to the deputy mayor. In May 2014 Ford announced that he would take a break from his duties and his re-election campaign to enter a rehabilitation program. Although he won his local riding and retained his seat, he died of cancer in March 2016.

PERCEPTIONS OF CORRUPT POLITICIANS AFFECT CANADIAN TRADE

Why would students of international business be worried about these revelations being recounted in the media in Canada and throughout the world? First, Canada is an exporting nation. As you learned from the first three chapters, exporting leads our economy. Our ability to be competitive exporters depends on the perceptions of international customers, as well as on other influences in the economic environment. Canada is a country that is highly regarded by many nations for the activities of our Armed Forces as peacekeepers and for the comparatively polite way that Canadian tourists behave abroad, and enjoys favourable and confident opinions in nations around the globe. Political scandals based on unethical dealings that are played out daily in the international news raise concerns of international business people dealing with Canada.

ANOTHER PERSPECTIVE

Corruption Perceptions Index

In the days after the *Maclean's* cover story about corruption in Quebec, that province's politicians, political party executives, and business leaders in the province countered that identifying corruption must not be a certainty because, by its nature, it is secretive. The "participants" in corruption go to great lengths to hide their activities—"how could *Maclean's* or anybody quantify corruption and determine one region was more or less corrupt than another?" The answer is the Corruption Perceptions Index.

Launched in 1995, the Corruption Perceptions Index is produced by Transparency International (TI). TI was founded by former executives of various NGOs such as the World Bank. In producing the Corruption Perceptions Index, TI uses various indexes, surveys, and opinion lists to create a comparative numerical score and rank 170+ countries. TI also publishes an annual Global Corruption Report, a Global Corruption Barometer and a Bribe Payers Index. For the past several years, Canada has been at the highest end in terms of being perceived as free of corruption. The Corruption Perceptions Index can be seen online at www.transparency.org. In 2013, the three most corrupt countries were Somalia, North Korea, and Afghanistan. The countries with the least corruption are Denmark and New Zealand (tied for first spot) and Finland (#3). Canada ranks #9, tied with Australia. Our two largest trading partners are the United States (#19) and China (#80).

Source: "Corruptions Perceptions Index 2016," Surveys, January 25, 2017, Transparency International, http://www.transparency.org/news/feature/corruption_perceptions_index_2016

HUMAN RIGHTS

Beyond employment issues, multinational companies may find themselves having to adjust as political situations change. Because Canada has signed CISG and Bill S-21, as discussed in Chapter 2, Canadian multinationals may find themselves part of the changing political and economic landscapes in their subsidiary host countries, where questions of human rights can arise in international business. Basic human rights still are not respected in many nations. Rights that we take for granted in developed nations, such as freedom of association, freedom of speech, freedom of assembly, freedom of movement, freedom from political repression, and so on, are by no means universally accepted (see Chapter 2 for details).

In 2011 and 2012, Canada was caught up in human rights issues through its participation in a coalition of countries operating in Afghanistan. Since the early days of NATO forces' involvement in Afghanistan in 2002, and throughout the participation of Canadian combat troops and Canadian government agencies such as CIDA (Canadian International Development Agency), there have been widespread accusations against corrupt Afghan officials who are making it

Afghan villagers. © *Tracing Tea/Shutterstock*

challenging for Canadian aid efforts (money and activities) to have results that improve the lives of the Afghan people.

As Canada winds down its presence in Afghanistan, corruption in the areas of water management and energy production are particularly troublesome since our government's main focus in assisting the Afghan people has been to rebuild the water dams and rebuild the schools in the areas occupied by Canadian Forces.

Ethics in the Changing Social-Cultural Environment

What is considered normal practice in one culture may be considered unethical in others. Examples of these "ranges" of ethical/unethical behaviour may include things such as how gift giving might be considered bribery; how you interact with law enforcement officers; whether companies only concern themselves with obeying precise regulations, or do they go further and adhere to the moral principals of the societies within which they operate; or how women are treated and issues of child labour.

Because they work for an institution that transcends national borders and cultures, managers in a multinational firm need to be particularly sensitive to these differences and able to choose the ethical action in those circumstances where variation across societies creates the potential for ethical problems. In the international business setting, the most common ethical issues involve exchanges of money, employment practices, human rights, environmental regulations, corruption, and the moral obligation of multinational corporations. The challenge today and beyond is that these ethical issues and challenges are intensified by fast-moving developments facilitated by the technological environment.

ANOTHER PERSPECTIVE

The Issue of Giving Meaning Across Cultures

One difficulty in making ethical decisions across cultural borders is that expatriate managers may interpret a local cultural practice in the way such behaviour would be understood in their home culture. If the manager does not attempt to understand the practice's meaning in the local culture, the manager may miss a huge step in ethical analysis. For example, Western standards would fail to properly interpret Muslim women's practice of covering their heads and faces in conservative Muslim cultures. Remember to consider context when conducting an ethical analysis. In such a process, a local informant can be helpful. At the same time, be aware of the ethical trap of cultural relativism captured in the adage, "When in Rome, do as the Romans do."

Source: Example from H. Lane, M. Maznevski, M. Mendenhall, and J. McNett, *The Blackwell Handbook of Global Management: A Guide to Managing Complexity* (Oxford: Wiley-Blackwell, 2004).

Ethics in the Changing Technological Environment

Developments and applications of sophisticated technology can create ethical nightmares reaching far across the globe and touching many governments and organizations. This became evident in the fall of 2016, leading up to the American presidential election when the idea of "fake news" was first presented and began affecting voter opinion. "Fake news" is information sourced from opinion sites. Stories lack research and, therefore, journalistic integrity. Although politicians at all levels tried to deal with an overwhelming volume of commentary on issues, the sheer number of stories, images, and videos on social media sites (Facebook, YouTube, and Instagram) made it challenging to get the real stories out—the "real" stories authored by legitimate journalists and news organizations.[6]

The growing popularity of social media has affected how employees connect with one another and the world. More and more people who work for very large corporate organizations connect through social media to share comments, photos, and videos of their work environment. This can promote an understanding of "how the other half lives" and serve to reduce ignorance about the welfare of the employees of the globally distributed parts of a company, its subsidiaries, and its outsourcing partners.

Ethics in the Changing Economic Environment

The economic environment sees currency fluctuations and international NGOs playing a more significant role in national and regional economies.

In April 2016 a number of media outlets reported a story of how wealthy Canadians had successfully been hiding investments in offshore tax havens—a situation first being revealed when the details of a Panamanian law firm (Mossack Fonseca) became public. According to Statistics Canada (as reported by *The Toronto Star* and other newspapers) "Canadians have declared $199 billion in offshore tax haven investments around the world." However the International Consortium of Investigative Journalists and the German newspaper *Süddeutsche Zeitung* argued that this amount is "a small fraction of the Canadian offshore wealth that goes undeclared."[7] The story about the activities of the Panamanian law firm, and the consequential revealing of how billions of tax dollars have avoided being paid to the governments of various wealthy citizens, became known as "The Panama Papers."

Corporations have also been criticized for not paying taxes. See the Management Focus on tax avoidance to understand the impact this can have on a government and a country's economy.

Ethics in the Changing Competitive Environment
EMPLOYMENT PRACTICES

In March 2017 Kon Leong, CEO at ZL Technologies in San Francisco, wrote in the *Harvard Business Review* a thought-provoking article titled "Is Your Company Using Employee Data Ethically?" Leong suggests that large enterprises gathered data, related to employee messaging and social media posts, originally from the perspective of producing "evidence for litigation, to preserve business records, and to respond to regulators' demands for information." A corollary of such data gathered (usually by high-performance computers running advanced AI software), as propositioned by Leong, is that such data is "...visualizing employee interactions, mapping domain expertise, replaying past events, tracking employee sentiment..." and can help managers manage certain HR issues more effectively.[8] When the competitive environment

MANAGEMENT FOCUS

Avoiding Paying Taxes—Cheating the Government

Very few people talk about wanting to pay taxes—for most citizens in most countries it is a natural inclination to avoid paying taxes, particularly when people object to the way the government spends the tax dollars on activities and programs that are contrary to the personal beliefs of individual citizens. Yet most students reading this textbook, and in a college or university course in Canada where this course is being taught, are the beneficiary of tax dollars in the context of how the government collects personal income tax and corporate tax and uses that money to subsidize educational costs—costs such as the building, the salary of the professor, the transportation system that gets you to class, etc.

Sometimes national and regional governments operate in areas where there are not enough medium- and large-sized companies paying corporate tax; therefore the government has a difficult time obtaining tax revenue to provide educational and health care services to the citizens. When the government does not have the means to collect enough taxes it has to make choices and often one of the primary ways governments cut costs is to cut education funding—meaning cuts to the number of teachers and cuts to facilities, technology, and other things necessary for students to obtain an education.

Recently (in 2012 and 2013), a number of leading American IT companies, such as Apple and Google, have been harshly criticized for using various strategies to avoid paying taxes in the United States, for example by outsourcing, offshoring, and listing income under foreign subsidiaries. The irony of the situation is bitter since both Apple and Google produce products and services that make it easier for students to carry out their studies, yet by avoiding paying millions in tax, these actions deprive the government of tax dollars that could be used to fund education.

Tax avoidance is not limited to the United States. In May 2013, *The Economist* magazine reported that "Google came under fire from British politicians, one of whom publicly accused the Internet giant of using unethical methods to avoid paying its fair share of tax." In the United States, the Senate's Permanent Subcommittee on Investigations reported that "between 2009 and 2012 Apple avoided paying tax in America on at least $74 billion of profits by setting up subsidiaries in Ireland that had no purpose other than to ensure these profits were shielded from tax."

Questions

1. Tax avoidance has been a hot topic in the United States. Has it become a topic in Canada as well? Research some news stories to see if you can find some Canadian companies criticized for avoiding Canadian taxes.

2. The federal government in Canada is now making more stringent efforts to collect tax from companies paying late, or not paying the full amount. Can you find out through an online search what the government is doing to recover money owed?

Source: "Biting Criticism," *The Economist*, May 21, 2013, http://www.economist.com/blogs/schumpeter/2013/05/apples-tax-arrangements, accessed June 5, 2017.

increases in intensity, and continued advances in the technological environment conspire to challenge companies to increase employee productivity, it is very helpful for enterprises of all types to know more about the true nature of how their employees feel about the company and how their communications through social media may contribute to the overall way the business is perceived by the public.

OUTSOURCING

Employment practices are increasingly influenced by outsourcing trends, which have arisen due to the globally competitive nature of creating low-priced products and services. Many large- and medium-sized enterprises feel the pressure from shareholders and investors, who make decisions to buy or sell shares based on the profitability of the enterprise. Maintaining profitability by employing solely within the country of the home office is challenging when the production of parts and manufacturing could be distributed globally among many capable and low-cost producers.

There are a number of ethical considerations that must be addressed by companies that decide to cut the costs of operations (manufacturing, data processing, assembling components, etc.) through outsourcing, offshoring and other strategies and tactics. When outsourced firms provide products and services at a lower cost, one of the most obvious considerations is discovering how the provider of the outsourced activity is "doing it cheaper."

- Are they using cheaper materials than what you would have used?
- Are the materials cheaper because the process to access the materials cut some safety or regulatory process?
- Are they employing cheaper labour? Is this just because they pay a low wage, or do they also cut out any benefits, which are a costly part of North American and European businesses?
- Are they cutting safety standards and processes?
- Do they get away with bypassing pollution and environmental considerations?

Outsourcing and offshoring become ethical issues when the nature of the activity is contrary to the ethical expectations of the citizens of the home country and in violation of the rules and regulations that govern how enterprises must operate both at home and abroad. As was mentioned in Chapter 2, Canada has rules and regulations that apply to Canadian companies operating outside Canada.

With an unusual twist on the effects of outsourcing being contrary to the goals and objectives of the enterprise comes the January 2017 story about the University of California (UC) being accused of outsourcing its IT jobs. *The Highlander*, a student newspaper out of the University of California, published a January 2017 editorial stating that UC had been "firing its IT staff and replacing them with workers from other countries... [which] sends a devastating message to many of the UC's students... studying right now to become software engineers." The student newspaper challenged that such outsourcing actions are "... sending a vote of no confidence in its own ability to educate, if it sees hired foreign workers as a better set of employees than people trained in this state." It is reasonable for all medium- and large-sized enterprises to seek operationally efficiency in a competitive environment, but the point made by critics of UC's actions is that the university is funded by tax dollars and that such ruthless cost savings is unwarranted and "paints the University of California as greedy and exploitative."[9]

ENVIRONMENTAL POLLUTION

Ethical issues arise when environmental regulations in host nations are far inferior to those in the home nation. Many developed nations have substantial regulations governing the emission of pollutants, the dumping of toxic chemicals, the use of toxic materials in the workplace, and so on. Those regulations are often lacking in developing nations, and, according to critics, the result can be higher levels of pollution from the operations of multinationals than would be allowed at home.

Sri Lanka, a country known by many Canadians as a source of new immigrants for many years, is struggling with pollution caused by companies manufacturing cheap goods for export. In November 2013, a Sri Lankan court issued a *"writ of mandamus"* compelling the Central Environmental Authority to bring justice to the residents of Rathupaswala. The people of Rathupaswala had taken legal action against glove manufacturer Venigros Private Limited alleging that the company had polluted the water in the Rathupaswala area of Gampaha district. The residents of Rathupaswala began the legal process after their protests led to a deadly conflict with law enforcement authorities. When police and the Sri Lankan military clashed with the protestors, three youths were shot and killed, and a number of others were injured.[10]

Protests about how companies fail to adhere to government regulations, or how they avoid burdensome legislation, are not confined to developing countries but in fact happen worldwide. Truckers in California set up picket lines at the entrance to the Port of Oakland in November 2013 to protest new air pollution regulations that would make it more difficult to operate their transport trucks delivering goods to the port. The Oakland truckers were fearful that they would not be able to comply with new state regulations that would require them to invest in newer cleaner equipment—specifically $35,000 to $50,000 diesel engines. These protests followed complaints in 2010 when the truckers had to outfit their trucks with $20,000 diesel filters.[11]

Should a multinational feel free to pollute in a developing nation? (To do so hardly seems ethical.) Is there a danger that amoral management might move production to a developing nation precisely because costly pollution controls are not required, and the company is therefore free to despoil the environment and perhaps endanger local people in its quest to lower production costs and gain a competitive advantage? What is the right and moral thing to do in such circumstances? Pollute to gain an economic advantage, or make sure that foreign subsidiaries adhere to common standards regarding pollution controls?

A CORPORATE RIGHT TO POLLUTE?

Asarco is a U.S.-based subsidiary of the giant Mexican mining conglomerate Grupo Mexico. Asarco has copper-mining operations near the towns of Hayden and Winkelman in Arizona. According to some documents dating back to 1912, the original operator of the property was granted special considerations to discharge a "limitless amount of smoke, dust, and fumes" without the threat of being responsible for the consequences. Moving forward to May 2005, the powerful American United Steelworkers union is backing residents of Hayden and Winkelman as they fight a legal battle with the Mexican owner. Asarco has gone to court in Arizona to assert that it is obvious pollution would be evident in the immediate area surrounding the mine, and anybody who lives in the region is wilfully exposing themselves to a risky situation and therefore has no claim against the operators producing any harm or effects.

These questions take on added importance because some parts of the environment are a public good that no one owns, but anyone can despoil. No one owns the atmosphere or the oceans, but polluting both, no matter where the pollution originates, harms all.[12] The atmosphere and oceans can be viewed as a global commons from which everyone benefits but for which no one is specifically responsible. In such cases, a phenomenon known as the tragedy of the commons becomes applicable. The tragedy of the commons occurs when a resource held in common by all, but owned by no one, is overused by individuals, resulting in its degradation.

In the modern world, corporations can contribute to the global tragedy of the commons by moving production to locations where they are free to pump pollutants into the atmosphere or dump them in oceans or rivers, thereby harming these valuable global commons. While such action may be legal, is it ethical? Again, such actions seem to violate basic societal notions of ethics and social responsibility.

The Power of Multinationals

Helping to end apartheid—the institutionalized racial segregation and discrimination in South African—is an example of the potential power of multinationals. By 1985, South Africa faced economic and political sanctions, and many multinational companies began to pull out of the country. After several bloody uprisings, the existing government was forced to dismantle the system.

Although change has come in South Africa, many repressive regimes still exist in the world. Is it ethical for multinationals to do business in them? It is often argued that inward investment by a multinational can be a force for economic, political, and social progress that ultimately improves the rights of people in repressive regimes. This position was first discussed in Chapter 2, when we noted that economic progress in a nation can create pressure for democratization. In general, this belief suggests it is ethical for a multinational to do business in nations that lack the democratic structures and human rights records of developed nations. Investment in China, for example, is frequently justified on the grounds that although China's human rights record is often questioned by human rights groups, and although the country is not a democracy, continuing inward investment will help boost economic growth and raise living standards. These developments will ultimately create pressures from the Chinese people for more participative government, political pluralism, and freedom of expression and speech.

But there is a limit to this argument. As was the case with South Africa's apartheid rule, some regimes are so repressive that investment cannot be justified on ethical grounds. A current example would be Myanmar (formally known as Burma). Ruled by a military dictatorship for more than 40 years, Myanmar has one of the worst human rights records in the world. Beginning in the mid-1990s, many Western companies exited Myanmar, judging the human rights violations to be so extreme that doing business there could not be justified on ethical grounds.

Power itself is morally neutral. It is how power is wielded that matters. It can be distributed in a positive and ethical manner to increase social welfare, or it can be applied in a manner that is ethically and morally suspect. Consider the case of News Corporation, one of the largest media conglomerates in the world. The power of media companies derives from their ability to shape public perceptions by the material they choose to publish. News Corporation founder and CEO Rupert Murdoch has long considered China to be one of the most promising media markets in the world and has sought permission to expand News Corporation's operations in China, particularly the satellite broadcasting operations of Star TV. Some critics believe that Murdoch used the power of News Corporation in an unethical way to attain this objective.[13]

Some multinationals have acknowledged a moral obligation to use their power to enhance social welfare where they do business. BP, one of the world's largest oil companies, has made it part of the company policy to undertake "social investments" in the countries where it does business.[14] In Algeria, BP has been investing in a major project to develop gas fields near the desert town of Salah. When the company noticed the lack of clean water in Salah, it built two desalination plants to provide drinking water for the local community and distributed containers to residents so they could take water from the plants to their homes. There was no economic reason for BP to make this social investment, but the company believes it is morally obligated to use its power in constructive ways. The action, while a small thing for BP, is a very important thing for the local community. It still has its lessons to learn, however, after the calamitous Deepwater Horizon oil spill in April 2010.

LO2 Ethical Dilemmas

The ethical obligations of a multinational corporation toward employment conditions, human rights, corruption, environmental pollution, and the use of power are not always clear cut. There may be no agreement about accepted ethical principles. From an international business perspective, some argue that what is ethical depends upon one's cultural perspective.[15]

Managers must confront very real ethical dilemmas. Using concepts discussed in Chapter 3, we can provide an imagined—but highly likely—situation faced by a Canadian executive visiting a foreign subsidiary in a poor nation. The executive discovers the subsidiary has hired a 12-year-old girl to work on a factory floor. Using child labour is in direct violation of the company's own ethical code, so the Canadian instructs the local manager to replace the child with an adult. The local manager dutifully complies.

What the Canadian executive does not know is that the girl is an orphan, who is the only breadwinner for herself and her six-year-old brother. Unable to find another job, she turns to prostitution. Two years later she dies of AIDS. Meanwhile, her brother takes up begging. He encounters the Canadian executive while begging outside the local McDonald's. Oblivious that this was the man responsible for his fate, the boy begs him for money. The Canadian quickens his pace and walks rapidly past the outstretched hand into the McDonald's, where he orders a quarter-pound cheeseburger with fries and a milkshake. A year later the boy contracts tuberculosis and dies.

Had the visiting Canadian understood the gravity of the girl's situation, would he still have requested her replacement? Perhaps not! Would it have been better, therefore, to stick with the status quo and allow the girl to continue working? Probably not, because that would have violated the reasonable prohibition against child labour found in the company's own ethical code. What then would have been the right thing to do? What was the obligation of the executive given this ethical dilemma? As was mentioned in Chapter 3, the Levi Strauss company confronted a similar scenario and came up with a solution. But are there other potential solutions?

There is no easy answer to these questions. That is the nature of **ethical dilemmas**— they are situations in which none of the available alternatives seems ethically acceptable.[16] In this case, employing child labour was not acceptable, but given that she was employed, neither was denying the child her only source of income. What the Canadian executive needed, what all managers need, was a moral compass, or perhaps an ethical algorithm, that would guide him through such an ethical dilemma to find an acceptable solution. Later in this chapter we will outline what such a moral compass might look like. For now, it is enough to note that ethical dilemmas exist because many real-world decisions are complex, difficult to frame, and involve first-, second-, and third-order consequences that are hard to quantify. Doing the right thing, or even knowing what the right thing might be, is often far from easy.

LO3 The Roots of Unethical Behaviour

Examples abound of managers behaving in a manner that might be judged unethical in an international business setting. In the mid-1990s, a group of American investors became interested in restoring the SS *United States*, once a luxurious ocean liner.[17] The first step in the restoration project involved stripping the ship of its asbestos lining.

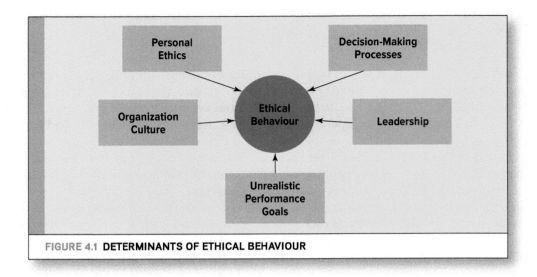

FIGURE 4.1 **DETERMINANTS OF ETHICAL BEHAVIOUR**

Asbestos is a highly toxic material that produces a fine dust. If the dust is inhaled, it can result in lung disease, cancer, and death. Accordingly, very tight standards in developed countries govern the removal of asbestos. A bid from a U.S. company, based on the standards established in the United States, priced the job at more than $100 million. A company in Ukraine offered to do the job for $2 million, so the ship was towed to the Ukrainian port of Sevastopol. By agreeing to do the work for $2 million, it is implied that the Ukrainian company could not have adopted standards even remotely close to those required in the United States. As a consequence, its employees were at a significant risk of developing asbestos-related disease. If this was the case, the desire to limit costs had resulted in the American investors acting in an unethical manner, for they were knowingly rewarding a company that exposed its workers to a significant health risk.

Why do managers behave in a manner that is unethical? There is no simple answer to this question because the causes are complex. But a few generalizations can be made (see Figure 4.1).[18]

Managers should be aware that business ethics are not divorced from personal ethics, which are the generally accepted principles of right and wrong governing the conduct of individuals. Ethical systems and how they exert themselves were discussed in Chapter 3. An individual with a strong sense of personal ethics is less likely to behave in an unethical manner in a business setting. It follows that the first step to establishing a strong sense of business ethics is for a society to emphasize strong personal ethics.

Home-country managers working abroad in multinational firms (expatriate managers) may experience more than the usual degree of pressure to violate their personal ethics. They are away from their ordinary social context and supporting culture, and they are psychologically and geographically distant from the parent company. They may be based in a culture that does not place the same value on ethical norms important in the manager's home country. Also, they may be surrounded by local employees who have less rigorous ethical standards.

Also, many studies of unethical behaviour in a business setting have concluded that business people sometimes do not realize they are behaving unethically, primarily because they simply fail to ask, "Is this decision or action ethical?"[19] Instead, they apply a straightforward business evaluation to what they perceive to be a business decision, forgetting that the decision may also have an important ethical dimension.

The fault lies in four places. First, the intense competitiveness of the international business environment puts pressure on companies to squeeze out every advantage they have and to cut costs in the most extreme way. Cutting costs are necessary to increase revenue and sustain profit—particularly for medium- and large-sized publicly traded companies that have skittish shareholders who will quickly dump their stock if the margins are not favourable.

Second, the fault also lies in processes that do not incorporate ethical considerations into business decision making. Those decisions were probably made on the basis of good economic logic. Subcontractors were probably chosen on the basis of business variables such as cost, delivery, and product quality, and the key managers simply failed to ask, "How does this subcontractor treat its workforce?" If they thought about the question at all, they probably reasoned that it was the subcontractor's concern, not theirs. For an example of a business decision that may have been unethical, see the Management Focus describing Pfizer's decision to test an experimental drug on children suffering from meningitis in Nigeria.

Unfortunately, the intense competitive international business climate, affecting all businesses of all sizes, puts a lot of pressure on all levels of management. The pressure to produce and sell products at cheaper and cheaper prices can encourage people to avoid thoroughly thinking through the ethical consequences of business decisions. This competitive pressure brings us to the third cause of unethical behaviour in businesses—an organization culture that de-emphasizes business ethics by reducing all decisions to the purely economic.

The term **organization culture** refers to the values and norms that are shared among employees of an organization. You will recall from Chapter 3 that values are abstract ideas about what a group believes to be good, right, and desirable, while norms are the social rules and guidelines that prescribe appropriate behaviour in particular situations. Just as societies have cultures, so do business organizations. Together, values and norms shape the culture of a business organization, and that culture has an important influence on the ethics of business decision making.

Author Robert Bryce has explained how the organization culture at now-bankrupt multinational energy company Enron was built on values that emphasized greed and deception.[20] According to Bryce, the tone was set by top managers who engaged in self-dealing to enrich themselves and their own families. Bryce tells how former Enron CEO Kenneth Lay made sure his own family benefited handsomely from Enron. Much of Enron's corporate travel business was handled by a travel agency partly owned by Lay's sister. When an internal auditor recommended that the company could do better by using another travel agency, he soon found himself out of a job. In 1997, Enron acquired a company owned by Kenneth Lay's son, Mark Lay, which was trying to establish a business trading paper and pulp products. At the time, Mark Lay and another company he controlled were targets of a federal criminal investigation of bankruptcy fraud and embezzlement. As part of the deal, Enron hired Mark Lay as an executive with a three-year contract that guaranteed him at least $1 million in pay over that period, plus options to purchase about 20 000 shares of Enron. Bryce also details how Lay's daughter used an Enron jet to transport her king-sized bed to France. With Kenneth Lay as an example, it is perhaps not surprising that self-dealing soon became endemic at Enron. The most notable example was Chief Financial Officer Andrew Fastow, who set up "off-balance-sheet" partnerships that not only hid Enron's true financial condition from investors, but also paid tens of millions of dollars directly to Fastow. (Fastow was subsequently indicted by the government for criminal fraud and went to jail.)

Testing Drugs in the Developing World

The drug-development process is long, risky, and expensive. It can take ten years and cost in excess of $500 million to develop a new drug. Moreover, between 80 and 90 percent of drug candidates fail in clinical trials. Pharmaceutical companies rely upon a handful of successes to pay for their failures. Among the most successful of the world's pharmaceutical companies is New York–based Pfizer. Developing a new drug involves risks and costs, and pharmaceutical companies will jump at opportunities to reduce both; in 1996 Pfizer thought it saw one such opportunity.

Pfizer had been developing a novel antibiotic, Trovan, that was proving to be useful in treating a wide range of bacterial infections. Wall Street analysts were predicting that Trovan could be a blockbuster, one of a handful of drugs capable of generating sales of more than $1 billion a year. In 1996, Pfizer was pushing to submit data on Trovan's efficacy to the Food and Drug Administration (FDA) for review. A favourable review would allow Pfizer to sell the drug in the United States, the world's largest market. Pfizer wanted the drug to be approved for both adults and children, but it was having trouble finding sufficient numbers of sick children in the United States on whom to test the drug. Then, in early 1996, a researcher at Pfizer read about an emerging epidemic of bacterial meningitis in Kano, Nigeria. This seemed like a quick way to test the drug on a large number of sick children.

Within weeks, a team of six doctors had flown to Kano and were administering the drug, in oral form, to children with meningitis. Desperate for help, Nigerian authorities had given the go-ahead for Pfizer to give the drug to children (the epidemic would ultimately kill nearly 16 000 people). Over the next few weeks, Pfizer treated 198 children. The protocol called for half the patients to get Trovan and half to get a comparison antibiotic already approved for the treatment of children. After a few weeks, the Pfizer team left, the experiment complete. Trovan seemed to be about as effective and safe as the already approved antibiotic. The data from the trial were put into a package with data from other trials of Trovan and delivered to the FDA.

Questions were soon raised about the nature of Pfizer's experiment. Critics alleged that the Pfizer team kept children on Trovan even after they failed to show a response to the drug, instead of switching them quickly to another drug. The result, according to critics, was that some children died who might have been saved had they been taken off Trovan sooner. Questions were also raised about the safety of the oral formulation of Trovan, which some doctors feared might lead to arthritis in children. Fifteen children who took Trovan showed signs of joint pain during the experiment, three times the rate of children taking the other antibiotic. Then there were questions about consent. The FDA requires that patient (or parent) consent be given before patients are enrolled in clinical trials, no matter where in the world the trials are conducted. Critics argue that in the rush to get the trial established in Nigeria, Pfizer did not follow proper procedures, and that many parents of the infected children did not know their children were participating in a trial for an experimental drug. Many of the parents were illiterate, could not read the consent forms, and had to rely upon the questionable translation of the Nigerian nursing staff. Pfizer rejected these charges and contends that it did nothing wrong.

Trovan was approved by the FDA for use in adults in 1997, but it was never approved for use in children. Launched in 1998, by 1999 there were reports that up to 140 patients in Europe suffered liver damage after taking Trovan. The FDA subsequently restricted the use of Trovan to those cases where the benefits of treatment outweighed the risk of liver damage. European regulators banned sales of the drug. In 2003, two dozen Nigerian families sued Pfizer in a federal court in New York. The families claim their children either died or were injured because Pfizer did not adequately inform them of the risks and alternatives for treatment with Trovan. The case was ultimately settled out of court.

Did Pfizer behave unethically by rushing to take advantage of an epidemic in Nigeria to test an experimental drug on children? Should it have been less opportunistic and proceeded more

MANAGEMENT FOCUS *Continued*

carefully? Were corners cut with regard to patient consent in the rush to establish a trial? And did doctors keep patients on Trovan too long, when they should have switched them to another medication? Is it ethical to test an experimental drug on children in a crisis setting in the developing world, where the overall standard of health care is so much lower than in the developed world and proper protocols might not be followed? These questions are all raised by the Pfizer case, and they remain unanswered, by the company at least.

Questions

1. The FDA requires that patient (or parent) consent be given before patients are enrolled in clinical trials, no matter where in the world the trials are conducted. Sometimes such consent cannot be easily obtained due to language barriers or literacy problems (meaning the parents can't read and/or sign consent). Should the trials proceed anyway if there is a chance of benefit to the children?

2. If it is true that between 80 and 90 percent of drug candidates fail in clinical trials, should we wait until advances in the "technological environment" remove the need for human testing trials, even if thousands could die from treatable diseases in the meantime?

Sources: J. Stephens, "Where Profits and Lives Hang in the Balance," *Washington Post*, December 17, 2000, p. A1; A. Brichacek, "What Price Corruption?" *Pharmaceutical Executive*, 21, no. 11 (November 2001), p. 94; and S. Hensley, "Court Revives Suit Against Pfizer on Nigeria Study," *The Wall Street Journal*, October 13, 2004, p. B4.

The lesson from the Enron debacle is that an organizational culture can legitimize behaviour that society would judge as unethical, particularly when this is mixed with a focus on unrealistic performance goals, such as maximizing short-term economic performance no matter the costs. In such circumstances, there is a greater than average probability that managers will violate their own personal ethics and engage in unethical behaviour.

The fourth cause of unethical behaviour in business is pressure from the parent company to meet unrealistic performance goals that can be attained only by cutting corners or acting in an unethical manner. For example, to meet centrally mandated performance goals, expatriate managers might give bribes to win contracts or might implement working conditions and environmental controls that are below acceptable standards. Local managers might encourage the expatriate to adopt such behaviour. And due to its geographical distance, the parent company may be unable to see how expatriate managers are meeting goals, or may choose not to see how they are doing so, allowing such behaviour to flourish and persist.

You don't have to look far to find examples of employees behaving unethically due to sales expectations from head office and the pressure to reach sales targets. In March 2017, TD Bank was dealing with damage to its reputation, and a decline in their stock price, following revelations that employees claimed they had violated regulations in order to make sales. Specific allegations reported by the *Financial Times* (unproven in court) were that "employees increased customers' lines of credit, overdraft protection amounts and credit card borrowing limits—all without authorisation—in order to reach sales targets."[21]

The examples of many unethical situations at many levels within a company suggest a fifth root cause of unethical behaviour—leadership. Leaders help to establish the culture of an organization, and they set the example that others follow. Other employees in a business often take their cue from business leaders, and if those leaders do not behave in an ethical manner, they might not either. It is not what leaders say that matters, but what they do.

Leaders set the tone of corporate culture. In what is perhaps the best example of this can be seen in the wake of the 2016 U.S. presidential elections. A number of media outlets are concerned President Trump's direct communications through Twitter to anyone he thinks challenges the ethical behaviour of his team may erode respect for the office of the president. That it is the man himself—not someone hired to be the voice of @POTUS—who casually addresses those who question or disagree with him and his team may result in his team believing that rigorously following ethical expectations is not a priority in the White House corporate environment. One widely analyzed example of Trump's team members flaunting ethical guidelines was when White House Senior Advisor Kellyanne Conway endorsed the clothing and jewellery line of Ivanka Trump during a television interview. In almost all jurisdictions there are regulations that prohibit people in public office (and their aides and advisors) from endorsing products that may provide personal gain to the people in office. The Office of Government Ethics said publicly that they thought the White House (office of the President) should take some sort of disciplinary action against Conway but at the time of this writing, the White House has not done so.

LO4 | Philosophical Approaches to Ethics

We shall look at several different approaches to business ethics here, beginning with some that can best be described as straw men, which either deny the value of business ethics or apply the concept in a very unsatisfactory way. Having discussed, and dismissed, the straw men, we will move on to consider approaches that are favoured by most moral philosophers and form the basis for current models of ethical behaviour in international businesses.

Straw Men

Straw man approaches to business ethics are raised by business ethics scholars primarily to demonstrate that they offer inappropriate guidelines for ethical decision making in a multinational enterprise. Four such approaches to business ethics are commonly discussed in the literature. These approaches can be characterized as the Friedman doctrine, cultural relativism, the righteous moralist, and the naive immoralist. All of these approaches have some inherent value, but all are unsatisfactory in important ways. Nevertheless, some companies tend to adopt these approaches.

The straw man analogy comes from the straw that was put inside scarecrows—the point being that it is not a serious effort to really fake people into thinking it is real man—anybody can see it is just straw stuffed into some worn out clothes. In arguments, this straw man phrase is used when people want to make a point, but it is a weak point and not likely to be convincing or stand up to scrutiny.

THE FRIEDMAN DOCTRINE

Nobel Prize-winning economist Milton Friedman wrote an article in 1970 that has since become a classic straw man that business ethics scholars outline only to then tear down.[22] Friedman's basic position is that the only social responsibility of business is to increase profits, so long as the company stays within the rules of law. He explicitly rejects the idea that businesses should undertake social expenditures beyond those

COUNTRY FOCUS

Nigeria: Child Lead-Poisoning Crisis

In many places in which mining is conducted in Africa there are circumstances in which the extraction processes result in toxic materials coming into contact with the labourers. For example, high levels of lead are often found in gold mining. The Zamfara State in northwestern Nigeria has high levels of lead in the gold ore and this has affected the heath of the people handling the ore during processing. Human Rights Watch said that in Zamfara children, working in the gold mines, are exposed to the lead dust. Since the time of the Romans (who used lead in their plumbing), contact with lead has been known to affect the body's neurological, biological, and cognitive functions. The concentration of lead in many gold ore bodies is rarely high enough to be fatal, but medical workers in Nigeria have reported that the lead concentration in the Zamfara State ore is very toxic and the mortality rate among children in the villages close to the mine site is 40 percent.

Questions

1. If the Nigerian government was pressured to eliminate child workers in the mining industry (a) would the Nigerian government have enough money to put those displaced child miners in school? and (b) would the mining companies hire "of age" workers, be able to pay them "adult" wages, and still have operational costs low enough to run the mine?

2. If the Nigerian government replaced child workers in the mine with adult workers, would they also be able to provide health and safety equipment to reduce exposure to lead poisoning and other toxins, and alleviate dangerous situations?

Source: "Nigeria: Child Lead Poisoning Crisis," February 7, 2012, Human Rights Watch, www.hrw.org/news/2012/02/07/nigeria-child-lead-poisoning-crisis.

mandated by the law and required for the efficient running of a business. For example, his arguments suggest that improving working conditions beyond the level required by the law *and* necessary to maximize employee productivity will reduce profits and are therefore not appropriate. His belief is that a firm should maximize its profits because that is the way to maximize the returns that accrue to the owners of the firm, its shareholders. If shareholders then wish to use the proceeds to make social investments, that is their right, according to Friedman, but managers of the firm should not make that decision for them.

Although Friedman is talking about social responsibility, rather than business ethics per se, most business ethics scholars equate social responsibility with ethical behaviour, and thus believe Friedman is also arguing against business ethics. However, the assumption that Friedman is arguing against ethics is not quite true, for Friedman does state,

> [T]here is one and only one social responsibility of business—to use its resources and engage in activities designed to increase its profits so long as it stays within the rules of the game, which is to say that it engages in open and free competition without deception or fraud.[23]

In other words, Friedman states that businesses should behave in an ethical manner and not engage in deception and fraud.

CULTURAL RELATIVISM

Another straw man often raised by business ethics scholars is **cultural relativism**, which is the belief that ethics are nothing more than the reflection of a culture—all ethics are culturally determined—and that accordingly, a firm should adopt the ethics of the culture in which it is operating.[24] This approach is often summarized by the maxim *when in Rome do as the Romans do.* As with Friedman's approach, cultural relativism does not stand up to a closer look. At its extreme, cultural relativism suggests that if a culture supports slavery, it is okay to use slave labour in a country. Clearly it is not. Cultural relativism implicitly rejects the idea that universal notions of morality transcend different cultures. As we shall argue later in the chapter, some universal notions of morality are found across cultures.

While dismissing cultural relativism in its most sweeping form, some ethicists argue there is residual value in this approach.[25] As noted in Chapter 3, societal values and norms do vary from culture to culture, customs do differ, so it might follow that certain business practices are ethical in one country, but not another. Indeed, the facilitating payments allowed in the U.S. Foreign Corrupt Practices Act can be seen as an acknowledgement that, in some countries, the payment of speed money to government officials is necessary to get business done, and if not ethically desirable, it is at least ethically acceptable.

However, not all ethicists or companies agree with this pragmatic view. For example, oil company BP explicitly states it will not make facilitating payments, no matter what the prevailing cultural norms are. In 2002, BP enacted a zero-tolerance policy for facilitation payments, primarily on the basis that such payments are a low-level form of corruption, and thus cannot be justified because corruption corrupts both the bribe giver and the bribe taker, and perpetuates the corrupt system. As BP notes on its Web site, as a result of its zero-tolerance policy:

> We operate in some of the world's highest-risk countries from an anti-bribery and corruption perspective.
>
> Our code of conduct explicitly prohibits engaging in bribery and corruption in any form. We have a responsibility to our employees, our shareholders and to the countries and communities in which we do business to be ethical and lawful in our work. . . .
>
> We expect our suppliers to comply with laws and act consistently with our code's principles. Our contracts with suppliers make these expectations clear.
>
> We also carry out checks once contracts are in place. For example, for a number of suppliers in higher-risk regions, our upstream business conducts audits to assess their compliance with our anti-bribery and corruption contractual requirements.
>
> Potential areas for improvement identified by the audits are shared with the suppliers and we often work with them to find the best ways to strengthen their procedures. The learnings from these audits help to reduce risk to both BP and our suppliers.[26]

BP's experience suggests that companies should not use cultural relativism as an argument for justifying behaviour that is clearly based upon suspect ethical grounds, even if that behaviour is both legal and routinely accepted in the country where the company is doing business.

THE RIGHTEOUS MORALIST

A **righteous moralist** claims that a multinational's home-country standards of ethics are the appropriate ones for companies to follow in foreign countries. This approach is typically associated with managers from developed nations. While this seems reasonable at first blush, the approach can create problems. Consider the following example. A North American bank manager was sent to Italy and was appalled to learn that the local branch's accounting department recommended grossly under-reporting the bank's profits for income tax purposes.[27] The manager insisted that the bank report its earnings accurately, North American–style. When he was called by the Italian tax department to the firm's tax hearing, he was told the firm owed three times as much tax as it had paid, reflecting the department's standard assumption that each firm under-reports its earnings by two-thirds. Despite his protests, the new assessment stood. In this case, the righteous moralist has run into a problem caused by the prevailing cultural norms in the country where he is doing business. How should he respond? The righteous moralist would argue for maintaining the position, while a more pragmatic view might be that in this case, the right thing to do is to follow the prevailing cultural norms because there is a big penalty for not doing so.

The main criticism of the righteous moralist approach is that its proponents go too far. While there are some universal moral principles that should not be violated, it does not always follow that the appropriate thing to do is adopt home-country standards. For example, Canadian laws set down strict guidelines with regard to minimum wage and working conditions. Does this mean it is ethical to apply the same guidelines in a foreign country, paying people the same as they are paid in Canada, providing the same benefits and working conditions? Probably not, because doing so might nullify the reason for investing in that country and therefore deny locals the benefits of inward investment by the multinational. Clearly, a more nuanced approach is needed.

THE NAIVE IMMORALIST

A **naive immoralist** asserts that if a manager of a multinational sees that firms from other nations are not following ethical norms in a host nation, that manager should not either. The classic example to illustrate the approach is known as the drug lord problem. In one variant of this problem, a Canadian mine manager in Congo routinely pays off the local tribal chief to guarantee that his plant will not be sabotaged and that none of his employees will be kidnapped. The manager argues that such payments are ethically defensible because everyone is doing it.

The objection is twofold. First, to simply say that an action is ethically justified if everyone is doing it is not sufficient. If firms in a country routinely employ 12-year-olds and make them work ten-hour days, is it therefore ethically defensible to do the same? Obviously not, and the company does have a clear choice. It does not have to abide by local practices, and it can decide not to invest in a country where the practices are particularly odious. Second, the multinational must recognize that it does have the ability to change the prevailing practice in a country. It can use its power for a positive moral purpose. This is what BP is doing by adopting a zero-tolerance policy with regard to facilitating payments. BP is stating that the prevailing practice of making facilitating payments in countries such as India is ethically wrong, and it is incumbent upon the company to use its power to try to change the standard. While some might argue that such an approach smells of moral imperialism and a lack of cultural sensitivity, if it is consistent with widely accepted moral standards in the global community, it may be ethically justified.

To return to the mine in Congo problem, an argument can be made that it is ethically defensible to make such payments, not because everyone else is doing so but because not doing so would cause greater harm (i.e., the tribal chief might seek retribution and engage in killings and kidnappings). Another solution to the problem is to refuse to invest in a country where the rule of law is so weak that tribal chiefs can demand protection money. This solution, however, is also imperfect, for it might mean denying the law-abiding citizens of that country the benefits associated with inward investment by the multinational (i.e., jobs, income, greater economic growth and welfare). Clearly, the tribal chief problem constitutes one of those intractable ethical dilemmas where there is no obvious right solution, and managers need a moral compass to help them find an acceptable solution to the dilemma.

Rights Theories

Developed in the twentieth century, **rights theories** recognize that human beings have fundamental rights and privileges that transcend national boundaries and cultures. Rights establish a minimum level of morally acceptable behaviour. One well-known definition of a fundamental right construes it as something that takes precedence over or "trumps" a collective good. Thus, we might say that the right to free speech is a fundamental right that takes precedence over all but the most compelling collective goals and overrides, for example, the interest of the state in civil harmony or moral consensus.[28] Moral theorists argue that fundamental human rights form the basis for the *moral compass* that managers should navigate by when making decisions that have an ethical component. More precisely, they should not pursue actions that violate these rights.

The notion that there are fundamental rights that transcend national borders and cultures was the underlying motivation for the United Nations **Universal Declaration of Human Rights**, which has been ratified by almost every country on the planet and lays down basic principles that should always be adhered to irrespective of the culture in which one is doing business.[29] Article 1 of this declaration states:

> Article 1: All human beings are born free and equal in dignity and rights. They are endowed with reason and conscience and should act towards one another in a spirit of brotherhood.

> Article 23 of this declaration, which relates directly to employment, states:

> 1. Everyone has the right to work, to free choice of employment, to just and favourable conditions of work, and to protection against unemployment.
> 2. Everyone, without any discrimination, has the right to equal pay for equal work.
> 3. Everyone who works has the right to just and favourable remuneration ensuring for himself and his family an existence worthy of human dignity, and supplemented, if necessary, by other means of social protection.
> 4. Everyone has the right to form and to join trade unions for the protection of his interests.

Clearly, the rights to "just and favourable work conditions," "equal pay for equal work," and remuneration that ensures an "existence worthy of human dignity" embodied in Article 23 imply that it is unethical to employ child labour in sweatshop settings and pay less than subsistence wages, even if that happens to be common practice in some countries. These are fundamental human rights that transcend national borders.

It is important to note that along with *rights* come *obligations*. Because we have the right to free speech, we are also obligated to make sure that we respect the free speech of others. The notion that people have obligations is stated in Article 29 of the Universal Declaration of Human Rights:

> Article 29: Everyone has duties to the community in which alone the free and full development of his personality is possible.

Within the framework of a theory of rights, certain people or institutions are obligated to provide benefits or services that secure the rights of others. Such obligations also fall upon more than one class of moral agent (a moral agent is any person or institution that is capable of moral action, such as a government or corporation).

For example, to escape the high costs of toxic waste disposal in the West, in the late 1980s several firms shipped their waste in bulk to African nations, where it was disposed of at a much lower cost. In 1987, five European ships unloaded toxic waste containing dangerous poisons in Nigeria. Workers wearing sandals and shorts unloaded the barrels for $2.50 a day and placed them in a dirt lot in a residential area. They were not told about the contents of the barrels.[30] Who bears the obligation for protecting the rights of workers and residents to safety in a case like this? According to rights theorists, the obligation rests not on the shoulders of one moral agent, but on the shoulders of all moral agents whose actions might harm or contribute to the harm of the workers and residents. Thus, it was the obligation not just of the Nigerian government but also of the multinational firms that shipped the toxic waste to make sure it did no harm to residents and workers. In this case, both the government and the multinationals apparently failed to recognize their basic obligation to protect the fundamental human rights of others.

Justice Theories

Justice theories focus on the attainment of a just distribution of economic goods and services. A **just distribution** is one that is considered fair and equitable. There is no one theory of justice, and several theories of justice conflict with each other in important ways.[31] Here we shall focus on one particular theory of justice that is both influential and has important ethical implications. The theory is attributed to philosopher John Rawls.[32] Rawls argues that all economic goods and services should be distributed equally except when an unequal distribution would work to everyone's advantage.

According to Rawls, valid principles of justice are those with which all persons would agree if they could freely and impartially consider the situation. Impartiality is guaranteed by a conceptual device that Rawls calls the *veil of ignorance*. Under the veil of ignorance, everyone is imagined to be ignorant of all of his or her particular characteristics, for example, race, sex, intelligence, nationality, family background, and special talents. Rawls then asks what system people would design under a veil of ignorance. Under these conditions, people would unanimously agree on two fundamental principles of justice.

DEBATE THE ISSUE

Ethical Analysis: *In a Different Voice*

In addition to utilitarian, rights, and justice approaches to business ethics, Carol Gilligan offers another way to think about our moral actions. Gilligan suggests we view our actions as a series of caring relationships that evolve over time, focused first on the self, then on dependent others, and, finally, on establishing equality of needs between self and others so that dynamic relationships can replace dependent ones. Do you think that such an approach (self, dependent other, dynamic equality) may be a helpful way of thinking about a multinational's evolving corporate involvement in a developing country?

Source: Carol Gilligan, 1982, *In a Different Voice.*

The first principle is that each person be permitted the maximum amount of basic liberty compatible with a similar liberty for others. Rawls takes these to be political liberty (e.g., the right to vote), freedom of speech and assembly, liberty of conscience and freedom of thought, the freedom and right to hold personal property, and freedom from arbitrary arrest and seizure.

The second principle is that once equal basic liberty is assured, inequality in basic social goods—such as income and wealth distribution, and opportunities—is to be allowed *only* if such inequalities benefit everyone. Rawls accepts that inequalities can be just if the system that produces inequalities is to the advantage of everyone. More precisely, he formulates what he calls the *difference principle,* which is that inequalities are justified if they benefit the position of the least-advantaged person. So, for example, wide variations in income and wealth can be considered just if the market-based system that produces this unequal distribution also benefits the least-advantaged members of society. One can argue that a well-regulated, market-based economy and free trade, by promoting economic growth, benefits the least-advantaged members of society. In principle at least, the inequalities inherent in such systems are therefore just (in other words, the rising tide of wealth created by a market-based economy and free trade lifts all boats, even those of the most disadvantaged).

In the context of international business ethics, Rawls' theory creates an interesting perspective. Managers could ask themselves whether the policies they adopt in foreign operations would be considered just under Rawls' veil of ignorance. Is it just, for example, to pay foreign workers less than workers in the firm's home country? Rawls' theory would suggest it is, so long as the inequality benefits the least-advantaged members of the global society (which is what economic theory suggests). Alternatively, it is difficult to imagine that managers operating under a veil of ignorance would design a system where foreign employees were paid subsistence wages to work long hours in sweatshop conditions and where they were exposed to toxic materials. Such working conditions are clearly unjust in Rawls' framework, and therefore, it is unethical to adopt them. Similarly, operating under a veil of ignorance, most people would probably design a system that imparts some protection from environmental degradation to important global commons, such as the oceans, atmosphere, and tropical rain forests. To the extent that this is the case, it follows that it is unjust, and by extension unethical, for companies to pursue actions that contribute toward extensive degradation of these commons. Thus, Rawls' veil of ignorance is a conceptual tool that contributes to the moral compass that managers can use to help them navigate through difficult ethical dilemmas.

LO5 Ethical Decision Making

What then is the best way for managers in a multinational firm to make sure that ethical considerations figure into international business decisions? How do managers decide upon an ethical course of action when confronted with decisions pertaining to working conditions, human rights, corruption, and environmental pollution? From an ethical perspective, how do managers determine the moral obligations that flow from the power of a multinational? In many cases, there are no easy answers to these questions, for many of the most vexing ethical problems arise because there are very real dilemmas inherent in them and no obvious correct action. Nevertheless, managers can and should do many things to make sure that basic ethical principles are adhered to and that ethical issues are routinely inserted into international business decisions.

Before proceeding to discuss five things that an international business and its managers can do to make sure ethical issues are considered in business decisions, it is useful to explain an overall reason why managers should consider ethics—namely "morale." As noted earlier in this chapter, the intense competitive environment of international business challenges employers to increase productivity so they can make more products with fewer resources. Fewer resources includes fewer people—which means increasing productivity of the employees. A key part of increasing the productivity of employees is enhancing morale so that employees feel motivated to work under more stressful conditions. If a company behaves in an unethical way to employees, customers, or suppliers, this will jeopardize morale and negatively affect productivity. Put simply, if your company does not "do the right thing," your employees with be disgruntled and your competitiveness will decline.

There are five things that an international business and its managers can do to make sure ethical issues are considered in business decisions:

1. Favour hiring and promoting people with a well-grounded sense of personal ethics.
2. Build an organizational culture that places a high value on ethical behaviour.
3. Make sure that leaders within the business not only articulate the rhetoric of ethical behaviour, but also act in a manner that is consistent with that rhetoric.
4. Put decision-making processes in place that require people to consider the ethical dimension of business decisions.
5. Develop moral courage.

Hiring and Promotion

It seems obvious that businesses should strive to hire people who have a strong sense of personal ethics and would not engage in unethical or illegal behaviour. Similarly, you would rightly expect a business to not promote people, and perhaps to fire people, whose behaviour does not match generally accepted ethical standards. But actually doing so is very difficult. How do you know that someone has a poor sense of personal ethics? In our society, we have an incentive to hide a lack of personal ethics from public view. Once people realize that you are unethical, they will no longer trust you.

Is there anything that businesses can do to make sure they do not hire people who subsequently turn out to have poor personal ethics, particularly given that people have an incentive to hide this from public view (indeed, the unethical person may lie about his or her nature)? Businesses can give potential employees psychological tests to try to discern their ethical predisposition, and they can check with prior employers regarding someone's reputation (e.g., by asking for letters of reference and talking to people who have worked with the prospective employee). The latter is common and does influence the hiring process. Promoting people who have displayed poor ethics should not occur in a company where the organization culture values the need for ethical behaviour and where leaders act accordingly.

Not only should businesses strive to identify and hire people with a strong sense of personal ethics, but it also is in the interests of prospective employees to find out as much as they can about the ethical climate in an organization. Who wants to work at a multinational such as Enron, which ultimately entered bankruptcy because unethical executives had established risky partnerships that were hidden from public view and that existed in part to enrich those same executives? Table 4.1 lists some questions job seekers might want to ask a prospective employer.

TABLE 4.1	A Job Seeker's Ethics Audit

Some probing questions to ask about a prospective employer:

1. Is there a formal code of ethics? How widely is it distributed? Is it reinforced in other formal ways such as through decision-making systems?
2. Are workers at all levels trained in ethical decision making? Are they also encouraged to take responsibility for their behaviour or to question authority when asked to do something they consider wrong?
3. Do employees have formal channels available to make their concerns known confidentially? Is there a formal committee high in the organization that considers ethical issues?
4. Is misconduct disciplined swiftly and justly within the organization?
5. Is integrity emphasized to new employees?
6. How are senior managers perceived by subordinates in terms of their integrity? How do such leaders model ethical behaviour?

Source: Linda K. Trevino, chair of the Department of Management and Organization, Smeal College of Business, Pennsylvania State University. Reported in K. Maher, "Career Journal. Wanted: Ethical Employer," *The Wall Street Journal*, July 9, 2002, p. B1. Reprinted with permission of *The Wall Street Journal*, Copyright © 2002 Dow Jones & Company, Inc. All Rights Reserved Worldwide. License numbers 4096670748633 and 4096670860533.

Organizational Culture and Leadership

To foster ethical behaviour, businesses need to build an organization culture that values ethical behaviour. Three things are particularly important in building an organization culture that emphasizes ethical behaviour. First, the businesses must explicitly articulate values that emphasize ethical behaviour. Many companies now do this by drafting a **code of ethics**, which is a formal statement of the ethical priorities a business adheres to. Often, the code of ethics draws heavily upon documents such as the U.N. Universal Declaration of Human Rights, which itself is grounded in Kantian and rights-based theories of moral philosophy. Others have incorporated ethical statements into documents that articulate the values or mission of the business. For example, the Canadian Marketing Association has a code of ethics to which all association members must adhere to. The Code of Ethics, displayed on the CMA Web site at www.the-cma.org, is written in language that adheres to existing provincial and federal regulations governing human rights, privacy, and ethics. For example:

H3.1 Marketers must not participate in any campaign involving the disparagement or exploitation of any person or group on the grounds of race, colour, ethnicity, religion, national origin, gender, sexual orientation, marital status or age.

N3.4 Unlisted Numbers: Marketers must not knowingly call any consumer or business who has an unlisted or unpublished telephone number, except where the telephone number was furnished by the consumer or business to that marketer, or by a third-party with the consumer's consent.

Note the CMA's refusal to disparage any person or group, a statement that is grounded in Kantian ethics. The CMA's principles send a very clear message about appropriate ethics to managers and employees.

Having articulated values in a code of ethics or some other document, leaders in the business must give life and meaning to those words by repeatedly emphasizing their importance *and then acting on them*. This means using every relevant opportunity to stress the importance of business ethics and making sure that key business decisions not only make good economic sense but also are ethical. Many companies have gone a step further, hiring independent auditors to make sure they are behaving in a manner consistent with their ethical codes. Hudson's Bay Company (HBC), for example, has hired independent auditors to make sure that suppliers used by the company are living up to HBC's code of conduct for vendors.

Decision-Making Processes

In addition to establishing the right kind of ethical culture in an organization, business people must be able to think through the ethical implications of decisions in a systematic way. To do this, they need a moral compass, and both rights theories and Rawls' theory of justice help to provide such a compass. Beyond these theories, some experts on ethics have proposed a straightforward practical guide—or ethical algorithm—to determine whether a decision is ethical.[33] According to these experts, a decision is acceptable on ethical grounds if a business person can answer yes to each of these questions:

1. Does my decision fall within the accepted values or standards that typically apply in the organizational environment (as articulated in a code of ethics or some other corporate statement)?
2. Am I willing to see the decision communicated to all stakeholders affected by it—for example, by having it reported in newspapers or on television?
3. Would the people with whom I have a significant personal relationship, such as family members, friends, or even managers in other businesses, approve of the decision?

Others have recommended a five-step process to think through ethical problems (this is another example of an ethical algorithm).[34]

STEP 1

In Step 1, business people should identify which stakeholders a decision would affect and in what ways. A firm's **stakeholders** are individuals or groups that have an interest, claim, or stake in the company, in what it does, and in how well it performs.[35] They can be divided into internal stakeholders and external stakeholders. **Internal stakeholders** are individuals or groups who work for or own the business. They include all employees, the board of directors, and shareholders. **External stakeholders** are all other individuals and groups that have some claim on the firm. Typically, this group comprises customers, suppliers, lenders, governments, unions, local communities, and the general public.

All stakeholders are in an exchange relationship with the company. Each stakeholder group supplies the organization with important resources (or contributions), and in exchange each expects its interests to be satisfied (by inducements).[36] For example, employees provide labour, skills, knowledge, and time and in exchange expect commensurate income, job satisfaction, job security, and good working conditions. Customers provide a company with its revenues and in exchange they want quality products that represent value for money. Communities provide businesses with local infrastructure and in exchange they want businesses that are responsible citizens and seek some assurance that the quality of life will be improved as a result of the business firm's existence.

Stakeholder analysis involves a certain amount of what has been called *moral imagination*.[37] This means standing in the shoes of a stakeholder and asking how a proposed decision might impact that stakeholder. For example, when considering outsourcing to subcontractors, managers might need to ask themselves how it might feel to be working under substandard health conditions for long hours.

ANOTHER PERSPECTIVE

Stakeholders

This text describes stakeholders as ". . . individuals or groups that have an interest, stake, or claim in the actions and overall performance of a company." Many business textbooks use the term stakeholders and it is commonly used among business people to describe the persons who "have a stake" in the company. . . . But where does the term come from? It comes from the practice of prospecting for a mine.

In Canada's Yukon during the 1890s, people who went out into the bush looking for a vein of gold were called prospectors. Retired Queen's Professor George Richardson explains that these prospectors would pan for gold sitting by a stream, and dig in the rock and soil looking for glints of the precious yellow metal and if they came across an area which looked promising, they would take wooden stakes and "stake their claim."

Richardson, who taught mining history, adds that the next step for prospectors would be to go to the local government office and have the details of their claim (location, date) registered in their name so that they could later proceed to mine the property and they would be given a legal right to do so without other people infringing on their territory.

Source: Interview with George Richardson.

STEP 2

Step 2 involves judging the ethics of the proposed strategic decision, given the information gained in Step 1. Managers need to determine whether a proposed decision would violate the *fundamental rights* of any stakeholders. For example, we might argue that the right to information about health risks in the workplace is a fundamental entitlement of employees. Similarly, the right to know about potentially dangerous features of a product is a fundamental entitlement of customers (something tobacco companies violated when they did not reveal to their customers what they knew about the health risks of smoking). Managers might also want to ask themselves whether they would allow the proposed strategic decision if they were designing a system under Rawls' veil of ignorance. For example, if the issue under consideration was whether to outsource work to a subcontractor with low pay and poor working conditions, managers might want to ask themselves whether they would allow for such action if they were considering it under a veil of ignorance, where they themselves might ultimately be the ones to work for the subcontractor.

The judgment at this stage should be guided by various moral principles that should not be violated. The principles might be those articulated in a corporate code of ethics or other company documents. In addition, certain moral principles that we have adopted as members of society—for instance, the prohibition on stealing—should not be violated. The judgment at this stage will also be guided by the decision rule that is chosen to assess the proposed strategic decision. Although maximizing long-run profitability is the decision rule that most businesses stress, it should be applied subject to the constraint that no moral principles are violated—that the business behaves in an ethical manner.

STEP 3

Step 3 requires managers to establish moral intent. This means the business must resolve to place moral concerns ahead of other concerns in cases where either the fundamental rights of stakeholders or key moral principles have been violated. At this stage, input from top management might be particularly valuable. Without the proactive encouragement of top managers, middle-level managers might tend to place the narrow economic interests of the company before the interests of stakeholders. They might do so in the (usually erroneous) belief that top managers favour such an approach.

STEP 4

Step 4 requires the company to engage in ethical behaviour based on the outcomes of the previous steps.

STEP 5

Step 5 requires the business to audit its decisions, reviewing them to make sure they were consistent with ethical principles, such as those stated in the company's code of ethics. This final step is critical and often overlooked. Without auditing past decisions, business people may not know if their decision process is working and if changes should be made to ensure greater compliance with a code of ethics.

ETHICS OFFICERS

To make sure that a business behaves in an ethical manner, a number of firms now have ethics officers. These individuals are responsible for making sure that all employees are trained to be ethically aware, that ethical considerations enter the business decision-making process, and that the company's code of ethics is adhered to. Ethics officers may also be responsible for auditing decisions to make sure they are consistent with this code. In many businesses, ethics officers act as an internal ombudsperson with responsibility for handling confidential inquiries from employees, investigating complaints from employees or others, reporting findings, and making recommendations for change.

NovaGold Resources Inc., a Vancouver-based Canadian mining company, devotes particular attention to their "Code of Business Conduct & Ethics" on the company Web site at www.novagold.com. NovaGold explains that one of the reasons for publicly posting their ethics code is because "[o]ur business is becoming increasingly complex, both in terms of the geographies in which we function and the laws with which we must comply." NovaGold, like many Canadian mining companies, has designated a specific person (their corporate Controller) within the senior executive team to handle ethics complaints and deal with public relations matters on ethical issues.

Moral Courage

Finally, it is important to recognize that employees in an international business may need significant *moral courage*. Moral courage enables managers to walk away from a decision that is profitable, but unethical. Moral courage gives an employee the strength to say no to a superior who instructs her to pursue actions that are unethical. And moral courage gives employees the integrity to go public to the media and blow the whistle on persistent unethical behaviour in a company. This moral courage does not come easily; there are well-known cases where individuals have lost their jobs because they blew the whistle on corporate behaviours they thought unethical, telling the media about what was occurring.[38]

However, companies can strengthen the moral courage of employees by committing themselves to not retaliate against employees who exercise moral courage, say no to superiors, or otherwise complain about unethical actions. For example, consider the following extract from Unilever's Code of Business Principles:

> Unilever is committed to a working environment that promotes diversity and equal opportunity and where there is mutual trust, respect for human rights and no discrimination....

Any breaches of the Code must be reported. The Board of Unilever will not criticise management for any loss of business resulting from adherence to these principles and other mandatory policies. Provision has been made for employees to be able to report in confidence and no employee will suffer as a consequence of doing so.[39]

Clearly this statement gives permission to employees to exercise moral courage. Companies can also set up ethics hotlines, which allow employees to anonymously register a complaint with a corporate ethics officer.

Summary of Decision-Making Steps

All of the steps discussed here—hiring and promoting people based upon ethical considerations as well as more traditional metrics of performance, establishing an ethical culture in the organization, instituting ethical decision-making processes, appointing ethics officers, and creating an environment that facilitates moral courage—can help to make sure that when making business decisions, managers are cognizant of the ethical implications and do not violate basic ethical prescripts. At the same time, it must be recognized that not all ethical dilemmas have a clean and obvious solution—that is why they are dilemmas. There are clearly things that international businesses should not do and there are things that they should do but there are also actions that present managers with true dilemmas. In these cases, a premium is placed on managers' ability to make sense out of complex situations and make balanced decisions that are as just as possible.

Ethical Decisions and Approaches to Corporate Social Responsibility

Corporate social responsibility (also referred to as CSR) is a term that has been used since the 1960s. It has taken on special significance in the age of social media and "citizen journalists," where the problems and difficulties of a company's operations can be exposed on a large scale in a very short period of time. Without a clear understanding of a corporation's social responsibility, any exposed issues in a competitive environment could have shareholders dumping stock and force some serious public relations work.

The concept of **corporate social responsibility** refers to the idea that business people should consider the social consequences of economic actions when making business decisions, and that there should be a presumption in favour of decisions that have both good economic and social consequences.[40]

CSR, also known as sustainably responsible business, social performance, corporate social performance, corporate citizenship, corporate conscience, and other variations and combinations, is a way that companies self-regulate their interactions with customers, suppliers, government, and employees to ensure that they are seen to be in compliance with the social-cultural environment and the political-legal-regulatory environment in the different geographic areas in which they operate.

CSR Moral Obligations

Multinational corporations have power that comes from their control over resources and their ability to move production from country to country. Although that power is constrained not only by laws and regulations, but also by the discipline of the market and the competitive process, it is nevertheless substantial. Some moral philosophers argue that with power comes the social responsibility for multinationals to give something back to the societies that enable them to prosper and grow. In its purest form, corporate social responsibility can be supported for its own sake simply because it is the right way for a business to behave. Advocates of this approach argue that businesses, particularly large successful businesses, need to recognize their *noblesse oblige* and give something back to the societies that have made their success possible. *Noblesse oblige* is a French term that refers to honourable and benevolent behaviour considered the responsibility of people of high (noble) birth. In a business setting, it is taken to mean benevolent behaviour that is the responsibility of successful enterprises. This has long been recognized by many business people, resulting in a substantial and venerable history of corporate giving to society and in businesses making social investments designed to enhance the welfare of the communities in which they operate.

In discussing how managers of companies, associations, and government agencies address CSR in terms of reaction to public relations incidents and circumstances made known in social media there are four common terms used.

The **obstructionist stance** is when an enterprise (company, trade association, or government agency) makes it difficult for customers (or journalists) to effectively complain about some unethical situation. For example, companies that are obstructionist require excessive paperwork to be completed before the complainant can obtain information. Obstructionist associations may deny they have authority to release information to an individual or a journalist by claiming the matter is covered by a privacy regulation. Companies and government agencies that are obstructionist may use stalling tactics and delay responding to a request in the hopes that they can "out wait" the person seeking information. Companies adopting an obstructionist response may also cite the "technological environment" and claim that the information requested is not available due to hardware or software problem, or they may cite "legacy software issues" or software incompatibility with a recent IT upgrade.

An example of the obstructionist stance occurred in 2010, when the CEO of Toyota in Japan was brought to the United States to testify to a congressional inquiry about many Toyota vehicles that had crashed, causing death and injury.

Prof. Tim Richardson was interviewed by BNN about the Toyota situation and a discussion of how Toyota reacted to the allegations. Richardson, who previously lived in Japan and is the former Executive Director of the Canada-Japan Trade Council, explained that the social-cultural environment is different in Japan and when a well-known corporate CEO is challenged by the media about some ethical situation the Japanese reaction is more shame oriented than guilt oriented. At the time the U.S. authorities were investigating the details, Toyota representatives in the U.S. and Japan were reported as avoiding providing details so that a true analysis could not be made of how the crashes were caused and a repair or recall could not be initiated.

When Richardson was interviewed on BNN in February 2010, he revealed that one of the

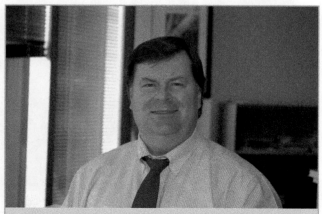

Prof. Tim Richardson spoke on BNN about the Toyota recall.
Courtesy of Prof. Tim Richardson

issues challenging the U.S. authorities was that the black box (properly termed the *event data recorder*) in the vehicles contained data that was encrypted. Toyota subsequently released the code information to the U.S. authorities.

The **defensive stance** is not as blatantly confrontational as the obstructionist stance, but it is still a negative response. Companies that adopt a defensive stance often respond to complaints with "it wasn't our fault." Another defensive tactic is to try to make the customer believe nothing can be done at all—that the problem is just too unsurmountable. Corporate managers who are encouraged to employ the defensive stance sometimes adopt this reaction based on their perception that their job is to make money for the company and that anything that distracts them from that achieving that objective is secondary. The defensive stance is often found in medium- and large-sized consumer products companies, where promotion is based on the bottom line of sales increases.

ANOTHER PERSPECTIVE

Corporate Social Responsibility Index

One of the indicators of how serious the concept of corporate social responsibility is taken is the prevalence of this term on the corporate Web sites of medium- and large-sized firms in Canada. Most of the major banks and consumer product companies have a section noting specific policies and actions the firm has taken to address corporate responsibilities in a social context in the communities in which the company operates. Royal Bank, perennially Canada's largest financial institution and one of the most profitable, has a complete section on its corporate Web site devoted to corporate social responsibility, noting that in recent years it ranked # 1 on the annual *Report on Business* listing. Canadian auto parts giant Magna describes their corporate social responsibility in terms of Community Activities, Environmental, and Health & Safety.

BlackBerry, like many tech companies, is often pressured to attend to matters of environmental considerations, ethics, and local community concerns. On BlackBerry's Web site (2013) they say that "it is important to give back to the local, national, and global communities in which we operate," a phrase echoed on many of the Web sites of companies lauding their corporate social responsibility activities.

Sources: RBC, Community & Sustainability, http://www.rbc.com/community-sustainability/, accessed June 9, 2017; Blackberry, Corporate Citizenship, http://ca.blackberry.com/company/about-us/corporate-responsibility/corporate-philanthropy.html, accessed June 9, 2017.

Royal Bank's sign at Spadina and Dundas, similar to the other banks on the other corners, reflects the social-cultural environment of the area. *Courtesy of Prof. Tim Richardson*

Companies also take the defensive stance when they obey the law to the exact letter but do not take fairness or compassion into account. Take, for example, situations where travel agencies and airlines go bankrupt and leave vacationing people stranded in a foreign destination. Depending on how the situation developed (perhaps if there was a corporate takeover or bankruptcy), the executives may not be required by law to help stranded vacationers, but morally they should stop selling tickets immediately before an event happens that could strand passengers far from home.

The **accommodative stance** is exhibited by firms that not only meet the standards expected, but go further. By exceeding customer expectations when responding to a problem, companies often receive the reward of repeat customer purchases and good public relations. This helps a company's brand in a competitive environment, particularly now that social media can also be helpful to a company. Some examples of being accommodative include companies allowing customers to exchange items for products that are not exactly the same, but similar, or allowing customers to return items for warranty even if they do not have the original receipt.

Companies that understand customer relationship management (CRM) and customer lifetime value (CLV) in an intense competitive environment appreciate that growing your business is sometimes less about market penetration than it is about market development—the distinction being that market penetration means simply gaining a greater number of customers whereas market development means making more money from each customer through repeat business and through upselling and cross-selling. One of the keys to successfully accomplishing market development is to have an accommodative stance when dealing with customer complaints and publicity issues.

The **proactive stance**, as the name suggests, is when companies, associations, and government agencies proactively reach out to customers, members, and citizens to tell them in advance when something has happened. They also explain how they will respond to mitigate any negative effects and keep operations and activities operational to the extent that emergency resources may allow.

An example of the proactive stance would be reaching out to customers to tell them in advance some information they need—such as letting a customer know that warranty period may expire several weeks in advance, or that a product will soon be withdrawn so they have the option to buy spare parts. A "proactive stance" (on a small scale) adopted by Telus is to let customers know how much data they have used as the month progresses so they do not surpass the limits of their data plan and incur additional charges. Allowing the customer to keep track of their phone usage protects Telus from having to respond to irate customers who receive bill amounts much higher than they expected.

IMPLICATIONS FOR BUSINESS

The material in this chapter has implications for how managers operate internationally in a globalized economy where advances in Internet-enabled communications and mass media allow worldwide audiences to be instantly aware of events anywhere and anytime. In addition to the "threat" that the technological environment can speedily broadcast news of an unethical situation, companies also have to deal with the consequences of an intensified competitive environment that both creates and worsens situations in which ethics are compromised to produce products and services at lower costs and sold at higher margins. Framing the background is a volatile political environment in which regional and national politicians have to create compromise from increasingly "blended cultures" and the stress that comes from having to accommodate different values and beliefs in a more diverse society.

The managerial implications for attending to ethical considerations put the burden on company executives to not only "do the right thing" but also appear to be doing the right thing for the media. As more and more medium- and small-sized companies "go public" and list their shares on the stock market, ethical issues that get raised in the media can negatively affect shareholder confidence and the subsequent stock price fluctuations may jeopardize the company's finances.

BENEFITS

One of the benefits of a company behaving ethically is the confidence of knowing that when the increasingly sophisticated consumer discovers some unethical circumstances within your competition, your product and your firm can withstand any subsequent scrutiny that may come with the global media seeking out other instances within the sector.

COSTS

It is being said these days that to succeed in business is not necessarily a matter of doing things well, but rather being in a position to handle the consequences when things do not go well—as inevitably happens. Having a clear conscience regarding the way your company has been handling a sensitive ethical situation in a region of conflict may serve you well when the CBC *National News* does an exposé on the circumstances, where all your competitors are implicated—while your company is praised for the way in which it handled things ethically from the beginning. It may have cost you more to have proper effluent pollution controls in place, or it may have been more expensive to provide special services to workers when other companies didn't, but your company will more than make up for these costs by selling product while your competitors are spending money on high-priced publicity to recover public opinion.

RISKS

Operating in a way that appears to be ethical is not an exact science; sometimes it is a matter of opinion. While bribery of government officials may not be tolerated or may even be illegal in the home country, bribery of government officials may be a natural way that services are rendered in the host country. In circumstances where a national government has a limited corporate tax base, certain government services might be considered on a "user pay" basis. So if somebody wanted special concessions from a regional administrator to allow permits for some activity to take place, it might be considered perfectly acceptable to directly pay that administrator a "bonus" for handling the required paperwork in a timely fashion. The risk you take is proportionate to the nature of the activity and unfortunately, there is no Manual that can be referenced to see if certain activities are ethically acceptable in the broader scheme of things. There is also the risk that media interpretation (should they find out there was a "bonus") might be broadcast in a way that does not include an understanding of the cultural or political environment, so perceptions might be twisted out of context.

Key Terms

accommodative stance

business ethics

code of ethics

Convention on Combating Bribery of Foreign Public Officials in International Business Transactions

corporate social responsibility

cultural relativism

defensive stance

ethical dilemma

ethical strategy

external stakeholders

internal stakeholders

just distribution

naive immoralist

obstructionist stance

organization culture

proactive stance

righteous moralist

rights theories

stakeholder

Universal Declaration of Human Rights

LO Learning Objectives Summary

This chapter has discussed the source and nature of ethical issues in international businesses, the different philosophical approaches to business ethics, and the steps managers can take to ensure that ethical issues are respected in international business decisions. The chapter made these points:

1. The term *ethics* refers to accepted principles of right or wrong that govern the conduct of a person, the members of a profession, or the actions of an organization. Business ethics are the accepted principles of right or wrong governing the conduct of business people, and an ethical strategy is one that does not violate these accepted principles. The most common ethical issues in international business involve employment practices, human rights, environmental regulations, corruption, and the moral obligation of multinational corporations.

2. The question of managers behaving ethically on behalf of their company is understood to be something that cannot be divorced from personal ethics. Home-country managers working abroad in multinational firms (expatriate managers) may experience more than the usual degree of pressure to violate their personal ethics.

3. Ethical issues and dilemmas in international business are rooted in the variations among political systems, law, economic development, and culture from country to country. Unethical behaviour is rooted in poor personal ethics, the psychological and geographical distances of a foreign subsidiary from the home office, a failure to incorporate ethical issues into strategic and operational decision making, a dysfunctional culture, and failure of leaders to act in an ethical manner.

4. Ethical dilemmas are situations in which none of the available alternatives seems ethically acceptable. Moral philosophers contend that approaches to business ethics such as the Friedman doctrine, cultural relativism, the righteous moralist, and the naive immoralist are unsatisfactory in important ways. The Friedman doctrine states that the only social responsibility of business is to increase profits, as long as the company stays within the rules of law. Cultural relativism contends that one should adopt the ethics of the culture in which one is doing business. The righteous moralist monolithically applies home-country ethics to a foreign situation, while the naive immoralist believes that if a manager of a multinational sees that firms from other nations are not following ethical norms in a host nation, that manager should not either. Rights theories recognize that human beings have fundamental rights and privileges that transcend national boundaries and cultures. These rights establish a minimum level of morally acceptable behaviour.

5. To make sure that ethical issues are considered in international business decisions, managers should (i) favour hiring and promoting people with a well-grounded sense of personal ethics; (ii) build an organization culture that places a high value on ethical behaviour; (iii) make sure that leaders within the business not only articulate the rhetoric of ethical behaviour, but also act in a manner that is consistent with that rhetoric; (iv) put decision-making processes in place that require people to consider the ethical dimension of business decisions; and (v) be morally courageous and encourage others to do the same.

Critical Thinking and Discussion Questions

1. Review the Management Focus on testing drugs in the developing world and discuss the following questions:
   a. Did Pfizer behave unethically by rushing to take advantage of a Nigerian epidemic to test an experimental drug on sick children? Should the company have proceeded more carefully?
   b. Is it ethical to test an experimental drug on children in emergency settings in the developing world where the overall standard of health care is much lower than in the developed world, and where proper protocols might not be followed?

2. A visiting North American executive finds that a foreign subsidiary in a poor nation has hired a 12-year-old girl to work on a factory floor, in violation of the company's prohibition on child labour. He tells the local manager to replace the child and tell her to go back to school. The local manager tells the North American executive that the child is an orphan with no other means of

support, and she will probably become a street child if she is denied work. What should the North American executive do?

3. Drawing upon John Rawls' concept of the veil of ignorance, develop an ethical code that will (a) guide the decisions of a large oil multinational toward environmental protection, and (b) influence the policies of a clothing company to outsourcing of manufacturing process.

4. Under what conditions is it ethically defensible to outsource production to the developing world where labour costs are lower when such actions also involve laying off long-term employees in the firm's home country?

5. Are facilitating payments ethical?

Research Task globalEDGE™ globaledge.msu.edu

Use the globalEDGE™ site to complete the following exercises:

1. Promoting respect for universal human rights is a central dimension of all countries' foreign policy. As history has repeatedly shown, human rights abuses are everybody's concern. Begun in 1977, the annual Country Reports on Human Rights Practices are designed to assess the state of democracy and human rights around the world, and call attention to violations. Find the annual Country Reports on Human Right Practices, and provide information on how the reports are prepared.

2. The Corruption Perceptions Index (CPI) is a comparative assessment of a country's integrity performance, along with related academic research on corruption. Provide a description of this index and its ranking. Identify the five countries with the lowest and five with the highest CPI scores according to this index.

3. The Canadian federal government and the provincial governments all have Web sites on which ethics, ethical codes, and ethical compliance are discussed. Find the ones for the federal agencies in the context of international business.

CLOSING CASE

ETCH-A-SKETCH ETHICS

The Ohio Art Company is perhaps best known as the producer of one of the top selling toys of all time, the venerable Etch-A-Sketch. More than 100 million of the familiar red rectangular drawing toys have been sold since 1960 when it was invented. The late 1990s, however, became a troubled time for the toy's maker. Confronted with sluggish toy sales, the Ohio Art Company lost money for two years. In December 2000, it made the strategic decision to outsource production of the Etch-A-Sketch toys to Kin Ki Industrial, a leading Chinese toy maker, laying off 100 U.S. workers in the process.

The closure of the Etch-A-Sketch line was not unexpected among employees. The company had already moved the production of other toy lines to China, and most employees knew it was just a matter of time before Etch-A-Sketch went too. Still, the decision was a tough one for the company, which did most of its manufacturing in its home base, the small Ohio town of Bryan (population 8000). As William Killgallon, the CEO of the Ohio Art Company, noted, the employees who made the product "were like family. It was a necessary financial decision we saw coming for some time, and we did it gradually, product by product. But that doesn't mean it's emotionally easy."

In a small town such as Bryan, the cumulative effect of outsourcing to China has been significant. The tax base is eroding from a loss of manufacturing and a population decline. The local paper is full of notices of home foreclosures and auctions. According to former employees, the biggest hole in their lives after Etch-A-Sketch moved came from the death of a community. For many workers, the company was their family, and now that family was gone.

The rationale for the outsourcing was simple enough. Pressured to keep the cost of Etch-A-Sketch under $10 by big retailers such as Walmart and Toys "R" Us, the Ohio Art Company had to get its costs down or lose money. In this case, unionized workers making $1500 a month were replaced by Chinese factory workers who made $75 a month. However, according to Killgallon, the main savings came not from lower wages, but from lower overhead costs for plant, maintenance, electricity, and payroll, and the ability to get out from the soaring costs of providing health benefits to U.S. manufacturing employees.

The choice of Kin Ki as manufacturer for Etch-A-Sketch was easy—the company had been making pocket-sized Etch-A-Sketch toys for nearly a decade and always delivered on cost. To help Kin Ki, the Ohio Art Company shipped some of its best equipment to the company, and it continues to send crucial raw materials, such as aluminum powder, which is hard to get in China.

The story would have ended there had it not been for an exposé in *The New York Times* in December 2003. The *Times* reporter painted a dismal picture of working conditions at the Kin Ki factory that manufactured the Etch-A-Sketch. According to official Kin Ki publications:

> Workers at Kin Ki make a decent salary, rarely work nights or weekends, and often "hang out along the streets, playing Ping Pong and watching TV." They all have work contracts, pensions, and medical benefits. The factory canteen offers tasty food. The dormitories are comfortable.

Not so, according to Joseph Kahn, the *Times* reporter. He alleged that real-world Kin Ki employees, mostly teenage migrants from internal Chinese provinces, work long hours for 40 percent less than the company claims. They are paid 24 cents per hour, below the legal minimum wage of 33 cents an hour in Shenzhen province where Kin Ki is located. Most do not have pensions, medical benefits, or employment contracts. Production starts at 7:30 a.m. and continues until 10 p.m., with breaks only for lunch and dinner. Saturdays and Sundays are treated as normal workdays. This translates into a work week of seven 12-hour days, or 84 hours a week, well above the standard 40-hour week set by authorities in Shenzhen. Local rules also allow for no more than 32 hours of overtime and stipulate that the employees must be paid 1.5 times the standard hourly wage, but Kin Ki's overtime rate is just 1.3 times base pay.

As for the "comfortable dormitories," the workers sleep head to toe in tiny rooms with windows that are covered with chicken wire. To get into and out of the factories, which are surrounded by high walls, workers must enter and leave through a guarded gate. As for the tasty food, it is apparently a mix of boiled vegetables, beans, and rice, with meat or fish served only twice a month.

The workers at Kin Ki have apparently become restless. They went on strike twice in 2003, demanding higher wages and better working conditions. The company responded by raising wages a few cents and allotting an extra dish of food to each worker per day (but still no more meat). However, Kin Ki simultaneously made "fried squid" of two workers who were ringleaders of the strike ("fried squid" is apparently a popular term for dismissal). Johnson Tao, a senior executive at the company, denies that the two ringleaders were dismissed for organizing the strikes. Rather, he noted that they were well-known troublemakers who left the factory of their own accord. Mr. Tao acknowledges the low wages at the company, stating, "I know that I need to increase wages to comply with the law. I have the intention of doing this and will raise all wages in 2004."

Meanwhile, in Ohio, William Killgallon, Ohio Art Company's CEO, stated to the *Times* reporter that he considered Kin Ki's executives to be honest and that he had no knowledge of labour problems there. But he said he intended to visit China soon to make sure "they understand what we expect."

Sources: Joseph Kahn, "Ruse in Toyland: Chinese Workers' Hidden Woe," *The New York Times*, December 7, 2003, pp. A1, A8; Joseph Kahn, "An Ohio Town Is Hard Hit as Leading Industry Moves to China," *The New York Times*, December 7, 2003, p. A8; Carol Hymowitz, "Toy Maker Survives by Moving an Icon from Ohio to China," *The Wall Street Journal*, October 21, 2003, p. B1; and John Seewer, "Etch A Sketch Enters Fourth Decade," *Columbian*, November 22, 2001, p. E3.

Case Discussion Questions

1. Was it ethical of the Ohio Art Company to move production to China? What were the economic and social costs and benefits of this decision? What would have happened if production had not been moved?

2. Assuming that the description of working conditions given in *The New York Times* is correct, is it ethical for the Ohio Art Company to continue using Kin Ki to manufacture Etch-A-Sketch toys?

3. Is it possible, as Mr. Killgallon claims, that the Ohio Art Company had no knowledge of labour problems at Kin Ki? Do you think company executives had any knowledge of the working conditions?

4. What steps can executives at the Ohio Art Company take to make sure they do not find the company profiled in *The New York Times* again as an enterprise that benefits from sweatshop labour?

© Glowimages/Getty Images

Chapter 5
International Trade Theories

OPENING CASE

CREATING THE WORLD'S BIGGEST FREE-TRADE ZONE

In his February 12, 2013, State of the Union address, President Barack Obama committed the United States to negotiating a free trade deal with the European Union (EU). The United States and the 28 countries that are members of the EU already make up the world's largest and richest trading partnership, accounting for about half of global GDP and one-third of all international trade. Nevertheless, the announcement was greeted with approval on both sides of the Atlantic and, unusually for this president, from both sides of the political divide in the United States.

Flash forward to April 2016 when more than 130 000 people presented a petition to Barack Obama to kill this same trade deal during his UK visit.

Why this sudden change? We will examine the negatives associated with free trade in the next chapter and in Chapter 8. Here we will deal with the theories underlying trade in general, and the reasons for much of the free trade movement in the past 50 years.

The reason for the initial enthusiasm can be traced to widespread acceptance of the key axiom of international trade theory—trade is a good thing for all countries involved in a free trade agreement. Free trade is a positive sum game; it is equivalent to the rising tide that lifts all boats. Since 2008, both the United States and the EU have been struggling with low economic growth, persistently high unemployment, and large government deficits. A new free trade deal could help economies on both sides of the Atlantic grow faster, thereby reducing unemployment, without costing another dime in government spending.

Canada signed such a deal in 2016. As President Jean-Claude Juncker said at the G20 Summit in September 2016: "Our new trade deal with Canada is the best and most progressive agreement we have ever, as a European Union, negotiated. On top of the new opportunities it creates for businesses and citizens, it also marks a new approach to investment protection that is transparent and that is impartial."

A trade deal is, in effect, a cost-free stimulus package. How big the economic impact will be remains to be seen. For both the United States and the EU average tariffs (taxes) on imported goods are already low, close to 3 percent by most measures. Further reduction could nonetheless stimulate additional trade, and there are some areas where tariffs are much higher, notably on agricultural goods.

Beyond tariff reductions, there are many nontariff barriers to international trade that could be reduced or eliminated as the result of a deal. One example is found in the automobile industry, where the EU and United States both employ equally strict but different safety standards. This means that to sell in both the EU and United States, automobile manufacturers must adhere to two different sets of regulations. Similarly, pharmaceutical firms currently have to submit new drugs to two sets of safety tests, one in the United States and one in the EU. Such regulatory requirements are functionally equivalent to an import tariff insofar as they raise the costs of business and international trade. By some calculations, nontariff barriers such as these are equivalent to a traditional import tariff of 10–20 percent. Initial estimates suggest that a comprehensive and ambitious agreement that covers both tariff and nontariff barriers to trade will boost annual GDP growth by about 0.5 percent per annum on both sides of the Atlantic, producing an additional $200 billion a year in economic activity.

Sources: H. Timmons, "Transatlantic Trading," *The Economist*, February 2, 2013; Andrew Walker, "EU and US Free Trade Talks Launched," *BBC News*, February 13, 2013; Paul Ames, "Parmesan Cheese: Thorn in US-EU Free Trade Deal?" *GlobalPost.com*, February 25, 2013; Henry Chu, "U.S., EU Resume Negotiations on Free Trade Agreement," *Los Angeles Times*, November 11, 2013; and https://ec.europa.eu/commission/priorities/balanced-eu-us-free-trade-agreement_en.

LO | LEARNING OBJECTIVES

By the end of this chapter you should be able to:

1. Explain why nations trade with each other.

2. Distinguish the different theories that explain trade flows between nations.

3. Express why many economists believe that unrestricted (free) trade between nations will raise the economic welfare of all countries that participate in a free trade system.

4. Summarize the arguments of those who maintain that government can play a proactive role in promoting national competitive advantage in certain industries.

5. Demonstrate the important implications that international trade theory holds for business practice.

Introduction

The proposed free trade deal between the United States and the European Union, and the existing deal between Canada and the European Union are examples of the benefits of free trade. These agreements include a reduction in tariff and nontariff barriers to the free flow of goods and services between the countries involved. It could boost economic growth rates and help bring down persistently high unemployment rates, all without costing anything in additional government spending. Economists have long argued that free trade stimulates economic growth and raises living standards across the board. As the opening case illustrates, the economic arguments concerning the benefits of free trade in goods and services are not abstract academic ones.

If there are losers in this process (and recent political discussions in the United States in 2016 and 2017 have focussed on this aspect), it is predominantly manufacturing employees in developed markets such as Canada and the United States, where the number of jobs is starting to fall. In the world of international trade, there are always winners and losers, but as economists have long argued, the benefits to the winners outweigh the costs borne by the losers, resulting in a net gain to society. Moreover, economists argue that in the long run, free trade stimulates economic growth and raises living standards across the board. For example, as Mexico or China (two countries that have been targets in the anti-free trade rhetoric) gets richer, the nation's citizens will consume more goods and services produced in Canada and the United States, raising Canadian and U.S. living standards. On balance, free trade, in the view of economists, is a win–win situation.

The economic arguments surrounding the benefits and costs of free trade in goods and services are not abstract academic ones. International trade theory has shaped the economic policy of many nations for the past 50 years. It was the driver behind the World Trade Organization and regional trading blocs such as the European Union and the North American Free Trade Agreement (NAFTA). The 1990s, in particular, saw a global move towards greater free trade. It is crucially important to understand, therefore, what these theories are and why they have been so successful in shaping the economic policy of so many nations and the competitive environment in which international businesses compete, especially given the recent backlash to free trade, which will be discussed in more detail in the coming chapters.

This chapter has two goals that go to the heart of the debate over the benefits and costs of free trade. The first is to review a number of theories that explain why it is beneficial for a country to engage in international trade. The second goal is to explain the pattern of international trade that we observe in the world economy. With regard to the pattern of trade, we will be primarily concerned with explaining the pattern of exports and imports of goods and services between countries. We will not be concerned with the pattern of foreign direct investment between countries; that is discussed in Chapter 7.

An Overview of Trade Theory

We open this chapter with a discussion of mercantilism. Propagated in the sixteenth and seventeenth centuries, mercantilism advocated that countries should simultaneously encourage exports and discourage imports. Although mercantilism is an old and largely discredited doctrine, its echoes remain in modern political debate and in the trade policies of many countries. Next we will look at Adam Smith's theory of absolute advantage. Proposed in 1776, Smith's theory was the first to explain why unrestricted free trade is beneficial to a country. **Free trade** refers to a situation where a government does not attempt to influence (through quotas or duties) what its citizens can buy from another country, or what they can produce and sell to another country. Smith argued that the invisible hand of the market mechanism, rather than government policy, should determine what a country imports and what it exports. His arguments imply that such a laissez-faire stance toward trade was in the best interests of a country. Building on Smith's work are two additional theories that we shall review. One is the theory of comparative advantage, advanced by the nineteenth century English economist David Ricardo. This theory is the intellectual basis of the modern argument for unrestricted free trade. In the twentieth century, Ricardo's work was refined by two Swedish economists, Eli Heckscher and Bertil Ohlin, whose theory is known as the Heckscher–Ohlin theory.

LO1   The Benefits of Trade

The great strength of the theories of Smith, Ricardo, and Heckscher–Ohlin is that they identify with precision the specific benefits of international trade. Common sense suggests that some international trade is beneficial. For example, nobody would suggest that Iceland should grow its own oranges. Iceland can benefit from trade by exchanging some of the products it can produce at a low cost (fish) for some products it cannot produce at all (oranges). Thus, by engaging in international trade, Icelanders are able to add oranges to their diet of fish.

The theories of Smith, Ricardo, and Heckscher–Ohlin go beyond this common-sense notion, however, to show why it is beneficial for a country to engage in international trade *even for products it is able to produce for itself.* This is a difficult concept for people to grasp. For example, many Canadians believe that to help save Canadian jobs from foreign competition, Canadian consumers should buy products produced in Canada by Canadian companies whenever possible. This same kind of nationalistic sentiment can be observed in many other countries, and particularly in the United States in 2106 and 2017.

However, the theories of Smith, Ricardo, and Heckscher–Ohlin tell us that a country's economy may gain if its citizens buy certain products from other nations that could be produced at home. The gains arise because international trade allows a country to specialize in the manufacture and export of products that can be produced most efficiently in that country, while importing products that can be produced more efficiently in other countries. Since we are recognized as pioneers in the mining industry, it may make sense for Canada to specialize in the production of heavy mining equipment and export our expertise to Chile, Papua New Guinea, and elsewhere. On the other hand, it may make sense for Canada to import textiles from India, since the efficient production of textiles requires a relatively cheap labour force—and cheap labour is not abundant in Canada.

This economic argument is often difficult for segments of a country's population to accept. With their future threatened by imports, Canadian textile companies and their employees have, in the past, tried to persuade the federal government to limit the importation of textiles by demanding quotas and tariffs. Recent World Trade Organization decisions have overruled independent country wishes to keep tariff barriers in place. In January 2005, tariffs on textiles were abolished for member WTO countries. Although such import controls may benefit particular groups, such as

American textile businesses and their employees, or domestic toy manufacturers in the case of imports of Chinese toys, the theories of Smith, Ricardo, and Heckscher–Ohlin suggest that the economy as a whole is hurt by this action. Limits on imports are often in the interests of domestic producers, but not domestic consumers, who end up paying higher prices.

ANOTHER PERSPECTIVE

Outsourcing: Putting Jobs into Growing Markets

Another way of looking at how outsourcing is hollowing out Western knowledge-based economies is to see the process from the perspective of developing nations. To them, outsourcing brings with it the benefits of trade. It is one of the positive outcomes of globalization. Multinational corporations doing some business in their markets can locate their production in the very markets into which they are selling. As India, the Philippines, and China develop a knowledge-based labour supply, companies such as Intel and Apple that are selling into these markets may want to locate some of their research and development and other knowledge-based activities in these markets as a commitment to a local presence, as a way to learn more about the customer, and as a way to establish sustained and sustaining relationships. Yes, there are cost savings, especially on labour, but long term, such cost savings may be secondary.

The Pattern of International Trade

The theories of Smith, Ricardo, and Heckscher–Ohlin also help to explain the pattern of international trade that we observe in the world economy. Some aspects of the pattern are easy to understand. Climate and natural-resource endowments explain why Ghana exports cocoa, Brazil exports coffee, Saudi Arabia exports oil, and China exports ginseng. But much of the observed pattern of international trade is more difficult to explain. For example, why does Japan export automobiles, consumer electronics, and machine tools? Why does Switzerland export chemicals, watches, and jewellery? David Ricardo's theory of comparative advantage offers an explanation in terms of international differences in labour productivity. The more sophisticated Heckscher–Ohlin theory emphasizes the interplay between the proportions in which the factors of production (such as land, labour, and capital) are available in different countries and the proportions in which they are needed for producing particular goods. This explanation rests on the assumption that countries have varying endowments of the factors of production. Tests of this theory, however, suggest it is a less powerful explanation of real-world trade patterns than once thought.

One early response to the failure of the Heckscher–Ohlin theory to explain the observed pattern of international trade was the *product life-cycle theory*. Proposed by Raymond Vernon, this theory suggests that early in their life cycle, most new products are produced in and exported from the country in which they were developed. As a new product becomes widely accepted internationally, however, production starts in other

Brazil has long had a national competitive advantage in the growing of coffee beans. © *Duncan Walker/ Getty Images*

countries. As a result, the theory suggests, the product may ultimately be exported back to the country of its original innovation.

In a similar vein, during the 1980s, economists such as Paul Krugman of the Massachusetts Institute of Technology developed what has come to be known as the *new trade theory*. New trade theory stresses that in some cases countries specialize in the production and export of particular products not because of underlying differences in factor endowments, but because in certain industries the world market can support only a limited number of firms. (This is argued to be the case for the commercial aircraft industry.) In such industries, firms that enter the market first build a competitive advantage that is difficult to challenge. Thus, the observed pattern of trade between nations may be due in part to the ability of firms within a given nation

COUNTRY FOCUS

Is China a Neo-mercantilist Nation?

China's rapid rise in economic power (it is now the world's second-largest economy) has been built on export-led growth. The country takes raw material imports and, using its cheap labour, converts them into products that it sells to developed nations. For years, the country's exports have been growing faster than its imports, leading some critics to claim that China is pursuing a neo-mercantilist policy, trying to amass record trade surpluses and foreign currency that will give it economic power over developed nations. By late 2013 its foreign exchange reserves exceeded $3.7 trillion, some 60 percent of which were held in U.S. denominated assets. Observers worry that if China ever decides to sell its holdings of U.S. currency, this could depress the value of the dollar against other currencies and increase the price of imports into America.

Throughout most of the 2000s China's exports have grown faster than its imports, leading some to argue that China has been limiting imports by pursuing an import substitution policy, encouraging domestic investment in the production of products such as steel, aluminum, and paper, which it had historically imported from other nations. The trade deficit with America has been a particular cause for concern, especially during the 2016 presidential election. This exceeded $350 billion. At the same time, China long resisted attempts to let its currency float freely against the U.S. dollar. Many claim that China's currency is too cheap, and that this keeps the prices of China's goods artificially low, which fuels the country's exports.

So is China a neo-mercantilist nation that is deliberately discouraging imports and encouraging exports in order to increase its trade surplus and accumulate foreign exchange reserves, which might give it economic power? The jury is out on this issue. Skeptics suggest that going forward, the country will have no choice but to increase its imports of commodities that it lacks, such as oil. They also note that China did start allowing the value of the yuan (China's currency) to appreciate against the dollar in July 2005, albeit at a slow pace. In July 2005 one U.S. dollar purchased 8.11 yuan. By January 2014, one U.S. dollar purchased 6.05 yuan, a decline of 25 percent. Despite this, China's trade surplus with the rest of the world remains persistently high and exceeded $240 billion in 2013.

Questions

1. Are there other countries you can think of that might be pursuing such a policy?
2. Who is affected if China is deliberately discouraging imports?

Sources: A. Browne, "China's Wild Swings Can Roil the Global Economy," *The Wall Street Journal*, October 24, 2005, p. A2; S. H. Hanke, "Stop the Mercantilists," *Forbes*, June 20, 2005, p. 164; G. Dyer and A. Balls, "Dollar Threat as China Signals Shift," *Financial Times*, January 6, 2006, p. 1; Tim Annett, "Righting the Balance," *The Wall Street Journal*, January 10, 2007, p. 15; "China's Trade Surplus Peaks," *Financial Times*, January 12, 2008, p. 1; W. Chong, "China's Trade Surplus to U.S. to Narrow," *China Daily*, December 7, 2009; A. Wang and K. Yao, "China's Trade Surplus Dips, Taking Heat off Yuan," *Reuters*, January 9, 2011; Aaron Back, "China's Trade Surplus Shrank in '11," *The Wall Street Journal*, January 11, 2012; and Richard Silk, "China's Foreign Exchange Reserves Jump Again," *The Wall Street Journal*, October 15, 2013.

to capture first-mover advantages. The United States dominates in the export of commercial jet aircraft because American firms such as Boeing were first movers in the world market. Boeing built a competitive advantage that has subsequently been difficult for firms from countries with equally favourable factor endowments to challenge.

In a work related to the new trade theory, Michael Porter of the Harvard Business School developed a theory, referred to as the theory of national competitive advantage, that attempts to explain why particular nations achieve international success in certain industries. Like the new trade theorists, in addition to factor endowments, Porter points out the importance of country factors such as domestic demand and domestic rivalry in explaining a nation's dominance in the production and export of particular products.

Trade Theory and Government Policy

Although all these theories agree that international trade is beneficial to a country, they lack agreement in their recommendations for government policy. Mercantilism makes a case for government involvement in promoting exports and limiting imports. The theories of Smith, Ricardo, and Heckscher–Ohlin form part of the case for unrestricted free trade. The argument for unrestricted free trade is that both import controls and export incentives (such as subsidies) are self-defeating and result in wasted resources. Both the new trade theory and Porter's theory of national competitive advantage can be interpreted as justifying some limited government intervention to support the development of certain export-oriented industries. We will discuss the pros and cons of this argument, known as strategic trade policy, as well as the pros and cons of the argument for unrestricted free trade in Chapter 6.

LO2 | Mercantilism

The first theory of international trade emerged in England in the mid-sixteenth century. Referred to as **mercantilism**, its principal assertion was that gold and silver were the mainstays of national wealth and essential to vigorous commerce. The main tenet of mercantilism was that it was in a country's best interests to maintain a trade surplus, to export more than it imported. By doing so, a country would accumulate gold and silver and, consequently, increase its national wealth and prestige. As the English mercantilist writer Thomas Mun put it in the year 1630:

> The ordinary means therefore to increase our wealth and treasure is by foreign trade, wherein we must ever observe this rule: to sell more to strangers yearly than we consume of theirs in value.[1]

Consistent with this belief, the mercantilist doctrine advocated government intervention to achieve a surplus in the balance of trade. The mercantilists saw no virtue in a large volume of trade per se. Rather, they recommended policies to maximize exports and minimize imports. To achieve this, imports were limited by tariffs and quotas, while exports were subsidized.

The classical economist David Hume pointed out an inherent inconsistency in the mercantilist doctrine in 1752. According to Hume, if England had a balance-of-trade surplus with France (it exported more than it imported) the resulting inflow of gold and silver would swell the domestic money supply and generate inflation in England. In France, however, the outflow of gold and silver would have the opposite effect.

France's money supply would contract, and its prices would fall. This change in relative prices between France and England would encourage the French to buy fewer English goods (because they were becoming more expensive) and the English to buy more French goods (because they were becoming cheaper). The result would be a deterioration in the English balance of trade and an improvement in France's trade balance, until the English surplus was eliminated. Hence, according to Hume, in the long run no country could sustain a surplus on the balance of trade and so accumulate gold and silver as the mercantilists had envisaged.

The flaw with mercantilism was that it viewed trade as a zero-sum game. (A **zero-sum game** is one in which a gain by one country results in a loss by another.) It was left to Adam Smith and David Ricardo to show the short-sightedness of this approach and to demonstrate that trade is a **positive-sum game**, or a situation in which all countries can benefit. The mercantilist doctrine is by no means dead.[2] For example, Jarl Hagelstam, a director at the Finnish Ministry of Finance, has observed that in most trade negotiations:

> The approach of individual negotiating countries, both industrialized and developing, has been to press for trade liberalization in areas where their own comparative competitive advantages are the strongest, and to resist liberalization in areas where they are less competitive and fear that imports would replace domestic production.[3]

Hagelstam attributes this strategy by negotiating countries to a neomercantilist belief held by the politicians of many nations. This belief, strongly present in the statements of U.S. President Donald Trump, equates political power with economic power and economic power with a balance-of-trade surplus. Thus, the trade strategy of many nations is designed to simultaneously boost exports and limit imports.

Absolute Advantage

In his 1776 landmark book *The Wealth of Nations*, Adam Smith attacked the mercantilist assumption that trade is a zero-sum game. Smith argued that countries differ in their ability to produce goods efficiently. In his time, the English, by virtue of their superior manufacturing processes, were the world's most efficient textile manufacturers. Due to the combination of favourable climate, good soils, and accumulated expertise, the French had the world's most efficient wine industry. The English had an *absolute advantage* in the production of textiles, while the French had an *absolute advantage* in the production of wine. Thus, a country has an **absolute advantage** in the production of a good when it is more efficient than any other country in producing it. For example, Canada has an absolute advantage in many raw materials from silver to timber.

According to Smith, countries should specialize in the production of goods for which they have an absolute advantage and then trade these for goods produced by other countries. Smith's basic argument, therefore, is that a country should never produce goods at home that it can buy at a lower cost from other countries. According to Smith, by specializing in the production of goods in which each has an absolute advantage, both countries benefit by engaging in trade.

Consider the effects of trade between Ghana and South Korea. The production of any good (output) requires resources (inputs) such as land, labour, and capital. Assume that Ghana and South Korea both have the same amount of resources and that these resources can be used to produce either rice or cocoa. Assume further that 200 units of resources are available in each country. Imagine that in Ghana it takes 10 resources to produce 1 tonne of cocoa and 20 resources to produce 1 tonne of rice. Thus, Ghana could produce

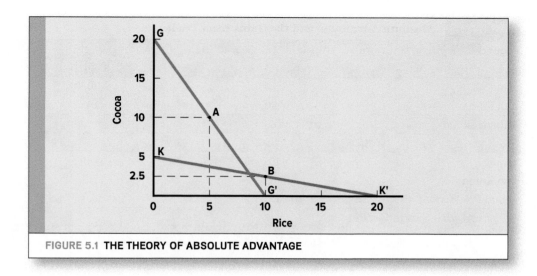

FIGURE 5.1 **THE THEORY OF ABSOLUTE ADVANTAGE**

20 tonnes of cocoa and no rice, 10 tonnes of rice and no cocoa, or some combination of rice and cocoa between these two extremes. The different combinations that Ghana could produce are represented by the line GG' in Figure 5.1. This is referred to as Ghana's production possibility frontier (PPF). Similarly, imagine that in South Korea it takes 40 resources to produce 1 tonne of cocoa and 10 resources to produce 1 tonne of rice. Thus, South Korea could produce 5 tonnes of cocoa and no rice, 20 tonnes of rice and no cocoa, or some combination between these two extremes. The different combinations available to South Korea are represented by the line KK' in Figure 5.1, which is South Korea's PPF. Clearly, Ghana has an absolute advantage in the production of cocoa. (More resources are needed to produce a tonne of cocoa in South Korea than in Ghana.) By the same token, South Korea has an absolute advantage in the production of rice.

Now consider a situation in which neither country trades with any other. Each country devotes half of its resources to the production of rice and half to the production of cocoa. Each country must also consume what it produces. Ghana would be able to produce 10 tonnes of cocoa and 5 tonnes of rice (point A in Figure 5.1), while South Korea would be able to produce 10 tonnes of rice and 2.5 tonnes of cocoa (point B in Figure 5.1). Without trade, the combined production of both countries would be 12.5 tonnes of cocoa (10 tonnes in Ghana plus 2.5 tonnes in South Korea) and 15 tonnes of rice (5 tonnes in Ghana and 10 tonnes in South Korea). If each country were to specialize in producing the good for which it had an absolute advantage and then trade with the other for the good it lacks, Ghana could produce 20 tonnes of cocoa, and South Korea could produce 20 tonnes of rice. Thus, specializing could increase the production of both goods. Production of cocoa would increase from 12.5 tonnes to 20 tonnes, while production of rice would increase from 15 tonnes to 20 tonnes. The increase in production that would result from specialization is therefore 7.5 tonnes of cocoa and 5 tonnes of rice. Table 5.1 summarizes these figures.

By engaging in trade and swapping 1 tonne of cocoa for 1 tonne of rice, producers in both countries could consume more of both cocoa and rice. Imagine that Ghana and South Korea swap cocoa and rice on a one-to-one basis; that is, the price of 1 tonne of cocoa is equal to the price of 1 tonne of rice. If Ghana decided to export 6 tonnes of cocoa to South Korea and import 6 tonnes of rice in return, its final consumption after trade would be 14 tonnes of cocoa and 6 tonnes of rice. This is 4 tonnes more cocoa than it could have consumed before specialization and trade and 1 tonne more rice.

TABLE 5.1	Absolute Advantage and the Gains from Trade	
Resources Required to Produce 1 Tonne of Cocoa and Rice		
	COCOA	RICE
Ghana	10	20
South Korea	40	10
Production and Consumption Without Trade		
	COCOA	RICE
Ghana	10.0	5.0
South Korea	2.5	10.0
Total Production	12.5	15.0
Production with Specialization		
	COCOA	RICE
Ghana	20.00	0.0
South Korea	0.0	20.0
Total Production	20.0	20.0
Consumption After Ghana Trades 6 Tonnes of Cocoa for 6 Tonnes of South Korean Rice		
	COCOA	RICE
Ghana	14.0	6.0
South Korea	6.0	14.0
Increase in Consumption as a Result of Specialization and Trade		
	COCOA	RICE
Ghana	4.0	1.0
South Korea	3.5	4.0

Similarly, South Korea's final consumption after trade would be 6 tonnes of cocoa and 14 tonnes of rice. This is 3.5 tonnes more cocoa than it could have consumed before specialization and trade and 4 tonnes more rice. Thus, as a result of specialization and

DEBATE THE ISSUE

Which Products Should Always be Produced at Home?

One of the key insights of international trade theory is that limits on imports are often in the interests of domestic producers, but not domestic consumers. This is especially true if Adam Smith's theory of absolute advantage is in play, where one country is better at producing a product than another country. The reason is that consumers typically want the best products they can get for the amount of money they are willing to pay.

But what about the comparative advantage theory that was originally conceptualized by David Ricardo and then refined by Eli Heckscher and Bertil Ohlin? Comparative advantage theory argues that a country should consider not producing products that it can actually produce reasonably well if the country can produce something else even more efficiently. In reality, not a single country has stopped all production of products they produce less efficiently than some other country. The reason is that countries always engage in a strategic balancing act! They prefer to be as efficient as possible (engage in international trade when advantageous) while also being as self-sufficient as possible (produce inside their country). So, what types of products should always be produced in the home country, and which products should always be considered for importing if other countries can produce them more efficiently?

trade, output of both cocoa and rice would be increased, and consumers in both nations would be able to consume more. Thus, we can see that trade is a positive-sum game; it produces net gains for all involved.

Comparative Advantage

David Ricardo took Adam Smith's theory one step further by exploring what might happen when one country has an absolute advantage in the production of all goods.[4] Smith's theory of absolute advantage suggests that such a country might derive no benefits from international trade. In his 1817 book *Principles of Political Economy*, Ricardo showed this was not the case. According to Ricardo's theory of **comparative advantage**, it makes sense for a country to specialize in the production of those goods that it produces most efficiently and to buy the goods that it produces less efficiently from other countries, even if this means buying goods from other countries that it could produce more efficiently itself.[5] While this may seem counterintuitive, especially to those in the political arena south of the border during 2016 and 2017, the logic can be explained with a simple example.

Assume that Ghana is more efficient in the production of both cocoa and rice; that is, Ghana has an absolute advantage in the production of both products. In Ghana it takes 10 resources to produce 1 tonne of cocoa and 13-1/3 resources to produce 1 tonne of rice. Thus, given its 200 units of resources, Ghana can produce 20 tonnes of cocoa and no rice, 15 tonnes of rice and no cocoa, or any combination in between on its PPF (the line GG' in Figure 5.2). In South Korea it takes 40 resources to produce 1 tonne of cocoa and 20 resources to produce 1 tonne of rice. Thus, South Korea can produce 5 tonnes of cocoa and no rice, 10 tonnes of rice and no cocoa, or any combination on its PPF (the line KK' in Figure 5.2). Again assume that without trade, each country uses half of its resources to produce rice and half to produce cocoa. Thus, without trade, Ghana will produce 10 tonnes of cocoa and 7.5 tonnes of rice (point A in Figure 5.2), while South Korea will produce 2.5 tonnes of cocoa and 5 tonnes of rice (point B in Figure 5.2).

In light of Ghana's absolute advantage in the production of both goods, why should it trade with South Korea? Although Ghana has an absolute advantage in the production of both cocoa and rice, it has a comparative advantage only in the

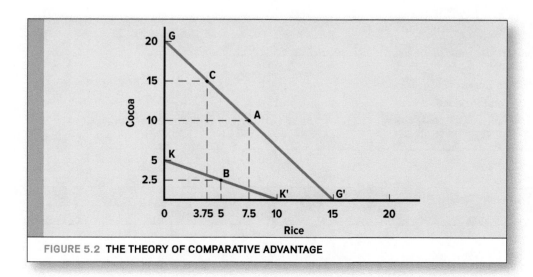

FIGURE 5.2 **THE THEORY OF COMPARATIVE ADVANTAGE**

production of cocoa: Ghana can produce 4 times as much cocoa as South Korea, but only 1.5 times as much rice. Ghana is *comparatively* more efficient at producing cocoa than it is at producing rice.

Without trade, the combined production of cocoa will be 12.5 tonnes (10 tonnes in Ghana and 2.5 in South Korea), and the combined production of rice will also be 12.5 tonnes (7.5 tonnes in Ghana and 5 tonnes in South Korea). Without trade, each country must consume what it produces. By engaging in trade, the two countries can increase their combined production of rice and cocoa, and consumers in both nations can consume more of both goods.

The Gains from Trade

Imagine that Ghana exploits its comparative advantage in the production of cocoa to increase its output from 10 tonnes to 15 tonnes. This uses up 150 units of resources, leaving the remaining 50 units of resources to use in producing 3.75 tonnes of rice (point C in Figure 5.2). Meanwhile, South Korea specializes in the production of rice, producing 10 tonnes. The combined output of both cocoa and rice has now increased. Before specialization, the combined output was 12.5 tonnes of cocoa and 12.5 tonnes of rice. Now it is 15 tonnes of cocoa and 13.75 tonnes of rice (3.75 tonnes in Ghana and 10 tonnes in South Korea). The source of the increase in production is summarized in Table 5.2.

TABLE 5.2	**Comparative Advantage and the Gains from Trade**	
Resources Required to Produce 1 Tonne of Cocoa and Rice		
	COCOA	**RICE**
Ghana	10	13.33
South Korea	40	20
Production and Consumption Without Trade		
	COCOA	**RICE**
Ghana	10.0	7.5
South Korea	2.5	5.0
Total Production	12.5	12.5
Production with Specialization		
	COCOA	**RICE**
Ghana	15.0	3.75
South Korea	0.0	10.0
Total Production	15.0	13.75
Consumption After Ghana Trades 4 Tonnes of Cocoa for 4 Tonnes of South Korean Rice		
	COCOA	**RICE**
Ghana	11.0	7.75
South Korea	4.0	6.0
Increase in Consumption as a Result of Specialization and Trade		
	COCOA	**RICE**
Ghana	1.0	0.25
South Korea	1.5	1.0

Not only is output higher, but also both countries can now benefit from trade. If Ghana and South Korea swap cocoa and rice on a one-to-one basis, with both countries choosing to exchange 4 tonnes of their export for 4 tonnes of the import, both countries are able to consume more cocoa and rice than they could before specialization and trade (see Table 5.2). Thus, if Ghana exchanges 4 tonnes of cocoa with South Korea for 4 tonnes of rice, it is still left with 11 tonnes of rice, which is 1 tonne more than it had before trade. The 4 tonnes of rice it gets from South Korea in exchange for its 4 tonnes of cocoa, when added to the 3.75 tonnes it now produces domestically, leaves it with a total of 7.75 tonnes of rice, which is one-fourth of a tonne more than it had before specialization. Similarly, after swapping 4 tonnes of rice with Ghana, South Korea still ends up with 6 tonnes of rice, which is more than it had before specialization. In addition, the 4 tonnes of cocoa it receives in exchange is 1.5 tonnes more than it produced before trade. Thus, consumption of cocoa and rice can increase in both countries as a result of specialization and trade.

The basic message of the theory of comparative advantage is that *potential world production is greater with unrestricted free trade than it is with restricted trade.* Ricardo's theory suggests that consumers in all nations can consume more if there are no trade restrictions. This occurs even in countries that lack an absolute advantage in the production of any good.

In other words, to an even greater degree than the theory of absolute advantage, *the theory of comparative advantage suggests that trade is a positive-sum game in which all countries that participate realize economic gains.* As such, this theory provides a strong rationale for encouraging free trade. So powerful is Ricardo's theory that it remains a major intellectual weapon for those who argue for free trade.

LO3 | Qualifications and Assumptions

The conclusion that free trade is universally beneficial is a rather bold one to draw from such a simple model. Our simple model includes many unrealistic assumptions:

1. We have assumed a simple world in which there are only two countries and two goods. In the real world, there are many countries and many goods.

2. We have assumed away transportation costs between countries.

3. We have assumed away differences in the prices of resources in different countries. We have said nothing about exchange rates, simply assuming that cocoa and rice could be swapped on a one-to-one basis.

4. We have assumed that resources can move freely from the production of one good to another within a country. In reality, this is not always the case.

5. We have assumed constant returns to scale; that is, that specialization by Ghana or South Korea has no effect on the amount of resources required to produce one tonne of cocoa or rice. In reality, both diminishing and increasing returns to specialization exist. The amount of resources required to produce a good might decrease or increase as a nation specializes in production of that good.

6. We have assumed that each country has a fixed stock of resources and that free trade does not change the efficiency with which a country uses its resources.

This static assumption makes no allowances for the dynamic changes in a country's stock of resources and in the efficiency with which the country uses its resources that might result from free trade.

7. We have assumed away the effects of trade on income distribution within a country.

Given these assumptions, can the conclusion that free trade is mutually beneficial be extended to the real world of many countries, many goods, transportation costs, volatile exchange rates, immobile domestic resources, nonconstant returns to specialization, and dynamic changes? Although a detailed extension of the theory of comparative advantage is beyond the scope of this book, economists have shown that the basic result derived from our simple model can be generalized to a world composed of many countries producing many different goods.[6] Despite the shortcomings of the Ricardian model, research suggests that the basic proposition that countries will export the goods that they are most efficient at producing is supported by the data.[7]

However, once all the assumptions are dropped, the case for unrestricted free trade, while still positive, has been argued by some economists associated with the "new trade theory" to lose some of its strength.[8] We return to this issue later in this chapter and in the next.

Trade and Extensions of the Ricardian Model

Let us explore the effect of relaxing two of the assumptions identified above in the simple comparative advantage model. Below we relax the assumption that resources move freely from the production of one good to another within a country and the assumption that trade does not change a country's stock of resources or the efficiency with which those resources are utilized.

IMMOBILE RESOURCES

In our simple comparative model of Ghana and South Korea, we assumed that producers (farmers) could easily convert land from the production of cocoa to rice, and vice versa. While this assumption may hold for some agricultural products, resources do not always shift quite so easily from producing one good to another. A certain amount of friction is involved. For example, embracing a free trade regime for an advanced economy such as Canada often implies that the country will produce less of some labour-intensive goods, such as textiles, and more of some knowledge-intensive goods, such as computer software or biotechnology products. Although the country as a whole will gain from such a shift, textile producers will lose. A textile worker in Quebec is probably not qualified to write software for Microsoft. Thus, the shift to free trade may mean that she becomes unemployed or has to accept another less attractive job, such as working at a fast-food restaurant.

Resources do not always move easily from one economic activity to another. The process also creates friction and human suffering. While the theory predicts that the benefits of free trade outweigh the costs by a significant margin, this is little comfort to those who bear the costs. Accordingly, political opposition to a free trade regime typically comes from those whose jobs are most at risk. In Canada, for example, textile workers and their unions have long opposed the move toward free trade precisely because this group has much to lose. Governments often ease the transition toward free trade by helping to retrain those who lose their jobs as a result. The pain caused by the movement toward a free trade regime is a short-term phenomenon, while the gains from trade once the transition has been made are both significant and enduring.

DIMINISHING RETURNS

The simple comparative advantage model developed earlier assumes **constant returns to specialization**. By constant returns to specialization we mean the units of resources required to produce a good (cocoa or rice) are assumed to remain constant no matter where one is on a country's production possibility frontier (PPF). Thus, we assumed that it always took Ghana 10 units of resources to produce 1 tonne of cocoa. However, it is more realistic to assume diminishing returns to specialization. Diminishing returns to specialization occurs when more units of resources are required to produce each additional unit. While 10 units of resources may be sufficient to increase Ghana's output of cocoa from 12 tonnes to 13 tonnes, 11 units of resources may be needed to increase output from 13 to 14 tonnes, 12 units of resources to increase output from 14 tonnes to 15 tonnes, and so on. Diminishing returns implies a convex PPF for Ghana (see Figure 5.3), rather than the straight line depicted in Figure 5.2.

It is more realistic to assume diminishing returns for two reasons. First, not all resources are of the same quality. As a country tries to increase its output of a certain good, it is increasingly likely to draw on more marginal resources whose productivity is not as great as those initially employed. The result is that it requires ever more resources to produce an equal increase in output. For example, some land is more productive than other land. As Ghana tries to expand its output of cocoa, it might have to utilize increasingly marginal land that is less fertile than the land it originally used. As yields per acre decline, Ghana must use more land to produce one tonne of cocoa.

A second reason for diminishing returns is that different goods use resources in different proportions. For example, imagine that growing cocoa uses more land and less labour than growing rice, and that Ghana tries to transfer resources from rice production to cocoa production. The rice industry will release proportionately too much labour and too little land for efficient cocoa production. To absorb the additional resources of labour and land, the cocoa industry will have to shift toward more labour-intensive methods of production. The effect is that the efficiency with which the cocoa industry uses labour will decline, and returns will diminish.

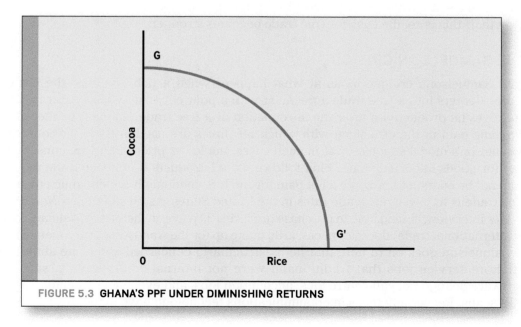

FIGURE 5.3 **GHANA'S PPF UNDER DIMINISHING RETURNS**

Diminishing returns show that it is not feasible for a country to specialize to the degree suggested by the simple Ricardian model outlined earlier. Diminishing returns to specialization suggest that the gains from specialization are likely to be exhausted before specialization is complete. In reality, most countries do not specialize, but instead, produce a range of goods. However, the theory predicts that it is worthwhile to specialize until that point where the resulting gains from trade are outweighed by diminishing returns. Thus, the basic conclusion that unrestricted free trade is beneficial still holds, although because of diminishing returns, the gains may not be as great as suggested in the constant returns case.

DYNAMIC EFFECTS AND ECONOMIC GROWTH

Our simple comparative advantage model assumed that trade does not change a country's stock of resources or the efficiency with which it utilizes those resources. This static assumption makes no allowances for the dynamic changes that might result from trade. If we relax this assumption, it becomes apparent that opening an economy to trade is likely to generate dynamic gains of two sorts.[9] First, free trade might increase a country's stock of resources as increased supplies of labour and capital from abroad become available for use within the country. This is occurring now in Eastern Europe, where many Western businesses are investing large amounts of capital in the former Communist countries.

Second, free trade might also increase the efficiency with which a country uses its resources. Gains in the efficiency of resource utilization could arise from a number of factors. For example, economies of large-scale production might become available as trade expands the size of the total market available to domestic firms. Trade might make better technology from abroad available to domestic firms; better technology can increase labour productivity or the productivity of land. Also, opening an economy to foreign competition might stimulate domestic producers to look for ways to increase their efficiency. Again, this phenomenon is arguably occurring in the once-protected markets of Eastern Europe, where many former state monopolies are increasing their efficiency to survive in the competitive world market. The theory suggests that opening an economy to free trade not only results in static gains of the type discussed earlier, but also results in dynamic gains that stimulate economic growth. If this is so, the case for free trade becomes stronger.

THE SAMUELSON CRITIQUE

Paul Samuelson's critique looks at what happens when a rich country—the United States—enters into a free trade agreement with a poor country—China—that rapidly improves its productivity after the introduction of a free trade regime (i.e., there is a dynamic gain in the efficiency with which resources are used in the poor country). Samuelson's model suggests that in such cases, the lower prices that U.S. consumers pay for goods imported from China following the introduction of a free trade regime may not be enough to produce a net gain for the U.S. economy if the dynamic effect of free trade is to lower real wage rates in the United States. As he stated in a *New York Times* interview, "Being able to purchase groceries 20 percent cheaper at Walmart (due to international trade) does not necessarily make up for the wage losses (in America)."[10]

Samuelson goes on to note that he is particularly concerned about the ability to offshore service jobs that traditionally were not internationally mobile, such as software debugging, call centre jobs, accounting jobs, and even medical diagnosis of MRI scans. Recent advances in communications technology have made this possible, effectively expanding the labour market for these jobs to include educated people in places such as India, the Philippines, and China. When coupled with rapid advances in the productivity of foreign labour due to better education, the effect on middle-class wages in the United States, according to Samuelson, may be similar to mass inward migration into the United States—it will lower the market-clearing wage rate, perhaps by enough to outweigh the positive benefits of international trade.

However, Samuelson concedes that free trade has historically benefited rich countries. Also, he notes that introducing protectionist measures (e.g., trade barriers) to guard against the theoretical possibility that free trade may harm the United States in the future may produce a situation that is worse than the disease they are trying to prevent. To quote Samuelson: "Free trade may turn out pragmatically to be still best for each region in comparison to lobbyist-induced tariffs and quotas, which involve both a perversion of democracy and non-subtle deadweight distortion losses."[11]

Some economists have been quick to dismiss Samuelson's fears.[12] While not questioning his analysis, they note that as a practical matter developing nations are unlikely to be able to upgrade the skill level of their workforce rapidly enough to give rise to the situation in Samuelson's model. In other words, they will quickly run into diminishing returns. To quote one such rebuttal: "The notion that India and China will quickly educate 300 million of their citizens to acquire sophisticated and complex skills at stake borders on the ludicrous. The educational sectors in these countries face enormous difficulties."[13] Notwithstanding such rebuttals, however, Samuelson's stature is such that his work will undoubtedly be debated for some time to come.

EVIDENCE FOR THE LINK BETWEEN TRADE AND GROWTH

Many economic studies have looked at the relationship between trade and economic growth. In general, these studies suggest that, as predicted by the theory, countries that adopt a more open stance toward international trade enjoy higher growth rates than those that close their economies to trade. Jeffrey Sachs and Andrew Warner created a measure of how "open" to international trade an economy was and then looked at the relationship between "openness" and economic growth for a sample of more than 100 countries from 1970 to 1990.[14] Among other findings, they reported:

> We find a strong association between openness and growth, both within the group of developing and the group of developed countries. Within the group of developing countries, the open economies grew at 4.49 percent per year, and the closed economies grew at 0.69 percent per year. Within the group of developed economies, the open economies grew at 2.29 percent per year, and the closed economies grew at 0.74 percent per year.[15]

A study by Wacziarg and Welch updated the Sachs and Warner data through the late 1990s. They found that over the period 1950–1998, countries that liberalized their trade regimes experienced, on average, increases in their annual growth rates of 1.5 percent compared to pre-liberalization times.[16] An exhaustive survey of 61 studies published between 1967 and 2009 concluded: "The macroeconomic evidence provides dominant support for the positive and significant effects of trade on output and growth."[17]

The message of this study seems clear: adopt an open economy and embrace free trade, and over time your nation will be rewarded with higher economic growth rates. Higher growth will raise income levels and living standards. This last point has recently been confirmed by a study that looked at the relationship between trade and growth in incomes. The study, undertaken by Jeffrey Frankel and David Romer, found that on average, a one percentage point increase in the ratio of a country's trade to its gross domestic product increases income per person by at least one-half percent.[18] For every 10 percent increase in the importance of international trade in an economy, average income levels will rise by at least 5 percent. Despite the short-term adjustment costs associated with adopting a free trade regime, trade would seem to produce greater economic growth and higher living standards in the long run, just as the theory of Ricardo would lead us to expect.[19]

Heckscher–Ohlin Theory

Ricardo's theory stresses that comparative advantage arises from differences in productivity. Thus, whether Ghana is more efficient than South Korea in the production of cocoa depends on how productively it uses its resources. Ricardo stressed labour productivity and argued that differences in labour productivity between nations underlie the notion of comparative advantage. Swedish economists Eli Heckscher (in 1919) and Bertil Ohlin (in 1933) put forward a different explanation of comparative advantage. They argued that comparative advantage arises from differences in national factor endowments.[20] By factor endowments they meant the extent to which a country is endowed with such resources as land, labour, and capital. Nations have varying factor endowments, and different factor endowments explain differences in factor costs. The more abundant a factor, the lower its cost. The Heckscher–Ohlin theory predicts that countries will export those goods that make intensive use of factors that are locally abundant, while importing goods that make intensive use of factors that are locally scarce. Thus, the Heckscher–Ohlin theory attempts to explain the pattern of international trade that we observe in the world economy. Like Ricardo's theory, the Heckscher–Ohlin theory argues that free trade is beneficial. Unlike Ricardo's theory, however, the Heckscher–Ohlin theory argues that the pattern of international trade is determined by differences in factor endowments, rather than differences in productivity.

The Heckscher–Ohlin theory also has commonsense appeal. Canada, for example, has abundant land, a growing population, and exportable products from fish to minerals. In contrast, China excels in the export of goods produced in labour-intensive manufacturing industries, such as textiles and footwear. This reflects China's relative abundance of low-cost labour. The United States, which lacks abundant low-cost labour, has been a primary importer of these goods. Note that it is relative, not absolute, endowments that are important; a country may have larger absolute amounts of land and labour than another country, but be relatively abundant in one of them.

The Leontief Paradox

The Heckscher–Ohlin theory has been one of the most influential theoretical ideas in international economics. Most economists prefer the Heckscher–Ohlin theory to Ricardo's theory because it makes fewer simplifying assumptions. Because of its influence, the theory has been subjected to many empirical tests. Beginning with a famous study published in 1953 by Wassily Leontief (winner of the Nobel Prize in economics in 1973), many of these tests have raised questions about the validity of the Heckscher–Ohlin theory.[21] Using the Heckscher–Ohlin theory, Leontief postulated that since the United States was relatively abundant in capital compared to other nations, the United States would be an exporter of capital-intensive goods and an importer of labour-intensive goods. To his surprise, however, he found that U.S. exports were less capital intensive than U.S. imports. Since this result was at variance with the predictions of the theory, it has become known as the Leontief paradox.

No one is quite sure why we observe the Leontief paradox. One possible explanation is that the United States has a special advantage in producing new products or goods made with innovative technologies. Such products may be less capital intensive than products whose technology has had time to mature and become suitable for mass production. Thus, the United States may be exporting goods that use skilled labour and innovative entrepreneurship heavily, such as computer software, while importing heavy manufacturing products that use large amounts of capital. Some more recent empirical studies tend to confirm this.[22] Further tests of the Heckscher–Ohlin theory using data for many countries tend to confirm the existence of the Leontief paradox.[23]

This leaves economists with a difficult dilemma. They prefer Heckscher–Ohlin on theoretical grounds, but the theory is a relatively poor predictor of real-world international trade patterns. On the other hand, the theory they regard as being too limited, Ricardo's theory of comparative advantage, predicts trade patterns with greater accuracy. The best solution to this dilemma may be to return to the Ricardian idea that trade patterns are largely driven by international differences in productivity. Thus, one might argue that the United States exports commercial aircraft and imports automobiles not because its factor endowments are especially suited to aircraft manufacture and not suited to automobile manufacture, but because the United States is more efficient at producing aircraft than automobiles. A key assumption in the Heckscher–Ohlin theory is that technologies are the same across countries. This may not be the case, and differences in technology may lead to differences in productivity, which in turn, drives international trade patterns.[24] Thus, Japan's success in exporting automobiles in the 1970s and 1980s was based not just on the relative abundance of capital, but also on its development of innovative manufacturing technology that enabled it to achieve higher productivity levels in automobile production than other countries that also had abundant capital.

More recent empirical work suggests that this theoretical explanation may be correct.[25] The new research shows that once differences in technology across countries are controlled for, countries do indeed export those goods that make intensive use of factors that are locally abundant, while importing goods that make intensive use of factors that are locally scarce. In other words, once the impact of differences of technology on productivity is controlled for, the Heckscher-Ohlin theory seems to gain predictive power.

The Product Life-Cycle Theory

Raymond Vernon proposed the product life-cycle theory in the mid-1960s.[26] Vernon's theory was based on the observation that for most of the twentieth century a very large proportion of the world's new products had been developed by U.S. firms and sold first in the U.S. market (e.g., mass-produced automobiles, televisions, instant cameras, photocopiers, personal computers, and semiconductor chips). To explain this, Vernon argued that the wealth and size of the U.S. market gave U.S. firms a strong incentive to develop new consumer products. In addition, the high cost of U.S. labour gave U.S. firms an incentive to develop cost-saving process innovations.

Just because a new product is developed by a U.S. firm and first sold in the U.S. market, it does not follow that the product must be produced in the United States. It could be produced abroad at some low-cost location and then exported back into the United States. However, Vernon argued that most new products were initially produced in America.

Vernon went on to argue that early in the life cycle of a typical new product, while demand is starting to grow rapidly in the United States, demand in other advanced countries is limited to high-income groups. The limited initial demand in other advanced countries does not make it worthwhile for firms in those countries to start producing the new product, but it does necessitate some exports from the United States to those countries.

Over time, demand for the new product starts to grow in other advanced countries (e.g., Great Britain, France, Germany, and Japan). As it does, it becomes worthwhile for foreign companies to begin producing for their home markets. In addition, U.S. firms might set up production facilities in those advanced countries where demand is growing. Consequently, production within other advanced countries begins to limit the potential for exports from the United States.

As the market in the United States and other advanced nations matures, the product becomes more standardized, and price becomes the main competitive weapon. As this occurs, cost considerations start to play a greater role in the competitive process. Producers based in advanced countries where labour costs are lower than in the United States (e.g., Italy, Spain) might now be able to export to the United States.

If cost pressures become intense, the process might not stop there. The cycle by which the United States lost its advantage to other advanced countries might be repeated once more, as developing countries (e.g., Thailand) begin to acquire a production advantage over advanced countries. Thus, the locus of global production initially switches from the United States to other advanced nations and then from those nations to developing countries.

Evaluating the Product Life-Cycle Theory

Historically, the product life-cycle theory seems to be an accurate explanation of international trade patterns. Consider photocopiers; the product was developed in the early 1960s by Xerox in the United States and sold initially to U.S. users. Originally Xerox exported photocopiers from the United States, primarily to Japan and the advanced countries of Western Europe. As demand began to grow in those countries, Xerox entered into joint ventures to set up production in Japan (Fuji-Xerox) and Great Britain (Rank-Xerox). In addition, once Xerox's patents on the photocopier process expired, other foreign competitors began to enter the market (e.g., Canon in Japan, Olivetti in Italy). As a consequence, exports from the United States declined, and U.S. users began to buy some of their photocopiers from lower-cost foreign sources, particularly Japan. More recently, Japanese companies have found that manufacturing costs are too high in their own country, so they have begun to switch production to developing countries such as Singapore and Thailand. Thus, initially the United States and now other advanced countries (e.g., Japan and Great Britain) have switched from being exporters of photocopiers to importers. This evolution in the pattern of international trade in photocopiers is consistent with the predictions of the product life-cycle theory, that mature industries tend to go out of the United States and into low-cost assembly locations.

However, the product life-cycle theory is not without weaknesses. Viewed from an Asian or European perspective, Vernon's argument that most new products are developed and introduced in the United States seems ethnocentric. Although it may be true that during U.S. dominance of the global economy (from 1945 to 1975), most new products were introduced in the United States, there have always been important exceptions. These exceptions appear to have become more common in recent years.

Many new products are now first introduced in Japan (e.g., video game consoles) or Europe (new wireless phones). Also, with the increased globalization and integration of the world economy discussed in Chapter 1, a growing number of new products (e.g., GPSs, tablets, and smart phones) are now introduced simultaneously in the United States, Japan, and the advanced European nations. This may be accompanied by globally dispersed production, with particular components of a new product being produced in those locations around the globe where the mix of factor costs and skills is most favourable (as predicted by the theory of comparative advantage). In sum, although Vernon's theory may be useful for explaining the pattern of international trade during the brief period of American global dominance, its relevance in the modern world seems more limited.

ANOTHER PERSPECTIVE

Emerging Markets Drive Consumer Electronics

For the first time in history, emerging markets have zoomed past mature markets as the primary engine driving consumer electronics technology consumption, according to a research published in Accenture's Consumer Products and Services Usage Survey. Some 16 000 respondents in four emerging markets were queried (China, India, Malaysia, and Singapore) and their responses were compared to data from four mature markets (France, Germany, Japan, and the United States). It was found that respondents in the emerging nations are twice as likely as their counterparts in the developed markets to purchase and use consumer technology over the next year. Furthermore, the emerging countries are more invested in mobile technologies—including applications on each device—than those in mature markets. The main factor in this paradigm shift is the rapid expansion of the middle class in emerging markets. More than half the world now earns at least a middle-class income. In emerging countries, that income is feeding a hunger for technology that far exceeds that of more gadget-saturated countries such as Japan and the United States. Further, because these countries are tapping into the market at a later stage of technological development, they are adapting newer, superior versions of smart phones, mobile gadgets, and social networking applications. The emerging market as consumer powerhouse is here to stay, and technology companies that wish to prosper in the future must service it well. Potentially billions of dollars in sales are at stake.

Source: "Emerging markets drive consumer electronics," *EET Asia*, March 10, 2010, www.eetasia.com/ ART_8800600190_499495_NT_53dc7f22.HTM.

The New Trade Theory

The new trade theory began to emerge in the 1970s when a number of economists pointed out that the ability of firms to attain economies of scale might have important implications for international trade.[27] **Economies of scale** are unit cost reductions associated with a large scale of output. Economies of scale have a number of sources, including the ability to spread fixed costs over a large volume and the ability of large-volume producers to utilize specialized employees and equipment that are more productive than less specialized employees and equipment. Economies of scale are a major source of cost reductions in many industries, from computer software to automobiles and from pharmaceuticals to aerospace. For example, Microsoft realizes economies of scale by spreading the fixed costs of developing new versions of its Windows operating system, which runs to about $5 billion, over the 250 million or so personal computers upon which each new system is ultimately installed. Similarly, automobile companies realize economies of scale by producing a high volume of automobiles from an assembly line where each employee has a specialized task.

New trade theory makes two important points: First, through its impact on economies of scale, trade can increase the variety of goods available to consumers and decrease the average cost of those goods. Second, in those industries when the output required to attain economies of scale represents a significant proportion of total world demand, the global market may be able to support only a small number of enterprises. Thus, world trade in certain products may be dominated by countries whose firms were first movers in their production.

Increasing Product Variety and Reducing Costs

Imagine first a world without trade. In industries where economies of scale are important, both the variety of goods that a country can produce and the scale of production are limited by the size of the market. If a national market is small, there may not be enough demand to enable producers to realize economies of scale for certain products. Accordingly, those products may not be produced, thereby limiting the variety of products available to consumers. Alternatively, they may be produced, but at such low volumes that unit costs and prices are considerably higher than they might be if economies of scale could be realized.

Now consider what happens when nations trade with each other. Individual national markets are combined into a larger world market. As the size of the market expands due to trade, individual firms may be able to better attain economies of scale. The implication, according to new trade theory, is that each nation may be able to specialize in producing a narrower range of products than it would in the absence of trade, yet by buying goods that it does not make from other countries, each nation can simultaneously increase the *variety* of goods available to its consumers and *lower the costs* of those goods—thus trade offers an opportunity for mutual gain even when countries do not differ in their resource endowments or technology.

Suppose there are two countries, each with an annual market for 1 million automobiles. By trading with each other, these countries can create a combined market for 2 million cars. In this combined market, due to the ability to better realize economies of scale, more varieties (models) of cars can be produced, and cars can be produced at a lower average cost, than in either market alone. For example, demand for a sports car may be limited to 55 000 units in each national market, while a total output of at least 100 000 per year may be required to realize significant scale economies. Similarly, demand for a minivan may be 80 000 units in each national market, and again a total output of at least 100 000 per year may be required to realize significant scale economies. Faced with limited domestic market demand, firms in each nation may decide not to produce a sports car, because the costs of doing so at such low volume are too great. Although they may produce minivans, the cost of doing so will be higher, as will prices, than if significant economies of scale had been attained. Once the two countries decide to trade, however, a firm in one nation may specialize in producing sports cars while a firm in the other nation may produce minivans. The combined demand for 110 000 sports cars and 160 000 minivans allows each firm to realize scale economies. Consumers in this case benefit from having access to a product (sports cars) that was not available before international trade and from the lower price for a product (minivans) that could not be produced at the most efficient scale before international trade. Trade is thus mutually beneficial because it allows for the specialization of production, the realization of scale economies, the production of a greater variety of products, and lower prices.

Economies of Scale, First-Mover Advantages, and the Pattern of Trade

A second theme in new trade theory is that the pattern of trade we observe in the world economy may be the result of economies of scale and first-mover advantages. As noted in Chapter 2, first-mover advantages are the economic and strategic advantages that accrue to early entrants into an industry. The ability to capture scale economies ahead of later entrants, and thus benefit from a lower cost structure, is an important first-mover advantage. New trade theory argues that for those products where economies of scale are significant and represent a substantial proportion of world demand, the first movers in an industry can gain a scale-based cost advantage that later entrants find almost impossible to match. Thus, the pattern of trade that we observe for such products may reflect first-mover advantages. Countries may dominate in the export of certain goods because economies of scale are important in their production, and because firms located in those countries were the first to capture scale economies, giving them a first-mover advantage.

For example, consider the commercial aerospace industry. In aerospace there are substantial scale economies that come from the ability to spread the fixed costs of developing a new jet aircraft over a large number of sales. It has cost Airbus Industrie more than $15 billion to develop its new super-jumbo jet, the 550-seat A380. According to the original business plan, to recoup those costs and break even Airbus would have to sell at least 250 A380 planes. Total demand for this class of aircraft was estimated to be between 400 and 600 units. Thus, the global market can probably profitably support only one producer of jet aircraft in the super-jumbo category. It follows that the European Union might come to dominate in the export of very large jet aircraft, primarily because a European-based firm, Airbus, was the first to produce a super-jumbo jet aircraft and realize scale economies. Other potential producers, such as Boeing, might be shut out of the market because they will lack the scale economies that Airbus will enjoy. By pioneering this market category, Airbus may have captured a *first-mover advantage* based on scale economies that will be difficult for rivals to match, and that will result in the European Union becoming the leading exporter of very large jet aircraft. (Boeing does not believe the market to be large enough to even profitably support one producer, hence its decision not to build a similar aircraft and instead to focus on its super-efficient 787.)

Implications of New Trade Theory

New trade theory has important implications. The theory suggests that nations may benefit from trade even when they do not differ in resource endowments or technology. Trade allows a nation to specialize in the production of certain products, attaining scale economies and lowering the costs of producing those products, while buying products that it does not produce from other nations that specialize in the production of other products. By this mechanism, the variety of products available to consumers in each nation is increased, while the average costs of those products should fall, as should their price, freeing resources to produce other goods and services.

The theory also suggests that a country may predominate in the export of a good simply because it was lucky enough to have one or more firms among the first to produce that good. Because they are able to gain economies of scale, the first movers in an industry may get a lock on the world market that discourages subsequent entry. First movers' ability to benefit from increasing returns creates a *barrier to entry*. In the commercial aircraft industry, the fact that Boeing and Airbus are already in the industry and have the benefits of economies of scale discourages new entry and reinforces the dominance of America and Europe in the trade of midsize and large jet aircraft. This dominance is further reinforced because global demand may not be sufficient to profitably support another producer of midsize and large jet aircraft in the industry. So although Japanese firms might be able to compete in the market, they have decided not to enter the industry but to ally themselves as major subcontractors with primary producers (e.g., Mitsubishi Heavy Industries is a major subcontractor for Boeing on the 777 and 787 programs).

New trade theory is at variance with the Heckscher–Ohlin theory, which suggests a country will predominate in the export of a product when it is particularly well endowed with those factors used intensively in its manufacture. New trade theorists argue that the United States is a major exporter of commercial jet aircraft not because it is better endowed with the factors of production required to manufacture aircraft, but because one of the first movers in the industry, Boeing, was a U.S. firm. The new trade theory is not at variance with the theory of comparative advantage. Economies of scale increase productivity. Thus, the new trade theory identifies an important source of comparative advantage.

LO4 | Use of the Theory

This theory is quite useful in explaining trade patterns. Empirical studies seem to support the predictions of the theory that trade increases the specialization of production within an industry, increases the variety of products available to consumers, and results in lower average prices.[28] With regard to first-mover advantages and international trade, a study by Harvard business historian Alfred Chandler suggests the existence of first-mover advantages is an important factor in explaining the dominance of firms from certain nations in specific industries.[29] The number of firms is very limited in many global industries, including the chemical industry, the heavy construction-equipment industry, the heavy truck industry, the tire industry, the consumer electronics industry, the jet engine industry, and the computer software industry.

Perhaps the most contentious implication of the new trade theory is the argument that it generates for government intervention and strategic trade policy.[30] New trade theorists stress the role of luck, entrepreneurship, and innovation in giving a firm first-mover advantages. According to this argument, the reason Boeing was the first mover in commercial jet aircraft manufacture—rather than firms such as Great Britain's DeHavilland and Hawker Siddeley, or Holland's Fokker, all of which could have been—was that Boeing was both lucky and innovative. One way Boeing was lucky is that DeHavilland lost its advantage when its Comet jet airliner, introduced two years earlier than Boeing's first jet airliner, the 707, was found to be full of serious technological flaws. Had DeHavilland not made some serious technological mistakes, Great Britain might have become the world's leading exporter of commercial jet aircraft. Boeing's innovativeness was demonstrated by its independent development of the technological know-how required to build a commercial jet airliner. Several new trade theorists have pointed out, however, that

Boeing's R&D was largely paid for by the U.S. government; the 707 was a spin-off from a government-funded military program (the entry of Airbus into the industry was also supported by significant government subsidies). Herein is a rationale for government intervention: by the sophisticated and judicious use of subsidies, could a government increase the chances of its domestic firms becoming first movers in newly emerging industries, as the U.S. government apparently did with Boeing (and the European Union did with Airbus)? Is this possible to do in the future, as some U.S. politicians, including the current president Donald Trump, suggest? If this is possible, and the new trade theory suggests it might be, we have an economic rationale for a proactive trade policy that is at variance with the free trade prescriptions of the trade theories we have reviewed so far. We will consider the policy implications of this issue in Chapter 6.

National Competitive Advantage: Porter's Diamond

Michael Porter of the Harvard Business School has conducted intensive research that attempted to determine why some nations succeed and others fail in international competition.[31] Porter and his team looked at 100 industries in ten nations. The book that contains the results of this work, *The Competitive Advantage of Nations*, has made an important contribution to thinking about trade. Like the work of the new trade theorists, Porter's work was driven by a belief that existing theories of international trade told only part of the story. For Porter, the essential task was to explain why a nation achieves international success in a particular industry. Why does Canada do so well in the manufacturing of heavy mining equipment? Canada has developed a competitive advantage in the mining industry because it has a vast wealth of natural resources and has learned how to extract them in relation to meeting local and international demands. Why does Switzerland excel in the production and export of precision instruments and pharmaceuticals? Why do Germany and the United States do so well in the chemical industry? These questions cannot be answered easily by the Heckscher–Ohlin theory, and the theory of comparative advantage offers only a partial explanation. The theory of comparative advantage would say that Switzerland excels in the production and export of precision instruments because it uses its resources very productively in these industries. Although this may be correct, this does not explain why Switzerland is more productive in this industry than Great Britain, Germany, or Spain. Porter tries to solve this puzzle.

Porter theorizes that four broad attributes of a nation shape the environment in which local firms compete and these attributes promote or impede the creation of competitive advantage (see Figure 5.4). These attributes are:

- *Factor endowments*—a nation's position in factors of production such as skilled labour or the infrastructure necessary to compete in a given industry.

- *Demand conditions*—the nature of home demand for the industry's product or service.

- *Relating and supporting industries*—the presence or absence of supplier industries and related industries that are internationally competitive.

- *Firm strategy, structure, and rivalry*—the conditions governing how companies are created, organized, and managed and the nature of domestic rivalry.

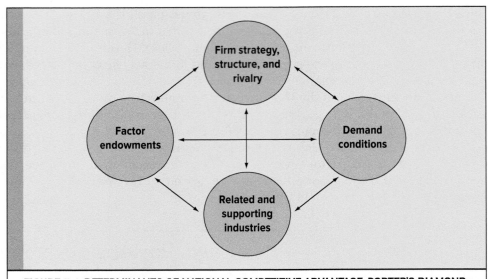

Porter speaks of these four attributes as constituting the *diamond*. He argues that firms are most likely to succeed in industries or industry segments where the diamond is most favourable. He also argues that the diamond is a mutually reinforcing system. The effect of one attribute is contingent on the state of others. For example, Porter argues favourable demand conditions will not result in competitive advantage unless the state of rivalry is sufficient to cause firms to respond to them.

Porter maintains that two additional variables can influence the national diamond in important ways: chance and government. Chance events, such as major innovations,

ANOTHER PERSPECTIVE

London Remains the Financial Capital of the World

A BNP Paribas Real Estate survey has found that 82 percent of respondents consider London to be the world's leading financial centre, helping to assuage fears that the financial crisis had weakened its position. Despite the turmoil in the financial sector over recent years, and in contrast to the somewhat pessimistic outlook of some commentators regarding the London market, BNP Paribas Real Estate's latest banking survey shows that London remains the world's leading financial centre. Eighty-two percent of respondents cited the capital as the global leader, compared to just 16 percent who specified New York. Indeed, the outlook for London is positive, with 60 percent of respondents confirming the UK as their focal point for growth over the next three years. London benefits from two key advantages that can never be taken away. First, London's central position in the time zones means that throughout the working day it is possible to speak to, and do business with, the markets in Hong Kong and Singapore in the morning and New York in the afternoon. No other financial centre in the world can provide such connectivity to the global markets. Second, London also remains the centre of the English-speaking world and is therefore a magnet for English-speaking talent.

Source: Excerpted from "London Remains the Financial Capital of the World," by Dan Bayley, *The Banker*, January 6, 2011, www.thebanker.com/Comment-Profiles/Bracken/London-remains-the-financial-capital-of-the-world. Reprinted with permission.

can reshape industry structure and provide the opportunity for one nation's firms to supplant another's. Government, by its choice of policies, can detract from or improve national advantage. For example, regulation can alter home demand conditions, antitrust policies can influence the intensity of rivalry within an industry, and government investments in education can change factor endowments.

Factor Endowments

Factor endowments lie at the centre of the Heckscher–Ohlin theory. While Porter does not propose anything radically new, he does analyze the characteristics of factors of production. He recognizes hierarchies among factors, distinguishing between basic factors (e.g., natural resources, climate, location, and demographics) and advanced factors (e.g., communication infrastructure, sophisticated and skilled labour, research facilities, and technological know-how). He argues that advanced factors are the most significant for competitive advantage. Unlike the naturally endowed basic factors, advanced factors are a product of investment by individuals, companies, and governments. Thus, government investments in basic and higher education, by improving the general skill and knowledge level of the population and by stimulating research at higher education institutions, can upgrade a nation's advanced factors.

The relationship between advanced and basic factors is complex. Basic factors can provide an initial advantage that is subsequently reinforced and extended by investment in advanced factors. Conversely, disadvantages in basic factors can create pressures to invest in advanced factors. An obvious example of this phenomenon is Japan, a country that lacks arable land and mineral deposits and yet through investment has built a substantial endowment of advanced factors. Porter notes that Japan's large pool of engineers (reflecting a much higher number of engineering graduates per capita than almost any other nation) has been vital to Japan's success in many manufacturing industries.

Demand Conditions

Porter emphasizes the role domestic demand plays in upgrading competitive advantage. Firms are typically most sensitive to the needs of their closest customers. Thus, the characteristics of home demand are particularly important in shaping the attributes of domestically made products and in creating pressures for innovation and quality. Porter argues that a nation's firms gain competitive advantage if their domestic consumers are sophisticated and demanding. Such consumers pressure local firms to meet high standards of product quality and to produce innovative products. Porter notes that Japan's sophisticated and knowledgeable camera buyers helped stimulate the Japanese camera industry to improve product quality and to introduce innovative models.

Related and Supporting Industries

The third broad attribute of national advantage in an industry is the presence of suppliers or related industries that are internationally competitive. The benefits of investments in advanced factors of production by related and supporting industries can spill over into an industry, thereby helping it achieve a strong competitive position internationally. Swedish strength in fabricated steel products (e.g., ball bearings and cutting tools) has drawn on strengths in Sweden's specialty steel industry. Technological leadership in the U.S. semiconductor industry until the mid-1980s provided the basis for U.S. success in personal computers and several other technically advanced electronic products. Similarly, Switzerland's success in pharmaceuticals is closely related to its previous international success in the technologically related dye industry.

One consequence of this process is that successful industries within a country tend to be grouped into clusters of related industries. This was one of the most pervasive findings of Porter's study. One such cluster is the German textile and apparel sector, which includes high-quality cotton, wool, synthetic fibres, sewing machine needles, and a wide range of textile machinery. Such clusters are important because valuable knowledge can flow between the firms within a geographic cluster, benefiting all within that cluster. Knowledge flows occur when employees move between firms within a region and when national industry associations bring employees from different companies together for conferences or workshops.[32]

Firm Strategy, Structure, and Rivalry

The fourth broad attribute of national competitive advantage in Porter's model is the strategy, structure, and rivalry of firms within a nation. Porter makes two important points here. First, different nations are characterized by different management ideologies, which either help them or do not help them to build national competitive advantage. For example, Porter notes the predominance of engineers in top management at German and Japanese firms. He attributes this to these firms' emphasis on improving manufacturing processes and product design. In contrast, Porter notes a predominance of people with finance backgrounds leading many U.S. firms. He links this to U.S. firms' lack of attention to improving manufacturing processes and product design, particularly during the 1970s and '80s. He also argues that the dominance of finance has led to a corresponding overemphasis on maximizing short-term financial returns. According to Porter, one consequence of these different management ideologies has been a relative loss of U.S. competitiveness in those engineering-based industries where manufacturing processes and product design issues are all-important (e.g., the automobile industry).

Porter's second point is that there is a strong association between vigorous domestic rivalry and the creation and persistence of competitive advantage in an industry.

ANOTHER PERSPECTIVE

Business Clusters and Trade Theory

Business clusters are everywhere. Fast-food restaurants tend to cluster, as do department stores. We have heavy manufacturing areas in and around Hamilton, Ontario. That similar businesses set up in the same geographic area might seem illogical at first, especially if they are sales organizations (if they were alone, they would face less competition). Modern trade theory suggests that businesses cluster to draw on resources they have created by clustering. These resources form a comparative advantage for the area. Think about the Waterloo, Ontario, corridor and the comparative advantage it offers high-tech firms that decide to locate there: many innovative people developing new ideas, a labour market that is educated and experienced and knows how to manage knowledge innovation. Informal networking among similarly focused people while at the health club or in a restaurant or bar creates additional stimulation, which drives further innovation. This explanation works for fast food, too, albeit with different drivers. Clusters create a pool of trained labour and an area that functions as a magnet for the hungry consumer who chooses a quick-service restaurant. Plus the robust competition such clusters create pushes innovation. Clustered companies learn from each other.

MANAGEMENT FOCUS

Moving U.S. White-Collar Jobs Offshore

Economists have long argued that free trade produces gains for all countries that participate in a free trading system. As the next wave of globalization sweeps through the U.S. economy, many people are wondering if this is true. During the 1980s and 1990s, free trade was associated with the movement of low-skill, blue-collar manufacturing jobs out of rich countries such as the United States and toward low-wage countries—textiles to Costa Rica, athletic shoes to the Philippines, steel to Brazil, electronic products to Thailand, and so on.

While many observers bemoaned the "hollowing out" of U.S. manufacturing, economists stated that high-skill and high-wage white-collar jobs associated with the knowledge-based economy would stay in the United States. Computers might be assembled in Thailand, so the argument went, but they would continue to be designed in Silicon Valley by highly skilled U.S. engineers, and software applications would be written in the United States by programmers at Apple, Microsoft, Adobe, Oracle, and the like.

Developments over the past several decades have people questioning this assumption. Many American companies have been moving white-collar, "knowledge-based" jobs to developing nations where they can be performed for a fraction of the cost. During the long economic boom of the 1990s, Bank of America had to compete with other organizations for the scarce talents of information technology specialists, driving annual salaries to more than $100,000. However, with business under pressure since then, the bank cut nearly 5000 jobs from its 25 000-strong, U.S.-based information technology workforce. Some of these jobs were transferred to India, where work that costs $100 an hour in the United States could be done for $20 an hour.

One beneficiary of Bank of America's downsizing is Infosys Technologies Ltd., a Bangalore, India, information technology firm where 250 engineers now develop information technology applications for the bank. Other Infosys employees are busy processing home loan applications for U.S. mortgage companies. Nearby in the offices of another Indian firm, Wipro Ltd., radiologists interpret 30 CT scans a day for Massachusetts General Hospital that are sent over the Internet. At yet another Bangalore business, engineers earn $10,000 a year designing leading-edge semiconductor chips for Texas Instruments. Nor is India the only beneficiary of these changes.

Some architectural work also is being outsourced to lower-cost locations. Flour Corp., a California-based construction company, employs some 1200 engineers and draftsmen in the Philippines, Poland, and India to turn layouts of industrial facilities into detailed specifications. For a Saudi Arabian chemical plant, Flour is designing, 200 young engineers based in the Philippines earning less than $3,000 a year collaborate in real time over the Internet with elite U.S. and British engineers who make up to $90,000 a year. Why does Flour do this? According to the company, the answer is simple. Doing so reduces the prices of a project by 15 percent, giving the company a cost-based competitive advantage in the global market for construction design. Most disturbing of all for future job growth in the United States, some high-tech start-ups are outsourcing significant work right from inception. For example, Zoho Corporation, a California-based start-up offering online web applications for small businesses, has about 20 employees in the United States and more than 1000 in India.

Questions

1. Do you see this trend continuing in the future. Can you think of any Canadian examples?
2. Are all white-collar jobs the same? Is there any differentiation in the types of white-collar jobs that are moving offshore?

Sources: P. Engardio, A. Bernstein, and M. Kripalani, "Is Your Job Next?" *Businessweek*, February 3, 2003, pp. 50–60; "America's Pain, India's Gain," *The Economist*, January 11, 2003, p. 57; M. Schroeder and T. Aeppel, "Skilled Workers Mount Opposition to Free Trade, Swaying Politicians," *The Wall Street Journal*, October 10, 2003, pp. A1, A11; D. Clark, "New U.S. Fees on Visas Irk Outsources," *The Wall Street Journal*, August 16, 2010, p. 6; and J. R. Hagerty, "U.S. Loses High Tech Jobs as R&D Shifts to Asia," *The Wall Street Journal*, January 18, 2012, p. B1.

Vigorous domestic rivalry induces firms to look for ways to improve efficiency, which makes them better international competitors. Domestic rivalry creates pressures to innovate, to improve quality, to reduce costs, and to invest in upgrading advanced factors. All this helps to create world-class competitors. Porter cites the case of Japan.

> Nowhere is the role of domestic rivalry more evident than in Japan, where it is all-out warfare in which many companies fail to achieve profitability. With goals that stress market share, Japanese companies engage in a continuing struggle to outdo each other. Shares fluctuate markedly. The process is prominently covered in the business press. Elaborate rankings measure which companies are most popular with university graduates. The rate of new product and process development is breathtaking.[33]

A similar point about the stimulating effects of strong domestic competition can be made with regard to the rise of Nokia to global pre-eminence in the market for cellular telephone equipment. For details, see the Management Focus.

Evaluating Porter's Theory

Porter contends that the degree to which a nation is likely to achieve international success in a certain industry is a function of the combined impact of factor endowments, domestic demand conditions, related and supporting industries, and domestic rivalry. He argues that the presence of all four components is usually required for this diamond to boost competitive performance (although there are exceptions). Porter also contends that government can influence each of the four components of the diamond—either positively or negatively. Factor endowments can be affected by subsidies, policies toward capital markets, policies toward education, and so on. Government can shape domestic demand through local product standards or with regulations that mandate or influence buyer needs. Government policy can influence supporting and related industries through regulation and affect firm rivalry through such devices as capital market regulation, tax policy, and antitrust laws.

If Porter is correct, we would expect his model to predict the pattern of international trade that we observe in the real world. Countries should be exporting products from those industries where all four components of the diamond are favourable, while importing in those areas where the components are not favourable. Is he correct? We simply do not know. Porter's theory has not been subjected to detailed empirical testing. Much about the theory rings true, but the same can be said for the new trade theory, the theory of comparative advantage, and the Heckscher-Ohlin theory. It may be that each of these theories, which complement each other, explains something about the pattern of international trade.

LO5 IMPLICATIONS FOR BUSINESS

Why does all this matter for business? There are at least three main implications for international businesses of the material discussed in this chapter: location implications, first-mover implications, and policy implications.

LOCATION IMPLICATIONS

Underlying most of the theories we have discussed is the notion that different countries have particular advantages in different productive activities. Thus, from a profit perspective, it makes sense for a firm to disperse its productive activities to those countries where, according to the theory of international trade, they can be performed most efficiently (transportation costs and tariffs permitting). If design can be performed most efficiently in France, that is where design facilities should be located; if the manufacture of basic components can be performed most efficiently in Singapore, that is where they should be manufactured; and if final assembly can be performed most efficiently in China, that is where final assembly should be performed. The result is a global web of productive activities, with different activities being performed in different locations around the globe depending on considerations of comparative advantage, factor endowments, and the like. If the firm does not do this, it may find itself at a competitive disadvantage relative to firms that do.

Consider the production of a laptop computer, a process with four major stages: (1) basic research and development of the product design; (2) manufacture of standard electronic components (e.g., memory chips); (3) manufacture of advanced components (e.g., flat-top colour display screens and microprocessors); and (4) final assembly. Basic R&D requires a pool of highly skilled and educated workers with good backgrounds in microelectronics. The two countries with a comparative advantage in basic microelectronics R&D and design are Japan and the United States, so most producers of laptop computers locate their R&D facilities in one or both of these countries.

The manufacture of standard electronic components is a capital-intensive process requiring semi-skilled labour, and cost pressures are intense. The best locations for such activities today are places such as Singapore, Taiwan, and Malaysia. These countries have pools of relatively skilled, low-cost labour. Thus, many producers of laptop computers have standard components, such as memory chips, produced at these locations.

The manufacture of advanced components such as microprocessors and display screens is a capital-intensive process requiring skilled labour. Because cost pressures are not so intense at this stage, these components can be—and are—manufactured in countries with high labour costs that also have pools of highly skilled labour (primarily Japan, South Korea, and the United States).

Finally, assembly is a relatively labour-intensive process requiring only low-skilled labour, and cost pressures are intense. As a result, final assembly may be carried out in a country such as Mexico, which has an abundance of low-cost, low-skilled labour. A laptop computer produced by a U.S. manufacturer may be designed in California, have its standard components produced in Taiwan and Singapore, have its advanced components produced in Japan and the United States, have its final assembly in Mexico, and be sold in the United States or elsewhere in the world. By dispersing production activities to different locations around the globe, the U.S. manufacturer is taking advantage of the differences between countries identified by the various theories of international trade.

FIRST-MOVER IMPLICATIONS

According to the new trade theory, firms that establish a first-mover advantage with regard to the production of a particular new product may subsequently dominate global trade in that product. This is particularly true in industries where the global market can profitably support only a limited number of firms, such as the aerospace market, but early commitments also seem to be important in less concentrated industries such as the market for cellular telephone equipment. For the individual firm, the clear message is that it pays to invest substantial financial resources in trying to build a first-mover, or early-mover, advantage, even if that means several years of substantial losses before a new venture becomes profitable. Although the details of how to achieve this are beyond the scope of this book, many publications offer strategies for exploiting first-mover advantages.[34]

POLICY IMPLICATIONS

The theories of international trade also matter to international businesses because firms are major players on the international trade scene. Business firms produce exports, and business firms import the products of other countries. Because of their pivotal role in international trade, businesses can influence government trade policy, lobbying to promote free trade or trade restrictions. The theories of international trade claim that promoting free trade is generally in the best interests of a country, although it may not always be in the best interest of an individual firm or its employees. Many firms recognize this and lobby for open markets (although those adversely affected often lobby for greater protectionism).

For example, in the early 1990s, when the U.S. government announced its intention to place a tariff on Japanese imports of liquid crystal display (LCD) screens, IBM and Apple Computer protested strongly.

Both IBM and Apple pointed out that (1) Japan was the lowest-cost source of LCD screens; (2) they used these screens in their own laptop computers; and (3) the proposed tariff, by increasing the cost of LCD screens, would increase the cost of laptop computers produced by IBM and Apple, thus making them less competitive in the world market. In other words, the tariff, designed to protect U.S. firms, would be self-defeating. In response to these pressures, the U.S. government reversed its position.

Unlike IBM and Apple, however, businesses do not always lobby for free trade. This is important to realize when examining the rise of the anti-free trade movement in the United States. In the United States, for example, restrictions on imports of steel have periodically been put into place in response to direct pressure by U.S. firms on the government. In some cases, the government has responded to pressure by getting foreign companies to agree to "voluntary" restrictions on their imports, using the implicit threat of more comprehensive formal trade barriers to get them to adhere to these agreements (historically, this has occurred in the automobile industry). In other cases, the government used what are called "antidumping" actions to justify tariffs on imports from other nations (these mechanisms will be discussed in detail in the next chapter).

As predicted by international trade theory, many of these agreements have been self-defeating, such as the voluntary restriction on machine tool imports agreed to in 1985. Shielded from international competition by import barriers, the U.S. machine tool industry had no incentive to increase its efficiency. Consequently, it lost many of its export markets to more efficient foreign competitors. Because of this misguided action, the U.S. machine tool industry shrunk during the period when the agreement was in force. For anyone schooled in international trade theory, this was not surprising.

Finally, Porter's theory of national competitive advantage also contains policy implications. Porter's theory suggests that it is in the best interest of business for a firm to invest in upgrading advanced factors of production, for example, to invest in better training for its employees and to increase its commitment to research and development. It is also in the best interests of business to lobby the government to adopt policies that have a favourable impact on each component of the national diamond. Thus, according to Porter, businesses should urge government to increase investment in education, infrastructure, and basic research (since all these enhance advanced factors) and to adopt policies that promote strong competition within domestic markets (since this makes firms stronger international competitors, according to Porter's findings).

Key Terms

absolute advantage	free trade
comparative advantage	mercantilism
constant returns to specialization	positive-sum game
economies of scale	zero-sum game

LO Learning Objectives Summary

1. This chapter reviewed a number of theories that explain why it is beneficial for a country to engage in international trade and explained the pattern of international trade observed in the world economy. The theories of Smith, Ricardo, and Heckscher-Ohlin all make strong cases for unrestricted free trade. In contrast, the mercantilist doctrine and, to a lesser extent, the new trade theory can be interpreted to support government intervention to promote exports through subsidies and to limit imports through tariffs and quotas.

2. In explaining the pattern of international trade, the different theories offer largely complementary explanations. Although no one theory may explain the apparent pattern of international trade, taken

together, the theory of comparative advantage, the Heckscher–Ohlin theory, the product life-cycle theory, the new trade theory, and Porter's theory of national competitive advantage do suggest which factors are important. Comparative advantage tells us that productivity differences are important; Heckscher–Ohlin tells us that factor endowments matter; the product life-cycle theory tells us that where a new product is introduced is important; the new trade theory tells us that increasing returns to specialization and first-mover advantages matter; and Porter tells us that all these factors may be important insofar as they affect the four components of the national diamond.

3. The theory of comparative advantage suggests that it makes sense for a country to specialize in producing those goods that it can produce most efficiently, while buying goods that it can produce relatively less efficiently from other countries—even if that means buying goods from other countries that it could produce more efficiently itself. It suggests that unrestricted free trade brings about increased world production, that is, that trade is a positive-sum game. New trade theory states that trade allows a nation to specialize in the production of certain goods, attaining scale economies and lowering the costs of producing those goods, while buying goods that it does not produce from other nations that are similarly specialized. By this mechanism, the variety of goods available to consumers in each nation is increased, while the average costs of those goods should fall.

4. Some new trade theorists have promoted the idea of strategic trade policy. The argument is that government, by the sophisticated and judicious use of subsidies, might be able to increase the chances of domestic firms becoming first movers in newly emerging industries. Porter's theory of national competitive advantage suggests that the pattern of trade is influenced by four attributes of a nation: *(a)* factor endowments, *(b)* domestic demand conditions, *(c)* related and supporting industries, and *(d)* firm strategy, structure, and rivalry. Government policy can shape domestic demand, and influence supporting and related industries through regulation, and influence rivalry through regulation and policies.

5. Theories of international trade are important to an individual business firm primarily because they can help the firm decide where to locate its various production activities. Firms involved in international trade can and do exert a strong influence on government policy toward trade. By lobbying government, business firms can promote free trade or trade restrictions.

Critical Thinking and Discussion Questions

1. "Mercantilism is a bankrupt theory that has no place in the modern world." Evaluate this statement.

2. "China is a neomercantilist nation. It protects industries where it has no competitive advantage in the world economy, while demanding that other countries open up those markets where Chinese producers have a competitive advantage." Evaluate this statement.

3. Unions in developed nations often oppose imports from low-wage countries and advocate trade barriers to protect jobs from what they often characterize as "unfair" import competition. Is such competition "unfair"? Do you think this argument is in the best interests of (a) the unions, (b) the people they represent, and/or (c) the country as a whole?

4. Drawing on the theory of comparative advantage to support your arguments, outline the case for free trade.

5. What are the potential costs of adopting a free trade regime? Do you think governments should do anything to reduce these costs? What?

6. Using the new trade theory and Porter's theory of national competitive advantage, outline the case for government policies that would build national competitive advantage in a particular industry. What kinds of policies would you recommend that the government adopt? Are these policies at variance with the basic free trade philosophy?

7. "The world's poorest countries are at a competitive disadvantage in every sector of their economies. They have nothing to export. They have no capital; their land is of poor quality; they often have too many people given available work opportunities; and they are poorly educated. Free trade cannot possibly be in the interests of such nations!" Evaluate this statement.

8. "In general, policies designed to limit competition from low-cost foreign competitors do not help a country to achieve greater economic growth." Evaluate this statement.

9. Is free trade fair? Discuss.

Research Task ~~globalEDGE™~~ globaledge.msu.edu

Use the globalEDGE™ site to complete the following exercises:

1. WTO's *International Trade Statistics* is an annual report that provides comprehensive, comparable, and up-to-date statistics on trade in merchandise and commercial services. This report allows for an assessment of world trade flows by country, region, and main product groups or service categories. Using the most recent statistics available, identify the top five countries that lead in the export and import of merchandise, respectively.

2. Your company is interested in importing Australian wine to Canada. As part of the initial analysis, you want to identify the strengths of the Australian wine industry. Provide a short description of the current status of Australian wine exports by variety, and a list of the top importing countries of Australian wines. A useful Web site is the CanadExport Web site at http://tradecommissioner.gc.ca/canadexport/index.aspx?lang=eng.

CLOSING CASE

THE RISE OF INDIA'S DRUG INDUSTRY

One of the great success stories in international trade in recent years has been the strong growth of India's pharmaceutical industry. The country used to be known for producing cheap knockoffs of patented drugs discovered by Western and Japanese pharmaceutical companies. This made the industry something of an international pariah. Because they made copies of patented products, and therefore violated intellectual property rights, Indian companies were not allowed to sell these products in developed markets. With no assurance that their intellectual property would be protected, foreign drug companies refused to invest in, partner with, or buy from their Indian counterparts, further limiting the business opportunities of Indian companies. In developed markets such as Canada and the United States, the best that Indian companies could do was to sell low-cost generic pharmaceuticals (generic pharmaceuticals are products whose patents have expired).

In 2005, however, India signed an agreement with the World Trade Organization that brought the country into compliance with WTO rules on intellectual property rights. Indian companies stopped producing counterfeit products. Secure in knowledge that their patents would be respected, foreign companies started to do business with their Indian counterparts. For India, the result has been dramatic growth in its pharmaceutical sector. The sector generated sales of close to $30 billion in 2012–2013, more than two and a half times the figure of 2005. Driving this growth have been surging exports, which grew at 15 percent per annum between 2006 and 2012. In 2000, pharmaceutical exports from India amounted to around $1 billion. By 2012–2013, the figure was around $14.7 billion!

Much of this growth has been the result of partnerships between Western and Indian firms. Western companies have been increasingly outsourcing manufacturing and packaging activities to India while scaling back some of these activities at home and in places such as Puerto Rico, which historically has been a major manufacturing hub for

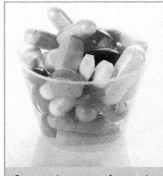

Generic drugs manufactured in India help that country to emerge as a major exporter of pharmaceuticals. © *Radius Images/Getty Images*

firms serving the North American market. India's advantages in manufacturing and packaging include relatively low wage rates, an educated workforce, and the widespread use of English as a business language. Western companies have continued to perform high value-added R&D, marketing, and sales activities, and these remain located in their home markets.

During India's years as an international pariah in the drug business, its nascent domestic industry set the foundations for today's growth. Local start-ups invested in the facilities required to discover and produce pharmaceuticals, creating a market for pharmaceutical scientists and workers in India. In turn, this drove the expansion of pharmaceutical programs in the country's universities, thereby increasing the supply of talent. Moreover, the industry's experience in the generic drug business during the 1990s and early 2000s has given it expertise in dealing with regulatory agencies in the United States and European Union. After 2005, this know-how made Indian companies more attractive as partners for Western enterprises. Combined with low labour costs, all these factors came together to make India an increasingly attractive location for the manufacturing of pharmaceuticals.

The U.S. Federal Drug Administration (FDA) responded to the shift of manufacturing to India by opening two offices there to oversee manufacturing compliance and make sure safety was consistent with FDA-mandated standards. Today, the FDA has issued approvals to produce pharmaceuticals for sale in the United States to some 900 plants in India, giving Indian companies a legitimacy that potential rivals in places such as China lack.

For Western enterprises, the obvious attraction of outsourcing drug manufacturing to India is that it lowers their costs, enabling them to protect their earnings in an increasingly difficult domestic environment where government health care regulation and increased competition have put pressure on the pricing of many pharmaceuticals. Arguably, this also benefits consumers, particularly in the United States, because lower pharmaceutical prices mean lower insurance costs, and ultimately lower out-of-pocket expenses than if those pharmaceuticals were still manufactured domestically. Offset against this economic benefit, of course, must be the cost of jobs lost in U.S. pharmaceutical manufacturing. Indicative of this trend, total manufacturing employment in this sector fell by 5 percent between 2008 and 2010.

Sources: H. Timmons, "A Pharmaceutical Future," *The New York Times*, July 7, 2010, pp. B1, B4; K. K. Sharma, "On the World Stage," *Business Today*, January 9, 2011, pp. 116–17; M. Velterop, "The Indian Perspective," *Pharmaceutical Technology Europe*, September 2010, pp. 40–41; "Pharma Exports Expected to Touch Rs 75,000 in 2012–2013," *Business Standard*, February 27, 2013; and Lynne Taylor, "India: Exports of Generics Growing 24% a Year," *PharmaTimes*, October 21, 2013.

Case Discussion Questions

1. How might (a) North American pharmaceutical companies and (b) Western consumers benefit from the rise of the Indian pharmaceutical industry?

2. Who might have lost out as a result of the recent rise of the Indian pharmaceutical industry?

3. Do the benefits from trade with the Indian pharmaceutical sector outweigh the losses?

4. What international trade theory (or theories) best explain the rise of India as a major exporter of pharmaceuticals?

Chapter 6

The Political Economy of International Trade

SUGAR SUBSIDIES DRIVE CANDY MAKERS ABROAD

Back in the 1930s at the height of the Great Depression, the U.S. government stepped in to support the U.S. sugar industry with a combination of subsidies, price supports, import quotas, and tariffs. These actions were meant to be temporary, but as of 2017, they are still in place. Under policies approved in the 2008 farm bill, the government guarantees 85 percent of the market for U.S. producers, primarily farmers growing sugar beets and cane. The remaining 15 percent is allocated for imports from certain countries at a preferential tariff rate. The government also sets a floor price for sugar. If the price falls below the floor, the government steps in to purchase excess supply, driving the price back up again. The surplus is then sold at a loss to producers of ethanol. A significant U.S. sugar harvest in 2013 required the government to spend some $300 million to prop up U.S. sugar prices. As a result of these policies, between 2010 and 2013, the U.S. sugar price has averaged between 64 percent and 92 percent higher than the world price of sugar.

American sugar producers say that the federal programs are necessary to keep big sugar-producing countries like Brazil, India, and Thailand from flooding the U.S. market and driving them out of business. Opponents of the practice include numerous small candy producers. Many of them complain about the high U.S. price for sugar. Increasingly, they have responded by moving production offshore. For example, the Spangler Candy Company, the maker of Dum Dums, has moved 200 jobs from Ohio to Juarez, Mexico, where it makes candy canes that are then imported back into the United States. Similarly, Adams & Brooks, a California-based candy company, has shifted two-thirds of its production across the border to Mexico in response to higher U.S. sugar prices.

A recent academic study suggests that the U.S. sugar policies primarily benefit 4700 sugar producers, while imposing costs of $2.9 billion to $3.5 billion per annum on U.S. consumers due to higher sugar prices. The same research predicts that removing the support programs would lead to the net creation of 17 000 to 20 000 new jobs in the United States, while dramatically reducing imports of products containing sugar.

Given the benefits of removing sugar support programs, and all the talk about deregulation and reducing the budget deficit in Congress, many observers thought that 2013 would be the year that the sugar programs were finally abandoned. The farm bill was up for renewal, and the sugar support programs were held up as an example of how wasteful government subsidies are. However, sugar producers spent some $20 million on political lobbying between 2011 and 2013. Partly due to their influence, the U.S. Senate voted 54 to 45 against any reform in the sugar programs. The majority included 20 out of 45 Republican senators, most of who publicly rail against this kind of government intervention. Apparently however, political expediency required that they support intervention in this case.

Sources: G. F. Will, "Congress Needs to Stop Subsidies to Sugar Farmers," *Washington Post*, June 7, 2013; R. Nixon, "American Candy Makers, Pinched by Inflated Sugar Prices, Look Abroad," *New York Times*, October 30, 2013; and J. Beghin, A. Elobeid, "The Impact of the U.S. Sugar Program Redux," *Iowa State Working Paper 13-WP 538*, May 2013, http://www.card.iastate.edu/products/publications/pdf/13wp538.pdf.

 LO **LEARNING OBJECTIVES**

By the end of this chapter you should be able to:

1. Identify the policy instruments used by governments to influence international trade flows.

2. Understand why governments sometimes intervene in international trade.

3. Summarize and explain the arguments against strategic trade policy.

4. Describe the development of the world trading system and the current trade issue.

5. Explain the implications for managers of developments in the world trading system.

Introduction

Our review of the classical trade theories of Smith, Ricardo, and Heckscher–Ohlin in Chapter 5 showed us that, in a world without trade barriers, trade patterns are determined by the relative productivity of different factors of production in different countries. Countries will specialize in products that they can make most efficiently, while importing products that they can produce less efficiently. Chapter 5 also laid out the intellectual case for free trade. Remember, free trade refers to a situation where a government does not attempt to restrict what its citizens can buy from another country or what they can sell to another country. As we saw in Chapter 5, the theories of Smith, Ricardo, and Heckscher–Ohlin predict that the consequences of free trade include both static economic gains (because free trade supports a higher level of domestic consumption and more efficient utilization of resources) and dynamic economic gains (because free trade stimulates economic growth and the creation of wealth).

This chapter looks at the political reality of international trade. Although many nations are nominally committed to free trade, they tend to intervene in international trade to protect the interests of politically important groups or promote the interests of key domestic producers. The opening case illustrates one such situation. Even though successive U.S. administrations have often promoted free trade policies, the government still has a long history of intervening in markets to protect some domestic producers. U.S. sugar producers are a case in point. There is little doubt that policies put in place in the 1930s to support the U.S. sugar industry are now out of date. They lead to higher sugar prices in the United States, effectively imposing a tax on U.S. consumers, while creating an incentive for U.S. candy manufacturers to move production offshore where sugar prices are lower, which leads to job losses in the United States. However, due to effective political lobbying by sugar producers, the policies seem likely to continue in place for some time to come.

ANOTHER PERSPECTIVE

Check Out Canadian Import Tariffs

You can find information about importing into Canada at the following link: http://www.cbsa-asfc. gc.ca./menu-eng.html, and click on the links on importing and exporting commerical goods. If you were the manager of a company in Australia and wanted to export to Canada, how might these tariffs affect your export strategy? How might they affect your relationship with your own Australian government?

In this chapter, we explore the political and economic reasons that governments have for intervening in international trade. When governments intervene, they often do so by restricting imports of goods and services into their nation, while adopting policies that promote exports. Normally their motives are to protect domestic producers and jobs from foreign competition while increasing the foreign market for products of domestic producers. However, in recent years, "social" issues have intruded into the decision-making process. In the United States, for example, there is a movement to try to ban imports of goods from countries that do not abide by the same labour, health, and environmental regulations as the United States. This is in addition to broad, sweeping pronouncements from some politicians that they are against free trade (or that they want the yet-to-be-defined fair trade).

We start this chapter by describing the range of policy instruments that governments use to intervene in international trade. This is followed by a detailed review of the various political and economic motives that governments have for intervention. In the third section of this chapter we consider how the case for free trade stands up in view of the various justifications given for government intervention in international trade. Then we look at the emergence of the modern international trading system, which is based on the General Agreement on Tariffs and Trade (GATT) and its successor, the

World Trade Organization (WTO). The GATT and WTO are the creations of a series of multinational treaties. Like the GATT before it, the WTO promotes free trade by limiting the ability of national governments to adopt policies that restrict imports into their nations. In the final section of this chapter, we discuss the implications of this material for business practice.

LO1 Instruments of Trade Policy

Trade policy uses seven main instruments: tariffs, subsidies, import quotas, voluntary export restraints, local content requirements, administrative policies, and antidumping duties. Tariffs are the oldest and simplest instrument of trade policy. As we shall see later in this chapter, they are also the instrument that GATT and WTO have been most successful in limiting. A fall in tariff barriers in recent decades (until political talk during 2016 and 2017 in the United States brought back the issue) has been accompanied by a rise in nontariff barriers, such as subsidies, quotas, voluntary export restraints, and antidumping duties.

Tariffs

A **tariff** is a tax levied on imports. Tariffs fall into two categories. **Specific tariffs** are levied as a fixed charge for each unit of a good imported (for example, $3 per barrel of oil). **Ad valorem tariffs** are levied as a proportion of the value of the imported good. The European Union had imposed such a tariff on imports of bananas from Latin America in the early 1990s; the tariff amounted to 15 to 20 percent by value on the first 2.5 million tonnes of imports of bananas from Latin America.

Tariffs are the simplest and most straightforward mechanism for governments to implement. U.S. President Donald Trump has spoken almost exclusively on his willingness to impose tariffs on products, in his search for making trade fairer to the United States. He has repeatedly stated that no government can stop a U.S. manufacturing plant from moving overseas (primarily to Mexico or China), but if that firm wishes to sell its newly manufactured product back into the United States, it will be hit by a tariff (sometimes reaching up to 30-40 percent).

A tariff raises the cost of imported products. In most cases, tariffs are put in place to protect domestic producers from foreign competition. For example, the Canadian lumber industry suffered during the decades-long acrimonious softwood lumber trade disputes between the United States and Canada. As of June 2010, Canadian forestry companies will no longer pay an export tax on lumber exported to the United States, which was imposed in the 2006 Softwood Lumber Agreement. The export tax was changed from 18 percent at the start of 2010 to zero. The original expiry date of the Softwood Lumber Agreement was 2013, but Canada and the United States agreed to extend the agreement for an additional two years, to October 2015, and a further extension to October 2016. As it stands currently, Canadian producers have complete access to the U.S. market, though this will undoubtedly change with the new Trump administration and its stated goal of renegotiating the North American Free Trade agreement (NAFTA).

Part of the reason that the previously contentious issue is no longer in the news is that the dynamics of supply and demand have shifted: demand has begun to shift as more wood is sent to China, and supply has been restricted by forests killed by the pine beetle in British Columbia and by the regulatory reductions of trees that can be cut down in Ontario.

ANOTHER PERSPECTIVE

Canadian Government Subsidies to Foreign Companies

Increasingly there is pressure exerted by the WTO on governments that seek to offer "sweeteners" to entice foreign companies to come and set up shop. Before the era of free trade, Canada and the U.S. signed the historic Auto Pact in 1965 whereby U.S. carmakers, in exchange for tariff-free access, had to assemble in Canada at least one vehicle for every one sold in the country. This exclusive relationship ended in 1999 when the World Trade Organization overruled parts of the Auto Pact.

Still, we have seen other types of incentives offered by the Canadian government to foreign car manufacturers, such as Toyota in Cambridge, Ontario, and to auto makers generally as a result of the market slowdown beginning in 2008.

The WTO is gradually seeking to phase out member country government incentives, including tax breaks and other fiscal motivators. Canada is not immune. Do you think that the WTO is overstepping its bounds? There are many Web sites expressing opinions on this topic. Check out the WTO's Web site at www.wto.org and briefly search for their rulings on these and other matters.

In general, two conclusions can be derived from economic analysis of the effect of import tariffs.[1] First, tariffs are generally pro-producer and anti-consumer. While they protect producers from foreign competitors, this restriction of supply also raises domestic prices. For example, a study by Japanese economists calculated that tariffs on imports of foodstuffs, cosmetics, and chemicals into Japan cost the average Japanese consumer about $890 per year in the form of higher prices.[2] Almost all studies find that import tariffs impose significant costs on domestic consumers in the form of higher prices.[3]

Second, import tariffs reduce the overall efficiency of the world economy. They reduce efficiency because a protective tariff encourages domestic firms to produce products at home that, in theory, could be produced more efficiently abroad. The consequence is an inefficient utilization of resources. For example, tariffs on the importation of rice into South Korea have led to an increase in rice production in that country; however, rice farming is an unproductive use of land in South Korea. It would make more sense for the South Koreans to purchase their rice from lower-cost foreign producers and to utilize the land now employed in rice production in some other way, such as growing foodstuffs that cannot be produced more efficiently elsewhere or for residential and industrial purposes.

Sometimes tariffs are levied on exports of a product from a country. Export tariffs are far less common than import tariffs. In general, export tariffs have two objectives: first, to raise revenue for the government, and second, to reduce exports from a sector, often for political reasons. For example, in 2004 China imposed a tariff on textile exports. The primary objective was to moderate the growth in exports of textiles from China, thereby alleviating tensions with other trading partners.

Subsidies

A **subsidy** is a government payment to a domestic producer. Subsidies take many forms, including cash grants, low-interest loans, tax breaks, and government equity participation in domestic firms. By lowering production costs, subsidies help domestic producers in two ways: (1) competing against foreign imports and (2) gaining export markets. In response to a severe sales slump following the global financial crisis, both

COUNTRY FOCUS

Are the Chinese Illegally Subsidizing Auto Exports?

Trade issues involving the United States and China which end up playing a part in U.S. presidential elections did not begin with the 2016 campaign. In late 2012, during that presidential election campaign, the Obama administration filed a complaint against China with the World Trade Organization. The complaint claims that China is providing export subsidies to its auto and auto parts industries. The subsidies include cash grants for exporting, grants for R&D, subsidies to pay interest on loans, and preferential tax treatment.

The United States estimates the value of the subsidies to be at least $1 billion between 2009 and 2011. The complaint also points out that in the years 2002 through 2011, the value of China's exports of autos and auto parts increased more than ninefold from $7.4 billion to $69.1 billion. The United States was China's largest market for exports of auto parts during this period. The United States is asserting that, to some degree, this growth may have been helped by subsidies. The complaint goes on to claim that these subsidies have hurt producers of automobiles and auto parts in the United States. This is a large industry in the United States, employing over 800 000 people and generating some $350 billion in sales.

While some in the labour movement applauded the move, the response from U.S. auto companies and auto parts producers was muted. One reason for this is that many U.S. producers do business in China and, in all probability, want to avoid retaliation from the Chinese government. GM, for example, has a joint venture and two wholly owned subsidiaries in China and is doing very well there. In addition, some U.S. producers benefit by purchasing cheap Chinese auto parts, so any retaliatory tariffs imposed on those imports might actually raise their costs.

More cynical observers saw the move as nothing more than political theatre. The week before the complaint was filed, the Republican presidential candidate, Mitt Romney, had accused the Obama administration of "failing American workers" by not labelling China a currency manipulator. So perhaps the complaint was in part simply another move on the presidential campaign chessboard.

Questions

1. What types of government actions might be interpreted as subsidies? Give examples.
2. How easy is it to define what would be a "Chinese company"? Is this easier or more difficult in the case of the auto industry?

Sources: James Healey, "U.S. Alleges Unfair China Auto Subsidies in WTO Action," *USA Today*, September 17, 2012; and M. A. Memoli, "Obama to Tell WTO That China Illegally Subsidizes Auto Imports," *Los Angeles Times*, September 17, 2012.

---

the Canadian and U.S. governments gave subsidies to automobile makers worth billions of dollars. While the purpose of the subsidies was to help them survive a very difficult economic climate, one of the consequences was to give subsidized companies an unfair competitive advantage in the global auto industry.

Agriculture tends to be one of the largest beneficiaries of subsidies in most countries. In May 2002, President George W. Bush signed into law a bill that contained subsidies of more than $180 billion for U.S. farmers spread over 10 years. This was followed in 2007 by a farm bill that contained $286 billion in subsidies for the next 10 years.

Outside of agriculture, subsidies are much lower, but they are still significant. One study found that government subsidies to manufacturing industries in most industrialized countries amounted to between 2 and 3.5 percent of the value of industrial output. The average rate of subsidy in the United States was 0.5 percent; in

Japan it was 1 percent, and in Europe it ranged from just below 2 percent in Great Britain and Germany to as much as 6 to 7 percent in Sweden and Ireland.[4] These figures, however, almost certainly underestimate the true value of subsidies, since they are based only on cash grants and ignore other kinds of subsidies (e.g., equity participation or low-interest loans).

The main gains from subsidies accrue to domestic producers, whose international competitiveness is increased as a result of them. Advocates of strategic trade policy (which, as you will recall from Chapter 5, is an outgrowth of the new trade theory) favour subsidies to help domestic firms achieve a dominant position in those industries where economies of scale are important and the world market is not large enough to profitably support more than a few firms (e.g., aerospace). According to this argument, subsidies can help a firm achieve a first-mover advantage in an emerging industry (just as Canadian government subsidies, in the form of substantial interest-free loans, allegedly helped Bombardier). If this is achieved, further gains to the domestic economy arise from the employment and tax revenues that a major global company can generate.

Subsidies must be paid for. Governments typically pay for subsidies by taxing individuals. Therefore, whether subsidies generate national benefits that exceed their national costs is debatable. In practice, many subsidies are not successful at increasing the international competitiveness of domestic producers. Rather, they tend to protect the inefficient and promote excess production. Agricultural subsidies, for example, (1) allow inefficient farmers to stay in business; (2) encourage countries to overproduce heavily subsidized agricultural products; (3) encourage countries to produce products that could be grown more cheaply elsewhere and imported; and, therefore, (4) reduce international trade in agricultural products. One recent study estimated that if advanced countries abandoned subsidies to farmers, global trade in agricultural products would be 50 percent higher and the world as a whole would be better off to the tune of $160 billion.[5] This increase in wealth arises from the more efficient use of agricultural land.

Import Quotas and Voluntary Export Restraints

An **import quota** is a direct restriction on the quantity of some good that may be imported into a country. The restriction is usually enforced by issuing import licences to a group of individuals or firms. For example, the United States has a quota on cheese imports. The only firms allowed to import cheese are certain trading companies, each of which is allocated the right to import a maximum number of kilograms of cheese each year. In some cases, the right to sell is given directly to the governments of exporting countries. This is the case for sugar and textile imports in the United States.

A variant on the import quota is the voluntary export restraint (VER). A **voluntary export restraint** is a quota on trade imposed by the exporting country, typically at the request of the importing country's government. One of the most famous examples is the limitation on auto exports to the United States enforced by Japanese automobile producers in 1981. A response to direct pressure from the U.S. government, this VER limited Japanese imports to no more than 1.68 million vehicles per year. The agreement was revised in 1984 to allow 1.85 million Japanese vehicles per year. The agreement was allowed to lapse in 1985, but the Japanese government indicated its intentions at that time to continue to restrict exports to the United States to 1.85 million vehicles per year.[6] Foreign producers agree to VERs because they fear far more damaging punitive tariffs or import quotas might follow if they do not. Agreeing to a VER is seen as a way of making the best of a bad situation by appeasing protectionist pressures in a country.

As with tariffs and subsidies, both import quotas and VERs benefit domestic producers by limiting import competition. As with all restrictions on trade, quotas do not benefit consumers. An import quota or VER always raises the domestic price of an imported good. When imports are limited to a low percentage of the market by a quota or VER, the price is bid up for that limited foreign supply. In the case of the automobile industry, for example, the VER increased the price of the limited supply of Japanese imports. According to a study by the U.S. Federal Trade Commission, the automobile industry VER cost U.S. consumers about $1 billion per year between 1981 and 1985. That $1 billion per year went to Japanese producers in the form of higher prices.[7] The extra profit that producers make when supply is artificially limited by an import quota is referred to as a quota rent.

If a domestic industry lacks the capacity to meet demand, an import quota can raise prices for *both* the domestically produced and imported good. This happened in the U.S. sugar industry, where an import quota has long limited the amount foreign producers can sell in the U.S. market. According to one study, as a result of import quotas the price of sugar in the United States has been as much as 40 percent greater than the world price.[8] These higher prices have translated into greater profits for U.S. sugar producers, who have lobbied politicians to keep the lucrative agreement in place. They argue that U.S. jobs in the sugar industry will be lost to foreign producers if the quota system is scrapped.

Another industry that has long operated with import quotas is the textile industry, which has a complex set of multinational agreements that govern the amount one country can export to others. In this industry, quotas on imports into the United States have restricted the supply of certain apparel products and increased their price by as much as 70 percent.[9] Quotas also encourage firms to engage in strategic actions designed to circumvent quotas. The United States is not alone in imposing quotas on textile imports. Most other developed nations have similar quotas. In 1995, the World Trade Organization struck an agreement to phase out the lion's share of textile product quotas in the United States and elsewhere. On January 1, 2005, much to the chagrin of U.S. textile producers, the final quota in the United States was lifted, giving the world "unrestricted access" to the U.S. market.[10]

See the accompanying Management Focus to understand how Nova Scotia-based Clearwater Seafoods has brought a global perspective to fishing quotas.

Local Content Requirements

A **local content requirement** demands that some specific fraction of a good be produced domestically. The requirement can be expressed either in physical terms (e.g., 75 percent of component parts for this product must be produced locally) or in value terms (e.g., 75 percent of the value of this product must be produced locally). Local content regulations have been widely used by developing countries to shift their manufacturing base from the simple assembly of products whose parts are manufactured elsewhere into the local manufacture of component parts. They have also been used in developed countries to try to protect local jobs and industry from foreign competition. For example, a little-known law in the United States, the Buy America Act, specifies that government agencies must give preference to American products when putting contracts for equipment out to bid unless the foreign products

MANAGEMENT FOCUS

Clearwater Seafoods

Colin Macdonald, a co-founder and now Chairman of Clearwater Seafoods, has brought a global perspective to the fishing business they began in Nova Scotia in 1976.

Once a low-tech industry, things have changed in the fishing business. Captain's logbooks have been replaced by notebook computers while global positioning systems both track the vessels and navigate over the ocean bottom.

Aside from the integration of technology and the diversity of products and markets, Clearwater also benefits from vertical integration. The company controls the process from harvesting to processing, and from marketing to delivery, which produces price efficiencies for both the company and its customers.

It is truly a global company. For many years it has been focusing on demand for premium shellfish and rising per capita consumption of sea food generally driven by consumers in emerging economies, especially in Asia. The company distributes its products worldwide, using local sales and marketing teams to position the company in both mature and emerging markets. It has sales offices in major centres in Canada, the United States, Europe, as well as four offices in China.

Fishing is subject to quotas, and thus the right of being allowed to harvest a certain amount of fish becomes a valuable property. For example, in 2003, Clearwater acquired the right to certain scallop quotas from High Liner Foods Inc. This increased Clearwater's share of the Canadian sea scallop supply—called the *total allowable catch*, or TAC, from 36 percent to 50 percent. Quota ownership is a very important part of Clearwater's competitive advantage. It owns between 50 and 100 percent of the supply (TAC) for sea scallops, offshore lobsters, cold water shrimps, arctic surf clams, Jonah crabs, and Argentine scallops. Owning such a high percentage of the fish quota allows the company to "control its own destiny" and ensures a consistent supply of product to customers. In 2012, an independent appraisal of the company's fishing quotas placed a value of $453 million on these rights.

Questions

1. Are there other industries, either in Canada or other countries, that have quota systems applied to their industry in a similar fashion as the fishing industry?
2. How can a company serving a global marketplace keep track of changing consumer preferences, which is particularly the case in the food industry?

Sources: Clearwater, *Annual Report, 2004,* https://www.clearwater.ca/site/media/Parent/2004CSIFAnnualReport(1).pdf; K. Cox, "Clearwater Trawls For Fresh Opportunities," *The Globe and Mail,* May 22, 2004; Clearwater, *Annual Report, 2006,* https://www.clearwater.ca/site/media/Parent/ClearwaterAR06(1).pdf; Clearwater, *Annual Report, 2009,* https://www.clearwater.ca/site/media/Parent/2009ARa(1)(1).pdf.

have a significant price advantage. The law specifies a product as "American" if 51 percent of the materials by value are produced domestically. This amounts to a local content requirement. If a foreign company, or an American one, wishes to win a contract from a U.S. government agency to provide some equipment, it must ensure that at least 51 percent of the product by value is manufactured in the United States.

For a domestic producer of parts, local content regulations provide protection in the same way an import quota does: by limiting foreign competition. The aggregate economic effects are also the same; domestic producers benefit, but the restrictions on imports raise the prices of imported components. In turn, higher prices for imported components are passed on to consumers of the final product in the form of higher final prices. So as with all trade policies, local content regulations tend to benefit producers and not consumers.

Is Having a Local Content Requirement a Good Idea?

Local content requirements refer to a specific fraction of a product that needs to be manufactured domestically. Basically, LCRs establish a minimum level of local content required under trade law when giving foreign companies the right to manufacture in a particular place. In the wake of the economic downturn in 2008, many economists feared that some governments would institute protectionist policies similar to the tariff escalations during the Great Depression of the 1930s. However, most public policy officials avoided traditional forms of protection (e.g., tariffs, quotas). This led some observers to underestimate the degree of protectionism. Instead, what had happened was that so-called nontariff barriers in the form of local content requirements (LCR) had become increasingly popular. As a (1) citizen of a specific country and (2) as a global customer, do you think local content requirements help you as a citizen of a country, as a global customer, as both, or as neither?

Source: G. C. Hufbauer and J. J. Scott, *Local Content Requirements: A Global Problem*, Washington, DC: Peterson Institute for International Economics, 2013.

Administrative Policies

In addition to the formal instruments of trade policy, governments of all types sometimes use informal or administrative policies to restrict imports and boost exports. **Administrative trade policies** are bureaucratic rules designed to make it difficult for imports to enter a country. Some would argue that the Japanese are the masters of this kind of trade barrier. In recent years, Japan's formal tariff and nontariff barriers have been among the lowest in the world. However, critics charge that the country's informal administrative barriers to imports more than compensate for this. For example, the Netherlands exports tulip bulbs to almost every country in the world except Japan. In Japan, customs inspectors insist on checking every tulip bulb by cutting it vertically down the middle, and even Japanese ingenuity cannot put them back together again! Federal Express has had a tough time expanding its global express shipping services into Japan because Japanese customs inspectors insist on opening a large proportion of express packages to check for pornography, a process that can delay an "express" package for days. Japan is not the only country that engages in such policies. As with all instruments of trade policy, administrative instruments benefit producers and hurt consumers, who are denied access to possibly superior foreign products.

Antidumping Policies

In the context of international trade, **dumping** is variously defined as selling goods in a foreign market at below their costs of production, or as selling goods in a foreign market at below their "fair" market value. There is a difference between these two definitions; the "fair" market value of a good is normally judged to be greater than the costs of producing that good because the former includes a "fair" profit margin. Dumping is viewed as a method by which firms unload excess production in foreign markets. Some dumping may be the result of predatory behaviour, with producers using substantial profits from their home markets to subsidize prices in a foreign market with a view to driving indigenous competitors out of that market. Once this has been achieved, so the argument goes, the predatory firm can raise prices and earn substantial profits.

An alleged example of dumping occurred in 1997, when two South Korean manufacturers of semiconductors, LG Semicon and Hyundai Electronics, were accused of selling dynamic random access memory chips (DRAMs) in the U.S. market at below their costs of production. This action occurred in the middle of a worldwide glut of chip-making capacity. It was alleged that the firms were trying to unload their excess production in the United States.

Antidumping policies are designed to punish foreign firms that engage in dumping. The ultimate objective is to protect domestic producers from "unfair" foreign competition. Although antidumping policies vary somewhat from country to country, the majority are similar to U.S. policies. If a domestic producer believes that a foreign firm is dumping production in the U.S. market, it can file a petition with two government agencies, the Commerce Department and the International Trade Commission. In the Korean DRAM case, Micron Technology, a U.S. manufacturer of DRAMs, filed the petition. The government agencies then investigate the complaint. If they find it has merit, the Commerce Department may impose an antidumping duty on the offending foreign imports (antidumping duties are often called **countervailing duties**).

LO2 | The Case for Government Intervention

Now that we have reviewed the various instruments of trade policy that governments can use, it is time to take a more detailed look at the case for government intervention in international trade. Arguments for government intervention take two paths—political and economic. Political arguments for intervention are concerned with protecting the interests of certain groups within a nation (normally producers), often at the expense of other groups (normally consumers). or with achieving some political objective that lies outside the sphere of economic relationships, such as protecting the environment or human rights. Economic arguments for intervention are typically concerned with boosting the overall wealth of a nation (to the benefit of all, both producers and consumers).

Political Arguments for Intervention

Political arguments for government intervention cover a range of issues including protecting jobs, protecting industries deemed important for national security, retaliating to unfair foreign competition, protecting consumers from "dangerous" products, furthering the goals of foreign policy, and protecting the human rights of individuals in exporting countries.

PROTECTING JOBS AND INDUSTRIES

Perhaps the most common political argument for government intervention is that it is needed to protect jobs from unfair foreign competition.

Though this argument is closely tied to President Donald Trump, he is certainly not the first U.S. President to talk about tariffs and protecting jobs. The tariffs placed on imports of foreign steel by President George W. Bush in 2002 were designed to protect jobs (many steel producers were located in states that Bush needed to win re-election in 2004). A political motive also underlay establishment of the Common Agricultural Policy (CAP) by the European Union. The CAP was designed to protect the jobs of Europe's politically powerful farmers by restricting imports and guaranteeing prices.

However, the higher prices that resulted from the CAP have cost Europe's consumers dearly. This is true of many attempts to protect jobs and industries through government intervention. For example, the imposition of steel tariffs in 2002 raised steel prices for American consumers, such as automobile companies, making them less competitive in the global marketplace.

A related argument, and one that has found greater resonance in Canada is to protect entire industries, particularly cultural industries from foreign competition.

Over the past three decades, Canadian cultural content policies were implemented and amended to buffer Canadian cultural "institutions" from American print media, radio, and television advertisements and programming, much to the chagrin of U.S. businesses that view culture as an industry, not an "off limits" abstract heritage concept. The perceived need to protect all Canadian cultural pillars from encroachment by American media industries and values, has, in some circles, done Canada well, creating Canadian television stations, books, and magazines, which may not have otherwise occurred.

More broadly, in 1973, the Canadian Foreign Investment Review Act (FIRA) came into existence as a means to monitor and control foreign corporate acquisitions of Canadian companies. An unforeseen offshoot of this Act was that, in fact, it slowed growth in the oil patch sector and other Canadian industry sectors by categorically turning away investment. A second more insidious side effect is still being felt to this day. FIRA drove a political wedge between Eastern and Western Canada. Many potential oil-related acquisitions of Albertan firms by foreign firms were overturned due to this policy, restraining economic growth and expansion in Alberta.

The unpopularity of FIRA reached its peak during the early 1980s and evolved to a gentler version of protecting jobs and industries from foreign encroachment with the signing of the 1985 Investment Act. It, in part, paved the way for the 1988 North American Free Trade Agreement.

NATIONAL SECURITY

Countries sometimes argue that it is necessary to protect certain industries because they are important for national security. Defence-related industries often get this kind of attention (e.g., aerospace, advanced electronics, semiconductors, etc.). Although not as common as it used to be, this argument is still made. Those in favour of protecting the U.S. semiconductor industry from foreign competition, for example, argue that semiconductors are now such important components of defence products that it would be dangerous to rely primarily on foreign producers for them. In 1986, this argument helped persuade the U.S. federal government to support Sematech, a consortium of 14 U.S. semiconductor companies that accounted for 90 percent of the U.S. industry's revenues. Sematech's mission was to conduct joint research into manufacturing techniques to be parcelled out to members. The government saw the venture as so critical that Sematech was specially protected from antitrust laws. Initially, the U.S. government provided Sematech with $100 million per year in subsidies. By the mid-1990s, however, the U.S. semiconductor industry had regained its leading market position, largely through the personal computer boom and demand for microprocessor chips made by Intel. In 1994, the consortium's board voted to seek an end to U.S. federal funding, and since 1996 the consortium has been funded entirely by private money.[11]

More recently, at the end of 2013, Canada's Industry Minister James Moore announced that it would block the sale of Manitoba Telecom Service (MTS) Inc.'s Allstream division to Accelero Capital Holdings (a foreign buyer). The Minister said, in a brief statement, that after a review under the national security provisions of the Investment Canada Act, the transaction would not proceed. "MTS Allstream operates a national fibre optic network that provides critical telecommunications services to businesses and governments, including the government of Canada." The chief executive of MTS said that Ottawa did not provide a specific explanation for its concerns.[12]

RETALIATION

Some argue that governments should use the threat to intervene in trade policy as a bargaining tool to help open foreign markets and force trading partners to "play by the rules of the game." The U.S. government has used the threat of punitive trade sanctions to try to get the Chinese government to enforce intellectual property laws. Lax enforcement of these laws had given rise to massive copyright infringements in China that have been costing U.S. companies such as Microsoft hundreds of millions of dollars per year in lost sales revenues. After the United States threatened to impose 100 percent tariffs on a range of Chinese imports, and after harsh words between officials from the two countries, the Chinese agreed to tighter enforcement of intellectual property regulations.[13]

If it works, such a politically motivated rationale for government intervention may liberalize trade and bring with it resulting economic gains. It is a risky strategy, however. A country that is being pressured may not back down and instead may respond to the imposition of punitive tariffs by raising trade barriers of its own. This is exactly what the Chinese government threatened to do when pressured by the United States, although it ultimately backed down. If a government does not back down, however, the results could be higher trade barriers all around and an economic loss to all involved.

PROTECTING CONSUMERS

Many governments have long had regulations in place to protect consumers from "unsafe" products. The indirect effect of such regulations often is to limit or ban the importation of such products. One example is baby walkers, which could injure toddlers using them if the child fell down stairs or pulled dangerous objects onto themselves.[14] Injuries suffered by young children included burns, concussions, fractures, brain hemorrhages, and even death. In April 2004, the Canadian government imposed a permanent ban on the sale and import of baby walkers, making Canada the first country to ban such devices. In another example concerning children, 125 000 Healthy Care, Easy Clean, and Close to Me High Chairs were sold in Canada and 947 000 in the United States. The pegs on the backs of the chair where the tray could be stored protruded so that children could fall against them, which resulted in cuts and other injuries. In the United States, 14 children needed stitches and one child was reported injured in Canada. In September 2010, Fisher-Price recalled over 10 million tricycles, toys, and high chairs due to safety concerns. This massive recall affected consumers who purchased these items in Canada and the United States from 1997 to September 2010.[15] Health Canada's Web site issues warnings on current product recalls and can be found at http://hc-sc.gc.ca/cps-spc/advisories-avis/index-eng.php.

The conflict over the ban on the sale of importation of hormone-treated beef into the European Union may be a taste of things to come. In addition to the use of hormones to promote animal growth and meat production, the science of biotechnology has made it possible to genetically alter many crops so that they are resistant to common herbicides,

A genetically engineered cotton seed that protects against three common insects has been met with resistance in Europe due to a fear that these genetically altered seeds could potentially be harmful to humans. © *Kent Knudson/PhotoLink/Getty Images*

produce proteins that are natural insecticides, have dramatically improved yields, or can withstand inclement weather. Another example is a genetically engineered cotton seed produced by Monsanto (a technological agricultural company that specializes in the production of seeds for large acre crops). Use of this seed reduces or eliminates the need for traditional pesticide applications. As enticing as such innovations sound, they have met with intense resistance from consumer groups, particularly in Europe. In Canada, farmers and some groups of consumers have protested the introduction of such products, but those concerns do not seem to have translated to the average consumer.[16] The fear is that the widespread use of genetically altered seed corn could have unanticipated and harmful effects on human health and may result in "genetic pollution." (An example of genetic pollution would be when the widespread use of crops that produce "natural pesticides" stimulates the evolution of "super-bugs" that are resistant to those pesticides.) Such concerns have led Austria and Luxembourg to outlaw the importation, sale, or use of genetically altered organisms.[17]

FURTHERING FOREIGN POLICY OBJECTIVES

Governments sometimes use trade policy to support their foreign policy objectives.[18] A government may grant preferential trade terms to a country it wants to build strong relations with. Trade policy has also been used several times to pressure or punish "rogue states" that do not abide by international law or norms. Iraq has laboured under extensive trade sanctions since the UN coalition defeated the country in the 1991 Gulf War. Other than hurting the poor, trade sanctions seemed to have little effect in Iraq. The wealthier Iraqis procured products through the inflated black market. Therefore, economic punishment of "rogue states" does not always have its desired effect. The theory is that such pressure might persuade the "rogue state" to mend its ways or it might hasten a change of government. In the case of Iraq, the sanctions were seen as a way of forcing that country to comply with several UN resolutions. In another example, the United States has maintained long-running trade sanctions against Cuba, which have been eased recently by the Obama administration. Their principal function was to impoverish Cuba in the hope that the resulting economic hardship will lead to the downfall of Cuba's Communist government and its replacement with a more democratically inclined regime.

Other countries can undermine any unilateral trade sanctions. The U.S. sanctions against Cuba, for example, have not stopped other Western countries from trading with Cuba. The U.S. sanctions have done little more than help create a vacuum into which other trading nations, such as Canada and Germany, have stepped. In an attempt to halt this and further tighten the screws on Cuba, in 1996 the U.S. Congress passed the **Helms–Burton Act**. This Act allows Americans to sue foreign firms that use property in Cuba confiscated from them after the 1959 revolution. A similar Act, the **D'Amato Act**, aimed at Libya and Iran, was also passed that year.

The passage of Helms–Burton elicited protests from America's trading partners, including the European Union, Canada, and Mexico, all of which claim the law violates their sovereignty and is illegal under World Trade Organization rules. For example, Canadian companies that have been doing business in Cuba for years see no reason they should suddenly be sued in U.S. courts when Canada does not restrict trade with Cuba. They are not violating Canadian law and they are not U.S. companies, so why should they be subject to U.S. law? Despite such protests, the law is still on the books in the United States, although the U.S. government has been less than enthusiastic about enforcing it—probably because it is unenforceable.

PROTECTING HUMAN RIGHTS

Protecting and promoting human rights in other countries is an important element of foreign policy for many democracies. Governments sometimes use trade policy to try to improve the human rights policies of trading partners. For example, the U.S. government long had trade sanctions in place against the nation of Myanmar, in no small part due to the poor human rights practices in that nation. In late 2012 the U.S. said that it would ease trade sanctions against Myanmar in response to democratic reforms in that country. Similarly, in the 1980s and 1990s, Western governments used trade sanctions against South Africa as a way of pressuring that nation to drop its apartheid policies, which were seen as a violation of basic human rights.

But others contend that limiting trade with such countries would make matters worse, not better. They argue that the best way to change the internal human rights stance of a country is to engage it through international trade. At its core, the argument is simple: growing bilateral trade raises the income levels of both countries, and as a state becomes richer, its people begin to demand—and generally receive—better treatment with regard to their human rights. This is a variant of the argument in Chapter 2 that economic progress begets political progress (if political progress is measured by the adoption of a democratic government that respects human rights).

Economic Arguments for Intervention

With the development of the new trade theory and strategic trade policy (see Chapter 5), the economic arguments for government intervention have undergone a renaissance in recent years. Until the early 1980s, most economists saw little benefit in government intervention and strongly advocated a free trade policy. This position has changed at the margins with the development of strategic trade policy, although as we will see in the next section, there are still strong economic arguments for sticking to a free trade stance.

THE INFANT INDUSTRY ARGUMENT

The infant industry argument is by far the oldest economic argument for government intervention. Alexander Hamilton proposed it in 1792. According to this argument, many developing countries have a potential comparative advantage in manufacturing, but new manufacturing industries cannot initially compete with well-established industries in developed countries. To allow manufacturing to get a toehold, the argument is that governments should temporarily support new industries (with tariffs, import quotas, and subsidies) until they have grown strong enough to meet international competition.

This argument has had substantial appeal for the governments of developing nations during the past 50 years, and the GATT recognized the infant industry argument as a legitimate reason for protectionism. Nevertheless, many economists remain very critical of this argument. They make two main points. First, protection of manufacturing from foreign competition does no good unless the protection helps make the industry efficient. In case after case, however, protection seems to have done little more than foster the development of inefficient industries that have little hope of ever competing in the world market. Brazil, for example, built the world's 10th largest auto industry behind tariff barriers and quotas. Once those barriers were removed in the late 1980s, however, foreign imports soared and the Brazilian industry was forced to admit that after 30 years of protection, it was one of the world's most inefficient.[19]

Second, the infant industry argument relies on an assumption that firms are unable to make efficient long-term investments by borrowing money from the domestic or international capital market. Consequently, governments have been required to subsidize long-term investments. Given the development of global capital markets over the past decades, this assumption no longer looks as valid as it once did. Today, if a developing country really does have a potential comparative advantage in a manufacturing industry, firms in that country should be able to borrow money from the capital markets to finance the required investments. Given financial support, firms based in countries with a potential comparative advantage have an incentive to go through the necessary period of initial losses to make long-run gains without requiring government protection. Many Taiwanese and South Korean firms did this in industries such as textiles, semiconductors, machine tools, steel, and shipping. Thus, given efficient global capital markets, the only industries that would require government protection would be those that are not worthwhile.

STRATEGIC TRADE POLICY

Some new trade theorists have proposed the strategic trade policy argument.[20] We reviewed the basic argument in Chapter 5 when we considered the new trade theory. The new trade theory argues that in industries where the existence of substantial scale economies implies that the world market will profitably support only a few firms, countries may predominate in the export of certain products simply because they had firms that were able to capture first-mover advantages. The dominance of Boeing in the commercial aircraft industry is attributed to such factors.

The strategic trade policy argument consists of two components. First, it is argued that by appropriate actions, a government can help raise national income if it can somehow ensure that the firm or firms to gain first-mover advantages in such an industry are domestic rather than foreign enterprises. Thus, according to the strategic trade policy argument, a government should use subsidies to support promising firms that are active in newly emerging industries. Advocates of this argument point out that the substantial R&D grants the U.S. government gave Boeing in the 1950s and '60s probably helped tilt the field of competition in the newly emerging market for jet passenger planes in Boeing's favour. (Boeing's 707 jet airliner was derived from a military plane.) Similar arguments have been made with regard to Japan's dominance in the production of liquid crystal display screens (used in laptop computers). Although these screens were invented in the United States, the Japanese government, in cooperation with major electronics companies, targeted this industry for research support in the late 1970s and early '80s. The result was that Japanese firms, not U.S. firms, subsequently captured the first-mover advantages in this market.

The second component of the strategic trade policy argument is that it might pay government to intervene in an industry if it helps domestic firms overcome the barriers to entry created by foreign firms that have already reaped first-mover advantages. This argument underlies government support of Airbus Industrie, Boeing's major competitor. Formed in 1966 as a consortium of four companies from Great Britain, France, Germany, and Spain, Airbus had less than 5 percent of the world commercial aircraft market when it began production in the mid-1970s. By 2000, it had increased its share to about 45 percent and was threatening Boeing's dominance. How did Airbus achieve this? According to the U.S. government, the answer is a $13.5 billion subsidy from the governments of Great Britain, France, Germany, and Spain.[21] Without this subsidy, Airbus would never have been able to break into the world market.

In another example, the rise to dominance of the Japanese semiconductor industry, despite the first-mover advantages enjoyed by U.S. firms, is attributed to intervention by the Japanese government. In this case, the government did not subsidize the costs of domestic manufacturers. Rather, it protected the Japanese home market while pursuing policies that ensured Japanese companies got access to the necessary manufacturing and product know-how.

If these arguments are correct, they clearly suggest a rationale for government intervention in international trade. Governments should target technologies that may be important in the future and use subsidies to support development work aimed at commercializing those technologies. Furthermore, government should provide export subsidies until the domestic firms have established first-mover advantages in the world market. Government support may also be justified if it can help domestic firms overcome the first-mover advantages enjoyed by foreign competitors and emerge as viable competitors in the world market (as in the Airbus and semiconductor examples). In this case, a combination of home-market protection and export-promoting subsidies may be called for.

LO3 | The Revised Case for Free Trade

The strategic trade policy arguments of the new trade theorists suggest an economic justification for government intervention in international trade. This justification challenges the rationale for unrestricted free trade found in the work of classic trade theorists such as Adam Smith and David Ricardo. In response to this challenge to economic orthodoxy, a number of economists—including some of those responsible for the development of the new trade theory, such as Paul Krugman of MIT—have been quick to point out that although strategic trade policy looks nice in theory, in practice it may be unworkable. This response to the strategic trade policy argument constitutes the revised case for free trade.[22]

Retaliation and Trade War

Krugman argues that a strategic trade policy aimed at establishing domestic firms in a dominant position in a global industry is a beggar-thy-neighbour policy that boosts national income at the expense of other countries. A country that attempts to use such policies will probably provoke retaliation. In many cases, the resulting trade war between two or more interventionist governments will leave all countries involved worse off than if a hands-off approach had been adopted in the first place. If the U.S. government were to respond to the Airbus subsidy by increasing its own subsidies to Boeing, for example, the result might be that the subsidies would cancel each other out. In the process, both European and U.S. taxpayers would end up supporting an expensive and pointless trade war, and both Europe and the United States would be worse off.

Krugman may be right about the danger of a strategic trade policy leading to a trade war. The problem, however, is how to respond when one's competitors are already being supported by government subsidies; that is, how should Boeing and the United States respond to the subsidization of Airbus? According to Krugman, the answer is probably not to engage in retaliatory action, but to help establish rules that minimize the use of trade-distorting subsidies. This is what the World Trade Organization seeks to do.

Domestic Politics

Governments do not always act in the national interest when they intervene in the economy; politically important interest groups often influence them. The European Union's support for the Common Agricultural Policy (CAP), which arose because of the political power of French and German farmers, is an example. The CAP benefited inefficient farmers and the politicians who relied on the farm vote, but not consumers in the EU, who pay more for their foodstuffs. Thus, a further reason for not embracing strategic trade policy, according to Krugman, is that such a policy is almost certain to be captured by special interest groups within the economy, who will distort it to their own ends. Krugman concludes that in the United States:

> To ask the Commerce Department to ignore special-interest politics while formulating detailed policy for many industries is not realistic: to establish a blanket policy of free trade, with exceptions granted only under extreme pressure, may not be the optimal policy according to the theory but may be the best policy that the country is likely to get.[23]

LO4 Development of the World Trading System

There are strong economic arguments for supporting unrestricted free trade. While many governments have recognized the value of these arguments, they have been unwilling to unilaterally lower their trade barriers for fear that other nations might not follow suit. Consider the problem that two neighbouring countries, say Brazil and Argentina, face when assessing whether to lower barriers to trade between them. In principle, the government of Brazil might be in favour of lowering trade barriers, but it might be unwilling to do so for fear that Argentina will not do the same. Instead, the government might fear that the Argentineans will take advantage of Brazil's low barriers to enter the Brazilian market, while at the same time continuing to shut Brazilian products out of their market through high trade barriers. The Argentinean government might believe that it faces the same dilemma. The essence of the problem is a lack of trust. Both governments recognize that their respective nations will benefit from lower trade barriers between them, but neither government is willing to lower barriers for fear that the other might not follow.[24]

ANOTHER PERSPECTIVE

Are Free Trade Agreements Good?

The benefits of free trade agreements are often hard to see. At the same time, the benefits of protecting certain industries and/or companies from foreign competition are often very visible. Given these scenarios, many people often argue that free trade agreements are bad for their country. Perhaps as a result, many governments impose many tariffs, quotas, and other nontariff barriers to trade. For example, the common perception is that by establishing trade barriers, a country keeps the jobs at home instead of jobs being shipped overseas. This is the argument made during the 2016 U.S. Presidential election cycle.

Source: D. J. Boudreaux, "The Benefits of Free Trade: Addressing the Myths," Washington, DC; Mercatus Center, George Mason University, 2013.

Such a deadlock can be resolved if both countries negotiate a set of rules to govern cross-border trade and lower trade barriers. But who is to monitor the governments to make sure they play by the trade rules? And who is to impose sanctions on a government that cheats? Both governments could set up an independent body whose function is to act as a referee. This referee could monitor trade between the countries, make sure that no side cheats, and impose sanctions on a country if it does cheat in the trade game.

While it might sound unlikely that any government would compromise its national sovereignty by submitting to such an arrangement, since World War II an international trading framework has evolved that has exactly these features. For its first 50 years, this framework was known as the General Agreement on Tariffs and Trade. Since

1995, it has been known as the World Trade Organization (WTO). Here we look at the evolution and workings of the GATT and the WTO. We set the scene with a brief discussion of the pre-GATT history of world trade.

From Smith to the Great Depression

As we saw in Chapter 5, the theoretical case for free trade dates to the late eighteenth century and the work of Adam Smith and David Ricardo. Free trade as a government policy was first officially embraced by Great Britain in 1846, when the British Parliament repealed the Corn Laws. The Corn Laws placed a high tariff on imports of foreign corn. The objectives of the Corn Laws tariff were to raise government revenues and to protect British corn producers. There had been annual motions in Parliament in favour of free trade since the 1820s when David Ricardo was a member. However, agricultural protection was withdrawn only as a result of a protracted debate when the effects of a harvest failure in Great Britain were compounded by the imminent threat of famine in Ireland. Faced with considerable hardship and suffering among the populace, Parliament narrowly reversed its long-held position.

During the next 80 years or so, Great Britain, as one of the world's dominant trading powers, pushed the case for trade liberalization; but the British government was a voice in the wilderness. Its major trading partners did not reciprocate the British policy of unilateral free trade. The only reason Britain kept this policy for so long was that, as the world's largest exporting nation, it had far more to lose from a trade war than did any other country.

By the 1930s, however, the British attempt to stimulate free trade was buried under the economic rubble of the Great Depression. The Great Depression had roots in the failure of the world economy to mount a sustained economic recovery after the end of World War I in 1918. Things got worse in 1929 with the U.S. stock market collapse and the subsequent run on the U.S. banking system. Economic problems were compounded in 1930 when the U.S. Congress passed the Smoot-Hawley Act. Aimed at avoiding rising unemployment by protecting domestic industries and diverting consumer demand away from foreign products, the Smoot-Hawley Act erected an enormous wall of tariff barriers. Almost every industry was rewarded with its "made-to-order" tariff. A particularly odd aspect of the Smoot-Hawley tariff-raising binge was that the United States was running a balance-of-payment surplus at the time and it was the world's largest creditor nation. The Smoot-Hawley Act had a damaging effect on employment abroad. Other countries reacted to the U.S. action by raising their own tariff barriers. U.S. exports tumbled in response, and the world slid further into the Great Depression.[25]

1947–1979: GATT, Trade Liberalization, and Economic Growth

The economic damage caused by the beggar-thy-neighbour trade policies that the Smoot-Hawley Act ushered in exerted a profound influence on the economic institutions and ideology of the post-World War II world. The United States emerged from the war both victorious and economically dominant. After the debacle of the Great Depression, opinion in the U.S. Congress had swung strongly in favour of free trade. Under U.S. leadership, GATT was established in 1947.

The GATT was a multilateral agreement whose objective was to liberalize trade by eliminating tariffs, subsidies, import quotas, and the like. From its foundation in 1947 until it was superseded by the WTO, the GATT's membership grew from 19 to more than

120 nations. The GATT did not attempt to liberalize trade restrictions in one fell swoop; that would have been impossible. Rather, tariff reduction was spread over eight rounds.

In its early years, the GATT was, by most measures, very successful. For example, the average tariff declined by nearly 92 percent in the United States between the Geneva Round of 1947 and the Tokyo Round of 1973–79. Consistent with the theoretical arguments first advanced by Ricardo and reviewed in Chapter 5, the move toward free trade under the GATT appeared to stimulate economic growth. From 1953 to 1963, world trade grew at an annual rate of 6.1 percent, and world income grew at an annual rate of 4.3 percent. Performance from 1963 to 1973 was even better; world trade grew at 8.9 percent annually, and world income grew at 5.1 percent annually.[26]

1980–1993: Protectionist Trends

During the 1980s and early 1990s, the world trading system erected by the GATT came under strain as pressures for greater protectionism increased around the world. Three reasons caused the rise in such pressures during the 1980s. First, the economic success of Japan strained the world trading system. Japan was in ruins when the GATT was created. By the early 1980s, however, it had become the world's second largest economy and its largest exporter. Japan's success in such industries as automobiles and semiconductors by itself might have been enough to strain the world trading system. Things were made worse, however, by the widespread perception in the West that, despite low tariff rates and subsidies, Japanese markets were closed to imports and foreign investment by administrative trade barriers.

Second, the world trading system was strained by the persistent trade deficit in the world's largest economy, the United States. The consequences of the U.S. deficit included painful adjustments in industries such as automobiles, machine tools, semiconductors, steel, and textiles, where domestic producers steadily lost market share to foreign competitors. The resulting unemployment gave rise to renewed demands in the U.S. Congress for protection against imports.

A third reason for the trend toward greater protectionism was that many countries found ways to get around GATT regulations. Bilateral VERs circumvent GATT agreements, because neither the importing country nor the exporting country complain to the GATT bureaucracy in Geneva—and without a complaint, the GATT bureaucracy can do nothing. Exporting countries agreed to VERs to avoid more damaging punitive tariffs. One of the best-known examples is the VER between Japan and the United States, under which Japanese producers promised to limit their auto imports into the United States to defuse growing trade tensions. According to a World Bank study, 16 percent of the imports of industrialized countries in 1986 were subjected to nontariff trade barriers such as VERs.

The Uruguay Round and the World Trade Organization

Against the background of rising pressures for protectionism, in 1986 the GATT members embarked on their eighth round of negotiations to reduce tariffs, the Uruguay Round (so named because it occurred in Uruguay). This was the most difficult round of negotiations yet, primarily because it was also the most ambitious. Until then, GATT rules had applied only to trade in manufactured goods and commodities. In the Uruguay Round, member countries sought to extend GATT rules to cover trade in services. They also sought to write rules governing the protection of intellectual property, to reduce agricultural subsidies, and to strengthen the GATT's monitoring and enforcement mechanisms.

The Uruguay Round dragged on for seven years before an agreement was reached on December 15, 1993. The agreement was formally signed by member states at a meeting in Marrakech, Morocco, on April 15, 1994. It went into effect July 1, 1995. The Uruguay Round contained the following provisions: (1) tariffs on industrial goods were to be reduced by more than one-third, and tariffs were to be scrapped on over 40 percent of manufactured goods; (2) average tariff rates imposed by developed nations on manufactured goods were to be reduced to less than 4 percent of value, the lowest level in modern history; (3) there was to be a substantial reduction in agricultural subsidies; (4) for the first time, GATT fair trade and market access rules were to be extended to cover a wide range of services; (5) GATT rules were also to be extended to provide enhanced protection for patents, copyrights, and trademarks (intellectual property); (6) barriers on trade in textiles were to be significantly reduced over 10 years; and (7) a World Trade Organization (WTO) was to be created to implement the GATT agreement.

SERVICES AND INTELLECTUAL PROPERTY

In the long run, the extension of GATT rules to cover services and intellectual property may be particularly significant. Until 1995, GATT rules applied only to industrial goods (i.e., manufactured goods and commodities). In 2010, world trade in services amounted to $3,690 billion (compared to world trade in goods of $15,237 billion). Ultimately, extension of GATT rules to this important trading arena could significantly increase both the total share of world trade accounted for by services and the overall volume of world trade. The extension of GATT rules to cover intellectual property will make it much easier for high-technology companies to do business in developing nations where intellectual property rules historically have been poorly enforced (see Chapter 2 for details).

THE WORLD TRADE ORGANIZATION

The clarification and strengthening of GATT rules and the creation of the World Trade Organization also hold out the promise of more effective policing and enforcement of GATT rules. The WTO acts as an umbrella organization that encompasses the GATT along with two new sister bodies, one on services and the other on intellectual property. The WTO's General Agreement on Trade in Services (GATS) has taken the lead to extending free trade agreements to services. The WTO's Agreement on Trade-Related Aspects of Intellectual Property Rights (TRIPS) is an attempt to narrow the gaps in the way intellectual property rights are protected around the world and to bring them under common international rules. WTO has taken over responsibility for arbitrating trade disputes and monitoring the trade policies of member countries. While the WTO operates on the basis of consensus as the GATT did, in the area of dispute settlement member countries are no longer able to block adoption of arbitration reports. Arbitration panel reports on trade disputes between member countries are automatically adopted by the WTO unless there is a consensus to reject them. Countries that have been found by the arbitration panel to violate GATT rules may appeal to a permanent appellate body, but its verdict is binding. If offenders fail to comply with the recommendations of the arbitration panel, trading partners have the right to compensation or, in the last resort, to impose (commensurate) trade sanctions. Every stage of the procedure is subject to strict time limits. Thus, the WTO has something that the GATT never had—teeth.

WTO: Experience to Date

By 2017, the WTO had 164 members, including China and the Russian Federation, which joined in 2001 and 2012, respectively, and those countries collectively account for 97 percent of world trade. (As mentioned in Chapter 1, the accession process is underway for 21 countries to join the WTO.) Since its formation, the WTO has remained at the forefront of efforts to promote global free trade. Its creators expressed the hope that the enforcement mechanisms granted to the WTO would make it more effective at policing global trade rules than the GATT had been. The great hope was that the WTO might emerge as an effective advocate and facilitator of future trade deals, particularly in areas such as services. The experience so far has been encouraging, although a shift back toward some limited protectionism following the global financial crisis of 2008-09, and stalled talks after several historic packages were accepted in 2015 have raised a number of questions about the future direction of the WTO.

WTO AS GLOBAL POLICE

The first 20 years in the life of the WTO suggests that its policing and enforcement mechanisms are having a positive effect. Currently, they have received their 500th issue to arbitrate.[27] This record compares with a total of 196 cases handled by the GATT over almost half a century. Of the cases brought to the WTO, three-fourths had been resolved by informal consultations between the disputing countries. Resolving the remainder has involved more formal procedures, but these have been largely successful. In general, countries involved have adopted the WTO's recommendations. The fact that countries are using the WTO represents an important vote of confidence in the organization's dispute resolution procedures.

EXPANDING TRADE AGREEMENTS

As explained earlier, the Uruguay Round of GATT negotiations extended global trading rules to cover trade in services. The WTO was given the role of brokering future agreements to open up global trade in services. The WTO was also encouraged to extend its reach to encompass regulations governing foreign direct investment, something the GATT had never done. Two of the first industries targeted for reform were the global telecommunication and the financial services industries.

In February 1997, the WTO brokered a deal to get countries to agree to open their telecommunication markets to competition, allowing foreign operators to purchase ownership stakes in domestic telecommunication providers and establishing a set of common rules for fair competition. Under the pact, 68 countries accounting for more than 90 percent of world telecommunication revenues pledged to start opening their markets to foreign competition and to abide by common rules for fair competition in telecommunications. Most of the world's biggest markets—including the United States, the European Union, and Japan—were fully liberalized by January 1, 1998, when the pact went into effect. All forms of basic telecommunication service are covered, including voice telephony, data and fax transmissions, and satellite and radio communications. Many telecommunication companies responded positively to the deal, pointing out that it would give them a much greater ability to offer their business customers one-stop shopping—a global, seamless service for all their corporate needs and a single bill.[28]

This was followed in December 1997 with an agreement to liberalize cross-border trade in financial services.[29] The deal covers more than 95 percent of the world's financial services market. Under the agreement, which took effect at the beginning of March 1999, 102 countries pledged to open (to varying degrees) their banking, securities, and insurance sectors to foreign competition. In common with the telecommunication deal, the accord covers not just cross-border trade but also foreign direct investment. Seventy countries agreed to dramatically lower or eradicate barriers to foreign direct investment in their financial services sector. The United States and the European Union (with minor exceptions) are fully open to inward investment by foreign banks, insurance, and securities companies. As part of the deal, many Asian countries made important concessions that allow significant foreign participation in their financial services sectors for the first time.

The Future of the WTO: Unresolved Issues and the Doha Round

Since the successes of the 1990s, the World Trade Organization has struggled to make progress on the international trade front. Confronted by a slower-growing world economy after 2001, many national governments were reluctant to agree to a fresh round of policies designed to reduce trade barriers. Since then, political opposition to the WTO has been growing in many nations. As the public face of globalization, some politicians and nongovernmental organizations blame the WTO for a variety of ills, including high unemployment, environmental degradation, poor working conditions in developing nations, falling real wage rates among the lower paid in developed nations, and rising income inequality. The rapid rise of China as a dominant trading nation has also played a role here. Like sentiments regarding Japan over 30 years ago, many perceive China as failing to play by the international trading rules, even as it embraces the WTO. This has been a major charge made by the Trump administration in the U.S.

Against this difficult political backdrop, much remains to be done on the international trade front. Four issues at the forefront of the current agenda of the WTO are antidumping policies, the high level of protectionism in agriculture, the lack of strong protection for intellectual property rights in many nations, and continued high tariff rates on nonagricultural goods and services in many nations. We shall look at each in turn before discussing the latest round of talks between WTO members aimed at reducing trade barriers, the Doha Round, which began in 2001 and is still ongoing today.

ANOTHER PERSPECTIVE

Members Continue to Criticize Argentina's Import Licensing

Import licenses are permits granted before a product is imported. The administrative procedures for obtaining the licenses should be simple, neutral, equitable, and transparent. Where possible they should be given automatically and quickly, and even if they are non-automatic they should not obstruct trade unnecessarily. Australia, Turkey, the EU, Norway, Thailand, the United States, New Zealand, Costa Rica, Colombia, Peru, Chinese Taipei, Japan, Rep. Korea, Switzerland, and Canada said their producers and traders reported that their exports to Argentina have declined or been delayed by Argentina's licensing processes and requirements, which some described as "protectionist." Among the complaints, almost 600 products are now covered either explicitly or in practice by such licensing requirements, each requiring individual approval in order to be imported; non-automatic licenses are issued as part of a "trade-balancing" policy, on condition that the importer also exports or invests in local production; processing an application can take considerably longer than the 30–60 days maximums for non-automatic licensing; the licensing is more burdensome than necessary; and lastly that Argentina as a member of the G-20 group of leading economies is not living up to the group's declarations against increasing protectionism.

Source: World Trade Organization (WTO), "Members continue to criticize Argentina's import licensing," Import Licensing: Committee Meeting, April 27, 2012, www.wto.org/english/news_e/news12_e/impl_27apr12_e.htm.

ANTIDUMPING ACTIONS

Antidumping actions proliferated during the 1990s. WTO rules allow countries to impose antidumping duties on foreign goods that are being sold cheaper than at home, or below their cost of production, when domestic producers can show that they are being harmed. Unfortunately, the rather vague definition of what constitutes "dumping" has proved to be a loophole that many countries are exploiting to pursue protectionism.

Antidumping actions seem to be concentrated in certain sectors of the economy, such as basic metal industries (e.g., aluminum and steel), chemicals, plastics, and machinery and electrical equipment. These sectors account for approximately 70 percent of all antidumping actions reported to the WTO.[30] Since 1995, these four sectors have been characterized by periods of intense competition and excess productive capacity, which have led to low prices and profits (or losses) for firms in those industries. It is not unreasonable, therefore, to hypothesize that the high level of antidumping actions in these industries represents an attempt by beleaguered manufacturers to use the political process in their nations to seek protection from foreign competitors, who they claim are engaging in unfair competition. While some of these claims may have merit, the process can become very politicized as representatives of businesses and their employees lobby government officials to "protect domestic jobs from unfair foreign competition," and government officials, mindful of the need to get votes in future elections, oblige by pushing for antidumping actions. The WTO is clearly worried by the use of antidumping policies, suggesting that it reflects persistent protectionist tendencies and pushing members to strengthen the regulations governing the imposition of antidumping duties. To some extent, the WTO has been successful—as outlined in the Another Perspective, "Antidumping Compliance."

PROTECTIONISM IN AGRICULTURE

Another focus of the WTO has been the high level of tariffs and subsidies in the agricultural sector of many economies. Tariff rates on agricultural products are generally much higher than tariff rates on manufactured products or services. The implication is that consumers in these countries are paying significantly higher prices than necessary for agricultural products imported from abroad, which leaves them with less money to spend on other goods and services.

The historically high tariff rates on agricultural products reflect a desire to protect domestic agriculture and traditional farming communities from foreign competition. In addition to high tariffs, agricultural producers also benefit from substantial

---

ANOTHER PERSPECTIVE

Antidumping Compliance

The World Bank maintains the Temporary Trade Barriers Database (TTBD) Web site, which hosts newly collected, freely available, and detailed data on more than 30 different national governments' use of policies such as antidumping (AD), global safeguards (SG), China-specific transitional safeguard (CSG) measures, and countervailing duties (CVD). The information provided in this detailed database will cover over 95 percent of the global use of these particular import-restricting trade remedy instruments. The TTBD consists of the Global Antidumping Database, which has been freely and publicly available since 2005, and four other databases of temporary trade barriers. The database and analytical reports based on it can be found at http://econ.worldbank.org/ttbd/.

subsidies. According to estimates from the Organization for Economic Cooperation and Development (OECD), government subsidies on average account for about 17 percent of the cost of agricultural production in Canada, 21 percent in the United States, 35 percent in the European Union, and 59 percent in Japan.[31] In total, OECD countries spend more than $300 billion a year in agricultural subsidies.

Not surprisingly, the combination of high tariff barriers and subsidies introduces significant distortions into the production of agricultural products and international trade of those products. The net effect is to raise prices to consumers, reduce the volume of agricultural trade, and encourage the overproduction of products that are heavily subsidized (with the government typically buying the surplus). Because global trade in agriculture currently amounts to 10.5 percent of total merchandized trade, or about $750 billion per year, the WTO argues that removing tariff barriers and subsidies could significantly boost the overall level of trade, lower prices to consumers, and raise global economic growth by freeing consumption and investment resources for more productive uses. According to estimates from the International Monetary Fund, removal of tariffs and subsidies on agricultural products would raise global economic welfare by $128 billion annually.[32] Others suggest gains as high as $182 billion.[33]

The biggest defenders of the existing system have been the advanced nations of the world, which want to protect their agricultural sectors from competition by low-cost producers in developing nations. In contrast, developing nations have been pushing hard for reforms that would allow their producers greater access to the protected markets of the developed nations. Estimates suggest that removing all subsidies on agricultural production alone in OECD countries could return to the developing nations of the world three times more than all the foreign aid they currently receive from the OECD nations.[34] In other words, free trade in agriculture could help to jump-start economic growth among the world's poorer nations and alleviate global poverty.

PROTECTING INTELLECTUAL PROPERTY

Another issue that has become increasingly important to the WTO has been protecting intellectual property. The 1995 Uruguay agreement that established the WTO also contained an agreement to protect intellectual property (the Trade-Related Aspects of Intellectual Property Rights, or TRIPS, agreement). The TRIPS regulations oblige WTO members to grant and enforce patents lasting at least 20 years and copyrights lasting 50 years. Rich countries had to comply with the rules within a year. Poor countries, in which such protection was generally much weaker, had 5 years' grace, and the very poorest had 10 years. The basis for this agreement was a strong belief among signatory nations that the protection of intellectual property through patents, trademarks, and copyrights must be an essential element of the international trading system. Inadequate protections for intellectual property reduce the incentive for innovation. Because innovation is a central engine of economic growth and rising living standards, the argument has been that a multilateral agreement is needed to protect intellectual property.

Without such an agreement it is feared that producers in a country—let's say, India—might market imitations of patented innovations pioneered in a different country—say, the United States. This can affect international trade in two ways. First, it reduces the export opportunities in India for the original innovator in the United States. Second, to the extent that the Indian producer is able to export its pirated imitation to additional countries, it also reduces the export opportunities in those countries for the U.S. inventor. Also, one can argue that because the size of the total world market for the innovator is reduced, its incentive to pursue risky and expensive innovations is also reduced. The net effect would be less innovation in the world economy and less economic growth.

As noted in Chapter 2, intellectual property rights violation is also an endemic problem in several other industries, most notably computer software and music. The WTO believes that reducing piracy rates in areas such as drugs, software, and music recordings would have a significant impact on the volume of world trade and increase the incentive for producers to invest in the creation of intellectual property. A world without piracy would have more new drugs, computer software, and music recordings produced every year. In turn, this would boost economic and social welfare and global economic growth rates. It is thus in the interests of WTO members to make sure that intellectual property rights are respected and enforced. While the 1995 Uruguay agreement that created the WTO did make headway with the TRIPS agreement, some believe these requirements do not go far enough and further commitments are necessary.

MARKET ACCESS FOR NONAGRICULTURAL GOODS AND SERVICES

Although the WTO and the GATT have made big strides in reducing the tariff rates on nonagricultural products, much work remains. Although most developed nations have brought their tariff rates on industrial products down to an average of 3.8 percent of value, exceptions still remain. In particular, while average tariffs are low, high tariff rates persist on certain imports into developed nations, which limit market access and economic growth. A particular area for concern is high tariff rates on imports of selected goods from developing nations into developed nations.

In addition, tariffs on services remain higher than on industrial goods. The average tariff on business and financial services imported into the United States, for example, is 8.2 percent, into the EU it is 8.5 percent, and into Japan it is 19.7 percent.[35] Given the rising value of cross-border trade in services, reducing these figures can be expected to yield substantial gains.

The WTO would like to bring down tariff rates still further and reduce the scope for the selective use of high tariff rates. The ultimate aim is to reduce tariff rates to zero. Although this might sound ambitious, 40 nations have already moved to zero tariffs on information technology goods, so a precedent exists. Empirical work suggests that further reductions in average tariff rates toward zero would yield substantial gains. One estimate by economists at the World Bank suggests that a broad global trade agreement coming out of the current Doha negotiations could increase world income by $263 billion annually, of which $109 billion would go to poor countries.[36] Another estimate from the OECD suggests a figure closer to $300 billion annually.[37] Looking further out, the WTO would like to bring down tariff rates on imports of nonagricultural goods into developing nations. Many of these nations use the infant industry argument to justify the continued imposition of high tariff rates; however, ultimately these rates need to come down for these nations to reap the full benefits of international trade. For example, tariffs, by raising domestic prices, help to protect inefficient domestic producers and limit economic growth by reducing the real income of consumers who must pay more for transportation equipment and related services.

DOHA ROUND POST-2016

In 2001, the WTO launched a new round of talks between member states aimed at further liberalizing the global trade and investment framework. For this meeting, it picked the remote location of Doha in the Persian Gulf state of Qatar. The talks were originally scheduled to last three years, although they have already gone on for more almost 15 years, culminating in the Nairobi Ministerial. However, there are some who wonder if the Doha Round is over and, if so, if it was successful.[38]

The agenda includes cutting tariffs on industrial goods and services, phasing out subsidies to agricultural producers, reducing barriers to cross-border investment, and limiting the use of antidumping laws. Some difficult compromises were made to reach agreement on this agenda. The EU and Japan had to give significant ground on the issue of agricultural subsidies, which are used extensively by both entities to support politically powerful farmers. The United States bowed to pressure from virtually every other nation to negotiate revisions of antidumping rules, which the United States has used extensively to protect its steel producers from foreign competition. Europe had to scale back its efforts to include environmental policy in the trade talks, primarily because of pressure from developing nations that see environmental protection policies as trade barriers by another name. Excluded from the agenda was any language pertaining to attempts to tie trade to labour standards in a country.

Countries with big pharmaceutical sectors acquiesced to demands from African, Asian, and Latin American nations on the issue of drug patents. Specifically, the language in the agreement declares that WTO regulation on intellectual property "does not and should not prevent members from taking measures to protect public health." This language was meant to assure the world's poorer nations that they can make or buy generic equivalents to fight such killers as AIDS and malaria.

Clearly, it is one thing to agree to an agenda and quite another to reach a consensus on a new treaty. Nevertheless, if an agreement is reached, there are some clear potential winners. These include low-cost agricultural producers in the developing world and developed nations such as Australia and the United States. If the talks are ultimately successful, agricultural producers in these nations will ultimately see the global markets for their goods expand. Developing nations also gain from the lack of language on labour standards, which many saw as an attempt by rich nations to erect trade barriers. The sick and poor of the world also benefit from guaranteed access to cheaper medicines. There are also clear losers in this agreement, including EU and Japanese farmers, U.S. steelmakers, environmental activists, and pharmaceutical firms in the developed world. These losers can be expected to lobby their governments hard during the ensuing years to make sure the final agreement is more in their favour.[39] In general, though, if ultimately successful, the Doha Round of negotiations could significantly raise global economic welfare. As noted earlier, estimates suggest that a successful Doha Round would raise global incomes by as much as $300 billion annually, with 60 percent of the gain going to the world's poorer nations, which would help to pull 150 million people out of poverty.[40]

The talks are ongoing, and as seems normal in these cases, they are characterized by halting progress punctuated by significant setbacks and missed deadlines. Even after the Nairobi Ministerial Agreement in December 2015, there are still questions on how to proceed with reducing agricultural subsidies and tariffs.[41] Currently, the goal is to reduce tariffs for manufactured and agricultural goods by 60 to 70 percent and to cut subsidies to half of their current level—but getting nations to agree to these goals is proving exceedingly difficult.[42] In response to the apparent failure of the Doha Round negotiations to progress, many nations have pushed forward with bilateral free trade agreements.

Estimating the Gains from Trade

A study published by the Institute for International Economics tried to estimate the gains to the American economy from free trade. According to the study, due to reductions in tariff barriers under the GATT and WTO since 1947, by 2003 the gross domestic product (GDP) of the United States was 7.3 percent higher than would otherwise be the case. The benefits of that amounted to roughly $1 trillion a year, or $9,000 extra income for each American household per year.

The same study tried to estimate what would happen if America concluded free trade deals with all its trading partners, reducing tariff barriers on all goods and services to zero. Using several methods to estimate the impact, the study concluded that additional annual gains of between $450 billion and $1.3 trillion could be realized. This final march to free trade, according to the authors of the study, could safely be expected to raise incomes of the average American household by an additional $4,500 per year.

The authors also tried to estimate the scale and cost of employment disruption that would be caused by a move to universal free trade. Jobs would be lost in certain sectors and gained in others if the country abolished all tariff barriers. Using historical data as a guide, they estimated that 226 000 jobs would be lost every year due to expanded trade, although some two-thirds of those losing jobs would find reemployment after a year. Reemployment, however, would be at a wage that was 13 to 14 percent lower. The study concluded that the disruption costs would total some $54 billion annually. Offset against this, however, must be the higher economic growth resulting from free trade, which creates many new jobs and raises household incomes, creating another $450 billion to $1.3 trillion annually in net gains to the economy.

In other words, the estimated annual gains from trade are far greater than the estimated annual costs associated with job disruption, and more people benefit than lose as a result of a shift to a universal free trade regime.

Source: S. C. Bradford, P. L. E. Grieco, and G. C. Hufbauer, "The Payoff to America from Global Integration," in *The United States and the World Economy: Foreign Policy for the Next Decade*, C. F. Bergsten, ed. (Washington, DC: Peterson Institute for International Economics, 2005).

LO5   IMPLICATIONS FOR BUSINESS

What are the implications of all this for business practice? Why should the international manager care about the political economy of free trade or about the relative merits of arguments for free trade and protectionism? There are two answers to this question. The first concerns the impact of trade barriers on a firm's strategy. The second concerns the role that business firms can play in promoting free trade or trade barriers.

TRADE BARRIERS AND FIRM STRATEGY

To understand how trade barriers affect a firm's strategy, consider first the material we covered in Chapter 5. Drawing on the theories of international trade, we discussed how it makes sense for the firm to disperse its production activities to those countries where they can be performed most efficiently. Thus, it may make sense for a firm to design and engineer its product in one country, to manufacture components in another, to perform final assembly operations in yet another country, and then to export the finished product to the rest of the world.

Clearly, trade barriers constrain a firm's ability to disperse its productive activities in such a manner. First, and most obviously, tariff barriers raise the costs of exporting products to a country (or of exporting partly finished products between countries). This may put the firm at a competitive disadvantage vis-à-vis indigenous competitors in that country. In response, the firm may then find it economical to locate production facilities in that country so that it can compete on an even footing with indigenous competitors. Second, quotas and VERs may limit a firm's ability to serve a country from locations outside of that country. Again, the response by the firm might be to set up production facilities in that country—even though it may result in higher production costs. Such reasoning was one factor behind the rapid expansion of Japanese automaking capacity in the United States during the 1980s and 1990s. This followed the establishment of a VER agreement between the United States and Japan that limited U.S. imports of Japanese automobiles.

Third, to conform to local content regulations, a firm may have to locate more production activities in a given market than it would otherwise. Again, from the firm's perspective, the consequence might be to raise costs above the level that could be achieved if each production activity were dispersed to the optimal location for that activity. And finally, even when trade barriers do not exist, the firm may still want to locate some production activities in a given country to reduce the threat of trade barriers being imposed in the future.

All the above effects are likely to raise the firm's costs above the level that could be achieved in a world without trade barriers. The higher costs that result need not translate into a significant competitive disadvantage relative to other foreign firms, however, if the countries imposing trade barriers do so to the imported products of all foreign firms, irrespective of their national origin. But when trade barriers are targeted at exports from a particular nation, firms based in that nation are at a competitive disadvantage to firms of other nations. The firm may deal with such targeted trade barriers by moving production into the country imposing barriers. Another strategy may be to move production to countries whose exports are not targeted by the specific trade barrier.

Finally, the threat of antidumping action limits the ability of a firm to use aggressive pricing to gain market share in a country. Firms in a country can also use antidumping measures to limit aggressive competition from low-cost foreign producers.

POLICY IMPLICATIONS

As noted in Chapter 5, business firms are major players on the international trade scene. Because of their pivotal role in international trade, firms exert a strong influence on government policy toward trade. This influence can encourage protectionism or it can encourage the government to support the WTO and push for open markets and freer trade among all nations. Government policies with regard to international trade can have a direct impact on business.

Consistent with strategic trade policy, examples can be found of government intervention in the form of tariffs, quotas, antidumping actions, and subsidies helping firms and industries establish a competitive advantage in the world economy. In general, however, the arguments contained in this chapter and in Chapter 5 suggest that government intervention has three drawbacks. Intervention can be self-defeating, since it tends to protect the inefficient rather than help firms become efficient global competitors. Intervention is dangerous; it may invite retaliation and trigger a trade war. Finally, intervention is unlikely to be well-executed, given the opportunity for such a policy to be captured by special interest groups. Does this mean that business should simply encourage government to adopt a laissez-faire free trade policy?

Most economists would probably argue that the best interests of international business are served by a free trade stance, but not a laissez-faire stance. It is probably in the best long-run interests of the business community to encourage the government to aggressively promote greater free trade by, for example, strengthening the WTO. Business probably has much more to gain from government efforts to open protected markets to imports and foreign direct investment than from government efforts to support certain domestic industries in a manner consistent with the recommendations of strategic trade policy.

This conclusion is reinforced by a phenomenon we touched on in Chapter 1—the increasing integration of the world economy and internationalization of production that has occurred over the past two decades. We live in a world where many firms of all national origins increasingly depend on globally dispersed production systems for their competitive advantage. Such systems are the result of freer trade. Freer trade has brought great advantages to firms that have exploited it and to consumers who benefit from the resulting lower prices. Given the danger of retaliatory action, business firms that lobby their governments to engage in protectionism must realize that by doing so they may be denying themselves the opportunity to build a competitive advantage by constructing a globally dispersed production system. By encouraging their governments to engage in protectionism, their own activities and sales overseas may be jeopardized if other governments retaliate. This does not mean a firm should never seek protection in the form of antidumping actions and the like, but it should review its options carefully and think through the larger consequences.

Key Terms

ad valorem tariff

administrative trade policies

antidumping policies

countervailing duties

D'Amato Act

dumping

Helms–Burton Act

import quota

local content requirement

specific tariff

subsidy

tariff

voluntary export restraint (VER)

LO   Learning Objectives Summary

This chapter described how the reality of international trade deviates from the theoretical ideal of unrestricted free trade reviewed in Chapter 5. Trade policies such as tariffs, subsidies, antidumping regulations, and local content requirements tend to be pro-producer and anti-consumer. Gains accrue to producers (who are protected from foreign competitors), but consumers lose because they must pay more for imports.

1. There are several policy instruments used by governments to influence international trade flows. Trade policies such as tariffs, subsidies, antidumping regulations and local content requirements tend to be pro-producer (who are protected from foreign competitors) and anti-consumer (who must pay more for imports).

2. There are two types of arguments for government intervention in international trade: political and economic. Political arguments for intervention are concerned with protecting the interests of certain groups, often at the expense of other groups, or with promoting goals with regard to foreign policy, human rights, consumer protection, and the like. Economic arguments for intervention are about boosting the overall wealth of a nation. A common political argument for intervention is that it is necessary to protect jobs. However, political intervention often hurts consumers and it can be self-defeating. Countries sometimes argue that it is important to protect certain industries for reasons of national security. Some argue that government should use the threat to intervene in trade policy as a bargaining tool to open foreign markets. This can be a risky policy; if it fails, the result can be higher trade barriers. The infant industry argument for government intervention contends that to let manufacturing get a toehold, governments should temporarily support new industries. In practice, however, governments often end up protecting the inefficient.

3. Strategic trade policy suggests that with subsidies, government can help domestic firms gain first-mover advantages in global industries where economies of scale are important. Government subsidies may also help domestic firms overcome barriers to entry into such industries. The problems with strategic trade policy are twofold: (a) such a policy may invite retaliation, in which case all will lose, and (b) strategic trade policy may be captured by special interest groups, which will distort it to their own ends.

4. The GATT was a product of the postwar free trade movement. The GATT was successful in lowering trade barriers on manufactured goods and commodities. The move toward greater free trade under the GATT appeared to stimulate economic growth. The completion of the Uruguay Round of GATT talks and the establishment of the WTO have strengthened the world trading system by extending GATT rules to services, increasing protection for intellectual property, reducing agricultural subsidies, and enhancing monitoring and enforcement mechanisms.

5. Trade barriers act as a constraint on a firm's ability to disperse its various production activities to optimal locations around the globe. One response to trade barriers is to establish more production activities in the protected country. Business may have more to gain from government efforts to open protected markets to imports and foreign direct investment than from government efforts to protect domestic industries from foreign competition.

Critical Thinking and Discussion Questions

1. Do you think governments should take human rights considerations into account when granting preferential trading rights to countries? What are the arguments for and against taking such a position?

2. Whose interests should be the paramount concern of government trade policy—the interests of producers (businesses and their employees) or of consumers?

3. Given the arguments relating to the new trade theory and strategic trade policy, what kind of trade policy should business be pressuring government to adopt?

Research Task globaledge.msu.edu

Use the globalEDGE™ site to complete the following exercises:

1. Your company is considering exporting its products to Egypt, but management's current knowledge of the country's trade policies and barriers is limited. Conduct Web research to identify Egypt's current import policies with respect to fundamental issues such as tariffs and restrictions; prepare an executive summary of your findings.

2. The number of member nations of the WTO is increasing. Additionally, some nonmember countries have observer status, which requires accession negotiations to begin within five years of attaining the preliminary position. Identify the current total number of WTO members. Also, prepare a list of the observer countries.

CLOSING CASE

CHINA LIMITS EXPORTS OF RARE EARTH MATERIALS

Rare earth metals are a set of 17 chemical elements in the periodic table and include scandium, yttrium, cerium, and lanthanum. Small concentrations of these metals are a crucial ingredient in the manufacture of a wide range of high-technology products, including wind turbines, iPhones, industrial magnets, and the batteries used in hybrid cars. Extracting rare earth metals can be a dirty process due to the toxic acids that are used during the refining process. As a consequence, strict environmental regulations have made it extremely expensive to extract and refine rare earth metals in many countries.

Environmental restrictions in countries such as Australia, Canada, and the United States have opened the way for China to become the world's leading producer and exporter of rare earth metals. In 1990, China accounted for 27 percent of global rare earth production. By 2010, this figure had surged to 97 percent. In 2010, China sent shock waves through the high-tech manufacturing community when it imposed tight quotas on the exports of rare earths. In 2009, it exported around 50 000 tons of rare earths. The 2010 quota limited exports to 30 000 tons. The quota remained in effect for 2011 and was increased marginally to around 31 000 tons in 2012 and 2013.

The reason offered by China for imposing the export quota is that several of its own mining companies didn't meet environmental standards and had to be shut down. The effect, however, was to dramatically increase prices for rare earth metals outside of China, putting foreign manufacturers at a cost disadvantage. Many observers quickly concluded that the imposition of export quotas was an attempt by China to give its domestic manufacturers a cost advantage and to encourage foreign manufacturers to move more production to China so that they could get access to lower-cost supplies of rare earths. As news magazine *The Economist* concluded, "Slashing their exports of rare earth metals has little to do with dwindling supplies or environmental concerns. It's all about moving Chinese manufacturers up the supply chain, so they can sell valuable finished goods to the world rather than lowly raw materials." In other words, China may have been using trade policy to support its industrial policy.

Developed countries cried foul, claiming that the export quotas violate China's obligations under World Trade Organization rules. In July 2012, the WTO responded by launching its own investigation. Commenting on the investigation, a U.S. administration official said that the export quotas were part of a "deeply rooted industrial policy aimed at providing substantial competitive advantages for Chinese manufacturers at the expense of non-Chinese manufacturers."

In the meantime, the world is not sitting still. In response to the high prices for rare earth metals, many companies have been redesigning their products to use substitute materials. Toyota, Renault, and Tesla, for example—all major automotive consumers of rare earth products—have stated that they plan to stop using parts that have rare earth elements in their cars. Governments have also tried to encourage private mining companies to expand their production of rare earth metals. By 2012, there were some 350 rare earth mine projects under development outside of China and India. An example, Molycorp, a U.S. mining company, is quickly boosting its rare earth production at a California mine. As a consequence of such actions, China's recent share of rare earth output had slipped to 80 percent.

Sources: Chuin-Wei Yap, "China Revamps Rare-Earth Exports," *The Wall Street Journal*, December 28, 2011, p. C3; "The Difference Engine: More Precious than Gold," *The Economist*, September 17, 2010; "Of Metals and Market Forces," *The Economist*, February 4, 2012; and J. T. Areddy and C. W. Yap, "China Raises Rare-Earth Export Quota," *The Wall Street Journal*, August 22, 2012.

Case Discussion Questions

1. Which groups benefitted the most from China imposing an export quota on rare earth metals? Did it give the Chinese domestic manufacturers a significant cost advantage? Did it result in dramatically increased quality and environmental standards?

2. Given that 97 percent of rare earth metal production is now done in China, an increase from 27 percent to 97 percent between 1990 and 2010, do you think Canada should reconsider their environmental restrictions on product of such metals?

3. The restrictions imposed by China on rare earth metals has resulted in some companies (e.g., Toyota, Renault, Tesla) starting to look for alternatives. They plan to use parts that do not include rare earth metals. Is this a good solution?

© SvedOliver/Shutterstock

Chapter 7
Foreign Direct Investment

OPENING CASE

FOREIGN DIRECT INVESTMENT IN NIGERIA

For years now, the economy of Nigeria, Africa's most populous nation, was held back by political instability, poor government policies, a lack of infrastructure, and endemic corruption. This started to change in the 2000s. In halting steps, Nigeria has moved toward a more stable, democratic form of government. In 2007, for the first time in the history of the country, there was a peaceful transfer of civilian power following general elections. Since then, the government has pursued market-orientated reforms, including the removal of subsidies, privatization of some state-run businesses, lowering trade barriers, and deregulation. The government has tried to rid itself of corruption, albeit with mixed success. There has also been some attempt to improve the country's poor transportation and power infrastructure.

The reforms have had a positive impact. The GDP of Nigerian purchasing power parity almost tripled from $170 billion in 2000 to a high of $568 billion in 2014, before falling modestly to $481 billion in 2015. When estimates of the "informal" or "black economy" sector are taken into account, GDP may have been as large as $750 billion in 2014. Powering this growth during the early part of this decade were high oil prices. Nigeria is a significant oil producer, and high oil prices have helped to improve government finances, but the industrial and agricultural sectors of the economy are also growing.

One of the major engines of growth has been foreign direct investment. For years, foreign investors stayed away from Nigeria—scared off by the political instability and high levels of corruption—but that too is starting to change. Encouraged by better economic management and the promise of a large domestic market, inward foreign investment in Nigeria increased from $1.2 billion in 2000 to a peak of almost $9 billion recently. Among recent investors has been General Electric, which announced in 2013 that it would put more than $1 billion into Nigeria for the following five years. The investments include building a manufacturing plant to support the power generation and oil extraction industries, and a service centre for supporting GE equipment. GE believes that its investment will create 2300 jobs.

While the majority of investments are still targeted at Nigeria's large energy sector, there are signs that this too is beginning to shift. A case in point is Procter & Gamble, which in 2012 invested $250 million to construct a state-of-the-art plant to manufacture disposable diapers in Nigeria. Explaining the investment, a P&G spokesperson noted that "Nigeria has a very strong, dynamic and growing population of now over 167 million people with over 40 percent less than 15 years old. By 2050, Nigeria is projected to have the third-largest population in the world. This represents a rapidly growing number of consumers and a wonderful opportunity to serve." The P&G spokesperson also indicated that P&G would increase its investment if the Nigerian government was successful in further lowering import tariffs and consumption taxes, and resolved some of the infrastructure problems that were currently holding the country back.

Sources: K. Aderinokun, "Nigeria: We Want to Make Nigeria the Hub of Procter and Gamble's West African Operations," *AllAfrica*, August 21, 2012; N. Mazen, "General Electric Plans $1 Billion Investment in Nigerian Power," *Bloomberg*, January 31, 2013; CIA, *The World Factbook: Nigeria*; and Trading Economics, Nigeria GDP, http://www.tradingeconomics.com/nigeria/gdp.

LO | LEARNING OBJECTIVES

By the end of this chapter you should be able to:

1. Recognize current trends regarding foreign direct investment (FDI) in the world economy.

2. Explain the different theories of FDI.

3. Understand how political ideology shapes a government's attitudes toward FDI.

4. Describe the benefits and costs of FDI to home and host countries.

5. Explain the range of policy instruments that governments use to influence FDI.

6. Identify the implications for managers of the theory and government policies associated with FDI.

Introduction

Foreign direct investment (FDI) occurs when a firm invests directly in facilities to produce or market a product in a foreign country. According to the U.S. Department of Commerce, FDI occurs whenever a U.S. citizen, organization, or affiliated group takes an interest of 10 percent or more in a foreign business entity. Once a firm undertakes FDI, it becomes a *multinational enterprise*. Two examples of FDI are given in the opening case—the recent investments by General Electric and Procter & Gamble in production facilities in Nigeria.

FDI takes on two main forms; the first is a **greenfield investment**, which involves the establishment of a wholly new operation in a foreign country. Both GE's and P&G's investments in Nigeria were greenfield investments. The second involves acquiring or merging with an existing firm in the foreign country. Acquisitions can be a minority (where the foreign firm takes a 10 percent to 49 percent interest in the firm's voting stock), majority (foreign interest of 50 percent to 99 percent), or full outright stake (foreign interest of 100 percent).[1]

We begin this chapter by looking at the importance of foreign direct investment in the world economy. Next, we review the theories that have been used to explain foreign direct investment. The chapter then looks at government policy toward foreign direct investment. The chapter closes with a section on implications for business.

 Foreign Direct Investment in the World Economy

When discussing foreign direct investment, it is important to distinguish between the flow of FDI and the stock of FDI. The **flow of FDI** refers to the amount of FDI undertaken over a given time period (normally a year). The **stock of FDI** refers to the total accumulated value of foreign-owned assets at a given time. We also talk of **outflows of FDI**, meaning the flow of FDI out of a country, and **inflows of FDI**, meaning the flow of FDI into a country.

Trends in FDI

The past 35 years have seen a marked increase in both the flow and stock of FDI in the world economy. The average yearly outflow of FDI increased from $243 billion in 1990 to $1.5 trillion in 2015. Table 7.1 shows this growth in world FDI.

In general, over the past 35 years the flow of FDI has accelerated faster than the growth in world trade and world output. For example, between 1992 and 2012, the

TABLE 7.1	World FDI Outflows
Year	**FDI Outflows $billions**
1990	$243
2000	$1,163
2010	$1,392
2015	$1,474

Source: United Nations, FDI Outflows by Region and Economy, Table 2, http://unctad.org/en/Pages/DIAE/World%20 Investment%20Report/Annex-Tables.aspx

total flow of FDI from all countries increased around ninefold while world trade by value grew fourfold and world output by around 55 percent.[2] As a result of the strong FDI flows, by 2015 the global stock of FDI was about $25 trillion. Clearly, by any measure, FDI is a very important phenomena.

FDI has grown more rapidly than world trade and world output for several reasons. First, despite the general decline in trade barriers over the past 35 years, firms still fear protectionist pressures. Executives see FDI as a way of circumventing future trade barriers. Second, much of the increase in FDI has been driven by the political and economic changes that have been occurring in many of the world's developing nations. The general shift toward democratic political institutions and free market economies that we discussed in Chapter 2 has encouraged FDI. Across much of Asia, Eastern Europe, and Latin America, economic growth, economic deregulation, privatization programs that are open to foreign investors, and removal of many restrictions on FDI have made these countries more attractive to foreign multinationals. According to the United Nations, some 90 percent of the 2700 changes made worldwide between 1992 and 2009 in the laws governing foreign direct investment created a more favourable environment for FDI.[3]

The globalization of the world economy is also having a positive effect on the volume of FDI. Many firms now see the whole world as their market, and they are undertaking FDI in an attempt to make sure they have a significant presence in many regions of the world. For reasons that we shall explore later in this book, many firms now believe it is important to have production facilities based close to their major customers. This, too, creates pressure for greater FDI.

The Direction of FDI

Historically, most FDI has been directed at the developed nations around the world, as firms based in these countries invested in each other's markets. During the past few decades, the United States has been the favourite target of FDI inflows. It is an attractive target for FDI because of its large and wealthy domestic market, its dynamic and stable economy, and its openness to FDI. Investors include firms based in Great Britain, Japan, Germany, and Canada (see Table 7.2). While FDI flows to developed countries rose by 466% between 1990 and 2015, note the extreme variability of this number over time. Also note that much of this growth happened during the previous century, between 1990–2000.

Even though developed nations still account for the largest share of FDI inflows, FDI into developing nations has increased markedly. Between 1990 and 2015, FDI inflows increased by almost 2,150%. Most recent inflows into developing nations have been targeted at the emerging economies of Southeast Asia. Driving much of the

TABLE 7.2	FDI Inflows ($billions)	
Year	Developed Countries	Developing Countries
1990	$170	$34
2000	$1,120	$232
2010	$700	$625
2015	$962	$764

Source: United Nations, FDI Inflows by Region and Economy, Table 1, http://unctad.org/en/Pages/DIAE/World%20Investment%20 Report/Annex-Tables.aspx

increase has been the growing importance of China as a recipient of FDI, which attracted about $136 billion of FDI in 2015, up from just $3.4 billion in 1990. The reasons for the strong flow of investment into China are discussed in the accompanying Country Focus.

ANOTHER PERSPECTIVE

Zambia Experiences Large FDI Increase

Inward foreign investment into Zambia increased significantly recently, arresting a downward trend that followed the 2008 financial crisis. In 2011 there were record levels of FDI into the country, with 26 investments made and more than $2.3bn [billion] invested. This led to the creation of more than 10 000 jobs. When compared with 2010 data, the number of investments increased by 86 percent, the level of capital investment increased by 74 percent, and the number of jobs created increased by 273 percent. This assertion is attributed to the efforts made by the Zambian government to make the country more attractive to potential investors. Much of this increase in 2011 can be explained by large-scale investments in the metals sector, with eight investments in this sector creating more than 6500 jobs and garnering $1.8bn in investments.

Source: Paul Flynn, "Zambia experiences large FDI increase for 2011," *fDi Intelligence*, May 14, 2012, http://www.fdiintelligence.com/Trend-Tracker/Zambia-experiences-large-FDI-increase-for-2011

The Source of FDI

Since World War II, the United States has been the largest source country for FDI, a position it retained during the late 1990s although no longer true today in 2017. According to this UN Survey on prospective top host economies in the 2013–2015 period, other important host economies include India, Indonesia, Brazil, and Thailand. As we can see from Figure 7.1, this UNCTAD survey places Canada 16th, behind South Africa, Australia, and Poland. Note Canada was not on the list prior to 2013 as indicated by the numbers in parentheses.

That being said, it is noteworthy that Chinese firms have started to emerge as major foreign investors. In 2005, Chinese firms invested some $12 billion internationally. Since then, the figure has risen steadily, reaching $84 billion in 2012. Firms based in Hong Kong accounted for another $84 billion of outward FDI in 2012. Much of the outward investment by Chinese firms has been directed at extractive industries in less developed nations (e.g., China has been a major investor in African countries). A major motive for these investments has been to gain access to raw materials, of which China is one of the world's largest consumers. There are signs, however, that Chinese firms are starting to turn their attention to more advanced nations. In 2012, Chinese firms invested $6.5 billion in the United States, up from $146 million in 2003.[4]

The Form of FDI: Acquisitions versus Greenfield Investments

As noted earlier, FDI can take the form of a greenfield investment in a new facility or an acquisition of or a merger with an existing local firm. The data suggest the majority of cross-border investment is in the form of mergers and acquisitions rather than greenfield investments. However, FDI flows into developed nations differ markedly from those into developing nations. In the case of developing nations, only about

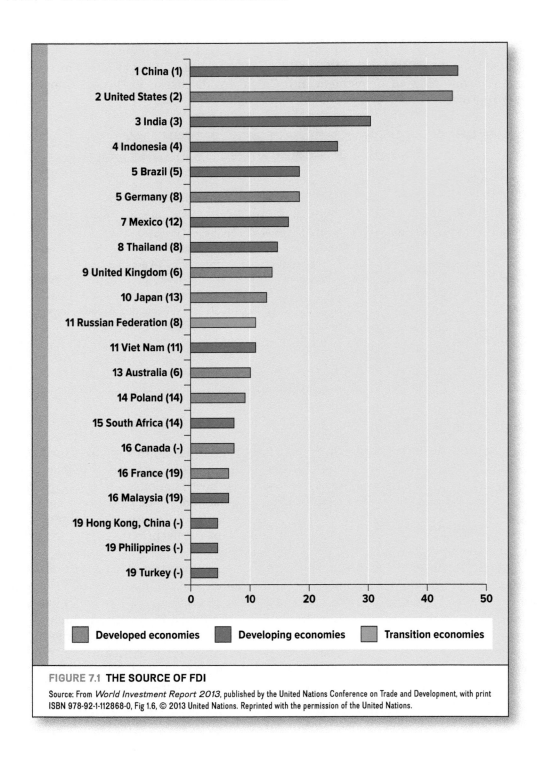

FIGURE 7.1 **THE SOURCE OF FDI**

Source: From *World Investment Report 2013*, published by the United Nations Conference on Trade and Development, with print ISBN 978-92-1-112868-0, Fig 1.6, © 2013 United Nations. Reprinted with the permission of the United Nations.

one-third of FDI is in the form of cross-border mergers and acquisitions. The lower percentage of mergers and acquisitions may simply reflect the fact that there are fewer target firms to acquire in developing nations.

When contemplating FDI, why do firms apparently prefer to acquire existing assets rather than undertake greenfield investments? We shall return to this and consider it in greater depth in Chapter 12, so for now we will make only a few basic observations. First, mergers and acquisitions are quicker to execute than greenfield investments.

This is an important consideration in the modern business world where markets evolve very rapidly. Many firms apparently believe that if they do not acquire a desirable target firm, then their global rivals will.

Second, foreign firms are acquired because those firms have valuable strategic assets, such as brand loyalty, customer relationships, trademarks or patents, distribution systems, production systems, and the like. It is easier and perhaps less risky for a firm to acquire those assets than to build them from the ground up through a greenfield investment.

Third, firms make acquisitions because they believe they can increase the efficiency of the acquired unit by transferring capital, technology, or management skills. Thus, there are some fairly compelling arguments favouring mergers and acquisitions over greenfield investments. But many mergers and acquisitions fail to realize their anticipated gains.[5] This is also explored further in Chapter 12.

As to the impact of FDI on a country, there are two schools of thought. The first says that while it is desirable, there is nothing special about it. One dollar of FDI is worth no more, or no less to a country, than any other type of investment. The second school of thought notes that along with the FDI investment itself can come a host of other positive spillover effects such as technology transfer. Thus, in theory, FDI can increase the productivity of all firms in a country and close "the knowledge gap," not just benefiting those companies that receive the FDI. The most current research actually reconciles these two schools of thought. It states that FDI on its own does not always positively increase economic growth in a country. For that to happen, the country itself must have a certain minimum threshold stock of human capital. In other words, for the technology transfer and other benefits to occur, the country must be at a certain stage of awareness, willingness, and capacity to obtain the full range of benefits from FDI.

DEBATE THE ISSUE

Which Is Better, an Acquisition or a Greenfield Investment?

A greenfield investment is an establishment of a new operation in a foreign country (i.e., a parent company starts a new venture in a foreign country by building new production facilities from the ground up). The acquisition approach refers to buying or merging operations with an existing firm in a foreign country. In the text of this chapter and Chapter 12, we discuss reasons for greenfield and acquisition-based investments in a foreign country. While mergers and acquisitions (M&A) are typically quicker to execute than building something from the ground up, literally, M&A often fail to gain the advantages expected. The failure rate of M&A is somewhere between 50 and 83 percent. At the same time, the trend shows that both the number of M&A and the sums of money spent on M&A are increasing consistently every year. If you were making the decision, would you prefer to make a greenfield investment or engage in either a merger or acquisition in a foreign country?

Source: Y. Weber, C. Oberg, and S. Tarba, "The M&A Paradox: Factors of Success and Failure in Mergers and Acquisitions," *Comprehensive Guide to Mergers & Acquisitions, A: Managing the Critical Success Factors Across Every Stage of the M&A Process* (Upper Saddle River, NJ: FT Press, 2013).

Canada's Case

For much of Canada's recent history, its FDI inflows have been far less than its outflows. In a global context, FDI inflows and outflows remain promising for Canada well into 2015 (see Figure 7.2). Figure 7.2 illustrates, from a global perspective, those factors that favour and impact FDI flows at home and abroad.

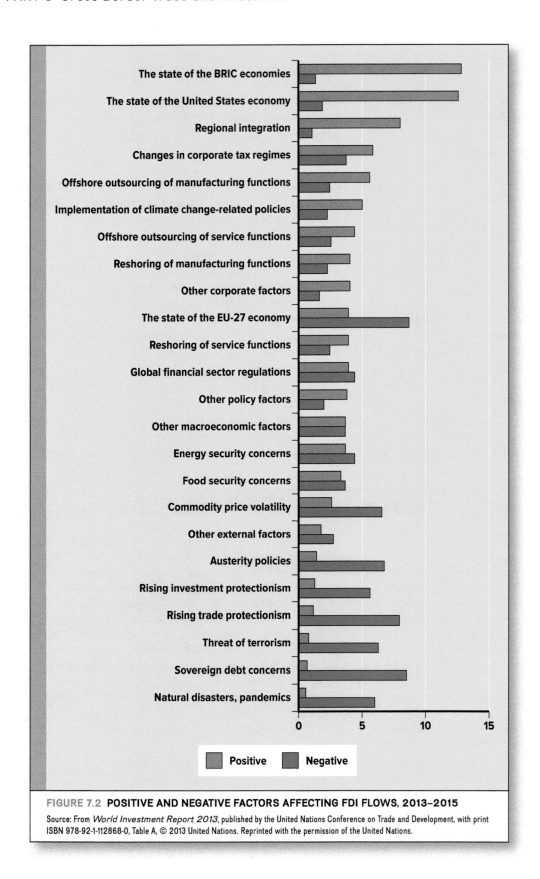

FIGURE 7.2 **POSITIVE AND NEGATIVE FACTORS AFFECTING FDI FLOWS, 2013–2015**

Source: From *World Investment Report 2013*, published by the United Nations Conference on Trade and Development, with print ISBN 978-92-1-112868-0, Table A, © 2013 United Nations. Reprinted with the permission of the United Nations.

In the field of international trade, until 2007 Canada and the United States shared the largest bilateral flow of goods, services, people, capital, and investments between any two countries in the world. Even though only by a hair, by the end of December 2007 China nudged passed Canada as top exporter to the United States with total exports of $321.5 billion (US$). This trend has continued to this day.

For the most part, Canadian gains in FDI outflow are due to the rise of Canadian affiliates and subsidiaries in the United States. Statistics Canada reports that most overseas investments made by Canadian companies in the last five years have gone to existing affiliates and subsidiaries for working capital purposes. This investment, which bolsters the Canadian corporate presence abroad, might also be a good omen that Canadian companies are strengthening their global supply and production networks. The acquisition of foreign assets and companies has been the main driver of Canadian FDI outflows consistently since 2002. As Canada's multicultural population grows, Canadian business is better equipped to expand its geographical reach beyond the United States.[6]

LO2 | Theories of Foreign Direct Investment

In this section we review several theories of foreign direct investment. These theories approach the phenomenon of foreign direct investment from three complementary perspectives. One set of theories seeks to explain why a firm will favour direct investment as a means of entering a foreign market when two other alternatives are open to it, exporting and licensing. Another set of theories seeks to explain why firms in the same industry often undertake foreign direct investment at the same time, and why certain locations are favoured over others as targets for foreign direct investment. These theories attempt to explain the observed *pattern* of foreign direct investment flows. A third theoretical perspective, known as the eclectic paradigm, attempts to combine the two other perspectives into a single holistic explanation of foreign direct investment (the term *eclectic* means picking the best aspects of other theories and combining them into a single explanation).

Why Foreign Direct Investment?

Why do firms go to all the trouble of establishing operations abroad through foreign direct investment when two alternatives are available for exploiting the profit opportunities in a foreign market: exporting and licensing? **Exporting** involves producing goods at home and then shipping them to the receiving country for sale. **Licensing** involves granting a foreign entity (the licensee) the right to produce and sell the firm's product in return for a royalty fee on every unit the foreign entity sells.

The question is an important one given that foreign direct investment can be both expensive and risky when compared to exporting and licensing. FDI is expensive because a firm must bear the costs of establishing production facilities in a foreign country or of acquiring a foreign enterprise. FDI is risky because of the problems associated with doing business in a different culture where the rules of the game may be very different. Relative to indigenous firms, there is a greater probability that a foreign firm undertaking FDI in a country for the first time will make costly mistakes

COUNTRY FOCUS

Foreign Direct Investment in China

Beginning in late 1978, China's leadership decided to move the economy away from a centrally planned socialist system to one that was more market driven. The result has been nearly four decades of sustained high economic growth rates of around 10 percent annually compounded. This growth attracted substantial foreign investment. Starting from a tiny base, foreign investment increased to an annual average rate of $2.7 billion between 1985 and 1990 and then surged to $40 billion annually in the late 1990s, making China the second biggest recipient of FDI inflows in the world after the United States. By the end of the last decade, China was attracting between $80 billion and $100 billion of FDI annually, with another $60 billion a year going into Hong Kong. In 2011, a record $124 billion was invested in China and another $78.4 billion in Hong Kong. Over the past 20 years, this inflow has resulted in the establishment of more than 300 000 foreign-funded enterprises in China. The total stock of FDI in mainland China grew from almost nothing in 1978 to $832 billion most recently (another $1.4 trillion of FDI stock was in Hong Kong).

The reasons for this investment are fairly obvious. With a population of more than 1.3 billion people, China represents the world's largest market. Historically, import tariffs made it difficult to serve this market via exports, so FDI was required if a company wanted to tap into the country's huge potential. China joined the World Trade Organization in 2001. As a result, average tariff rates on imports have fallen from 15.4 percent to about 8 percent today, reducing this motive for investing in China (although at 8 percent, tariffs are still above the average of 3.5 percent found in many developed nations). Notwithstanding tariff rates, many foreign firms believe that doing business in China requires a substantial presence in the country to build *guanxi*, the crucial relationship networks (see Chapter 4 for details). Furthermore, a combination of relatively inexpensive labour and tax incentives, particularly for enterprises that establish themselves in special economic zones, makes China an attractive base from which to serve Asian or world markets with exports (although rising labour costs in China are now making this less important).

Less obvious, at least to begin with, was how difficult it would be for foreign firms to do business in China. Blinded by the size and potential of China's market, many firms paid less attention than perhaps they should to the complexities of operating a business in China until after the investment had been made. China may have a huge population, but despite decades of rapid growth, it is still relatively poor. The lack of purchasing power translates into relatively immature market for many Western consumer goods outside of relatively affluent urban areas such as Shanghai. Other problems include a highly regulated environment, which can make it problematic to conduct business transactions, and shifting tax and regulatory regimes. For example, a few years ago, the Chinese government suddenly scrapped a tax credit scheme that had made it attractive to import capital equipment into China. This immediately made it more expensive to set up operations in the country. Then there are problems with local joint-venture partners that are inexperienced, opportunistic, or simply operate according to different goals. One manager explained that when he laid off 200 people to reduce costs, his Chinese partner hired them all back the next day. When he inquired why they had been hired back, the executive of the Chinese partner, which was government owned, explained that as an agency of the government, it had an "obligation" to reduce unemployment.

To continue to attract foreign investment, the Chinese government has committed itself to invest more than $800 billion in infrastructure projects by 2020. This should improve the nation's poor highway system. By giving preferential tax breaks to companies that invest in special regions, such as that around Chongqing, the Chinese have created incentives for foreign companies to invest in China's vast interior where markets are underserved. They have been pursuing a macroeconomic policy that includes an emphasis on maintaining steady economic growth, low inflation, and a stable currency—all of which are attractive to foreign investors. Given these developments, it seems likely that the country will continue to be an important magnet for foreign investors well into the future.

Questions

1. Do you see a continued trend of foreign investment into China? What would speed up and what would delay such investment?
2. What indicators (political, economic, and others) would a company look at to decide whether or not to invest in China?

Sources: Interviews by the author while in China; United Nations, *World Investment Report, 2009* (New York and Geneva: The United Nations, 2009); L. Ng and C. Tuan, "Building a Favorable Investment Environment: Evidence for the Facilitation of FDI in China," *The World Economy*, 2002, pp. 1095–114; and S. Chan and G. Qingyang, "Investment in China Migrates Inland," *Far Eastern Economic Review*, May 2006, pp. 52–57.

due to ignorance. When a firm exports, it need not bear the costs associated with foreign direct investment, and the risks associated with selling abroad can be reduced by using a native sales agent. Similarly, when a firm allows another enterprise to produce its products under licence, it need not bear the costs or risks of FDI, since these are borne by the licensee. So why do so many firms apparently prefer FDI over either exporting or licensing? A deeper examination of the issue reveals that the answer can be found in the limitations of exporting and licensing as means for capitalizing on foreign market opportunities.

LIMITATIONS OF EXPORTING

The viability of an exporting strategy is often constrained by transportation costs and trade barriers. When transportation costs are added to production costs, it becomes unprofitable to ship some products over a large distance. This is particularly true of products that have a low value-to-weight ratio and can be produced in almost any location (e.g., cement, soft drinks, etc.). For such products, relative to either FDI or licensing, the attractiveness of exporting decreases. For products with a high value-to-weight ratio, however, transport costs are normally a very minor component of total landed cost (e.g., electronic components, personal computers, medical equipment, computer software, etc.) and have little impact on the relative attractiveness of exporting, licensing, and FDI.

Transportation costs aside, much FDI is undertaken as a response to actual or threatened trade barriers such as import tariffs or quotas. By placing tariffs on imported goods, governments can increase the cost of exporting relative to foreign direct investment and licensing. Similarly, by limiting imports through quotas, governments increase the attractiveness of FDI and licensing. For example, the wave of FDI by Japanese auto companies in the United States during the 1980s and 1990s was partly driven by protectionist threats from the U.S. Congress and by quotas on the importation of Japanese cars. For Japanese auto companies, these factors decreased the profitability of exporting and increased that of foreign direct investment. Trade barriers do not have to be in place for foreign direct investment to be favoured over exporting. Often, the desire to reduce the "threat" that trade barriers might be imposed is enough to justify foreign direct investment as an alternative to exporting.

MANAGEMENT FOCUS

Four Seasons Hotels and Resorts

Few large companies can boast of continuity of management over a 50-year period, and Four Seasons Hotels and Resorts is one of the few corporations that is able to do just that. Often the entrepreneurial flair exhibited by a company founder turns to a more bureaucratic style of management as the company grows.

Isadore Sharp, chairman and chief executive officer, founded the first Four Seasons hotel in 1960 as a mid-priced inn on the fringes of downtown Toronto. In keeping with his entrepreneurial flair, and after a decade of being in business, he developed the formula of creating the Four Seasons brand as a luxury group of hotels and resorts. Today he is still the chairman of the company. By 2017 Four Seasons managed a total of 102 hotels and resorts in 43 countries. It entered the Chinese market as early as 2002. The company's eighth hotel in China opened in September 2013. Today it also has a further 60 projects in some stage of planning and development.

Aside from being properties of exceptional design and finish, the company is well known for its personal service, catering to the needs of the discriminating traveller. The service component has become such a feature of the company that Four Seasons has shifted its focus in the past decades. Once a major owner of the hotel properties, today it is mostly engaged in the management of the hotels that have the Four Seasons name. Under the terms of a typical management agreement, Four Seasons supervises all aspects of the day-to-day operations of the hotel on behalf of the property owner. This includes hiring, training, and supervising staff, providing sales and marketing services, undertaking purchasing and budgeting, as well as providing for the repair and maintenance of the physical structure of the hotel. In return for managing a property, Four Seasons earns a number of fees, including a base fee, an incentive fee based on the profits of the hotel or the resort, a sales and marketing fee, as well as additional fees if the company provided pre-opening design and consulting work. These fees provide an ongoing, relatively steady stream of revenue for the company. The company, through the Four Seasons Private Residences, Residence Clubs, and other brands, is also expanding into the luxury condominium market, tied to the many services offered in its hotel offerings.

A key component of the company is to provide a high level of standardized service throughout the world, as well as centralized purchasing and reservation systems, while at the same time ensuring that each property is unique. A Four Seasons Hotel should not look, or feel, like a cookie-cutter Holiday Inn, which is mostly the same whether you are in Atlanta or Calgary.

In 2007 the company, which had been publicly traded, was taken private in a partnership between Microsoft's Bill Gates and Prince Al-Waleed bin Talal, one of the original and major shareholders of Four Seasons. The former Canadian company became truly global, both in its reach and in its ownership.

Sources: Four Seasons, www.fourseasons.com and CBC/Radio-Canada, www.cbc.ca; Four Seasons History, 2000–2009: A Global Luxury Brand, http://www.fourseasons.com/about_four_seasons/2000_to_2009/; Press Room, http://press.fourseasons.com/; and About Four Seasons, http://www.fourseasons.com/about_four_seasons/

Questions

1. How can a company maintain its image, quality, and reputation when it is so widely spread out around the globe?
2. How susceptible do you think a luxury brand like Four Seasons is to the recent global economic slowdown which began in 2008, or to economic recessions generally?

LIMITATIONS OF LICENSING

A branch of economic theory known as **internalization theory** seeks to explain why firms often prefer foreign direct investment over licensing as a strategy for entering foreign markets (this approach is also known as the **market imperfections** approach).[7] According to internalization theory, licensing has three major drawbacks as a strategy for exploiting foreign market opportunities. First, *licensing may result in a firm's giving away valuable technological know-how to a potential foreign competitor.* For example, in the 1960s, RCA licensed its leading-edge colour television technology to a number of Japanese companies, including Matsushita and Sony. At the time, RCA saw licensing as a way to earn a good return from its technological know-how in the Japanese market without the costs and risks associated with foreign direct investment. However, Matsushita and Sony quickly assimilated RCA's technology and used it to enter the U.S. market to compete directly against RCA. As a result, RCA is now a minor player in its home market, while Matsushita and Sony have a much bigger market share.

A second problem is that *licensing does not give a firm the tight control over manufacturing, marketing, and strategy in a foreign country that may be required to maximize its profitability.* With licensing, control over manufacturing, marketing, and strategy are granted to a licensee in return for a royalty fee. However, for both strategic and operational reasons, a firm may want to retain control over these functions. The rationale for wanting control over the strategy of a foreign entity is that a firm might want its foreign subsidiary to price and market very aggressively as a way of keeping a foreign competitor in check. Unlike a wholly owned subsidiary, a licensee would probably not accept such an imposition, because it would likely reduce the licensee's profit, or it might even cause the licensee to take a loss.

The rationale for wanting control over the operations of a foreign entity is that the firm might wish to take advantage of differences in factor costs across countries, producing only part of its final product in a given country, while importing other parts from elsewhere where they can be produced at lower cost. Again, a licensee would be unlikely to accept such an arrangement, since it would limit the licensee's autonomy. Thus, for these reasons, when tight control over a foreign entity is desirable, foreign direct investment is preferable to licensing.

A third problem with licensing arises when the firm's competitive advantage is based not as much on its products as on the management, marketing, and manufacturing capabilities that produce those products. The problem here is that *such capabilities are often not amenable to licensing.* While a foreign licensee may be able to physically reproduce the firm's product under licence, it often may not be able to do so as efficiently as the firm could itself. As a result, the licensee may not be able to fully exploit the profit potential inherent in a foreign market.

For example, consider Toyota, a company whose competitive advantage in the global auto industry is acknowledged to come from its superior ability to manage the overall process of designing, engineering, manufacturing, and selling automobiles— that is, from its management and organizational capabilities. Indeed, Toyota is credited with pioneering the development of a new production process, known as *lean production,* that enables it to produce higher-quality automobiles at a lower cost than its global rivals.[8] Although Toyota could license certain products, its real competitive advantage comes from its management and process capabilities. These kinds of skills are difficult to articulate or codify; they certainly cannot be written down in a simple licensing contract. They are organization-wide and have been developed over the years. They are not embodied in any one individual but instead are widely dispersed throughout the company. Put another way, Toyota's skills are embedded in its organizational culture, and culture is something that cannot be licensed. Thus, if Toyota were to allow a foreign entity to produce its cars under licence, the chances are that the entity could not do so as efficiently as could Toyota. In turn, this would limit the ability of the foreign entity to fully develop the market potential of that product. Such reasoning underlies Toyota's preference for direct investment in foreign markets, as opposed to allowing foreign automobile companies to produce its cars under licence.

All of this suggests that when one or more of the following conditions holds, markets fail as a mechanism for selling know-how and FDI is more profitable than licensing: (1) when the firm has valuable know-how that cannot be adequately protected by a licensing contract; (2) when the firm needs tight control over a foreign entity to maximize its market share and earnings in that country; and (3) when a firm's skills and know-how are not amenable to licensing.

ADVANTAGES OF FOREIGN DIRECT INVESTMENT

It follows from the above discussion that a firm will favour foreign direct investment over exporting as an entry strategy when transportation costs or trade barriers make exporting unattractive. Furthermore, the firm will favour foreign direct investment over licensing (or franchising) when it wishes to maintain control over its technological know-how, or over its operations and business strategy, or when the firm's capabilities are simply not amenable to licensing.

The Pattern of Foreign Direct Investment

Observation suggests that firms in the same industry often undertake foreign direct investment about the same time. Also, there is a clear tendency for firms to direct their investment activities toward certain locations. The two theories we consider in this section attempt to explain the patterns that we observe in FDI flows.

STRATEGIC BEHAVIOUR

One theory used to explain foreign direct investment patterns is based on the idea that FDI flows are a reflection of strategic rivalry between firms in the global marketplace. An early variant of this argument was expounded by F. T. Knickerbocker, who looked at the relationship between FDI and rivalry in oligopolistic industries.[9] An **oligopoly** is an industry composed of a limited number of large firms (an industry in which four firms control 80 percent of a domestic market is considered an oligopoly). A critical competitive feature of such industries is interdependence of the major players: what one firm does can have an immediate impact on the major competitors, forcing a response in kind. Thus, if one firm in an oligopoly cuts prices, this can take market share away from its competitors, forcing them to respond with similar price cuts to retain their market share.

Such imitative behaviour can take many forms in an oligopoly. One firm raises prices, the others follow; someone expands capacity, and the rivals imitate lest they be left at a disadvantage in the future. Building on this, Knickerbocker argued that the same kind of imitative behaviour characterizes foreign direct investment. Consider an oligopoly in Canada in which three firms—A, B, and C—dominate the market. Firm A establishes a subsidiary in France. Firms B and C reflect that if this investment is successful, it may knock out their export business to France and give a first-mover advantage to firm A. Furthermore, firm A might discover some competitive asset in France that it could repatriate to Canada to torment firms B and C on their native soil. Given these possibilities, firms B and C decide to follow firm A and establish operations in France.

Imitative behaviour does lead to foreign direct investment. Several studies of U.S. enterprises suggest that firms based in oligopolistic industries do tend to imitate each other's FDI.[10] The same phenomenon has been observed among Japanese firms.[11] For example, Toyota and Nissan responded to investments by Honda in the United States and Europe by undertaking their own FDI in the United States and Europe.

Knickerbocker's theory can be extended to embrace the concept of multipoint competition. **Multipoint competition** arises when two or more enterprises encounter each other in different regional markets, national markets, or industries.[12] Economic theory suggests that, rather like chess players jockeying for advantage, firms will try to match each other's moves in different markets to try to hold each other in check. The idea is to ensure that a rival does not gain a commanding position in one market and then use the profits generated there to subsidize competitive attacks in other markets.

Although Knickerbocker's theory and its extensions can help to explain imitative FDI behaviour by firms in oligopolistic industries, it does not explain why the first firm in an oligopoly decides to undertake FDI rather than to export or license. Internalization theory addresses this phenomenon. The imitative theory also does not address the issue of whether FDI is more efficient than exporting or licensing for expanding abroad. Again, internalization theory addresses the efficiency issue. For these reasons, many economists favour internalization theory as an explanation for FDI, although most would agree that the imitative explanation tells an important part of the story.

THE PRODUCT LIFE CYCLE

We considered Raymond Vernon's product life-cycle theory in Chapter 5. However, we did not dwell on Vernon's contention that his theory also explains the pattern of FDI over time. Vernon argued that the same firm or firms that pioneered the product and introduced it in their home market often establish facilities abroad to produce a product for consumption in that market or for export to other markets. Thus, Xerox originally introduced the photocopier into the U.S. market, and it was Xerox that originally set up production facilities in Japan (Fuji-Xerox) and Great Britain (Rank-Xerox) to serve those markets.

Vernon's view is that firms undertake FDI at particular stages in the life cycle of a product they have pioneered. They invest in other advanced countries when local demand in those countries grows large enough to support local production (as Xerox did). They subsequently shift production to developing countries when product standardization and market saturation give rise to price competition and cost pressures. Investment in developing countries, where labour costs are lower, is seen as the best way to reduce costs.

There is merit to Vernon's theory; firms do invest in a foreign country when demand in that country will support local production, and they do invest in low-cost regions when cost pressures become intense.[13] But Vernon's theory fails to explain why it is profitable for a firm to undertake FDI at such times, rather than continuing to export from its home base, and rather than licensing a foreign firm to produce its product. Just because demand in a foreign country is large enough to support local production, it does not necessarily follow that local production is the most profitable option. It may still be more profitable to produce at home and export to that country (to realize the scale economies that arise from serving the global market from one location). Alternatively, it may be more profitable for the firm to license a foreign firm to produce its product for sale in that country. The product life-cycle theory ignores these options and, instead, simply argues that once a foreign market is large enough to support local production, FDI will occur. This limits its explanatory power and its usefulness to business (in that it fails to identify when it is profitable to invest abroad).

THE ECLECTIC PARADIGM

The **eclectic paradigm** has been championed by the British economist John Dunning.[14] Dunning argues that in addition to the various factors discussed above, location-specific advantages are also important in explaining both the rationale for, and the direction of foreign direct investment. By **location-specific advantages**, Dunning means the advantages that arise from utilizing resource endowments or assets that are tied to a particular foreign location and that a firm finds valuable to combine with its own unique assets (such as the firm's technological, marketing, or management capabilities). Dunning accepts the argument of internalization theory that it is difficult for a firm to license its own unique capabilities and know-how. Therefore, he argues that combining location-specific assets or resource endowments *and* the firm's own unique capabilities often requires foreign direct investment. That is, it requires the firm to establish production facilities where those foreign assets or resource endowments are located.

An obvious example of Dunning's arguments are natural resources, such as oil and other minerals, which are by their character specific to certain locations. Dunning suggests that to exploit such foreign resources a firm must undertake FDI. Clearly this explains the FDI undertaken by many of the world's oil companies, which have to invest where oil is located to combine their technological and managerial capabilities with this valuable location-specific resource. Another obvious example is valuable human resources, such as low-cost, highly skilled labour. The cost and skill of labour varies from country to country. Since labour is not internationally mobile, according to Dunning it makes sense for a firm to locate production facilities where the cost and skills of local labour are most suited to its particular production processes.

However, Dunning's theory has implications that go beyond basic resources such as minerals and labour. Consider Silicon Valley, which is the world centre for the computer and semiconductor industry. Many of the world's major computer and semiconductor companies, such as Twitter, Facebook, Amazon, Netflix, Apple Computer, Hewlett-Packard, and Intel, are located close to each other in the Silicon Valley region of California. As a result, much of the cutting-edge research and product development in computers and semiconductors takes place here. According to Dunning's arguments, knowledge being generated in Silicon Valley with regard to the design and manufacture of computers and semiconductors is available nowhere else in the world. As it is commercialized, that knowledge diffuses throughout the world, but the leading edge of knowledge generation in the computer and semiconductor industries is to be found in Silicon Valley. In Dunning's language, this means that Silicon Valley has a *location-specific advantage* in the generation of knowledge related to the computer and semiconductor industries. In part, this advantage comes from the sheer concentration of intellectual talent in this area, and in part it arises from a network of informal contacts that allow firms to benefit from each other's knowledge generation. Economists refer to such knowledge "spillovers" as **externalities**, and a well-established theory suggests that firms can benefit from such externalities by locating close to their source.[15]

Given this, it may make sense for foreign computer and semiconductor firms to invest in research and (perhaps) production facilities so that they can benefit from being in the location where the knowledge is first generated. Externalities may allow firms based there to learn about and use valuable new knowledge before those based elsewhere, thereby giving them a competitive advantage in the global marketplace. If this argument is correct, one would expect to see significant evidence of FDI by European, Japanese, South Korean, Canadian, and Taiwanese computer and semiconductor firms in the Silicon Valley region. In fact, evidence seems to show that firms from these countries are investing in the Silicon Valley region, precisely because they wish to benefit from the externalities that arise there.[16] In a similar vein, others have argued that direct investment by foreign firms in the U.S. biotechnology industry

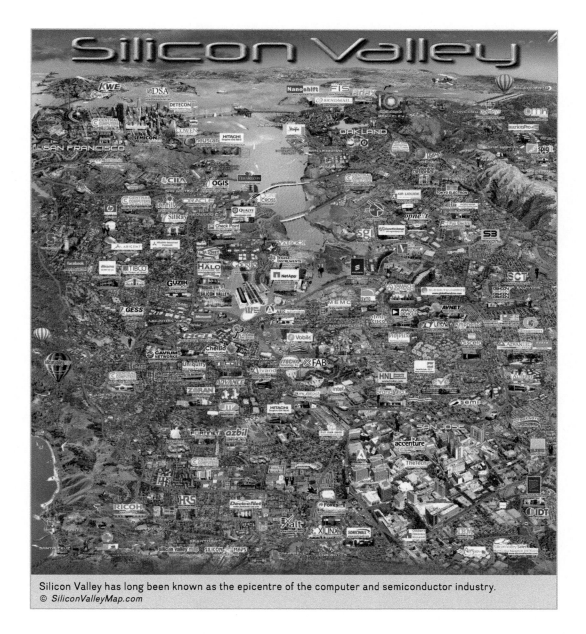

Silicon Valley has long been known as the epicentre of the computer and semiconductor industry.
© SiliconValleyMap.com

has been motivated by desires to gain access to the unique location-specific technological knowledge of U.S. biotechnology firms.[17] Dunning's theory, therefore, seems to be a useful addition to those outlined above, for it helps explain like no other how location factors affect the direction of FDI.

LO3 Political Ideology and Foreign Direct Investment

Government policy toward FDI has typically been driven by political ideology. Historically, ideology toward FDI has ranged from a radical stance that is hostile to all FDI to the noninterventionist principle of free market economics. In between these two extremes is an approach that might be called pragmatic nationalism.

The Radical View

The radical view traces its roots to Marxist political and economic theory. Radical writers argue that the multinational enterprise (MNE) is an instrument of imperialist domination. They see the MNE as a tool for exploiting host countries to the exclusive benefit of their capitalist-imperialist home countries. They argue that MNEs extract profits from the host country and take them to their home country, giving nothing of value to the host country. They note, for example, that key technology is tightly controlled by the MNE, and that important jobs in the foreign subsidiaries of MNEs go to home-country nationals rather than to citizens of the host country. Because of this, according to the radical view, FDI by the MNEs of advanced capitalist nations keeps the developing countries of the world relatively backward and dependent on advanced capitalist nations for investment, jobs, and technology. Thus, according to the extreme version of this view, no country should ever permit foreign corporations to undertake FDI, since they can never be instruments of economic development, only of economic domination. Moreover, where MNEs already exist in a country, they should be immediately nationalized.[18]

By the end of the 1980s, however, the radical position was in retreat almost everywhere. There seem to be three reasons for this: (1) the collapse of communism in Eastern Europe; (2) the generally abysmal economic performance of those countries that embraced the radical position, and a growing belief by many of these countries that FDI can be an important source of technology and jobs and can stimulate economic growth; and (3) the strong economic performance of those developing countries that embraced capitalism rather than radical ideology (e.g., Singapore, Hong Kong, and Taiwan). For example, even though the governing African National Congress party in South Africa contains many former Communists, the government has not adopted a radical stance and is encouraging foreign firms to undertake FDI. Twenty years ago this would not have occurred, but in the new world order ushered in by the collapse of communism it is a common position.

The Free Market View

The free market view has its roots in classical economics and the international trade theories of Adam Smith and David Ricardo (see Chapter 6). The free market view argues that international production should be distributed among countries according to the theory of comparative advantage. That is, countries should specialize in the production of those goods and services that they can produce most efficiently. Within this framework, the MNE is seen as an instrument for dispersing the production of goods and services to those locations where they can be produced most efficiently. Viewed this way, FDI by the MNE is a way to increase the overall efficiency of the world economy.

However, in practice, no country has adopted the free market view in its pure form (just as no country adopts the radical view in its pure form). Countries such as Great Britain, the United States, and Canada are among the most open to FDI, but governments of these three countries intervene. Great Britain does so by reserving the right to block foreign takeovers of domestic firms if the takeovers are seen as "contrary to national security interests" or if they have the potential for reducing competition. (In practice this right is rarely exercised.) U.S. controls on FDI are more limited and largely informal. For political reasons, the United States will occasionally restrict U.S. firms from undertaking FDI in certain countries (Cuba, North Korea, and Iran).

ANOTHER PERSPECTIVE

India to Allow FDI from Pakistan

Improving the economic ties between the two nations, India recently announced that it will allow FDI from Pakistan, paving the way for industries from the neighbouring country to set up businesses in the growing Indian market. This is a prime example of how free markets are promoting trade between countries that have not traditionally enjoyed stable political relationships with each other. Free markets promote the trade normalization process to allow foreign direct investment from Pakistan into India. Leading to further economic activity, talks are also underway to allow banks from both the countries to open branches in each other's territory. At present, India and Pakistan are engaged only in trade of goods, which has recently been liberalized. Several Pakistani industries and banks are keen on setting up business in India, which would be possible only when a policy decision on allowing cross-border FDI is taken.

Source: "India to allow FDI from Pakistan: Anand Sharma," *hinudustantimes*, August 13, 2012, http://www.hindustantimes.com/business/india-to-allow-fdi-from-pakistan-anand-sharma/story-uiTeMMavy5OTDjHtuAFR7O.html

Canada's approach to FDI was seen as socialist by many during the initial stages of the Foreign Investment Review Agency. The Foreign Investment Review Agency came about during the Trudeau era of mild socialism, during which time takeovers of Canadian industry were closely vetted and more often than not turned down. During the robust oil markets of the 1970s, foreign oil companies wanted a piece of Alberta's action, for example. FIRA's frequent interference in the free market processes helped to set the political stage for the ensuing and noticeable anti-Ottawa feelings of Albertan mistrust and suspicion, which to this day are alive and well. FIRA was abolished by Prime Minister Brian Mulroney during the 1980s and replaced by a milder form of foreign direct investment screening; however, Canada is still not entirely open for business to foreign entities. Airlines such as Air Canada, for example, will remain subject to the general abuse of dominance provision.[19]

In the Canadian broadcasting industry, regulated by the Canadian Radio-television and Telecommunications Commission, similar restrictions apply. On December 12, 2002, in a speech given by CRTC Chairperson Charles Dalfen to the Standing Committee on Canadian Heritage in Ottawa, he stated

. . . The Commission is instructed under the Broadcasting Act to give effect to certain directions of the Governor in Council. One of the most important of these is the direction dealing with the ineligibility of non-Canadians to hold broadcasting licences, which was originally issued in 1969, and was last amended in 1998.

Under this direction, the Commission can neither issue broadcasting licences nor grant amendments or renewals to applicants that are non-Canadian. The direction spells out the criteria that applicants must satisfy in order to qualify as Canadian. In the case of a corporation, these include the following: a minimum of 80% of the issued and outstanding voting shares of a licensee corporation and 80% of its voting rights must be owned and controlled by Canadians; the chief executive officer and a minimum of 80 percent of the corporation's directors must be Canadians who normally reside in Canada; and where the licensee is a subsidiary, 66 2/3% of the parent corporation's issued and outstanding voting shares and voting rights must be owned by Canadians. Where the foreign ownership of a parent corporation is over 20%, the parent corporation or its directors cannot influence the programming decisions of the licensee.[20]

The sum of these measures may be the reason that while bilateral investment treaties (BITs) have continued to grow worldwide until very recently and have continued to be broader in scope with increasing detail, the number of new BITs signed each year has actually been declining. There are examples of rapid global trade expansion everywhere one looks, and the increasing flow of capital is noted ad nauseam by celebrants and watchdogs alike. In the face of this, however, it is useful for the observer of global business to note that neither the force of expanding markets nor nations' support of them is absolute.

Pragmatic Nationalism

In practice, many countries have adopted neither a radical policy nor a free market policy toward FDI, but instead a policy that can best be described as pragmatic nationalism. The pragmatic nationalist view is that FDI has both benefits and costs. FDI can benefit a host country by bringing capital, skills, technology, and jobs, but those benefits often come at a cost. When products resulting from an investment are sold by a foreign company rather than a domestic company, the profits from that investment go abroad. Many countries are also concerned that a foreign-owned manufacturing plant may import many components from its home country, which has negative implications for the host country's balance-of-payments position.

Recognizing this, countries adopting a pragmatic stance pursue policies designed to maximize the national benefits and minimize the national costs. According to this view, FDI should be allowed only if the benefits outweigh the costs.

Another aspect of pragmatic nationalism is the tendency to aggressively court FDI seen to be in the national interest by, for example, offering subsidies to foreign MNEs in the form of tax breaks or grants. Countries often compete with each other to attract foreign investment, offering large tax breaks and subsidies to enterprises considering investment. For example, in Europe, Britain has been the most successful at attracting Japanese investment in the automobile industry, often in the face of major competition from other European nations. Nissan, Toyota, and Honda have major assembly plants in Britain. All three now use this country as their base for serving the rest of Europe—with obvious employment and balance-of-payments benefits for Britain.

Shifting Ideology

Recent years have seen a marked decline in the number of countries that adhere to a radical ideology. Although few countries have adopted a pure free market policy stance, an increasing number of countries are gravitating toward the free market end of the spectrum and have liberalized their foreign investment regime. This includes many countries that less than two decades ago were firmly in the radical camp (e.g., the former communist countries of Eastern Europe and many of the socialist countries of Africa) and several countries that until recently could best be described as pragmatic nationalists with regard to FDI (e.g., Japan, South Korea, Italy, Spain, and most Latin American countries). One result has been the surge in the volume of FDI worldwide, which, as we noted earlier, has been growing twice as fast as the growth in world trade. Another result has been an increase in the volume of FDI directed at countries that have recently liberalized their FDI regimes, such as China, India, and Vietnam.

As a counterpoint, there is recent evidence of the beginnings of what might become a shift to a more hostile approach to foreign direct investment. Venezuela and Bolivia have become increasingly hostile to foreign direct investment. In 2005 and 2006 the governments of both nations unilaterally rewrote contracts for oil and gas exploration, raising the royalty rate that foreign enterprises had to pay the government for oil and gas extracted in their territories. Following his election victory, in 2006 Bolivian

President Evo Morales nationalized the nation's gas fields and stated that he would evict foreign firms unless they agreed to pay about 80 percent of their revenues to the state and relinquish production oversight. In some developed nations, too, evidence of hostile reactions to inward FDI is increasing. In Europe in 2006 there was a hostile political reaction to the attempted takeover of Europe's largest steel company, Arcelor, by Mittal Steel, a global company controlled by an Indian entrepreneur, Lakshmi Mittal. In mid-2005 China National Offshore Oil Company withdrew a takeover bid for Unocal of the United States after highly negative reaction in Congress about the proposed takeover of a "strategic asset" by a Chinese company. As noted in previous chapters, the move to renegotiating trade agreements, and the lip service being paid to perceived positive aspects to trade barriers may, if they continue, place the 30-year-long movement toward lower barriers to cross-border investment in jeopardy.

LO4 Costs and Benefits of FDI to the Nation-State

To a greater or lesser degree, many governments can be considered pragmatic nationalists when it comes to FDI. Accordingly, their policy is shaped by a consideration of the costs and benefits of FDI. Here we explore the benefits and costs of FDI, first from the perspective of a host country, and then from the perspective of the home country. Later, we look at the policy instruments governments use to manage FDI.

Host-Country Effects: Benefits

There are three main benefits of inward FDI for a host country: the resource-transfer effect, the employment effect, and the balance-of-payments effect. In the following section we will explore the costs of FDI to host countries.

RESOURCE-TRANSFER EFFECTS

Foreign direct investment can make a positive contribution to a host economy by supplying capital, technology, and management resources that would otherwise not be available. If capital, technology, or management skills are scarce in a country, the provision of these skills by an MNE (through FDI) may boost that country's economic growth rate.

The argument with regard to capital is that many MNEs, by virtue of their large size and financial strength, have access to financial resources not available to host-country firms. These funds may be available from internal company sources, or, because of their reputation, large MNEs may find it easier to borrow money from capital markets than host-country firms would.

As for technology, you will recall from Chapter 2 that technology can stimulate a country's economic growth and industrialization.[21] Technology can take two forms, both of which are valuable. It can be incorporated in a production process (e.g., the technology for discovering, extracting, and refining oil) or it can be incorporated in a product (e.g., personal computers). However, many countries lack the research and development resources and skills required to develop their own indigenous product and process technology. This is particularly true of the world's less-developed nations. Such countries must rely on advanced industrialized nations for much of the technology required to stimulate economic growth, and FDI can provide it.

The foreign management skills provided through FDI may also produce important benefits for the host country. Beneficial spin-off effects arise when local personnel who are trained to occupy managerial, financial, and technical posts in the subsidiary of a foreign MNE subsequently leave the firm and establish indigenous firms. Similar benefits may arise if the superior management skills of a foreign MNE stimulate local suppliers, distributors, and competitors to improve their own management skills.

The beneficial effects may be reduced if most management and highly skilled jobs in the subsidiaries of foreign firms are reserved for home-country nationals. In such cases, citizens of the host country do not receive the benefits of training by the MNE. This may limit the spin-off effect. Consequently, the percentage of management and skilled jobs that go to citizens of the host country can be a major negotiating point between an MNE wishing to undertake FDI and a potential host government. In recent years, most MNEs have responded to host-government pressures on this issue by agreeing to reserve a large proportion of management and highly skilled jobs for citizens of the host country.

ANOTHER PERSPECTIVE

Does Foreign Direct Investment Promote Growth?

There are multiple reasons for companies to make foreign direct investments. Lowering the cost of production, increasing capacity (volume) of production, and strategically locating production facilities to serve world regions are some of the many reasons for FDI by a company. For the host countries that receive the investment by multinational corporations, the logic is that the influx of capital and increase in tax revenues will benefit the host country in the form of new infrastructure, increased knowledge, and general economic development. However, the evidence so far is very mixed on the value of FDI to the host, ranging from beneficial to detrimental.

Source: L. Alfaro, A. Chanda, S. Kalemli-Ozcan, and S. Sayek, "Does Foreign Direct Investment Promote Growth? Exploring the Role of Financial Markets on Linkages," *Journal of Development Economics*, March 2010, 91(2): 242-256, www.people.hbs.edu/lalfaro/fdiandlinkages.pdf

ANOTHER PERSPECTIVE

FDI Creates Jobs in Ghana

A total of 8351 jobs are expected to be created out of 117 new projects registered in the fourth quarter of 2011, representing 134.32 percent over 3564 expected jobs to be created in the corresponding quarter of 2010. According to the Ghana Investment Promotion Centre (GIPC), 7629 of the jobs representing 91.35 percent were for Ghanaians, while 722 representing 8.65 percent would go to expatriates. In terms of the sectors, agriculture recorded the highest with 3277 jobs followed by manufacturing, building, and construction and services with 1357, 930, and 918 jobs respectively. General trading and liaison were also expected to create 844 and 263 jobs respectively.

Source: "FDI Creates 8,351 Jobs," *Modern Ghana*, January 27, 2012, https://www.modernghana.com/news/374697/fdi-creates-8351-jobs.html

EMPLOYMENT EFFECTS

Another beneficial employment effect claimed for FDI is that it brings jobs to a host country that would otherwise not be created there. The effects of FDI on employment are both direct and indirect. Direct effects arise when a foreign MNE employs a number of host-country citizens. Indirect effects arise when jobs are created in local suppliers as a result of the investment and when jobs are created because of increased local spending by employees of the MNE. The indirect employment effects are often as large as, if not larger than, the direct effects. For example, when Toyota decided to open a new auto plant in France, estimates suggested the plant would create 2000 direct jobs and perhaps another 2000 jobs in support industries.[22]

Cynics argue that not all the "new jobs" created by FDI represent net additions in employment. In the case of FDI by Japanese auto companies in the United States, some argue that the jobs created by this investment have been

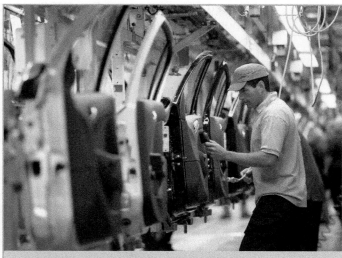

Job creation is a result of FDI. These French workers assemble cars at Toyota's Valenciennes manufacturing plant. © *Monty Rakusen/Getty Images*

more than offset by the jobs lost in U.S.-owned auto companies, which have lost market share to their Japanese competitors. Because of such substitution effects, the net number of new jobs created by FDI may not be as great as initially claimed by an MNE. The issue of the likely net gain in employment may be a major negotiating point between an MNE wishing to undertake FDI and the host government.

When FDI takes the form of an acquisition of an established enterprise in the host economy, as opposed to a greenfield investment, the immediate effect may be to reduce employment as the multinational tries to improve operating efficiency. However, even in such cases, research suggests that after the initial restructuring, enterprises acquired by foreign firms tend to grow their employment base at a faster rate than domestic rivals. For example, an OECD study found that between 1989 and 1996 foreign firms created new jobs at a faster rate than their domestic counterparts.[23] The same study found that foreign firms tended to pay higher wage rates than domestic firms, suggesting that the quality of employment was better. Another study looking at FDI in Eastern European transition economies found that although employment fell after acquisition of an enterprise by a foreign firm, often those enterprises were in competitive difficulties and would not have survived if they had not been acquired. After an initial period of adjustment and retrenchment, employment downsizing was often followed by new investments, and employment either remained stable or increased.[24]

BALANCE-OF-PAYMENTS EFFECTS

The effect of FDI on a country's balance-of-payments accounts is an important policy issue for most host governments. A country's **balance-of-payments accounts** keep track of both its payments to and its receipts from other countries. Governments normally are concerned when their country is running a deficit on the current account of their balance of payments. The **current account** tracks the export and import of goods and services. A current-account deficit, or trade deficit as it is often called, arises when a country is importing more goods and services than it is exporting. Governments typically prefer to see a current-account surplus rather than a deficit. The only way a current-account deficit can be supported in the long run is by selling assets to foreigners (for a detailed explanation of why this is the case, see Krugman and Obstfeld).[25] For example, the persistent U.S. current-account since the 1980s was financed by a steady sale of U.S. assets (stocks, bonds, real estate, and whole corporations) to foreigners. Because national governments invariably dislike seeing the assets of their country fall into foreign hands, they prefer their nation to run a current-account surplus. FDI can help a country achieve this goal in two ways.

First, if the FDI is a substitute for imports of goods or services, the effect can be to improve the current account of the host country's balance of payments. Much of the FDI by Japanese automobile companies in Canada and the United Kingdom, for example, substitutes for imports from Japan. Thus, the current account of Canadian balance of payments has improved somewhat because many Japanese companies are now supplying the Canadian market from production facilities in Canada, as opposed to facilities in Japan. Insofar as this has reduced the need to finance a current-account deficit by asset sales to foreigners, Canada has clearly benefited from this. A second potential benefit arises when the MNE uses a foreign subsidiary to export goods and services to other countries. According to a UN report, inward FDI by foreign multinationals has been a major driver of export-led economic growth in a number of developing and developed nations over the last decade.[26]

ANOTHER PERSPECTIVE

FDI—Modern Day Colonialism

FDI is seen by many as a boon to the expansion and equalization of world trade. Its critics tell a darker tale of exploitation, doom, and infringement on human rights. To them it is colonialism with a new face. FDI is not just about major retail or fast-food chains setting up shop in other countries. FDI can be carried out by an industry wishing to take advantage of a business situation in a potential host country.

For example, Barrick Gold Corporation, a Canadian-based mining operation, has operations in the Porgera Valley, Papua New Guinea, where large gold deposits are being mined. Critics of this facility have stated that during the 1990s the mine operators had shown negative cultural and environmental examples towards area Aboriginals.

Yet Barrick Gold works with local communities to develop plans compatible with host Aboriginal cultural and spiritual sites and traditions. It also provides significant employment opportunities. The company has set up formal and informal networks with government and social communities in and around the mining community. It also enables local Aboriginals to upgrade their work skills through training programs at educational institutions.

Though these are just some of the initiatives that the mining company has put in place, there are many who stand firm that this is yet another example of FDI producing a new form of paternalism.

Is such form of FDI acceptable in today's world?

Source: Barrick Gold Corporation, Community Relations, http://www.barrick.com/responsibility/society/community-relations/default.aspx

---

Host-Country Effects: Costs

Three main costs of inward FDI concern host countries: (1) the possible adverse effects of FDI on competition within the host nation, (2) adverse effects on the balance of payments, and (3) the perceived loss of national sovereignty and autonomy.

ADVERSE EFFECTS ON COMPETITION

Host governments sometimes worry that the subsidiaries of foreign MNEs operating in their country may have greater economic power than indigenous competitors. Because they may be part of a large international organization, the foreign MNE may be able to draw on funds generated elsewhere to subsidize its costs in the host market, which could drive indigenous companies out of business and allow the firm to monopolize the market. Once the market is monopolized, the foreign MNE could raise prices above those that would prevail in competitive markets, with harmful effects on the economic welfare of the host nation. This concern tends to be greater in countries that have few large firms of their own that are able to compete effectively with the subsidiaries of foreign MNEs (generally less-developed countries). It tends to be a relatively minor concern in most advanced industrialized nations.

Another variant of the competition argument is related to the infant industry concern we discussed in Chapter 6. Import controls may be motivated by a desire to let a local industry develop to a stage where it is capable of competing in world markets. The same logic suggests that FDI should be restricted. If a country with a potential comparative advantage in a particular industry allows FDI in that industry, indigenous firms may never have a chance to develop.

In practice, the above arguments are often used by inefficient indigenous competitors when lobbying their government to restrict direct investment by foreign MNEs. Although a host government may state publicly in such cases that its restrictions on inward FDI are designed to protect indigenous competitors from the market power of foreign MNEs, they may have been enacted to protect inefficient but politically powerful indigenous competitors from foreign competition.

ADVERSE EFFECTS ON THE BALANCE OF PAYMENTS

The possible adverse effects of FDI on a host country's balance-of-payments position are twofold. First, set against the initial capital inflow that comes with FDI must be the subsequent outflow of income as the foreign subsidiary repatriates earnings to its parent company. Such outflows show up as a debit on the current account of the balance of payments. The statements of U.S. President Donald Trump focus on this factor, as it relates to dealings with China and Chinese firms. A second concern arises when a foreign subsidiary imports a substantial number of its inputs from abroad, which also results in a debit on the current account of the host country's balance of payments.

NATIONAL SOVEREIGNTY AND AUTONOMY

Many host governments worry that FDI is accompanied by some loss of economic independence. The concern is that key decisions that can affect the host country's economy will be made by a foreign parent that has no real commitment to the host country and over which the host country's government has no real control. A quarter of a century ago this concern was expressed by several European countries, which feared that FDI by U.S. MNEs was threatening their national sovereignty. The same concerns have surfaced in the United States with regard to European and Japanese FDI. The main fear seems to be that if foreigners own assets in the United States, they can somehow "hold the country to economic ransom." Twenty-five years ago, when officials in the French government were making similar complaints about U.S. investments in France, many U.S. politicians dismissed the charge as silly. Now that the U.S. finds itself in the same position, some U.S. politicians no longer think the notion is silly. However, most economists dismiss such concerns as groundless and irrational. Political scientist Robert Reich has noted that such concerns are the product of outmoded thinking because they fail to account for the growing interdependence of the world economy.[27] In a world where firms from all advanced nations are increasingly investing in each other's markets, it is not possible for one country to hold another to "economic ransom" without hurting itself.

Home-Country Effects: Benefits

Although the cost and benefits of FDI for a host country have received the most attention, there are also costs and benefits to the home (or source) country. For example, does the U.S. economy benefit or lose from investments by a firm such as Starbucks in foreign markets? Some would argue that FDI is not always in the home country's national interest and should, therefore, be restricted. Others argue that the benefits far outweigh the costs, and that any restrictions would be contrary to national interests. To understand why people take these positions, let us look at the benefits and costs of FDI to the home (source) country.[28]

The benefits of FDI to the home country arise from three sources. First, the current account of the home country's balance of payments benefits from the inward flow of foreign earnings. Thus, Starbucks' investments in Asia directly benefit the U.S. economy because it repatriates profits earned in Asia to the United States. FDI can also boost the current account of the home country's balance of payments if the foreign subsidiary creates demands for home-country exports of capital equipment, intermediate goods, complementary products, and the like.

Second, benefits to the home country from outward FDI arise from employment effects. As with the balance of payments, positive employment effects arise when the foreign subsidiary creates demand for home-country exports of capital equipment, intermediate goods, complementary products, and the like. Third, benefits arise when the home-country MNE learns valuable skills from its exposure to foreign markets that can subsequently be transferred back to the home country. This amounts to a reverse resource-transfer effect. Through its exposure to a foreign market, an MNE can learn about superior management techniques and superior product and process technologies. These resources can then be transferred back to the home country, with a commensurate beneficial effect on the home country's economic growth rate.[29]

Home-Country Effects: Costs

Against these benefits must be set the apparent costs of FDI for the home (source) country. The most important concerns centre around the balance of payments and employment effects of outward FDI. The home country's trade position (its current account) may deteriorate if the purpose of the foreign investment is to serve the home market from a low-cost production location. For example, when a Canadian textile company closes its plants in Quebec and moves production to Mexico or to other countries, as many have, imports into Canada rise and the trade position deteriorates. The current account of the balance of payments also suffers if the FDI is a substitute for direct exports. Thus, insofar as Toyota's assembly operations in Canada are intended to substitute for direct exports from Japan, the current-account position of Japan will deteriorate.

With regard to employment effects, the most serious concerns arise when

When a Canadian textile company shuts down its plants and moves production to Mexico, as some have, imports into Canada rise and the trade position deteriorates. One objection raised by Canadian labour leaders to free trade is generally that Canadian firms will invest in other countries to take advantage of cheaper labour and then export back to the Canadian market.
© D. Normark/PhotoLink/Getty Images

FDI is seen as a substitute for domestic production. If the labour market in the home country is already very tight, this concern may not be great. However, if the home country is suffering from high unemployment, concern about the export of jobs may rise to the fore.

International Trade Theory and Foreign Direct Investment

When assessing the costs and benefits of FDI to the home country, keep in mind the lessons of international trade theory (see Chapter 5). International trade theory tells us that home-country concerns about the negative economic effects of offshore production may be misplaced. The term *offshore production* refers to FDI undertaken to serve the home market. Far from reducing home-country employment, such FDI may actually stimulate economic growth (and hence employment) in the home country by freeing home-country resources to concentrate on activities where the home country has a comparative advantage. In addition, home-country consumers benefit if the price of the particular product falls as a result of the FDI. Also, if a company were prohibited from making such investments on the grounds of negative employment effects while its international competitors reaped the benefits of low-cost production locations, it would undoubtedly lose market share to its international competitors. Under such a scenario, the adverse long-run economic effects for a country would probably outweigh the relatively minor balance-of-payments and employment effects associated with offshore production.

LO5 | Government Policy Instruments and FDI

We have now reviewed the costs and benefits of FDI from the perspective of both home country and host country. Before tackling the important issue of bargaining between the MNE and the host government, we need to discuss the policy instruments governments use to regulate FDI activity by MNEs. Both home (source) countries and host countries have a range of policy instruments available. We will look at each in turn.

Home-Country Policies

Through their choice of policies, home countries can both encourage and restrict FDI by local firms. We look at policies designed to encourage outward FDI first. These include foreign risk insurance, capital assistance, tax incentives, and political pressure. Then we will look at policies designed to restrict outward FDI.

ENCOURAGING OUTWARD FDI

Many investor nations now have government-backed insurance programs to cover major types of foreign investment risk. The types of risks insurable through these programs include expropriation (nationalization), war losses, and the inability to transfer profits home. Such programs are particularly useful in encouraging firms to undertake investments in politically unstable countries.[30] In addition, several advanced countries also have special funds or banks that make government loans to firms wishing to invest in developing countries. As a further incentive to encourage domestic firms to undertake FDI, many countries have eliminated double taxation of foreign income (i.e., taxation of income in both the host country and the home country). Last, and perhaps most significant, a number of investor countries (including the United States) have used their political influence to persuade host countries to relax their restrictions on inbound FDI. For example, in response to direct U.S. pressure, Japan relaxed many of its formal restrictions on inward FDI in the 1980s. Then, in response to further U.S. pressure, Japan moved toward relaxing its informal barriers to inward FDI. One beneficiary of this trend has been Toys "R" Us, which, after five years of intensive lobbying by company and U.S. government officials, opened its first retail stores in Japan in December 1991. Today, Toys "R" Us has over 160 stores in Japan.[31]

RESTRICTING OUTWARD FDI

Virtually all investor countries, including Canada, have exercised some control over outward FDI from time to time. One common policy has been to limit capital outflows out of concern for the country's balance of payments. From the early 1960s until 1979, for example, Great Britain had exchange-control regulations that limited the amount of capital a firm could take out of the country. Although the main intent of such policies was to improve the British balance of payments, an important secondary intent was to make it more difficult for British firms to undertake FDI.

In addition, countries have occasionally manipulated tax rules to try to encourage their firms to invest at home. The objective behind such policies is to create jobs at home rather than in other nations. At one time these policies were also adopted by Great Britain. The British advanced a corporation tax system that taxed British companies' foreign earnings at a higher rate than their domestic earnings. This tax code created an incentive for British companies to invest at home.

Finally, countries sometimes prohibit firms from investing in certain countries for political reasons. Such restrictions can be formal or informal. For example, formal rules prohibit U.S. firms from investing in countries such as Libya and Iran because these countries' political ideologies and actions are judged to be contrary to U.S. interests. Even the recent warming of Cuban and American relations have not opened the trade embargo and U.S. companies are still not allowed to invest in Cuba. Similarly, during the 1980s, informal pressure was applied to dissuade U.S. firms from investing in South Africa. In this case, the objective was to pressure South Africa to change its apartheid laws, which occurred during the early 1990s. Thus, this policy was successful.

Host-Country Policies

Host countries adopt policies designed both to restrict and to encourage inward FDI. As noted earlier in this chapter, political ideology has determined the type and scope of these policies in the past. In the last decade of the twentieth century, many countries moved quickly away from adhering to some version of the radical stance and prohibiting much FDI and toward a combination of free market objectives and pragmatic nationalism.

ENCOURAGING INWARD FDI

It is common for governments to offer incentives to foreign firms to invest in their countries. Such incentives take many forms, but the most common are tax concessions, low-interest loans, and grants or subsidies. Incentives are motivated by a desire to gain from the resource-transfer and employment effects of FDI. They are also motivated by a desire to capture FDI away from other potential host countries. For example, in the mid-1990s, the governments of Britain and France competed with each other on the incentives they offered Toyota to invest in their respective countries. In the United States, state governments often compete with each other to attract FDI. For example, Kentucky offered Toyota an incentive package worth $112 million to persuade it to build its U.S. automobile assembly plants there. The package included tax breaks, new state spending on infrastructure, and low-interest loans.[32] American cities similarly compete for business with the same packages of benefits. In Canada, cities are by law not allowed to offer such dramatic incentives and tax breaks, though provinces can and do bestow loans, grants, and other incentives on industries from the auto industry to the high-tech sector.

RESTRICTING INWARD FDI

Host governments use a wide range of controls to restrict FDI in one way or another. The two most common are ownership restraints and performance requirements. Ownership restraints can take several forms. In some countries, foreign companies are excluded from specific fields. For example, they are excluded from tobacco and mining in Sweden and from the development of certain natural resources in Brazil, Finland, and Morocco. In other industries, foreign ownership may be permitted although a significant proportion of the equity of the subsidiary must be owned by local investors. As a case in point, foreign ownership is restricted to 25 percent or less of an airline in Canada. However, the Canadian Parliament has passed an amendment to the Canadian Transportation Act. The amendment continues to specify a 25 percent cap, but the Governor in Council has been delegated the authority to increase this percentage to up to 49 percent.

Foreign firms are often excluded from certain sectors on the grounds of national security or competition. Particularly in less-developed countries, the belief seems to be that local firms might not be able to develop unless foreign competition is restricted by a combination of import tariffs and FDI controls. This is really a variant of the infant industry argument discussed in Chapter 6.

Also, ownership restraints seem to be based on a belief that local owners can help to maximize the resource-transfer and employment benefits of FDI for the host country. Until the early 1980s, the Japanese government prohibited most FDI but allowed joint ventures between Japanese firms and foreign MNEs if the MNE had a valuable technology. The Japanese government clearly believed such an arrangement would speed up the subsequent diffusion of the MNE's valuable technology throughout the Japanese economy.

Performance requirements can also take several forms. Performance requirements are controls over the behaviour of the MNE's local subsidiary. The most common performance requirements are related to local content, exports, technology transfer, and local participation in top management. As with certain ownership restrictions, the logic underlying performance requirements is that such rules help to maximize the benefits and minimize the costs of FDI for the host country. Virtually all countries employ some form of performance requirements when it suits their objectives. However, performance requirements tend to be more common in less-developed countries than in advanced industrialized nations. For example, one study found that some 30 percent of the affiliates of U.S. MNEs in less-developed countries were subject to performance requirements, while only 6 percent of the affiliates in advanced countries were faced with such requirements.[33]

International Institutions and the Liberalization of FDI

Until the 1990s there was no consistent involvement by multinational institutions in the governing of FDI. This changed with the formation of the World Trade Organization in 1995. As noted in Chapter 6, the role of the WTO embraces the promotion of international trade in services. Because many services have to be produced where they are sold, exporting is not an option (for example, one cannot export McDonald's hamburgers or consumer banking services). Given this, the WTO has become involved in regulations governing FDI. As might be expected for an institution created to promote free trade, the thrust of the WTO's efforts has been to push for the liberalization of regulations governing FDI, particularly in services. Under the auspices of the WTO, two extensive multinational agreements were reached in 1997 to liberalize trade in telecommunications and financial services. Both these agreements contained detailed clauses that require signatories to liberalize their regulations governing inward FDI, essentially opening their markets to foreign telecommunication and financial services companies.

However, the WTO has had less success trying to initiate talks aimed at establishing a universal set of rules designed to promote the liberalization of FDI. Led by Malaysia and India, developing nations have so far rejected any attempts by the WTO to start such discussions. In an attempt to make progress on this issue, in 1995 the **Organisation for Economic Co-operation and Development (OECD)** initiated talks between its members. (The OECD is a Paris-based intergovernmental organization of "wealthy" nations whose purpose is to provide its 35 member states with a forum in which governments can compare their experiences, discuss the problems they share, and seek solutions that can then be applied within their own national contexts. The members include most European Union countries, the United States, Canada, Japan, and South Korea.) The aim of the talks was to draft a **Multilateral Agreement on Investment (MAI)** that would make it illegal for signatory states to discriminate against foreign investors. This would liberalize rules governing FDI between OECD states. Unfortunately for those promoting the agreement, the talks broke down in early 1998, primarily because the United States refused to sign the agreement. According to the United States, the proposed agreement contained too many exceptions that would weaken its powers. For example, the proposed agreement would not have barred discriminatory taxation of foreign-owned companies, and it would have allowed countries to restrict foreign television programs and music in the name of preserving culture. Also campaigning against the MAI were environmental and labour groups, who criticized the proposed agreement on the grounds that it contained no binding environmental or labour agreements. Despite these problems, negotiations on a revised MAI treaty may be restarted. Also, as noted earlier, individual nations have continued to unilaterally remove restrictions to inward FDI as a wide range of countries from South Korea to South Africa try to encourage foreign firms to invest in their economies.[34]

LO6 | IMPLICATIONS FOR BUSINESS

Several implications for business are inherent in the material discussed in this chapter. We deal first with the implications of the theory, and then turn our attention to the implications of government policy.

THE THEORY OF FDI

The implications of the theories of FDI for business practice are straightforward. The location-specific-advantages argument associated with John Dunning does help explain the *direction* of FDI. However, this argument does not explain *why* firms prefer FDI to licensing or to exporting. In this regard, from both an explanatory and a business perspective, perhaps the most useful theories are those that focus on the limitations of exporting and licensing. These theories are useful because they

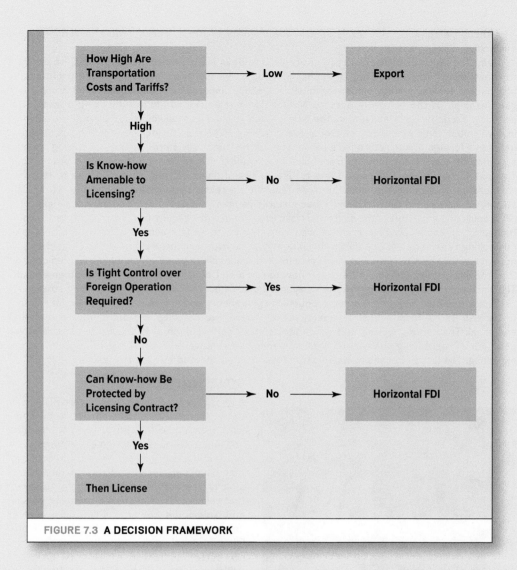

FIGURE 7.3 A DECISION FRAMEWORK

identify with some precision how the relative profitability of foreign direct investment, exporting, and licensing vary with circumstances. The theories suggest that exporting is preferable to licensing and foreign direct investment as long as transport costs are minor and trade barriers are trivial. As transport costs and/or trade barriers increase, exporting becomes unprofitable, and the choice is between FDI and licensing. Because FDI is more costly and more risky than licensing, other things being equal, the theories argue that licensing is preferable to FDI. Other things are seldom equal, however. Although licensing may work, it is not an attractive option when one or more of the following conditions exist: (1) the firm has valuable know-how that cannot be adequately protected by a licensing contract; (2) the firm needs tight control over a foreign entity to maximize its market share and earnings in that country; and (3) a firm's skills and capabilities are not amenable to licensing. Figure 7.3 presents these considerations as a decision tree.

Firms for which licensing is not a good option tend to be clustered in three types of industries:

1. High-technology industries, where protecting firm-specific expertise is of paramount importance and licensing is hazardous.

2. Global oligopolies, where competitive interdependence requires that multinational firms maintain tight control over foreign operations so that they can launch coordinated attacks against their global competitors.

3. Industries where intense cost pressures require that multinational firms maintain tight control over foreign operations (so that they can disperse manufacturing to locations around the globe where factor costs are most favourable to minimize costs).

Although empirical evidence is limited, the majority of the evidence seems to support these conjectures.[35]

Firms for which licensing is a good option tend to be in industries whose conditions are opposite to those specified above. That is, licensing tends to be more common (and more profitable) in fragmented, low-technology industries in which globally dispersed manufacturing is not an option. A good example is the fast-food industry. McDonald's has expanded globally by using a franchising strategy. Franchising is essentially the service-industry version of licensing, although it normally involves much longer-term commitments than licensing. With franchising, the firm licenses its brand name to a foreign firm in return for a percentage of the franchisee's profits. The franchising contract specifies the conditions that the franchisee must fulfill if it is to use the franchisor's brand name. Thus, McDonald's allows foreign firms to use its brand name so long as they agree to run their restaurants on exactly the same lines as McDonald's restaurants elsewhere in the world. This strategy makes sense for McDonald's because (1) like many services, fast food cannot be exported; (2) franchising economizes the costs and risks associated with opening up foreign markets; (3) unlike technological know-how, brand names are relatively easy to protect using a contract; (4) there is no compelling reason for McDonald's to have tight control over franchisees; and (5) McDonald's know-how, in terms of how to run a fast-food restaurant, is amenable to being specified in a written contract (e.g., the contract specifies the details of how to run a McDonald's restaurant). As another example, Tim Hortons has expanded aggressively beyond Canada's borders by using a franchising strategy.

Finally, it should be noted that the product life-cycle theory and Knickerbocker's theory of FDI tend to be less useful from a business perspective. These two theories are descriptive rather than analytical. They do a good job of describing the historical evolution of FDI, but they do a relatively poor job of identifying the factors that influence the relative profitability of FDI, licensing, and exporting. The issue of licensing as an alternative to FDI is ignored by both of these theories.

By using a franchising strategy, McDonald's has expanded globally, but can continue to guarantee (relatively) that a Big Mac anywhere in Asia is the same as a Big Mac in Canada or the United States.
© Dave Moyer

GOVERNMENT POLICY

A host government's attitude toward FDI should be an important variable in decisions about where to locate foreign production facilities and where to make a foreign direct investment. Other things being equal, investing in countries that have permissive policies toward FDI is clearly preferable to investing in countries that restrict FDI. Canada's investment policies and tolerance towards FDI have evolved considerably since the early days of Pierre Elliot Trudeau's government of the 1970s, and no better indicator of this is Canada's willingness to sign the FTA of 1988 and the subsequent 1994 NAFTA. This same recognition of the importance of international trade expansion is also evidenced in Canada's active role within the World Trade Organization.

However, often the issue is not this straightforward. Despite the move toward a free market stance in recent years, many countries still have a rather pragmatic stance toward FDI, and sometimes (as has been seen since 2016) outright hostility to FDI. In such cases, a firm considering FDI must often negotiate the specific terms of the investment with the country's government. Such negotiations centre on two broad issues. If the host government is trying to attract FDI, the central issue is likely to be the kind of incentives the host government is prepared to offer to the MNE and what the firm will commit in exchange. If the host government is uncertain about the benefits of FDI and might restrict access, the central issue is likely to be the concessions that the firm must make to be allowed to go forward with a proposed investment.

To a large degree, the outcome of any negotiated agreement depends on the relative bargaining power of both parties. Each side's bargaining power depends on three factors:

- the value each side places on what the other has to offer;
- the number of comparable alternatives available to each side; and
- each party's time horizon.

From the perspective of a firm negotiating the terms of an investment with a host government, the firm's bargaining power is high when the host government places a high value on what the firm has to offer, the number of comparable alternatives open to the firm is greater, and the firm has a long time in which to complete the negotiations. The converse also holds. The firm's bargaining power is low when the host government places a low value on what the firm has to offer, the number of comparable alternatives open to the firm is fewer, and the firm has a short time in which to complete the negotiations.[36]

Key Terms

balance-of-payments accounts

current account

eclectic paradigm

exporting

externalities

flow of FDI

foreign direct investment (FDI)

greenfield investment

inflows of FDI

internalization theory

licensing

location-specific advantages

market imperfections

Multilateral Agreement on Investment (MAI)

multipoint competition

oligopoly

Organisation for Economic Co-operation and Development (OECD)

outflows of FDI

stock of foreign direct investment

LO Learning Objectives Summary

This chapter reviewed theories that attempt to explain the pattern of FDI between countries and to examine the influence of governments on firms' decisions to invest in foreign countries. The chapter made the following points:

1. The past few decades have seen a large increase in both the flow and stock of FDI in the world economy. Any theory seeking to explain FDI must explain why firms go to the trouble of acquiring or establishing operations abroad when the alternatives of exporting and licensing are available to them.

2. High transportation costs or tariffs imposed on imports help explain why many firms prefer FDI or licensing over exporting. Firms often prefer FDI to licensing when: (a) a firm has valuable know-how that cannot be adequately protected by a licensing contract; (b) a firm needs tight control over a foreign entity in order to maximize its market share and earnings in that country; and (c) a firm's skills and capabilities are not amenable to licensing. Knickerbocker's theory suggests that much FDI is explained by imitative behaviour by rival firms in an oligopolistic industry. Dunning has argued that location-specific advantages are of considerable importance in explaining the nature and direction of FDI. According to Dunning, firms undertake FDI to exploit resource endowments or assets that are location specific.

3. Political ideology is an important determinant of government policy toward FDI. Ideology ranges from a radical stance that is hostile to FDI to a noninterventionist, free market stance. Between the two extremes is an approach best described as pragmatic nationalism.

4. Benefits of FDI to a host country arise from resource-transfer effects, employment effects, and balance-of-payments effects. The costs of FDI to a host country include adverse effects on competition and balance of payments, and a perceived loss of national sovereignty. The benefits of FDI to the home (source) country include improvement in the balance of payments as a result of the inward flow of foreign earnings, positive employment effects when the foreign subsidiary creates demand for home-country exports, and benefits from a reverse resource-transfer effect. A reverse resource-transfer effect arises when the foreign subsidiary learns valuable skills abroad that can be transferred back to the home country. The costs of FDI to the home country include adverse balance-of-payments effects that arise from the initial capital outflow and from the export substitution effects of FDI. Costs also arise when FDI exports jobs abroad.

5. Home countries can adopt policies designed to both encourage and restrict FDI. Host countries try to attract FDI by offering incentives and try to restrict FDI by dictating ownership restraints and requiring that foreign MNEs meet specific performance requirements.

6. Internalization theories identify the profitability of FDI, exporting, and licensing. A host government's attitude to FDI is an important variable to consider in making the "go global" decision.

Critical Thinking and Discussion Questions

1. In the 1980s, Japanese FDI in the United States grew more rapidly than Japanese FDI in Canada. Why do you think this is the case? What are the implications of this trend?

2. Compare and contrast these explanations of FDI: internalization theory, Vernon's product life-cycle theory, and Knickerbocker's theory of FDI. Which theory do you think offers the best explanation of the historical pattern of FDI? Why?

3. Read the opening case on Nigeria. What are the benefits to the country of FDI?

4. You are the international manager of a Canadian business that has just developed a revolutionary new software application that can perform the same functions as a Microsoft application but costs only half as much to manufacture. Your CEO has asked you to formulate a recommendation for how to expand into Western Europe. Your options are (a) to export from Canada; (b) to license a European firm to manufacture and market the computer in Europe; or (c) to set up a wholly owned subsidiary in Europe. Evaluate the pros and cons of each alternative and suggest a course of action to your CEO.

5. Explain how the politics of a host government might influence the process of negotiating access between the host government and a foreign MNE.

Research Task   globalEDGE™   globaledge.msu.edu

Use the globalEDGE™ site to complete the following exercises:

1. The UNCTAD *World Investment Report* and *World Investment Directory* provide quick electronic access to comprehensive statistics on foreign direct investment (FDI) and the operations of transnational corporations. Gather a list of the largest transnational corporations in terms of their foreign direct investment; also, identify their home country (i.e., headquarters country). Provide a commentary about the characteristics of countries that have the greatest number of transnational firms.

2. Your company is considering opening a new factory in Latin America, and management is evaluating the specific country locations for this direct investment. The pool of candidate countries has been narrowed to Argentina, Mexico, and Brazil. Prepare a short report comparing the foreign direct investment environment and regulations of these three countries.

CLOSING CASE

FOREIGN RETAILERS IN INDIA

For years now, there has been intense debate in India about the wisdom of relaxing the country's restrictions on foreign direct investment into its retail sector. The Indian retailing sector is highly fragmented and dominated by small enterprises. Estimates suggest that barely 6 percent of India's almost $500 billion in retail sales take place in organized retail establishments. The rest takes place in small shops, most of which are unincorporated businesses run by individuals or households. In contrast, organized retail establishments account for more than 20 percent of sales in China, 36 percent of sales in Brazil, and 85 percent of all retail sales in the United States. In total, retail establishments in India employ some 34 million people, accounting for more than 7 percent of the workforce.

Advocates of opening up retailing in India to large foreign enterprises such as Wal-Mart, Carrefour, Ikea, and Tesco, make a number of arguments. They believe that foreign retailers can be a positive force for improving the efficiency of India's distribution systems. Companies like Wal-Mart and Tesco are experts in supply chain management. Applied to India, such know-how could take significant costs out of the economy. Logistics costs are around 14 percent of GDP in India, much higher than the 8 percent in the United States. While this is partly due to a poor road system, it is also the case that most distribution is done by small trucking enterprises, often with a single truck, that have few economies of scale or scope. Large foreign retailers tend to establish their own trucking operations and can reap significant gains from tight control of their distribution system.

Foreign retailers will also probably make major investments in distribution infrastructure such as cold storage facilities and warehouses. Currently, there is a chronic lack of cold storage facilities in India. Estimates suggest that about 25 to 30 percent of all fruits and vegetables spoil before they reach the market due to inadequate cold storage. Similarly, there is a lack of warehousing capacity. A lot of wheat, for example, is simply stored under tarpaulins, where it is at risk of rotting. Such problems raise foods costs to consumers and impose significant losses on farmers.

Farmers have emerged as significant advocates of reform. This is not surprising because they stand to benefit from working with foreign retailers. Similarly, reform-minded politicians argue that foreign retailers will help to keep food processing in check, which benefits all. Ranged against them is a powerful coalition of small shop owners and left-wing politicians, who argue that the entry of large, well-capitalized foreign retailers will result in the significant job losses and force many small retailers out of businesses.

In 1997, it looked as if the reformers had the upper hand when they succeeded in changing the rules to allow foreign enterprises to participate in wholesale trading. Taking advantage of this reform, in 2009 Wal-Mart started to open up wholesale stores in India under the name Best Price. The stores are operated by a joint venture with Bharti, an Indian conglomerate. These stores are only allowed to sell to other businesses, such as hotels, restaurants, and small retailers. By 2012, the venture had 20 stores in India. Customers of these stores note that unlike many local competitors, they always have products in stock, and they are not constantly changing their prices. Farmers, too, like the joint venture because the wholesalers have worked closely with them to secure consistent supplies and have made investments in warehouses and cold storage. The joint venture also pays farmers better prices—something it can afford to do because far less produce goes to waste in its system.

For its part, in 2011 the Indian government indicated that it would soon introduce legislation to allow foreign enterprises like Wal-Mart entry into the retail sector. On the basis on this promise, Wal-Mart and Bharti were planning to expand downstream from wholesale into retail establishments, but their plans were put on hold in late 2011 when the Indian government announced that the legislation had been shelved for the time being. Apparently, opposition to such reform had reached such a pitch that implementing it was not worth the political risk. Opponents argued that global experience showed that FDI leads to job losses, although they cited no data to support this claim. Whether India will further relax regulations limiting inward FDI into retail remains to be seen.

Sources: V. Bajaj, "Wal-Mart Debate Rages in India," *The New York Times,* December 6, 2011, pp. B1, B2; S. G. Mozumder, "Walmart Is Not Coming to India Just to Sell," *India Abroad,* December 16, 2011, pp. A18–A19; and R. Kohli and J. Bhaqwati, "Organized Retailing in India: Issues and Outlook," Columbia Program on Indian Economic Policies, working paper no. 2011-1, January 22, 2011.

Case Discussion Questions

1. Why do you think that the Indian retail sector is so fragmented?
2. What are the potential benefits to India of entry by foreign retail establishments?
3. Who stands to lose as a result of foreign entry into the Indian retail sector?
4. Why do you think reform of FDI regulations in India has been so difficult?

© Cultura Creative/Alamy

Chapter 8

Regional Economic Integration

TOMATO WARS

U.S. President Donald Trump should take note of this opening case. Often quotas or other government involvement in trade has unintended consequences for all the parties involved.

When the North America Free Trade Agreement (NAFTA) went into effect in December 1992 and tariffs on imported tomatoes were dropped, U.S. tomato producers in Florida feared that they would lose business to lower-cost producers in Mexico. So they lobbied the government to set a minimum floor price for tomatoes imported from Mexico. The idea was to stop Mexican producers from cutting prices below the floor to gain share in the U.S. market. In 1996 the United States and Mexico agreed on the basic floor price of 21.69 cents a pound. At the time, both sides declared themselves to be happy with the deal.

As it turns out, the deal didn't offer much protection for U.S. tomato growers. In 1992, the year before NAFTA was passed, Mexican producers exported 800 million pounds of tomatoes to the United States. By 2011 they were exporting 2.8 billion pounds of tomatoes, an increase of 3.5-fold. The value of Mexican tomato exports almost tripled to $2 billion during the same period. In contrast, tomato production in Florida has fallen by 41 percent since NAFTA went into effect. Florida growers complained that they could not compete against low wages and lax environmental oversight in Mexico. They also alleged that Mexican growers were dumping tomatoes in the United States market at below the cost of production, with the goal of driving U.S. producers out of business. In 2012, Florida growers petitioned the U.S. Department of Commerce to scrap the 1996 minimum-price agreement, which would then allow them to file an antidumping case against Mexican producers. In September 2012 the Commerce Department announced a preliminary decision to scrap the agreement.

At first glance, it looked as if the Florida growers were going to get their way. It soon became apparent, however, that the situation was more complex than it appeared initially. Some 370 business and trade groups in the United States wrote or signed letters to the Commerce Department in favour of continuing the 1996 agreement. Among the letter writers was Kevin Ahern, the CEO of Ahern Agribusiness in San Diego, a company that sells about $20 million a year in tomato seeds and transplants to Mexican farmers. In a letter sent to *The New York Times*, Ahern said, "Yes, Mexico produces their tomatoes on average at a lower cost than Florida; that's what we call competitive advantage." Ahern claimed that without the agreement, his business would suffer. Another U.S. company, NatureSweet Ltd., grows cherry and grape tomatoes under 1200 acres of greenhouses in Mexico for the U.S. market. It employs 5000 people, although all but 100 work in Mexico. The CEO, Bryant Ambelang, said that his company couldn't survive without NAFTA. In his view, Mexican-grown tomatoes were more competitive because of lower labour costs, good weather, and more than a decade of investment in greenhouse technology. In a similar vein, Scott DeFife, a representative of the U.S. National Restaurant Association, stated that "people want tomato-based dishes all the time. You plan over the course of the year where you are going to get your supply in the winter, the spring, the fall." DeFife stated that without tomatoes from Mexico, a winter freeze in Florida, for example, would send prices shooting up.

Faced with a potential backlash from U.S. importers and U.S. producers with interests in Mexico, the Commerce Department pulled back from its initial conclusion that the agreement should be scrapped. Instead, in early 2013 it reached an agreement with Mexican growers to raise the minimum floor price from 21.69 cents a pound to 31 cents a pound. The new agreement also established even higher prices for specialty tomatoes and tomatoes grown in controlled environments. This was clearly aimed at Mexican growers, who have invested billions to grow tomatoes in greenhouses. Florida tomatoes are largely picked green and treated with gas to change their colour.

Sources: E. Malkin, "Mexico Finds Unlikely Allies in Trade Fight," *The New York Times*, December 25, 2012, p. B1; S. Strom, "United States and Mexico Reach Tomato Deal, Averting a Trade War," *The New York Times*, February 3, 2013; and J. Margolis, "NAFTA 20 Years After: Florida's Tomato Growers Struggling," *The World*, December 17, 2012.

LO | LEARNING OBJECTIVES

By the end of this chapter you should be able to:

1. Describe the different levels of regional economic integration.
2. Understand the economic and political arguments for regional economic integration.
3. Understand the economic and political arguments against regional economic integration.
4. Explain the history, current scope, and future prospects of the world's most important regional economic agreements.
5. Understand the implications for business that are inherent in regional economic integration agreements.

Introduction

This chapter takes a close look at the arguments for regional economic integration through the establishment of trading blocs such as the European Union and the North American Free Trade Agreement. By **regional economic integration** we mean agreements among countries in a geographic region to reduce, and ultimately remove, tariff and nontariff barriers to the free flow of goods, services, and factors of production between each other. The opening case illustrates some of the issues surrounding the creation of a trading bloc. By creating a single market, NAFTA aimed to lower the price for goods and services in the United States, Canada, and Mexico. Such a policy is good for consumers, because it lowers prices, but it presents challenges to some producers who have to adapt to a more competitive environment. As the opening case explains, while NAFTA has resulted in a surge in tomato imports from Mexico, which has arguably benefited U.S. consumers, food producers, and retailers, it has hurt tomato growers in Florida, who have steadily lost business to Mexican producers.

The past two decades have witnessed an unprecedented proliferation of regional trade blocs that promote regional economic integration. World Trade Organization members are required to notify the WTO of any regional trade agreements in which they participate. By 2013, nearly all of the WTO's members had notified the organization of participation in one or more regional trade agreements. The total number of regional trade agreements currently in force is more than 440.[1]

Consistent with the predictions of international trade theory and particularly the theory of comparative advantage (see Chapter 5), agreements designed to promote freer trade within regions are believed to produce gains from trade for all member countries. As we saw in Chapter 6, the General Agreement on Tariffs and Trade and its successor, the World Trade Organization, also seek to reduce trade barriers. With 164 member states, the WTO has a worldwide perspective. By entering into regional agreements, groups of countries aim to reduce trade barriers more rapidly than can be achieved under the auspices of the WTO.

But circumstances change. As we also noted in Chapter 6, there are arguments that have been successfully made against free trade both in the United States and in England. Both U.S. presidential candidates, to different degrees, argued that free trade was costing U.S. jobs. And in June of 2016, a vote was held in England to decide whether the United Kingdom should leave or remain in the European Union. The vote to leave won with 52 percent versus 48 percent voting to stay. This came to be known as Brexit (a merging of the words "Britain" with "Exit").

Until very recently, the movement toward regional economic integration in Europe has been deemed to be very successful. On January 1, 1993, the European Union (EU) formally removed many barriers to doing business across borders within the EU in an attempt to create a single market with 340 million consumers. However, the EU did not stop there. The member states of the EU have launched a single currency, the euro; they are moving toward a closer political union. On May 1, 2004, the EU expanded from 15 to 25 countries, and in 2007 two more countries joined—Bulgaria and Romania—making the total 27. In mid-2013 Croatia became the 28th country. Today, the EU has a population of over 500 million and a gross domestic product of over $16 trillion, making it larger than the United States in economic terms.

Similar moves toward regional integration are being pursued elsewhere in the world. Canada, Mexico, and the United States have implemented the North American Free Trade Agreement (NAFTA). Ultimately, this aims to remove all barriers to the

The euro—the common currency for the EU member states—replaced all the different currencies across the European Union in January 2002. *(left) © PhotoLink/Getty Images; (right) © Getty Images*

free flow of goods and services among the three countries. While the implementation of NAFTA has resulted in job losses in some sectors of the American economy, in aggregate and consistent with the predictions of international trade theory, most economists argue that the benefits of greater regional trade outweigh any costs. South America, too, has moved toward regional integration. In 1991, Argentina, Brazil, Paraguay, and Uruguay implemented an agreement known as Mercosur to start reducing barriers to trade between each other, and although progress within Mercosur has been halting, the institution is still in place. There have also been attempts at regional economic integration in Central America, the Andean region of South America, Southeast Asia, and parts of Africa.

While the move toward regional economic integration is generally seen as a good thing, some worry that it will lead to a world in which regional trade blocs compete against each other. In this future scenario, free trade will exist within each bloc, but each bloc will protect its market from outside competition with high tariffs. The spectre of the EU and NAFTA turning into economic fortresses that shut out foreign producers through high tariff barriers is worrisome to those who believe in unrestricted free trade. If such a situation were to materialize, the resulting decline in trade between blocs could more than offset the gains from free trade within blocs. And the current political climate on both sides of the Atlantic makes it unlikely that any new large trading blocs will be formed.

With these issues in mind, this chapter will explore the economic and political debate surrounding regional economic integration, paying particular attention to the economic and political benefits and costs of integration; review progress toward regional economic integration around the world; note the current trends; and map the important implications of regional economic integration for the practice of international business. Before tackling these objectives, we first need to examine the levels of integration that are theoretically possible.

LO1 Levels of Economic Integration

Several levels of economic integration are possible in theory (see Figure 8.1). From least integrated to most integrated, they are a free trade area, a customs union, a common market, an economic union, and, finally, a full political union.

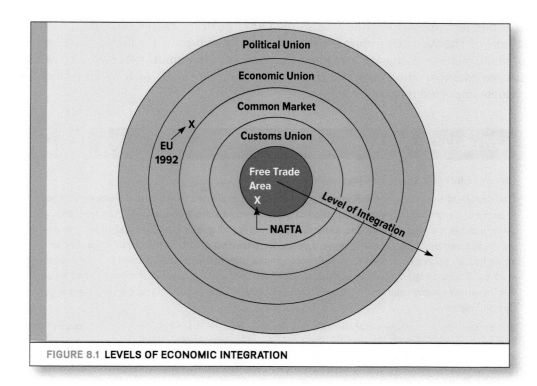

FIGURE 8.1 **LEVELS OF ECONOMIC INTEGRATION**

In a **free trade area**, all barriers to the trade of goods and services among member countries are removed. In the theoretically ideal free trade area, no discriminatory tariffs, quotas, subsidies, or administrative impediments are allowed to distort trade between members. Each country, however, is allowed to determine its own trade policies with regard to nonmembers. Thus, for example, the tariffs placed on the products of nonmember countries may vary from member to member. Free trade agreements are the most popular form of regional economic integration, accounting for almost 90 percent of regional agreements.[2]

The most enduring free trade area in the world is the **European Free Trade Association (EFTA)**. Established in January 1960, EFTA currently joins four countries—Norway, Iceland, Liechtenstein, and Switzerland—down from seven in 1995 (three former EFTA members, Austria, Finland, and Sweden, joined the EU on January 1, 1996). EFTA was founded by those western European countries that initially decided not to be part of the European Community (the forerunner of the EU). Its original members included Austria, Great Britain, Denmark, Finland, and Sweden, all of which are now members of the EU. The emphasis of EFTA has been on free trade in industrial goods. Agriculture was left out of the arrangement, each member being allowed to determine its own level of support. Members are also free to determine the level of protection applied to goods coming from outside EFTA. Other free trade areas include the North American Free Trade Agreement, which we shall discuss in depth later in this chapter.

The customs union is one step farther along the road to full economic and political integration. A **customs union** eliminates trade barriers between member countries and adopts a common external trade policy. Establishment of a common external trade policy necessitates significant administrative machinery to oversee trade relations with nonmembers. Most countries that enter into a customs union desire even greater economic integration down the road. The EU began as a customs union, but it has now moved beyond this stage. Other customs unions include the current version of the Andean Community (formerly known as the Andean Pact) among Bolivia, Colombia, Ecuador, and Peru. The Andean Community established free trade between member countries and imposes a common tariff, of 5 to 20 percent, on products imported from outside.[3]

ANOTHER PERSPECTIVE

Economic Integration in the Classical World

Traditionally, the success of the Roman Empire has been explained by economic historians as an example of centralized, forced reallocation of goods. Recent scholarship, though, suggests that there was not a single empire-wide, centralized market for all goods, but that local markets were connected and that most exchanges were voluntary, based on reciprocity and exchange. Ancient Rome had an economic system that was an enormous, integrated conglomeration of interdependent markets. Transportation and communication took time, and the discipline of the market was loose. But there were many voluntary economic connections between even far-flung parts of the early Roman Empire.

Sources: Karl Polanyi, *The Livelihood of Man* (New York: Academic Press, 1977); and Peter Temin, "Market Economy in the Early Roman Empire," University of Oxford, Discussion Papers in Economic and Social History.

The next level of economic integration, a **common market**, has no barriers to trade among member countries, includes a common external trade policy, and allows factors of production to move freely among members. Labour and capital are free to move because there are no restrictions on immigration, emigration, or cross-border flows of capital among member countries. Establishing a common market demands a significant degree of harmony and cooperation on fiscal, monetary, and employment policies. Achieving this degree of cooperation has proven very difficult. For years, the European Union functioned as a common market, although it has now moved beyond this stage. Mercosur—the South American grouping of Argentina, Brazil, Paraguay, and Uruguay—hopes to eventually establish itself as a common market. Venezuela was accepted as a full member of Mercosur subject to ratification by the governments of the four existing members. As of 2016, Paraguay has yet to ratify Venezuela's membership.

An economic union entails even closer economic integration and cooperation than a common market. Like the common market, an **economic union** involves the free flow of products and factors of production among member countries and the adoption of a common external trade policy, but it also requires a common currency, harmonization of members' tax rates, and a common monetary and fiscal policy. Such a high degree of integration demands a coordinating bureaucracy and the sacrifice of significant amounts of national sovereignty to that bureaucracy. The EU is an economic union, although an imperfect one because not all members of the EU have adopted the euro, the currency of the EU; differences in tax rates and regulations across countries still remain; and some markets, such as the market for energy, are still not fully deregulated.

The move toward economic union raises the issue of how to make a coordinating bureaucracy accountable to the citizens of member nations. The answer is through **political union** in which a central political apparatus coordinates the economic, social, and foreign policy of the member states. The EU is on the road toward at least partial political union. The European Parliament, which is playing an ever more important role in the EU, has been directly elected by citizens of the EU countries since the late 1970s. In addition, the Council of Ministers (the controlling, decision-making body of the EU) is composed of government ministers from each EU member. The United States provides an example of even closer political union; in the United States, independent states are effectively combined into a single nation. If the EU holds together after Brexit, the EU may move toward a similar federal structure, though this is far from certain.

LO2 | The Case for Regional Integration

The case for regional integration is both economic and political but is typically not accepted by many groups within a country, which explains why most attempts to achieve regional economic integration have been contentious and halting. In this section, we examine the economic and political cases for integration and two impediments to integration. In the next section, we look at the case against integration.

DEBATE THE ISSUE

Should Regional Economic Integration Be Based on Culture?

A free trade area is a group of countries committed to removing all barriers to the free flow of goods and services while at the same time pursuing independent external trade policies. A free trade area can be of the form of a customs union, common market, economic union, or political union. The European Union is an economic union—although some would say that the EU is striving for the approach of a political union as well. The EU, in reality, is an imperfect economic union because not all members of the EU have adopted the common currency, the euro, and countries differ in a variety of economic measures (e.g., taxes, regulations). But the most obvious reason the EU is an imperfect market is that the cultures of the independent countries in many cases are very different, from the Nordic countries to the southern European countries to the former eastern bloc European countries, and so on. Do you think regional economic integration should be more based on similarity in culture of the nations involved, or are market-based economic indicators the most appropriate?

The Economic Case for Integration

The economic case for regional integration is straightforward. We saw in Chapter 5 how economic theories of international trade predict that unrestricted free trade will allow countries to specialize in the production of goods and services that they can produce most efficiently. The result is greater world production than would be possible with trade restrictions. We also saw in that chapter how opening a country to free trade stimulates economic growth in the country, which creates dynamic gains from trade. Further, we saw in Chapter 7 how foreign direct investment (FDI) can transfer technological, marketing, and managerial know-how to host nations. Given the central role of knowledge in stimulating economic growth, opening a country to FDI also is likely to stimulate economic growth. In sum, economic theories suggest that free trade and investment is a positive-sum game, in which all participating countries stand to gain.

Given this, the theoretical ideal is a total absence of barriers to the free flow of goods, services, and factors of production among nations. However, as we saw in Chapters 6 and 7, a case can be made for government intervention in international trade and FDI. Because many governments have accepted part or all of the case for intervention, unrestricted free trade and FDI have proved to be only an ideal. Although international institutions such as GATT and the WTO have been moving the world toward a free trade regime, success has been less than total. In a world of many nations and many political ideologies, it is very difficult to get all countries to agree to a common set of rules.

Against this background, regional economic integration can be seen as an attempt to achieve additional gains from the free flow of trade and investment between countries beyond those attainable under international agreements such as the WTO. It is easier to establish a free trade and investment regime among a limited number of adjacent countries than among the world community. Problems of coordination and policy harmonization are largely a function of the number of countries that seek agreement. The greater the number of countries involved, the greater the number of perspectives that must be reconciled, and the harder it will be to reach agreement. Thus, attempts at regional economic integration are motivated by a desire to exploit the gains from free trade and investment while avoiding the difficulties inherent in larger agreements.

The Political Case for Integration

The political case for regional economic integration has also loomed large in most attempts to establish free trade areas, customs unions, and the like. Linking neighbouring economies and making them increasingly dependent on each other creates incentives for political cooperation between the neighbouring states. This reduces the potential for violent conflict between the states. In addition, by grouping their economies, the countries can enhance their political weight in the world.

These considerations underlay establishment of the European Community (EC) in 1957 (the EC was the forerunner of the European Union). Europe had suffered two devastating wars in the first half of the century, both arising out of the unbridled ambitions of nation-states. Those who have sought a united Europe have always had a desire to make another war in Europe unthinkable. Many Europeans also believed that after World War II the European nation-states were no longer large enough to hold their own in world markets and world politics. The need for a united Europe to deal with the United States and the politically alien Soviet Union loomed large in the minds of many of the EC's founders.[4] A long-standing joke in Europe is that the European Commission should erect a statue to Joseph Stalin, for without the aggressive policies of the former dictator of the old Soviet Union, the countries of Western Europe may have lacked the incentive to cooperate and form the European Community.

Impediments to Integration

Despite the strong economic and political arguments for integration, it has never been easy to achieve or sustain for two main reasons. First, although economic integration benefits the majority, it has its costs. While a nation as a whole may benefit significantly from a regional free trade agreement, certain groups may lose. Moving to a free trade regime involves some painful adjustments. For example, because of the 1994 establishment of NAFTA, some Canadian and U.S. workers in such industries as textiles, which employ low-cost, low-skilled labour, lost their jobs as Canadian and U.S. firms moved production to Mexico. The promise of significant net benefits to the Canadian and U.S. economies as a whole is little comfort to those who lost as a result of NAFTA. It is understandable then, that such groups have been at the forefront of opposition to NAFTA and continue to oppose any widening of the agreement.

A second impediment to integration arises from concerns over national sovereignty. For example, Mexico's concerns about maintaining control of its oil interests resulted in an agreement with Canada and the United States to exempt the Mexican oil industry from any liberalization of foreign investment regulations achieved under NAFTA. Concerns about national sovereignty arise because close economic integration demands that countries give up some degree of control over such key policy issues as monetary policy, fiscal policy (e.g., tax policy), and trade policy. This has been a major stumbling block in the European Union. To achieve full economic union, the European Union introduced a common currency to be controlled by a central EU bank. Although most member states have signed on to such a deal, Great Britain remained an important holdout. A politically important segment of public opinion in that country opposed a common currency on the grounds that it would require relinquishing control of the country's monetary policy to the European Union, which many British perceived as a bureaucracy run by foreigners. In 1992 the British won the right to opt out of any single currency agreement, and the British government had never reversed its decision at the time of the Brexit vote. Those who promoted Britain to leave the EU cited sovereignty and democracy as the primary issues, wanting Britain to take back full control of its own borders and also to reduce the number of people moving there to live and/or work in that country.

ANOTHER PERSPECTIVE

China Complains to WTO against the U.S. Solar Protectionism

The United States Department of Commerce (DOC) recently imposed import tariffs from 31 percent to 250 percent on Chinese solar panel manufacturers, accusing Beijing of dumping the solar cells in the United States. It all started in October [2012], when seven solar firms, including SolarWorld A.G. (ETR:SWV), filed a complaint with the U.S. International Trade Commission and Commerce accusing the Chinese solar cell manufacturers of improper trade practices. The United States immediately started investigating the matter, which eventually led to trade barriers. This compelled China to start its own investigation into the United States in November. According to China's mission to WTO headquarters in Geneva, the U.S. investigation process was inconsistent with "WTO rules and rulings in many aspects." If the U.S. import subsidies were meant to support the local solar industry, which has witnessed four bankruptcies in the past year, then it has missed its target by miles. The U.S. actions could have initiated a trade war between the two biggest economies of the world. The United States and other western economies are going through a period of financial recovery. Their focus is on cutting down expenses and creating more jobs. Under such circumstances, according to WTO chief Pascal Lamy, the wrong thing to do is to erect more trade barriers, which can provide short-term relief at the cost of long-term damage.

Source: Excerpted from, "Trade war looming as China rebukes US support for solar," *Boston Globe*, May 25, 2012, https://www.bostonglobe.com/business/2012/05/25/trade-war-looming-china-rebukes-support-for-solar/6nbtN6oTJkwaZ9KvD79NPN/story.html

---

LO3 The Case against Regional Integration

Although the tide has been running strongly in favour of regional free trade agreements in recent years, some economists have expressed concern that the benefits of regional integration have been oversold, while the costs have often been ignored.[5] They point

MANAGEMENT FOCUS

NAFTA—Friend or Foe of Canadian Business?

January 1, 2014, heralded a significant milestone in trade and economic relations among Canada, the United States, and Mexico. The North American Free Trade Agreement (NAFTA) turned twenty years old. NAFTA forms the world's largest trading blocs.

NAFTA has certainly made the news in 2016 and 2017, with U.S. President Donald Trump citing the agreement as a cause for massive losses in U.S. manufacturing employment to Mexico. He has threatened to both "rip up" the agreement, or to renegotiate this twenty-year-old agreement. Often lost in this debate over U.S. jobs moving to Mexico is Canada's role in the agreement.

The North American Free Trade Agreement (NAFTA), like all free trade entities, had its share of critics and fans, individual, corporate, and government alike. On the one hand it is viewed as the root cause of job exoduses from Canada to Mexico. Yet on the other hand it is seen to be a vehicle for universal prosperity for all within its realm. These same types of pro and con feelings permeate the worlds of free trade negotiations. Those who viewed NAFTA in a negative light focused on alleged poor track record on a multitude of issues ranging from worsening environmental standards, to job losses, to Mexico's *maquilladoras*, or work zones of cheap labour that are commonly found along the Texas–Mexican borders, while Canadian government officials have praised the merits of the agreement.

Small and large businesses have failed and will continue to fail as either an indirect or direct result of NAFTA. Then again, businesses either succeeded or failed before NAFTA as well. Competitive advantage makes a business survive and succeed and an inability to adapt makes it stall and end. For consumers in all three countries, NAFTA increasingly provides more choices at competitive prices. Lower tariffs mean that families pay less for the products they buy and have a greater selection of goods and services, which increases their standard of living.

A good analysis of the situation comes from the Council of Foreign Relations. They note:

> Like the United States and Mexico, Canada, the leading exporter of goods to the United States, has experienced economic growth since NAFTA's implementation. If anything, Canada has seen the strongest gains, though again it is difficult to attribute direct causation, particularly given that Canada and the United States had a free trade deal that predated NAFTA. Canada's GDP has grown at a faster rate than either Mexico's or the United States' since 1994. Between 1994 and 2003, Canada's economy showed average annual growth rates of 3.6 percent, compared to 3.3 percent in the United States and 2.7 percent in Mexico. Canadian employment levels have also shown steady gains in recent years, with overall employment rising from 14.9 million to 15.7 million in the early 2000s. Even Canadian manufacturing employment held steady, though Schott and Hufbauer note that Canadian economists remain concerned about the "productivity gap" between the Canadian and U.S. economies. U.S. labor productivity has consistently outpaced Canada's, and the gap has broadened since NAFTA was put in place.

Snapshots of the success stories of NAFTA abound. Here is one Canadian company's success story.

Baultar Inc., www.baultar.com, of Windsor, Quebec, manufactures and designs flooring and seats for for the passenger transportation market. It employs 95 people. Mexico has been a major market for the company. To strengthen its competitive position, Baultar transferred its manufacturing and installation expertise to a Mexican company. Thanks to this partnership, the company landed a major contract with the STC (Sistema de Transporte Colectivo). Baultar's activities in Mexico were supported by Export Development Canada (EDC) and Canada's Trade Commissioner Service. Baultar's foray into the Mexican market was assisted by a team of Canadian government officials, assisting the company through the labyrinth of export details for setting up a greenfield operation in Mexico.

Ability combined with willingness to adjust to new competitive situations is paramount to staying afloat in today's dynamic business world. Coupled with the abundance of readily available Canadian government export advisory and financial services, Canadian companies are testing their mettle in new markets.

Questions

1. Do you think that Baultar could have accessed the Mexican market without NAFTA? Why, or why not?
2. Outside of North America, what trade pacts would influence the company (see especially the section "The Future of the European Union")?

Sources: International Trade Canada, "Why Trade Matters," at http://www.martec.ca/newsreports/stories-en%20 2003-Jun-30.pdf; SBA Online Women's Business Centre; Baultar at http://www.baultar.com/about-us/history/; http://www.ftaa-alca.org/busfac/clist_e.asp; http://en.wikipedia.org/wiki/Free_Trade_Area_of_the_Americas; M. Copeland, "Canadian company buys Waco-based American Amicable, takes over ALICO Building," *Waco Tribune-Herald*, April 29, 2010; www.cfr.org/world/naftas-economic-impact/p15790#p7; and http://www.washingtonpost.com/wp-dyn/content/article/2008/03/24/AR2008032401562_2.html.

out that the benefits of regional integration are determined by the extent of trade creation, as opposed to trade diversion. **Trade creation** occurs when high-cost domestic producers are replaced by low-cost foreign producers from within the free trade area. It may also occur when higher-cost external producers are replaced by lower-cost external producers within the free trade area. **Trade diversion** occurs when lower-cost external suppliers are replaced by higher-cost suppliers within the free trade area. A regional free trade agreement will benefit the world only if the amount of trade it creates exceeds the amount it diverts.

Suppose Canada and Mexico imposed tariffs on imports from all countries, and then they set up a free trade area, scrapping all trade barriers between themselves but maintaining tariffs on imports from the rest of the world. If Canada began to import textiles from Mexico, would this change be for the better? If Canada previously produced all its own textiles at a higher cost than Mexico, then the free trade agreement has shifted production to the cheaper source. According to the theory of comparative advantage, trade has been created within the regional grouping, and there would be no decrease in trade with the rest of the world. Clearly, the change would be for the better. If, however, Canada previously imported textiles from Costa Rica, which produced them at less cost than either Mexico or Canada, then trade has been diverted from a low-cost source—a change for the worse. The Management Focus discusses NAFTA after ten years with respect to these issues.

In theory, WTO rules should ensure that a free trade agreement does not result in trade diversion. These rules allow free trade areas to be formed only if the members set tariffs that are not higher or more restrictive to outsiders than the ones previously in effect. However, as we saw in Chapter 6, GATT and the WTO do not cover some nontariff barriers. As a result, regional trade blocs could emerge whose markets are protected from outside competition by high nontariff barriers. In such cases, the trade diversion effects might outweigh the trade creation effects. The only way to guard against this possibility, according to those concerned about this potential, is to increase the scope of the WTO so it covers nontariff barriers to trade. There is no sign that this is going to occur anytime soon, however, so the risk remains that regional economic integration will result in trade diversion.

LO4 | Regional Economic Integration in Europe

Europe has two trade blocs—the European Union and the European Free Trade Association. Of the two, the EU is by far the more significant, not just in terms of membership (the EU has 28 members [27 when Britain leaves] and EFTA has 4), but also in terms of economic and political influence in the world economy. For many years people saw the EU as an emerging economic and political superpower of the same order as the United States and Japan. With Brexit, the long-term future is debatable, yet currently it is still a major trading bloc. Accordingly, we will concentrate our attention on the EU.[6]

Evolution of the European Union

The European Union is the product of two political factors: (1) the devastation of two world wars on Western Europe and the desire for a lasting peace; and (2) the European nations' desire to hold their own on the world's political and economic stage.

The original forerunner of the European Union, the European Coal and Steel Community, was formed in 1951 by Belgium, France, West Germany, Italy, Luxembourg, and the Netherlands. Its objective was to remove barriers to intragroup shipments of coal, iron, steel, and scrap metal. With the signing of the Treaty of Rome in 1957, the European Community was established. The name changed again in 1994 when the European Community became the European Union following the ratification of the Maastricht Treaty (discussed later).

The Treaty of Rome provided for the creation of a common market. Article 3 of the treaty laid down the key objectives of the new community, calling for the elimination of internal trade barriers and the creation of a common external tariff and requiring member states to abolish obstacles to the free movement of factors of production among the members. To facilitate the free movement of goods, services, and factors of production, the treaty provided for any necessary harmonization of the member states' laws. Furthermore, the treaty committed the EC to establish common policies in agriculture and transportation.

The community grew in 1973, when Great Britain, Ireland, and Denmark joined. These three were followed in 1981 by Greece; in 1986 by Spain and Portugal; and in 1995 by Austria, Finland, and Sweden—bringing the total membership to 15. (East Germany became part of the EC after the reunification of Germany in 1990.) Another ten countries joined the EU on May 1, 2004—eight of them from Eastern Europe plus the small Mediterranean nations of Malta and Cyprus. Bulgaria and Romania joined in 2007, and in mid-2013 Croatia became the 28th country. Today, the EU has a population of over 500 million and a gross domestic product of over $16 trillion, making it larger than the United States in economic terms. (see Map 8.1).

Political Structure of the European Union

The economic policies of the European Union are formulated and implemented by a complex and still-evolving political structure. The four main institutions in this structure are the European Commission, the Council of the European Union, the European Parliament, and the Court of Justice.

The European Commission is responsible for proposing EU legislation, implementing it, and monitoring compliance with EU laws by member states. Headquartered in Brussels, Belgium, the Commission has more than 23 000 employees.

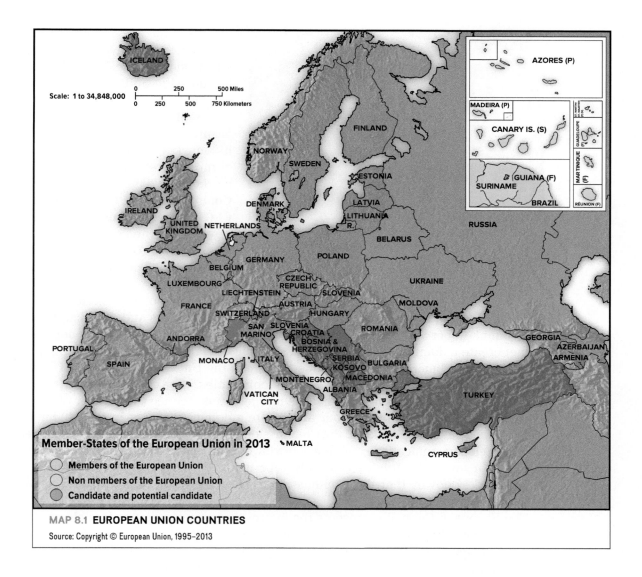

Member-States of the European Union in 2013

- ○ Members of the European Union
- ○ Non members of the European Union
- ● Candidate and potential candidate

MAP 8.1 EUROPEAN UNION COUNTRIES

Source: Copyright © European Union, 1995–2013

It is run by a group of 28 commissioners appointed by each member country for five-year renewable terms. Each country appoints only one commissioner. A president and vice-presidents are chosen from among these commissioners for five-year renewable terms. The Commission has a monopoly in proposing European Union legislation. The Commission starts the legislative ball rolling by making a proposal, which goes to the Council of Ministers and then to the European Parliament. The Council of Ministers cannot legislate without a Commission proposal in front of it. The Commission is also responsible for implementing aspects of EU law, although in practice much of this must be delegated to member states. Another responsibility of the Commission is to monitor member states to make sure they are complying with EU laws. In this policing role, the Commission will normally ask a state to comply with any EU laws that are being broken. If this persuasion is not sufficient, the Commission can refer a case to the Court of Justice.

The European Commission's role in competition policy has become increasingly important to business in recent years. Since 1990, when the office was formally assigned a role in competition policy, the EU's competition commissioner has been steadily gaining influence as the chief regulator of competition policy in the member

In 2000, a proposed merger between Time Warner of the United States and EMI of the United Kingdom failed after the European Commission expressed the concern that the merger would monopolize the music recording industry.
© filonmar/Getty Images

nations of the EU. As with antitrust authorities in the United States, which include the Federal Trade Commission and the Department of Justice, the role of the competition commissioner is to ensure that no one enterprise uses its market power to drive out competitors and monopolize markets. In 2009, for example, the Commission fined Intel a record €1.06 billion for abusing its market power in the computer chip market. (See Another Perspective for details.) The previous record for a similar abuse was €497 million imposed on Microsoft in 2004 for blocking competition in markets for server computers and media software. The commissioner also reviews proposed mergers and acquisitions to make sure they do not create a dominant enterprise with substantial market power.[7] For example, in 2000 a proposed merger between Time Warner of the United States and EMI of the United Kingdom, both music recording companies, was withdrawn after the Commission expressed concerns that the merger would reduce the number of major record companies from five to four and create a dominant player in the $40 billion global music industry. Similarly, the Commission blocked a proposed merger between two U.S. telecommunication companies, WorldCom and Sprint, because their combined holdings of Internet infrastructure in Europe would give the merged companies so much market power that the Commission argued the combined company would dominate that market.

The European Council represents the interests of member states. It is clearly the ultimate controlling authority within the European Union since draft legislation from the Commission can become EU law only if the Council agrees. The Council is composed of one representative from the government of each member state. The membership, however, varies depending on the topic being discussed. When agricultural issues are being discussed, the agriculture ministers from each state attend Council meetings; when transportation is being discussed transportation ministers attend, and so on. Before 1993, all Council issues had to be decided by unanimous agreement between member states. This often led to marathon Council sessions and a failure to make progress or reach agreement on proposals submitted from the Commission. In an attempt to clear the resulting logjams, the Single European Act formalized the use of majority voting rules on issues "which have as their object the establishment and functioning of a single market." Most other issues, however, such as tax regulations and immigration policy, still require unanimity among Council members if they are to become law.

The European Parliament is directly elected by the populations of the member states. The Parliament, which meets in Strasbourg, France, is primarily a consultative rather than legislative body. It debates legislation proposed by the Commission and forwarded to it by the Council. It can propose amendments to that legislation, which the Commission and ultimately the Council are not obliged to take up but often will. Recently the power of the Parliament has been increasing, although not by as much as parliamentarians would like. The European Parliament now has the right to vote on the appointment of commissioners and has veto power over some laws (such as the EU budget and single-market legislation).

The Court of Justice, which comprises one judge from each country, is the supreme appeals court for EU law. Like commissioners, the judges are required to act as independent officials, rather than as representatives of national interests. The Commission or a member country can bring other members to the court for failing to meet treaty obligations. Similarly, member countries, companies, or institutions can bring the Commission or Council to the court for failure to act according to an EU treaty.

ANOTHER PERSPECTIVE

The European Commission and Intel

In May 2009, the European Commission announced that it had imposed a record €1.6 billion ($1.45 billion) fine on Intel for anti-competitive behaviour. This fine was the result of an investigation into Intel's competitive conduct during the period from October 2002 to December 2007. During this time period, Intel's market share of microprocessor sales to personal computer manufacturers consistently exceeded 70 percent. According to the Commission, Intel illegally used its market power to ensure that its major rival, AMD, was at a competitive disadvantage, thereby harming "millions of European consumers."

The Commission charged that Intel granted major rebates to PC manufacturers—including Acer, Dell, Hewlett-Packard, Lenovo, and NEC—on the condition that they purchased all or almost all of their supplies from Intel. Intel also made payments to some manufacturers in exchange for them postponing, cancelling, or putting restrictions on the introduction or distribution of AMD-based products.

Under the order, Intel had to change its practices immediately, pending any appeal. The company was also required to write a bank guarantee for the fine, although that guarantee is held in a bank until the appeal process is exhausted.

For its part, Intel immediately appealed the ruling. The company insisted that it had never coerced computer makers and retailers with inducements and maintained that Intel had never paid to stop AMD products from reaching the market in Europe. Although Intel acknowledges that it did offer rebates, it claimed that they were never conditional on specific actions by manufacturers and retailers aimed to limit AMD. Intel appealed in mid-2012, but lost the case in June 2014.

Sources: M. Hachman, "EU Hits Intel with $1.45 Billion Fine for Antitrust Violations," *PCMAG.com*, May 13, 2009; J. Kanter, "Europe Fines Intel $1.45 billion in Antitrust Case," *The New York Times*, May 14, 2009; and J. Mick, "Intel Loses Appeal of $1.4B USD European Union Fine for Illegal Behavior," *Dailytech.com*, June 12, 2014, http://www.dailytech.com/Intel+Loses+Appeal+of+14B+USD+European+Union+Fine+for+Illegal+Behavior/article35051.htm

---

The Single European Act

Two revolutions occurred in Europe in the late 1980s. The first was the collapse of communism in Eastern Europe. The second revolution was much quieter, but its impact on Europe and the world may have been just as profound as the first. It was the 1987 adoption of the Single European Act by the EC member nations. This act committed the EC countries to work toward establishment of a single market by December 31, 1992.

THE STIMULUS FOR THE SINGLE EUROPEAN ACT

The Single European Act was born of a frustration among EC members that the community was not living up to its promise. By the early 1980s, it was clear that the EC had fallen short of its objectives to remove barriers to the free flow of trade and investment between member countries and to harmonize the wide range of technical and legal standards for doing business.

Against this background, many of the EC's prominent business people mounted an energetic campaign in the early 1980s to end the EC's economic divisions. The EC responded by creating the Delors Commission. Under the chairmanship of Jacques Delors, the former French finance minister and president of the EC Commission, the Delors Commission produced a discussion paper in 1985 proposing that all impediments to the formation of a single market be eliminated by December 31, 1992. The result was the Single European Act, which was independently ratified by the parliaments of each member country and became EC law in 1987.

THE OBJECTIVES OF THE ACT

The purpose of the Single European Act was to have a single market in place by December 31, 1992. The act proposed the following changes:[8]

- Remove all frontier controls between EC countries, thereby abolishing delays and reducing the resources required for complying with trade bureaucracy.

- Apply the principle of "mutual recognition" to product standards. A standard developed in one EC country should be accepted in another, provided it meets basic requirements in such matters as health and safety.

- Open public procurement to non-national suppliers, reducing costs directly by allowing lower-cost suppliers into national economies and indirectly by forcing national suppliers to compete.

- Lift barriers to competition in the retail banking and insurance businesses, which should drive down the costs of financial services, including borrowing, throughout the EC.

- Remove all restrictions on foreign-exchange transactions between member countries by the end of 1992.

- Abolish restrictions on cabotage—the right of foreign truckers to pick up and deliver goods within another member state's borders—by the end of 1992. Estimates suggested this would reduce the cost of haulage within the EC by 10 to 15 percent.

All those changes were predicted to lower the costs of doing business in the EC, but the single-market program was also expected to have more complicated supply-side effects. For example, the expanded market was predicted to give EC firms greater opportunities to exploit economies of scale. In addition, it was thought that the increase in competitive intensity brought about by removing internal barriers to trade and investment would force EC firms to become more efficient. To signify the importance of the Single European Act, the European Community also decided to change its name to the European Union once the act took effect.

The Single European Act has had a significant impact on the EU economy.[9] The act provided the impetus for the restructuring of substantial sections of European industry. Many firms have shifted from national to pan-European production and distribution systems in an attempt to realize scale economies and better compete in

COUNTRY FOCUS

The Greek Sovereign Debt Crisis

When the euro was established, some critics worried that free-spending countries in the euro zone (such as Italy and Greece) might borrow excessively, running up large public-sector deficits that they could not finance. This would then rock the value of the euro, requiring their more sober brethren, such as Germany or France, to step in and bail out the profligate nation. In 2010, this worry became a reality as a financial crisis in Greece hit the value of the euro.

The financial crisis had its roots in a decade of free spending by the Greek government, which ran up a high level of debt to finance extensive spending in the public sector. Much of the spending increase could be characterized as an attempt by the government to buy off powerful interest groups in Greek society, from teachers and farmers to public-sector employees, rewarding them with high pay and extensive benefits. To make matters worse, the government misled the international community about the level of its indebtedness. In October 2009, a new government took power and quickly announced that the 2009 public-sector deficit, which had been projected to be around 5 percent, would actually be 12.7 percent. The previous government had apparently been cooking the books.

This shattered any faith that international investors might have had in the Greek economy. Interest rates on Greek government debt quickly surged to 7.1 percent, about 4 percentage points higher than the rate on German bonds. Two of the three international rating agencies also cut their ratings on Greek bonds and warned that further downgrades were likely. The main concern now was that the Greek government might not be able to refinance some €20 billion of debt that would mature in April or May 2010. A further concern was that the Greek government might lack the political willpower to make the large cuts in public spending necessary to bring down the deficit and restore investor confidence.

Nor was Greece alone in having large public-sector deficits. Three other euro zone countries—Spain, Portugal, and Ireland—also had large debt loads, and interest rates on their bonds surged as investors sold out. This raised the specter of financial contagion, with large-scale defaults among the weaker members of the euro zone. If this did occur, the EU and IMF would most certainly have to step in and rescue the troubled nations. With this possibility, once considered very remote, investors started to move money out of euros, and the value of the euro started to fall on the foreign exchange market.

Recognizing that the unthinkable might happen—and that without external help, Greece might default on its government debt, pushing the EU and the euro into a major crisis—in May 2010 the euro zone countries, led by Germany, along with the IMF agreed to lend Greece up to €110 billion. These loans were judged sufficient to cover Greece's financing needs for three years. In exchange, the Greek government agreed to implement a series of strict austerity measures. These included tax increases, major cuts in public-sector pay, reductions in benefits enjoyed by public-sector employees (e.g., the retirement age was increased to 65 from 61, and limits were placed on pensions), and reductions in the number of public-sector enterprises from 6000 to 2000. However, the Greek economy contracted so fast in 2010 and 2011 that tax revenues plunged. By the end of 2011, the Greek economy was almost 29 percent smaller than it had been in 2005, while unemployment approached 20 percent. The contracting tax base limited the ability of the government to pay down debt. By early 2012, yields on 10-year Greek government debt reached 34 percent, indicating that many investors now expected Greece to default on its sovereign debt. This forced the Greek government to seek further aid from the euro zone countries and the IMF. As a condition for a fresh €130 billion bailout plan, the Greek government had to get holders of Greek government bonds to agree to the biggest sovereign debt restructuring in history, In effect, bondholders agreed to write off 53.5 percent of the debt they held. While the Greek government did not technically default on its sovereign debt, to many it seemed as if the EU and IMF had orchestrated an orderly partial default. By early 2014, it looked as if the Greek economy had finally turned a corner and was on the way to recovery. Yields on 10-year bonds had fallen below

8 percent, and the government was running a budget surplus before interest payments. In 2015, the possibility of the Greek economy starting to grow and fears of default receded. However, in early 2017, Greece again requested financial support from the EU and IMF.

Questions

1. Are there other countries today (both within and outside of the EU) that have large debts? Could such a situation happen to them?
2. Given Brexit, do you think that debt and/or currency crises are more likely in the euro zone in the future?

Sources: N. Chrysoloras, C. Ruhe, and R. Berguin, "EU Pressures Greece to Resolve Issues as New Debt Crisis Looms," *Bloomberg*, March 19, 2017, https://www.bloomberg.com/politics/articles/2017-03-20/greece-edges-toward-another-crisis-as-bailout-quarrel-persists; "A Very European Crisis," *The Economist*, February 6, 2010, pp. 75–77; L. Thomas, "Is Debt Trashing the Euro?" *The New York Times*, February 7, 2010, pp. 1, 7; "Bite the Bullet," *The Economist*, January 15, 2011, pp. 77–79; "The Wait Is Over," *The Economist*, March 17, 2012, pp. 83–84; and "Aegean Stables," *The Economist*, January 11, 2014.

a single market. The results have included faster economic growth than would otherwise have been the case.

However, over 20 years after the formation of a single market, the reality still falls short of the ideal. As you will see in the closing case, for example, we saw how until 2011 sports organizations such as soccer's Premier League had still been able to segment the EU into different national markets for auctioning off broadcast rights. Thus, although the EU is undoubtedly moving toward a single marketplace, established legal, cultural, and language differences among nations mean that implementation has been uneven.

The Establishment of the Euro

In February 1992, EC members signed a treaty (the **Maastricht Treaty**) that committed them to adopting a common currency by January 1, 1999.[10] The euro is now used by 19 of the 28 member states of the European Union; these 19 states are members of what is often referred to as the euro zone. It encompasses 330 million EU citizens and includes the powerful economies of Germany and France. Many of the countries that joined the EU on May 1, 2004, and the two that joined in 2007 originally planned to adopt the euro when they fulfilled certain economic criteria—a high degree of price stability, a sound fiscal situation, stable exchange rates, and converged long-term interest rates (the current members had to meet the same criteria). However, the events surrounding the EU sovereign debt crisis of 2010–2012 persuaded many of these countries to put their plans on hold, at least for the time being.

The establishment of the euro has rightly been described as an amazing political feat. There are few precedents for what the Europeans are doing. Establishing the euro required the participating national governments not only to give up their own currencies, but also to give up control over monetary policy. Governments do not routinely sacrifice national sovereignty for the greater good, indicating the importance that the Europeans attach to the euro. By adopting the euro, the European Union has created the second largest currency zone in the world after that of the U.S. dollar. Some believe that ultimately the euro could come to rival the dollar as the most important currency in the world.

Three EU countries decided not to participate and are exempt from adopting the euro: initially, Britain and Denmark. As of 2017, Sweden has yet to meet the conditions to adopt this single currency. Once it does, the euro will replace their national currency.[11]

The initial 12 countries agreeing to the euro locked their exchange rates against each other January 1, 1999. Euro notes and coins were not actually issued until January 1, 2002. In the interim, national currencies circulated in each of the 12 countries. However, in each participating state the national currency stood for a defined amount of euros. After January 1, 2002, euro notes and coins were issued and the national currencies were taken out of circulation. By mid-2002, all prices and routine economic transactions within the euro zone were in euros.

BENEFITS OF THE EURO

Europeans decided to establish a single currency in the EU for a number of reasons. First, they believe that business and individuals will realize significant savings from having to handle one currency, rather than many. These savings come from lower foreign exchange and hedging costs.

Second, and perhaps more importantly, the adoption of a common currency will make it easier to compare prices across Europe. This should increase competition because it will be much easier for consumers to shop around.

Third, faced with lower prices, European producers will be forced to look for ways to reduce their production costs to maintain their profit margins. The introduction of a common currency, by increasing competition, should ultimately produce long-run gains in the economic efficiency of European companies.

Fourth, the introduction of a common currency should give a strong boost to the development of a highly liquid pan-European capital market. Such a capital market should lower the cost of capital and lead to an increase in both the level of investment and the efficiency with which investment funds are allocated. This could be especially helpful to smaller companies that have historically had difficulty borrowing money from domestic banks. For example, the capital market of Portugal is very small and illiquid, which makes it extremely difficult for bright Portuguese entrepreneurs with a good idea to borrow money at a reasonable price. However, in theory, such companies should soon be able to tap a much more liquid pan-European capital market. Currently, Europe has no continent-wide capital market, such as the NASDAQ market in the United States, that funnels investment capital to dynamic young growth companies. The euro's introduction could facilitate establishment of such a market. The long-run benefits of such a development should not be underestimated.

Finally, the development of a pan-European, euro-denominated capital market will increase the range of investment options open to both individuals and institutions. For example, it will now be much easier for individuals and institutions based in, let's say, Holland, to invest in Italian or French companies. This will enable European investors to better diversify their risk, which again lowers the cost of capital and should also increase the efficiency with which capital resources are allocated.[12]

COSTS OF THE EURO

The drawback, for some, of a single currency is that national authorities have lost control over monetary policy. Thus, it is crucial to ensure that the EU's monetary policy is well managed. The Maastricht Treaty called for establishment of the independent European Central Bank (ECB), similar in some respects to the U.S. Federal Reserve, with a clear mandate to manage monetary policy so as to ensure price stability. The ECB, based in Frankfurt, is meant to be independent from political pressure—although critics question this. Among other things, the ECB sets interest rates and determines monetary policy across the euro zone.

The implied loss of national sovereignty to the ECB underlies the decision by Great Britain, Denmark, and Sweden to stay out of the euro zone, and in Great Britain's case, led to a vote in 2016 to exit the EU. Many in these countries are suspicious of the ECB's ability to remain free from political pressure and to keep inflation under tight control.

In theory, the design of the ECB should ensure that it remains free of political pressure. The ECB is modelled on the German Bundesbank, which historically has been the most independent and successful central bank in Europe. The Maastricht Treaty prohibits the ECB from taking orders from politicians. The executive board of the bank, which consists of a president, vice president, and four other members, carries out policy by issuing instructions to national central banks. The policy itself is determined by the governing council, which consists of the executive board plus the central bank governors from the 19 euro zone countries. The governing council votes on interest rate changes. Members of the executive board are appointed for eight-year nonrenewable terms, insulating them from political pressures to get reappointed. Nevertheless, the jury is still out on the issue of the ECB's independence, and it will take some time for the bank to establish its credentials.

According to critics, another drawback of the euro is that the EU is not what economists would call an optimal currency area. In an **optimal currency area**, similarities in the underlying structure of economic activity make it feasible to adopt a single currency and use a single exchange rate as an instrument of macroeconomic policy. Many of the European economies in the euro zone, however, are very dissimilar. For example, Finland and Portugal have different wage rates, tax regimes, and business cycles, and they may react very differently to external economic shocks. A change in the euro exchange rate that helps Finland may hurt Portugal. Obviously, such differences complicate macroeconomic policy. For example, when euro economies are not growing in unison, a common monetary policy may mean that interest rates are too high for depressed regions and too low for booming regions.

One way of dealing with such divergent effects within the euro zone is for the EU to engage in fiscal transfers, taking money from prosperous regions and pumping it into depressed regions. Such a move, however, opens a political can of worms. Would the citizens of Germany forgo their "fair share" of EU funds to create jobs for underemployed Greece workers? Not surprisingly, there is strong political opposition to such practices.

THE EURO EXPERIENCE: 1999 TO THE SOVEREIGN DEBT CRISIS

Since its establishment January 1, 1999, the euro has had a volatile trading history against the world's major currency, the U.S. dollar. After starting life in 1999 at €1 = $1.17, the euro steadily fell until it reached a low of €1 = $0.83 in October 2000, leading critics to claim the euro was a failure. A major reason for the fall in the euro's value was that international investors were investing money in booming U.S. stocks and bonds and taking money out of Europe to finance this investment. In other words, they were selling euros to buy dollars so that they could invest in dollar-denominated assets. This increased the demand for dollars and decreased the demand for the euro, driving the value of the euro down.

The fortunes of the euro began improving in late 2001 when the dollar weakened; the currency stood at a robust all-time high of €1 = $1.54 in early March 2008. One reason for the rise in the value of the euro was that the flow of capital into the United States stalled as the U.S. financial markets fell during 2007 and 2008.[13] Many investors were now taking money out of the United States, selling dollar-denominated assets such as U.S. stocks and bonds, and purchasing euro-denominated assets. Falling demand for U.S. dollars and rising demand for euros translated into a fall in the value of the dollar against the euro. Furthermore, in a vote of confidence in both the euro and the ability of the ECB to manage monetary policy within the euro zone, many foreign central banks added more euros to their supply of foreign currencies. In the first three years of its life, the euro never reached the 13 percent of global reserves made up by the deutsche mark and other former euro zone currencies. The euro did not jump that hurdle until early 2002, but by 2011 it stood at 26.3 percent.[14]

Since 2008, however, the euro has weakened, reflecting persistent concerns over slow economic growth and large budget deficits among several EU member states, particularly Greece, Portugal, Ireland, Italy, and Spain. During the 2000s, all of these governments sharply increased their government debt to finance public spending. Government debt as a percentage of GDP hit record levels in many of these nations. By 2010, private investors became increasingly concerned that many of these nations would not be able to service their sovereign debt, particularly given the economic slowdown following the 2008–2009 global financial crisis. They sold off government bonds of troubled nations, driving down bond prices and driving up the cost of government borrowing (bond prices and interest rates are inversely related). This led to fears that several national governments, particularly Greece, might default on their sovereign debt, plunging the euro zone into an economic crisis. To try and stave off such a sovereign debt crisis, in May 2010 the euro zone nations and the International Monetary Fund (IMF) agreed to a €110 billion bailout package to help rescue Greece. In November 2010, the EU and IMF agreed to a bailout package for Ireland of €85 billion; in May 2011, euro zone countries and the IMF instituted a €78 billion bailout plan for Portugal. In return for these loans, all three countries had to agree to sharp reductions in government spending, which meant slower economic growth and high unemployment until government debt was reduced to more sustainable levels. While Italy and Spain did not request bailout packages, both countries were forced by falling bond prices to institute austerity programs that required big reductions in government spending. The euro zone nations also set up a permanent bailout fund—the European Stability Mechanism—worth about €500 billion, which was designed to restore confidence in the euro.

As might be expected, the economic turmoil led to a decline in the value of the euro. By early 2012, the dollar euro exchange rate stood at €1 = $1.32, some way below its 2008 level but still significantly better than the exchange rate in early 2000. It has continued to fall to €1 = $1.12 in mid 2017 due to broader economic concerns and the ongoing crisis in Greece.

More troubling perhaps for the long run success of the euro, many of the newer EU nations that had committed to adopting the euro put their plans on hold. Countries like Poland and the Czech Republic had no desire to join the euro zone and then have their taxpayers help bail out the profligate governments of countries like Greece. To compound matters, the sovereign debt crisis had exposed a deep flaw in the euro zone—it was difficult for fiscally more conservative nations like Germany to limit profligate spending by the governments of other nations that might subsequently create strains and impose costs on the entire euro zone. The Germans in particular found themselves in the unhappy position of having to underwrite loans to bail out the governments of Greece, Portugal, and Ireland. This started to erode support for the euro in the stronger EU states. To try and correct this flaw, 25 of the EU's 28 nations signed a fiscal pact in January 2012 that made it more difficult for member states to break tight new rules on government deficits (the UK and Czech Republic abstained). Whether such actions will be sufficient to get the euro back on track remains to be seen.

ANOTHER PERSPECTIVE

Can the Euro Survive?

With the current eurozone crisis (both from the Greek debt crisis and the more recent Brexit vote) the question is, will the euro survive? The answer lies in examining several interesting facts of the European Union. First, the lack of a European treasury is the missing piece of the puzzle. Without it, the ECB is limited in the assistance it can provide to eurozone member states. In theory, the ECB could bail out those member states burdened with excessive debt by printing more money. However, that would require the approval of all member states (not just the 18 euro zone that use the euro as their national currency) that make up the EU.

Some of the EU members also think it is unfair to bail out those states that have lived beyond their means for many years now. It is difficult to compare the difficulties within the EU to those of other nations that have faced similar problems and survived. That's because the EU is not a cohesive nation. The member nations of the EU are separated geographically. In addition, they literally and figuratively don't even speak the same language. Both the United States and Canada have a vested interest in EU; the collapse of the EU, or the euro, would have an impact on both of these economies, which are major export destinations for these North American economies.

Source: William Larson, "Can The Euro Survive 2012?" *Seeking Alpha*, May 7, 2012, http://seekingalpha.com/article/565381-can-the-euro-survive-2012

The Future of the European Union

Up until 2016, a major issue facing the EU over the past few years has been that of enlargement. Enlargement of the EU into Eastern Europe has been a possibility since the collapse of communism at the end of the 1980s, and by the end of the 1990s, 13 countries had applied to become EU members. To qualify for EU membership, the applicants had to privatize state assets, deregulate markets, restructure industries, and tame inflation. They also had to enshrine complex EU laws into their own systems, establish stable democratic governments, and respect human rights.[15] In December 2002, the EU formally agreed to accept the applications of 10 countries, and they joined May 1, 2004. The new members include the Baltic countries, the Czech Republic, and the larger nations of Hungary and Poland. The only new members not in Eastern Europe were the Mediterranean island nations of Malta and Cyprus. Their inclusion in the EU expanded the union to 25 states, stretching from the Atlantic to the borders of Russia; added 23 percent to the landmass of the EU; brought 75 million new citizens into the EU, building an EU with a population of 450 million people; and created a single continental economy with a GDP of close to €11 trillion. In 2007, Bulgaria and Romania joined, bringing total membership to 27 nations, and Croatia in 2013 brought the total to 28.

The new members were not able to adopt the euro until at least 2007 (and 2010 in the case of the 2007 entrants), and free movement of labour among the new and existing members was prohibited until then (Lithuania adopted the euro as of early 2015). Consistent with theories of free trade, the enlargement should create added benefits for all members. However, given the small size of the Eastern European economies (together they amount to only 5 percent of the GDP of current EU members), the initial impact has been small. The biggest notable change might be in the EU bureaucracy and decision-making processes, where budget negotiations among 28 nations are bound to prove more problematic than negotiations among 15 nations.

Left standing at the door is Turkey. Turkey, which has long lobbied to join the union, presents the EU with some difficult issues. The country has had a customs union with the EU since 1995, and about half of its international trade is already with the EU. However, full membership has been denied because of concerns over human rights issues. In December 2004, the EU agreed to allow Turkey to start accession talks in October 2005, but those talks are not moving along rapidly, particularly after the 2016 military coup in Turkey and the EU's continued concern with that country's human rights abuses.

A more recent addition is Canada. A Canada–European free trade agreement was recently announced, the Comprehensive Economic and Trade Agreement, known as CETA. In October 2016, Prime Minister Trudeau signed the agreement, which was ratified by the European Parliament in early 2017, but not by the 28 countries of the EU. This 1600-page document had taken seven years to negotiate. When the ratification by member countries will happen is anybody's guess. Nonetheless, the agreement, when implemented, will have a major effect on this country.

And 2016 also saw the vote by Britain to leave the European Union (Brexit). The "leave" side won by 52 percent to 48 percent, confounding most pundits who thought that the vote to remain was a "slam dunk." The referendum turnout was high, with more than 30 million people voting. The then-prime minister David Cameron resigned the day after the referendum, with Theresa May becoming the new prime minister. Both prime ministers had been against leaving the EU, but Teresa May has vowed to honour the referendum, noting that "Brexit means Brexit."

As in all matters involving trade, nothing will happen quickly. The prime minister has said that she will start the process in late March of 2017 by invoking Article 50 of the Lisbon Treaty, which gives any party that wishes to leave the EU two years to agree to terms. However, recently the UK's Supreme Court has voted that Parliament must have a vote before Article 50 is invoked. Effectively, what this means is that a split is unlikely before at least the middle of 2019.

And the aftermath of this? All of the major players, at least currently, state that they want free trade to continue, and that what pushed the Brexit vote was not any anti-free trade sentiment, but rather one of protecting national sovereignty. If this remains the case, it is likely that the next level of economic integration, a customs union, will take place. Failing that, it is likely that Britain will negotiate a series of bilateral trade agreements with its major trading partners, including both Canada and the United States.

Regional Economic Integration in the Americas

No other attempt at regional economic integration comes close to the EU in its boldness or its potential implications for the world economy, although regional economic integration has been on the rise in the Americas until very recently. The most significant attempt, and the agreement that was again in the news during the 2016 U.S. presidential election, is the North American Free Trade Agreement. In addition to NAFTA, several other trade blocs are in the offing in the Americas, the most significant of which appear to be the Andean Community and Mercosur. Also, negotiations are underway to establish a hemisphere-wide Free Trade Area of the Americas (FTAA), although currently they seem to be stalled.

The North American Free Trade Agreement

In 1988 the governments of the United States and Canada agreed to enter into a free trade agreement, which took effect January 1, 1989. The agreement's goal was to eliminate all tariffs on bilateral trade between Canada and the United States by 1998. This was followed in 1991 by talks among the United States, Canada, and Mexico aimed at establishing a North American Free Trade Agreement for the three countries. The talks concluded in August 1992 with an agreement in principle, and by late 1993, the agreement had been ratified by the governments of all three countries.

NAFTA'S CONTENTS

The agreement became law January 1, 1994.[16] The contents of the original NAFTA agreement included the following:

- Abolition within ten years of tariffs on 99 percent of the goods traded between Mexico, Canada, and the United States.
- Removal of most barriers on the cross-border flow of services, allowing financial institutions, for example, unrestricted access to the Mexican market by 2000.
- Protection of intellectual property rights.
- Removal of most restrictions on foreign direct investment between the three member countries, although special treatment (protection) will be given to Mexican energy and railway industries, American airline and radio communications industries, and Canadian culture.
- Application of national environmental standards, provided such standards have a scientific basis. Lowering of standards to lure investment is described as being inappropriate.
- Establishment of two commissions with the power to impose fines and remove trade privileges when environmental standards or legislation involving health and safety, minimum wages, or child labour are ignored.

THE CASE FOR NAFTA

In 1991, proponents argued that NAFTA was an opportunity to create an enlarged and more efficient productive base for the entire region. They did recognize that one likely effect of NAFTA would be that many U.S. and Canadian firms would move some production to Mexico to take advantage of lower labour costs (average hourly labour costs in Mexico are about one-tenth those found in Canada and the United States).

Movement of production to Mexico would most likely occur in low-skilled, labour-intensive manufacturing industries where Mexico might have a comparative advantage, such as in textiles. Proponents argued that many would benefit from such a trend. Mexico would benefit because it would receive much-needed investment and employment. The United States and Canada would benefit because the increased incomes of the Mexicans would allow them to import more U.S. and Canadian goods, thereby increasing demand and making up for the jobs lost in industries that moved production to Mexico. U.S. and Canadian consumers would benefit from the lower prices of products produced in Mexico. In addition, the international competitiveness of U.S. and Canadian firms that moved production to Mexico to take advantage of lower labour costs would be enhanced, enabling them to better compete with Asian and European rivals.

THE CASE AGAINST NAFTA

Those who opposed NAFTA in 1991 claimed that ratification would be followed by a mass exodus of jobs from the United States and Canada into Mexico as employers sought to profit from Mexico's lower wages and less strict environmental and labour laws. According to one extreme opponent, Ross Perot, an independent presidential candidate and businessman who ran in the 1992 U.S. election, up to 5.9 million U.S. jobs would be lost to Mexico after NAFTA. Most economists, however, dismissed these numbers as being absurd and alarmist. They argued that Mexico would have to run a bilateral trade surplus with the United States of close to $300 billion for job loss on such a scale to occur—and $300 billion is about the size of Mexico's present GDP. In other words, such a scenario is implausible.

More sober estimates of the impact of NAFTA ranged from a net creation of 170 000 jobs in the United States (due to increased Mexican demand for U.S. goods and services) and an increase of $15 billion per year to the U.S. and Mexican GDP, to a net loss of 490 000 U.S. jobs. To put these numbers in perspective, employment in the U.S. economy was predicted to grow by 18 million from 1993 to 2003. As most economists repeatedly stressed, NAFTA would have a small impact

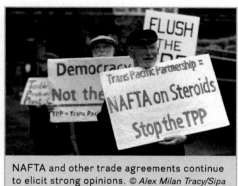

NAFTA and other trade agreements continue to elicit strong opinions. © *Alex Milan Tracy/Sipa USA/Newscom*

on both Canada and the United States. It could hardly be any other way, since the Mexican economy is only 5 percent of the size of the U.S. economy.

Signing NAFTA required the largest leap of economic faith from Mexico rather than Canada or the United States. Falling trade barriers would expose Mexican firms to highly efficient U.S. and Canadian competitors that, when compared to the average Mexican firm, have far greater capital resources, access to highly educated and skilled workforces, and much greater technological sophistication. The short-run outcome was likely to be painful economic restructuring and unemployment in Mexico. But if economic theory is any guide, there would be dynamic gains in the long run in the efficiency of Mexican firms as they adjust to the rigours of a more competitive marketplace. To the extent that this happened, an acceleration of Mexico's long-run rate of economic growth would follow, and Mexico might become a major market for Canadian and U.S. firms.[17]

Environmentalists also voiced concerns about NAFTA. They pointed to the sludge in the Rio Grande River and the smog in the air over Mexico City and warned that Mexico could degrade clean air and toxic waste standards across the continent. They claimed that the lower Rio Grande was the most polluted river in the United States, increasing in chemical waste and sewage along its course from El Paso, Texas, to the Gulf of Mexico.

There was also opposition in Mexico to NAFTA from those who feared a loss of national sovereignty. Mexican critics argued that their country would be dominated by U.S. firms that would not really contribute to Mexico's economic growth, but instead use Mexico as a low-cost assembly site, while keeping their high-paying, high-skilled jobs north of the border. (Interestingly, this is currently one of the arguments used by President Donald Trump in regards to U.S. sovereignty.)

NAFTA: THE RESULTS

But studies of NAFTA's impact suggest its initial effects were at best muted, and both advocates and detractors may have been guilty of exaggeration.[18] On average, studies indicate that NAFTA's overall impact has been small but positive.[19] From 1993 to 2005, trade among NAFTA's partners grew by 250 percent.[20] Canada and Mexico are now among the top three trading partners of the United States (the other is China), suggesting the economies of the three NAFTA nations have become more closely integrated. In 1990, U.S. trade with Canada and Mexico accounted for about a quarter of total U.S. trade. By 2005, the figure was close to one-third. Canada's trade with its NAFTA partners increased from about 70 percent to more than 80 percent of all Canadian foreign trade between 1993 and 2005, while Mexico's trade with NAFTA increased from 66 percent to 80 percent over the same period. All three countries also experienced strong productivity growth over this period. In Mexico, labour productivity has increased by 50 percent since 1993, and the passage of NAFTA may have contributed to this. However, estimates suggest that employment effects of NAFTA have been small. The most pessimistic estimates suggest the United States lost 110 000 jobs per year due to NAFTA between 1994 and 2000—and many economists dispute this figure—which is tiny compared to the more than 2 million jobs a year created in the United States during the same period.

Perhaps the most significant impact of NAFTA has not been economic, but political. Many observers credit NAFTA with helping to create the background for increased political stability in Mexico. For most of the post-NAFTA period, Mexico has been viewed as a stable democratic nation with a steadily growing economy, something that is beneficial to the United States, which shares a 2000-mile border with the country.[21] However, recent events have cast a cloud over Mexico's future. In late 2006, newly elected Mexican President Felipe Calderon initiated a crackdown on Mexico's increasingly powerful drug cartels (whose main business has been the illegal trafficking of drugs across the border into the United States). Calderon sent 6500 troops into the Mexican state of Michoacan to end escalating drug violence there. The cartels responded by escalating their own violence, and the country is now gripped in what amounts to an all-out war. Fuelled by the lucrative business of selling drugs to the United States and armed with guns purchased in the United States, the cartels have been fighting each other and the Mexican authorities in an increasingly brutal conflict that claimed 9000 lives in 2009 and another 16 736 in 2013, and which many feared would spill into the United States.[22] Unfortunately, this violence continues to grip the country under President Nieto and there appears to be no near-term, realistic solution.

THE FUTURE

The NAFTA agreement is now over twenty years old, which is a very long time for any political agreement to still have widespread support. Up until very recently, the issue confronting NAFTA is that of enlargement. A number of other Latin American countries had indicated their desire to eventually join NAFTA. The governments of both Canada and the United States adopted a wait-and-see attitude with regard to most countries.

Since NAFTA was approved in 1993, there have been changes to the agreement. Often, one partner has taken a case to court for decisions. Any and all changes took time to initiate, negotiate, and finalize. The agreement is in the news again due to changing political environment.

During the U.S. presidential race in 2016, almost all candidates questioning NAFTA. None was a more vocal opponent than Donald Trump, who was forthright in his wish to "rip up NAFTA." In the current political environment, it is difficult to predict what will happen to this several-decades-old agreement. As of this writing in mid-2017, President. Trump has acted on his promise to take another look at NAFTA and preliminary discussions about renegotiating are underway.

Getting NAFTA approved in 1993 was a bruising political experience, and no government is eager to repeat the process. However both Prime Minister Trudeau and Mexico's President Nieto have spoken of a willingness to sit down with the U.S. to discuss this two-decade-old agreement.

The Andean Community

Bolivia, Chile, Ecuador, Colombia, and Peru signed an agreement in 1969 to create the Andean Pact. The **Andean Pact** was largely based on the EU model, but was far less successful at achieving its stated goals. The integration steps begun in 1969 included an internal tariff reduction program, a common external tariff, a transportation policy, a common industrial policy, and special concessions for the smallest members, Bolivia and Ecuador.

By the mid-1980s, the Andean Pact had all but collapsed and had failed to achieve any of its stated objectives. There was no tariff-free trade among member-countries, no common external tariff, and no harmonization of economic policies. Political and economic problems seem to have hindered cooperation among member-countries. The countries of the Andean Pact have had to deal with low economic growth, hyperinflation, high unemployment, political unrest, and crushing debt burdens. In addition, the dominant political ideology in many of the Andean countries during this period tended toward the radical/socialist end of the political spectrum. Because such an ideology is hostile to the free market economic principles on which the Andean Pact was based, progress toward closer integration could not be expected.

The tide began to turn in the late 1980s when, after years of economic decline, the governments of Latin America began to adopt free market economic policies. In 1990, the heads of the five current members of the Andean Community—Bolivia, Ecuador, Peru, Colombia, and Venezuela—met in the Galápagos Islands. The resulting Galápagos Declaration effectively relaunched the Andean Pact, which was renamed the Andean Community in 1997. The declaration's objectives included the establishment of a free trade area by 1992, a customs union by 1994, and a common market by 1995. This last milestone has not been reached. A customs union was implemented in 1995—although Peru opted out and Bolivia received preferential treatment until 2003. The Andean Community now operates as a customs union. In December 2005, it signed an agreement with Mercosur to restart stalled negotiations on the creation of a free trade area between the two trading blocs. Those negotiations are proceeding at a slow pace. In late 2006, Venezuela withdrew from the Andean Community as part of that country's attempts to join Mercosur.

Mercosur

Mercosur originated in 1988 as a free trade pact between Brazil and Argentina. The modest reductions in tariffs and quotas accompanying this pact reportedly helped bring about an 80 percent increase in trade between the two countries in the late 1980s.[23] Encouraged by this success, the pact was expanded in March 1990 to include

Paraguay and Uruguay. The initial aim was to establish a full free trade area by the end of 1994 and a common market sometime thereafter. The four countries of Mercosur have a combined population of 200 million. With a market of this size, Mercosur could have a significant impact on the economic growth rate of the four economies. In December 1995, Mercosur's members agreed to a five-year program under which they hoped to perfect their free trade area and move toward a full customs union.[24]

For its first eight years or so, Mercosur seemed to be making a positive contribution to the economic growth rates of its member states. Trade between Mercosur's four core members quadrupled between 1990 and 1998. The combined GDP of the four member states grew at an annual average rate of 3.5 percent between 1990 and 1996, a performance that is significantly better than the four attained during the 1980s.[25]

However, Mercosur has its critics, including Alexander Yeats, a senior economist at the World Bank, who wrote a stinging critique of Mercosur that was "leaked" to the press in October 1996.[26] According to Yeats, the trade diversion effects of Mercosur outweighed its trade creation effects. Yeats pointed out that the fastest-growing items in intra-Mercosur trade were cars, buses, agricultural equipment, and other capital-intensive goods that were produced relatively inefficiently in the four member countries. In other words, Mercosur countries, insulated from outside competition by tariffs that ran as high as 70 percent of value on motor vehicles, were investing in factories that built products that were too expensive to sell to anyone but themselves. The result, according to Yeats, was that Mercosur countries might not be able to compete globally once the group's external trade barriers come down. In the meantime, capital was being drawn away from more efficient enterprises. In the near term, countries with more efficient manufacturing enterprises lost because Mercosur's external trade barriers kept them out of the market.

The leak of Yeats's report caused a storm at the World Bank, which typically does not release reports that are critical of member states (the Mercosur countries are members of the World Bank). It also drew strong protests from Brazil, one of the primary targets of the critique. Still, in tacit admission that at least some of Yeats's arguments have merit, a senior Mercosur diplomat let it be known that external trade barriers would gradually be reduced, forcing member countries to compete globally. Many external Mercosur tariffs, which averaged 14 percent, were lower than they were before the group's creation, and there were plans for a hemispheric Free Trade Area of the Americas to be established by 2005 (which would combine Mercosur, NAFTA, and other American nations).

Mercosur hit a significant roadblock in 1998, when its member states slipped into recession and intrabloc trade slumped. Trade fell further in 1999 following a financial crisis in Brazil that led to the devaluation of the Brazilian real, which immediately made the goods of other Mercosur members 40 percent more expensive in Brazil, their largest export market. At this point, progress toward establishing a customs union all but came to a halt. Things deteriorated further in 2001 when Argentina, beset by economic stresses, suggested that the customs union be "temporarily suspended." Argentina wanted to suspend Mercosur's tariff so that it could abolish duties on imports of capital equipment, while raising those on consumer goods to 35 percent (Mercosur had established a 14 percent import tariff on both sets of goods). Brazil agreed to this request, effectively putting an end for now to Mercosur's quest to become a fully functioning customs union.[27]

Hope for a revival arose in 2003 when new Brazilian President Lula da Silva announced his support for a revitalized and expanded Mercosur modelled after the EU with a larger membership, a common currency, and a democratically elected Mercosur

Parliament.[28] As of this writing, Mercosur comprises the 4 sovereign member states of Argentina, Brazil, Paraguay, and Uruguay. As a customs union, they negotiate as a bloc with potential trading partners such as Canada.[29]

Golden BRIC Countries

The acronym BRIC (also sometimes called the Golden BRIC or The Big Four) refers to Brazil, Russia, India, and China. These countries were given this title by an investment banker at Goldman Sachs more than a decade ago. They are important for a number of reasons:

- They are the four largest national economies outside of the OECD.
- They are all seen to be at roughly the same stage of economic development.
- With the exception of Russia, they sustained themselves well through the economic crisis that began in 2008.
- They are the only developing economies with annual GDPs of over $1 trillion (US$).
- All four countries combined account for about 40 percent of the world's total foreign-exchange reserves.
- They all have large domestic markets, and trade among BRIC countries is rapidly increasing.

However while the economic importance of the BRIC countries is significant, it far exceeds their political importance in world affairs. Unlike the countries that make up the G7, there are large differences between BRIC countries. Two are democracies, while two have authoritarian regimes. Only two of the four have a permanent seat on the UN's Security Council. Country incomes vary widely, from Russia's $15,000 per person annually, to India's $3000 per person annually. They are neither a formal economic bloc like the European Union, nor do they share a common currency. However, their economic growth will continue through this century, and with economic growth will come growing political power as well.

Central American Common Market, CAFTA, and CARICOM

Two other trade pacts in the Americas have not made much progress. In the early 1960s, Costa Rica, El Salvador, Guatemala, Honduras, and Nicaragua attempted to set up a **Central American Common Market**. It collapsed in 1969 when war broke out between Honduras and El Salvador after a riot at a soccer match between teams from the two countries. Since then, the member countries have made some progress toward reviving their agreement (the five founding members were joined by the Dominican Republic). The proposed common market was given a boost in 2003 when the U.S. signalled its intention to enter into bilateral free trade negotiations with the group. The negotiations culminated in a 2004 agreement to establish a free trade agreement between the six countries and the United States. Known as the **Central America Free Trade Agreement**, or CAFTA, the aim is to lower trade barriers between the United States and the six countries for most goods and services.

A customs union was to have been created in 1991 between the English-speaking Caribbean countries under the auspices of the Caribbean Community. Referred to as **CARICOM**, it was established in 1973. However, it repeatedly failed to progress toward economic integration. A formal commitment to economic and monetary union was adopted by CARICOM's member states in 1984, but since then, little progress has been made. In October 1991, the CARICOM governments failed, for the third consecutive time, to meet a deadline for establishing a common external tariff. Despite this, CARICOM expanded to 15 members by 2005. In early 2006, six CARICOM members established the **Caribbean Single Market and Economy (CSME)**. Modelled on the EU's single market, CSME's goal is to lower trade barriers and harmonize macroeconomic and monetary policy between member states.[30]

Free Trade Area of the Americas

At a hemisphere-wide Summit of the Americas in December 1994, a Free Trade Area of the Americas (FTAA) was proposed. It took more than three years for the talks to start, but in April 1998, 34 heads of state travelled to Santiago, Chile, for the second Summit of the Americas, where they formally inaugurated talks to establish an FTAA by January 1, 2005—something that did not occur. The continuing talks have addressed a wide range of economic, political, and environmental issues related to cross-border trade and investment. Although both the United States and Brazil were early advocates of the FTAA, support from both countries seems to be mixed at this point. Because the United States and Brazil have the largest economies in North and South America, respectively, strong U.S. and Brazilian support is a precondition for establishment of the free trade area.

The major stumbling blocks were twofold. First, the United States wanted its southern neighbours to agree to tougher enforcement of intellectual property rights and lower manufacturing tariffs, which they were not eager to embrace. Second, Brazil and Argentina wanted the United States to reduce its subsidies to U.S. agricultural producers and scrap tariffs on agricultural imports, which the U.S. government was not inclined to do. Observers at the time agreed that the United States and Brazil would have had to reach an agreement on these crucial issues.[31]

One last attempt to get talks going again, was in November 2005 at a summit of 34 heads of state from North and South America. It failed when opponents, led by Venezuela's populist President Hugo Chavez, blocked efforts by the Bush administration to set an agenda for further talks on FTAA. In voicing his opposition, Chavez condemned the U.S. free trade model as a "perversion" that would unduly benefit the United States to the detriment of poor people in Latin America, whom Chavez claimed would not benefit from free trade details.[32] Such views, even with the death of Hugo Chavez, make it unlikely that there will be much progress on establishing a FTAA in the near term. There have been no talks since 2005, and further action is unlikely.

The Trans-Pacific Partnership Agreement (TPP)

While President Donald Trump announced that the Trans-Pacific Partnership (TPP) was "dead" within the first week of his administration, it is useful to briefly review the history of this agreement.

The agreement began is 2006 with just four countries: Brunei, Chile, New Zealand and Singapore. It removed tariffs on a wide range of goods. It eventually grew to include 12 countries that border the Pacific Ocean, representing roughly 40 percent of the world's economic output. Like all trade agreements, the TPP aimed to cut tariffs and boost trade between the countries, with an eventual goal to become a common market, similar to the EU. All 12 nations needed to ratify the agreement for it to come into effect. To take effect, the deal would have had to be ratified by February 2018. Without the participation of the United States, this is highly unlikely to happen.

A common complaint against free trade agreements, which was noted in Chapter 6, is that they are often negotiated in secret. While it is true that any negotiations, especially those involving multiple parties, needs to have an element of privacy for frank discussions and negotiations to occur, in the case of the TPP this secrecy was implemented to a very high degree. For many, the first time they heard that such an agreement was being negotiated was after parties agreed to it (but had yet to ratify it). The TPP has no Web site, and the easiest place to read the full agreement is on the government of New Zealand's Web site https://www.mfat.govt.nz/en/about-us/who-we-are/treaties/trans-pacific-partnership-agreement-tpp/text-of-the-trans-pacific-partnership. In this case, the argument that the agreement was conducted in secret has some merit.

Regional Economic Integration Elsewhere

Numerous attempts at regional economic integration have been tried throughout Asia and Africa. However, few exist in anything other than name. Perhaps the most significant is the Association of Southeast Asian Nations (ASEAN). In addition, the Asia-Pacific Economic Cooperation (APEC) forum has recently emerged as the seed of a potential free trade region.

Association of Southeast Asian Nations (ASEAN)

Formed in 1967, the **Association of Southeast Asian Nations (ASEAN)** includes Brunei, Cambodia, Indonesia, Laos, Malaysia, Myanmar, Philippines, Singapore, Thailand, and Vietnam. Laos, Myanmar, Vietnam, and Cambodia have all joined recently, creating a regional grouping of 500 million people with a combined GDP of some $740 billion (see Map 8.2). The basic objective of ASEAN is to foster freer trade among member countries and to achieve cooperation in their industrial policies. Progress so far has been limited, however.

Until recently, only 5 percent of intra-ASEAN trade consisted of goods whose tariffs had been reduced through an ASEAN preferential trade arrangement. In 2003, an ASEAN Free Trade Area (AFTA) among the six original members of ASEAN came into full effect. The AFTA cut tariffs on manufacturing and agricultural products to less than 5 percent. However, there were some significant exceptions to this tariff reduction. Malaysia, for example, refused to bring down tariffs on imported cars until 2005 and then agreed to lower the tariff only to 20 percent, not the 5 percent called for under the AFTA. Malaysia wanted to protect Proton, an inefficient local carmaker, from foreign competition. Similarly, the Philippines has refused to lower tariff rates on petrochemicals, and rice—the largest agricultural product in the region—will remain subject to higher tariff rates until at least 2020.[33]

Notwithstanding such issues, ASEAN and AFTA are at least progressing toward establishing a free trade zone. Vietnam joined the AFTA in 2006, Laos and Myanmar in 2008, and Cambodia in 2010. The goal was to reduce import tariffs among the six original members to zero by 2010 and to do so by 2015 for the newer members (although important exceptions to that goal, such as tariffs on rice, will persist).

ASEAN also recently signed a free trade agreement with China that removes tariffs on 90 percent of traded goods. This went into effect January 1, 2010. Trade between China and ASEAN members more than tripled during the first decade of the twenty-first century, and this agreement should spur further growth.[34]

Asia-Pacific Economic Cooperation (APEC)

The Asia-Pacific Economic Cooperation (APEC) was founded in 1990 at the suggestion of Australia. APEC currently has 21 member economies, including such economic powerhouses as the United States, Japan, and China. Collectively, the member economies account for about 55 percent of the world's GNP, 49 percent of world trade, and much of the growth in the world economy. The stated aim of APEC is to increase multilateral cooperation in view of the economic rise of the Pacific nations and the growing

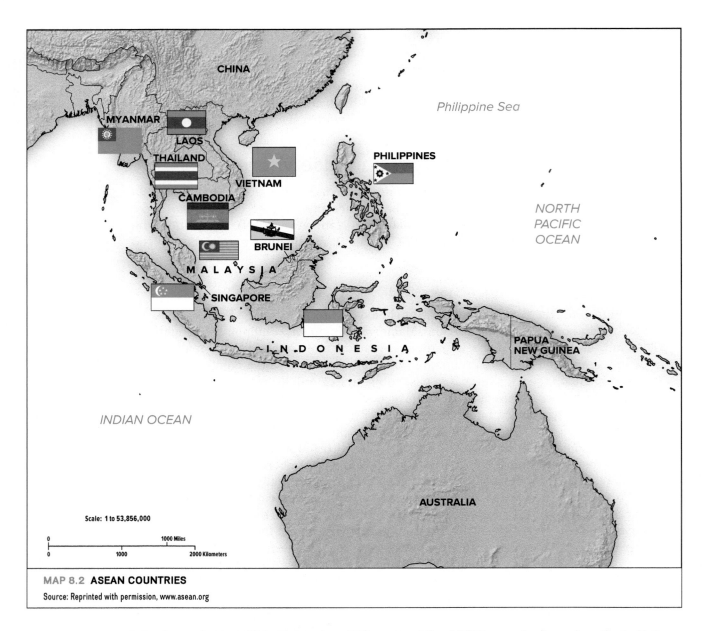

MAP 8.2 ASEAN COUNTRIES

Source: Reprinted with permission, www.asean.org

interdependence within the region. U.S. support for APEC was also based on the belief that it might prove a viable strategy for heading off any moves to create Asian groupings from which it would be excluded.

Interest in APEC was heightened considerably in November 1993 when the heads of APEC member economies met for the first time at a two-day conference in Seattle. Debate before the meeting speculated on the likely future role of APEC. One view was that APEC should commit itself to the ultimate formation of a free trade area. Such a move would transform the Pacific Rim from a geographical expression into the world's largest free trade area. Another view was that APEC would produce no more than hot air and lots of photo opportunities for the leaders involved. As it turned out, the APEC meeting produced little more than some vague commitments from member economies to work together for greater economic integration and a general lowering of trade barriers. However, member economies did not rule out the possibility of closer economic cooperation in the future.[35]

The economic leaders have met again on a number of occasions. At a 1997 meeting, member economies formally endorsed proposals designed to remove trade barriers in 15 sectors, ranging from fish to toys. However, the vague plan committed APEC to doing no more than holding further talks, which is all that has been accomplished to date. Commenting on the vagueness of APEC pronouncements, the influential Brookings Institution, a U.S.-based economic policy institution, noted APEC "is in grave danger of shrinking into irrelevance as a serious forum." Despite the slow progress, APEC is worth watching. If it eventually does transform itself into a free trade area, it will probably be the world's largest.[36]

Regional Trade Blocs in Africa

African countries have been experimenting with regional trade blocs for half a century. There are now nine trade blocs on the African continent. Many countries are members of more than one group. Although the number of trade groups is impressive, progress toward the establishment of meaningful trade blocs has been slow.

Many of these groups have been dormant for years. Significant political turmoil in several African nations has persistently impeded any meaningful progress. Also, deep suspicion of free trade exists in several African countries. The argument most frequently heard is that because these countries have less developed and less diversified economies, they need to be "protected" by tariff barriers from unfair foreign competition. Given the prevalence of this argument, it has been hard to establish free trade areas or customs unions.

The most recent attempt to reenergize the free trade movement in Africa occurred in early 2001, when Kenya, Uganda, and Tanzania, member states of the East African Community (EAC), committed themselves to relaunching their bloc, 24 years after it collapsed. The three original countries, with 80 million inhabitants, intend to establish a customs union, regional court, legislative assembly, and, eventually, a political federation.

ANOTHER PERSPECTIVE

Economic Integration in Africa

Many efforts are pushing regional economic integration in Africa, and they tend to fall into geographic groupings. One huge benefit of economic integration would be a reduction in the perceived political risk for trade among African countries and a development of African-based distribution channels. Now, largely because of the perceived risk, companies that manufacture for export tend to ship their finished goods to industrialized countries, which then export their imports back to other African countries. A manufactured good from Kenya, say a solar panel, might be shipped to London to be sent to Nigeria. Integration would lead to a more direct alternative, across the continent. Political scientists suggest that integrated political and economic unions need a shared national hardship to push the collaboration. For the EU it was the devastation of World War II. Craig Jackson, a legal scholar of integration forces, suggests that the devastation in Africa due to poverty and underdevelopment is the kind of force that might push toward the development of the African Union.

Source: www.law.cam.ac.uk/rcil/jackson.rtf+African+economic+integration&hl=en&ie=UTF-8/

Their program includes cooperation on immigration, road and telecommunication networks, investment, and capital markets. However, while local business leaders welcomed the relaunch as a positive step, they were critical of the EAC's failure in practice to make progress on free trade. At the EAC treaty's signing in November 1999, members gave themselves four years to negotiate a customs union, with a draft slated for the end of 2001. But that fell far short of earlier plans for an immediate free trade zone, shelved after Tanzania and Uganda, fearful of Kenyan competition, expressed concerns that the zone could create imbalances similar to those that contributed to the breakup of the first community.[37] Nevertheless, in 2005 the EAC did start to implement a customs union. In 2007, Burundi and Rwanda joined the EAC and South Sudan joined the group in 2016, bringing the total inhabitants in the union to 173 million. The EAC established a common market in 2010 and continues to work toward the goal of a monetary union.

LO5   IMPLICATIONS FOR BUSINESS

Currently the most significant developments in regional economic integration, in this case against the priciple of more open borders, are occurring in the European Union and NAFTA. Although some of the Latin American trade blocs, APEC, and the proposed FTAA may have greater economic significance in the future, at present the European Union and NAFTA have more profound and immediate implications for business practice. Accordingly, in this section we will concentrate on the business implications of those two groups. Similar conclusions, however, could be drawn with regard to the creation of a single market anywhere in the world.

OPPORTUNITIES

The creation of a single market offers significant opportunities because markets that were formerly protected from foreign competition are opened. For example, in Europe before 1992 the large French and Italian markets were among the most protected. These markets are now much more open to foreign competition in the form of both exports and direct investment. Nonetheless, the spectre of "Fortress Europe" suggests that to fully exploit such opportunities, it may pay non-EU firms to set up EU subsidiaries. Many major U.S. firms have long had subsidiaries in Europe. Those that do not would be advised to consider establishing them now, lest they run the risk of being shut out of the EU by nontariff barriers. In fact, non-EU firms rapidly increased their direct investment in the EU in anticipation of the creation of a single market. Between 1985 and 1989, for example, approximately 37 percent of the FDI inflows into industrialized countries was directed at the EC. By 1991, this figure had risen to 66 percent, and FDI inflows into the EU have been substantial ever since (see Chapter 7).[38]

Additional opportunities arise from the inherent lower costs of doing business in a single market— as opposed to 28 national markets in the case of the European Union or 3 national markets in the case of NAFTA. Free movement of goods across borders, harmonized product standards, and simplified tax regimes make it possible for firms based in the European Union and the NAFTA countries to realize potentially significant cost economies by centralizing production in those EU and NAFTA locations where the mix of factor costs and skills is optimal. Rather than producing a product in each of the 28 EU countries or the 3 NAFTA countries, a firm may be able to serve the whole EU or North American market from a single location. This location must be chosen carefully, of course, with an eye on local factor costs and skills.

Over the past century, companies have seen the value in being close to their markets and one such company, 3M, has been in business in Canada for over 50 years, since creating its first subsidiary operation in London, Ontario.[39] The growth of free markets since that time has in some ways heightened the need for companies to centralize locations closest to their biggest markets. In response to changes created by the EU after 1992, the St. Paul-based 3M Company has been consolidating its European manufacturing and distribution facilities to take advantage of economies of scale.[40] Thus, a plant in Great Britain now produces 3M's printing products and a German factory its reflective traffic control materials for all of the EU. In each case, 3M chose a location for centralized production after carefully considering the likely production costs in alternative locations within the EU. The ultimate goal of 3M is to dispense with all national distinctions, directing R&D, manufacturing, distribution, and marketing for each product group from an EU headquarters.[41] Similarly, Unilever, one of Europe's largest companies, began rationalizing its production in advance of 1992 to attain scale economies. Unilever concentrated its production of dishwashing powder for the EU in one plant, bath soap in another, and so on.[42]

Even after the removal of barriers to trade and investment, enduring differences in culture and competitive practices often limit the ability of companies to realize cost economies by centralizing production in key locations and producing a standardized product for a single multi-country market.

THREATS

The emergence of single markets in the EU and North America creates opportunities for business, but it also presents threats. For one thing, the business environment within each grouping will become more competitive. Lowering barriers to trade and investment between countries is likely to lead to increased price competition throughout the EU and NAFTA. For example, before 1992 a Volkswagen Golf cost 55 percent more in Great Britain than in Denmark and 29 percent more in Ireland than in Greece.[43] Over time, such price differentials will vanish in a single market. This is a direct threat to any firm doing business in EU or NAFTA countries. To survive in the tougher single-market environment, firms must take advantage of the opportunities offered by the creation of a single market to rationalize their production and reduce their costs. Otherwise, they will be severely disadvantaged.

A further threat to firms outside these trading blocs arises from the likely long-term improvement in the competitive position of many firms within the areas. This is particularly relevant in the EU, where many firms are currently limited by a high cost structure in their ability to compete globally with North American and Asian firms. The creation of a single market and the resulting increased competition in the European Union is beginning to produce serious attempts by many EU firms to reduce their cost structure by rationalizing production. This could transform many EU companies into efficient global competitors. The message for non-EU businesses is that they need to prepare for the emergence of more capable European competitors by reducing their own cost structures.

Another threat to firms outside of trading areas is the threat of being shut out of the single market by the creation of a "trade fortress." The charge that regional economic integration might lead to a fortress mentality is most often levelled at the EU. As noted earlier in the chapter, although the free trade philosophy underpinning the EU theoretically argues against the creation of any fortress in Europe, there are signs that the EU may raise barriers to imports and investment in certain "politically sensitive" areas, such as autos. Non-EU firms might be well advised, therefore, to set up their own EU operations as quickly as possible. This could also occur in the NAFTA countries, but it seems less likely.

The emerging role of the European Commission in competition policy suggests the EU is increasingly willing and able to intervene and impose conditions on companies proposing mergers and acquisitions. This is a threat insofar as it limits the ability of firms to pursue the corporate strategy of their choice. While this constrains the strategic options for firms, in taking such action, the Commission is trying to maintain the level of competition in Europe's single market, which should benefit consumers.

Finally, there is the political risk of changes to these free trade agreements. It must be remembered that free trade is not dead, and that despite Brexit, for example, there is still a European Common Market of 27 countries. But agreements change, especially NAFTA, and the wise business maintains awareness of a shifting political landscape.

Key Terms

Andean Pact

Association of Southeast Asian Nations (ASEAN)

Caribbean Single Market and Economy (CSME)

CARICOM

Central America Free Trade Agreement (CAFTA)

Central American Common Market

common market

customs union

economic union

European Free Trade Association (EFTA)

free trade area

Maastricht Treaty

maquilladoras

optimal currency area

political union

regional economic integration

trade creation

trade diversion

LO Learning Objectives Summary

1. A number of levels of economic integration are possible in theory. In order of increasing integration, they include a free trade area, a customs union, a common market, an economic union, and full political union. In a free trade area, barriers to trade among member countries are removed, but each country determines its own external trade policy. In a customs union, internal barriers to trade are removed and a common external trade policy is adopted. A common market is similar to a customs union, except that a common market also allows factors of production to move freely among countries. An economic union involves even closer integration, including the establishment of a common currency and the harmonization of tax rates. A political union is the logical culmination of attempts to achieve ever-closer economic integration.

2. The argument for regional economic integration states it is an attempt to achieve economic gains from the free flow of trade and investment between neighbouring countries. The argument recognizes integration is not easily achieved or sustained. Although integration brings benefits to the majority, it is never without costs for the minority. Concerns over national sovereignty often slow or stop integration attempts.

3. The argument against regional integration suggests it will not increase economic welfare if the trade creation effects in the free trade area are outweighed by the trade diversion effects.

4. The Single European Act sought to create a true single market by abolishing administrative barriers to the free flow of trade and investment among EU countries. Eighteen EU members now use a common currency, the euro. The economic gains from a common currency come from reduced exchange costs, reduced risk associated with currency fluctuations, and increased price competition within the EU. Increasingly, the European Commission is taking an activist stance with regard to competition policy, intervening to restrict mergers and acquisitions that it believes will reduce competition in the EU. Although no other attempt at regional economic integration comes close to the EU in terms of potential economic and political significance, various other attempts are being made in the world. The most notable include NAFTA in North America, the Andean Community and Mercosur in Latin America, ASEAN in Southeast Asia, and perhaps APEC.

5. The creation of single markets in the EU and North America means that many markets that were formerly protected from foreign competition are now more open. This creates major investment and export opportunities for firms within and outside these regions. The free movement of goods across borders, the harmonization of product standards, and the simplification of tax regimes make it possible for firms based in a free trade area to realize potentially enormous cost economies by centralizing production in those locations within the area where the mix of factor costs and skills is optimal. Lowering barriers to trade and investment among countries within a trade group will probably be followed by increased price competition.

Critical Thinking and Discussion Questions

1. "NAFTA is likely to continue to produce net benefits for the Canadian, Mexican, and U.S. economies." Evaluate this statement.

2. What are the economic and political arguments for regional economic integration? Given these arguments, why don't we see more integration in the world economy?

3. What effect did creating a single market and a single currency within the European Union have on competition within the European Union? Why?

4. How should a firm with self-sufficient production facilities in several EU countries respond to the creation of a single market? What are the constraints on its ability to respond in a manner that minimizes production costs?

5. Do you see Mercosur expanding beyond its current four countries? Why or why not?

6. Would establishment of the TPP be good for the two most advanced economies in the hemisphere, the United States and Canada? How might the establishment of the TPP impact the strategy of North American firms?

Research Task globalEDGE™ **globaledge.msu.edu**

Use the globalEDGE™ site to complete the following exercises:

1. Your company is considering opening an office in Germany, Switzerland, or another country in the European Union. The size of the investment is significant, and top management wishes to have a clearer picture of the current and probable future economic status of the EU. Prepare an executive summary describing the features you consider as crucial in making such a decision.

2. Bringing the Free Trade Area of the Americas back to life could be a threat, as well as an opportunity, for your company. Identify the countries likely to participate in the negotiations for the FTAA. What would the main themes of the negotiation process?

CLOSING CASE

I WANT MY GREEK TV!

It's now over two decades since the member-states of the European Union (EU) started to implement a treaty calling for the establishment of a single market for goods and services across the union, and yet progress toward this goal is still not complete. A case in point: the TV broadcasts of Premier League soccer. The English Premier League, which is one of the most lucrative broadcasting sports franchises in Europe, if not the world, has for years segmented Europe into different national markets, charging different prices for broadcasting rights depending on local demand. Not surprisingly, the rights are most expensive in the United Kingdom, where the league has contracted with British Sky Broadcasting Group and ESPN to screen games.

Karen Murphy, the owner of the Red, White & Blue pub in Portsmouth, England, didn't want to pay the £7,000 annual subscription fee that Sky demanded for access to the Premier League feed. Instead, she purchased a TV signal decoder card and used it to unscramble the feed from a Greek TV broadcaster, Nova, which had purchased the rights to broadcast Premier League soccer in Greece. This cost her just £800 a year. In 2005, it also brought a lawsuit from the Premier League. The initial judgment in a British court upheld the right of the Premier League to segment the market and charge a higher price to UK subscribers. Murphy was fined £8,000. She appealed the ruling, claiming the practice violated the EU's Single Market Act, which the United Kingdom had signed in 1992.

The case eventually landed in the European Court of Justice, the EU's highest court. The Premier League argued before the court that the EU needs individual national TV markets to satisfy the "cultural preferences" of viewers. The court did not agree. In a bombshell for the

Customers watching soccer in a British pub. © *andresr/Getty Images*

Premier League, on February 3, 2011, the court stated, "Territorial exclusivity agreements relating to the transmission of football matches are contrary to European Union law. European law does not make it possible to prohibit the live transmission of Premier League matches in pubs by means of foreign decoder cards." In short, Murphy can continue to purchase her feed from Nova. This decision was a legal opinion prepared by the court's advocate general, so technically it is still possible that the full court might overturn it, but in four out of five cases this does not happen.

This was not the first time the EU court had issued a ruling that affected Premier League soccer. In 1995, the court upheld the right of a Belgian soccer player to play in another EU country, stating athletes had the same freedom of movement as other EU workers. Ironically, this ruling, which also affirmed the principle of a single market, benefited Premier League clubs, enabling them to sign foreign players, rapidly transforming the league into the best in the world. The new ruling, however, creates significant challenges for the league. Revenue from broadcasting is a major source of income for Premier League clubs. The current deal giving British broadcasting rights to Sky and ESPN is worth some £1.782 billion to the league between 2010 and 2013.

In February 2012 the EU court affirmed the ruling. Many consumers may now follow Murphy and buy TV decoders so that they can watch lower-cost feeds. If enough do this, the income loss from arbitrage by consumers may force the Premier League to move toward pan-European broadcasting and pricing. This will reduce income to the clubs, which could have a profound impact on the players they can recruit and the wages they can afford. In short, the ruling, while benefiting consumers such as Murphy and her customers at the Red, White & Blue pub, is a dark cloud hanging over the future of British soccer.

Sources: O. Gibson, "Round One to the Pub Lady," *The Guardian*, February 4, 2011, p. 5; J. W. Miller, "European TV Market for Sports Faces Turmoil from Legal Ruling," *The Wall Street Journal*, February 4, 2011; J. Wilson, "What the Legal Wrangle Means for Armchair Fans," *The Daily Telegraph*, February 4, 2011, p. 8; and "Portsmouth pub landlady Karen Murphy has Premier League TV conviction quashed," *Metro*, February 24th, 2012.

Case Discussion Questions

1. Why do you think the English Premier League has historically charged different prices for broadcasting rights in different European markets?

2. Do you think the European Court of Justice was right to rule that the league could not stop people from buying Premier League soccer feeds from other countries? Explain your reasoning?

3. Who benefits from the EU ruling? Who will be the losers?

4. If you were running the English Premier League, what would your strategy be on broadcast rights going forward?

Sustainability in Practice

FOREIGN INVESTMENT FOR SUSTAINABLE COMMUNITY DEVELOPMENT

The following case studies describe the microcredit programs at the Grameen Bank and at the world banking group ABN AMRO. The first case study explains how the Grameen Bank uses microcredit within Bangladesh as a sustainable development tool to help build local economies and reduce poverty. The second case study describes how Oikocredit Canada is successfully merging economic development with returns to investors.

MULTINATIONALS LEARNING FROM THE GRAMEEN EXAMPLE

The Grameen Bank has shown that innovative business models can deliver services in novel ways that create business profit as well as opportunities for the poor. Set up in 1976 to overturn conventional banking mentality, Grameen Bank provides services to the rural poor through microcredit.

The bank demonstrates how a traditional service can be repackaged to reach new customers in the segment that has been called the "market at the bottom of the pyramid." Nontraditional business models need to be innovative and based on lower margins from larger markets. But if successful, they can begin to overcome many of the barriers to meeting the needs of these markets—such as a lack of electricity, poor educational systems, limited infrastructure, and finance for large-scale products and services.

In many countries, including Bangladesh, poor people lack access to institutional credit because the rural banking system operates on "no collateral, no credit" policy. The Grameen scheme provides credit to the poorest of the poor in rural Bangladesh without any collateral. Instead, it relies on supervision, accountability, participation, and creativity.

Since formally becoming a bank in 1983, and as of December 2015, Grameen has 8.81 million borrowers, 97 percent of whom are women. With 2568 branches, GB provides services in 81 392 villages, covering more than 97 percent of the total villages in Bangladesh.

As a result of its success, Grameen has diversified, creating additional products and services that conventional business does not provide, such as renewable energy schemes, telecommunications services, and information technology development.

Grameen Bank simultaneously provides credit to a new market while contributing to sustainable development. The needs of the rural poor are far from satisfied, but this market holds considerable promise. Services that are better tailored to the need of clients lead to better performance and sustainability among clients, which in turn can lead to better performance and sustainability for the company.

On a broader scale, these management structures contribute to sustainable development by building the capacity of the poor to govern themselves and the organizations to which they belong.

FOREIGN INVESTMENT IN MICROCREDIT: THE OIKOCREDIT CANADA EXAMPLE

Oikocredit is a worldwide organization. Its mandate can best be described using its own words from the Web site www.oikocredit.ca:

> Our organisation manages one of the world's largest sources of private capital for development finance. The financial resources come from investments by individuals, organizations and churches. We pay our shareholders a modest annual dividend. Oikocredit finances and invests in microfinance institutions, co-operatives and small and medium enterprises in developing countries, aimed at positive social impact.

Yet, Oikocredit is more than an investment institution. We are movement for social change.

Through our members and our Support Associations in Canada and around the world, we are helping to change the conversation about development. We are helping to introduce the idea that international development is not charity bestowed by the wealthy. It is solidarity between investors and borrowers. In our view, investment can help to transform lives in the developing world.

And this investment can bring returns to an ever increasing range of small savers. In Ontario, for example, Oikocredit has partnered with a credit union to offer Oikocredit Global Impact Guaranteed Investment Certificates (GICs). Any member of a credit union can invest in these certificates, backed by the Deposit Insurance Corporation of Ontario, and hold them individually, or in tax advantaged plans like a Registered Retirement Savings Plan (RRSP). Investors earn a guaranteed return on their money, while "doing good" at the same time.

Sources: The Grameen Bank information was adapted by Dr. Debra Rowe and is used with permission. Other information from Oikocredit Canada at www.oikocredit.ca.

© Liens/Getty Images

Chapter 9

The Foreign Exchange Market

THE WILD RIDE OF THE BRAZILIAN REAL

For many years Brazil was a country battered by persistently high inflation. As a result the value of its currency, the real, depreciated steadily against the U.S. dollar. This changed in the early 2000s when the Brazilian government was successful in bringing down annual inflation rates into the single digits. Lower inflation, coupled with policies that paved the way for the expansion of the Brazilian economy, resulted in a steady appreciation of the real against the U.S. dollar. In May 2004, 1 real bought $0.3121; by August 2008, 1 real bought $0.65, an appreciation of more than 100 percent.

The appreciation of the real against the dollar was a mixed bag for Embraer, the world's largest manufacturer of regional jets of up to 110 seats and one of Brazil's most prominent industrial companies. Embraer purchases many of the parts that go into its jets, including the engines and electronics, from U.S. manufacturers. As the real appreciated against the dollar, these parts cost less when translated into reals, which benefited Embraer's profit margins. However, the company also prices its aircraft in U.S. dollars, as do all manufacturers in the global market for commercial jet aircraft. So, as the real appreciated against the dollar, Embraer's dollar revenues were compressed when exchanged back into reals.

To try and deal with the impact of currency appreciation on its revenues, in the mid-2000s Embraer started to hedge against future appreciation of the real by buying forward contracts (forward contracts give the holder the right to exchange one currency—in this case dollars—for another—in this case reals—at some point in the future at a predetermined exchange rate). If the real had continued to appreciate, this would have been a great strategy for Embraer because the company could have locked in the rate at which sales made in dollars were exchanged back into reals. Unfortunately for Embraer, as the global financial crisis unfolded in 2008, investors fled to the dollar, which they viewed as a safe haven, and the real depreciated against the dollar. Between August 2008 and November 2008, the value of the real fell by almost 40 percent against the dollar. But for the hedging, this depreciation would have actually increased Embraer's revenues in reals. Embraer, however, had locked itself into a much higher real/dollar exchange rate, and the company was forced to take a $121 million loss on what was essentially a bad currency bet.

Since the shock of 2008, Embraer has cut back on currency hedging, and most of its dollar sales and purchases are not hedged. This makes Embraer's sales revenues very sensitive to the real/dollar exchange rate. By 2010, the Brazilian real was once more appreciating against the U.S. dollar, which pressured Embraer's revenues. By 2012, however, the Brazilian economy was stagnating, while inflation was starting to increase again. This led to a sustained fall in the value of the real, which fell from 1 real = $0.644 in July 2011 to 1 real = $0.40 by January 2014, a depreciation of 38 percent. What was bad for the Brazilian currency, however, was good for Embraer, whose stock price surged to the highest price since February 2008 on speculation that the decline on the real would lead to a boost in Embraer's revenues when expressed in reals. Since then the real has dropped further to $0.32 in early 2017, while Embraer's stock has pulled back from its all time highs due to competition and factors unrelated to the Brazilian currency.

Sources: D. Godoy, "Embraer Rallies as Brazilian Currency Weakens," *Bloomberg*, May 31, 2013; K. Kroll, "Embraer Fourth Quarter Profits Plunge 44% on Currency Woes," *Cleveland.com*, March 27, 2009; "A fall from Grace: Brazil's Mediocre Economy," *The Economist*, June 8, 2013; and "Brazil's Economy: The Deterioration," *The Economist*, December 7, 2013.

LO ∣ LEARNING OBJECTIVES

By the end of this chapter you should be able to:

1. Describe the functions of the foreign exchange market.

2. Understand the nature of the foreign exchange market.

3. Understand the different theories explaining how currency exchange rates are determined and their relative merits.

4. Identify the merits of different approaches toward exchange rate forecasting and understand the issues surrounding currency convertibility.

5. Compare and contrast the differences among translation, transaction, and economic exposure, and what managers can do to manage each type of exposure.

Introduction

Like many enterprises in the global economy, the Brazilian aircraft manufacturer Embraer is affected by changes in the value of currencies on the foreign exchange market. As described in the opening case, Embraer's revenues are helped when the Brazilian currency is weak against the U.S. dollar, and vice versa. The case illustrates that what happens in the foreign exchange market can have a fundamental impact on the sales, profits, and strategy of an enterprise. Accordingly, it is very important for managers to understand the foreign exchange market, and what the impact of changes in currency exchange rates might be for their enterprise.

This chapter has three main objectives. The first is to explain how the foreign exchange market works. The second is to examine the forces that determine exchange rates and to discuss the degree to which it is possible to predict future exchange rate movements. The third objective is to map the implications for international business of exchange rate movements and the foreign exchange market. This chapter is the first of two that deal with the international monetary system and its relationship to international business. In the next chapter we will explore the institutional structure of the international monetary system. The institutional structure is the context within which the foreign exchange market functions. As we shall see, changes in the institutional structure of the international monetary system can exert a profound influence on the development of foreign exchange markets.

The **foreign exchange market** is a market for converting the currency of one country into that of another country. An **exchange rate** is simply the rate at which one currency is converted into another. For example, Kia uses the foreign exchange market to convert the dollars it earns from selling cars in the United States into the Korean won. Without the foreign exchange market, international trade and international investment on the scale that we see today would be impossible; companies would have to resort to barter. The foreign exchange market is the lubricant that enables companies based in countries that use different currencies to trade with each other.

We know from earlier chapters that international trade and investment have their risks. Some of these risks exist because future exchange rates cannot be perfectly predicted. The rate at which one currency is converted into another can change over time. For example, at the start of 2001, one U.S. dollar bought 1.065 euros, but by the end of 2013 one U.S. dollar only bought about 0.74 euros. The U.S. dollar had fallen sharply in value against the euro. This made American goods cheaper in Europe, boosting export sales. At the same time, it made European goods more expensive in the United States, which hurt the sales and profits of European companies that sold goods and services to the United States.

However currency markets are volatile. The strengthening U.S. dollar beginning in late 2016 resulted in the rise in price of U.S. goods when sold in Europe. By early 2017 the U.S. dollar had risen again and one U.S. dollar was about about 0.94 euros.

One function of the foreign exchange market is to provide some insurance against the risks that arise from such volatile changes in exchange rates, commonly referred to as foreign exchange risk. Although the foreign exchange market offers some insurance against foreign exchange risk, it cannot provide complete insurance. It is not unusual for international businesses to suffer losses because of unpredicted changes in exchange rates. Currency fluctuations can make seemingly profitable trade and investment deals unprofitable, and vice versa.

We begin this chapter by looking at the functions and the form of the foreign exchange market. This includes distinguishing among spot exchanges, forward exchanges, and currency swaps. Then we will consider the factors that determine exchange rates. We will also look at how foreign trade is conducted when a country's currency cannot be exchanged for other currencies; that is, when its currency is not convertible. The chapter closes with a discussion of these items in terms of their implications for business.

LO1   The Functions of the Foreign Exchange Market

The foreign exchange market serves two main functions. The first is to convert the currency of one country into the currency of another. The second is to provide some insurance against **foreign exchange risk**, by which we mean the adverse consequences of unpredictable changes in exchange rates.[1]

ANOTHER PERSPECTIVE

Should Countries Be Free to Set Currency Policy?

Exchange rates are critically important in the global economy. They affect the price of every country's imports and exports, companies' foreign direct investment, and—directly or indirectly—people's spending behaviours. In recent years, disagreements among countries over exchange rates have become much more widespread. Some government officials and analysts even suggest that there is a "currency war" among certain countries. For example, U.S. President Donald Trump, and others, have accused China of manipulating its currency, to the detriment of the United States. The main issue here is whether or not some countries are using exchange rate policies to undermine free currency markets and whether they intentionally, in essence, devalue their currency to gain a trade advantage at the expense of other countries. A weaker currency makes exports inexpensive (or at least cheaper) to foreigners, which can lead to higher exports and job creation in the export sector.

Source: R. M. Nelson, "Current Debates over Exchange Rates: Overview and Issues for Congress," *Congressional Research Service*, November 12, 2013.

Currency Conversion

Each country has a currency in which the prices of goods and services are quoted. In the United States, it is the dollar ($); in Great Britain, the pound (£); in the rest of Europe, the euro (€); in Canada, the Canadian dollar (CAD$); and so on. In general, within the borders of a particular country, one must use the national currency. A Canadian tourist cannot walk into a store in Edinburgh, Scotland, and use Canadian dollars to buy a bottle of Scotch whisky. Dollars are not recognized as legal tender in Scotland; the tourist must use British pounds. Fortunately, the tourist can go to a bank and exchange her dollars for pounds. Then she can buy the whisky.

When a tourist changes one currency into another, she is participating in the foreign exchange market. Exchange rates allow us to compare the relative price of goods and services in different countries. A Canadian tourist wishing to buy a bottle of Scotch whisky in Glasgow learns that she must pay £30 for the bottle, knowing that the same bottle costs $45 in Canada. Is this a good deal? Imagine the pound/Canadian dollar exchange rate is 1.70. Upon calculation of this exchange rate, the tourist calculates the exchange rate for the £30 bottle of whisky. (The calculation is 1.70 × 30.) She finds that the bottle of Scotch costs the equivalent of $51.00 (CAD$). She is surprised that a bottle of Scotch whisky could cost less in Canada than in Scotland. (This is true; alcohol is heavily taxed in Great Britain.)

Tourists are minor participants in the foreign exchange market; companies engaged in international trade and investment are major ones. International businesses have four main uses of foreign exchange markets. First, the payments a company receives for its exports, the income it receives from foreign investments, or the income it receives from licensing agreements with foreign firms may be in foreign currencies. To use those funds in its home country, the company must convert them to

Using forwards, swaps, and other derivatives can insure a company against exchange rate risk. © PhotoLink/Getty Images

its home country's currency. Consider the Scotch distillery that exports its whisky to Canada. The distillery is paid in dollars (most likely in U.S. dollars) but since those dollars cannot be spent in Great Britain, they must be converted to British pounds. (The Canadian firm would have first converted Canadian dollars to U.S. dollars on the foreign exchange markets and paid the U.S./Canadian dollar exchange rate at the time of the conversion.)

Second, international businesses use foreign exchange markets when they must pay a foreign company for its products or services in its country's currency. For example, Dell Computer buys many components for its computers from Malaysian firms. The Malaysian companies are required to be paid in Malaysia's currency, the ringgit, so Dell must convert money from dollars into ringgit.

Third, international businesses use foreign exchange markets when they have spare cash that they wish to invest for short terms in money markets. Imagine that a Canadian company has $10 million it wants to invest for three months in its U.S. dollar account. The best rate it might earn on this amount in its U.S. dollar account is 2 percent. Investing in an Australian money market account, however, may earn it 10 percent. Thus, in this example, the company may change its $10 million to Australian dollars and invest it into its existing Australian operations. Note, however, that the rate of return it earns on this investment depends not only on the Australian dollar interest rate, but also on the changes in the value of the Australian

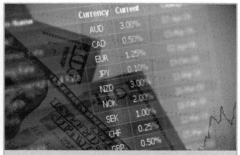

The foreign exchange market enables companies based in countries that use different currencies to trade with each other. © Paul Paladin/Alamy

MANAGEMENT FOCUS

Hedging in the Canadian Gold Producers' World

Barrick is the largest producer of gold in the world. Its operations, which include mines and exploration and development projects, are found on four continents.

In a field where many mining companies are small, operating one or two mines or exploring for one or two new mines, Barrick is certainly the leader. It is worth almost $30 billion (CAD$), meaning that it is worth more than such household names as Canadian Tire or Air Canada.

Gold has been a store of value for centuries.
© Image Source/Alamy

Barrick drew headlines around the world in 2009 when it announced that it would stop its gold hedging program. Gold had been rising for the previous few years, and Barrick did not participate in this price movement. Therefore, in late 2009, Barrick's chief financial officer, Jamie Sokalsky, announced the end of the gold hedging program, at a time when gold had risen to about $1000 an ounce. "We made this decision to gain full leverage to the gold price on all future production, based on an increasingly positive outlook for gold," he said. "By eliminating the gold hedge book, the company will participate in future gold price movements." And Barrick was not alone. Other gold producers such as Newmont Mining Corp. and AngloGold Ashanti Ltd. also announced ending their gold hedging programs.

Gold did continue to rise, though it did not quadruple in price as it had during Barrick's hedging program. But the company did not seem to benefit greatly from this movement. Commenting a year after Barrick stopped its hedging, John Daly in *The Globe and Mail* noted that when the company eliminated its hedging program, its shares were about $42. A year later they had increased by 5 percent. However, over that same period, gold increased about 20 percent, from $1000 an ounce to almost $1200 an ounce. While economic theory says that gold producers' shares should rise at least in the same proportion as the underlying metal, this did not happen. The worldwide economic problems in 2010 saw investors fleeing stocks, including gold producers, for safer investments, such as Treasury bills and gold itself. This led to deeply depressed stock prices felt around the globe.

Unfortunately, while Barrick did not participate fully in gold's rise, it has participated in the recent decline of gold prices. At the beginning of 2013, gold was about $1700 an ounce, and Barrick shares traded in the $35 a share range. By the end of the year, gold dropped to about $1350 an ounce, and Barrick's shares declined to the $20 range. Since then gold has declined further, and Barrick's shares have remained below the $25 range.

Interestingly, the decline in gold prices has lead some mining firms, including Barrick, to once again talk about hedging their gold holding, though this time it is to lock in current prices in the belief that gold may fall further in the future. Speaking in early 2014, the new Chairman John Thornton said, "As an outsider, I always thought it made great sense to hedge. I can't understand for the life of me why that wouldn't be an active topic that you would be carefully following at all times."

By 2016, hedging was almost becoming more acceptable in the gold industry. Canadian firm New Gold Inc. announced it was starting a hedging program in March 2016. A few days later mining company B2Gold Corp. announced it was starting to hedge, as were some other firms in Australia and Africa.

MANAGEMENT FOCUS *Continued*

Questions

1. Undertaking a hedging program is a management decision. Are company managers likely to undertake a program (such as hedging) once they have so publicly announced that they are scrapping it, even in the face of changing economic circumstances?

2. Hedging programs are not free (it is estimated that it cost Barrick over $5.6 billion to exit its hedges). When do you think a company should enter a currency or other commodity hedging program? What factors should a manager consider?

Sources: F. Freeman, "Gold," *Handbook of Canadian Security Analysis*, Volume 1 (Toronto: John Wiley, 1997); Kristine Owram, "Barrick Gold posts US 5.4 billion net loss on windup of gold hedging program", *The Canadian Press*, October 29, 2009; John Daly, "As Barrick tones up, investors fail to notice", *The Globe and Mail*, August 16, 2010; "Gold-Hedging Talk creeps in, but miners prefer exposure," *Moneybeat(blog)*, August 14, 2013; http://www.barrick.com/operations/default.aspx; https://www.bloomberg.com/news/articles/2013-12-05/barrick-s-thornton-weighs-return-to-gold-hedging; and http://business.financialpost.com/news/mining/once-reviled-gold-hedging-makes-an-unexpected-return

dollar against the U.S. dollar in the intervening period. Large Canadian companies normally have huge U.S. dollar reserves and thus do not always have to convert back to the "home currency"—the Canadian dollar.

Finally, **currency speculation** is another use of foreign exchange markets. Currency speculation typically involves the short-term movement of funds from one currency to another in the hope of profiting from shifts in exchange rates. Consider again the Canadian company with $10 million (US$) to invest for three months. Suppose the company suspects that the U.S. dollar will be overvalued against the Japanese yen. That is, it expects the U.S. dollar to depreciate (fall) against that of the yen. Imagine the current dollar/yen exchange rate is US$1 = ¥120. The company exchanges $10 million into yen receiving 1.2 billion yen ($10 million × 120 = 1.2 billion yen). Over the next three months, the value of the dollar depreciates against the yen until $1 = ¥100. Now the company exchanges its 1.2 billion yen back into dollars and finds that it has $12 million. The company has made a $2 million profit on currency speculation in three months on an initial investment of $10 million. However, currency speculation does not always yield gains. Had the currencies moved in the other direction in this example, then the Canadian company could have lost $2 million (US$).

ANOTHER PERSPECTIVE

Key into Exchange Rate Language

The language used to describe exchange rates can be confusing, even though the ideas themselves are simple. Here's why: any given observation describes a changing relationship (the movement in the currencies) that itself describes two relationships (the exchange rates for both currencies). The important thing to remember is that an exchange rate is described in terms of other exchange rates.

The language we use to describe these moving phenomena works in a similar, dual way: the euro gains against the dollar, so the euro is strengthening, or becoming dearer, from a dollar perspective. Meanwhile, the same observation indicates its mirror image, that the dollar is weakening, becoming cheaper against the euro, from a euro perspective.

The World and the Canadian Dollar

As for the Canadian dollar, the reality is that it is a secondary currency.[2] However, it is increasingly being recognized as a "petrocurrency."[3] That is, Canadian currency is linked to the raw materials, including oil and natural gas, that Canada exports. Thus, the movements of the Canadian dollar have become increasingly correlated with price of oil. As a result, the Canadian dollar is not immune to speculation as it does rise and fall. Money market traders will take advantage of such moves irrespective of the nationality of the currency, but more people around the world relate to the U.S. dollar, Swiss franc, yen, pound sterling, and euro, than to the Canadian dollar. Canadian businesses normally all but forget about using the Canadian dollar in most international business deals. Commercial payments usually occur in universally accepted U.S. dollars. Although less frequent than U.S. dollar international payments, yen, euros, and Swiss francs are also used. When doing business abroad, smaller Canadian companies likely will settle in U.S. dollars, but only on a transaction per transaction basis. Large Canadian companies operate internationally through established U.S. dollar accounts or other major currency accounts, and are less concerned about the Canadian dollar and its fluctuations than small Canadian businesses. Although larger firms may have to make an initial one-time currency conversion from Canadian dollars into U.S. dollars or other major currency accounts, once done, the state of the Canadian dollar is of little or no concern to the execution of foreign business transactions.

However, small Canadian businesses can be highly susceptible to exchange rate fluctuations when exporting to the United States and fear that a rise in the Canadian dollar will increase the cost to the U.S. consumer and damage export-related profits. If an American were to purchase a Canadian product for $100 (CAD$) in a mid-June 2008, exchange rate of 1.02296 (CAD$ = US$0.98), the product would cost the American US$97.76.[4] If the Canadian dollar were to fall to $1.00 (US$) then the American would purchase the same product at parity for $100.00 (US$). Such a move could stand to erode Canadian exports to the United States and increase the unemployment rate in Canada.

However, many Canadian business people do not buy into this storyline that plays with the idea that an increasing value of Canadian dollar results in lost exports, which results in lost jobs. During the twentieth century, before the onset of the euro, several countries had very expensive currencies, such as Germany with the deutschmark. Yet, in spite of the highly unfavourable German deutschmark exchange rate, which made the acquisition of German products very expensive in relation to similar domestic products in other countries, the Germans still managed to capture huge market share of the automobile market, heavy machinery market, and so on.

This German success was achieved through efficient manufacturing processes, the execution of aggressive international sales and marketing strategies, and continuous quality improvement practices that made and make foreign buyers flock to German products. Quality and an understanding of the needs of foreign buyers all but cancelled out unfavourable deutschemark foreign exchange rate concerns. German manufacturers were not oblivious to the risk of losing business due to high exchange rates. They worked with that knowledge and created a competitive advantage through higher-quality products than those of other foreign companies competing for the same market share.

Insuring Against Foreign Exchange Risk

A second function of the foreign exchange market is to provide insurance to protect against the possible adverse consequences of unpredictable changes in exchange rates (foreign exchange risk). To explain how the market performs this function, we must first distinguish among spot exchange rates, forward exchange rates, and currency swaps.

SPOT EXCHANGE RATES

When two parties agree to exchange currency and execute the deal immediately, the transaction is referred to as a spot exchange. Exchange rates governing such "on the spot" trades are referred to as *spot exchange rates*. The **spot exchange rate** is the rate at which a foreign exchange dealer converts one currency into another currency on a particular day. Thus, when our Canadian tourist in Glasgow goes to a bank to convert her Canadian dollars into pounds, the exchange rate is the spot rate for that day.

Spot exchange rates are reported on a real-time basis on many financial Web sites. An exchange rate can be quoted in two ways: as the amount of foreign currency one U.S. dollar will buy or as the value of a dollar for one unit of foreign currency. Thus, at the end of 2013, one U.S. dollar bought about €0.74, and one euro bought about $1.35 U.S. dollars. The first of these exchange rate quotations (dollar per foreign currency) is said to be in *direct* (or American) terms, the second (foreign currency units per dollar) in *indirect* terms.

Spot rates change continually, often on a day-by-day basis (although the magnitude of the changes over such short time periods is small). The value of a currency is determined by the interaction between the demand and supply of that currency relative to the demand and supply of other currencies. For example, if lots of people want U.S. dollars and dollars are in short supply, and few people want British pounds and pounds are in plentiful supply, the spot exchange rate for converting dollars into pounds will change. The dollar is likely to appreciate against the pound (or, conversely, the pound will depreciate against the dollar). Imagine the spot exchange rate is £1 = US$1.60 when the market opens. As the day progresses, dealers demand more dollars and fewer pounds. By the end of the day, the spot exchange rate might be £1 = US$1.58. The dollar has appreciated, and the pound has depreciated.

FORWARD EXCHANGE RATES

The fact that spot exchange rates change continually as determined by the relative demand and supply for different currencies can be problematic for an international business. A large Canadian company with an active U.S. dollar account that imports laptop computers from Japan knows that in 30 days it must pay yen to a Japanese supplier when a shipment arrives. The company will pay the Japanese supplier 200,000 yen for each laptop computer, and the current dollar/yen exchange rate is $1 = ¥99.00. At this rate, each computer costs the importer $2020.20 (i.e., 200,000 yen/99). The importer knows she can sell the computers the day they arrive for $2200.00 each, which yields a gross profit of $179.80 on each computer ($2200.00 − $2020.20). However, the importer will not have the funds to pay the Japanese supplier until the computers have been sold. If over the next 30 days the dollar unexpectedly depreciates again the yen, say to $1 = ¥90, the importer will still have to pay the Japanese company ¥200,000 per computer, but in dollar terms that would be equivalent to $2222.22 per computer, which is more than she can sell the computers for. A depreciation in the value of the dollar against the yen from $1 = ¥99.00 to $1 = ¥90.00 would transform a profitable deal into an unprofitable one.

To avoid this risk, the Canadian importer might want to engage in a forward exchange in U.S. dollars. A **forward exchange** occurs when two parties agree to exchange currency and execute the deal at some specific date in the future. Exchange rates governing such future transactions are referred to as **forward exchange rates**. For most major currencies, forward exchange rates are quoted for 30 days, 90 days, and 180 days into the future. Returning to our computer importer example, let us assume the 30-day forward exchange rate for converting dollars into yen is $1 = ¥95.00. The importer enters into a 30-day forward exchange transaction with a foreign exchange dealer at this rate and is guaranteed that she will have to pay no more than $2105.26 for each computer (2105.26 = 200,000/95.0). This guarantees her a profit of $94.74 per computer ($2200.00 − $2105.26). She also insures herself against the possibility that an unanticipated change in the dollar/yen exchange rate will turn a profitable deal into an unprofitable one. In this example, the spot exchange rate ($1 = ¥99) and the 30-day forward one ($1 = ¥95) differ. Such differences are normal; they reflect the expectations of the foreign exchange market about future currency movements. In our example, the fact that $1 bought more yen with a spot exchange than with a 30-day forward exchange indicates foreign exchange dealers expected the dollar to depreciate against the yen in the next 30 days. When this occurs, we say the dollar is selling at a *discount* on the 30-day forward market (i.e., it is worth less than on the spot market). Of course, the opposite can also occur. If the 30-day forward exchange rate were $1 = ¥103.30, for example, $1 would buy more yen with a forward exchange than with a spot exchange. In such a case, we say the dollar is selling at a *premium* on the 30-day forward market. This reflects the foreign exchange dealers' expectations that the dollar will appreciate against the yen over the next 30 days.

DEBATE THE ISSUE

Should Currency Speculation Be Allowed?

Currency speculation involves the short-term movement of funds from one currency to another in the hopes of profiting from shifts in exchange rates. Sometimes this speculation is done as what is called a carry trade. This involves borrowing in one currency where interest rates are low and then using the proceeds to invest in another currency where interest rates are high. In effect, it can be argued that currency speculation tactics may have a strong negative effect on some countries' economic foundation (e.g., Iceland, Thailand). For years, Iceland was a respected country for its unmatchable standards of living. The 2008 economic turmoil threw the island nation's currency off the cliff. The hedge funds closed in, and the government had to try to fight off the predators. Several years later, Iceland is still feeling the effect of these currency woes, albeit the country is now in recovery mode and progressing in a positive direction. But, the issue remains that large-scale currency speculation has the potential to adversely affect global markets. So, should currency speculation be allowed?

Source: A. Jung and C. Pauly, "Currency Woes: Crashing the Party of Icelandic Prosperity," *Spiegel Online International*, April 10, 2008.

CURRENCY SWAPS

The above discussion of spot and forward exchange rates might lead you to conclude that the option to buy forward is very important to companies engaged in international trade—and you would be right. Forward transactions account for about two-thirds of all foreign exchange transactions, with spot exchanges accounting for about one-third. However, the vast majority of these forward exchanges are not forward exchanges of the type we have been discussing, but rather a more sophisticated instrument known as currency swap.

A **currency swap** is the simultaneous purchase and sale of a given amount of foreign exchange for two different value dates. Swaps are transacted between international businesses and their banks, between banks, and between governments when it is desirable to move out of one currency into another for a limited period without incurring foreign exchange risk. A common kind of swap is spot against forward. Consider a company such as Apple Computer. Apple assembles laptop computers in the United States, but the screens are made in Japan. Apple also sells some of the finished laptops in Japan. So, like many companies, Apple both buys from and sells to Japan. Imagine Apple needs to change US$1 million into yen to pay its supplier of laptop screens today. Apple knows that in 90 days it will be paid ¥99,000,000 by the Japanese importer that buys its finished laptops. It will want to convert these yen into dollars for use in the United States. Let us say today's spot exchange rate $1 = ¥99.00 and the 90-day forward exchange rate $1 = ¥90.00. Apple sells $1 million to its bank in return for ¥99.00 million. Now Apple can pay its Japanese supplier. At the same time, Apple enters into a 90-day forward exchange deal with its bank for converting ¥99 million into dollars. Thus, in 90 days Apple will receive $1,100,000 (¥99,000,000/90 = $1,100,000). Since the yen is trading at a premium on the 90-day forward market, Apple ends up with more dollars than it started with (although the opposite could also occur). The swap deal is just like a conventional forward deal in one important respect: it enables Apple to insure itself against foreign exchange risk. By engaging in a swap, Apple knows today that the ¥99.00 million payment it will receive in 90 days will yield $1.1 million.

LO2 | The Nature of the Foreign Exchange Market

So far we have dealt with the foreign exchange market only as an abstract concept. It is now time to take a closer look at the nature of this market. The foreign exchange market is not located in any one place. It is a global network of banks, brokers, and foreign exchange dealers connected by electronic communications systems. When companies wish to convert currencies, they typically go through their own banks rather than entering the market directly. The foreign exchange market has been growing at a rapid pace, reflecting a general growth in the volume of cross-border trade and investment (see Chapter 1). Current estimates for the average total value of foreign exchange trading is over $1.5 trillion per day.[5] The world's key money trading centres are London, New York, Tokyo, and Singapore. Major secondary trading centres include Zurich, Frankfurt, Paris, Hong Kong, San Francisco, and Sydney. Much to the dismay of pundits' claim of Toronto's status as a world-class city, Toronto does not figure on the map as a second-tier global financial city.

As seen earlier in this chapter, the Canadian dollar is not widely used in cross-border trade, investment, and payments. In exchange-traded currencies, if an individual or a company wants to trade large quantities of the Canadian dollar, they cannot even do this within Canada. Instead, they would have to trade it through the Chicago Mercantile Exchange located in Chicago but accessed by computers from any point in the world. London's dominance in the foreign exchange market is due to both history and geography. As the capital of the world's first major industrial trading nation, London had become the world's largest centre for international banking by the end of the nineteenth century, a position it has retained. Today London's central position between Tokyo and Singapore to the east and New York to the west has made it the critical link between the East Asian and New York markets. Due to time zone

Even though the British pound has declined in importance as a vehicle currency, London remains the key location for global foreign exchange. © *Ingram Publishing*

differences, London opens soon after Tokyo closes for the night and is still open for the first few hours of trading in New York.

Two features of the foreign exchange market are of particular note. The first is that the market never sleeps. Tokyo, London, and New York are simultaneously closed for only 3 hours out of every 24. During these three hours, trading continues in a number of minor centres, particularly San Francisco and Sydney, Australia. The second feature of the market is the extent of integration of the various trading centres. High-speed computer links between trading centres around the globe have effectively created a single market. The integration of financial centres implies there can be no significant difference in exchange rates quoted in the trading centres. For example, if the yen/dollar exchange rate quoted in London at 3 P.M. is ¥99.00 = $1, the yen/dollar exchange rate quoted in New York at the same time (10 A.M. New York time) will be identical. If the New York yen/dollar exchange rate were ¥105 = $1, a dealer could make a profit through **arbitrage**, buying a currency low and selling it high. For example, if the prices differed in London and New York as given, a dealer in New York could take $1 million and use that to purchase ¥105 million. She could then immediately sell the ¥105 million for dollars in London, where the transaction would yield $1,060,606.61, allowing the trader to book a profit of $60,606.06 on the transaction. If all dealers tried to cash in on the opportunity, however, the demand for yen in New York would rise, resulting in an appreciation of the yen against the dollar such that the price differential between New York and London would quickly disappear. Since foreign exchange dealers are continually watching their computer screens for arbitrage opportunities, the few that arise tend to be small, and they disappear in minutes.

Another feature of the foreign exchange market is the important role played by the U.S. dollar. Although a foreign exchange transaction can, in theory, involve any two currencies, most transactions involve U.S. dollars on one side. This is true even when a dealer wants to sell one non-dollar currency and buy another. A dealer wishing to sell the Korean won for Canadian dollars, for example, will usually sell the won for U.S. dollars, and then use the U.S. dollars to buy the Canadian dollars. Although this may seem a roundabout way of doing things, it is actually cheaper than trying to find a holder of Canadian dollars who wants to buy won. Because the volume of international transactions involving U.S. dollars is so great, it is not hard to find dealers who wish to trade U.S. dollars for won or Canadian dollars.

Due to its central role in so many foreign exchange deals, the U.S. dollar is a vehicle currency. After the dollar, the most important vehicle currencies are the euro and the British pound—reflecting the importance of these trading entities in the world economy. Since the implementation of the euro, it has replaced the German mark as the world's second most important vehicle currency. The British pound used to be second in importance to the dollar as a vehicle currency, but its importance has diminished in recent years. Despite this, London still retains its leading position in the global foreign exchange market.

ANOTHER PERSPECTIVE

The Chinese Yuan In Toronto?

Given China's importance in international trade, it is very likely that the role of the yuan will continue to expand in the foreign exchange market. A study from the Brookings Institution suggests that in the long run, the ascendance of the yuan to reserve-currency standing is likely. A so-called reserve currency is a currency that is held in significant quantities by governments and institutions as a part of their foreign exchange reserves and that is commonly used in international financial transactions. China is the only country whose currency does not have reserve status. Getting there will require overcoming two main challenges. First, it will take exchange rate flexibility and financial market development to improve the cost–benefit trade-off of the yuan. Second, it will take strengthening the Chinese banking system.

Perhaps the first step was taken by Prime Minister Stephen Harper in late 2014 who announced an agreement with China to establish Canada as the first trading hub in the Americas for the yuan. In this way Canadian companies would be able to deal directly with Chinese companies in their own currency, making it easier and less expensive for everybody to do business. Toronto, as the financial centre of Canada, has been positioning itself through 2015–2017 to become Canada's hub for Chinese currency transactions.

Source: P. da Costa, "China renminbi as reserve currency: yuan a bet?" *Reuters*, February 8, 2012, http://blogs.reuters.com/macroscope/2012/02/08/china-renminbi-as-reserve-currency-yuan-a-bet/; J. Ecker, "Yuan trading-hub status a major win for Canada," *The Globe and Mail*, Nov. 11, 2014, http://www.theglobeandmail.com/report-on-business/international-business/yuan-trading-hub-status-a-major-win-for-canada/article21541747/; Toronto Financial Service Alliance, http://www.tfsa.ca/renminbi/faqs/

LO3 Economic Theories of Exchange Rate Determination

At the most basic level, exchange rates are determined by the demand and supply of one currency relative to the demand and supply of another. For example, if the demand for dollars outstrips the supply of them and if the supply of Japanese yen is greater than the demand for them, the dollar/yen exchange rate will change. The dollar will appreciate against the yen (or the yen will depreciate against the dollar). However, differences in relative demand and supply explain the determination of exchange rates only in a superficial sense. This simple explanation does not tell us what factors underlie the demand for and supply of a currency. Nor does it tell us when the demand for dollars will exceed the supply (and vice versa) or when the supply of Japanese yen will exceed demand for them (and vice versa). Neither does it tell us under what conditions a currency is in demand or under what conditions it is not demanded. In this section, we will review economic theory's answers to these questions. This will give us a deeper understanding of how exchange rates are determined.

If we understand how exchange rates are determined, we may be able to forecast exchange rate movements. Since future exchange rate movements influence export opportunities, the profitability of international trade and investment deals, and the price competitiveness of foreign imports, this is valuable information for an international business. Unfortunately, there is no simple explanation. The forces that determine exchange rates are complex, and no theoretical consensus exists, even among academic economists who study the phenomenon every day. Nonetheless, most economic theories of exchange rate movements seem to agree that three factors have an important impact on future exchange rate movements in a country's currency: the country's price inflation, its interest rate, and market psychology.[6]

Prices and Exchange Rates

To understand how prices are related to exchange rate movements, we first need to discuss an economic proposition known as the law of one price. Then we will discuss the theory of purchasing power parity (PPP), which links changes in the exchange rate between two countries' currencies to changes in the countries' price levels.

THE LAW OF ONE PRICE

The **law of one price** states that in competitive markets free of transportation costs and barriers to trade (such as tariffs), identical products sold in different countries must sell for the same price when their price is expressed in terms of the same currency.[7] For example, if the exchange rate between the British pound and the U.S. dollar is £1 = US$2.00, a jacket that retails for $75 (US$) in New York should sell for £35 in London (since $75/2.00 = £35). Consider what would happen if the jacket cost £30 in London ($60 in U.S. currency). At this price, it would pay a trader to buy jackets in London and sell them in New York (an example of arbitrage). The company initially could make a profit of $15 on each jacket by purchasing it for £30 ($60) in London and selling it for $75 in New York (we are assuming away transportation costs and trade barriers). However, the increased demand for jackets in London would raise their price in London, and the increased supply of jackets in New York would lower their price there. This would continue until prices were equalized. Thus, prices might equalize when the jacket cost £44 ($88) in London and $88 in New York (assuming no change in the exchange rate of £1 = US$2.00).

ANOTHER PERSPECTIVE

The Internet and the Law of One Price

The law of one price applies to Internet buying across national borders because Internet research can provide accurate pricing information across markets. Many Americans are trying to invoke the law of one price with pharmaceuticals, which, they have discovered, sell at lower costs in Canada than in the United States. There are several barriers, though—transportation costs and a U.S. law, designed to protect U.S. consumers, that forbids the import of pharmaceuticals. As these barriers fall, we should see the law of one price force down U.S. prescription drug costs. Similarly, this cost has been offset by the rise of the Canadian dollar, relative to the U.S. dollar.

PURCHASING POWER PARITY

If the law of one price were true for all goods and services, the purchasing power parity (PPP) exchange rate could be found from any individual set of prices. By comparing the prices of identical products in different currencies, it would be possible to determine the "real" or PPP exchange rate that would exist if markets were efficient. (An **efficient market** has no impediments to the free flow of goods and services, such as trade barriers.)

A less extreme version of the PPP theory states that given **relatively efficient markets**—that is, markets in which few impediments to international trade exist—the price of a "basket of goods" should be roughly equivalent in each country. To express the PPP theory in symbols, let $P_{\$}$ be the U.S. dollar price of a basket of particular goods and $P_{¥}$ be the price of the same basket of goods in Japanese yen. The PPP theory predicts that the dollar/yen exchange rate, $E_{\$/¥}$, should be equivalent to:

$$E_{\$/¥} = P_{\$}/P_{¥}$$

Thus, if a basket of goods costs $200 in the United States and ¥20,000 in Japan, PPP theory predicts that the dollar/yen exchange rate should be US$200/¥20,000 or $0.01 per Japanese yen (i.e., US$1 = ¥100).

The next step in the PPP theory is to argue that the exchange rate will change if relative prices change. For example, imagine there is no price inflation in the United States, while prices in Japan are increasing by 10 percent a year. At the beginning of the year, a basket of goods costs $200 in the United States and ¥16,666, so the dollar/yen exchange rate, according to PPP theory, should be US$1 = ¥83.33. At the end of the year, the basket still costs $200 in the United States but it costs ¥18,332 in Japan. PPP theory predicts that the exchange rate should change as a result. More precisely, by the end of the year:

$$E_{\$/¥} = US\$200/¥18,332$$

Thus, ¥1 = US$0.0109098 (or US$1 = ¥91.66). Because of 10 percent price inflation, the Japanese yen as depreciated by 10 percent against the dollar. One U.S. dollar will by 10 percent more yen at the end of the year than at the beginning.

MONEY SUPPLY AND PRICE INFLATION

In essence, PPP theory predicts that changes in relative prices will result in a change in exchange rates. Theoretically, a country in which price inflation is running wild should expect to see its currency depreciate against that of countries in which inflation rates are lower. If we can predict what a country's future inflation rate is likely to be, we can also predict how the value of its currency relative to other currencies—its exchange rate—is likely to change. The growth rate of a country's money supply determines its likely future inflation rate.[8] Thus, in theory at least, we can use information about the growth in money supply to forecast exchange rate movements.

Inflation is a monetary phenomenon. It occurs when the quantity of money in circulation rises faster than the stock of goods and services; that is, when the money supply increases faster than output increases. Imagine what would happen if everyone in the country was suddenly given $10,000 by the government. Many people would rush out to spend their extra money on those things they had always wanted—new cars, new furniture, better clothes, and so on. There would be a surge in demand for goods and services. Car dealers, department stores, and other providers of goods and services would respond to this upsurge in demand by raising prices. The result would be price inflation.

A government increasing the money supply is analogous to giving people more money. An increase in the money supply makes it easier for banks to borrow from the government and for individuals and companies to borrow from banks. The resulting increase in credit causes increases in demand for goods and services. Unless the output of goods and services is growing at a rate similar to that of the money supply, the result will be inflation. This relationship has been observed time after time in country after country.

So now we have a connection between the growth in a country's money supply, price inflation, and exchange rate movements. Put simply, when the growth in a country's money supply is faster than the growth in its output, price inflation is fuelled.

TABLE 9.1	Macroeconomic Data for Bolivia, April 1984–October 1985		
Month	Money Supply (Billions of Pesos)	Price Level Relative to 1982 (Average = 1)	Exchange Rate (Pesos Per Dollar)
1984			
April	270	21.1	3576
May	330	31.1	3512
June	440	32.3	3342
July	599	34.0	3570
August	718	39.1	7038
September	889	53.7	13,685
October	1194	85.5	15,205
November	1495	112.4	18,469
December	3296	180.9	24,515
1985			
January	4630	305.3	73,016
February	6455	863.3	141,101
March	9089	1078.6	128,137
April	12,885	1205.7	167,428
May	21,309	1635.7	272,375
June	27,778	2919.1	481,756
July	47,341	4854.6	885,476
August	74,306	8081.0	1,182,300
September	103,272	12,647.6	1,087,440
October	132,550	12,411.8	1,120,210

Source: From Juan-Antino Morales, "Inflation Stabilization in Bolivia," in *Inflation Stabilization: The Experience of Israel, Argentina, Brazil, Bolivia, and Mexico*, ed. Michael Bruno et al. (Cambridge, MA: MIT Press, 1998).

The PPP theory tells us that a country with a high inflation rate will see a depreciation in its currency exchange rate. In one of the clearest historical examples, in the mid-1980s, Bolivia experienced hyperinflation—an explosive and seemingly uncontrollable price inflation in which money loses value very rapidly. Table 9.1 presents data on Bolivia's money supply, inflation rate, and its peso's exchange rate with the U.S. dollar during the period of hyperinflation. The exchange rate is actually the "black market" exchange rate; the Bolivian government prohibited converting the peso to other currencies during the period. The data show that the growth in money supply, the rate of price inflation, and the depreciation of the peso against the dollar all moved in step with each other. This is just what PPP theory and monetary economics predict. Between April 1984 and July 1985, Bolivia's money supply increased by 17 433 percent, prices increased by 22 908 percent, and the value of the peso against the U.S. dollar fell by 24 662 percent. In October 1985, the Bolivian government instituted a dramatic stabilization plan—which included the introduction of a new currency and tight control of the money supply—and by 1987 the country's annual inflation rate was down to 16 percent.[9]

Another way of looking at the same phenomenon is that an increase in a country's money supply, which increases the amount of currency available, changes the relative demand and supply conditions in the foreign exchange market. If the U.S. money supply is growing more rapidly than U.S. output, dollars will be relatively more plentiful than the currencies of countries where monetary growth is closer to output growth. As a result of this relative increase in the supply of dollars, the dollar will depreciate on the foreign exchange market against the currencies of countries with slower monetary growth.

Government policy determines whether the rate of growth in a country's money supply is greater than the rate of growth in output. A government can increase the money supply simply by telling the country's central bank to print more money. Governments tend to do this to finance public expenditure (building roads, paying government workers, paying for defence, etc.). A government could finance public expenditure by raising taxes, but because nobody likes paying more taxes and politicians do not like to be unpopular, they have a natural preference for printing money. Unfortunately, there is no magic money tree. The inevitable result of excessive growth in money supply is price inflation. However, this has not stopped governments around the world from printing money, with predictable results. If an international business is attempting to predict future movements in the value of a country's currency on the foreign exchange market, it should examine that country's policy toward monetary growth. If the government seems committed to controlling the rate of growth in money supply, the country's future inflation rate may be low (even if the current rate is high) and its currency should not depreciate too much on the foreign exchange market. If the government seems to lack the political will to control the rate of growth in money supply, the future inflation rate may be high, which is likely to cause its currency to depreciate. Historically, many Latin American governments have fallen into this latter category, including Argentina, Bolivia, and Brazil. More recently, many of the newly democratic states of Eastern Europe made the same mistake.

EMPIRICAL TESTS OF PPP THEORY

PPP theory predicts that exchange rates are determined by relative prices, and that changes in relative prices will result in a change in exchange rates. A country in which price inflation is running wild should expect to see its currency depreciate against that of countries with lower inflation rates. This is intuitively appealing, but is it true? There are several good examples of the connection between a country's price inflation and exchange rate position (such as Bolivia). However, extensive empirical testing of PPP theory has yielded mixed results.[10] While PPP theory seems to yield relatively accurate predictions in the long run, it does not appear to be a strong predictor of short-run movements in exchange rates covering time spans of five years or less.[11] In addition, the theory seems to best predict exchange rate changes for countries with high rates of inflation and underdeveloped capital markets. The theory is less useful for predicting short-term exchange rate movements between the currencies of advanced industrialized nations that have relatively small differentials in inflation rates.

The failure to find a strong link between relative inflation rates and exchange rate movements has been referred to as the purchasing power parity puzzle. Several factors may explain the failure of PPP theory to predict exchange rates more accurately.[12] PPP theory assumes away transportation costs and barriers to trade. In practice, these factors are significant and they tend to create significant price differentials between countries. Transportation costs are certainly not trivial for many goods. Moreover, as we saw in Chapter 6, governments routinely intervene in international trade, creating tariff and nontariff barriers to cross-border trade. Barriers to trade limit the ability of traders to use arbitrage to equalize prices for the same product in different countries, which is required for the law of one price to hold. Government intervention in cross-border trade, by violating the assumption of efficient markets, weakens the link between relative price changes and changes in exchange rates predicted by PPP theory.

In addition, the PPP theory may not hold if many national markets are dominated by a handful of multinational enterprises that have sufficient market power to influence prices, control distribution channels, and differentiate their product offerings between nations.[13] In fact, this situation seems to prevail in a number of industries. In the detergent industry, two companies, Procter & Gamble and Unilever, dominate the market in nation after nation. Applied Materials Inc. is still the leader in the semiconductor equipment.[14] Apple Inc. is the largest technology company in the world.[15] In such cases, dominant enterprises may be able to exercise a degree of pricing power, setting different prices in different markets to reflect varying demand conditions. This is referred to as price discrimination (we consider the topic from a strategic perspective in Chapter 14).

For price discrimination to work, arbitrage must be limited. According to this argument, enterprises with some market power may be able to control distribution channels and therefore limit the unauthorized resale (arbitrage) of products purchased in another national market. They may also be able to limit resale (arbitrage) by differentiating otherwise identical products among nations along some line, such as design or packaging. For example, even though the version of Microsoft Office sold in China may be less expensive than the version sold in the United States, the use of arbitrage to equalize prices may be limited because few Americans would want a version that was based on Chinese characters. The design differentiation between Microsoft Office for China and for the United States means that the law of one price would not work for Microsoft Office, even if transportation costs were trivial and tariff barriers between the United States and China did not exist. If the inability to practice arbitrage were widespread enough, it would break the connection between changes in relative prices and exchange rates predicted by the PPP theorem and help explain the limited empirical support for this theory.

Another factor of some importance is that governments also intervene in the foreign exchange market to attempt to influence the value of their currencies. We will look at why and how they do this in Chapter 10. For now, the important thing to note is that governments regularly intervene in the foreign exchange market, and this further weakens the link between price changes and changes in exchange rates. One more factor explaining the failure of PPP theory to predict short-term movements in foreign exchange rates is the impact of investor psychology and other factors on currency purchasing decisions and exchange rate movements. We will discuss this issue in more detail later in this chapter.

Interest Rates and Exchange Rates

Economic theory tells us that interest rates reflect expectations about likely future inflation rates. In countries where inflation is expected to be high, interest rates also will be high, because investors want compensation for the decline in the value of their money. This relationship was first formalized by economist Irvin Fisher and is referred to as the Fisher Effect. The Fisher Effect states that a country's "nominal" interest rate (i) is the sum of the required "real" rate of interest (r) and the expected rate of inflation over the period for which the funds are to be lent (I). More formally,

$$i = r + I$$

For example, if the real rate of interest in a country is 5 percent and annual inflation is expected to be 10 percent, the nominal interest rate will be 15 percent. As predicted by the Fisher Effect, a strong relationship seems to exist between inflation rates and interest rates.[16]

We can take this one step further and consider how it applies in a world of many countries and unrestricted capital flows. When investors are free to transfer capital between countries, real interest rates will be the same in every country. If differences in real interest rates did emerge between countries, arbitrage would soon equalize them. For example, if the real interest rate in Canada was 10 percent and only 6 percent in the United States, it would pay investors to borrow money in the United States and invest it in Canada. The resulting increase in the demand for money in the United States would raise the real interest rate there, while the increase in the supply of foreign money in Canada would lower the real interest rate there. This would continue until the two sets of real interest rates were equalized. (In practice, differences in real interest rates may persist due to government controls on capital flows; investors are not always free to transfer capital between countries.)

It follows from the Fisher Effect that if the real interest rate is the same worldwide, any difference in interest rates between countries reflects differing expectations about inflation rates. Thus, if the expected rate of inflation in the United States is greater than that in Canada, U.S. nominal interest rates will be greater than Canadian nominal interest rates.

Since we know from PPP theory that there is a link (in theory at least) between inflation and exchange rates, and since interest rates reflect expectations about inflation, it follows that there must also be a link between interest rates and exchange rates. This link is known as the **International Fisher Effect** (IFE). The International Fisher Effect states that for any two countries, the spot exchange rate should change in an equal amount but in the opposite direction to the difference in nominal interest rates between the two countries. The change in the spot exchange rate between the United States and Canada, for example, can be modelled as follows:

$$(S_1 - S_2)/S_2 \times 100 \times i_\$ - i_{CAD}$$

where $i_\$$ and i_{CAD} are the respective nominal interest rates in the United States and Canada, S_1 is the spot exchange rate at the beginning of the period, and S_2 is the spot exchange rate at the end of the period. If the U.S. nominal interest rate is higher than Canada's, reflecting greater expected inflation rates, the value of the U.S. dollar against the Canadian dollar should fall by that interest rate differential in the future. So if the interest rate in the United States is 10 percent and in Canada it is 6 percent, we would expect the value of the U.S. dollar to depreciate by 4 percent against the Canadian dollar.

Do interest rate differentials help predict future currency movements? The evidence is mixed; as in the case of PPP theory, in the long run, there seems to be a relationship between interest rate differentials and subsequent changes in spot exchange rates. However, considerable short-run deviations occur. Like PPP, the International Fisher Effect is not a good predictor of short-run changes in spot exchange rates.[17]

Investor Psychology and Bandwagon Effects

Empirical evidence suggests that neither PPP theory nor the International Fisher Effect are particularly good at explaining short-term movements in exchange rates. One reason may be the impact of investor psychology on short-run exchange rate

COUNTRY FOCUS

Quantitative Easing, Inflation, and the Value of the U.S. Dollar

In the fall of 2010, the U.S. Federal Reserve decided to expand the U.S. money supply by entering the open market and purchasing $600 billion in U.S. government bonds from bondholders, a technique known as *quantitative easing*. Where did the $600 billion come from? The Fed simply created new bank reserves and used this cash to pay for the bonds. It had, in effect, printed money. The Fed took this action in an attempt to stimulate the U.S. economy, which, in the aftermath of the 2008–09 global financial crisis, was struggling with low economic growth and high unemployment rates. The Fed had already tried to stimulate the economy by lowering short-term interest rates, but these were already close to zero, so it decided to lower medium- to longer-term rates; its tool for doing this was to pump $600 billion into the economy, increasing the supply of money and lowering its price, the interest rate.

Critics were quick to attack the Fed's moves. Many claimed that the policy of expanding the money supply would fuel inflation and lead to a decline in the value of the U.S. dollar on the foreign exchange market. Some even called the policy a deliberate attempt by the Fed to debase the value of the U.S. currency, thereby driving down its value and promoting U.S. exports, which if true would be a form of mercantilism.

On closer inspection, however, these charges seem to be unfounded, for two reasons. First, at the time, the core U.S. inflation rate was the lowest in 50 years. In fact, the Fed actually feared the risk of deflation (a persistent fall in prices), which is a very damaging phenomenon. When prices are falling, people hold off their purchases because they know that goods will be cheaper tomorrow than they are today. This can result in a collapse in aggregate demand and high unemployment. The Fed felt that a little inflation—say, 2 percent per year—might be a good thing. Second, U.S. economic growth had been weak, unemployment was high, and there was excess productive capacity in the economy. Consequently, if the injection of money into the economy did stimulate demand, this would not translate into price inflation, because the first response of businesses would be to expand output to utilize their excess capacity. Defenders of the Fed argued that the important point, which the critics seemed to be missing, was that expanding the money supply only leads to higher price inflation when unemployment is relatively low and there is not much excess capacity in the economy, a situation that did not exist in the fall of 2010. As for the currency market, its reaction was muted. At the beginning of November 2010, just before the Fed announced its policy, the index value of the dollar against a basket of other major currencies stood at 72.0623. In the following three years the dollar rose, mostly staying in a channel between 75 and 85 cents. In short, currency traders did not seem to be selling off the dollar or reflecting worries about high inflation rates.

Questions

1. Look at current online and printed newspapers and magazines to see what economists and analysts are saying about quantitative easing. When do they forecast this to end?
2. Canada, along with many other countries, has also followed the U.S. lead and undertaken its own program of quantitative easing. How is this different from what is described above?

Sources: P. Wallsten and S. Reddy, "Fed's Bond Buying Plan Ignites Growing Criticism," *The Wall Street Journal*, November 15, 2010; and S. Chan, "Under Attack, the Fed Defends Policy of Buying Bonds," *International Herald Tribune*, November 17, 2010.

movements. Increasing evidence reveals that psychological factors play an important role in determining the expectations of market traders as to likely future exchange rates.[18] In turn, expectations have a tendency to become self-fulfilling prophecies.

According to a number of studies, investor psychology and bandwagon effects play a major role in determining short-run exchange rate movements.[19] However, these effects can be hard to predict. Investor psychology can be influenced by political factors and by microeconomic events, such as the investment decisions of individual firms, many of which are only loosely linked to macroeconomic fundamentals, such as relative inflation rates. Also, bandwagon effects can be both triggered and exacerbated by the idiosyncratic behaviour of politicians. Something like this seems to have occurred in Southeast Asia during 1997 when one after another, the currencies of Thailand, Malaysia, South Korea, and Indonesia lost between 50 percent and 70 percent of their value against the U.S. dollar in a few months. The collapse in the value of the Korean currency did not occur because South Korea had a higher inflation rate than the United States. It occurred because of an excessive buildup of dollar-denominated debt among South Korean firms. By mid-1997, it was clear that these companies were having trouble servicing this debt. Foreign investors, fearing a wave of corporate bankruptcies, took their money out of the country, exchanging won for U.S. dollars. As this began to depress the exchange rate, currency traders jumped on the bandwagon and speculated against the won (selling it short).

Summary

Relative monetary growth, relative inflation rates, and nominal interest rate differentials are all moderately good predictors of long-run changes in exchange rates. They are poor predictors of short-run changes in exchange rates, however, perhaps because of the impact of psychological factors, investor expectations, and bandwagon effects on short-term currency movements. This information is useful for an international business. Insofar as the long-term profitability of foreign investments, export opportunities, and the price competitiveness of foreign imports are all influenced by long-term movements in exchange rates, international businesses would be advised to pay attention to countries' differing monetary growth, inflation, and interest rates. International businesses that engage in foreign exchange transactions on a day-to-day basis could benefit by knowing some predictors of short-term foreign exchange rate movements. Unfortunately, short-term exchange rate movements are difficult to predict.

LO4 | Exchange Rate Forecasting

A company's need to predict future exchange rate variations raises the issue of whether it is worthwhile for the company to invest in exchange rate forecasting services to aid decision making. Two schools of thought address this issue. The efficient market school argues that forward exchange rates do the best possible job of forecasting future spot exchange rates, and, therefore, investing in forecasting services would be a waste of money. The other school of thought, the inefficient market school, argues that companies can improve the foreign exchange market's estimate of future exchange rates (as contained in the forward rate) by investing in forecasting services. In other words, this school of thought does not believe the forward exchange rates are the best possible predictors of future spot exchange rates.

The Efficient Market School

Forward exchange rates represent market participants' collective predictions of likely spot exchange rates at specified future dates. If forward exchange rates are the best possible predictor of future spot rates, it would make no sense for companies to spend additional money trying to forecast short-run exchange rate movements. Many economists believe the foreign exchange market is efficient at setting forward rates.[20] An efficient market is one in which prices reflect all available public information. (If forward rates reflect all available information about likely future changes in exchange rates, there is no way a company can beat the market by investing in forecasting services.)

If the foreign exchange market is efficient, forward exchange rates should be unbiased predictors of future spot rates. This does not mean the predictions will be accurate in any specific situation. It means inaccuracies will not be consistently above or below future spot rates; they will be random. Many empirical tests have addressed the efficient market hypothesis. Although most of the early work seems to confirm the hypothesis (suggesting that companies should not waste their money on forecasting services), more recent studies have challenged it.[21] There is some evidence that forward rates are not unbiased predictors of future spot rates, and that more accurate predictions of future spot rates can be calculated from publicly available information.[22]

The Inefficient Market School

Citing evidence against the efficient market hypothesis, some economists believe the foreign exchange market is inefficient. An **inefficient market** is one in which prices do not reflect all available information. In an inefficient market, forward exchange rates will not be the best possible predictors of future spot exchange rates.

If this is true, it may be worthwhile for international businesses to invest in forecasting services (as many do). The belief is that professional exchange rate forecasts might provide better predictions of future spot rates than forward exchange rates do. However, the track record of professional forecasting services is not that good. An analysis of the forecasts of 12 major forecasting services between 1978 and 1982 concluded the forecasters in general did not provide better forecasts than the forward exchange rates.[23] Also, forecasting services did not predict the 1997 currency crisis that swept through Southeast Asia, nor did they predict the rise in the value of the U.S. dollar that occurred during late 2008, a period when the United States fell into a deep financial crisis that some thought would lead to a decline in the value of the dollar (it appears that the dollar rose because it was seen as a relatively safe currency in a time when many nations were experiencing economic trouble).

Approaches to Forecasting

Assuming the inefficient market school is correct that the foreign exchange market's estimate of future spot rates can be improved, on what basis should forecasts be prepared? Here again, there are two schools of thought. One adheres to fundamental analysis, while the other uses technical analysis.

FUNDAMENTAL ANALYSIS

Fundamental analysis draws on economic theory to construct sophisticated econometric models for predicting exchange rate movements. The variables contained in these models typically include those we have discussed, such as relative money supply growth rates, inflation rates, and interest rates. In addition, they may include variables related to balance-of-payments positions.

Running a deficit on a balance-of-payments current account (a country is importing more goods and services than it is exporting) creates pressures that result in the depreciation of the country's currency on the foreign exchange market.[24] (For background on the balance of payments, see Chapter 7.) Consider what might happen if the United States was running a persistent current account balance-of-payments deficit. Since the United States would be importing more than it was exporting, people in other countries would be increasing their holdings of U.S. dollars. If these people were willing to hold their dollars, the dollar's exchange rate would not be influenced. However, if these people converted their dollars into other currencies, the supply of dollars in the foreign exchange market would increase (as would demand for the other currencies). This shift in demand and supply would create pressures that could lead to the depreciation of the dollar against other currencies.

This argument hinges on whether people in other countries are willing to hold dollars, which in turn depends on such factors as U.S. interest rates, the return on holding other dollar-denominated assets such as stocks in U.S. companies, and, most importantly, inflation rates. So, in a sense, the balance-of-payments situation is not a fundamental predictor of future exchange rate movements. For example, between 1998 and 2001, the U.S. dollar appreciated against most major currencies despite a growing balance-of-payments deficit. Relatively high real interest rates in the United States, coupled with low inflation and a booming U.S. stock market that attracted inward investment from foreign capital, made the dollar very attractive to foreigners, so they did not convert their dollars into other currencies. On the contrary, they converted other currencies into dollars to invest in U.S. financial assets, such as bonds and stocks, because they believed they could earn a high return by doing so. Capital flows into the United States fuelled by foreigners who wanted to buy U.S. stocks and bonds kept the dollar strong despite the current account deficit. But what makes financial assets such as stocks and bonds attractive? The answer is prevailing interest rates and inflation rates, both of which affect underlying economic growth and the real return to holding U.S. financial assets. Given this, we are back to the argument that the fundamental determinants of exchange rates are monetary growth, inflation rates, and interest rates.

TECHNICAL ANALYSIS

Technical analysis uses price and volume data to determine past trends, which are expected to continue into the future. This approach does not rely on a consideration of economic fundamentals. Technical analysis is based on the premise that there are analyzable market trends and waves and that previous trends and waves can be used to predict future trends and waves. Since there is no theoretical rationale for this assumption of predictability, many economists compare technical analysis to fortune-telling. Despite this skepticism, technical analysis has gained favour in recent years.[25]

Currency Convertibility

Until this point, we have assumed that the currencies of various countries are freely convertible into other currencies. This assumption is invalid. Many countries restrict the ability of residents and nonresidents to convert the local currency into a foreign currency, making international trade and investment more difficult.

Convertibility and Government Policy

Due to government restrictions, a significant number of currencies are not freely convertible into other currencies. A country's currency is said to be **freely convertible** when the country's government allows both residents and nonresidents to purchase unlimited amounts of a foreign currency with it. A currency is said to be **externally convertible** when only nonresidents may convert it into a foreign currency without any limitations. A currency is **nonconvertible** when neither residents nor nonresidents are allowed to convert it into a foreign currency.

Free convertibility is the exception rather than the rule. Many countries restrict residents' ability to convert the domestic currency into a foreign currency (a policy of external convertibility). Restrictions range from the relatively minor (such as restricting the amount of foreign currency they may take with them out of the country on trips) to the major (such as restricting domestic businesses' ability to take foreign currency out of the country). External convertibility restrictions can limit domestic companies' ability to invest abroad, but they present few problems for foreign companies wishing to do business in that country. For example, even if the Japanese government tightly controlled the ability of its residents to convert the yen into U.S. dollars, all U.S. businesses with deposits in Japanese banks may at any time convert all their yen into dollars and take them out of the country. Thus, a U.S. company with a subsidiary in Japan is assured that it will be able to convert the profits from its Japanese operation into dollars and take them out of the country.

ANOTHER PERSPECTIVE

No Letup in Capital Flight Despite Ban

Billions of dollars are flying out of Pakistan through unofficial channels and the government and the State Bank of Pakistan seems to have failed to control the trend, as many politicians, officials, and money changers are allegedly involved in the illegality. There are a number of networks allegedly included in the illegitimate cross-border trade of foreign exchange, violating the relevant laws. More than one billion dollars in foreign exchange is being transferred to Dubai and some other countries per year through clandestine channels. Investors seem unwilling to invest in Pakistan and they have been transferring their assets and funds to foreign countries for the past decade.

Source: "No letup in capital flight despite ban," *The Nation*, July 23, 2011, www.nation.com.pk/pakistan-news-newspaper-daily-english-online/politics/23-Jul-2011/No-letup-in-capital-flight-despite-ban

---

Serious problems arise, however, under a policy of nonconvertibility. This was the practice of the former Soviet Union, and it continued to be the practice in Russia until 2006. When strictly applied, nonconvertibility means that although a U.S. company doing business in a country such as Russia may be able to generate significant ruble profits, it may not convert those rubles into dollars and take them out of the country. Obviously this is not desirable for international business.

Governments limit convertibility to preserve their foreign exchange reserves. A country needs an adequate supply of these reserves to service its international debt commitments and to purchase imports. Governments typically impose convertibility restrictions on their currency when they fear that free convertibility will lead to a run on their foreign exchange reserves. This occurs when residents and nonresidents rush to convert their holdings of domestic currency into a foreign currency—a phenomenon generally referred to as **capital flight**. Capital flight is most likely to occur when the value of the domestic currency is depreciating rapidly because of hyperinflation, or when a country's economic prospects are shaky in other respects. Under such circumstances, both residents and nonresidents tend to believe that their money is more likely to hold its value if it is converted into a foreign currency and invested abroad. Not only will a run on foreign exchange reserves limit the country's ability to service its international debt and pay for imports, but it will also lead to a precipitous depreciation in the exchange rate as residents and nonresidents unload their holdings of domestic currency on the foreign exchange markets (thereby increasing the market supply of the country's currency). Governments fear that the rise in import prices resulting from currency depreciation will lead to further increases in inflation. This fear provides another rationale for limiting convertibility.

Countertrade

Companies can deal with the nonconvertibility problem by engaging in countertrade. Countertrade is discussed in detail in Chapter 13, so we will merely introduce the concept here. **Countertrade** refers to a range of barter-like agreements by which goods and services can be traded for other goods and services. Countertrade can make sense when a country's currency is nonconvertible. For example, consider the deal that General Electric struck with the Romanian government in 1984, when that country's currency was nonconvertible. When General Electric won a contract for a $150-million generator project in Romania, it agreed to take payment in the form of Romanian goods that could be sold for $150 million on international markets. In a similar case, the Venezuelan government negotiated a contract with Caterpillar in 1986 under which Venezuela would trade 350 000 tonnes of iron ore for Caterpillar heavy construction equipment. Caterpillar subsequently traded the iron ore to Romania in exchange for Romanian farm products, which it then sold on international markets for dollars.[26]

To deal with nonconvertability problems, companies will barter instead. Venezuela traded iron ore for Caterpillar construction equipment. Caterpillar in turn sold the iron ore to Romania for farm products, which it then sold on international markets for dollars. © *Don Farrall/Photodisc/ Getty Images*

How important is countertrade? One estimate is that 20 to 30 percent of world trade in 1985 involved some form of countertrade agreements. Since then, however, more currencies have become freely convertible, and the percentage of world trade that involves countertrade has fallen to well under 10 percent.

LO5 IMPLICATIONS FOR BUSINESS

This chapter contains a number of clear implications for business. First, it is critical that international businesses understand the influence of exchange rates on the profitability of trade and investment deals. Adverse changes in exchange rates can make apparently profitable deals unprofitable. As noted, the risk introduced into international business transactions by changes in exchange rates is referred to as foreign exchange risk. Foreign exchange risk is usually divided into three main categories: translation exposure, transaction exposure, and economic exposure.

TRANSLATION EXPOSURE

Translation exposure is the impact of currency exchange rate changes on the reported financial statements of a company. Translation exposure is concerned with the present measurement of past events. The resulting accounting gains or losses are said to be unrealized—they are "paper" gains and losses—but they are still important. Consider a U.S. firm with a subsidiary in Mexico. If the value of the Mexican peso depreciates significantly against the dollar this would substantially reduce the dollar value of the Mexican subsidiary's equity. In turn, this would reduce the total dollar value of the firm's equity reported in its consolidated balance sheet. This would raise the apparent leverage of the firm (its debt ratio), which could increase the firm's cost of borrowing and potentially limit its access to the capital market. Similarly, if an American firm has a subsidiary in the European Union, and if the value of the euro depreciates rapidly against that of the dollar over a year, this will reduce the dollar value of the euro profit made by the European subsidiary, resulting in negative translation exposure. In fact, many U.S. firms suffered from significant negative translation exposure in Europe during 2000 precisely because the euro did depreciate rapidly against the dollar. In 2002–07, the euro rose in value against the dollar. This positive translation exposure boosted the dollar profits of American multinationals with significant operations in Europe.

TRANSACTION EXPOSURE

Transaction exposure is the extent to which the income from individual transactions is affected by fluctuations in foreign exchange values. Such exposure includes obligations for the purchase or sale of goods and services at previously agreed prices and the borrowing or lending of funds in foreign currencies. For example, suppose in 2015 an airline agreed to purchase ten aircraft for €120 million each for a total price of €1.2 billion, with delivery scheduled for 2020 and payment due then. When the contract was signed in 2015 the country's currency (let's call it a dollar/euro exchange rate) stood at $1 = €1.10 so the airline anticipated paying $1.09 billion for the ten aircraft when they were delivered (€1.2 billion/1.1 = $1.09 billion). However, imagine that the value of the dollar depreciated against the euro over the intervening period, so that $1 only bought €0.80 in 2020 when payment was due ($1 = €0.80). Now the total cost is $1.5 billion (€1.2 billion/0.80 = $1.5 billion), an increase of $0.41 billion! The transaction exposure here is $0.41 billion, which is the money lost due to an adverse movement in exchange rates between the time when the deal was signed and when the aircraft were paid for.

ECONOMIC EXPOSURE

Economic exposure is the extent to which a firm's future international earning power is affected by changes in exchange rates. Economic exposure is concerned with the long-run effect of changes in exchange rates on future prices, sales, and costs. This is distinct from transaction exposure, which is concerned with the effect of exchange rate changes on individual transactions, most of which are short-term affairs that will be executed within a few weeks or months. Consider the effect of wide swings in the value of the dollar on many U.S. firms' international competitiveness. The rapid rise in the value of the dollar on the foreign exchange market in the 1990s hurt the price competitiveness of many U.S. producers in world markets. U.S. manufacturers that relied heavily on exports (such as Caterpillar) saw their export volume and world market share decline. The reverse phenomenon occurred in 2000–07, when the dollar declined against most major currencies. The fall in the value of the dollar helped increase the price competitiveness of U.S. manufacturers in world markets.

REDUCING TRANSLATION AND TRANSACTION EXPOSURE

A number of tactics can help firms minimize their transaction and translation exposure. These tactics primarily protect short-term cash flows from adverse changes in exchange rates. We have already discussed two of these tactics in the chapter: entering into forward exchange rate contracts and currency swaps. In addition to buying forward and using swaps, firms can minimize their foreign exchange exposure through leading and lagging payables and receivables—that is, paying suppliers and collecting payment from customers early or late depending on expected exchange rate movements. A lead strategy involves attempting to collect foreign currency receivables (payments from customers) early when a foreign currency is expected to depreciate and paying foreign currency payables (to suppliers) before they are due when a currency is expected to appreciate. A lag strategy involves delaying collection of foreign currency receivables if that currency is expected to appreciate and delaying payables if the currency is expected to depreciate. Leading and lagging involve accelerating payments from weak-currency to strong-currency countries and delaying inflows from strong-currency to weak-currency countries.

Lead and lag strategies can be difficult to implement, however. The firm must be in a position to exercise some control over payment terms. Firms do not always have this kind of bargaining power, particularly when they are dealing with important customers who are in a position to dictate payment terms. Also, because lead and lag strategies can put pressure on a weak currency, many governments limit leads and lags. For example, some countries set 180 days as a limit for receiving payments for exports or making payments for imports.

REDUCING ECONOMIC EXPOSURE

Reducing economic exposure requires strategic choices that go beyond the realm of financial management. The key to reducing economic exposure is to distribute the firm's productive assets to various locations so the firm's long-term financial well-being is not severely affected by adverse changes in exchange rates. This is a strategy that firms both large and small sometimes pursue. For example, fearing that the euro will continue to strengthen against the U.S. dollar, some European firms who do significant business in the United States have set up local production facilities in that market to ensure that a rising euro does not put them at a competitive disadvantage relative to their local rivals. Similarly, Toyota has production plants distributed around the world in part to make sure that a rising yen does not price Toyota cars out of local markets.

OTHER STEPS FOR MANAGING FOREIGN EXCHANGE RISK

A firm needs to develop a mechanism for ensuring it maintains an appropriate mix of tactics and strategies for minimizing its foreign exchange exposure. Although there is no universal agreement as to the components of this mechanism, a number of common themes stand out.[27] First, central control of exposure is needed to protect resources efficiently and ensure that each subunit adopts the correct mix of tactics and strategies. Many companies have set up in-house foreign exchange centres. Although such centres may not be able to execute all foreign exchange deals—particularly in large, complex multinationals where myriad transactions may be pursued simultaneously—they should at least set guidelines for the firm's subsidiaries to follow.

Second, firms should distinguish between, on one hand, transaction and translation exposure and, on the other, economic exposure. Many companies seem to focus on reducing their transaction and translation exposure and pay scant attention to economic exposure, which may have more profound long-term implications.[28] Firms need to develop strategies for dealing with economic exposure. For example, Black & Decker, the maker of power tools, has a strategy for actively managing its economic risk. The key to Black & Decker's strategy is flexible sourcing. In response to foreign exchange movements, Black & Decker can move production from one location to another to offer the most competitive pricing. Black & Decker manufactures in more than a dozen locations around the world—in Europe, Australia, Brazil, Mexico, and Japan. More than 50 percent of the company's productive assets are based outside North America. Although each of Black & Decker's factories focuses on one or two products to achieve economies of scale, there is considerable overlap. On average, the company runs its factories at no more than 80 percent capacity, so most are able to switch rapidly from producing one product to producing another or to add a product. This allows a factory's production to be changed in response to foreign exchange movements. For example, if the dollar depreciates against other currencies, the amount of imports into the United States from overseas subsidiaries can be reduced and the amount of exports from U.S. subsidiaries to other locations can be increased.[29]

Third, the need to forecast future exchange rate movements cannot be overstated, though, as we saw earlier in the chapter, this is a tricky business. No model comes close to perfectly predicting future movements in foreign exchange rates. The best that can be said is that in the short run, forward exchange rates provide the best predictors of exchange rate movements, and in the long run, fundamental economic factors—particularly relative inflation rates—should be watched because they influence exchange rate movements. Some firms attempt to forecast exchange rate movements in-house; others rely on outside forecasters. However, all such forecasts are imperfect attempts to predict the future.

Fourth, firms need to establish good reporting systems so the central finance function (or in-house foreign exchange centre) can regularly monitor the firm's exposure positions. Such reporting systems should enable the firm to identify any exposed accounts, the exposed position by currency of each account, and the time periods covered.

Finally, on the basis of the information it receives from exchange rate forecasts and its own regular reporting systems, the firm should produce monthly foreign exchange exposure reports. These reports should identify how cash flows and balance sheet elements might be affected by forecasted changes in exchange rates. The reports can then be used by management as a basis for adopting tactics and strategies to hedge against undue foreign exchange risks. Surprisingly, some of the largest and most sophisticated firms do not take such precautionary steps, exposing themselves to very large foreign exchange risks. The Management Focus in this chapter details currency hedging in the Canadian gold industry.

Key Terms

arbitrage	forward exchange rates
capital flight	freely convertible currency
countertrade	fundamental analysis
currency speculation	inefficient market
currency swap	International Fisher Effect
efficient market	law of one price
exchange rate	nonconvertible currency
externally convertible currency	relatively efficient markets
foreign exchange market	spot exchange rate
foreign exchange risk	technical analysis
forward exchange	

LO   Learning Objectives Summary

1. One function of the foreign exchange market is to convert the currency of one country into the currency of another. International businesses participate in the foreign exchange market to facilitate international trade and investment, to invest spare cash in short-term money market accounts abroad, and to engage in currency speculation. A second function of the foreign exchange market is to provide insurance against foreign exchange risk. The spot exchange rate is the exchange rate at which a dealer converts one currency into another currency on a particular day. Foreign exchange risk can be reduced by using forward exchange rates. A forward exchange rate is an exchange rate governing future transactions. Foreign exchange risk can also be reduced by engaging in currency swaps. A swap is the simultaneous purchase and sale of a given amount of foreign exchange for two different value dates.

2. The foreign exchange market is not located in any one place. It is dominated by the U.S. dollar. The market exists 24 hours a day and is highly integrated. Arbitrage helps keep prices identical.

3. The law of one price holds that in competitive markets that are free of transportation costs and barriers to trade, identical products sold in different countries must sell for the same price when their price is expressed in the same currency. Purchasing power parity (PPP) theory states the price of a basket of particular goods should be roughly equivalent in each country. PPP theory predicts that the exchange rate will change if relative prices change. The rate of change in countries' relative prices depends on their relative inflation rates. A country's inflation rate seems to be a function of the growth in its money supply. The PPP theory of exchange rate changes yields relatively accurate predictions of long-term trends in exchange rates, but not of short-term movements. The failure of PPP theory to predict exchange rate changes more accurately may be due to the existence of transportation costs, barriers to trade and investment, and the impact of psychological factors such as bandwagon effects on market movements and short-run exchange rates. Interest rates reflect expectations about inflation. In countries where inflation is expected to be high, interest rates also will be high. The International Fisher Effect states that for any two countries, the spot exchange rate should change in an equal amount but in the opposite direction to the difference in nominal interest rates.

4. The most common approach to exchange rate forecasting is fundamental analysis. This relies on variables such as money supply growth, inflation rates, nominal interest rates, and balance-of-payments positions to predict future changes in exchange rates. In many countries, the ability of residents and nonresidents to convert local currency into a foreign currency is restricted by government policy. A government restricts the convertibility of its currency to protect the country's foreign exchange reserves and to halt any capital flight. Particularly bothersome for international business is a policy of nonconvertibility, which prohibits residents and nonresidents from exchanging local currency for foreign currency. A policy of nonconvertibility makes it very difficult to engage in international trade and investment in the country. One way of coping with the nonconvertibility problem is to engage in countertrade—to trade goods and services for other goods and services.

5. Tactics that insure against transaction and translation exposure include buying forward, using currency swaps, leading and lagging payables and receivables, manipulating transfer prices, and adjusting capital budgeting to reflect foreign exchange exposure. Reducing a firm's economic exposure requires strategic choices about how the firm's productive assets are distributed around the globe. To manage foreign exchange exposure effectively, the firm must exercise centralized oversight over its foreign exchange hedging activities, recognize the difference between transaction exposure and economic exposure, forecast future exchange rate movements, establish good reporting systems within the firm to monitor exposure positions, and produce regular foreign exchange exposure reports that can be used as a basis for action.

Critical Thinking and Discussion Questions

1. The interest rate on one-year Canadian government securities is 6 percent and expected inflation rate for the coming year is 2 percent. The U.S. one-year government security instrument interest rate is 4 percent with expected inflation for this coming year of 1 percent. Assume the exchange rate for the US$/CAD$ as of mid-June of this year is US$1 = CAD$1.02296 (US$100 = CAD$102.27). What is the spot exchange rate a year from now? What is the forward exchange rate a year from now? Explain the logic of your answers.
2. Two countries, Canada and the United States, produce just one good: beef. Suppose the price of beef in the United States is $3 per kilogram and in Canada it is $4 per kilogram.
   a. According to the PPP theory, what should the spot exchange rate be?
   b. Suppose the price of beef is expected to rise to $3.50 per kilogram in the United States and to $4.75 per kilogram in Canada. What should the one-year forward US$/CAD$ exchange rate be?
   c. Given your answers to parts *a* and *b*, if the current interest rate in the United States is 10 percent, what would you expect the current interest rate to be in Canada?

Research Task   globalEDGE™   **globaledge.msu.edu**

Use the globalEDGE™ site to complete the following exercises:

1. You are assigned the duty of ensuring the availability of 100,000 yen for a payment that is scheduled for next month. Your company possesses only U.S. dollars, so identify the spot and forward exchange rates. What factors affect your decision of utilizing spot versus forward exchange rates? Which one would you choose? How many dollars do you have to spend to acquire the amount of yen required?

2. As an entrepreneur, you are interested in expanding your business to Bulgaria. As part of your initial analysis, you would like to know if it is too risky. PRS Group provides country risk analysis (www.prsgroup.com). While a majority of its reports are available only for purchase, the site provides sample data for free (under International Country Risk Guide). Using this sample data, provide a short report of the current status of Bulgaria's country risk based on economical risk, external conflicts, and exchange rate stability.

CLOSING CASE

THE RISE (AND FALL) OF THE JAPANESE YEN

For most of the first decade of the 21st century, the Japanese yen was relatively weak against the U.S. dollar. This was a boon for Japan's export-led economy. On January 1, 2008, it took 122 yen to buy one U.S. dollar. For the next four years, the yen strengthened relentlessly against the dollar, hitting an all-time record high of ¥75.31 to the dollar on

October 31, 2011. The reasons for the rise of the yen were complex and had little to do with the strength of the Japanese economy because there has been very little of that in evidence.

The weakness of the yen during the early to mid-2000s was due to the so-called carry trade. This financial strategy involved borrowing in Japanese yen, where interest rates were close to zero, and investing the loans in higher yielding assets, typically U.S. Treasury bills, which carried interest rates 3 to 4 percentage points greater. Investors made profits from the interest rate differential. At its peak, financial institutions had more than a trillion dollars invested in the carry trade. Because the strategy involved selling borrowed yen to purchase dollar-denominated assets, it drove the value of the yen lower. The interest rate differential existed because the Japanese economy was weak, prices were falling, and the Bank of Japan had been lowering interest rates in an attempt to boost growth and get Japan out of a dangerous deflationary cycle.

When the global financial crisis hit in 2008 and 2009, the Federal Reserve in the United States responded by injecting liquidity into battered financial markets, effectively lowering U.S. interest rates on U.S. Treasury bonds. As these fell, the interest rate differential between Japanese and U.S. assets narrowed sharply, and the carry trade became unprofitable. Financial institutions unwound their positions, selling dollar-denominated assets and buying yen to pay back their original loans. The increased demand drove up the value of the yen.

For Japanese exporters, the 40 percent increase in the value of the yen against the dollar (and the euro) between early 2008 and 2012 was a painful experience. A strong yen hurts the price competitiveness of Japanese exports and reduces the value of profits earned overseas when translated back into yen. Take Toyota as an example: In February 2012, the company stated that its profit for the year ending March 31, 2012, would be about ¥200 billion, 51 percent lower than in the prior year. Toyota makes nearly half of the cars it sells globally at its Japanese plants, so it has been particularly hard hit by a rise in the value of the yen.

In late 2012, things started to change when the pro-business Liberal Democratic Party won national elections and Shinzo Abe was appointed prime minister. Abe had campaigned on a platform that included taking actions to weaken the value of the yen in order to help Japan's exporters. Even before the election, Japan's central bank had accelerated purchases of government securities, thereby expanding the money supply, and had agreed to a higher inflation target. Under Abe's leadership, this policy had explicit government support. One consequence of the policy was to reduce the value of the yen against other currencies. Indeed, between October 2012 and December 2013, the yen lost more than 25 percent of its value against the U.S. dollar. The yen was trading at ¥104 to the U.S. dollar in late December 2013. While this helped Japan's exporters, the policy was criticized by other major industrial nations as unilateral action that came dangerously close to precipitating a currency war.

Sources: C. Dawson and Y. Takahashi, "Toyota Shows Optimism Despite Gloom," *The Wall Street Journal*, February 8, 2012; Y. Takahashi, "Nissan's CEO Says Yen Still Not Weak Enough," *The Wall Street Journal*, February 27, 2010; "The Yen's 40 Year Win Streak May Be Ending," *The Wall Street Journal*, January 27, 2012; and "U.S., Europe Seek to Cool Currency Jitters," *The Wall Street Journal*, February 11, 2013.

Case Discussion Questions

1. Why did the yen carry trade work during the early 2000s? Why did it stop working after 2008?

2. What drove an increase in the value of the yen between 2008 and 2011?

3. Why did the policy of the Abe government to purchase government securities help to drive down the value of the yen? What was the mechanism at work here?

4. Do you think the Japanese government was engaging in currency manipulation? If so, what should other nations do about it at the time?

5. Who in Japan benefits from devaluation of the yen? Who does this hurt in Japan?

6. What does this case teach you about the way foreign exchange markets work?

© Sirithana Tiranardvanich/Dreamstime.com

Chapter 10
The Global Monetary System

THE IMF AND ICELAND'S ECONOMIC RECOVERY

When the global financial crisis hit in 2008, tiny Iceland suffered more than most. The country's three biggest banks had been expanding at a breakneck pace since 2000 when the government privatized the banking sector. With a population of around 320 000, Iceland was too small for the banking sector's ambitions, so the banks started to expand into other Scandinavian countries and the UK. They entered local mortgage markets, purchased foreign financial institutions, and opened foreign branches, attracting depositors by offering high interest rates. The expansion was financed by debt, much of it structured as short-term loans that had to be regularly refinanced. By early 2008, the three banks held debts that amounted to almost six times the value of the entire economy of Iceland! So long as they could periodically refinance this debt, it was not a problem. However, in 2008, global financial markets imploded following the bankruptcy of Lehman Brothers and the collapse of the U.S. housing market. In the aftermath financial markets froze. The Icelandic banks found that they could not refinance their debt, and they faced bankruptcy.

The Icelandic government lacked the funds to bail out the banks, so it decided to let the big three fail. In quick succession the local stock market plunged 90 percent and unemployment increased ninefold. The krona, Iceland's currency, plunged on foreign exchange markets, pushing up the price of imports, and inflation soared to 18 percent. Iceland appeared to be in free fall. The economy shrank by almost 7 percent in 2009 and another 4 percent in 2010.

To stem the decline, the government secured $10 billion in loans from the International Monetary Fund (IMF) and other countries. The Icelandic government stepped in to help local depositors, seizing the domestic assets of the Icelandic banks and using IMF and other loans to backstop deposit guarantees. Far from implementing austerity measures to solve the crisis, the Icelandic government looked for ways to shore up consumer spending. For example, the government provided means-tested subsidies to reduce the mortgage interest expenses of borrowers. The idea was to stop domestic consumer spending from imploding and further depressing the economy.

With the financial system stabilized, thanks to the IMF and other foreign loans, what happened next is an object lesson in the value of having a floating currency. The fall in the value of the krona helped boost Iceland's exports, such as fish and aluminum, while depressing demand for costly imports, such as automobiles. By 2009 the krona was worth half as much against the U.S. dollar and euro as it was in 2007 before the crisis. Iceland's exports surged and imports slumped. While the high cost of imports did stoke inflation, booming exports started to pump money back into the Icelandic economy. In 2011 the economy grew again at a 3.1 percent annual rate. This was followed by 2.7 percent growth in 2012 and 4 percent growth in 2013, while unemployment fell from a high of nearly 10 percent to 4.4 percent at the end of 2013. This trend of stable unemployment and rising productivity has continued into 2017.

Sources: Charles Forelle, "In European Crisis, Iceland Emerges as an Island of Recovery," *The Wall Street Journal*, May 19, 2012, pp. A1, A10; "Coming in from the Cold," *The Economist*, December 16, 2010; Charles Duxbury, "Europe Gets Cold Shoulder in Iceland," *The Wall Street Journal*, April 26, 2012; and "Iceland," *The World Factbook 2013* (Washington, DC: Central Intelligence Agency, 2013).

LO | LEARNING OBJECTIVES

By the end of this chapter you should be able to:

1. Describe the historical development of the modern global monetary system.

2. Explain the role played by the World Bank and the IMF in the international monetary system.

3. Compare and contrast the differences between a fixed and a floating exchange rate system.

4. Identify exchange rate regimes used in the world today and why countries adopt different exchange rate regions.

5. Understand the debate surrounding the role of the IMF in the management of financial crises.

6. Explain the implications of the global monetary system for currency management and business strategy.

Introduction

What happened in Iceland goes to the heart of the material covered in this chapter. Here we look at the international monetary system and its role in determining exchange rates. The **international monetary system** refers to the institutional arrangements that countries adopt to govern exchange rates. In Chapter 9, we assumed the foreign exchange market was the primary institution for determining exchange rates and the impersonal market forces of demand and supply determined the relative value of any two currencies (i.e., their exchange rate). Furthermore, we explained that the demand and supply of currencies is influenced by their respective countries' relative inflation rates and interest rates. When the foreign exchange market determines the relative value of a currency, we say that the country is adhering to a **floating exchange rate** regime. The world's four major trading currencies—the U.S. dollar, the European Union's euro, the Japanese yen, and the British pound—are all free to float against each other. Thus, their exchange rates are determined by market forces and fluctuate against each other on a day-to-day, if not minute-to-minute, basis. As we saw in the opening case, the Icelandic currency, the krona, is also free to float against other currencies, a fact that some claim helped Iceland recover from the 2008 financial crisis in that country. However, the exchange rates of many currencies are not determined by the free play of market forces; other institutional arrangements are adopted.

Many of the world's developing nations peg their currencies, primarily to the dollar or the euro. A **pegged exchange rate** means the value of the currency is fixed relative to a reference currency, such as the U.S. dollar, and then the exchange rate between that currency and other currencies is determined by the reference currency exchange rate.

Other countries, while not adopting a formal pegged rate, try to hold the value of their currency within some range against an important reference currency such as the U.S. dollar. This is often referred to as a **dirty-float system**. It is a float because in theory, the value of the currency is determined by market forces, but it is a dirty float (as opposed to a clean float) because the central bank of a country will intervene in the foreign exchange market to try to maintain the value of its currency if it depreciates too rapidly against an important reference currency. This has been the policy adopted by the Chinese since July 2005. The value of the Chinese currency, the yuan, has been linked to a basket of other currencies—including the dollar, yen, and euro—and it is allowed to vary in value against individual currencies, but only within limits.

Still other countries have operated with a **fixed exchange rate** system, in which the values of a set of currencies are fixed against each other at some mutually-agreed-upon exchange rate. Before the introduction of the euro in 2000, several member states of the European Union operated with fixed exchange rates within the context of the European Monetary System (EMS). For a quarter of a century after World War II, the world's major industrial nations participated in a fixed exchange rate system. Although this system collapsed in 1973, some still argue that the world should attempt to re-impose it.

Pegged, dirty-float, and fixed exchange rate systems all require some degree of government intervention in the foreign exchange market to maintain the value of a currency. A currency may come under pressure when the nation experiences significant economic or political problems. A **central bank** is the generic name given to a country's primary monetary authority, such as the Federal Reserve System in the United States or the Bank of Canada in Canada. It usually has the responsibility for issuing currency, administering monetary policy, holding member banks' deposits, and facilitating the nation's banking industry.

In this chapter, we will explain how the international monetary system works and point out its implications for international business. To understand how the international monetary system works, we must review the system's evolution. We will begin with a discussion of the gold standard and its breakup during the 1930s. Then we will discuss the 1944 Bretton Woods conference. This established the basic framework for the post-World War II international monetary system. The Bretton Woods system called for fixed exchange rates against the U.S. dollar. Under this fixed exchange rate system, the value of most currencies in terms of U.S. dollars was fixed for long periods and allowed to change only under a specific set of circumstances. The Bretton Woods conference also created two major international institutions that play a role in the international monetary system—the International Monetary Fund (IMF) and the World Bank. The IMF was given the task of maintaining order in the international monetary system; the World Bank's role was to promote development.

Today, both these institutions continue to play major roles in the world economy and in the international monetary system. The IMF was actively involved in helping Greece, Ireland, and Portugal manage their financial crises in 2010. There has been a vigorous debate about the role of the IMF and, to a lesser extent, the World Bank, and the appropriateness of their policies for many developing nations. Several prominent critics claim that in some cases IMF policies make things worse, not better. The debate over the role of the IMF took on new urgency given the institution's extensive involvement in the economies of developing countries during the late 1990s and early 2000s. We shall discuss the issue in some depth.

The Bretton Woods system of fixed exchange rates collapsed in 1973. Since then, the world has operated with a mixed system in which some currencies are allowed to float freely, but many are either managed by government intervention or pegged to another currency. We will explain the reasons for the failure of the Bretton Woods system as well as the nature of the present system. We will also discuss how pegged exchange rate systems work. Almost four decades after the breakdown of the Bretton Woods system, the debate continues over what kind of exchange rate regime is best for the world. Some economists advocate a system in which major currencies are allowed to float against each other. Others argue for a return to a fixed exchange rate regime similar to the one established at Bretton Woods. This debate is intense and important, and we will examine the arguments of both sides.

Finally, we will discuss the implications of all this material for international business. We will see how the exchange rate policy adopted by a government can have an important impact on the outlook for business operations in a given country. If government exchange rate policies result in currency devaluation, for example, exporters based in that country may benefit as their products become more price competitive in foreign markets. Alternatively, importers will suffer from an increase in the price of their products. We will also look at how the policies adopted by the IMF can affect the economic outlook for a country and, accordingly, the costs and benefits of doing business in that country.

LO1 The Gold Standard

The gold standard had its origin in the use of gold coins as a medium of exchange, unit of account, and store of value—a practice that dates to ancient times. When international trade was limited in volume, payment for goods purchased from another country was typically made in gold or silver. However, as the volume of international trade expanded in the wake of the Industrial Revolution, a more convenient means was needed. The solution adopted was to arrange for payment in paper currency and for governments to agree to convert the paper currency into gold on demand at a fixed rate.

Mechanics of the Gold Standard

Pegging currencies to gold and guaranteeing convertibility is known as the **gold standard**. By 1880, most of the world's major trading nations, including Great Britain, Germany, Japan, and the United States, had adopted the gold standard.

For example, under the gold standard, one U.S. dollar was defined as equivalent to 23.22 grains of "fine" (pure) gold. Thus, one could, in theory, demand that the U.S. government convert that one dollar into 23.22 grains of gold. Because there are 480 grains in an ounce, one ounce of gold cost $20.67 (480/23.22). The amount of a currency needed to purchase one ounce of gold was referred to as the gold par value. The British pound was valued at 113 grains of fine gold. In other words, one ounce of gold cost £4.25 (480/113). From the gold par values of pounds and dollars, we can calculate what the exchange rate was for converting pounds into dollars; it was £1 = $4.87 (i.e., $20.67 / £4.25).

Strength of the Gold Standard

The great strength claimed for the gold standard was that it contained a powerful mechanism for achieving balance-of-trade equilibrium by all countries.[1] A country is said to be in balance-of-trade equilibrium when the income its residents earn from exports is equal to the money its residents pay to people in other countries for imports (the current account of its balance of payments is in balance). Suppose there are only two countries in the world, Japan and the United States. Imagine Japan's trade balance is in surplus because it exports more to the United States than it imports from the United States. Japanese exporters are paid in U.S. dollars, which they exchange for Japanese yen at a Japanese bank. The Japanese bank submits the dollars to the U.S. government and demands payment of gold in return. (This is a simplification of what would occur, but it will make our point.)

Under the gold standard, when Japan has a trade surplus, there will be a net flow of gold from the United States to Japan. These gold flows automatically reduce the U.S. money supply and swell Japan's money supply. As we saw in Chapter 9, there is a close connection between money supply growth and price inflation. An increase in money supply will raise prices in Japan, while a decrease in the U.S. money supply will push U.S. prices downward. The rise in the price of Japanese goods will decrease demand for these goods, while the fall in the price of U.S. goods will increase demand for these goods. Thus, Japan will start to buy more from the United States, and the United States will buy less from Japan, until a balance-of-trade equilibrium is achieved.

This adjustment mechanism seems so simple and attractive that even today, more than 60 years after the final collapse of the gold standard, some people believe the world should return to a gold standard.

The Period Between the Wars: 1918–1939

The gold standard worked reasonably well from the 1870s until the start of World War I. During the war, several governments financed part of their massive military expenditures by printing money.

Great Britain, which abandoned the gold standard at the beginning of World War I, returned to the gold standard by pegging the pound to gold at the prewar gold parity level of £4.25 per ounce, despite substantial inflation between 1914 and 1925. This priced British goods out of foreign markets, which pushed the country into a deep depression. When foreign holders of pounds lost confidence in Great Britain's commitment to maintaining its currency's value, they began converting their holdings of pounds into gold. The British government saw that it could not satisfy the demand for gold without seriously depleting its gold reserves, so it suspended convertibility in 1931.

The United States followed suit and left the gold standard in 1933 but returned to it in 1934, raising the dollar price of gold from $20.67 per ounce to $35 per ounce. Since more dollars were needed to buy an ounce of gold than before, the implication was that the dollar was worth less. This effectively amounted to a devaluation of the dollar relative to other currencies. A number of other countries adopted a similar tactic, and in the cycle of competitive devaluations that soon emerged, no country could win.

The Canadian dollar was under the gold standard from 1854 to 1914. With the beginning of World War I, it went off the gold standard from 1914 to 1926 and temporarily went back on from 1926 to 1931.

The Currency Act was first proclaimed on August 1, 1854, and until World War I, Canada remained on the gold standard whereby the value of the Canadian dollar was fixed in terms of gold. It was also valued at par with the U.S. dollar, with a British sovereign valued at $4.8666 (CAD$), and both U.S. and British gold coins were legal tender in Canada. Paper money was freely convertible into gold without restriction and there were no controls on the export or import of gold.[2]

The start of World War I marked the end of the gold standard era. Most countries suspended the convertibility of domestic bank notes into gold and the free movement of gold between countries. As fear mounted in the days immediately before the declaration of war on August 4, 1914, there were heavy withdrawals of gold from Canadian banks. In an "atmosphere of incipient financial panic,"[3] there were concerns about the possibility of bank runs from bank customers rushing to redeem their paper money in gold. Since there was not enough gold to cover for paper money, an emergency meeting was held in Ottawa, on August 3, 1914, between the federal government and the Canadian Bankers Association to discuss the crisis. Later that day, an order-in-council was issued to provide protection for banks, which were threatened by insolvency, by giving bank notes issued by banks legal tender status. This allowed the banks to meet their depositor demands with their own bank notes rather than with dominion notes or gold. The government also increased the amount of notes that banks were legally permitted to issue. The government was also empowered to make advances to banks by issuing dominion notes against securities deposited with the minister of finance. This provision enabled banks to increase the amount of their bank notes in circulation. A second order-in-council, issued on August 10, 1914, suspended the redemption of dominion notes into gold.[4]

With Canada's return to the gold standard, from 1926 to 1931, currency supplied by the chartered banks lost its legal tender status, although the government, in the event of an emergency, could restore this status under the Finance Act. Consequently, legal tender in Canada once again consisted of British gold sovereigns and other current British gold coins; U.S. gold eagles ($10), double eagles, and half eagles; and Canadian gold coins (denominations of $5 and $10) and dominion notes. To a lesser degree, legal tender status was also accorded silver, nickel, and bronze coins minted in Canada.[5]

On April 10, 1933, an order-in-council officially suspended the redemption of dominion notes for gold, thus ending Canada's relationship with the gold standard.[6]

DEBATE THE ISSUE

Should We Go Back to the Gold Standard?

Porter Stansberry, founder of Stansberry & Associates Investment Research, says, "The purpose of gold is to make sure credit growth is restrained and limited to real growth and productivity." Since 1971, the amount of debt in the United States has skyrocketed, while the value of the dollar has tumbled. Moving away from gold "allows people who have borrowed money to pay it back in currency that's worth less," Stansberry says. Unfortunately, "it's hugely disruptive to our economy." His idea is that the United States and other countries should go back to a gold (or silver) standard.

On the other hand, "Why should we limit the amount of currency floating in circulation by a rock we have to dig out of the ground and store?" asks James Altucher of Formula Capital. "Gold is ultimately a limited resource. Why should we arbitrarily pick this yellow rock and limit the world's economy by it? Innovation happens because we've been able to extend credit . . . beyond what gold would allow us. And it's through debt and lending that companies grow." Who do you agree with—Stansberry, who argues for the gold standard, or Altucher, who argues for today's currency system?

Source: Aaron Task, "40 Years Later: Should America Go Back to the Gold Standard?" *Yahoo! Finance*, August 19, 2011, http://finance.yahoo.com/blogs/daily-ticker/40-years-later-america-back-gold-standard-114623756.html

The net result in Canada was the shattering of any remaining confidence in the system. With countries devaluing their currencies at will, one could no longer be certain how much gold a currency could buy. By the start of World War II in 1939, the gold standard was dead.

LO2 | The Bretton Woods System: Birth of the IMF and the World Bank

In 1944, at the height of World War II, representatives from 44 countries met at Bretton Woods, New Hampshire, to design a new international monetary system. With the collapse of the gold standard and the Great Depression of the 1930s fresh in their minds, these statesmen were determined to build an enduring economic order that would facilitate postwar economic growth. There was general consensus that fixed exchange rates were desirable.

The agreement reached at Bretton Woods established two multinational institutions— the International Monetary Fund (IMF) and the World Bank. The task of the IMF would be to maintain order in the international monetary system and that of the World Bank would be to promote general economic development. The Bretton Woods agreement also called for a system of fixed exchange rates that would be policed by the IMF. Under the agreement, all countries were to fix the value of their currency in terms of gold but were not required to exchange their currencies for gold. Only the dollar remained convertible into gold—at a price of $35 per ounce. Each country decided what it wanted its exchange rate to be vis-à-vis the dollar and then calculated the gold par value of the currency based on that selected dollar exchange rate.

Another aspect of the Bretton Woods agreement was a commitment not to use devaluation as a weapon of competitive trade policy. However, if a currency became too weak to defend, a devaluation of up to 10 percent would be allowed without any formal approval by the IMF. Larger devaluations required IMF approval.

The Role of the IMF

The IMF Articles of Agreement were heavily influenced by the worldwide financial collapse, competitive devaluations, trade wars, high unemployment, hyperinflation in Germany and elsewhere, and general economic disintegration that occurred between the two world wars. The aim of the Bretton Woods agreement, of which the IMF was the main custodian, was to try to avoid a repetition of that chaos through a combination of discipline and flexibility.

ANOTHER PERSPECTIVE

Criticisms of the IMF and the World Bank

There have been many criticisms levelled at the IMF and the World Bank, some of which have some justification. Critics note that IMF loans have gone to repressive regimes that have had numerous human rights abuses, from Chile in the 1970s and 1980s to the Sudan for the past 40 years. The IMF, in response, believes that economic stability, which it provides, is a necessary first step towards democracy and other freedoms.

More fundamentally, some economists believe that the IMF's policies actually harm countries. In some cases the IMF has promoted "austerity programs" that increase taxes even when a country's economy is weak, in order for the country to balance its budget. Such economic moves obviously produce dissatisfaction among those who are unwilling to undergo "short-term pain for long-term gains."

DISCIPLINE

A fixed exchange rate regime imposes discipline in two ways. First, the need to maintain a fixed exchange rate puts a brake on competitive devaluations and brings stability to the world trade environment. Second, a fixed exchange rate regime imposes monetary discipline on countries, thereby curtailing price inflation. For example, consider what would happen under a fixed exchange rate regime if Great Britain rapidly increased its money supply by printing pounds. As explained in Chapter 9, the increase in money supply would lead to price inflation. Given fixed exchange rates, inflation would make British goods uncompetitive in world markets, while the prices of imports would become more attractive in Great Britain. The result would be a widening trade deficit in Great Britain, with the country importing more than it exports. To correct this trade imbalance under a fixed exchange rate regime, Great Britain would be required to restrict the rate of growth in its money supply to bring price inflation back under control. Thus, fixed exchange rates are seen as a mechanism for controlling inflation and imposing economic discipline on countries.

FLEXIBILITY

Although monetary discipline was a central objective of the Bretton Woods agreement, it was recognized that a rigid policy of fixed exchange rates would be too inflexible. It would probably break down just as the gold standard had. In some cases, a country's attempts to reduce its money supply growth and correct a persistent balance-of-payments deficit could force the country into recession and create high unemployment. The architects of the Bretton Woods agreement wanted to avoid high unemployment, so they built limited flexibility into the system. Two major features of the IMF Articles of Agreement fostered this flexibility: IMF lending facilities and adjustable parities.

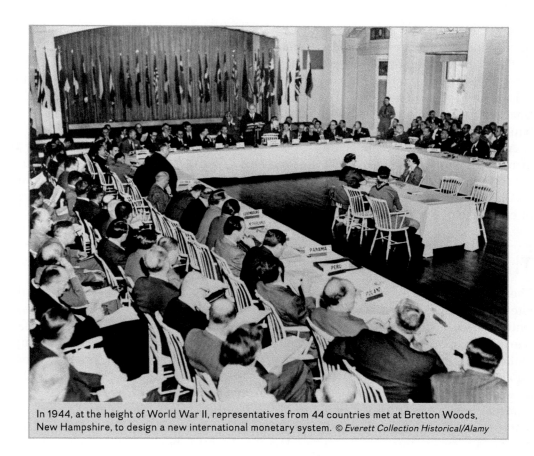

In 1944, at the height of World War II, representatives from 44 countries met at Bretton Woods, New Hampshire, to design a new international monetary system. © *Everett Collection Historical/Alamy*

The IMF stood ready to lend foreign currencies to members to tide them over during short periods of balance-of-payments deficits, when a rapid tightening of monetary or fiscal policy would hurt domestic employment. A pool of gold and currencies contributed by IMF members provided the resources for these lending operations. A persistent balance-of-payments deficit can lead to a depletion of a country's reserves of foreign currency, forcing it to devalue its currency. By providing deficit-laden countries with short-term foreign currency loans, IMF funds would buy time for countries to bring down their inflation rates and reduce their balance-of-payments deficits. The belief was that such loans would reduce pressures for devaluation and allow for a more orderly and less painful adjustment.

The Role of the World Bank

The official name for the World Bank is the International Bank for Reconstruction and Development (IBRD). When the Bretton Woods participants established the World Bank, the need to reconstruct the war-torn economies of Europe was foremost in their minds. The bank's initial mission was to help finance the building of Europe's economy by providing low-interest loans. As it turned out, the World Bank was overshadowed in this role by the Marshall Plan, under which the United States lent money directly to European nations to help them rebuild. So the bank turned its attention to "development" and began lending money to Third World nations. In the 1950s, the bank concentrated on public-sector projects. Power stations, road building, and other transportation investments were much in favour. During the

1960s, the bank also began to lend heavily in support of agriculture, education, population control, and urban development.

The bank lends money under two schemes. Under the IBRD scheme, money is raised through bond sales in the international capital market. Borrowers pay what the bank calls a market rate of interest—the bank's cost of funds plus a margin for expenses. This "market" rate is lower than commercial banks' market rate. Under the IBRD scheme, the bank offers low-interest loans to risky customers whose credit rating is often poor.

A second scheme is overseen by the International Development Agency (IDA), an arm of the bank created in 1960. Resources to fund IDA loans are raised through subscriptions from wealthy members such as the United States, Japan, and Germany. IDA loans go only to the poorest countries. Borrowers have 50 years to repay at an interest rate of 1 percent a year.

The Collapse of the Fixed Exchange Rate System

The system of fixed exchange rates established at Bretton Woods worked well until the late 1960s, when it began to show signs of strain. The system finally collapsed in 1973, and since then we have had a managed-float system. To understand why the system collapsed, one must appreciate the special role of the U.S. dollar in the system. As the only currency that could be converted into gold, and as the currency that served as the reference point for all others, the dollar occupied a central place in the system. Any pressure on the dollar to devalue could wreak havoc with the system, and that is what occurred.

Most economists trace the breakup of the fixed exchange rate system to the U.S. macroeconomic policy package of 1965–1968.[7] To finance both the Vietnam conflict and his welfare programs, U.S. President Lyndon Johnson backed an increase in U.S. government spending that was not financed by an increase in taxes. Instead, it was financed by an increase in the money supply, which led to a rise in price inflation from less than 4 percent in 1966 to close to 9 percent by 1968. At the same time, the rise in government spending stimulated the economy. With more money in their pockets, people spent more—particularly on imports—and the U.S. trade balance began to deteriorate.

The increase in inflation and the worsening of the U.S. foreign trade position gave rise to speculation in the foreign exchange market that the dollar would be devalued. Things came to a head in spring 1971 when U.S. trade figures showed that for the first time since 1945, the United States was importing more than it was exporting. This set off massive purchases of German deutschmarks in the foreign exchange market by speculators who guessed that the mark would be revalued against the dollar. On a single day, May 4, 1971, the Bundesbank (Germany's central bank) had to buy $1 billion to hold the dollar/deutschmark exchange rate at its fixed exchange rate given the great demand for deutschmarks. On the morning of May 5, the Bundesbank purchased another $1 billion during the first hour of foreign exchange trading. At that point, the Bundesbank faced the inevitable and allowed its currency to float.

In the weeks following the decision to float the deutschmark, the foreign exchange market became increasingly convinced that the dollar would have to be devalued. However, devaluation of the dollar was no easy matter. Under the Bretton Woods provisions, any other country could change its exchange rates against all currencies simply by fixing its dollar rate at a new level. But as the key currency in the system, the dollar could be devalued only if all countries agreed to simultaneously revalue against the dollar. And many countries did not want this, because it would make their products more expensive relative to U.S. products.

To force the issue, President Nixon announced in August 1971 that the dollar was no longer convertible into gold. He also announced that a new 10 percent tax on imports would remain in effect until U.S. trading partners agreed to revalue their currencies against the dollar. This brought the trading partners to the bargaining table, and in December 1971 an agreement was reached to devalue the dollar by about 8 percent against foreign currencies. The import tax was then removed.

The problem was not solved, however. The U.S. balance-of-payments position continued to deteriorate throughout 1972, while the nation's money supply continued to expand at an inflationary rate. Speculation continued to grow that the dollar was still overvalued and that a second devaluation would be necessary. In anticipation, foreign exchange dealers began converting dollars to deutschmarks and other currencies. After a massive wave of speculation in February 1973, which culminated with European central banks spending $3.6 billion on March 1 to try to prevent their currencies from appreciating against the dollar, the foreign exchange market was closed. When the foreign exchange market reopened March 19, the currencies of Japan and most European countries were floating against the dollar, although many developing countries continued to peg their currency to the dollar, and many do to this day. At that time, the switch to a floating system was viewed as a temporary response to unmanageable speculation in the foreign exchange market. But it is now nearing 50 years since the Bretton Woods system of fixed exchange rates collapsed, and the temporary solution looks permanent.

The Bretton Woods system had an Achilles' heel: the system could not work if its key currency, the U.S. dollar, was under speculative attack. The Bretton Woods system could work only as long as the U.S. inflation rate remained low and the United States did not run a balance-of-payments deficit. Once these things occurred, the system soon became strained to the breaking point.

The Floating Exchange Rate Regime

The floating exchange rate regime that followed the collapse of the fixed exchange rate system was formalized in January 1976 when IMF members met in Jamaica and agreed to the rules for the international monetary system that are in place today.

The Jamaica Agreement

The Jamaica meeting revised the IMF's Articles of Agreement to reflect the new reality of floating exchange rates. The main elements of the Jamaica agreement include the following:

1. Floating rates were declared acceptable. IMF members were permitted to enter the foreign exchange market to even out "unwarranted" speculative fluctuations.

2. Gold was abandoned as a reserve asset. The IMF returned its gold reserves to members at the current market price, placing the proceeds in a trust fund to help poor nations. IMF members were permitted to sell their own gold reserves at the market price.

3. Total annual IMF quotas—the amount member countries contribute to the IMF— were increased to $41 billion (US$). (Since then they have been increased to $300 billion while the membership of the IMF has been expanded to include 189 countries.) Non-oil-exporting, less-developed countries were given greater access to IMF funds.

Exchange Rates Since 1973

Since March 1973, exchange rates have become much more volatile and less predictable than they were between 1945 and 1973.[8] This volatility has been partly due to a number of unexpected shocks to the world monetary system, including:

1. The oil crisis in 1971, when the Organization of Petroleum Exporting Countries (OPEC) quadrupled the price of oil. The harmful effect of this on the U.S. inflation rate and trade position resulted in a further decline in the value of the dollar.

2. The loss of confidence in the dollar that followed the rise of U.S. inflation in 1977 and 1978.

3. The oil crisis of 1979, when OPEC once again increased the price of oil dramatically—this time it was doubled.

4. The unexpected rise in the dollar between 1980 and 1985, despite a deteriorating balance-of-payments picture.

5. The rapid fall of the U.S. dollar against the Japanese yen and German deutschmark between 1985 and 1987, and against the yen between 1993 and 1995.

6. The partial collapse of the European Monetary System in 1992.

7. The 1997 Asian currency crisis, when the Asian currencies of several countries, including South Korea, Indonesia, Malaysia, and Thailand, lost between 50 percent and 80 percent of their value against the U.S. dollar in a few months.

8. The decline of the value of the US dollar in the mid- to late-2000s.

9. The global financial crisis of 2008–10 and the sovereign debt crisis in the European Union during 2010–11.

Figure 10.1 summarizes the volatility of the U.S. dollar from 1973. The USD Index measures the performance of the U.S. dollar against a basket of currencies.

An interesting phenomenon in Figure 10.1 is the rapid rise in the value of the dollar between 1980 and 1985 and its subsequent fall between 1985 and 1988. A similar, though less pronounced, rise and fall in the value of the dollar occurred between 1995

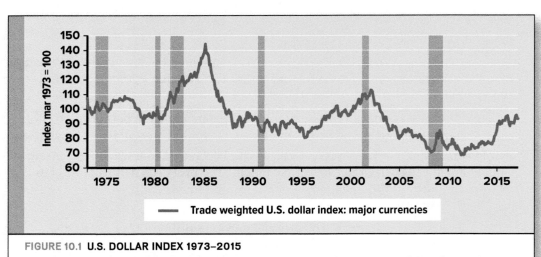

FIGURE 10.1 U.S. DOLLAR INDEX 1973–2015

Source: Board of Governors of the Federal Reserve System (US), Trade Weighted U.S. Dollar Index: Major Currencies [DTWEXM], retrieved from FRED, Federal Reserve Bank of St. Louis; https://fred.stlouisfed.org/series/DTWEXM, March 27, 2017. FRED® Graphs ©Federal Reserve Bank of St. Louis. 2017. All rights reserved. All FRED® Graphs appear courtesy of Federal Reserve Bank of St. Louis. https://fred.stlouisfed.org/

and 2012. We briefly discuss the rise and fall of the dollar during these periods because this tells us something about how the international monetary system has operated in recent years.

The rise in the value of the dollar between 1980 and 1985 occurred when the United States was running a large and growing trade deficit, importing substantially more than it exported. Conventional wisdom would suggest that the increased supply of dollars in the foreign exchange market as a result of the trade deficit should lead to a reduction in the value of the dollar, but as shown in Figure 10.1, it increased in value. Why?

A number of favourable factors overcame the unfavourable effect of a trade deficit. Strong economic growth in the United States attracted heavy inflows of capital from foreign investors seeking high returns on capital assets. High real interest rates attracted foreign investors seeking high returns on financial assets. At the same time, political turmoil in other parts of the world, along with relatively slow economic growth in the developed countries of Europe, helped create the view that the United States was a good place to invest. These inflows of capital increased the demand for dollars in the foreign exchange market, which pushed the value of the dollar upward against other currencies.

The fall in the value of the dollar between 1985 and 1988 was caused by a combination of government intervention and market forces. The rise in the dollar, which priced U.S. goods out of foreign markets and made imports relatively cheap, had contributed to a dismal trade picture. In 1985, the United States posted a then record-high trade deficit of more than $160 billion. This led to growth in demands for protectionism in the United States. In September 1985, the finance ministers and central bank governors of the so-called Group of Five major industrial countries (Great Britain, France, Japan, Germany, and the United States) met at the Plaza Hotel in New York and reached what was later referred to as the Plaza Accord. They announced that it would be desirable for most major currencies to appreciate vis-à-vis the U.S. dollar and pledged to intervene in the foreign exchange markets, selling dollars, to encourage this objective. The dollar had already begun to weaken during summer 1985, and this announcement further accelerated the decline.

The dollar continued to decline until 1987. The governments of the Group of Five began to worry that the dollar might decline too far, so the finance ministers of the Group of Five met in Paris in February 1987 and reached a new agreement known as the Louvre Accord. They agreed that exchange rates had been realigned sufficiently and pledged to support the stability of exchange rates around their current levels by intervening in the foreign exchange markets when necessary to buy and sell currency. Although the dollar continued to decline for a few months after the Louvre Accord, the rate of decline slowed, and by early 1988 the decline had ended.

Except for a brief speculative flurry around the time of the Persian Gulf War in 1991, the dollar was relatively stable for the first half of the 1990s. However, in the late 1990s, the dollar again began to appreciate against most major currencies, including the euro after its introduction, even though the United States was still running a significant balance-of-payments deficit. Once again, the driving force for the appreciation in the value of the dollar was that foreigners continued to invest in U.S. financial assets, primarily stocks and bonds, and the inflow of money drove up the value of the dollar on foreign exchange markets. The inward investment was due to a belief that U.S. financial assets offered a favourable rate of return.

By 2002, however, foreigners had started to lose their appetite for U.S. stocks and bonds, and the inflow of money into the United States slowed. Instead of reinvesting dollars earned from exports to the United States in U.S. financial assets, they exchanged those dollars for other currencies, particularly euros, to invest them in non-dollar-denominated assets. One reason for this was the continued growth in the U.S. trade deficit.

The U.S. deficit meant that even more dollars were flowing out of the United States into foreign hands, and those foreigners were less inclined to reinvest those dollars in the United States at a rate required to keep the dollar stable. This growing reluctance of foreigners to invest in the United States was in turn due to several factors. First, there was a slowdown in U.S. economic activity during 2001–2002. Second, the U.S. government's budget deficit expanded rapidly after 2001. This led to fears that ultimately the budget deficit would be financed by an expansionary monetary policy that could lead to higher price inflation. Third, from 2003 onward, U.S. government officials began to "talk down" the value of the dollar, in part because the administration believed that a cheaper dollar would increase exports and reduce imports, thereby improving the U.S. balance of trade position. Foreigners saw this as a signal that the U.S. government would not intervene in the foreign exchange markets to prop up the value of the dollar, which increased their reluctance to reinvest dollars earned from export sales in U.S. financial assets.

As a result of these factors, demand for dollars weakened, and the value of the dollar slid on the foreign exchange markets. Though it has recovered in recent years, due in part to continued global turmoil elsewhere around the globe, some believe that it could fall in the coming years, particularly if large holders of U.S. dollars, such as oil-producing states and China, decide to diversify their foreign exchange holdings (see the accompanying Country Focus for a discussion of this possibility with respect to oil-producing states).

Interestingly, from mid-2008 through early 2009, the dollar staged a moderate rally against major currencies, despite the fact that the American economy was suffering from a serious financial crisis. The reason seems to be that despite America's problems, things were even worse in many other countries, and foreign investors saw the dollar as a safe haven and put their money in low-risk U.S. assets, particularly low-yielding U.S. government bonds. This rally faltered in mid-2009 as investors became worried about the level of U.S. indebtedness.

ANOTHER PERSPECTIVE

Iran Presses Ahead with U.S. Dollar Attack

The Iranian Oil Bourse started trading oil in currencies other than the U.S. dollar in March 20, 2012. Iran has the third-largest oil reserves in the world and pricing oil in currencies other than dollars is a provocative move aimed at Washington. Iran announced in February 2017 that it would not use the U.S. dollar in financial statements. A switch to non-dollar terms for its oil payments could lead to a new oil price that would be denominated in euro, yen, or even the yuan or rupee, and will add both currency risk and overall volatility.

India is already in talks with Iran over how it can pay for its oil in rupees. Even more surprisingly, reports have suggested that India is even considering paying for its oil in gold bullion. However, it is more likely that the country will pay in rupees, a currency that is not freely convertible.

Sources: Garry White, "Iran presses ahead with dollar attack," *The Telegraph*, February 12, 2012, http://www.telegraph.co.uk/finance/commodities/9077600/Iran-presses-ahead-with-dollar-attack.html; D. Dudley, "Iran to ditch the dollar in wake of Trump's 'Muslim ban'," *Forbes*, January 30, 2017, https://www.forbes.com/sites/dominicdudley/2017/01/30/iran-to-ditch-dollar/#2d32ec726715, accessed June 21, 2017; and B. McKernan, "Iran to stop using US dollar in response to Donald Trump's 'Muslim ban'," *The Independent*, http://www.independent.co.uk/news/world/middle-east/iran-stop-using-us-dollar-currency-donald-trump-muslim-ban-immigration-refugee-iraq-syria-libya-a7556846.html, accessed June 21, 2017.

Thus, we see that in recent history, the value of the dollar has been determined by both market forces and government intervention. Under a floating exchange rate regime, market forces have produced a volatile dollar exchange rate. Governments have responded by intervening in the market—buying and selling dollars—in an attempt to limit the market's volatility and to correct what they see as overvaluation or potential undervaluation of the dollar. In addition to direct intervention, the value of the dollar has frequently been influenced by statements from government officials. The frequency of government intervention in the foreign exchange markets explains why the current system is often referred to as a managed-float system or a dirty-float system.

LO3 Fixed versus Floating Exchange Rates

The breakdown of the Bretton Woods system has not stopped the debate about the relative merits of fixed versus floating exchange rate regimes. Disappointment with the system of floating rates in recent years has led to renewed debate about the merits of fixed exchange rates. In this section, we review the arguments for fixed and floating exchange rate regimes.[9] We will discuss the case for floating rates before discussing why many commentators are disappointed with the experience under floating exchange rates and yearn for a system of fixed rates.

The Case for Floating Exchange Rates

The case for floating exchange rates has two main elements: monetary policy autonomy and automatic trade balance adjustments.

MONETARY POLICY AUTONOMY

It is argued that under a fixed system, a country's ability to expand or contract its money supply as it sees fit is limited by the need to maintain exchange rate parity. Monetary expansion can lead to inflation, which puts downward pressure on a fixed exchange rate (as predicted by the PPP theory; see Chapter 9). Similarly, monetary contraction requires high interest rates (to reduce the demand for money). Higher interest rates lead to an inflow of money from abroad, which puts upward pressure on a fixed exchange rate. Thus, to maintain exchange rate parity under a fixed system, countries were limited in their ability to use monetary policy to expand or contract their economies.

Advocates of a floating exchange rate regime argue that removing the obligation to maintain exchange rate parity would restore monetary control to a government. If a government faced with unemployment wanted to increase its money supply to stimulate domestic demand and reduce unemployment, it could do so unencumbered by the need to maintain its exchange rate. While monetary expansion might lead to inflation, this would lead to a depreciation in the country's currency. If PPP theory is correct, the resulting currency depreciation on the foreign exchange markets should offset the effects of inflation. Although domestic inflation would have an impact on the exchange rate under a floating exchange rate regime, it should have no impact on businesses' international cost competitiveness due to exchange rate depreciation. The rise in domestic costs should be exactly offset by the fall in the value of the country's currency on the foreign exchange markets. Similarly, a government could use monetary policy to contract the economy without worrying about the need to maintain parity.

TRADE BALANCE ADJUSTMENTS

Under the Bretton Woods system, if a country developed a permanent deficit in its balance of trade (importing more than it exported), that could not be corrected by domestic policy, the IMF would have to agree to a currency devaluation. Critics of this system argue that the adjustment mechanism works much more smoothly under a floating exchange rate regime. They argue that if a country is running a trade deficit, the imbalance between the supply and demand of that country's currency in the foreign exchange markets (supply exceeding demand) will lead to depreciation in its exchange rate. In turn, by making its exports cheaper and its imports more expensive, an exchange rate depreciation should correct the trade deficit.

The Case for Fixed Exchange Rates

The case for fixed exchange rates rests on arguments about monetary discipline, speculation, uncertainty, and the lack of connection between the trade balance and exchange rates.

MONETARY DISCIPLINE

We have already discussed the nature of monetary discipline inherent in a fixed exchange rate system when we discussed the Bretton Woods system. The need to maintain a fixed exchange rate parity ensures that governments do not expand their money supplies at inflationary rates. While advocates of floating rates argue that each country should be allowed to choose its own inflation rate (the monetary autonomy argument), advocates of fixed rates argue that governments all too often give in to political pressures and expand the monetary supply far too rapidly, causing unacceptably high price inflation. A fixed exchange rate regime would ensure that this does not occur.

SPECULATION

Critics of a floating exchange rate regime also argue that speculation can cause fluctuations in exchange rates. They point to the dollar's rapid rise and fall during the 1980s, which they claim had nothing to do with comparative inflation rates and the U.S. trade deficit, but everything to do with speculation. They argue that when foreign exchange dealers see a currency depreciating, they tend to sell the currency in the expectation of future depreciation regardless of the currency's longer-term prospects. As more traders jump on the bandwagon, the expectations of depreciation are realized. Such destabilizing speculation tends to accentuate the fluctuations around the exchange rate's long-run value. It can damage a country's economy by distorting export and import prices. Thus, advocates of a fixed exchange rate regime argue that such a system will limit the destabilizing effects of speculation.

UNCERTAINTY

Speculation also adds to the uncertainty surrounding future currency movements that characterizes floating exchange rate regimes. The unpredictability of exchange rate movements in the post-Bretton Woods era has made business planning difficult, and it makes exporting, importing, and foreign investment risky activities. Given a volatile exchange rate, international businesses do not know how to react to the changes—and often they do not react. Why change plans for exporting, importing, or foreign

COUNTRY FOCUS

The U.S. Dollar, Oil Prices, and Recycling Petrodollars

Between 2004 and 2008, global oil prices surged. They peaked at $147 a barrel in July 2008, up from about $20 in 2001, before falling sharply back to a $34 to $48 range by early 2009. Since then, they have increased again, rising to around $50 a barrel in early 2017. The initial rise in oil prices was due to a combination of greater-than-expected demand for oil, particularly from rapidly developing giants such as China and India; tight supplies; and perceived geopolitical risks in the Middle East, the world's largest oil-producing region.

The surge in oil prices was a windfall for oil-producing countries. Collectively, they earned well over $1 trillion a year at the 2008 price peak—some 64 percent of which went to members of OPEC. Saudi Arabia, the world's largest oil producer, reaped a major share. Because oil is priced in U.S. dollars, the rise in oil prices has translated into a substantial increase in the dollar holdings of oil producers (the dollars earned from the sale of oil are often referred to as *petrodollars*). In essence, rising oil prices represent a net transfer of dollars from oil consumers in countries such as the United States to oil producers in Russia, Saudi Arabia, and Venezuela. What have they been doing with these dollars?

One option for producing countries was to spend their petrodollars on public-sector infrastructure, such as health services, education, roads, and telecommunications systems. Among other things, this could boost economic growth in those countries and pull in foreign imports, which would help to counterbalance the trade surpluses enjoyed by oil producers and support global economic growth. Spending did indeed pick up in many oil-producing countries. The last time oil prices increased sharply in 1979, oil producers significantly ramped up spending on infrastructure, only to find themselves saddled with excessive debt when oil prices collapsed a few years later. This time they were more cautious—an approach that seems wise given the rapid fall in oil prices during late 2008.

Another option was for oil producers to invest a good chunk of the dollars they earn from oil sales in dollar-denominated assets, such as U.S. bonds, stocks, and real estate. This did happen. OPEC members in particular funnelled dollars back into U.S. assets, mostly low-risk government bonds. The implication is that by recycling their petrodollars, oil producers helped to finance the large and growing current account deficit of the United States, enabling it to pay its large oil import bill.

A third possibility for oil producers was to invest in non-dollar-denominated assets, including European and Japanese bonds and stocks. This, too, happened. Also, some OPEC investors have purchased not just small equity positions, but entire companies. For example, Dubai International Capital purchased the Tussauds Group, a British theme-park firm, and DP World of Dubai purchased P&O, Britain's biggest port and ferries group.

Despite examples such as these, between 2005 and 2008 at least, the bulk of petrodollars appear to have been recycled into dollar-denominated assets. In part, this was because U.S. interest rates increased throughout 2004–2007 and in part because the US was viewed as a safe haven in economically troubled times. However, if the flow of petrodollars should dry up, with oil-rich countries investing in other currencies, such as euro-denominated assets, the dollar could fall significantly.

Questions

1. Should producing countries attempt to diversify their oil-based economies? How could they do this? What economic sectors could they focus on?

2. The worldwide economic slowdown has affected real estate prices and projects in oil-producing countries. Give some examples of projects that were started, or planned, in the peak economic times which have stalled or never got off the ground.

Sources: "Oil producers' surpluses: Recycling the Petrodollars," *The Economist*, November 12, 2005, pp. 101–02; S. Johnson, "Dollar's Rise Aided by OPEC Holdings," *Financial Times*, December 5, 2005, p. 17; and "The petrodollar puzzle," *The Economist*, June 9, 2007, p. 86.

investment after a 6 percent fall in the dollar this month, when the dollar may rise 6 percent next month? This uncertainty, according to the critics, dampens the growth of international trade and investment. They argue that a fixed exchange rate, by eliminating such uncertainty, promotes the growth of international trade and investment. Advocates of a floating system reply that the forward exchange market insures against the risks associated with exchange rate fluctuations (see Chapter 9), so the adverse impact of uncertainty on the growth of international trade and investment has been overstated.

TRADE BALANCE ADJUSTMENTS AND ECONOMIC RECOVERY

Those in favour of floating exchange rates argue that floating rates help adjust trade imbalances. Critics question the closeness of the link between the exchange rate and the trade balance. They claim trade deficits are determined by the balance between savings and investment in a country, not by the external value of its currency.[10] They argue that depreciation in a currency will lead to inflation (due to the resulting increase in import prices). This inflation will wipe out any apparent gains in cost competitiveness that come from currency depreciation. In other words, a depreciating exchange rate will not boost exports and reduce imports, as advocates of floating rates claim; it will simply boost price inflation. In support of this argument, those who favour fixed rates point out that the 40 percent drop in the value of the dollar between 1985 and 1988 did not correct the U.S. trade deficit. In reply, advocates of a floating exchange rate regime argue that between 1985 and 1992, the U.S. trade deficit fell from over $160 billion to about $70 billion, and they attribute this in part to the decline in the value of the dollar.

Who Is Right?

Which side is right in the vigorous debate between those who favour a fixed exchange rate and those who favour a floating exchange rate? Economists cannot agree on this issue. From a business perspective, this is unfortunate because business, as a major player on the international trade and investment scene, has a large stake in the resolution of the debate. Would international business be better off under a fixed regime, or are flexible rates better? The evidence is not clear.

We do, however, know that a fixed exchange rate regime modelled along the lines of the Bretton Woods system will not work. Speculation ultimately broke the system, a phenomenon that advocates of fixed rate regimes claim is associated with floating exchange rates! Nevertheless, a different kind of fixed exchange rate system might be more enduring and might foster the stability that would facilitate more rapid growth in international trade and investment. In the next section, we look at potential models for such a system and the problems with such systems.

LO4 Exchange Rate Regimes in Practice

Governments around the world pursue a number of different exchange rate policies. These range from a pure "free float," where the exchange rate is determined by market forces, to a pegged system that has some aspects of the pre-1973 Bretton Woods system of fixed exchange rates. Some 21 percent of the IMF's members allow their currency to float freely. Another 23 percent intervene in only a limited way (the so-called *managed float*). A further 5 percent of IMF members now have no separate legal tender of their own (this figure excludes the European Union countries that have adopted the euro). These are typically smaller states, mostly in Africa or the Caribbean, that have no domestic currency and have adopted a foreign currency as legal tender within their borders, typically the U.S. dollar or the euro. The remaining countries use more inflexible systems, including a fixed peg arrangement (43 percent) under which they peg their currencies to other currencies, such as the U.S. dollar or the euro, or to a basket of currencies. Other countries have adopted a system under which their exchange rate is allowed to fluctuate against other currencies within a target zone (an adjustable, or crawling, peg system). In this section, we will look more closely at the mechanics and implications of exchange rate regimes that rely on a currency peg or target zone.

Pegged Exchange Rates

Under a pegged exchange rate regime, a country will peg the value of its currency to that of a major currency so that, for example, as the U.S. dollar rises in value, its own currency rises too. Pegged exchange rates are popular among many of the world's smaller nations. As with a full fixed exchange rate regime, the great virtue claimed for a pegged exchange rate is that it imposes monetary discipline on a country and leads to low inflation For example, if Belize pegs the value of the Belizean dollar to that of the U.S. dollar so that US$1 = B$1.97, then the Belizean government must make sure the inflation rate in Belize is similar to that in the United States. An inflation rate in Belize that is greater than the U.S. inflation rate will lead to pressure to devalue the Belizean dollar (i.e., to alter the peg). To maintain the peg, the Belizean government would be required to rein in inflation. Of course, for a pegged exchange rate to impose monetary discipline on a country, the country whose currency is chosen for the peg must also pursue sound monetary policy.

Evidence shows that adopting a pegged exchange rate regime does moderate inflationary pressures in a country. An IMF study concluded that countries with pegged exchange rates had an average annual inflation rate of 8 percent, compared with 14 percent for intermediate regimes and 16 percent for floating regimes.[11] However, many countries operate with only a nominal peg and in practice are willing to devalue their currency rather than pursue a tight monetary policy. It can be very difficult for a smaller country to maintain a peg against another currency if capital is flowing out of the country and foreign exchange traders are speculating against the currency. Something like this occurred in 1997 when a combination of adverse capital flows and currency speculation forced several Asian countries, including Thailand and Malaysia, to abandon pegs against the U.S. dollar and let their currencies float freely. Malaysia and Thailand would not have been in that position had they dealt with a number of problems that began to arise in their economies during the 1990s, including excessive private-sector debt and expanding current account trade deficits.

Currency Boards

Hong Kong's experience during the 1997 Asian currency crisis, however, has added a new dimension to the debate over how to manage a pegged exchange rate. During late 1997 when other Asian currencies were collapsing, Hong Kong maintained the value of its currency against the U.S. dollar at around US$1 = HK$7.8 despite several concerted speculative attacks. Hong Kong's currency board has been credited with this success. A country that introduces a **currency board** commits itself to converting its domestic currency on demand into another currency at a fixed exchange rate. To make this commitment credible, the currency board holds reserves of foreign currency equal at the fixed exchange rate to at least 100 percent of the domestic currency issued. The system used in Hong Kong means its currency must be fully backed by the U.S. dollar at the specified exchange rate. This is still not a true fixed exchange rate regime, because the U.S. dollar, and by extension the Hong Kong dollar, floats against other currencies, but it has some features of a fixed exchange rate regime.

Under this arrangement, the currency board can issue additional domestic notes and coins only when there are foreign exchange reserves to back it. This limits the ability of the government to print money and, thereby, create inflationary pressures. Under a strict currency board system, interest rates adjust automatically. If investors want to switch out of domestic currency into, for example, U.S. dollars, the supply of domestic currency will shrink. This will cause interest rates to rise until it eventually becomes attractive for investors to hold the local currency again. In the case of Hong Kong, the interest rate on three-month deposits climbed as high as 20 percent in late 1997 as investors switched out of Hong Kong dollars and into U.S. dollars. However, the dollar peg held, and interest rates declined again.

Since its establishment in 1983, the Hong Kong currency board has weathered several storms. This success seems to be persuading other countries in the developing world to consider a similar system. Argentina introduced a currency board in 1991, and Bulgaria, Estonia, and Lithuania have all gone down this road in recent years (seven IMF members had currency boards in 2006). Despite growing interest in the arrangement, however, critics are quick to point out that currency boards have their drawbacks.[12] If local inflation rates remain higher than the inflation rate in the country to which the currency is pegged, the currencies of countries with currency boards can become uncompetitive and overvalued. Also, under a currency board system, government lacks the ability to set interest rates. Interest rates in Hong Kong, for example, are effectively set by the U.S. Federal Reserve. Despite these drawbacks, Hong Kong's success in avoiding the currency collapse that afflicted its Asian neighbours suggests that other developing countries may adopt a similar system.

LO5 Crisis Management by the IMF

Many observers initially believed that the collapse of the Bretton Woods system in 1973 would diminish the role of the IMF within the international monetary system. The IMF's original function was to provide a pool of money from which members could borrow, in the short term, to adjust their balance-of-payments position and maintain their exchange rate. Some believed the demand for short-term loans would be considerably diminished under a floating exchange rate regime. A trade deficit would presumably lead to a decline in a country's exchange rate, which would help reduce imports and boost exports. No temporary IMF adjustment loan would be needed. Consistent with this, after 1973, most industrialized countries tended to let the foreign exchange market determine exchange rates in response to demand and supply. No major industrial country has borrowed funds from the IMF since the mid-1970s, when Great Britain and Italy did. Since the early 1970s, the rapid development of global capital markets has allowed developed countries such as Great Britain and the United States to finance their deficits by borrowing private money, as opposed to drawing on IMF funds.

Despite these developments, the activities of the IMF have expanded over the past 30 years. By 2016, the IMF had 188 members, 52 of which had some kind of IMF program in place. In 1997, the institution implemented its largest rescue packages until that date, committing more than $110 billion in short-term loans to three troubled Asian countries—South Korea, Indonesia, and Thailand. This was followed by additional IMF rescue packages in Turkey, Russia, Argentina, and Brazil. IMF loans increased again in late 2008 as the global financial crisis took hold. Between 2008 and 2010, the IMF made more than $100 billion in loans to troubled economies such as Latvia, Greece, and Ireland. In April 2009, in response to the growing financial crisis, major IMF members agreed to triple the institution's resources from $250 billion to $750 billion, thereby giving the IMF the financial leverage to act aggressively in times of global financial crisis.

The IMF's activities have expanded because periodic financial crises have continued to hit many economies in the post–Bretton Woods era. The IMF has repeatedly lent money to nations experiencing financial crises, requesting in return that the governments enact certain macroeconomic policies. Critics of the IMF claim these policies have not always been as beneficial as the IMF might have hoped and, in some cases, may have made things worse. Following the IMF loans to several Asian economies, these criticisms reached new levels, and a vigorous debate was waged as to the appropriate role of the IMF. In this section, we shall discuss some of the main challenges the IMF has had to deal with over the past three decades and review the ongoing debate over the role of the IMF.

Financial Crises in the Post–Bretton Woods Era

A number of broad types of financial crises have occurred over the past quarter century, many of which have required IMF involvement. A **currency crisis** occurs when a speculative attack on the exchange value of a currency results in a sharp depreciation in the value of the currency or forces authorities to expend large volumes of international currency reserves and sharply increase interest rates to defend the prevailing exchange rate. A **banking crisis** refers to a loss of confidence in the banking system that leads to a run on banks as individuals and companies withdraw their deposits. A **foreign debt crisis** is a situation in which a country cannot service its foreign debt obligations, whether private or government debt. These crises tend to have common underlying macroeconomic causes: high inflation, a widening current account deficit, excessive expansion of domestic borrowing, and asset price inflation (such as sharp increases in stock and property prices).[13] At times, elements of currency, banking, and debt crises may be present simultaneously, as in the 1997 Asian crisis or the 2010 crisis in Ireland.

To assess the frequency of financial crises, the IMF looked at the macroeconomic performance of a group of 53 countries from 1975 to 1997 (22 of these countries were developed nations, and 31 were developing countries).[14] The IMF found there had been 158 currency crises, including 55 episodes in which a country's currency declined by more than 25 percent. There were also 54 banking crises. The IMF's data suggest that developing nations were more than twice as likely to experience currency and banking crises as developed nations. It is not surprising, therefore, that most of the IMF's loan activities since the mid-1970s have been targeted toward developing nations.

For another example of a crisis, consider what happened in South Korea during the 1997 Asian crisis. The Asian crisis was triggered by excessive private borrowing during the 1990s in a number of Asian countries, including Thailand, Malaysia, Indonesia, and South Korea. All of these countries were experiencing an economic boom. Much of this borrowing was used to make speculative investments in property and industrial capacity. The result was the creation of excess capacity.

ANOTHER PERSPECTIVE

Canada's Monetary Policy

Canada's monetary policy is made up of two key components. The first is to pursue a flexible exchange rate, not tied or pegged to any other currency. This allows Canada to pursue a monetary policy that best suits its own purpose and is separate from that of its large neighbour, the United States. Secondly, the monetary policy is built on keeping inflation under control, within a target range of 1–3 percent.

For more information visit the Bank of Canada's Web site at http://www.bank-banque-canada. ca. Search for the monetary policy page.

In 1997, several Asian currencies started to fall sharply as international investors realized that there was a speculative investment bubble in the region. They took their money out of local currencies, changed it into U.S. dollars, and the local currencies started to fall precipitously. The currency declines started in Thailand and then, in a process of contagion, quickly spread to other countries in the region. Stabilizing the currencies required massive help from the IMF. In the case of South Korea, local enterprises had built up huge debt loads as they invested heavily in new industrial capacity. By 1997, they found they had too much industrial capacity and could not generate the income required to service their debt. South Korean banks and companies had also made the mistake of borrowing in dollars, much of it in the form of short-term loans that would come due within a year. Thus, when the Korean won started to decline in the fall of 1997 in sympathy with the problems elsewhere in Asia, South Korean companies saw their debt obligations balloon. Several large companies were forced to file for bankruptcy. This triggered a decline in the South Korean currency and stock market that was difficult to halt. The South Korean central bank tried to keep the dollar/won exchange rate above $1 = W1000 but found that this only depleted its foreign exchange reserves. On November 17, 1997, the South Korean central bank gave up the defence of the won, which quickly fell to $1 = W1500.

MANAGEMENT FOCUS

Using Gold As A Method of Payment

As this chapter notes, gold has been used as a currency or method of payment for centuries. However it has always been inconvenient to make very small payments using gold, though people through the ages have tried. For example, many old gold coins are "clipped," where a certain amount of gold was clipped or removed from a gold coin, to create a smaller price in order to make a payment.

A Toronto-based company aims to change this. In 2014, BitGold was formed as a company that promoted the buying and selling of smaller quantities of gold, using gold as a method of payment, and storing gold. All of these transactions would take place electronically. Despite the unfortunate choice of name (people have confused the company with Bitcoin, which has had a notorious past in its rise to become a global currency), BitGold quickly found itself operating across the world. Part of its quick rise to success came from a steady source of initial funding: from the Soros family and from a few Canadian Pension Plans.

In 2015, the company acquired Goldmoney Inc. and rolled its operations under this one banner. Today in early 2017, the company has just under 1.4 million customers holding $1.37 billion in assets in over 150 countries. The company's mission is "to provide secure and accessible gold-based savings to everyone, while also making gold useful for everyday payments. Goldmoney helps people around the world build and protect their savings, transfer value instantly, and empower their business with the tools they need to succeed." In early 2017 the company announced that its products achieved recognition as compliant with the new Shariah gold standard established by the Accounting and Auditing Organisation for Islamic Financial Institutions, AAOIFI, in conjunction with the World Gold Council. This can be expected to broaden the use of gold in the Muslim world in the future.

Questions

1. How can Goldmoney continue to grow in the future? Are there other products they could offer?
2. What type of company is Goldmoney or what type of company could it become? Currently in Canada it is regulated as a Dealer in Precious Metals. But could it become a bank? A money transfer service like Western Union? Could its products become a form of currency like the U.S. dollar?

Sources: Interview with firm in 2015 and 2016. https://www.goldmoney.com/about, *Goldmoney Insights*, January 23, 2017 (press release).

With its economy on the verge of collapse, the South Korean government requested $20 billion in standby loans from the IMF on November 21. As the negotiations progressed, it became apparent that South Korea was going to need far more than $20 billion. Among other problems, the country's short-term foreign debt was found to be twice as large as previously thought at close to US$100 billion, while the country's foreign exchange reserves were down to less than US$6 billion. On December 3, 1997, the IMF and South Korean government reached a deal to lend US$55 billion to the country. The agreement with the IMF called for the South Koreans to open their economy and banking system to foreign investors. South Korea also pledged to restrain Korea's largest enterprises, the *chaebol*, by reducing their share of bank financing and requiring them to publish consolidated financial statements and undergo annual independent external audits. On trade liberalization, the IMF said South Korea would comply with its commitments to the World Trade Organization to eliminate trade-related subsidies and restrictive import licensing and would streamline its import certification procedures, all of which was aimed at opening the South Korean economy to greater foreign competition.[15]

Evaluating the IMF's Policy Prescriptions

All IMF loan packages come with conditions attached. Until very recently, the IMF has insisted on a combination of tight macroeconomic policies, including cuts in public spending, higher interest rates, and tight monetary policy. It has also often pushed for the deregulation of sectors formerly protected from domestic and foreign competition, privatization of state-owned assets, and better financial reporting from the banking sector. These policies are designed to cool overheated economies by reining in inflation and reducing government spending and debt. This set of policy prescriptions has resulted in tough criticisms from many observers, and the IMF itself has started to change its approach.[16]

INAPPROPRIATE POLICIES

One criticism is that the IMF's traditional policy prescriptions represent a "one-size-fits-all" approach to macroeconomic policy that is inappropriate for many countries. In the case of the 1997 Asian crisis, critics argue that the tight macroeconomic policies imposed by the IMF were not well suited to countries that were suffering from a private-sector debt crisis with deflationary undertones, not from excessive government spending and inflation.[17]

In South Korea, for example, the government had been running a budget surplus for years (it was 4 percent of South Korea's GDP in 1994–1996), and inflation was low at about 5 percent. South Korea had the second strongest financial position of any country in the Organisation for Economic Co-operation and Development. Despite this, critics say, the IMF insisted on applying the same policies that it applies to countries suffering from high inflation. The IMF required South Korea to maintain an inflation rate of 5 percent. However, given the collapse in the value of its currency and the subsequent rise in price for imports such as oil, critics claimed inflationary pressures would inevitably increase in South Korea. So to hit a 5 percent inflation rate, the South Koreans would be forced to apply an unnecessarily tight monetary policy. Short-term interest rates in South Korea did jump from 12.5 percent to 21 percent immediately after the country signed its initial deal with the IMF. Increasing interest rates made it even more difficult for companies to service their already excessive short-term debt obligations, and critics used this as evidence to argue that the cure prescribed by the IMF may actually increase the probability of widespread corporate defaults, not reduce them.

At the time the IMF rejected this criticism. According to the IMF, the central task was to rebuild confidence in the won. Once this was achieved, the won would recover from its oversold levels, reducing the size of South Korea's dollar-denominated debt burden when expressed in won, making it easier for companies to service their debt. The IMF also argued that by requiring South Korea to remove restrictions on foreign direct investment, foreign capital would flow into the country to take advantage of cheap assets. This, too, would increase demand for the Korean currency and help to improve the dollar/won exchange rate.

South Korea did recover fairly quickly from the crisis, supporting the position of the IMF. While the economy contracted by 7 percent in 1998, by 2000 it had rebounded and grew at a 9 percent rate (measured by growth in GDP). Inflation, which peaked at 8 percent in 1998, fell to 2 percent by 2000, and unemployment fell from 7 percent to 4 percent over the same period. The won hit a low of $1 = W1812 in early 1998, but by 2000 was back to an exchange rate of around $1 = W1200, at which it seems to have stabilized.

ANOTHER PERSPECTIVE

UK Commits Further £10bn to IMF Bailout Fund

In April 2012, Britain committed a further £10bn to the International Monetary Fund's bailout war chest. Although the loan from the UK is sizeable, the Chancellor did not have to seek Parliamentary approval because it narrowly falls within the headroom he already has to provide to the Fund. It means that Britain's exposure to the IMF, which is deeply involved with the euro bailouts, will rise from just under £30bn currently to around £40bn. While in Washington at the time, then-Chancellor Osborne said: "The UK sees itself as part of the solution to the global debt crisis rather than adding to it. We will be part of the global effort." Mr. Osborne believed that a strong IMF was needed. He wanted the UK to be one of the many countries to support the IMF and become part of the global effort to increase the resources of the IMF. However, the Chancellor faced controversy back in the UK because their Parliament did not have to put the funding to a vote.

Source: Philip Aldrick, "Britain pledges additional £10bn towards IMF war chest," *The Telegraph*, April 20, 2012, http://www.telegraph.co.uk/finance/financialcrisis/9216956/Britain-pledges-additional-10bn-towards-IMF-war-chest.html; "Chancellor George Osborne criticised over UK £10bn IMF loan," BBC News, http://www.bbc.com/news/business-17794990, accessed June 21, 2017.

MORAL HAZARD

A second criticism of the IMF is that its rescue efforts are exacerbating a problem known to economists as moral hazard. **Moral hazard** arises when people behave recklessly because they know they will be saved if things go wrong. Critics point out that many Japanese and Western banks were far too willing to lend large amounts of capital to overleveraged Asian companies during the boom years of the 1990s. These critics argue that the banks should now be forced to pay the price for their rash lending policies, even if that means some banks must close.[18] Only by taking such drastic action, the argument goes, will banks learn the error of their ways and not engage in rash lending in the future. By providing support to these countries, the IMF is reducing the probability of debt default and in effect bailing out the banks whose loans gave rise to this situation.

This argument ignores two critical points. First, if some Japanese or Western banks with heavy exposure to the troubled Asian economies were forced to write off their loans due to widespread debt default, the impact would have been difficult to contain. The failure of large Japanese banks, for example, could have triggered a meltdown in the Japanese financial markets. That would almost inevitably lead to a serious decline in stock markets around the world, which was the very risk the IMF was trying to avoid by stepping in with financial support. Second, it is incorrect to imply that some banks have not had to pay the price for rash lending policies. The IMF insisted on the closure of banks in South Korea, Thailand, and Indonesia after the 1997 Asian financial crisis. Foreign banks with short-term loans outstanding to South Korean enterprises have been forced by circumstances to reschedule those loans at interest rates that do not compensate for the extension of the loan maturity.

LACK OF ACCOUNTABILITY

The final criticism of the IMF is that it has become too powerful for an institution that lacks any real mechanism for accountability.[19] The IMF has determined macroeconomic policies in those countries, yet according to critics such as noted economist Jeffrey Sachs, the IMF, with a staff of less than 1000, lacks the expertise required to do a good job. Evidence of this, according to Sachs, can be found in the fact that the IMF was singing the praises of the Thai and South Korean governments only months before both countries lurched into crisis. Then the IMF put together a draconian program for South Korea without having deep knowledge of the country. Sachs's solution to this problem is to reform the IMF so it makes greater use of outside experts and so its operations are open to greater outside scrutiny.

OBSERVATIONS

As with many debates about international economics, it is not clear which side is correct about the appropriateness of IMF policies. There are cases where one can argue that IMF policies have been counterproductive, or only had limited success. For example, one might question the success of the IMF's involvement in Turkey given that the country has had to implement some 18 IMF programs since 1958! But the IMF can also point to some notable accomplishments, including its success in containing the Asian crisis, which could have rocked the global international monetary system to its core, and its actions in 2008–10 to contain the global financial crisis, quickly stepping in to rescue Iceland, Ireland, Greece, and Latvia. Similarly, many observers give the IMF credit for its deft handling of politically difficult situations, such as the Mexican peso crisis, and for successfully promoting a free market philosophy.

Several years after the IMF's intervention, the economies of Asia and Mexico recovered. Certainly they all averted the kind of catastrophic implosion that might have occurred had the IMF not stepped in, and although some countries still faced considerable problems, it is not clear that the IMF should take much blame for this. The IMF cannot force countries to adopt the policies required to correct economic mismanagement. While a government may commit to taking corrective action in return for an IMF loan, internal political problems may make it difficult for a government to act on that commitment. In such cases, the IMF is caught between a rock and a hard place, because if it decided to withhold money, it might trigger financial collapse and the kind of contagion that it seeks to avoid.

Finally, it is notable that in recent years the IMF has started to change its policies. In response to the global financial crisis of 2008–09, the IMF began to urge countries to adopt policies that included fiscal stimulus and monetary easing—the direct opposite of what the fund traditionally advocated. Some economists in the fund are also now arguing that higher inflation rates might be a good thing, if the consequence is greater growth in aggregate demand, which would help to pull nations out of recessionary conditions. The IMF, in other words, is starting to display the very flexibility in policy responses that its critics claim it lacks. While the traditional policy of tight controls on fiscal policy and tight monetary policy targets might be appropriate for countries suffering from high inflation rates, the Asian economic crisis and the 2008–09 global financial crisis were caused not by high inflation rates, but by excessive debt, and the IMF's "new approach" seems tailored to deal with this.[20]

LO6 IMPLICATIONS FOR BUSINESS

The implications for international businesses of the material discussed in this chapter fall into three main areas: currency management, business strategy, and corporate–government relations.

CURRENCY MANAGEMENT

An obvious implication with regard to currency management is that companies must recognize that the foreign exchange market does not work quite as depicted in Chapter 9. The current system is a mixed system in which a combination of government intervention and speculative activity can drive the foreign exchange market. Companies engaged in significant foreign exchange activities need to be aware of this and to adjust their foreign exchange transactions accordingly.

We have seen how speculative buying and selling of currencies can create very volatile movements in exchange rates (as exhibited by the rise and fall of the dollar during the 1980s) under the present system. Contrary to the predictions of the purchasing power parity theory (see Chapter 9), we have seen that exchange rate movements during the 1980s, at least with regard to the dollar, did not seem to be strongly influenced by relative inflation rates. Insofar as volatile exchange rates increase foreign exchange risk, this is not good news for business. On the other hand, as we saw in Chapter 9, the foreign exchange market has developed a number of instruments, such as the forward market and swaps, that can help to insure against foreign exchange risk. Not surprisingly, use of these instruments has increased markedly since the breakdown of the Bretton Woods system in 1973.

BUSINESS STRATEGY

The volatility of the present global exchange rate regime presents a conundrum for international businesses. Exchange rate movements are difficult to predict, and yet their movement can have a major impact on a business's competitive position. Faced with uncertainty about the future value of currencies, firms can utilize the forward exchange market. However, the forward exchange market is far from perfect as a predictor of future exchange rates (see Chapter 9). It is also difficult if not impossible to get adequate insurance coverage for exchange rate changes that might occur several years in the future. The forward market tends to offer coverage for exchange rate changes a few months—not years—ahead. Given this, it makes sense to pursue strategies that will increase the company's strategic flexibility in the face of unpredictable exchange rate movements.

Maintaining strategic flexibility can take the form of dispersing production to different locations around the globe as a real hedge against currency fluctuations. Consider the case of Daimler/Chrysler (now Daimler AG and Chrysler Group LLC), Germany's export-oriented automobile and aerospace company. In June 1995, the company stunned the German business community when it announced it expected to post a severe loss in 1995 of about $720 million (US$). The cause was Germany's strong currency, which had appreciated by 4 percent against a basket of major currencies since the beginning of 1995 and had risen by more than 30 percent against the U.S. dollar since late 1994. By mid-1995, the exchange rate against the U.S. dollar stood at US$1 = DM1.38. Daimler's management believed it could not make money with an exchange rate under US$1 = DM1.60. Daimler's senior managers concluded that the appreciation of the mark against the dollar was probably permanent, so they decided to move substantial production outside of Germany and increase purchasing of foreign components. The idea was to reduce the vulnerability of the company to future exchange rate movements. The Mercedes-Benz division implemented this move. Even before its acquisition of Chrysler Corporation in 1998, Mercedes planned to produce 10 percent of its cars outside of Germany by 2000, mostly in the United States.[21] Similarly, the move by Japanese automotive companies to expand their production capacity in Canada, beginning in 1986 in Cambridge, Ontario, (Toyota) and Alliston, Ontario, (Honda), and throughout Europe can be seen in the context of the increase in the value of the yen between 1985 and 1995, which raised the price of Japanese exports. For the Japanese companies, building production capacity overseas is a hedge against continued appreciation of the yen (as well as against trade barriers).

Another way of building strategic flexibility involves contracting out manufacturing. This allows a company to shift suppliers from country to country in response to changes in relative costs brought about by exchange rate movements. However, this kind of strategy works only for low-value-added manufacturing (e.g., textiles), in which the individual manufacturers have few if any firm-specific skills that contribute to the value of the product. It is inappropriate for high-value-added manufacturing, in which firm-specific technology and skills add significant value to the product (e.g., the heavy equipment industry) and in which switching costs are correspondingly high. For high-value-added manufacturing, switching suppliers will lead to a reduction in the value that is added, which may offset any cost gains arising from exchange rate fluctuations.

The roles of the IMF and the World Bank in the present international monetary system also have implications for business strategy. Increasingly, the IMF has been acting as the macroeconomic police of the world economy, insisting that countries seeking significant borrowings adopt IMF-mandated macroeconomic policies. These policies typically include anti-inflationary monetary policies and reductions in government spending. In the short run, such policies usually result in a sharp contraction of demand. International businesses selling or producing in such countries need to be aware of this and plan accordingly. In the long run, the kind of policies imposed by the IMF can promote economic growth and an expansion of demand, which create opportunities for international business.

CORPORATE–GOVERNMENT RELATIONS

As major players in the international trade and investment environment, businesses can influence government policy toward the international monetary system. For example, intense government lobbying by U.S. exporters helped convince the U.S. government that intervention in the foreign exchange market was necessary. Similarly, much of the impetus behind establishment of the exchange rate mechanism of the European monetary system came from European business people, who understood the costs of volatile exchange rates.

With this in mind, business can and should use its influence to promote an international monetary system that facilitates the growth of international trade and investment. Whether a fixed or floating regime is optimal is a subject for debate. However, exchange rate volatility such as the world experienced during the 1980s and 1990s creates an environment less conducive to international trade and investment than one with more stable exchange rates. Therefore, it would seem to be in the interests of international business to promote an international monetary system that minimizes volatile exchange rate movements, particularly when those movements are unrelated to long-run economic fundamentals.

Key Terms

banking crisis	floating exchange rates
central bank	foreign debt crisis
currency board	gold standard
currency crisis	international monetary system
dirty-float system	moral hazard
fixed exchange rates	pegged exchange rate

LO Learning Objectives Summary

1. The gold standard is a monetary standard that pegs currencies to gold and guarantees convertibility to gold. It was thought that the gold standard contained an automatic mechanism that contributed to the simultaneous achievement of a balance-of-payments equilibrium by all countries. The gold standard broke down during the 1930s as countries engaged in competitive devaluations. The fixed exchange rate system collapsed in 1973, primarily due to speculative pressure on the dollar following a rise in U.S. inflation and a growing U.S. balance-of-trade deficit. Since 1973, the world has operated with a floating exchange rate regime, and exchange rates have become more volatile and far less predictable. Volatile exchange rate movements have helped reopen the debate over the merits of fixed and floating systems.

2. The Bretton Woods system of fixed exchange rates was established in 1944. The U.S. dollar was the central currency of this system; the value of every other currency was pegged to its value. Significant exchange rate devaluations were allowed only with the permission of the IMF. The role of the IMF was to maintain order in the international monetary system (a) to avoid a repetition of the competitive devaluations of the 1930s and (b) to control price inflation by imposing monetary discipline on countries. Bretton Woods participants also created the World Bank, whose initial mission was to provide low interest loans to help rebuild the European economy. Eventually the Bank expanded its mission to "development" in general, lending to Third World Nations.

3. The case for a floating exchange rate regime claims (a) such a system gives countries autonomy regarding their monetary policy and (b) floating exchange rates facilitate smooth adjustment of trade imbalances. The case for a fixed exchange rate regime claims (a) the need to maintain a fixed exchange rate imposes monetary discipline on a country; (b) floating exchange rate regimes are vulnerable to speculative pressure; (c) the uncertainty that accompanies floating exchange rates dampens the growth of international trade and investment; and (d) far from correcting trade imbalances, depreciating a currency on the foreign exchange market tends to cause price inflation.

4. In today's international monetary system, some countries have adopted floating exchange rates, some have pegged their currency to another currency such as the U.S. dollar, and some have pegged their currency to a basket of other currencies, allowing their currency to fluctuate within a zone around the basket.

5. In the post–Bretton Woods era, the IMF has continued to play an important role in helping countries navigate their way through financial crises by lending significant capital to embattled governments and by requiring them to adopt certain macroeconomic policies. An important debate continues over the appropriateness of IMF-mandated macroeconomic policies. Critics charge that the IMF often imposes inappropriate conditions on developing nations that are the recipients of its loans.

6. The current managed-float system of exchange rate determination has increased the importance of currency management in international businesses. The volatility of exchange rates under the current managed-float system creates both opportunities and threats. One way of responding to this volatility is for companies to build strategic flexibility and limit their economic exposure by dispersing production to different locations around the globe by contracting out manufacturing (in the case of low-value-added manufacturing) and other means.

Critical Thinking and Discussion Questions

1. Why did the gold standard collapse? Is there a case for returning to some type of gold standard? What is it?

2. What opportunities might current IMF lending policies to developing nations create for international businesses? What threats might they create?

3. Do you think the standard IMF policy prescriptions of tight monetary policy and reduced government spending are always appropriate for developing nations experiencing a currency crisis? How might the IMF change its approach? What would the implications be for international businesses?

4. Debate the relative merits of fixed and floating exchange rate regimes. From the perspective of an international business, what are the most important criteria in a choice between the systems? Which system is the more desirable for an international business?

5. Imagine that Canada, the United States, and Mexico decide to adopt a fixed exchange rate system similar to the ERM of the European Monetary System. What would be the likely consequences of such a system for (a) international businesses and (a) the flow of trade and investment among the three countries?

6. Do you notice any shifts in geographic regions of retail gold buying since 2013?

Research Task   globalEDGE™   globaledge.msu.edu

Use the globalEDGE™ site to complete the following exercises:

1. Latvia has been a member state of the European Union (EU) since 2004. This means that the country adheres to the European System of Accounts 1995 (ESA95)—a classification system that ensures the comparability of national statistics in the EU. To gain a better sense of how this system of accounts funct ions, visit the Bank of Latvia Web site and provide an overview of the ESA95 sectors in Latvia. What do you notice about this classification system? What are the particular sectors of the Latvian economy?

2. The International Capital Markets division of the International Monetary Fund (IMF) publishes the *Global Financial Stability Report,* a semi-annual report that provides an assessment of global financial markets. Find the Global Financial Stability Map in the most recent report. Provide a description of the indicators used to construct the map, and briefly summarize what the most current map illustrates in terms of changes in financial stability risks.

CLOSING CASE

CURRENCY TROUBLE IN MALAWI

When the former World Bank economist Bingu wa Mutharika became president of the East African nation of Malawi in 2004, it seemed to be the beginning of a new age for one of the world's poorest countries. In landlocked Malawi, most of the population subsists on less than a dollar a day. Mutharika was their champion. He introduced a subsidy program for fertilizer to help poor farmers and gave them seeds. Agricultural output expanded, and the economy boomed, growing by 7 percent per year between 2005 and 2010. International donors loved him, and aid money started to pour in from the United Kingdom and the United States. By 2011, foreign aid was accounting for more than half of Malawi's annual budget.

In 2009, to no one's surprise, Mutharika was reelected president. Then things started to fall apart. Mutharika became increasingly dictatorial. He pushed aside the country's central bankers and ministers to take full control of economic policy. He called himself "Economist in Chief." Critics at home were harassed and jailed. Independent newspapers were threatened. When a cable from the British ambassador describing Mutharika as "autocratic and intolerant of criticism" was leaked, he expelled the British ambassador. Britain responded by freezing aid worth $550 million over four years. When police in mid-2011 killed 20 antigovernment protestors, other aid donors withdrew their support, including most significantly the United States. Mutharika told the donors they could go to hell. To compound matters, tobacco sales, which usually accounted for 60 percent of foreign currency revenues, plunged on diminishing international demand and the decreasing quality of the local product, which had been hurt by a persistive drought.

By late 2011, Malawi was experiencing a full-blown foreign currency crisis. The International Monetary Fund urged Mutharika to devalue the kwacha, Malawi's currency, to spur tobacco and tea exports. The kwacha was pegged to the U.S. dollar at 170 kwacha to the dollar. The IMF wanted Malawi to adopt an exchange rate of 280 kwacha to the dollar, which was closer to the black market exchange rate. Mutharika refused, arguing that this would cause price inflation and hurt Malawi's poor. He also refused to meet with an IMF delegation, saying that the delegates were "too junior." The IMF put a $79 million loan program it had with Malawi on hold, further exacerbating the foreign currency crisis. Malawi was in a tailspin.

In early April 2012, Mutharika had a massive heart attack. He was rushed to the hospital in the capital Lilongwe, but ironically, the medicines that he needed were out of stock—the hospital lacked the foreign currency to buy them! Mutharika died. Despite considerable opposition from Mutharika supporters who wanted his brother to succeed him, Joyce Banda, the vice president, was sworn in as president. Although no one has stated this publicly, it seems clear that intense diplomatic pressure from the United Kingdom and United States persuaded Mutharika's supporters to relent. Once in power, Banda announced that Malawi would devalue the kwacha by 40 percent. For its part, the IMF unblocked its loan program, while foreign donors, including the UK and United States, stated that they would resume their programs.

Sources: P. McGroarty, "Currency Woes Curb Business in Malawi," *The Wall Street Journal*, April 4, 2012; P. McGroarty, "Malawi Hopes New Leader Spurs Recovery," *The Wall Street Journal*, April 8, 2012; J. Herskovitz, "Malawi Paid Price for Ego of Economist in Chief," *Reuters*, April 16, 2012; and A. R. Martinez and F. Jomo, "Malawi to Devalue Kwacha 40% to Unlock Aid," *Bloomberg Businessweek*, April 27, 2012.

Case Discussion Questions

1. What were the causes of Malawi's currency troubles?

2. Why did Mutharika resist IMF calls for currency devaluation? If he had lived and remained in power, what do you think would have happened to the economy of Malawi assuming that he did not change his position?

3. What do you think the economic consequences were once Malawi's currency was devalued? Does your research verify your answer?

© Andre Jenny/Alamy

Chapter 11
Global Strategy

IKEA'S SUPPLY CHAIN

Walk into an IKEA store in Canada or anywhere in the world, and you would recognize it instantly. The warehouse-type stores all sell the same broad range of affordable home furnishings, kitchens, and accessories. Most of the products are instantly recognizable as IKEA merchandise, with their clean yet tasteful lines and functional design. The outside of the store will be wrapped in the blue and yellow colors of the Swedish flag. The store itself will be laid out as a maze that requires customers to walk through every department before they reach the checkout stations. Immediately before the checkout, there is an in-store warehouse where customers can pick up the items they purchased. The furniture is all flat-packed for ease of transportation and requires assembly by the customer. If you look at the customers in the store, you will see that many of them are in there 20s and 30s. IKEA sells to the same basic customer set the world over: young upwardly mobile people who are looking for tasteful yet inexpensive "disposable" furniture.

A global network of more than 1050 suppliers based in 53 countries manufactures most of the 9500 or so products that IKEA sells. IKEA itself focuses on the design of products and works closely with suppliers to bring down manufacturing costs. Developing a new product line can be a painstaking process that takes years. IKEA's designers will develop a prototype design—a small couch, for example—look at the price that rivals charge for a similar piece, and then work with suppliers to figure out a way to cut prices by 40 percent without compromising on quality. IKEA also manufactures about 10 percent of what it sells in-house and uses the knowledge gained to help its suppliers improve their productivity, thereby lowering costs across the entire supply chain.

It's a formula that has worked remarkably well. From its roots in Scandinavia, IKEA has grown to become the largest furniture retailer in the world with almost 300 stores in 26 countries and revenues of more than 27 billion euros. IKEA is particularly strong in Europe, where it has 227 stores, but it also has around 50 stores in North America. Its strongest growth recently has been in China, where it had 17 stores in 2013, and Russia, where it had 14 stores.

Look a little closer, however, and you will see subtle differences between the IKEA offerings in North America, Europe, and China. In Canada and the United States, sizes are different to reflect the North American demand for bigger beds, furnishings, and kitchenware. This adaptation to local tastes and preferences was the result of a painful learning experience for IKEA. When the company first entered the United States in the late 1980s, it thought that consumers would flock to their stores the same way that they had in western Europe. At first they did, but they didn't buy as much, and sales fell short of expectations. IKEA discovered that its European-style sofas were not big enough, wardrobe drawers were not deep enough, glasses were too small, and kitchens didn't fit U.S. appliances. So the company set about redesigning its offerings to better match American tastes and was rewarded with accelerating sales growth.

Lesson learned, when IKEA entered China in the 2000s, it made adaptations to the local market. The store layout reflects the layout of many Chinese apartments, where most people live, and because many Chinese apartments have balconies, IKEA's Chinese stores include a balcony section. IKEA has also had to shift its locations in China, where car ownership lags behind that in Europe and North America. In the West, IKEA stores are located in suburban areas and have lots of parking space. In China, stores are located near public transportation, and IKEA offers a delivery service so that Chinese customers can get their purchases home.

Sources: J. Leland, "How the Disposable Sofa Conquered America," *The New York Times Magazine*, October 5, 2005, p. 45; "The Secret of IKEA's Success," *The Economist*, February 24, 2011; B. Torekull, *Leading by Design: The IKEA Story* (New York: Harper Collins, 1998); and P. M. Miller, "IKEA with Chinese Characteristics," *Chinese Business Review*, July–August 2004, pp. 36–69.

LO | LEARNING OBJECTIVES

By the end of this chapter you should be able to:

1. Explain the concept of strategy.

2. Recognize how firms can profit by expanding globally.

3. Understand how pressures for cost reductions and pressures for local responsiveness influence strategic choice.

4. Identify the different strategies for competing globally and their pros and cons.

5. Explain the pros and cons of using strategic alliances to support global strategies.

Introduction

Our primary concern thus far has been with aspects of the larger environment in which international businesses compete. As we have described it in the preceding chapters, this environment has included the different political, economic, and cultural institutions found in nations, the international trade and investment framework, and the international monetary system. Now our focus shifts from the environment to the firm itself and, in particular, to the actions managers can take to compete more effectively as an international business. In this chapter, we look at how firms can increase their profitability by expanding their operations in foreign markets. We discuss the different strategies that firms pursue when competing internationally. We consider the pros and cons of these strategies. We discuss the various factors that affect a firm's choice of strategy. We also look at why firms often enter into strategic alliances with their global competitors, and we discuss the benefits, costs, and risks of strategic alliances. In subsequent chapters we shall build on the framework established here to discuss a variety of topics including the design of organization structures and control systems for international businesses, strategies for entering foreign markets, the use and misuse of strategic alliances, strategies for exporting, and the various manufacturing, marketing, R&D, human resource, accounting, and financial strategies pursued by international businesses.

The strategy of furniture retailer IKEA, which was discussed in the opening case, gives us a preview of some of the key issues discussed in this chapter. IKEA's business-level strategy is to target young, upwardly mobile people and offer them affordable, tastefully designed, furniture and accessories. IKEA differentiates its offering by design. At the same time, the company does everything it can to lower the costs of the products it sells, thereby enabling it to underprice its rivals and still make good profits. IKEA developed its basic formula for competing in Scandinavia in the 1950s and 1960s. This formula, or business model, includes self-service, warehouse-type stores; a maze-like store layout that funnels customers through every department and maximizes impulse purchases; the design of furniture so that it can be flat-packed; an in-store warehouse; and so on. IKEA initially expanded into other countries by using exactly the same segmentation strategy and retailing formula and selling the same set of products. We refer to such a standardized approach as a *global strategy*. One of its great virtues is that it can help a company attain a low-cost position through the realization of economies of scale. However, as the opening case makes clear, while this worked in the western European region, it did not work in Canada and the United States where IKEA had to adapt its product design to the tastes and preferences of North American consumers. In other words, IKEA found that it needed to localize some of its offerings. As we shall see in this chapter, there is often a tension between the desire to standardize a product offering in order to attain low costs and the need to localize the offering to better match the tastes and preferences of local consumers, which can make it more difficult to attain scale economies and raise costs.

LO1 Strategy and the Firm

Before we discuss the strategies that multinational enterprises can pursue, we need to review basic principles of strategy. A firm's **strategy** can be defined as the actions that managers take to attain the goals of the firm. For most firms, the preeminent goal is to maximize long-term profitability. A firm makes a profit if the price it can charge for its output is greater than its costs of producing that output. **Profit** (II) is thus defined as the difference between total revenues (TR) and total costs (TC), or

$$II = TR - TC$$

Total revenues (TR) are equal to price (II) times the number of units sold by the firm (Q) or TR = II × Q. Total costs (TC) are equal to cost per unit (C) times the number of units sold or TC = C × Q. Total profit (II) is equal to profit per unit (π) times the number of units sold, or II = π × Q.

Profitability is a ratio or rate of return concept. A simple example would be the rate of return on sales (ROS), which is defined as profit (II) over total revenues, or

$$ROS = II/TR$$

Thus, a firm might operate with the goal of maximizing its profitability, as defined by its ROS, and its strategy would be the actions that its managers take to attain that goal. (A more common goal is to maximize the firm's return on investment, or ROI, which is defined as ROI = II/I where I represents the total capital, including both equity and debt, that has been invested in the firm.)

Managers can increase the profitability of the firm by pursuing strategies that lower costs or by pursuing strategies that add value to the firm's products, which enables the firm to raise prices. Managers can increase the rate at which the firm's profits grow over time by pursuing strategies to sell more products in existing markets or by pursuing strategies to enter new markets. As we shall see, expanding internationally can help managers boost the firm's profitability and increase the rate of profit growth over time.

Value Creation

Two basic conditions determine a firm's profits (II): the amount of value customers place on the firm's goods or services (sometimes referred to as perceived value) and the firm's costs of production. In general, the more value customers place on a firm's products, the higher the price the firm can charge for those products. Note, however, that the price a firm charges for a good or service is typically less than the value placed on that good or service by the customer. This is so because the customer captures some of that value in the form of what economists call a consumer surplus.[1] The customer is able to do this because the firm is competing with other firms for the customer's business, so the firm must charge a lower price than it could were it a monopoly supplier. Also, it is normally impossible to segment the market to such a degree that the firm can charge each customer a price that reflects that individual's assessment of the value of a product, which economists refer to as a customer's reservation price. For these reasons, the price that gets charged tends to be less than the value placed on the product by many customers.

Figure 11.1 illustrates these concepts. The value of a product to a consumer is V; the price that the firm can charge for that product given competitive pressures and its ability to segment the market is P; and the costs of producing that product are C. The firm's profit per unit sold (π) is equal to P − C, while the consumer surplus is equal to V − P. The firm makes a profit so long as P is greater than C, and its profit will be greater the lower C is *relative* to P. The difference between V and P is in part determined by the intensity of competitive pressure in the marketplace. The lower the intensity of competitive pressure, the higher the price that can be charged relative to V.[2]

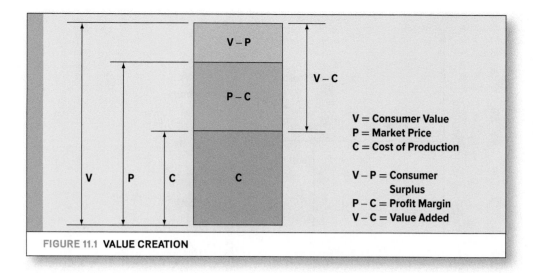

FIGURE 11.1 **VALUE CREATION**

The **value creation** of a firm is measured by the difference between V and C (V – C); a company creates value by converting inputs that cost C into a product on which consumers place a value of V. A company can create more value for its customers either by lowering production costs, C, or by making the product more attractive through superior design, functionality, quality, and the like, so that consumers place a greater value on it (V increases) and, consequently, are willing to pay a higher price (P increases). This discussion suggests that a firm has high profits when it creates more value for its customers and does so at a lower cost. We refer to a strategy that focuses on lowering production costs as a *low-cost strategy*. We refer to a strategy that focuses on increasing the attractiveness of a product as a *differentiation strategy*.[3] Michael Porter has argued that *low cost* and *differentiation* are two basic strategies for creating value and attaining a competitive advantage in an industry.[4] According to Porter, superior profitability goes to those firms that can create superior value, and the way to create superior value is to drive down the cost structure of the business and/or differentiate the product in some way so that consumers value it more and are prepared to pay a premium price. Superior value creation relative to rivals does not necessarily require a firm to have the lowest cost structure in an industry, or to create the most valuable product in the eyes of consumers. However, it does require that the gap between value (V) and cost of production (C) be greater than the gap attained by competitors.

Strategic Positioning

Porter notes that it is important for a firm to be explicit about its choice of strategic emphasis with regard to value creation (differentiation) and low cost, and to configure its internal operations to support that strategic emphasis.[5] Figure 11.2 illustrates his point. The convex curve in Figure 11.2 is what economists refer to as an *efficiency frontier*. The efficiency frontier shows all of the different positions that a firm can adopt with regard to adding value to the product (*V*) and low cost (*C*) assuming that its internal operations are configured efficiently to support a particular position (note that the horizontal axis in Figure 11.2 is reverse scaled—moving along the axis to the right implies lower costs). The efficiency frontier has a convex shape because of diminishing returns. Diminishing returns imply that when a firm already has significant value built into its product offering, increasing value by a relatively small amount

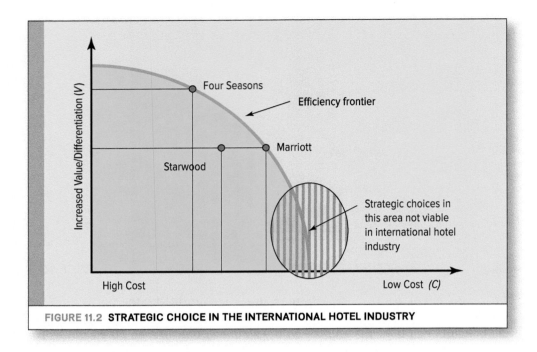

FIGURE 11.2 **STRATEGIC CHOICE IN THE INTERNATIONAL HOTEL INDUSTRY**

requires significant additional costs. The converse also holds, when a firm already has a low-cost structure, it has to give up a lot of value in its product offering to get additional cost reductions.

Figure 11.2 plots three hotel firms with a global presence that cater to international travellers: Four Seasons (a chain started in Canada), Marriott International, and Starwood (Starwood owns the Sheraton and Westin chains). Four Seasons positions itself as a luxury chain and emphasizes the value of its product offering, which drives up its costs of operations. Marriott and Starwood are positioned more in the middle of the market. Both emphasize sufficient value to attract international business travellers, but are not luxury chains like Four Seasons. In Figure 11.2, Four Seasons and Marriott are shown to be on the efficiency frontier, indicating that their internal operations are well configured to their strategy and run efficiently. Starwood is inside the frontier, indicating that its operations are not running as efficiently as they might be and that its costs are too high. This implies that Starwood is less profitable than Four Seasons and Marriott and that its managers must take steps to improve the company's performance.

Porter emphasizes that it is very important for management to decide where the company wants to be positioned with regard to value (*V*) and cost (*C*), to configure operations accordingly, and to manage them efficiently to make sure the firm is operating on the efficiency frontier. However, not all positions on the efficiency frontier are viable. In the international hotel industry, for example, there might not be enough demand to support a chain that emphasizes very low cost and strips all the value out of its product offering, as Figure 11.2 indicates. International travellers are relatively affluent and expect a degree of comfort (value) when they travel away from home.

A central tenet of the basic strategy paradigm is that to maximize its profitability, a firm must do three things: (1) pick a position on the efficiency frontier that is viable in the sense that there is enough demand to support that choice; (2) configure its internal operations, such as manufacturing, marketing, logistics, information systems, human resources, and so on, so that they support that position; and (3) make sure that the firm has the right organization structure in place to execute its strategy. *The strategy, operations, and organization of the firm must all be consistent with each other if it is to attain a competitive advantage and garner superior profitability.* By operations we mean the different value creation activities a firm undertakes, which we shall review next.

The Firm as a Value Chain

It is useful to think of the firm as a value chain composed of a series of distinct value creation activities including production, marketing and sales, materials management, research and development (R&D), human resources, information systems, and the firm infrastructure. We can categorize these value creation activities as primary activities and support activities (see Figure 11.3).[6]

PRIMARY ACTIVITIES

Primary activities have to do with the design, creation, and delivery of the product; its marketing; and its support and after-sale service. In the value chain illustrated in Figure 11.3, the primary activities are broken into four functions: research and development, production, marketing and sales, and service.

Research and development is concerned with the design of products and production processes. Although we think of R&D as being associated with the design of physical products and production processes in manufacturing enterprises, many service companies also undertake R&D. For example, banks compete with each other by developing new financial products and new ways of delivering those products to customers. Banking apps on cell phones and smart debit cards are two recent examples of new-product development in the banking industry. Earlier examples of innovation in the banking industry include automated teller machines, credit cards, and online banking. Through superior product design, R&D can increase the functionality of products, which makes them more attractive to consumers (raising V). Alternatively, R&D may result in more efficient production processes, thereby lowering production costs (lowering C). Either way, the R&D function can create value.

Production is concerned with the creation of a good or service. For physical products, when we talk about production we generally mean manufacturing. For services such as banking or retail operations, "production" typically occurs when the

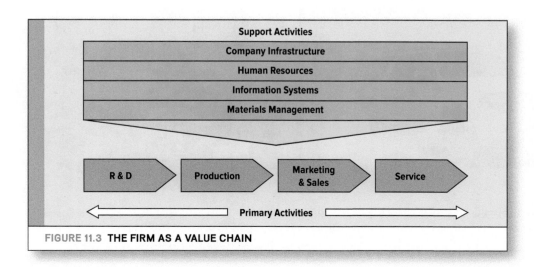

FIGURE 11.3 **THE FIRM AS A VALUE CHAIN**

service is delivered to the customer (for example, when a bank originates a loan for a customer it is engaged in "production" of the loan). For a media company such as MTV, production involves the creation and delivery of content (programming). The production activity of a firm creates value by performing its activities efficiently so lower costs result (lower C) or by performing them in such a way that a more reliable and higher-quality product is produced (which results in higher V).

The marketing and sales functions of a firm can help to create value in several ways. Through brand positioning and advertising, the marketing function can increase the value (V) that consumers perceive to be contained in a firm's product. If these create a favourable impression of the firm's product in the minds of consumers, they increase the price that can be charged for the firm's product. For example, Ford produced a high-value version of its Ford Expedition SUV. Sold as the Lincoln Navigator and priced around $10,000 higher, the Navigator has the same body, engine, chassis, and design as the Expedition, but through skilled advertising and marketing, supported by some fairly minor features changes (e.g., more accessories and the addition of a Lincoln-style engine grille and nameplate), Ford has fostered the perception that the Navigator is a "luxury SUV." This marketing strategy has increased the perceived value (V) of the Navigator relative to the Expedition, and enables Ford to charge a higher price for the vehicle (P).

Marketing and sales can also create value by discovering consumer needs and communicating them back to the R&D function of the company, which can then design products that better match those needs. For example, the allocation of research budgets at Pfizer, the world's largest pharmaceutical company, is determined by the marketing function's assessment of the potential market size associated with solving unmet medical needs. Thus, Pfizer is currently directing significant monies to R&D efforts aimed at finding treatments for Alzheimer's disease, principally because marketing has identified the treatment of Alzheimer's as a major unmet medical need in nations around the world where the population is aging.

The role of the enterprise's service activity is to provide after-sale service and support. This function can create a perception of superior value (V) in the minds of consumers by solving customer problems and supporting customers after they have purchased the product. For example, Caterpillar, the U.S.-based manufacturer of heavy earthmoving equipment, can get spare parts to any point in the world within

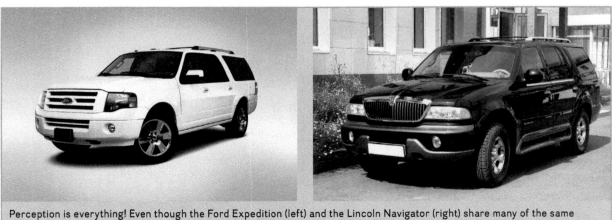

Perception is everything! Even though the Ford Expedition (left) and the Lincoln Navigator (right) share many of the same attributes, such as the body and engine, customers are willing to pay about $10,000 more for the Navigator's little extras.
(left) © Drive Images/Alamy; (right) © Artzzz/Dreamstime.com

24 hours, thereby minimizing the amount of downtime customers have to suffer if their Caterpillar equipment malfunctions. This is an extremely valuable capability in an industry where downtime is very expensive. It has helped to increase the value that customers associate with Caterpillar products and thus the price that Caterpillar can charge for its products.

SUPPORT ACTIVITIES

The support activities of the value chain provide inputs that allow the primary activities to take place (see Figure 11.3). The materials management (or logistics) function controls the transmission of physical materials through the value chain, from procurement through production and into distribution. The efficiency with which this is carried out can significantly lower cost (lower C), thereby creating more value.

Similarly, the human resource function can help create more value in a number of ways. It ensures that the company has the right mix of skilled people to perform its value creation activities effectively. The human resource function also ensures that people are adequately trained, motivated, and compensated to perform their value creation tasks.

Information systems refer to the (normally) electronic systems for managing inventory, tracking sales, pricing products, selling products, dealing with customer service inquiries, and so on. Information systems, when coupled with the communications features of the Internet, can alter the efficiency and effectiveness with which a firm manages its other value creation activities. Dell Computer, for example, has used its information systems to attain a competitive advantage over rivals. When customers place an order for a Dell product over the firm's Web site, that information is immediately transmitted, via the Internet, to suppliers, who then configure their production schedules to produce and ship that product so that it arrives at the right assembly plant at the right time. These systems have reduced the amount of inventory that Dell holds at its factories to under two days, which is a major source of cost savings. As we shall see, good information systems are very important in the global arena.

ANOTHER PERSPECTIVE

Education as a Part of Your Value Chain

The concept of value chain can be used to examine the role your undergraduate education plays in your life plans. If you examine your personal development plans (education, internship, physical and emotional/spiritual fitness, extracurricular activities) and think about them in terms of primary and support activities, how does your choice of major fit into your personal development strategy? How do your choices of how you spend your time fit into your value chain? Do you ever spend time doing things that don't support the strategic goals of your "personal value chain"?

The final support activity is the company infrastructure. By infrastructure we mean the context within which all the other value creation activities occur. The infrastructure includes the organizational structure, control systems, and culture of the firm. Because top management can exert considerable influence in shaping these aspects of a firm, top management should also be viewed as part of the firm's infrastructure. Through strong leadership, top management can consciously shape the infrastructure of a firm and through that the performance of all other value creation activities within it.

The Role of Strategy

There have been many developments in the growth of the Canadian economy since Confederation. One of the most significant phases of Canadian economic prosperity can be attributed to the post-World War II period during which Canada became a "branch plant" of the United States. Until that time, Canada was an exporter of raw materials and an importer of finished products. In its shift to a branch-plant economy, Canada suffered from weak research and development initiatives, both in the government and private sectors. This made Canada less competitive in international markets, while at the same time, making it more dependent on U.S. trade.

Many international markets are now extremely competitive due to the liberalization of the world trade and investment environment. In industry after industry, capable competitors confront each other around the globe. To be profitable in such an environment, a firm must both reduce the costs of value creation (lower C) and differentiate its product offering so that consumers value that product more (raise V) and are willing to pay more for the product than it costs to produce it. Thus, strategy is often concerned with identifying and taking actions that will *lower the costs* of value creation and/or will *differentiate* the firm's product offering through superior design, quality, service, functionality, and so on.

For an example of how this works, consider Brockville, Ontario-based Canarm Ltd. (www.canarm.com), a manufacturer and marketer of ceiling fans and lighting products, commercial ventilation products, and agricultural products. Canarm began as a small sheet metal shop and was originally known as Danor Manufacturing Co. Ltd. By 1963 they had moved their operations to Brockville, the location of their present operations. Today, this privately owned company employs over 300 full-time employees. Not exactly small, but no corporate giant either, though it added 40 000 square feet of new space to its Brockville facility in 2011. Canarm is a multinational firm with production facilities in China and retailers in North America and Europe.

With the energy crisis in the early 1970s, there was a pressing need to conserve energy. Slow-moving fans pushed pent hot air gathered at ceiling levels down to floor level. By using this low-energy solution, warm air could be salvaged in the winter and, in the summer, fans could circulate the air to cool rooms. In 1975, Danor imported industrial, three metal-blade, 140-cm (56-inch) ceiling fans from Hong Kong manufacturers.

By 1981, the Canadian prime interest rate had soared to 22 percent, and commercial businesses were forced to reduce their spending budget. Also, Asian manufacturers had an excess supply of ceiling fans with barely any international buyers. The metal-blade industrial ceiling fan was being replaced by more decorative wooden blades, opening up the market for ceiling fans. After extensive market research, Danor targeted restaurants and residential homeowners with these imported fans, and they redesigned their retail chains and lighting showrooms to attract this expanding market niche.

Canarm's residential lighting and ceiling fans are imported from China, and the company has had a relationship with China for 30 years. Canarm's success was shown in 2013, when it was named one of Canada's 50 Best Managed Companies by the *National Post.*

The choice of the Asian manufacturers was influenced by their combination of low labour costs and skilled work force. The firm's objective at this point was to lower production costs (lower C) by locating value creation activities at an appropriate location.

IN SUM: STRATEGIC FIT

In sum, as we have repeatedly stressed, for a firm to attain superior performance and earn a high return on capital, its strategy (as captured by its desired strategic position on the efficiency frontier) must make sense given market conditions (there must be sufficient demand to support that strategic choice). The operations of the firm must be configured in a way that supports the strategy of the firm, and the organization architecture of the firm must match the operations and strategy of the firm. In other words, market conditions, strategy, operations, and organization must all be consistent with each other, or fit each other, for superior performance to be attained.

Of course, the issue can quickly become complex. For example, the firm can influence market conditions through its choice of strategy—it can create demand by leveraging core skills to create new market opportunities. In addition, shifts in market conditions caused by new technologies, government action such as deregulation, demographics, or social trends can mean that the strategy of the firm no longer fits the market. In such circumstances, the firm must change its strategy, operations, and organization to fit the new reality—which can be an extraordinarily difficult challenge. And last but by no means least, international expansion adds another layer of complexity to the strategic challenges facing the firm. We shall now consider this.

LO2 | Profiting from Global Expansion

As suggested by the Canarm example, expanding globally allows firms to increase their profitability in ways not available to purely domestic enterprises. Firms that operate internationally are able to:

1. Realize location economies by dispersing individual value creation activities to those locations around the globe where they can be performed most efficiently and effectively.

2. Realize greater cost economies from experience effects by serving an expanded global market from a central location, thereby reducing the costs of value creation.

3. Earn a greater return from the firm's distinctive skills or core competencies by leveraging those skills and applying them to other entities within the firm's global network of operations.

4. Earn a greater return by leveraging any valuable skills developed in foreign operations and transferring them to other entities within the firm's global network of operations.

As we will see, however, a firm's ability to increase its profitability by pursuing these strategies is to some extent constrained by the need to customize its product offering, marketing strategy, and business strategy to differing national conditions by the imperative of localization.

Location Economies

We know from earlier chapters that countries differ along a range of dimensions including social, technological, economic, political, and legal, and that these differences can either raise or lower costs of doing business in a country. The theory of international trade also teaches us that due to differences in factor costs, certain countries have a comparative advantage in the production of certain products. Japan might excel in the production of cars, electronic devices, and computers; Canada in the production of energy products; the United States in the production of civilian aircraft, pharmaceuticals, and semiconductors; Switzerland in the production of food, metals, and precision instruments; and South Korea in the production of wireless telecommunications equipment and motor vehicles.[7]

What does all this mean for a firm trying to survive in a competitive global market? It means that, trade barriers and transportation costs permitting, the firm will benefit by basing each value creation activity it performs at that location where economic, political, and cultural conditions, including relative factor costs, are most conducive to the performance of that activity. Thus, if the best designers for a product live in France, then a firm should base its design operations there. If the most productive labour force for assembly operation is in Mexico, assembly operations should be based in Mexico. If the best marketers are in the United States, the marketing strategy should be formulated in the United States. If the best film animation production facilities are in Canada, the film animation strategy should be formulated in Canada. And so on.

ANOTHER PERSPECTIVE

Location Economies at Work in Ways We May Not Realize

When we call a company's customer service department, we expect that call centre to be in Canada, especially when someone who answers the phone has a neutral or "Canadian" accent. Besides that, the call centre representative may know about how cold it is in Edmonton, the flooding situation in New Brunswick, the results of the mayoral election in Calgary, and the Maple Leafs' loss the night before. These employees sound like they live in Canada, but that isn't always the case. They may actually be located in India, East Africa, or the Caribbean. Call centre employers hire people with "neutral" accents and once hired, have their employees read local Canadian newspapers prior to their shift. Think about having a job as an Indian pretending to be from British Columbia. What do you think of the ethics of such intentional deception?

Firms that pursue such a strategy can realize what we refer to as **location economies**, the economies that arise from performing a value creation activity in the optimal location for that activity, wherever in the world that might be (transportation costs and trade barriers permitting). Locating a value creation activity in the optimal location for that activity can have one of two effects. *It can lower the costs of value creation and help the firm to achieve a low-cost position, and/or it can enable a firm to differentiate its product offering from those of competitors.* In terms of Figure 11.1, it can lower C or increase V (which in general supports higher pricing, P), both of which boost the profitability of the enterprise. We can apply these considerations to Canarm, discussed earlier. Canarm moved its manufacturing operations out of Canada to China and Taiwan to take advantage of low labour costs, thereby lowering the costs of value creation (C). Canarm thinks that the optimal location for performing manufacturing operations is Asia. The firm has configured its value chain accordingly. By doing so, Canarm hopes to be able to simultaneously lower its cost structure and differentiate its product offering. In turn, differentiation should allow Canarm to charge a premium price for its product offering.

CREATING A GLOBAL WEB

Generalizing from the Canarm example, one result of this kind of thinking is the creation of a **global web** of value creation activities, with different stages of the value chain being dispersed to those locations around the globe where perceived value is maximized or where the cost of value creation are minimized.

In theory, a firm that realizes location economies by dispersing each of its value creation activities to its optimal location should have a competitive advantage vis-à-vis a firm that bases all its value creation activities at a single location. It should be able to better differentiate its product offering (thereby raising perceived value, V) and lower its cost structure (C) than its single-location competitor. In a world where competitive pressures are increasing, such a strategy may become an imperative for survival (as it seems to have been for Canarm).

SOME CAVEATS

Introducing transportation costs and trade barriers complicates this picture somewhat. Due to favourable factor endowments, New Zealand may have a comparative advantage for automobile assembly operations, but high transportation costs would make it an uneconomical location from which to serve global markets. A consideration of transportation costs and trade barriers helps explain why many U.S. firms are now shifting their production from Asia to Mexico. Mexico has three distinct advantages over many Asian countries as a location for value creation activities. First, low labour costs make it a good location for labour-intensive production processes. In recent years, wage rates have increased significantly in Japan, Taiwan, and Hong Kong, but they have remained low in Mexico. Second, Mexico's proximity to the large U.S. market reduces transportation costs. This is particularly important in the case of products with high weight-to-value ratios (e.g., automobiles). And third, the North American Free Trade Agreement (see Chapter 8) removed many trade barriers between Mexico, the United States, and Canada, increasing Mexico's attractiveness as a production site for the North American market. Although value added and the costs of value creation are important, transportation costs and trade barriers also must be considered in location decisions.

Another caveat concerns the importance of assessing political and economic risks when making location decisions. Even if a country looks very attractive as a production location when measured against all the standard criteria, if its government is unstable or totalitarian, the firm might be advised not to base production there. (Political risk is discussed in Chapter 2.) Similarly, if the government appears to be pursuing inappropriate economic policies, that might be another reason for not basing production in that location, even if other factors look favourable.

Experience Effects

The **experience curve** refers to systematic reductions in production costs that have been observed to occur over the life of a product.[8] A number of studies have observed that a product's costs decline by some quantity about each time cumulative output doubles. The relationship was first observed in the aircraft industry, where each time cumulative output of airframes was doubled, unit costs typically declined to 80 percent of their previous level.[9] Thus, production cost for the fourth airframe would be 80 percent of production cost for the second airframe, the eighth airframe's production costs 80 percent of the fourth's, the sixteenth's 80 percent of

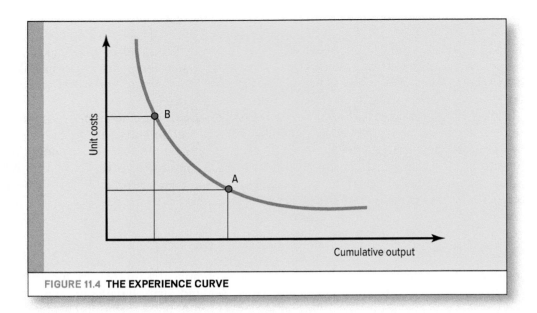

FIGURE 11.4 **THE EXPERIENCE CURVE**

the eighth's, and so on. Figure 11.4 illustrates this experience curve relationship between production costs and output. Two things explain this: learning effects and economies of scale.

LEARNING EFFECTS

Learning effects refer to cost savings that come from learning by doing. Labour, for example, learns by repetition how to carry out a task such as assembling airframes most efficiently. Labour productivity increases over time as individuals learn the most efficient ways to perform particular tasks. Equally important, in new production facilities, management typically learns how to manage the new operation more efficiently over time. Hence, production costs eventually decline due to increasing labour productivity and management efficiency.

Learning effects tend to be more significant when a technologically complex task is repeated, since there is more that can be learned about the task. Thus, learning effects will be more significant in an assembly process involving 1000 complex steps than in one of only 100 simple steps. No matter how complex the task, however, learning effects typically disappear after a while. It has been suggested that they are really important only during the start-up period of a new process and that they cease after two or three years.[10] Any decline in the experience curve after such a point is due to economies of scale.

ECONOMIES OF SCALE

Economies of scale refer to the reductions in unit cost achieved by producing a large volume of a product. Economies of scale have a number of sources. One of the most important seems to be the ability to spread fixed costs over a large volume.[11] Fixed costs are the costs required to set up a production facility, develop a new product, and the like, and they can be substantial. For example, establishing a new production line to manufacture semiconductor chips costs about $1 billion. According to one estimate, developing a new drug costs about $500 million and takes about ten years.[12] The only way to recoup such high fixed costs is to sell the product worldwide, which reduces unit costs by spreading them over a larger volume. The more rapidly that cumulative sales volume is built up, the more rapidly fixed costs can be amortized, and the more rapidly unit costs fall.

Another source of scale economies arises from the ability of large firms to employ increasingly specialized equipment or personnel. This theory goes back more than 200 years to Adam Smith, who argued that the division of labour is limited by the extent of the market. As a firm's output expands, it is better able to fully utilize specialized equipment and can justify hiring specialized personnel. For example, consider a metal stamping machine that is used in the production of body parts for automobiles. The machine can be purchased in a customized form, which is optimized for the production of a particular type of body part—say door panels—or a general-purpose form that will produce any kind of body part. The general-purpose form is less efficient and costs more to purchase than the customized form, but it is more flexible. Since these machines are very expensive, costing millions of dollars each, they have to be used continually to recoup a return on their costs. Fully utilized, a machine can turn out about 200 000 units a year. If an automobile company sells only 100 000 cars per year, it will not be worthwhile to purchase the specialized equipment, and it will have to purchase general-purpose machines. This will give it a higher cost structure than a firm that sells 200 000 cars per year, and for which it is economical to purchase a specialized stamping machine. Thus, because a firm with a large output can more fully utilize specialized equipment (and personnel), it should have a lower unit cost than a generalized firm.

A similar idea is known as **economies of scope** (as opposed to economies of scale) While economies of scale involve increasing the scale of a single product, or a single product type, economies of scope involves lowering overall costs across two or more products or product types. These economies come from using the specialized competencies of the firm across different product lines or businesses. Examples include Honda's small-engine competency realized in the motorcycle, auto, and lawn mower businesses, and Canon's image reproduction capability applied to cameras, photocopiers, and printers.

STRATEGIC SIGNIFICANCE

The strategic significance of the experience curve is clear. Moving down the experience curve allows a firm to reduce its cost of creating value (to lower C in Figure 11.1). The firm that moves down the experience curve most rapidly will have a cost advantage vis-à-vis its competitors. Thus, firm A in Figure 11.4, because it is farther down the experience curve, has a clear cost advantage over firm B.

Many of the underlying sources of experience-based cost economies are plant based. This is true for most learning effects as well as for the economies of scale derived by spreading the fixed costs of building productive capacity over a large output. Thus, one key to progressing downward on the experience curve as rapidly as possible is to increase the volume produced by a single plant as rapidly as possible. Because global markets are larger than domestic markets, a firm that serves a global market from a single location is likely to build accumulated volume more quickly than a firm that serves only its home market or that serves multiple markets from multiple production locations. Thus, serving a global market from a single location is consistent with moving down the experience curve and establishing a low-cost position (i.e., lowering the costs of value creation, C). In addition, to get down the experience curve rapidly, a firm may need to price and market aggressively so demand will expand rapidly. It will also need to build sufficient production capacity for serving a global market. Also, the cost advantages of serving the world market from a single location

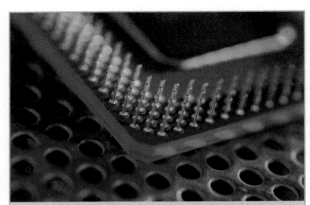

The only way to recoup the high fixed cost of a high-priced product, such as microprocessors, is to sell the product worldwide, which reduces average unit costs by spreading fixed costs over a larger volume. © *Getty Images*

will be even more significant if that location is the optimal one for performing the particular value creation activity. This will be detailed in our closing case about Ford, a company with numerous production facilities around the globe.

Once a firm has established a low-cost position, it can act as a barrier to new competition. Specifically, an established firm that is well down the experience curve, such as firm A in Figure 11.4, can price so that it is still making a profit while new entrants, which are farther up the curve, such as firm B in the figure, suffer losses at that price.

The classic example of the successful pursuit of such a strategy concerns the Japanese consumer electronics company Matsushita. Along with Sony and Philips, Matsushita was in the race to develop a commercially viable videocassette recorder in the 1970s. Although Matsushita initially lagged behind Philips and Sony, it was able to get its VHS format accepted as the world standard and to reap enormous experience-curve-based cost economies in the process. This cost advantage subsequently constituted a formidable barrier to new competition. Matsushita's strategy was to build global volume as rapidly as possible. To ensure it could accommodate worldwide demand, the firm increased its production capacity 33-fold from 205 000 units in 1977 to 6.8 million units by 1984. By serving the world market from a single location in Japan, Matsushita was able to realize significant learning effects and economies of scale. These allowed Matsushita to drop its prices 50 percent within five years of selling its first VHS-formatted VCR. As a result, Matsushita was the world's major VCR producer by 1983, accounting for about 45 percent of world production and enjoying a significant cost advantage over its competitors. The next largest firm, Hitachi, accounted for only 11.1 percent of world production in 1983.[13] Today, firms such as Intel are the masters of this kind of strategy. The costs of building a state-of-the-art facility to manufacture microprocessors are so large (now in excess of $2 billion) that to make this investment pay Intel *must* pursue experience curve effects, serving world markets from a limited number of plants to maximize the cost economies that derive from scale and learning effects.

Leveraging Core Competencies

The term **core competence** refers to skills within the firm that competitors cannot easily match or imitate.[14] These skills may exist in any of the firm's value creation activities—production, marketing, R&D, human resources, general management, and so on. Such skills are typically expressed in product offerings that other firms find difficult to match or imitate, and thus the core competencies are the bedrock of a firm's competitive advantage. They enable a firm to reduce the costs of value creation (C) and/or to create perceived value (V) in such a way that premium pricing is possible. McDonald's has a core competence in managing fast-food operations (it seems to be one of the most skilled firms in the world in this industry); and Umbra has a core competence in creating and manufacturing contemporary accessories for the home.

For such firms, global expansion is a way of further exploiting the value creation potential of their skills and product offerings by applying those skills and products in a larger market. The potential for creating value from such a strategy is greatest when the skills and products of the firm are most unique, when the value placed on them by consumers is great, and when there are very few capable competitors with similar skills and/or products in foreign markets. Firms with unique and valuable skills can often realize enormous returns by applying those skills, and the products they produce, to foreign markets where indigenous competitors lack similar skills and products.

In earlier eras, U.S. firms such as Kellogg, Coca-Cola, H. J. Heinz, and Procter & Gamble expanded overseas to exploit their skills in developing and marketing name-brand consumer products. These skills and the resulting products, which were developed in the U.S. market during the 1950s and '60s, yielded enormous returns when applied to European markets, where most indigenous competitors lacked similar marketing skills and products. Their near-monopoly on consumer marketing skills allowed these U.S. firms to dominate many European consumer product markets during the 1960s and '70s. Similarly, in the 1970s and '80s, many Japanese firms expanded globally to exploit their skills in production, materials management, and new-product development—skills that many of their indigenous North American and European competitors seemed to lack at the time. Today, retail companies such as Wal-Mart, and financial companies such as Citicorp and American Express are transferring the valuable skills they developed in their core home market to other developed and emerging markets where indigenous competitors lack those skills. Another example, SNC-Lavalin. It is active in such traditional engineering fields as chemicals, petroleum, and mining, but also in more service-oriented fields as project financing, investment, and facilities management.

Leveraging Subsidiary Skills

Implicit in our earlier discussion of core competencies is the idea that valuable skills are developed first at home and then transferred to foreign operations. However, for more mature multinationals that have already established a network of subsidiary operations in foreign markets, the development of valuable skills can just as well occur in foreign subsidiaries.[15] Skills can be created anywhere within a multinational's global network of operations, wherever people have the opportunity and incentive to try new ways of doing things. The creation of skills that help to lower the costs of production, or to enhance perceived value and support higher product pricing, is not the monopoly of the corporate centre.

Leveraging the skills created within subsidiaries and applying them to other operations within the firm's global network may create value. McDonald's is increasingly finding that its foreign franchisees are a source of valuable new ideas. Faced with slow growth in France, its local franchisees have begun to experiment not only with the menu, but also with the layout and theme of restaurants. Gone are the ubiquitous golden arches; gone too are many of the utilitarian chairs and tables and other plastic features of the fast-food giant. McDonald's customizes the look and feel of their restaurants to reflect the local style, and even advertises this fact on their Web site.[16] The menu, too, has been changed to include premier sandwiches, such as chicken on focaccia bread, priced some 30 percent higher than the average hamburger. In France at least, the strategy seems to be working. Following the change, increases in same-store sales rose from 1 percent annually to 3.4 percent. Impressed with the impact, McDonald's executives are considering similar changes at other McDonald's restaurants in markets where same-store sales growth is sluggish, including the United States.[17]

For the managers of the multinational enterprise, this phenomenon creates important new challenges. First, they must have the humility to recognize that valuable skills that lead to competencies can arise anywhere within the firm's global network, not just at the corporate centre. Second, they must establish an incentive system that encourages local employees to acquire new skills. This is not as easy as it sounds. Creating new skills involves a degree of risk. Not all new skills add value. For every valuable idea created by a McDonald's subsidiary in a foreign country, there may be several failures. The management of the multinational must install incentives that encourage employees to take the necessary risks. The company must reward people for successes and not sanction them unnecessarily for taking risks that did not pan out. Third, managers must have a process for identifying when valuable new skills have been created in a subsidiary. And finally, they need to act as facilitators, helping to transfer valuable skills within the firm.

PROFITABILITY AND PROFIT GROWTH SUMMARY

We have seen how firms that expand globally can increase their profitability and profit growth by entering new markets where indigenous competitors lack similar competencies, by lowering costs and adding value to their product offering through the attainment of location economies, by exploiting experience curve effects, and by transferring valuable skills between their global network of subsidiaries. For completeness it should be noted that strategies that increase profitability may also expand a firm's business, and thus enable it to attain a higher rate of profit growth. For example, by simultaneously realizing location economies and experience effects, a firm may be able to produce a more highly valued product at a lower unit cost, thereby boosting profitability. The increase in the perceived value of the product may also attract more customers, thereby growing revenues and profits as well. Furthermore, rather than raising prices to reflect the higher perceived value of the product, the firm's managers may elect to hold prices low to increase global market share and attain greater scale economies (in other words, they may elect to offer consumers better "value for money"). Such a strategy could increase the firm's rate of profit growth even further, since consumers will be attracted by prices that are low relative to value. The strategy might also increase profitability if the scale economies that result from market share gains are substantial. In sum, managers need to keep in mind the complex relationship between profitability and profit growth when making strategic decisions about pricing.

LO3 Pressures for Cost Reductions and Local Responsiveness

Firms that compete in the global marketplace typically face two types of competitive pressure. They face pressures for cost reductions and pressures to be locally responsive (see Figure 11.5). These competitive pressures place conflicting demands on a firm. Responding to pressures for cost reductions requires that a firm try to minimize its unit costs. Attaining such a goal may necessitate that a firm base its productive activities at the most favourable low-cost location, wherever in the world that might be. It may also necessitate that a firm offer a standardized product to the global marketplace. This helps the firm spread the fixed costs of developing a product offering over as large a volume as possible, thereby lowering its average unit costs.

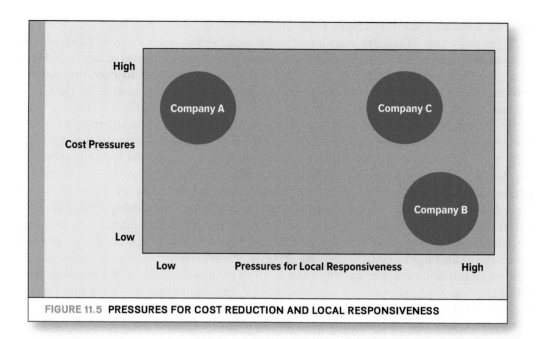

FIGURE 11.5 **PRESSURES FOR COST REDUCTION AND LOCAL RESPONSIVENESS**

Offering a standardized product also enables the firm to attain other scale economies and ride down the experience curve as quickly as possible. In contrast, responding to pressures to be locally responsive requires that a firm differentiate its product offering and marketing strategy from country to country in an attempt to accommodate the diverse demands that arise from national differences in consumer tastes and preferences, business practices, distribution channels, competitive conditions, and government policies. Because customizing product offerings to different national requirements can involve significant duplication and a lack of product standardization, the result may be to raise costs.

Some firms, such as firm A in Figure 11.5, face high pressures for cost reductions and low pressures for local responsiveness. Others, such as firm B, face low pressures for cost reductions and high pressures for local responsiveness. Many others are in the position of firm C in Figure 11.5. They face high pressures for cost reductions and high pressures for local responsiveness. Dealing with these conflicting and contradictory pressures is a difficult strategic challenge for a firm, primarily because being locally responsive tends to raise costs. In the remainder of this section, we shall look at the source of pressures for cost reductions and local responsiveness. In the next section, we look at the strategies that firms adopt to deal with these pressures.

Pressures for Cost Reductions

In competitive global markets, international businesses often face pressures for cost reductions. Responding to pressures for cost reduction requires a firm to try to lower the costs of value creation. A manufacturer, for example, might mass-produce a standardized product at the optimal locations in the world, wherever that might be, to realize economies of scale, learning effects, and location economies. Alternatively, a firm might outsource certain functions to low-cost foreign suppliers in an attempt to reduce costs. Thus, many computer companies have outsourced their telephone-based customer service functions to India, where qualified technicians who speak English can be hired for a lower wage rate than in the United States. In the same manner, a retailer such as Wal-Mart might push its suppliers (manufacturers) to do the same. (The pressure that Wal-Mart has placed on its suppliers to reduce prices has been cited as a major cause of the trend among North American manufacturers to shift production to China.[18]) A service business such as a bank might respond to cost pressures by moving some back-office functions, such as information processing, to developing nations where wage rates are lower.

Pressures for cost reduction can be particularly intense in industries producing commodity-type products where meaningful differentiation on nonprice factors is difficult and price is the main competitive weapon. This tends to be the case for products that serve universal needs. **Universal needs** exist when the tastes and preferences of consumers in different nations are similar if not identical. This is the case for conventional commodity products such as bulk chemicals, petroleum, steel, sugar, and the like. It also tends to be the case for many industrial and consumer products—for example, handheld calculators, semiconductor chips, personal computers, and liquid crystal display screens. Pressures for cost reductions are also intense in industries where major competitors are based in low-cost locations, where there is persistent excess capacity, and where consumers are powerful and face low switching costs. The liberalization of the world trade and investment environment in recent decades, by facilitating greater international competition, has generally increased cost pressures.[19]

Pressures for Local Responsiveness

Pressures for local responsiveness arise from a number of sources including (1) differences in consumer tastes and preferences; (2) differences in infrastructure and traditional practices; (3) differences in distribution channels; and (4) host-government demands.

DIFFERENCES IN CONSUMER TASTES AND PREFERENCES

Strong pressures for local responsiveness emerge when consumer tastes and preferences differ significantly between countries, as they may for historic or cultural reasons. In such cases, product and/or marketing messages have to be customized to appeal to the tastes and preferences of local consumers. This typically creates pressure to delegate production and marketing functions to national subsidiaries.

Pickup trucks may be used in the south and west of the United States as a second or third car, but in Europe they're seen purely as utility vehicles, which affects the marketing message being sent. © Steve Allen/Getty Images

The automobile industry in the 1980s and early 1990s moved toward the creation of "world cars." The idea was that global companies such as General Motors, Ford, and Toyota would be able to sell the same basic vehicle the world over, sourcing it from centralized production locations. If successful, the strategy would have enabled automobile companies to reap significant gains from global scale economies. However, this strategy has frequently run aground upon the hard rocks of consumer reality. Consumers in different automobile markets seem to have different tastes and preferences, and these require different types of vehicles. For example, some North American consumers show a strong demand for pickup trucks. This is particularly true in Western Canada and the Southern and Western United States, where many families have a pickup truck as a second or third car. But in European countries, pickup trucks are seen purely as utility vehicles and are purchased primarily by firms rather than individuals. As a consequence, the marketing message needs to be tailored to the different nature of demand in North America and Europe.

As a counterpoint, in a now classic article, Harvard Business School Professor Theodore Levitt argued that consumer demands for local customization are on the decline worldwide.[20] According to Levitt, modern communication and transportation technologies have created the conditions for a convergence of the tastes and preferences of consumers from different nations. The result is the emergence of enormous global markets for standardized consumer products. Levitt cites worldwide acceptance of McDonald's hamburgers, Coca-Cola, Gap clothing, and Apple products, all of which are sold as standardized products, as evidence of the increasing homogeneity of the global marketplace.

Levitt's argument, however, has been characterized as extreme by many commentators. For example, Christopher Bartlett and Sumantra Ghoshal have observed that, in the consumer electronics industry, consumers reacted to an overdose of standardized global products by showing a renewed preference for products that are differentiated to local conditions.[21] They note that Amstrad, the British computer and electronics firm, got its start by recognizing and responding to local consumer needs. Amstrad captured a major share of the British audio player market by moving away from the standardized, inexpensive music centres marketed by global firms such as Sony and Matsushita. Amstrad's product was encased in teak rather than metal cabinets and had a control panel tailor-made to appeal to British consumers' preferences. In response, Matsushita reversed its earlier bias toward standardized global design and placed more emphasis on local customization.

DIFFERENCES IN INFRASTRUCTURE AND TRADITIONAL PRACTICES

Pressures for local responsiveness emerge when there are differences in infrastructure and/or traditional practices between countries. In such circumstances, the product may need to be customized to the distinctive infrastructure and practices of different nations. This may necessitate the delegation of manufacturing and production functions to foreign subsidiaries. For example, in North America, consumer electrical systems are based on 110 volts, while in some European countries 240-volt systems are standard. Thus, domestic electrical appliances have to be customized for this difference in infrastructure. Traditional practices also often vary across nations. For example, in Great Britain, people drive on the left side of the road, thus creating a demand for right-hand drive cars, whereas in neighbouring France, people drive on the right side of the road, thus creating a demand for left-hand drive cars. Obviously automobiles have to be customized for this difference in traditional practices.

While many of the country differences in infrastructure are rooted in history, some are quite recent. For example, in the wireless telecommunication industry, technical standards vary around the world. A technical standard known as GSM is common in Europe, while an alternative standard, referred to as CDMA, is more common in Canada, the United States, and parts of Asia. Equipment designed for GSM will not work on a CDMA network, and vice versa. Thus, companies such as Apple, Samsung, and Sony, which manufacture wireless handsets and infrastructure such as fibre optics, need to customize their product offering according to the technical standard prevailing in a given country.

DIFFERENCES IN DISTRIBUTION CHANNELS

A firm's marketing strategies may have to be responsive to differences in distribution channels between countries. This may necessitate the delegation of marketing functions to national subsidiaries. In Germany, for example, a handful of food retailers dominate the market, but the market is very fragmented in neighbouring Italy. Thus, retail chains have considerable buying power in Germany but relatively little in Italy. Dealing with these differences requires varying marketing approaches for detergent firms. Similarly, in the pharmaceutical industry, the British and Japanese distribution systems are radically different from the U.S. system. British and Japanese doctors will not accept or respond favourably to an American-style high-pressure sales force. Thus, pharmaceutical firms have to adopt different marketing practices in Great Britain and Japan compared to the United States (soft sell versus hard sell).

HOST-GOVERNMENT DEMANDS

Economic and political demands imposed by host-country governments may necessitate a degree of local responsiveness. For example, the politics of health care around the world require that pharmaceutical firms manufacture in multiple locations. Pharmaceutical firms are subject to local clinical testing, registration procedures, and pricing restrictions, all of which require that the manufacturing and marketing of a drug should meet local requirements. Because governments and government agencies control a significant proportion of the health care budget in most countries, they can demand a high level of local responsiveness. Yet at the same time, outsiders attempt to benefit from changes in local conditions. For several years, patients in the United States used online pharmacies to purchase Canadian drugs at a lower price than in the United States. This practice has declined recently not because of government rules, but rather due to the sharp appreciation of the Canadian dollar versus the U.S. dollar.

Threats of protectionism, economic nationalism, and local content rules (which require that a certain percentage of a product be manufactured locally), all dictate that international businesses manufacture locally. Consider Bombardier, the Canadian-based manufacturer of railcars and aircraft. Bombardier's transportation division has operations in 28 countries.[22] Critics of the firm argue that the resulting duplication of manufacturing facilities leads to high costs and explains why Bombardier makes lower profit margins on its railcar operations than on its other business lines. Managers at Bombardier argue that in Europe, informal rules with regard to local content favour people who use local workers. To sell railcars in Germany, they claim, you must manufacture in Germany. The same goes for Belgium, Austria, and France. To address its cost structure in Europe, Bombardier has centralized its engineering and purchasing functions, but it has no plans to centralize manufacturing.[23]

LO4 Choosing a Strategy

Firms use four basic strategies to enter and compete in the international environment: an international strategy, a multidomestic strategy, a global strategy, and a transnational strategy.[24] Each of these strategies has its advantages and disadvantages. The appropriateness of each strategy varies with the extent of pressures for cost reductions and local responsiveness. Figure 11.6 illustrates when each of these strategies is most appropriate.

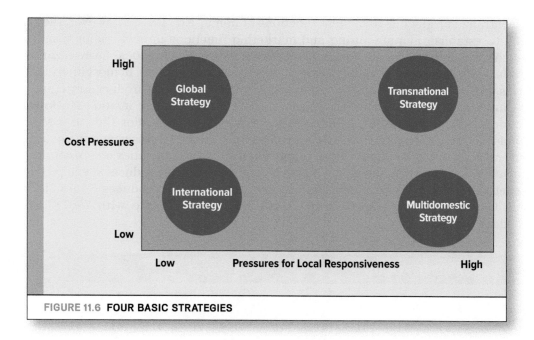

FIGURE 11.6 **FOUR BASIC STRATEGIES**

In this section we describe each strategy, identify when it is appropriate, and discuss the pros and cons of each.

DEBATE THE ISSUE

More Customized Products in the Global Marketplace?

The Coca-Cola Company's (TCCC) Minute Maid Pulpy became the cola giant's 14th brand to reach US$1 billion in global retail sales. As opposed to cola carbonates, which often rely on global brand recognition and cross-generational formulas for success, Minute Maid Pulpy has relied on product development and innovations inspired by local flavours and textures. Minute Maid released Minute Maid Pulpy toward the end of 2004, which contained less than 24 percent actual fruit juice, but TCCC was able to retail the product at a much lower price point. In China and throughout the Asia-Pacific region, consumer notions of freshness and health are connected much more to the consumption of actual fruit. Minute Maid Pulpy acknowledged this by including pieces of fruit in the drink, thereby creating a thicker texture that would not appeal to most North American consumers but has proven very popular in this region of the world. In customizing the product, Minute Maid Pulpy went from the 10th most popular fruit/vegetable juice brand in China in 2004 to 1st by the time it had achieved $1 billion in total sales in 2011. But isn't the world becoming more globalized? Do we still need large multinational corporations customizing their products to local markets?

Source: J. Feliciano, "Flavours and Textures: How Local Consumer Taste Palates Are Defining Global Soft Drinks," *Euromonitor International*, May 1, 2012, http://blog.euromonitor.com/2012/05/flavours-and-textures-how-local-consumer-taste-palates-are-defining-global-soft-drinks.html

International Strategy

Firms that pursue an international strategy try to create value by transferring valuable skills and products to foreign markets where indigenous competitors lack those skills and products. Most international firms have created value by transferring differentiated product offerings developed at home to new markets overseas. Accordingly, they tend to centralize product development functions at home (e.g., R&D). However, they also tend to establish manufacturing and marketing functions in each major country in which they do business. But while they may undertake some local customization of product offering and marketing strategy, this tends to be limited. In most international firms, the head office retains tight control over marketing and product strategy.

Canadian firms that operate with an international strategy include McDonald's, Barrick Gold Corporation, Gildan Activewear Inc., Bombardier Inc., and McCain Foods (Canada). McCain Foods develops its commitment to preserving the quality of the environment and extends those practices to all of their facilities on six continents. However, the company develops, markets, and customizes products specific to their target market. For instance, McCain Foods in Great Britain produces Gourmet Chips with Cornish Sea Salt and Gourmet Mash Maris Piper Potato with West Country Cheddar Cheese.[25]

MANAGEMENT FOCUS

Developing New Yogurt Brands

Yogurt is a big business in Canada. From 1996 to 2015 yogurt consumption among Canadians tripled. One of the beneficiaries of this growing trend is Longueil, Quebec-based Ultima Foods, which is owned by the Agropur and Agrifoods dairy cooperatives. Ultima is perhaps best known for its Yoplait brand, which it produced under a long-term license agreement with food giant General Mills. During discussions to renew the contract, Ultima Foods decided it would launch its own brand, as General Mills wanted direct control over Yoplait marketing in Canada and the U.S.

Instead, Ultima spent $60 million on research and development and $10 million to increase production capacity at its Granby, Quebec. plant to produce Iögo (pronounced "yo-go,") a new, made-in-Canada brand with over 40 products in 2012.

Things have certainly turned out for the better for Ultima. In December 2016, Ultima Foods announced the signing of a new seven-year agreement with General Mills to make yogurt products for its Canadian business. "General Mills' decision to pursue a significant portion of their yogurt production with Ultima Foods demonstrates their recognition of the high quality of our processes, the expertise of our teams, as well as our total commitment to always do better," said Martin Parent, President of Ultima Foods.

Questions

1. Is it always possible for a company to create a new product if it is not happy with a licensing or other type of agreement with a global partner?

2. Do you think that the creation of its own yogurt brand helped or hurt future negotiations with General Mills

Sources: Per Capita Consumption of Dairy Products (1997-2016), Government of Canada, http://www.dairyinfo.gc.ca/pdf/dpconsumption_e.pdf; Canada's Dairy Industry at a Glance, Government of Canada, http://www.dairyinfo.gc.ca/index_e.php?s1=cdi-ilc&s2=aag-ail; R. Harris, "Iögo emerges from cross-border marketing shuffle," *Marketing Magazine*, September 14, 2012, http://www.marketingmag.ca/advertising/iogo-emerges-from-cross-border-marketing-shuffle-62006; Ultima Foods, News Releases, http://www.ultimayog.ca/news-and-media/news-releases

An international strategy makes sense if a firm has a valuable core competence that indigenous competitors in foreign markets lack, and if the firm faces relatively weak pressures for local responsiveness and cost reductions (as is the case for Microsoft). In such circumstances, an international strategy can be very profitable. However, when pressures for local responsiveness are high, firms pursuing this strategy lose to firms that emphasize customizing the product offering and market strategy to local conditions. In addition, due to the duplication of manufacturing facilities, firms that pursue an international strategy tend to suffer from high operating costs. This makes the strategy inappropriate in manufacturing industries where cost pressures are high.

COUNTRY FOCUS

A Government Strategy for Business in Canada?

In a world that promotes free trade and downplays the role of government supports, the Canadian federal government and the provincial governments are quick to say that their role is not to "pick winners" in the economy. And yet this does occur. Federal aid to the auto industry in 2009 was presented, as it was in the United States, as a way of digging the economy out of the global economic slowdown.

At the provincial level, in mid-December 2013, the Ontario government announced a government "investment" of about $220 million in Cisco Canada, a move that was projected to add 1700 jobs. Opposition leaders quickly noted that Novartis, which received $4 million two years previously, has announced that it was closing a plant in a Toronto suburb. And in late 2016, Bombardier received a complicated series of funding measures from Quebec and Ottawa, including a direct $1 billion investment, in a deal that some are saying totals $2.6 billion.

While the federal and provincial governments seem to be focused on companies, municipalities are taking a different approach by focusing on economic sectors. Ottawa-Carlton focuses on the high-tech sector. The city of Toronto focuses on ten economic sectors, ranging from financial services and fashion and apparel to food and beverage. It offers customized research, policy advice, and liaison with other agencies and promotes international alliances for these sectors.

Questions

1. Should government continue to subsidize certain firms? If so, what criteria should they use (job creation, importance to the economy, other factors)?
2. Which do you think is a better strategy for governments: a company focused strategy or an economic sector strategy? Defend your argument.

Sources: "Ottawa prepared to review any foreign bid for Blackberry," *The Canadian Press*, October 6, 2013; M. Babbage, "Cisco to invest up to $4 billion and create 1700 jobs in Ontario," *The Canadian Press*, December 13, 2013; City of Toronto, www.toronto.ca, Economic Development & Culture Division, Strategic Growth Sector Development Contacts, accessed December 2013; and B. Haynes, "Brazil to challenge Canada at WTO over Bombardier funding," *Reuters*, December 19, 2016, http://www.reuters.com/article/us-brazil-canada-wto-idUSKBN1481FA

Multidomestic Strategy

Firms pursuing a multidomestic strategy orient themselves toward achieving maximum local responsiveness. The key distinguishing feature of multidomestic firms is that they extensively customize both their product offering and their marketing strategy to match different national conditions. Consistent with this, they also tend to establish a complete set of value creation activities, including production, marketing, and R&D in each major national market in which they do business. As a consequence, they are generally unable to realize value from experience curve effects and location economies. Accordingly, many multidomestic firms have a high cost structure. They also tend to do a poor job of leveraging core competencies within the firm.

A multidomestic strategy makes most sense when there are high pressures for local responsiveness and low pressures for cost reductions. The high-cost structure associated with the duplication of production facilities makes this strategy inappropriate in industries where cost pressures are intense. Another weakness associated with this strategy is that many multidomestic firms have developed into decentralized federations in which each national subsidiary functions in a largely autonomous manner. This was demonstrated by the failure of Philips NV to establish its V2000 VCR format as the standard in the industry during the late 1970s. Its U.S. subsidiary refused to adopt the V2000 format; instead, it bought VHS-format VCRs produced by Matsushita and put its own label on them!

Global Strategy

Firms that pursue a global strategy focus on increasing profitability by reaping the cost reductions that come from experience curve effects and location economies. That is, they are pursuing a low-cost strategy. The production, marketing, and R&D activities of firms pursuing a global strategy are concentrated in a few favourable locations.

Global firms tend not to customize their product offering and marketing strategy to local conditions because customization raises costs (it involves shorter production runs and the duplication of functions). Instead, global firms prefer to market a standardized product worldwide so they can reap the maximum benefits from the economies of scale that underlie the experience curve. They may also use their cost advantage to support aggressive pricing in world markets.

This strategy makes most sense where there are strong pressures for cost reductions and where demands for local responsiveness are minimal. Increasingly, these conditions prevail in many industrial goods industries. In the semiconductor industry, for example, global standards have created enormous demands for standardized global products. Accordingly, firms such as Intel and Motorola all pursue a global strategy. However, as we noted earlier, these conditions are not found in many consumer goods markets where demands for local responsiveness remain high (e.g., processed food products). The strategy is inappropriate when demands for local responsiveness are high.

Transnational Strategy

Christopher Bartlett and Sumantra Ghoshal have argued that in today's environment, competitive conditions are so intense that to survive in the global marketplace, firms must exploit experience-based cost economies and location economies, they must transfer core competencies within the firm, and they must do all of this while paying attention to pressures for local responsiveness.[26] They note that in the modern multinational enterprise, core competencies do not just reside in the home country. Valuable skills can develop in any of the firm's worldwide operations. Thus, Bartlett and Ghoshal maintain that the flow of skills and product offerings should not be all one way, from home firm to foreign subsidiary, as in the case of firms pursuing an international strategy. Rather, the flow should also be from foreign subsidiary to home country, and from foreign subsidiary to foreign subsidiary—a process they refer to as **global learning**.[27] Bartlett and Ghoshal refer to the strategy pursued by firms that are trying to simultaneously create value in these different ways as a **transnational strategy**.

A transnational strategy makes sense when a firm faces high pressures for cost reductions, high pressures for local responsiveness, and significant opportunities for leveraging valuable skills within a multinational's global network of operations. In some ways, firms that pursue a transnational strategy are trying to simultaneously achieve cost and differentiation advantages. In terms of the framework summarized in Figure 11.1, they are trying to simultaneously lower C and increase V. As attractive as this may sound, the strategy is not easy to pursue. Pressures for local responsiveness and cost reductions place conflicting demands on a firm. Being locally responsive raises costs. How can a firm effectively pursue a transnational strategy? Some clues can be derived from the case of Caterpillar. In the 1980s, the need to compete with low-cost competitors such as Komatsu and Hitachi of Japan forced Caterpillar to look for greater cost economies. At the same time, variations in construction practices and government regulations across countries meant that Caterpillar had to remain responsive to local demands. Therefore, Caterpillar was confronted with significant pressures for cost reductions and for local responsiveness.

To deal with cost pressures, Caterpillar redesigned its products to use many identical components and invested in a few large-scale component-manufacturing facilities, sited at favourable locations, to fill global demand and realize scale economics. The firm also augmented the centralized manufacturing of components with assembly plants in each of its major global markets. At these plants, Caterpillar added local product features, tailoring the finished product to local needs. By pursuing this strategy, Caterpillar realized many of the benefits of global manufacturing while also responding to pressures for local responsiveness by differentiating its product among national markets.[28] Caterpillar started to pursue this strategy in the early 1980s and by 1997 had doubled output per employee, significantly reducing its overall cost structure. Meanwhile, Komatsu and Hitachi, which are still wedded to a Japan-centric global strategy, have seen their cost advantages evaporate and have been steadily losing market share to Caterpillar.

Unilever, once a classic multidomestic firm, has had to shift toward more of a transnational strategy. A rise in competition that increased cost pressures forced Unilever to look for ways of rationalizing its detergent business. During the 1980s, Unilever had 17 largely self-contained detergent operations in Europe alone. The duplication of assets and marketing was enormous. Because Unilever was so fragmented, it could take as long as four years for the firm to introduce a new product across Europe. Now Unilever has integrated its European operations into a single entity, with detergents manufactured in a handful of cost-efficient plants, and standard packaging and advertising used across Europe. According to the firm, the result was an annual cost saving of more than $200 million. At the same time, due to national differences in distribution channels and brand awareness, Unilever recognizes that it must still remain locally responsive, even while it tries to realize economies from consolidating production and marketing at the optimal locations.[29] Bartlett and Ghoshal admit that building an organization that is capable of supporting a transnational strategic posture is complex and difficult. Simultaneously trying to achieve cost efficiencies, global learning (the leveraging of skills), and local responsiveness places contradictory demands on an organization. The organizational problems associated with pursuing what are essentially conflicting objectives constitute a major impediment to the pursuit of a transnational strategy. Firms that attempt to pursue a transnational strategy can become bogged down in an organizational morass that leads only to inefficiencies.

Also, Bartlett and Ghoshal may be overstating the case for the transnational strategy. They present the transnational strategy as the only viable strategy. While no one doubts that in some industries the firm that can adopt a transnational strategy will have a competitive advantage, in other industries, global, multidomestic, and international strategies remain viable. In the semiconductor industry, for example, pressures for local customization are minimal and competition is purely a cost game, in which case a global strategy, not a transnational strategy, is optimal. This is the

TABLE 11.1	The Advantages and Disadvantages of the Four Strategies	
Strategy	**Advantages**	**Disadvantages**
Global	Exploit experience curve effects Exploit location economies	Lack of local responsiveness
International	Transfer core competencies to foreign markets	Lack of local responsiveness Inability to realize location economies Failure to exploit experience curve effects
Multidomestic	Customize product offerings and marketing in accordance with local responsiveness	Inability to realize location economies Failure to exploit experience curve effects Failure to transfer core competencies to foreign markets
Transnational	Exploit experience curve effects Exploit location economies Customize product offerings and marketing in accordance with local responsiveness Reap benefits of global learning	Difficult to implement due to organizational problems

case in many industrial goods markets where the product serves universal needs. On the other hand, the argument can be made that to compete in certain consumer goods markets, such as the automobile and consumer electronics industry, a firm has to try to adopt a transnational strategy.

Summary

The advantages and disadvantages of each of the four strategies discussed above are summarized in Table 11.1. While a transnational strategy appears to offer the most advantages, implementing a transnational strategy raises difficult organizational issues. As shown in Figure 11.6, the appropriateness of each strategy depends on the relative strength of pressures for cost reductions and for local responsiveness.

LO5 Strategic Alliances

Strategic alliances refer to cooperative agreements between potential or actual competitors. In this section, we are concerned specifically with strategic alliances between firms from different countries. Strategic alliances run the range from formal joint ventures, in which two or more firms have equity stakes (e.g., Fuji Xerox), to short-term contractual agreements, in which two companies agree to cooperate on a particular task (such as developing a new product). Collaboration between competitors is fashionable; the last decades of the 20th century saw an explosion in the number of strategic alliances, and this seems to have continued into the 21st century.

The Advantages of Strategic Alliances

Firms ally themselves with actual or potential competitors for various strategic purposes.[30] First, strategic alliances may facilitate entry into a foreign market. For example, many firms believe that if they are to successfully enter the Chinese market, they need a local partner who understands business conditions and who has good connections. Thus Warner Brothers entered into a joint venture with two Chinese partners to produce and distribute films in China. As a foreign film company, Warner found that if it wanted to produce films on its own for the Chinese market, it had to go through a complex approval process for every film, and it had to farm out distribution to a local company, which made doing business in China very difficult. Due to the participation of Chinese firms, however, the joint-venture films will go through a streamlined approval process and the venture will be able to distribute any films it produces. Also, the joint venture will be able to produce films for Chinese TV, something that foreign firms are not allowed to do.[31]

Strategic alliances also allow firms to share the fixed costs (and associated risks) of developing new products or processes. An alliance between Boeing and a number of Japanese companies to build Boeing's latest commercial jetliner, the 787, was motivated by Boeing's desire to share the estimated $8 billion investment required to develop the aircraft.

Third, an alliance is a way to bring together complementary skills and assets that neither company could easily develop on its own.[32] In 2003, for example, Microsoft and Toshiba established an alliance aimed at developing embedded microprocessors (essentially tiny computers) that can perform a variety of entertainment functions in an automobile (e.g., run a backseat DVD player or a wireless Internet connection). The processors run a version of Microsoft's Windows CE operating system. Microsoft brings its software engineering skills to the alliance and Toshiba its skills in developing microprocessors.[33]

Fourth, it can make sense to form an alliance that will help the firm establish technological standards for the industry that will benefit the firm. For example, in 2011 Nokia, one of the leading makers of smart phones, entered into an alliance with Microsoft under which Nokia agreed to license and use Microsoft's Windows Mobile operating system in Nokia's phones. The motivation for the alliance was in part to help establish Windows Mobile as the industry standard for smart phones as opposed to the rival operating systems such as Apple's iPhone and Google's Android. Unfortunately for Microsoft, the Nokia's Windows phones failed to gain sufficient market share. In 2013, Microsoft decided to acquire Nokia's mobile phone business and bring it in house so that it could ensure a continued aggressive push into the smartphone hardware business.

The Disadvantages of Strategic Alliances

The advantages we have discussed can be very significant. Despite this, some commentators have criticized strategic alliances on the grounds that they give competitors a low-cost route to new technology and markets.[34] For example, Robert Reich and Eric Mankin argued that in the 1980s many strategic alliances between United States and Japanese firms were part of an implicit Japanese strategy to keep higher-paying, higher-value-added jobs in Japan while gaining the project engineering and production process skills that underlie the competitive success of many U.S. companies.[35] They argued that Japanese success in the machine tool and semiconductor industries was built on U.S. technology acquired through strategic alliances. And they argued that U.S. managers were aiding the Japanese in achieving their goals by entering alliances that channel new inventions to Japan and provide a U.S. sales and distribution network for the resulting products. Although such deals may generate short-term profits, Reich and Mankin argue, in the long run the result is to "hollow out" U.S. firms, leaving them with no competitive advantage in the global marketplace.

Reich and Mankin have a point. Alliances have risks. Unless a firm is careful, it can give away more than it receives. But there are so many examples of apparently successful alliances between firms—including alliances between U.S. and Japanese firms—that Reich and Mankin's position seems extreme. It is difficult to see how the many alliances noted above fit Reich and Mankin's thesis. In these cases, both partners seem to have gained from the alliance. Why do some alliances benefit both firms while others benefit one firm and hurt the other? The next section answers this question.

Making Alliances Work

The failure rate for international strategic alliances seems to be high. One study of 49 international strategic alliances found that two-thirds run into serious managerial and financial troubles within two years of their formation, and that although many of these problems are solved, 33 percent are ultimately rated as failures by the parties involved.[36] The success of an alliance seems to be a function of three main factors: partner selection, alliance structure, and the manner in which the alliance is managed.

Partner Selection

One key to making a strategic alliance work is to select the right ally. A good ally, or partner, has three characteristics. First, a good partner helps the firm achieve its strategic goals, whether they are market access, sharing the costs and risks of product development, or gaining access to critical core competencies. The partner must have capabilities that the firm lacks and that it values. Second, a good partner shares the firm's vision for the purpose of the alliance. If two firms approach an alliance with radically different agendas, the chances are great that the relationship will not be harmonious, will not flourish, and will end in divorce. Third, a good partner is unlikely to try to opportunistically exploit the alliance for its own ends; that is, to expropriate the firm's technological know-how while giving away little in return. In this respect, firms with reputations for "fair play" probably make the best allies. For example, General Electric is involved in so many strategic alliances that it would not pay the company to trample over individual alliance partners. This would tarnish GE's reputation of being a good ally and would make it more difficult for GE to attract alliance partners. Since GE attaches great importance to its alliances, it is unlikely to engage in the kind of opportunistic behaviour that Reich and Mankin highlight. Similarly, their reputations make it less likely (but by no means impossible) that such Japanese firms as Sony, Toshiba, and Fuji, which have histories of alliances with non-Japanese firms, would opportunistically exploit an alliance partner.

To select a partner with these three characteristics, a firm needs to conduct comprehensive research on potential alliance candidates. To increase the probability of selecting a good partner, the firm should:

1. Collect as much pertinent, publicly available information on potential allies as possible.

2. Collect data from informed third parties. These include firms that have had alliances with the potential partners, investment bankers who have had dealings with them, and former employees.

3. Get to know the potential partner as well as possible before committing to an alliance. This should include face-to-face meetings between senior managers (and perhaps middle-level managers) to ensure that the chemistry is right.

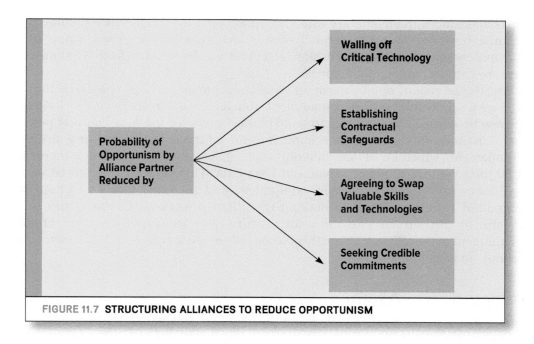

FIGURE 11.7 **STRUCTURING ALLIANCES TO REDUCE OPPORTUNISM**

Alliance Structure

Having selected a partner, the alliance should be structured so that the firm's risks of giving too much away to the partner are reduced to an acceptable level. Figure 11.7 depicts four safeguards against opportunism by alliance partners. (Opportunism includes the theft of technology and/or markets that Reich and Mankin describe.) First, alliances can be designed to make it difficult (if not impossible) to transfer technology not meant to be transferred. The design, development, manufacture, and service of a product manufactured by an alliance can be structured so as to wall off sensitive technologies to prevent their leakage to the other participant. In the alliance between General Electric and Snecma to build commercial aircraft engines, for example, GE reduced the risk of excess transfer by walling off certain sections of the production process. The modularization effectively cut off the transfer of what GE regarded as key competitive technology while permitting Snecma access to final assembly. Similarly, in the alliance between Boeing and the Japanese to build the 767, Boeing walled off research, design, and marketing functions considered central to its competitive position, while allowing the Japanese to share in production technology. Boeing also walled off new technologies not required for 767 production.[37]

Second, contractual safeguards can be written into an alliance agreement to guard against the risk of opportunism by a partner. For example, TRW, Inc. has three strategic alliances with large Japanese auto component suppliers to produce seat belts, engine valves, and steering gears for sale to Japanese-owned auto assembly plants in the United States. TRW has clauses in each of its alliance contracts that bar the Japanese firms from competing with TRW to supply U.S.-owned auto companies with component parts. By doing this, TRW protects itself against the possibility that the Japanese companies are entering into the alliances merely to gain access to TRW's home market.

Third, both parties to an alliance can agree in advance to swap skills and technologies that the other covets, thereby ensuring a chance for equitable gain.

Cross-licensing agreements are one way to achieve this goal. For example, in an alliance between Motorola and Toshiba, Motorola has licensed some of its microprocessor technology to Toshiba, and in return, Toshiba has licensed some of its memory chip technology to Motorola.

Fourth, the risk of opportunism by an alliance partner can be reduced if the firm extracts a significant credible commitment from its partner in advance. The long-term alliance between Xerox and Fuji to build photocopiers for the Asian market perhaps best illustrates this. Rather than enter into an informal agreement or a licensing arrangement (which Fuji Photo initially wanted), Xerox insisted that Fuji invest in a 50/50 joint venture to serve Japan and East Asia. This venture constituted such a significant investment in people, equipment, and facilities that Fuji Photo was committed from the outset to making the alliance work to earn a return on its investment. By agreeing to the joint venture, Fuji essentially made a credible commitment to the alliance. Given this, Xerox felt secure in transferring its photocopier technology to Fuji.[38]

Managing the Alliance

Once a partner has been selected and an appropriate alliance structure has been agreed on, the task facing the firm is to maximize its benefits from the alliance. As in all international business deals, an important factor is sensitivity to cultural differences (see Chapter 3). Many differences in management style are attributable to cultural differences, and managers need to make allowances for these in dealing with their partner. Beyond this, maximizing the benefits from an alliance seems to involve building trust between partners and learning from partners.[39]

BUILDING TRUST

Managing an alliance successfully requires building interpersonal relationships between the firms' managers, or what is sometimes referred to as *relational capital.*[40] This is one lesson that can be drawn from the successful strategic alliance between Ford and Mazda. Ford and Mazda set up a framework of meetings within which their managers not only discussed matters pertaining to the alliance but also had time to get to know each other better. The belief was that the resulting friendships helped build trust and facilitated harmonious relations between the two firms. Personal relationships also fostered an informal management network between the firms. This network was then used to help solve problems arising in more formal contexts (such as in joint committee meetings between personnel from the two firms).

LEARNING FROM PARTNERS

After a five-year study of 15 strategic alliances between major multinationals, Gary Hamel, Yves Doz, and C. K. Prahalad concluded that a major determinant of how much a company gains from an alliance is its ability to learn from its alliance partner.[41] They focused on a number of alliances between Japanese companies and Western (European or American) partners. In every case in which a Japanese company emerged from an alliance stronger than its Western partner, the Japanese company had made a greater effort to learn. Few Western companies studied seemed to want to learn from their Japanese partners. They tended to regard the alliance purely as a cost-sharing or risk-sharing device, rather than as an opportunity to learn how a potential competitor does business.

Consider the alliance between General Motors and Toyota constituted in 1985 to build the Chevrolet Nova. This alliance was structured as a formal joint venture, called New United Motor Manufacturing, Inc., and each party had a 50 percent equity stake. The venture owned an auto plant in Fremont, California. According to one Japanese manager, Toyota quickly achieved most of its objectives from the alliance: "We learned about U.S. supply and transportation. And we got the confidence to manage U.S. workers."[42] All that knowledge was then transferred to Georgetown, Kentucky, where Toyota opened its own plant in 1988. On the other hand, possibly all GM got was a new product, the Chevrolet Nova. Some GM managers complained that the knowledge they gained through the alliance with Toyota has never been put to good use inside GM. They believe they should have been kept together as a team to educate GM's engineers and workers about the Japanese system. Instead, they were dispersed to various GM subsidiaries.

To maximize the learning benefits of an alliance, a firm must try to learn from its partner and then apply the knowledge within its own organization. It has been suggested that all operating employees should be well briefed on the partner's strengths and weaknesses and should understand how acquiring particular skills will bolster their firm's competitive position. Hamel, Doz, and Prahalad note that this is already standard practice among Japanese companies. They made this observation:

> We accompanied a Japanese development engineer on a tour through a partner's factory. This engineer dutifully took notes on plant layout, the number of production stages, the rate at which the line was running, and the number of employees. He recorded all this despite the fact that he had no manufacturing responsibility in his own company, and that the alliance did not encompass joint manufacturing. Such dedication greatly enhances learning.[43]

For such learning to be of value, it must be diffused throughout the organization (as was seemingly not the case at GM after the GM–Toyota joint venture). To achieve this, the managers involved in the alliance should educate their colleagues about the skills of the alliance partner.

IMPLICATIONS FOR BUSINESS

There are many layers of business strategy required for success. Corporate success hinges on efficiency; effectiveness; communication; management; technologies; strategy, goals and vision; people; operations management; finances; product or service, and more. When benchmarked against domestic and international competitors, the picture becomes clearer. Companies who adapt, innovate, and make sacrifices are more likely to survive and expand than those who do not. Take for example the case of Air Canada, which has undergone a decades-long flirtation with bankruptcy. After making huge concessions and changes, which included employee wage reductions, it appears geared for a journey into the black.

INTERNATIONAL BUSINESS REQUIREMENTS

Many Canadian companies have made the tactical error of using Canadian marketing companies to lay the groundwork for foreign product launches. Failure to understand the strategic significance of speaking to foreign consumers from their culture base is a frequent recipe for disappointing results. For example, in spite of certain breweries' initiatives to market their beer to other countries, local tastes and loyalties to existing brands prevail. Foreign brewers have difficulty accessing this market, in spite of best efforts.

Key Terms

core competence	profit
economies of scope	profitability
experience curve	strategic alliances
global learning	strategy
global web	transnational strategy
learning effects	universal needs
location economies	value creation

LO Learning Objectives Summary

1. A strategy can be defined as the actions that managers take to attain the goals of the firm. For most firms, the preeminent goal is to maximize shareholder value. Maximizing shareholder value requires firms to focus on increasing their profitability and the growth rate of profits over time. International expansion may enable a firm to earn greater returns by transferring the product offerings derived from its core competencies to markets where indigenous competitors lack those product offerings and competencies.

2. It may pay a firm to base each value creation activity it performs at that location where factor conditions are most conducive to the performance of that activity. We refer to this strategy as focusing on the attainment of location economies. By rapidly building sales volume for a standardized product, international expansion can assist a firm in moving down the experience curve by realizing learning effects and economies of scale. A multinational firm can create additional value by identifying valuable skills created within its foreign subsidiaries and leveraging those skills within its global network of operations.

3. The best strategy for a firm to pursue often depends on a consideration of the pressures for cost reductions and for local responsiveness.

4. Firms pursuing an international strategy transfer the products derived from core competencies to foreign markets, while undertaking some limited local customization. Firms pursuing a localization strategy customize their product offering, marketing strategy, and business strategy to national conditions. Firms pursuing a global standardization strategy focus on reaping the cost reductions that come from experience curve effects and location economies. Many industries are now so competitive that firms must adopt a transnational strategy. This involves a simultaneous focus on reducing costs, transferring skills and products, and boosting local responsiveness. Implementing such a strategy may not be easy.

5. Strategic alliances are cooperative agreements between actual or potential competitors. The advantages of alliances are that they facilitate entry into foreign markets, enable partners to share the fixed costs and risks associated with new products and processes, facilitate the transfer of complementary skills between companies, and help firms establish technical standards. A disadvantage of a strategic alliance is that the firm risks giving away technological know-how and market access to its alliance partner in return for very little. The disadvantages associated with alliances can be reduced if the firm selects partners carefully, paying close attention to the firm's reputation and the structure of the alliance so as to avoid unintended transfers of know-how. Keys to making alliances work seem to be building trust and informal communications networks between partners and taking proactive steps to learn from alliance partners.

Critical Thinking and Discussion Questions

1. "In a world of zero transportation costs, no trade barriers, and trivial differences between nations with regard to factor conditions, firms must expand internationally if they are to survive." Evaluate this statement.

2. Are the following industries global industries or multidomestic industries: bulk chemicals, pharmaceuticals, branded food products, moviemaking, television manufacturing, personal computers, airline travel?

3. Discuss how the need for control over foreign operations varies with the strategy and core competencies of a firm. What are the implications of this for the choice of entry mode?

4. What do you see as the main organizational problems likely to be associated with implementation of a transnational strategy?

Research Task globalEDGE™ **globaledge.msu.edu**

Use the globalEDGE™ site to complete the following exercises:

1. Several classifications and rankings of multinational corporations are prepared by a variety of sources. Find one such ranking system and identify the criteria that are used in ranking the top global companies. Extract the list of the highest ranked 25 companies, paying particular attention to the home countries of the companies.

2. The top management of your company, a manufacturer and marketer of laptop computers, has decided to pursue international expansion opportunities in Eastern Europe. To achieve some economies of scale, your management is aiming toward a strategy of minimum local adaptation. Focusing on an Eastern European country of your choice, prepare an executive summary that features those aspects of the product where standardization will simply not work, and adaptation to local conditions will be essential.

CLOSING CASE

FORD'S GLOBAL STRATEGY

When Ford CEO Alan Mulally arrived at the company in 2006 after a long career at Boeing, he was shocked to learn that the company produced one Ford Focus for Europe and a totally different one for the United States. "Can you imagine having one Boeing 737 for Europe and one 737 for the United States?" he said at the time. Due to this product strategy, Ford was unable to buy common parts for the vehicles, could not share development costs, and couldn't use its European Focus plants to make cars for the United States, or vice versa. In a business where economies of scale are important, the result was high costs. Nor were these problems limited to the Ford Focus. The strategy of designing and building different cars for different regions was the standard approach at Ford.

Ford's long-standing strategy of regional models was based upon the assumption that consumers in different regions had different tastes and preferences, which required considerable local customization. Americans, it was argued, loved their trucks and SUVs, while Europeans preferred smaller, fuel-efficient cars. Notwithstanding such differences, Mulally still could not understand why small car models like the Focus, or the Escape SUV, which were sold in different regions, were not built on the same platform and did not share common parts. In truth, the strategy probably had more to do with the autonomy of different regions within Ford's organization—a fact that was deeply embedded in Ford's history as one of the oldest multinational corporations.

When the global financial crisis rocked the world's automobile industry in 2008–2009 and precipitated the steepest drop in sales since the Great Depression, Mulally decided that Ford had to change its long-standing practices in order to get its costs under control. Moreover, he felt that there was no way that Ford would be able to compete effectively in the large developing markets of China and India unless Ford leveraged its global scale to produce low-cost cars. The result was Mulally's One Ford strategy, which aims to create a handful of car platforms that Ford can use everywhere in the world.

Under this strategy, new models—such as the 2013 Fiesta, Focus, and Escape—share a common design, are built on a common platform, use the same parts, and will be built in identical factories around the world. Ultimately, Ford hopes to boost global production by reducing its core platforms from fifteen to nine by 2017. In 2006, Ford had 15 platforms that accounted for sales of 6.6 million vehicles. By pursuing this strategy, Ford can share the costs of design and tooling, and it can attain much greater scale economies in the production of component parts. Ford has stated that it will take about one-third out of the $1 billion cost of developing a new car model and should significantly reduce its $50 billion annual budget for component parts. Moreover, because the different factories producing these cars are identical in all respects, useful knowledge acquired through experience in one factory can quickly be transferred to other factories, resulting in systemwide cost savings.

What Ford hopes is that this strategy will bring down costs sufficiently to enable Ford to make greater profit margins in developed markets and be able to achieve good profit margins at lower price points in hypercompetitive developing nations, such as China (now the world's largest car market), where Ford currently trails its global rivals such as General Motors and Volkswagen.

Sources: M. Ramsey, "Ford SUV Marks New World Car Strategy," *The Wall Street Journal*, November 16, 2011; B. Vlasic, "Ford Strategy Will Call for Stepping Up Expansion, Especially in Asia," *The New York Times*, June 7, 2011; and "Global Manufacturing Strategy Gives Ford Competitive Advantage," Ford Motor Company Web site, http://media.ford.com/article_display.cfm?article_id=13633

Case Discussion Questions

1. How would you characterize the strategy for competing internationally that Ford was pursuing prior to the arrival of Alan Mulally in 2006? What were the benefits of this strategy? What were the costs? Why was Ford pursuing this strategy?

2. What strategy is Mulally trying to get Ford to pursue with his One Ford initiative? What are the benefits of this strategy? Can you see any drawbacks?

3. Does the One Ford initiative imply that Ford will now ignore national and regional differences in demand?

Chapter 12
Entering Foreign Markets

OPENING CASE

MARKET ENTRY AT STARBUCKS

A little more than forty years ago, Starbucks was a single store in Seattle's Pike Place Market selling premium-roasted coffee. Today, it is a global roaster and retailer of coffee with almost 20 000 stores, 40 percent of which are in 62 countries outside of the United States. Starbucks set out on its current course in the 1980s when the company's director of marketing, Howard Schultz, came back from a trip to Italy enchanted with the Italian coffeehouse experience. Schultz, who later became CEO, persuaded the company's owners to experiment with the coffeehouse format—and the Starbucks experience was born. The strategy was to sell the company's own premium roasted coffee and freshly brewed espresso-style coffee beverages, along with a variety of pastries, coffee accessories, teas, and other products, in a tastefully designed coffeehouse setting. From the outset, the company focused on selling "a third place experience," rather than just the coffee. The formula led to spectacular success in the United States, where Starbucks went from obscurity to one of the best-known brands in the country in a decade. Thanks to Starbucks, coffee stores became places for relaxation, chatting with friends, reading the newspaper, holding business meetings, or (more recently) browsing the Web.

In 1995, with 700 stores across the United States, Starbucks began exploring foreign opportunities. The first target market was Japan. The company established a joint venture with a local retailer, Sazaby Inc. Each company held a 50 percent stake in the venture, Starbucks Coffee of Japan. Starbucks initially invested $10 million in this venture, its first foreign direct investment. The Starbucks format was then licensed to the venture, which was charged with taking over responsibility for growing Starbucks' presence in Japan.

To make sure the Japanese operations replicated the "Starbucks experience" in North America, Starbucks transferred some employees to the Japanese operation. The licensing agreement required all Japanese store managers and employees to attend training classes similar to those given to U.S. employees. The agreement also required that stores adhere to the design parameters established in the United States. In 2001, the company introduced a stock option plan for all Japanese employees, making it the first company in Japan to do so. Skeptics doubted that Starbucks would be able to replicate its North American success overseas, but by the end of 2013 Starbucks' had some 1000 stores and a profitable business in Japan.

After Japan, the company embarked on an aggressive foreign investment program. In 1998, it purchased Seattle Coffee, a British coffee chain with 60 retail stores, for $84 million. An American couple, originally from Seattle, had started Seattle Coffee with the intention of establishing a Starbucks-like chain in Britain. In the late 1990s, Starbucks opened stores in Taiwan, Singapore, Thailand, New Zealand, South Korea, Malaysia, and—most significantly—China. In Asia, Starbucks' most common strategy was to license its format to a local operator in return for initial licensing fees and royalties on store revenues. As in Japan, Starbucks insisted on an intensive employee-training program and strict specifications regarding the format and layout of the store.

By 2002, Starbucks was pursuing an aggressive expansion in mainland Europe. As its first entry point, Starbucks chose Switzerland. Drawing on its experience in Asia, the company entered into a joint venture with a Swiss company, Bon Appetit Group, Switzerland's largest food service company. Bon Appetit was to hold a majority stake in the venture, and Starbucks would license its format to the Swiss company using a similar agreement to those it had used successfully in Asia. This was followed by a joint venture in other countries.

By 2014, Starbucks was emphasizing the rapid growth of its operations in China, where it now had 1000 stores and plans to roll out another 500 in three years. The success of Starbucks in China has been attributed to a smart partnering strategy. China is not one homogeneous market; the culture of northern China is very different from that of the east, and consumer spending power inland is not on par with that of the big coastal cities. To deal with this complexity, Starbucks entered into three different joint ventures: in the north, with Beijong Mei Da coffee; in the east with Taiwan-based Uni-President; and in the south with Hong Kong–based Maxim's Caterers. Each partner brought different strengths and local expertise that helped the company gain insights into the tastes and preferences of local Chinese customers, allowing the chain to adapt accordingly. Starbucks now believes that China will become its second largest market after the United States by 2020.

Sources: Starbucks 10K, various years; C. McLean, "Starbucks Set to Invade Coffee-Loving Continent," *Seattle Times*, October 4, 2000, p. E1; J. Ordonez, "Starbucks to Start Major Expansion in Overseas Market," *The Wall Street Journal*, October 27, 2000, p. B10; S. Homes and D. Bennett, "Planet Starbucks," *Businessweek*, September 9, 2002, pp. 99–110; "Starbucks Outlines International Growth Strategy," *Business Wire*, October 14, 2004; A. Yeh, "Starbucks Aims for New Tier in China," *Financial Times*, February 14, 2006, p. 17; C. Matlack, "Will Global Growth Help Starbucks?" *Businessweek*, July 2, 2008; and H. H. Wang, "Five Things Starbucks Did to Get China Right," *Forbes*, July 10, 2012.

| LO | **LEARNING OBJECTIVES** |

By the end of this chapter you should be able to:

1. Explain the three basic decisions that firms contemplating foreign expansion must make: which markets to enter, when to enter those markets, and on what scale.

2. Compare and contrast the different modes that firms use to enter foreign markets.

3. Identify the factors that influence a firm's choice of entry mode.

4. Recognize the pros and cons of acquisitions versus greenfield ventures as an entry strategy.

Introduction

This chapter is concerned with two closely related topics: (1) the decision of which foreign markets to enter, when to enter them, and on what scale; and (2) the choice of entry mode. Any firm contemplating foreign expansion must first struggle with the issue of which foreign markets to enter and the timing and scale of entry. The choice of which markets to enter should be driven by an assessment of relative long-run growth and profit potential. Chapter 11 focused on the role of strategy in creating opportunities for Canadian companies doing business abroad. Some of those strategies can be found in the chapter opening case about Starbucks. Enticed by its long-term growth potential, Starbucks entered China back in 1999. The company now believes that China will ultimately become its second largest market after the United States, and accordingly, it has been investing heavily in that nation.

The choice of mode for entering a foreign market is another major issue with which international businesses must wrestle. The various modes for serving foreign markets are exporting, licensing or franchising to host-country firms, establishing joint ventures with a host-country firm, setting up a new wholly owned subsidiary in a host country to serve its market, and acquiring an established enterprise in the host nation to serve that market. Each of these options has advantages and disadvantages. The magnitude of the advantages and disadvantages associated with each entry mode is determined by a number of factors, including transport costs, trade barriers, political risks, economic risks, business risks, costs, and firm strategy. The optimal entry mode varies by situation, depending on these factors. Thus, whereas some firms may best serve a given market by exporting, other firms may better serve the market by setting up a new wholly owned subsidiary or by acquiring an established enterprise. Starbucks, for example, seems to have had a preference for entering into joint ventures with local partners and then licensing its format to the joint venture. Starbucks has done this in order to benefit from its joint-venture partners' local expertise, which has helped the company to better configure its store format and menu to the tastes and preferences of local customers. In China, for example, its partners urged Starbucks to capitalize on the tea-drinking culture of the country by using popular local ingredients such as green tea. This helped to get consumers through the door, and once they frequented the stores, they quickly developed a taste for Starbucks coffee.

LO1 Basic Entry Decisions

In this section, we look at three basic decisions that a firm contemplating foreign expansion must make: which markets to enter, when to enter those markets, and on what scale.[1]

Which Foreign Markets?

The 196 nation-states in the world do not all hold the same profit potential for a firm contemplating foreign expansion. Ultimately, the choice must be based on an assessment of a nation's long-run profit potential. This potential is a function of several factors, many of which we have already studied in earlier chapters. In Chapter 2, we looked in detail at the economic and political factors that influence the potential attractiveness of a foreign market. There we noted that the attractiveness of a country as a potential market for an international business depends on balancing the benefits, costs, and risks associated with doing business in that country.

Chapter 2 also noted that the long-run economic benefits of doing business in a country are a function of factors such as the size of the market (in terms of demographics), the present wealth (purchasing power) of consumers in that market, and the likely future wealth of consumers. While some markets are very large when measured by number of consumers (e.g., China and India), low living standards may imply limited purchasing power and a relatively small market when measured in economic terms. We also argued that the costs and risks associated with doing business in a foreign country are typically lower in economically advanced and politically stable democratic nations, and they are greater in less-developed and politically unstable nations.

However, this calculation is complicated by the fact that the potential long-run benefits bear little relationship to a nation's current stage of economic development or political stability. Long-run benefits depend on likely future economic growth rates, and economic growth appears to be a function of a free market system and a country's capacity for growth (which may be greater in less-developed nations). This leads to the conclusion that, other things being equal, the benefit–cost–risk trade-off is likely to be most favourable in politically stable, developed and developing nations that have free market systems, and where there is not a dramatic upsurge in either inflation rates or private-sector debt. The trade-off is likely to be least favourable in politically unstable developing nations that operate with a mixed or command economy or in developing nations where speculative financial bubbles have led to excess borrowing (see Chapter 2 for further details).

By applying the reasoning processes alluded to above and discussed in more detail in Chapter 2, a firm can rank countries in terms of their attractiveness and long-run profit potential. Preference is then given to entering markets that rank highly. One other fact we have not yet discussed is the value an international business can create in a foreign market. This depends on the suitability of its product offering to that market and the nature of indigenous competition.[2] If the international business can offer a product that has not been widely available in that market and that satisfies an unmet need, the value of that product to consumers is likely to be much greater than if the international business simply offers the same type of product that indigenous competitors and other foreign entrants are already offering. Greater value translates into an ability to charge higher prices and/or to build sales volume more rapidly.

Timing of Entry

Once attractive markets have been identified, it is important to consider the **timing of entry**. We say that entry is early when an international business enters a foreign market before other foreign firms and late when it enters after other international businesses have established themselves. The advantages frequently associated with entering a market early are commonly known as *first-mover advantages*.[3] One first-mover advantage is the ability to pre-empt rivals and capture demand by establishing a strong brand name. A second advantage is the ability to build sales volume in that country and ride down the experience curve ahead of rivals, giving the early entrant a cost advantage over later entrants. This cost advantage may enable the early entrant to cut prices below that of later entrants, thereby driving them out of the market. A third advantage is the ability of early entrants to create switching costs that tie customers into their products or services. Such switching costs make it difficult for later entrants to win business.

Entering a foreign market before other international businesses also has disadvantages. These are often referred to as **first-mover disadvantages**.[4] These disadvantages may give rise to pioneering costs. **Pioneering costs** is the price that an early entrant has to bear that a later entrant can avoid. Pioneering costs arise when the business system in a foreign country is so different from that in a firm's home market that the enterprise has to devote considerable effort, time, and expense to learning the rules of the game. Pioneering costs include the costs of business failure if the firm, due to its ignorance of the foreign environment, makes major mistakes. A certain liability is associated with being a foreigner, and this liability is greater for foreign firms that enter a national market early.[5] Recent research seems to confirm that the probability of survival increases if an international business enters a national market after several other foreign firms have already done so.[6] The late entrant may benefit by observing and learning from the mistakes made by early entrants.

Pioneering costs also include the costs of promoting and establishing a product offering, including the costs of educating customers. These costs can be particularly significant when the product being promoted is unfamiliar to local consumers. In contrast, later entrants may be able to ride on an early entrant's investments in learning and customer education by watching how the early entrant proceeded in the market, by avoiding costly mistakes made by the early entrant, and by exploiting the market potential created by the early entrant's investments in customer education. For example, KFC introduced the Chinese to American-style fast food, but a later entrant, McDonald's, has capitalized on the market in China.

An early entrant may be at a severe disadvantage, relative to a later entrant, if regulations change in a way that diminishes the value of an early entrant's investments. This is a serious risk in many developing nations where the rules that govern business practices are still evolving. Early entrants can find themselves at a disadvantage if a subsequent change in regulations invalidates prior assumptions about the best business model for operating in that country.

Scale of Entry and Strategic Commitments

Another issue that an international business needs to consider when contemplating market entry is the scale of entry. Entering a market on a large scale involves the commitment of significant resources.

The consequences of entering on a significant scale are associated with the value of the resulting strategic commitments.[7] A **strategic commitment** has a long-term

MANAGEMENT FOCUS

Gildan's International Growth Strategy

Gildan Activewear employs 48 000 people around the globe, but is a name that is not well known to many Canadian consumers. Part of this comes from the products that the company makes: T-shirts, fleece shirts, socks, and underwear. But it has high visibility in two sectors. The first is what is known as the printwear business, which means specially ordered shirts with company, team, or other logos on them. It is the leader in this field in both Canada and the United States, and is extending its printwear abilities in global markets. The second area of visibility is through licensing agreements to produce New Balance and Under Armor branded products.

The company has a truly global supply chain system. The company's headquarters are in Montreal. Its printwear operations are in Barbados. Its branded apparel operates out of South Carolina, United States. The manufacturing facilities that support both of these operations are located in Central America, the Caribbean basin, and Bangladesh. Finally, the company's yarn spinning takes place in North Carolina and Georgia, in the United States.

The company is highly dependent on the price of its raw material: cotton. A few years ago cotton prices rose, then fell back to historic averages. The company made a strategic decision to lower its selling prices when cotton costs fell back to normal levels, even though this would mean lower profit margins for at least half a year as the company worked through the consumption of inventory that was purchased when cotton prices had reached an all-time high. This strategy had, obviously, negative short-term consequences, but positioned the company well in the medium-term. It worked well, as the lower prices ended up increasing demand, and Gildan was able to increase its market share in the U.S. printwear segment. This also helped international printwear sales where sales increased by 30 percent in the latest full fiscal year.

For the future, Gildan is planning upgrades to a textile manufacturing facility in Honduras and a new sewing facility in the Dominican Republic. These investments are expected to help the company's position as a low-cost producer in the 2016–17 period. In February 2017, the company announced that it completed the acquisition of the American Apparel Brand, thus widening the company's brands even further.

Questions

1. What are the benefits of having a global supply chain such as Gildan's? What are the risks?
2. The company is very sensitive to the price of its key raw material: cotton. Are there any steps it could take to reduce its risk (see Chapter 9)?

Sources: Gildan, *Annual Report 2012*, http://www.gildancorp.com/documents/Annual-Report-2012/annual_report_2012_en.pdf (accessed December 2013); News Release: "Gildan Activewear Announces Record Results," November 21, 2013 (accessed December 2013); Press Release: "Gildan Announces Completion of Acquisition of American Apparel Brand Montreal," February 8, 2017.

impact and is difficult to reverse. Deciding to enter a foreign market on a significant scale is a major strategic commitment. Strategic commitments, such as large-scale market entry, can have an important influence on the nature of competition in a market.

Significant strategic commitments are neither unambiguously good nor bad. Rather, they affect the competitive playing field and unleash a number of changes, some of which may be desirable and some of which will not be. It is important for a firm to think through the implications of large-scale entry into a market and act accordingly. Of particular relevance is trying to identify how actual and potential competitors might react to large-scale entry into a market. Also, the large-scale entrant is more likely than the small-scale entrant to be able to capture first-mover advantages associated with demand pre-emption, scale economies, and switching costs.

ANOTHER PERSPECTIVE

What's the Market Entry Logic Here?

Often the initial market entry decision is greatly influenced by culture. The assumption at work here is that the more similar the culture (and this often means language) the easier the entry and the more assured the results. We see companies based in Canada enter Australia and New Zealand while they ignore Mexico. Looking at recent figures, Australia has about 25 million people, New Zealand 5 million, and Mexico 130 million.

What do you think about these decisions?

Balanced against the value and risks of the commitments associated with large-scale entry are the benefits of a small-scale entry. Small-scale entry allows a firm to learn about a foreign market while limiting the firm's exposure to that market. Small-scale entry is a way to gather information about a foreign market before deciding whether to enter on a significant scale and how best to enter. By giving the firm time to collect information, small-scale entry reduces the risks associated with a subsequent large-scale entry. But the lack of commitment associated with small-scale entry may make it more difficult for the small-scale entrant to build market share and to capture first-mover or early-mover advantages. The risk-averse firm that enters a foreign market on a small scale may limit its potential losses, but it may also miss the chance to capture first-mover advantages.

Evaluating the Level of Risk

There are no "right" decisions here, just decisions that are associated with different levels of risk and reward. Entering a large developing nation such as China or India before most other international businesses in the firm's industry, and entering on a large scale, will be associated with high levels of risk. In such cases, the liability of being foreign is increased by the absence of prior foreign entrants whose experience can be a useful guide. At the same time, the potential long-term rewards associated with such a strategy are great. The early large-scale entrant into a major developing nation may be able to capture significant first-mover advantages that will bolster its long-run position in that market.[8] In contrast, entering developed nations such as Australia or Canada after other international businesses in the firm's industry, and entering on a small scale to first learn more about those markets, will be associated with much lower levels of risk. However, the potential long-term rewards are also likely to be lower because the firm is essentially forgoing the opportunity to capture first-mover advantages and because the lack of commitment signalled by small-scale entry may limit its future growth potential.

The previous section has been written largely from the perspective of a business based in a developed country considering entry into foreign markets. In a seminal article, Christopher Bartlett and Sumantra Ghoshal pointed out the ability that businesses based in developing nations have to enter foreign markets and become global players.[9] Although such firms tend to be late entrants into foreign markets, and although their resources may be limited, Bartlett and Ghoshal argue that such late movers can still succeed against well-established global competitors by pursuing appropriate strategies. In particular, Bartlett and Ghoshal argue that companies based in developing nations should benchmark their operations and

Being the first to enter a developing nation such as China is risky, but potentially rewarding. © Alex Woo/Getty Images

performance against competing foreign multinationals. They suggest that the local company may be able to differentiate itself from a foreign multinational, for example, by focusing on market niches that the multinational ignores or is unable to serve effectively if it has a standardized global product offering. Having improved its performance through learning and differentiating its product offering, the firm from a developing nation may then be able to pursue its own international expansion strategy. Even though the firm may be a late entrant into many countries, by benchmarking and then differentiating itself from early movers in global markets, the firm from the developing nation may build a strong international business presence.

DEBATE THE ISSUE

Is First-Mover Advantage Always a Good Thing?

Timing of entry into a foreign market is one of the most critical aspects of going international. Popularized by Marvin Lieberman and David Montgomery in 1988, first-mover advantage was an idea that resonated with every company. But, 10 years later, in 1998, Lieberman and Montgomery actually backed off their own idea that taking advantage of being the first mover was always a good strategy. By that time, it was too late: Venture capitalists, companies, people, and many scholars had already latched on to the positive things about being first in a new foreign market and stressed this approach over any other timing of entry. Now we are some about two decades into the twenty-first century, and companies realize that first-mover advantages also come with pioneering costs. If you had a choice of being the first-mover into a new emerging foreign market (e.g., Turkey) and being the fifth company entering that market with your product, what would you choose and why?

Sources: M. B. Lieberman and D. B. Montgomery, "First-Mover Advantages," *Strategic Management Journal*, 9, no. S1 (1988), pp. 41–58; and M. B. Lieberman and D. B. Montgomery, "First-Mover (Dis)Advantages: Retrospective and Link with the Resource-Based View," *Strategic Management Journal*, 19, no. 12 (1998), pp. 1111–25.

LO2 Entry Modes

Once a firm decides to enter a foreign market, the question arises as to the best mode of entry. Firms can use six different modes to enter foreign markets: exporting, turnkey projects, licensing, franchising, establishing joint ventures with a host-country firm, or setting up a new wholly owned subsidiary in the host country. Each entry mode has advantages and disadvantages. Managers need to consider these carefully when deciding which to use.[10]

Exporting

Many manufacturing firms begin their global expansion as exporters and later switch to another mode for serving a foreign market. We take a close look at the mechanics of exporting in the next chapter. Here we focus on the advantages and disadvantages of exporting as an entry mode.

ADVANTAGES

Exporting has two distinct advantages. First, it avoids the often-substantial costs of establishing manufacturing operations in the host country. Second, exporting may help a firm achieve experience curve and location economies (see Chapter 11). By manufacturing the product in a centralized location and exporting it to other national markets, the firm may realize substantial scale economies from its global sales volume. This is how Sony came to dominate the global HDTV market, how Panasonic came to dominate the DVD player market, how many Japanese automakers made inroads into the U.S. market, and how South Korean firms such as Samsung gained market share in the cell phone market.

DISADVANTAGES

Exporting has a number of drawbacks. First, exporting from the firm's home base may not be appropriate if there are lower-cost locations for manufacturing the product abroad (i.e., if the firm can realize location economies by moving production elsewhere). Thus, particularly for firms pursuing global or transnational strategies, it may be preferable to manufacture where the mix of factor conditions is most favourable from a value creation perspective and to export to the rest of the world from that location. This is not so much an argument against exporting as an argument against exporting from the firm's home country. Many U.S. and Canadian electronics firms have moved most of their manufacturing to the Far East because of the availability of low-cost, highly skilled labour there. They then export from that location to the rest of the world, including the United States and Canada.

A second drawback to exporting is that high transport costs can make exporting uneconomical, particularly for bulk products. One way of getting around this is to manufacture bulk products regionally. This strategy enables the firm to realize some economies from large-scale production and at the same time to limit its transport costs. For example, many multinational chemical firms manufacture their products regionally, serving several countries from one facility.

Another drawback is that tariff barriers can make exporting uneconomical. Similarly, the threat of tariff barriers can make exporting very risky.

A fourth drawback to exporting arises when a firm delegates its marketing in each country where it does business to a local agent. (This is common for firms that are just beginning to export.) Foreign agents often carry the products of competing firms and so have divided loyalties. In such cases, the foreign agent may not do as good a job as the firm would if it managed its marketing itself.

One way around this is to set up a wholly owned subsidiary in the country to handle local marketing. By doing this, the firm can exercise tight control over marketing in the country while reaping the cost advantages of manufacturing the product in a single location.

Turnkey Projects

Firms that specialize in the design, construction, and start-up of turnkey plants are common in some industries. In a **turnkey project**, the contractor agrees to handle every detail of the project for a foreign client, including the training of operating personnel. At completion of the contract, the foreign client is handed the "key" to a plant that is ready for full operation—hence, the term *turnkey*. This is a means of exporting process technology to other countries. Turnkey projects are most common in the chemical, pharmaceutical, petroleum refining, and metal refining industries, all of which use complex, expensive production technologies.

ADVANTAGES

The know-how required to assemble and run a technologically complex process, such as refining petroleum or steel, is a valuable asset. Turnkey projects are a way of earning great economic returns from that asset. The strategy is particularly useful where FDI is limited by host-government regulations. For example, the governments of many oil-rich countries have set out to build their own petroleum refining industry, so they restrict FDI in their oil and refining sectors. But because many of these countries lacked petroleum refining technology, they gained it by entering into turnkey projects with foreign firms that had the technology. Such deals are often attractive to the selling firm because without them, the firm would have no way to earn a return on its valuable know-how in that country. A turnkey strategy can also be less risky than conventional FDI. In a country with unstable political and economic environments, a longer-term investment might expose the firm to unacceptable political and/or economic risks (e.g., the risk of nationalization or of economic collapse).

DISADVANTAGES

Three main drawbacks are associated with a turnkey strategy. First, the firm that enters into a turnkey deal will have no long-term interest in the foreign country. This can be a disadvantage if that country subsequently proves to be a major market for the output of the process that has been exported. One way around this is to take a minority equity interest in the operation.

Second, the firm that enters into a turnkey project with a foreign enterprise may inadvertently create a competitor. For example, many of the Western firms that sold oil refining technology to firms in Saudi Arabia, Kuwait, and other Gulf states now find themselves competing with these firms in the world oil market. Third, if the firm's process technology is a source of competitive advantage, then selling this technology through a turnkey project is also selling competitive advantage to potential and/or actual competitors.

Licensing

A **licensing agreement** is an arrangement whereby a licensor grants the rights to intangible property to another entity (the licensee) for a specified period, and in return, the licensor receives a royalty fee from the licensee.[11] Intangible property includes patents, inventions, formulas, processes, designs, copyrights, and trademarks.

For example, to enter the Japanese market, Xerox, inventor of the photocopier, established a joint venture with Fuji Photo that is known as Fuji Xerox. Xerox then licensed its xerographic know-how to Fuji Xerox. In return, Fuji Xerox paid Xerox a royalty fee equal to 5 percent of the net sales revenue that Fuji Xerox earned from the sales of photocopiers based on Xerox's patented know-how. In the Fuji Xerox case, the licence was originally granted for 10 years, and it has been renegotiated and extended several times since and now includes 13 countries.[12] The licensing agreement between Xerox and Fuji Xerox also limited Fuji Xerox's direct sales to the Asian Pacific region (although Fuji Xerox does supply Xerox with photocopiers that are sold in North America under the Xerox label).[13]

ADVANTAGES

In the typical international licensing deal, the licensee puts up most of the capital necessary to get the overseas operation going. Thus, a primary advantage of licensing is that the firm does not have to bear the development costs and risks associated with opening a foreign market. Licensing is very attractive for firms lacking the capital to develop operations overseas. In addition, licensing can be attractive when a firm is unwilling to commit substantial financial resources to an unfamiliar or politically volatile foreign market. Licensing is also often used when a firm wishes to participate in a foreign market but is prohibited from doing so by barriers to investment. This was one of the original reasons for the formation of the Fuji–Xerox joint venture. Xerox wanted to participate in the Japanese market but was prohibited from setting up a wholly owned subsidiary by the Japanese government. So Xerox set up the joint venture with Fuji and then licensed its know-how to the joint venture.

Finally, licensing is frequently used when a firm possesses some intangible property that might have business applications, but it does not want to develop those applications itself. For example, Bell Laboratories at AT&T originally invented the transistor circuit in the 1950s, but AT&T decided it did not want to produce transistors, so it licensed the technology to a number of other companies, such as Texas Instruments. Similarly, Coca-Cola has licensed its famous trademark to clothing manufacturers, which have incorporated the design into their clothing.

DISADVANTAGES

Licensing has three serious drawbacks. First, it does not give a firm the tight control over manufacturing, marketing, and strategy that is required for realizing experience curve and location economies (as global and transnational firms must do; see Chapter 11). Licensing typically involves each licensee setting up its own production operations. This severely limits the firm's ability to realize experience curve and location economies by producing its product in a centralized location. When these economies are important, licensing may not be the best way to expand overseas.

Second, competing in a global market may require a firm to coordinate strategic moves across countries by using profits earned in one country to support competitive attacks in another (see Chapter 11). Licensing limits a firm's ability to do this. A licensee is unlikely to allow a multinational firm to use its profits (beyond those due in the form of royalty payments) to support a different licensee operating in another country.

A third problem with licensing is one that we encountered in Chapter 7 when we reviewed the economic theory of FDI. This is the risk associated with licensing technological know-how to foreign companies. Technological know-how constitutes the basis of many multinational firms' competitive advantage. Most firms wish to maintain control over how their know-how is used, and a firm can quickly lose control over its technology by licensing it. Many firms have made the mistake of thinking they could maintain control within the framework of a licensing agreement. RCA Corporation, for example, once licensed its colour TV technology to Japanese firms including Matsushita and Sony. The Japanese firms quickly assimilated the technology, improved on it, and used it to enter the U.S. market, taking substantial market share away from RCA.

There are ways of reducing the risks of this occurring. One way is by entering into a **cross-licensing agreement** with a foreign firm. Under a cross-licensing agreement, a firm might license some valuable intangible property to a foreign partner, but in addition to a royalty payment, the firm might also request that the foreign partner license some of its valuable know-how to the firm. Such agreements are believed to reduce the risks associated with licensing technological know-how, since the licensee realizes that if it violates the licensing contract (by using the knowledge obtained to compete directly with the licensor), the licensor can do the same to it. Cross-licensing agreements enable firms to hold each other hostage, which reduces the probability that they will behave opportunistically toward each other.[14] Such cross-licensing agreements are increasingly common in high-technology industries.

Another way of reducing the risk associated with licensing is to follow the Fuji–Xerox model and link an agreement to license know-how with the formation of a joint venture in which the licensor and licensee take important equity stakes. Such an approach aligns the interests of licensor and licensee, since both have a stake in ensuring that the venture is successful. Thus, the risk that Fuji Photo might appropriate Xerox's technological know-how, and then compete directly against Xerox in the global photocopier market, was reduced by the establishment of a joint venture in which both Xerox and Fuji Photo had an important stake.

DEBATE THE ISSUE

Exporting or Licensing?

In this chapter, we discuss as series of advantages and disadvantages of exporting and licensing (as well as turnkey projects, franchising, joint ventures, and wholly owned subsidiaries as other entry mode choices). Exporting refers to the sale of products produced in one country to residents of another country. Licensing refers to an arrangement in which a licensor grants the rights to intangible property to the licensee for a specified period and receives a royalty fee in return. Both of these modes of entry into a foreign market have unique advantages and disadvantages. Oftentimes, selecting exporting or licensing depends on myriad factors—one being the global mindset of the business owner. Assume you have a choice to enter three emerging markets—Bolivia, Chile, and Peru, which are neighbouring countries in South America. You have a great product, with lots of technological innovation and a lightweight packaging. Would you opt for exporting or licensing, and why?

Franchising

Franchising is similar to licensing, although franchising tends to involve longer-term commitments than licensing. **Franchising** is a specialized form of licensing in which the franchiser not only sells intangible property (normally a trademark) to the franchisee, but also insists that the franchisee agree to abide by strict rules as to how it does business. The franchiser will also often assist the franchisee to run the business on an ongoing basis. As with licensing, the franchiser typically receives a royalty payment, which amounts to some percentage of the franchisee's revenues. Whereas licensing is pursued primarily by manufacturing firms, franchising is employed primarily by service firms.[15] McDonald's is a good example of a firm that has grown by using a franchising strategy. McDonald's has strict rules as to how franchisees should operate a restaurant. These rules extend to control over the menu, cooking methods, staffing policies, and design and location of a restaurant. McDonald's also organizes the supply chain for its franchisees and provides management training and financial assistance.[16]

ADVANTAGES

The advantages of franchising as an entry mode are very similar to those of licensing. The firm is relieved of many of the costs and risks of opening a foreign market on its own. Instead, the franchisee typically assumes those costs and risks. This creates a good incentive for the franchisee to build a profitable operation as quickly as possible. Thus, using a franchising strategy, a service firm can build a global presence quickly and at a relatively low cost and risk, as McDonald's has.

DISADVANTAGES

The disadvantages are less pronounced than in the case of licensing. Since franchising is often used by service companies, there is no reason to consider the need for coordination of manufacturing to achieve experience curve and location economies. But franchising may inhibit the firm's ability to take profits out of one country to support competitive attacks in another.

A more significant disadvantage of franchising is quality control. The foundation of franchising arrangements is that the firm's brand name conveys a message to consumers about the quality of the firm's product. Thus, a business traveller checking in at a Hilton hotel in Hong Kong can reasonably

Boston Pizza has come a long way from its 1964 Edmonton founding to become one of Canada's premier franchises, combining both a sports bar and family restaurant under the same roof. © *Yelena Rodriguez/Dreamstime.com*

expect the same quality of room, food, and service that she would receive in Toronto. The Hilton name is supposed to guarantee consistent product quality. This presents a problem in that foreign franchisees may not be as concerned about quality as they are supposed to be, and the result of poor quality can extend beyond lost sales in a particular foreign market to a decline in the firm's worldwide reputation. For example, if the business traveller has a bad experience at the Hilton in Hong Kong, she may never go to another Hilton hotel and may urge her colleagues to do likewise. The geographical distance of the firm from its foreign franchisees can make poor quality difficult to detect. In addition, the sheer numbers of franchisees—in the case of McDonald's, tens of thousands—can make quality control difficult. Due to these factors, quality problems may persist.

One way around this disadvantage is to set up a subsidiary in each country in which the firm expands. The subsidiary might be wholly owned by the company or a joint venture with a foreign company. The subsidiary assumes the rights and obligations to establish franchises throughout the particular country or region. McDonald's, for example, establishes a master franchisee in many countries. Typically, this master franchisee is a joint venture between McDonald's and a local firm. The proximity and the smaller number of franchises to oversee reduce the quality control challenge. In addition, because the subsidiary (or master franchisee) is at least partly owned by the firm, the firm can place its own managers in the subsidiary to help ensure that it is doing a good job of monitoring the franchises. This organizational arrangement has proven very satisfactory for McDonald's, KFC, Hilton Hotel Corp., Four Seasons Hotels and Resorts, and others.

Joint Ventures

A **joint venture** entails establishing a firm that is jointly owned by two or more otherwise independent firms. Fuji–Xerox, for example, was set up as a joint venture between Xerox and Fuji Photo. Establishing a joint venture with a foreign firm has long been a popular mode for entering a new market. The most typical joint venture is a 50–50 arrangement in which there are two parties, each of which holds a 50 percent ownership stake (as is the case with the Fuji–Xerox joint venture) and contributes a team of managers to share operating control. Some firms, however, have sought joint ventures in which they have a majority share and thus tighter control.[17]

ADVANTAGES

Joint ventures have a number of advantages. First, a firm benefits from a local partner's knowledge of the host country's competitive conditions, culture, language, political systems, and business systems. Thus, for many U.S. firms, joint ventures have involved the U.S. company providing technological know-how and products and the local partner providing the marketing expertise and the local knowledge necessary for competing in that country. This was the case with the Fuji–Xerox joint venture.

Second, when the development costs and/or risks of opening a foreign market are high, a firm might gain by sharing these costs and/or risks with a local partner.

Third, in many countries, political considerations make joint ventures the only feasible entry mode. Again, this was a consideration in the establishment of the Fuji–Xerox venture. Research suggests joint ventures with local partners face a low risk of being subject to nationalization or other forms of adverse government interference.[18] This appears to be because local equity partners, who may have some influence on host-government policy, have a vested interest in speaking out against nationalization or government interference.

ANOTHER PERSPECTIVE

Technology and Knowledge Transfer: A Benefit and a Danger

A joint venture is like a party where everyone brings something and takes something. In a joint venture located in a developing country, the company with the business brings knowledge about the business and its processes, while often the local partner brings knowledge about the market and long-standing relationships, along with personnel. In its early preparation for entry into South Korea, KFC (then known as Kentucky Fried Chicken) selected a joint-venture partner, began training the partner, and began to bring in its systems and layout, including the pressure-cooked process, special equipment, and the 11 herbs and spices, to share with its new Korean partner. Imagine the Americans' surprise when they found hundreds of Kentucky Fried Chicken stores already up and running in and around Seoul. They were tiny mom-and-pop shops, a result of a family's U.S. vacation, and although they didn't prepare chicken the same way or offer the same product line, they did confuse the public about the KFC concept for a while. Even today, you can find little Kentucky Fried Chicken stalls in the middle of Seoul.

DISADVANTAGES

Despite these advantages, there are major disadvantages with joint ventures. First, as with licensing, a firm that enters into a joint venture risks giving control of its technology to its partner. Thus, a proposed joint venture in 2002 between Boeing and Mitsubishi Heavy Industries to build a new wide-body jet (the 787) raised fears that

Boeing might unwittingly give away its commercial airline technology to the Japanese. However, joint-venture agreements can be constructed to minimize this risk. One option is to hold majority ownership in the venture. This allows the dominant partner to exercise greater control over its technology. But it can be difficult to find a foreign partner who is willing to settle for minority ownership. Another option is to "wall off" technology that is central to the core competence of the firm, while sharing other technology.

A second disadvantage is that a joint venture does not give a firm the tight control over subsidiaries that it might need to realize experience curve or location economies. Nor does it give a firm the tight control over a foreign subsidiary that it might need for engaging in coordinated global attacks against its rivals. Consider the entry of Texas Instruments (TI) into the Japanese semiconductor market. When TI established semiconductor facilities in Japan, it did so for the dual purpose of checking Japanese manufacturers' market share and limiting their cash available for invading TI's global market. In other words, TI was engaging in global strategic coordination. To implement this strategy, TI's subsidiary in Japan had to be prepared to take instructions from corporate headquarters regarding competitive strategy. The strategy also required the Japanese subsidiary to run at a loss if necessary. Few if any potential joint-venture partners would have been willing to accept such conditions because it would have necessitated a willingness to accept a negative return on investment. Thus, to implement this strategy, TI set up a wholly owned subsidiary in Japan.

A third disadvantage with joint ventures is that the shared ownership arrangement can lead to conflicts and battles for control between the investing firms if their goals and objectives change or if they take different views as to what the strategy should be. This has apparently not been a problem with the Fuji–Xerox joint venture. According to Tony Kobayashi, the former CEO of Fuji–Xerox, a primary reason is that both Xerox and Fuji Photo adopted an arm's-length relationship with Fuji–Xerox, giving the venture's management considerable freedom to determine its own strategy.[19] However, much research indicates that conflicts of interest over strategy and goals often arise in joint ventures. These conflicts tend to be greater when the venture is between firms of different nationalities, and they often end in the dissolution of the venture.[20] Such conflicts tend to be triggered by shifts in the relative bargaining power of venture partners. For example, in the case of ventures between a foreign firm and a local firm, as a foreign partner's knowledge about local market conditions increases, it depends less on the expertise of a local partner. This increases the bargaining power of the foreign partner and ultimately leads to conflicts over control of the venture's strategy and goals.[21]

Wholly Owned Subsidiaries

In a **wholly owned subsidiary**, the firm owns 100 percent of the stock. Establishing a wholly owned subsidiary in a foreign market can be done in one of two ways. The firm can either set up a new operation in that country, often referred to as a greenfield venture, or it can acquire an established firm in that host nation and use that firm to promote its products.[22]

ADVANTAGES

There are three clear advantages of wholly owned subsidiaries. First, when a firm's competitive advantage is based on technological competence, a wholly owned subsidiary will often be the preferred entry mode because it reduces the risk of losing control over that competence. (See Chapter 7 for more details.) Many high-tech firms prefer this entry mode for overseas expansion (e.g., firms in the semiconductor, electronics, and pharmaceutical industries).

Second, a wholly owned subsidiary gives a firm tight control over operations in different countries. This is necessary for engaging in global strategic coordination (i.e., using profits from one country to support competitive attacks in another).

Third, a wholly owned subsidiary may be required if a firm is trying to realize location and experience curve economies (as firms pursuing global and transnational strategies try to do). As we saw in Chapter 11, when cost pressures are intense, it may make sense for a firm to configure its value chain in such a way that the value added at each stage is maximized. Thus, a national subsidiary may specialize in manufacturing only part of the product line or certain components of the end product, exchanging parts and products with other subsidiaries in the firm's global system. Establishing such a global production system requires a high degree of control over the operations of each affiliate. The various operations must be prepared to accept centrally determined decisions as to how they will produce, how much they will produce, and how their output will be priced for transfer to the next operation. Since licensees or joint-venture partners are unlikely to accept such a subservient role, establishment of wholly owned subsidiaries may be necessary.

DISADVANTAGES

Establishing a wholly owned subsidiary is generally the most costly method of serving a foreign market. Firms doing this must bear the full costs and risks of setting up overseas operations. The risks associated with learning to do business in a new culture are less if the firm acquires an established host-country enterprise. However, acquisitions raise additional problems, including those associated with trying to marry divergent corporate cultures. These problems may more than offset any benefits derived by acquiring an established operation. Because the choice between greenfield ventures and acquisition is such an important one, we shall discuss it in more detail later in the chapter.

LO3 Selecting an Entry Mode

As the preceding discussion demonstrated, advantages and disadvantages are associated with all the entry modes; they are summarized in Table 12.1. Due to these advantages and disadvantages, trade-offs are inevitable when selecting an entry mode. For example, when considering entry into an unfamiliar country with a track record for nationalizing foreign-owned enterprises, a firm might favour a joint venture with a local enterprise. Its rationale might be that the local partner will help it establish operations in an unfamiliar environment and will speak out against nationalization should the possibility arise. However, if the firm's core competence is based on proprietary technology, entering a joint venture might risk losing control of that technology to the joint-venture partner, in which case the strategy may seem unattractive. Despite the existence of such trade-offs, it is possible to make some generalizations about the optimal choice of entry mode.[23]

Core Competencies and Entry Mode

We saw in Chapter 11 that firms often expand internationally to earn greater returns from their core competencies, transferring the skills and products derived from their core competencies to foreign markets where indigenous competitors lack those skills. We say that such firms are pursuing an international strategy. The optimal entry mode

TABLE 12.1	Advantages and Disadvantages of Entry Modes	
Entry Mode	**Advantages**	**Disadvantages**
Exporting	Ability to realize location and experience curve economies	High transport costs Trade barriers Problems with local marketing agents
Turnkey contract	Ability to earn returns from process technology skills in countries where FDI is restricted	Creating efficient competitors Lack of long-term market presence
Licensing	Low development costs and risks	Lack of control over technology Inability to realize location and experience curve economies Inability to engage in global strategic coordination
Franchising	Low development costs and risks	Lack of control over quality Inability to engage in global strategic coordination
Joint venture	Access to local partner's knowledge Sharing development costs and risks Politically acceptable	Lack of control over quality technology Inability to realize location and experience economies
Wholly owned subsidiary	Protection of technology Ability to engage in global strategic coordination Ability to realize location and experience economies	High costs and risks

for these firms depends to some degree on the nature of their core competencies. A distinction can be drawn between firms whose core competency is in technological know-how and those whose core competency is in management know-how.

TECHNOLOGICAL KNOW-HOW

As was observed in Chapter 7, if a firm's competitive advantage (its core competence) is based on control over proprietary technological know-how, licensing and joint-venture arrangements should be avoided to minimize the risk of losing control over that technology. Thus, if a high-tech firm sets up operations in a foreign country to profit from a core competency in technological know-how, it will probably do so through a wholly owned subsidiary.

This rule should not be viewed as hard and fast, however. One exception is when a licensing or joint-venture arrangement can be structured so as to reduce the risks of a firm's technological knowledge being expropriated by licensees or joint-venture partners. We will see how this might be achieved later in the chapter when we examine the structuring of strategic alliances. Another exception exists when a firm perceives its technological advantage to be only transitory, when it expects rapid imitation of its core technology by competitors. In such cases, the firm might want to license its technology as rapidly as possible to foreign firms to gain global acceptance for its technology before the imitation occurs.[24] Such a strategy has some advantages. By licensing its technology to competitors, the firm may deter them from developing their own, possibly superior, technology. Further, by licensing its technology, the firm may establish its technology as the dominant design in the industry. This may ensure a steady stream of royalty payments. However, the attractions of licensing are probably outweighed by the risks of losing control over technology, and thus licensing should be avoided.

MANAGEMENT KNOW-HOW

The competitive advantage of many service firms is based on management know-how (e.g., McDonald's, Starbucks). For such firms, the risk of losing control over the management skills to franchisees or joint-venture partners is not that great. These firms' valuable asset is their brand name, and brand names are generally well protected by international laws pertaining to trademarks. Given this, many of the issues arising in the case of technological know-how are of less concern here. As a result, many service firms favour a combination of franchising and subsidiaries to control the franchises within particular countries or regions. The subsidiaries may be wholly owned or joint ventures, but most service firms have found that joint ventures with local partners work best for the controlling subsidiaries. A joint venture is often politically more acceptable and brings a degree of local knowledge to the subsidiary.

Pressures for Cost Reductions and Entry Mode

The greater the pressures for cost reductions are, the more likely a firm will want to pursue some combination of exporting and wholly owned subsidiaries. By manufacturing in those locations where factor conditions are optimal and then exporting to the rest of the world, a firm may be able to realize substantial location and experience curve economies. The firm might then want to export the finished product to marketing subsidiaries based in various countries. These subsidiaries will typically be wholly owned and have the responsibility for overseeing distribution in their particular countries. Setting up wholly owned marketing subsidiaries is preferable to joint-venture arrangements and to using foreign marketing agents because it gives the firm the tight control over marketing that might be required for coordinating a globally dispersed value chain. It also gives the firm the ability to use the profits generated in one market to improve its competitive position in another market. In other words, firms pursuing global or transnational strategies tend to prefer establishing wholly owned subsidiaries.

LO4   Establishing a Wholly Owned Subsidiary: Greenfield Venture or Acquisition?

A firm can establish a wholly owned subsidiary in a country by building a subsidiary from the ground up, the so-called greenfield strategy, or by acquiring an established enterprise in the target market. The volume of cross-border acquisitions has been growing at a rapid rate for two decades.

Pros and Cons of Acquisitions

BENEFITS OF ACQUISITIONS

Acquisitions have three major points in their favour. First, they are quick to execute. By acquiring an established enterprise, a firm can rapidly build its presence in the target foreign market. When the German automobile company Daimler-Benz decided it needed a bigger presence in the U.S. automobile market, it did not increase that presence by building new factories to serve the United States, a process that would have taken years. Instead, it acquired the number three U.S. automobile company, Chrysler, and merged the two operations to form DaimlerChrysler (Daimler spun off Chrysler into a private equity firm in 2007). When the Spanish telecommunications service provider Telefonica wanted to build a service presence in Latin America, it did so through a series of acquisitions, purchasing telecommunications companies in Brazil and Argentina. In these cases, the firms made acquisitions because they knew that was the quickest way to establish a sizable presence in the target market.

Second, in many cases firms make acquisitions to pre-empt their competitors. The need for pre-emption is particularly great in markets that are rapidly globalizing, such as telecommunications, where a combination of deregulation within nations and liberalization of regulations governing cross-border foreign direct investment has made it much easier for enterprises to enter foreign markets through acquisitions. In such markets, there can be concentrated waves of acquisitions as firms race each other to attain global scale. In the telecommunications industry, for example,

---

COUNTRY FOCUS

Trade Missions: Helping Canadian Companies Enter Global Markets

Trade missions are trips by businesses and various government officials to foreign countries to promote that country's businesses in general, and specifically the businesses that take part in the trade mission.

Why should companies go to all this trouble? As the Canadian Trade Commission Service notes:

Trade missions put Canadian companies on the map by showcasing our capabilities and competitiveness. Participants will learn about doing business in the host market(s), and gain exposure to the social and business cultures while experiencing first-hand the services offered by Canada's trade commissioners on the ground.

A trade mission offers:

* access to key economic and government decision makers;
* greater public profile at home and abroad;
* unparalleled networking opportunities with the local business community;
* business-to-business meetings with potential partners; and,
* an opportunity to initiate, develop, or complete deals.

Past Canadian trade missions have ranged from low technology sectors, such as infrastructure, to high technology. As an example, during 2017, three Canadian Women's Trade Missions are planned for Las Vegas, Orlando, and Atlanta.

You can find a list of past Canadian trade missions at http://www.tradecommissioner.gc.ca. Please search for previous trade missions.

Questions

1. In an era of global electronic communications, is there still a need for face-to-face meetings that occur through trade missions? Why or why not?
2. Review the list of past trade missions and suggest countries and economic sectors that would benefit from a future trade mission. Give reasons for your selections.

Source: Global Affairs Canada, About Trade Missions, Government of Canada, http://www.international.gc.ca/trade-missions-commerciale/about-a_propos.aspx?lang=eng&_ga=2.171607456.1449038137.1496172166-1947447324.1494524905.

regulatory changes at the end of the last century triggered what could be called a feeding frenzy, with firms entering each other's markets via acquisitions to establish a global presence. These included the $60 billion acquisition of Air Touch Communications in the United States by the British company Vodafone, which was the largest acquisition ever; the $13 billion acquisition of One 2 One in Britain by the German company Deutsche Telekom; and the $6.4 billion acquisition of Excel Communications in the United States by Teleglobe of Canada, all of which occurred in 1998 and 1999.[25] A similar wave of cross-border acquisitions occurred in the global automobile industry over the same time period, with Daimler acquiring Chrysler, Ford acquiring Volvo, and Renault acquiring Nissan.

Third, managers may believe acquisitions to be less risky than greenfield ventures. When a firm makes an acquisition, it buys a set of assets that are producing a known revenue and profit stream. In contrast, the revenue and profit stream that a greenfield venture might generate is uncertain because it does not yet exist. When a firm makes an acquisition in a foreign market, it not only acquires a set of tangible assets, such as factories, logistics systems, customer service systems, and so on, but it also acquires valuable intangible assets including a local brand name and managers' knowledge of the business environment. Such knowledge can reduce the risk of mistakes caused by ignorance of the national culture.

Despite the arguments for making acquisitions, acquisitions often produce disappointing results.[26] For example, a study by Mercer Management Consulting looked at 150 acquisitions worth more than $500 million each.[27] The Mercer study concluded that 50 percent of these acquisitions eroded shareholder value, while another 33 percent created only marginal returns. Only 17 percent were judged to be successful. Similarly, a study by KPMG, an accounting and management consulting company, looked at 700 large acquisitions. The study found that while some 30 percent of these actually created value for the acquiring company, 31 percent destroyed value, and the remainder had little impact.[28] A similar study by McKenzie & Co. estimated that some 70 percent of mergers and acquisitions failed to achieve expected revenue synergies.[29] In a seminal study of the post-acquisition performance of acquired companies, David Ravenscraft and Mike Scherer concluded that, on average, the profits and market shares of acquired companies declined following acquisition.[30] They also noted that a smaller but substantial subset of those companies experienced traumatic difficulties, which ultimately led to their being sold by the acquiring company. Ravenscraft and Scherer's evidence suggests that many acquisitions destroy rather than create value. While most of this research has looked at domestic acquisitions, the findings probably also apply to cross-border acquisitions.[31]

WHY DO ACQUISITIONS FAIL?

Acquisitions fail for several reasons. First, the acquiring firms often overpay for the assets of the purchased firm. The price of the target firm can get bid up if more than one firm is interested in its purchase, as is often the case. In addition, the management of the acquiring firm is often too optimistic about the value that can be created via a takeover and is thus willing to pay a significant premium over a target firm's market capitalization. This is called the "hubris hypothesis" of why acquisitions fail. The hubris hypothesis postulates that top managers typically overestimate their ability to create value from an acquisition, primarily because they have an exaggerated sense of their own capabilities.[32] For example, Daimler paid $40 billion for Chrysler in 1998, a premium of 40 percent over the market value of Chrysler before the takeover bid. Daimler paid this much because it thought it could use Chrysler to help it grow market share in the United States. At the time, Daimler's management issued bold announcements about the "synergies" that would be created from combining the operations of the two companies. Executives believed they could attain greater scale economies from the global presence, take costs out of the German and American operations, and boost the profitability of the combined entity. However, within a year of the acquisition, Daimler's German management was faced with a crisis at Chrysler, which was suddenly losing money due to weak sales in the United States. In retrospect, Daimler's management had been far too optimistic about the potential for future demand in the U.S. auto market and about the opportunities for creating value from "synergies." Daimler acquired Chrysler at the end of a multi-year boom in U.S. auto sales and paid a large premium over Chrysler's market value just before demand slumped. In May 2007, when Daimler sold Chrysler to Cerberus Capital Management, it had to pay an additional $650 million (US$) to close the deal.[33]

Second, many acquisitions fail because there is a clash between the cultures of the acquiring and acquired firm. After an acquisition, many acquired companies experience high management turnover, possibly because their employees do not like the acquiring company's way of doing things.[34] This happened at DaimlerChrysler; many senior managers left Chrysler in the first year after the merger. Apparently, Chrysler executives disliked the dominance in decision making by Daimler's German managers, while the Germans resented that Chrysler's American managers were paid two to three times as much as their German counterparts. These cultural differences created tensions, which ultimately exhibited themselves in high management turnover at Chrysler.[35] The loss of management talent and expertise can materially harm the performance of the acquired unit.[36] This may be particularly problematic in an international business, where managers of the acquired unit may have valuable local knowledge that may be difficult to replace.

Third, many acquisitions fail because attempts to realize synergies by integrating the operations of the acquired and acquiring entities often run into roadblocks and take much longer than forecast. Differences in management philosophy and company culture can slow the integration of operations. These problems are likely to be exacerbated by differences in national culture. Bureaucratic haggling between managers also complicates the process. Again, this reportedly occurred at DaimlerChrysler, where grand plans to integrate the operations of the two companies were bogged down by endless committee meetings and by simple logistical considerations such as the six-hour time difference between Detroit and Germany. By the time an integration plan had been worked out, Chrysler was losing money, and Daimler's German managers suddenly had a crisis on their hands.

Finally, many acquisitions fail due to inadequate pre-acquisition screening.[37] Many firms decide to acquire other firms without thoroughly analyzing the potential benefits and costs. They often move with undue haste to execute the acquisition, perhaps because they fear another competitor may pre-empt them. After the acquisition, however, many acquiring firms discover that instead of buying a well-run business, they have purchased a troubled organization. This may be a particular problem in cross-border acquisitions because the acquiring firm may not fully understand the target firm's different national culture and business system.

ANOTHER PERSPECTIVE

Risks and Entering Foreign Markets

Business is all about risk—the right risks. These risks increase and become more interesting with entry into foreign markets. Scholar David Conklin discusses the idea of managing risk through planned uncertainty. By "planned uncertainty," he means an awareness of contingencies, with possible what-if scenarios developed in advance. The key idea here is that through an ongoing monitoring of the various risk areas, decision makers can have much of the data they may need to address a number of possible outcomes. Of course, we have to know what uncertainty to plan for, and we don't know what we don't know. Planning for everything is impossible, but what Conklin suggests is that planned uncertainty is a way of thinking. Given that we don't know the future, this way of thinking may be helpful in career development and other parts of our lives.

Source: D. Conklin, "Analyzing and Managing Country Risks," *Ivey Business Journal: Improving the Practice of Management,* January/February, 1992. Also, see "Indices" for countries on globalEDGE.msu.edu (e.g., for Indonesia, globaledge.msu.edu/countries/indonesia/indices).

REDUCING THE RISKS OF FAILURE

These problems can all be overcome if the firm is careful about its acquisition strategy.[38] Screening the foreign enterprise to be acquired, including a detailed audit of operations, financial position, and management culture, can help to make sure the firm (1) does not pay too much for the acquired unit; (2) does not uncover any nasty surprises after the acquisition; and (3) acquires a firm whose organization culture is not antagonistic to that of the acquiring enterprise. It is also important for the acquirer to allay any concerns that management in the acquired enterprise might have. The objective should be to reduce unwanted management attrition after the acquisition. Finally, managers must move rapidly after an acquisition to put an integration plan in place and to act on that plan. Some people in both the acquiring and acquired units will try to erect roadblocks to slow or stop any integration efforts, particularly when losses of employment or management power are involved, and managers should have a plan for dealing with such impediments before they arise.

Pros and Cons of Greenfield Ventures

The big advantage of establishing a greenfield venture in a foreign country is that it gives the firm a much greater ability to build the kind of subsidiary company that it wants. For example, it is much easier to build an organization culture from scratch than it is to change the culture of an acquired unit. Similarly, it is much easier to establish a set of operating routines in a new subsidiary than it is to convert the operating routines of an acquired unit. This is a very important advantage for many international businesses, where transferring products, competencies, skills, and know-how from the established operations of the firm to the new subsidiary are principal ways of creating value. For example, McCain Foods Ltd. faces a mature market in developed countries, where low-carbohydrate foods are the craze, so they are expanding aggressively in developing countries. When McCain, "the world leader of producing French fries," first ventured into the Chinese market in 1996, they did so by establishing a sales office for importing French fries and vegetables. Then McCain invested $43.3-million to construct a potato processing plant in the northeast city of Harbin, China, in August 2004.

Whether to proceed or not with greenfield investments in China proved to be a challenge for McCain. The New Brunswick-based company completed a six-year agronomy program to guarantee that the quality of Chinese potatoes would meet McCain's high standards. Potatoes need to be a specific size and shape to be processed at the McCain plant, and the levels of sugar and moisture must be consistent. McCain now operates 53 production facilities in six continents and the company's frozen food products can be found in over 130 countries around the world. They are also the world's largest makers of frozen French fries, producing nearly 33 percent of the world's supply. This intensive groundwork and research proved worthwhile in reaching an investment decision to build a processing plant in China. Fast-food outlets such as McDonald's and KFC are opening and McCain hopes to supply this growing market.[39]

Set against the significant advantage of building a customized subsidiary are the disadvantages of establishing a greenfield venture. Greenfield ventures are slower to establish. They are also risky. As with any new venture, a degree of uncertainty is associated with future revenue and profit prospects. However, if the firm has already been successful in other foreign markets and understands what it takes to do business in other countries, these risks may not be that great. For example, having already gained great knowledge about operating internationally, the risk to McDonald's of entering yet another country is probably not that great. Also, greenfield ventures are less risky than acquisitions in the sense that there is less potential for unpleasant surprises. A final disadvantage is the possibility of being pre-empted by more aggressive global competitors, who enter via acquisitions and build a big market presence that limits the market potential for the greenfield venture.

Greenfield or Acquisition?

The choice between acquisitions and greenfield ventures is not an easy one to make. Both modes have their advantages and disadvantages. In general, the choice will depend on the circumstances confronting the firm. If the firm is seeking to enter a market where there are already well-established incumbent enterprises and where global competitors are also interested in establishing a presence, it may pay the firm to enter via an acquisition. In such circumstances, a greenfield venture may be too slow to establish a sizable presence. However, if the firm is going to make an acquisition, its management should be cognizant of the risks associated with acquisitions that were discussed earlier and consider these when determining which firms to purchase. It may be better to enter by the slower route of a greenfield venture than to make a bad acquisition.

If the firm is considering entering a country where there are no incumbent competitors to be acquired, then a greenfield venture may be the only mode. Even when incumbents exist, if the competitive advantage of the firm is based on the transfer of organizationally embedded competencies, skills, routines, and culture, it may still be preferable to enter via a greenfield venture. Things such as skills and organizational culture, which are based on significant knowledge that is difficult to articulate and codify, are much easier to embed in a new venture than they are in an acquired entity, where the firm may have to overcome the established routines and culture of the acquired firm. Thus, as our earlier examples suggest, firms such as McDonald's and McCain prefer to enter foreign markets by establishing greenfield ventures.

IMPLICATIONS FOR BUSINESS

Several means of entering foreign markets have been detailed in this chapter. For example, in some instances if a Canadian firm were considering overseas expansion, and depending on how aggressively it wanted the business, a host country could stipulate that the Canadian firm relinquish majority ownership in favour of host-country majority ownership (equity joint venture). Table 12.2, although representative of common problems and potential solutions to market entry modes in any and all countries, refers to China in this instance.

Certain businesses have found that equity joint ventures can be helpful in enhancing business goals after entering China, while others find that export and contractual joint ventures are more flexible. Export and contractual joint ventures can be useful to those companies with "made in Canada" technology, products, or manufacturing processes. Export and contractual joint ventures allow for low risk, minimal upfront cash outlay from the exporter, and a quick exit from the local market should business or political conditions change.

For the host country, there is a greater preference for equity joint ventures over export and contractual joint ventures. Equity joint ventures usually benefit the host country, as larger amount of profits, technology, and management expertise remain in the host country, unlike export and contractual joint ventures, which tend to favour the exporting country.

Equity joint ventures require large cash outlays. Export and contractual joint ventures normally involve little upfront investment, other than a commitment from the Canadian company to train employees, while ensuring that the product will function in the Chinese environment. The benefits derived from such an arrangement could accrue to the Canadian company for many years as training and maintenance needs arise in China.

In addition to the above, there is the most basic strategy of exporting, getting the goods from one country to another, for orders that occasionally arise. This strategy could make use of existing Canadian-based corporate sales staff already travelling to China, and who could provide useful market feedback to the Canadian head office from their roster of Chinese customers. As another

TABLE 12.2	Common Problems and Solutions Regardless of Entry Mode	
Areas of Main Concern	**Evaluation**	**How Did the Company Deal with It?**
Culture difference	Large but manageable	Companies had executives who were extremely fond of the Chinese culture. Hire local Chinese to bridge the gap.
Foreign exchange	Extremely important	Help the Chinese apply for Export Development Corporation funding.
Quality of local employees	Very important	High-quality local employees are available. Higher pay to attract quality people.
Training needs for the Chinese	Extremely important	Written into the employment contract for the Chinese employees to get training in Canada. Very good motivational tool.
High cost of doing business in China	The cost is reasonable	Hiring as many local Chinese as possible to lower the cost.
Expatriates	Not critical	None of the operations required full-time expatriate to be stationed in China.
		Each company had an individual who spent about six months out of a year in China.
Finding connections to help navigate the system	Very important	Connections and local employees help to do it.

Source: Adapted from The Department of Foreign Affairs and International Trade Canada, 2004.

means of entering foreign markets, companies might also consider retaining host country–based distributors who could be privy to greater market information than those employees who occasionally take business trips to China.

Many Canadian companies are leery of forming equity joint ventures with China because of China's frequently shifting regulations, issues with the convertibility of its currency, lack of skilled labour, and poor-quality raw materials. Despite the perceived shortcomings of equity joint ventures, many Canadian companies have found that their sales in China were considerably higher using this form of investment over others.

There is no magic formula for Canadian companies seeking to do business in China. Companies with limited resources and international business experience should normally consider starting with a basic export strategy and then increasing its presence in the host country as required.

All companies should be adequately prepared and know the playing field. Companies should exhibit aggressiveness where appropriate, and above all must show a strong commitment while being patient.

Key Terms

cross-licensing agreement

first-mover disadvantages

franchising

joint venture

licensing agreement

pioneering costs

strategic commitment

timing of entry

turnkey project

wholly owned subsidary

LO   Learning Objectives Summary

1. Basic entry decisions include identifying which markets to enter, when to enter those markets, and on what scale. The most attractive foreign markets tend to be found in politically stable developed and developing nations that have free market systems and where there is not a dramatic upsurge in either inflation rates or private-sector debt. There are several advantages associated with entering a national market early, before other international businesses have established themselves. These advantages must be balanced against the pioneering costs that early entrants often have to bear, including the greater risk of business failure. Large-scale entry into a national market constitutes a major strategic commitment that is likely to change the nature of competition in that market and limit the entrant's future strategic flexibility. Although making major strategic commitments can yield many benefits, there are also risks associated with such a strategy.

2. There are six modes of entering a foreign market: exporting, creating turnkey projects, licensing, franchising, establishing joint ventures, and setting up a wholly owned subsidiary. Exporting has the advantages of facilitating the realization of experience curve economies and of avoiding the costs of setting up manufacturing operations in another country. Disadvantages include high transport costs, trade barriers, and problems with local marketing agents. Turnkey projects allow firms to export their process know-how to countries where FDI might be prohibited, thereby enabling the firm to earn a greater return from this asset. The disadvantage is that the firm may inadvertently create efficient global competitors in the process. The main advantage of licensing is that the licensee bears the costs and risks of opening a foreign market. Disadvantages include the risk of losing technological know-how to the licensee and a lack of tight control over licensees. The main advantage of franchising is that the franchisee bears the costs and risks of opening a foreign market. Disadvantages centre on problems of quality control of distant franchisees. Joint ventures have the advantages of sharing the costs and risks of opening a foreign market and of gaining local knowledge and political influence. Disadvantages include the risk of losing control over technology and a lack of tight control. The advantages of wholly owned subsidiaries include tight control over technological know-how. The main disadvantage is that the firm must bear all the costs and risks of opening a foreign market.

3. The optimal choice of entry mode depends on the firm's strategy. When technological know-how constitutes a firm's core competence, wholly owned subsidiaries are preferred to maintain control over the technology. When management know-how constitutes a firm's core competence, foreign franchises controlled by joint ventures seem to be optimal. When the firm is pursuing a global standardization or transnational strategy, the need for tight control over operations to realize location and experience curve economies suggests wholly owned subsidiaries are the best entry mode.

4. When establishing a wholly owned subsidiary in a country, a firm must decide whether to do so by a greenfield venture strategy or by acquiring an established enterprise in the target market. Acquisitions are quick to execute, may enable a firm to pre-empt its global competitors, and involve buying a known revenue and profit stream. Acquisitions may fail when the acquiring firm overpays for the target, when the cultures of the acquiring and acquired firms clash, when there is a high level of management attrition after the acquisition, and when there is a failure to integrate the operations of the acquiring and acquired firm. The advantage of a greenfield venture in a foreign country is that it gives the firm a much greater ability to build the kind of subsidiary company that it wants. For example, it is much easier to build an organization culture from scratch than it is to change the culture of an acquired unit.

Critical Thinking and Discussion Questions

1. Review the opening case. Summarize Starbucks' core strategy. Does this strategy make sense? Why?

2. "Licensing proprietary technology to foreign competitors is the best way to give up a firm's competitive advantage." Evaluate this statement.

3. What kinds of companies stand to gain the most from entering into strategic alliances with potential competitors? Why?

4. Discuss how the need for control over foreign operations varies with firms' strategies and core competencies. What are the implications for the choice of entry mode?

5. A small Canadian firm that has developed some valuable new medical products using its unique biotechnology know-how is trying to decide how best to serve the European Community market. Its choices are:

   a. Manufacture the product at home and let foreign sales agents handle marketing.

   b. Manufacture the products at home and set up a wholly owned subsidiary in Europe to handle marketing.

   c. Enter into a joint venture with a large European pharmaceutical firm. The product would be manufactured in Europe by the 50/50 joint venture and marketed by the European firm.

   The cost of investment in manufacturing facilities will be a major one for the Canadian firm, but it is not outside its reach. If these are the firm's only options, which one would you advise it to choose? Why?

Research Task   globalEDGE™   globaledge.msu.edu

Use the globalEDGE™ site to complete the following exercises:

1. *Entrepreneur* magazine publishes an annual list of its ranking of America's top 200 franchisers seeking international franchisees. Provide a list of the top ten companies that pursue franchising as a mode of international expansion. Study one of these companies in detail and provide a description of its business model, its international expansion pattern, what qualifications it looks for in its franchisees, and what type of support and training it provides.

2. The U.S. Commercial Service prepares reports, titled the *Country Commercial Guide,* for each country of interest to U.S. investors. Use the *Guide* to gather information on Brazil. Imagine that your company is producing laptop computers and is considering entering this country. Select the most appropriate entry method, supporting your decision with the information collected from the commercial guide.

CLOSING CASE

JCB IN INDIA

JCB, the venerable British manufacturer of construction equipment, has long been a relatively small player in a global market that is dominated by the likes of Caterpillar and Komatsu, but there is one exception to this: India. While the company is present in 150 countries, of the 69 100 machines it sold globally in 2012, around one-third were in India. For JCB, India is truly the jewel in the crown.

The story of JCB in India dates back to 1979 when the company entered into a joint venture with Escorts, an Indian engineering conglomerate, to manufacture backhoe loaders for sale in India. Escorts held a majority 60 percent stake in the venture, and JCB 40 percent. The joint venture was a first for JCB, which historically had exported as much as two-thirds of its production from Britain to a wide range of nations. However, high tariff barriers made direct exports to India difficult.

JCB would probably have preferred to go it alone in India, but government regulations at the time required foreign investors to create joint ventures with local companies. JCB believed the Indian construction market was ripe for growth and could become very large. The company's managers believed that it was better to get a foothold in the nation, thereby gaining an advantage over global competitors, rather than wait until the growth potential was realized.

By the end of the 1990s the joint venture was selling some 2000 backhoes in India and had an 80 percent share of the Indian market. After years of deregulation, the Indian economy was booming. However, JCB felt that the joint venture limited its ability to expand. For one thing, much of JCB's global success was based upon the utilization of leading-edge manufacturing technologies and relentless product innovation, but the company was very hesitant about transferring this know-how to a venture where it did not have a majority stake and therefore lacked control. The last thing JCB wanted was for these valuable technologies to leak out of the joint venture into Escorts, which was one of the largest manufacturers of tractors in India and might conceivably become a direct competitor in the future. Moreover, JCB was unwilling to make the investment in India required to take the joint venture to the next level unless it could capture more of the long-run returns.

In 1999, JCB took advantage of changes in government regulations to renegotiate the terms of the venture with Escorts, purchasing 20 percent of its partner's equity to give JCB majority control. In 2003, JCB took this to its logical end when it responded to further relaxation of government regulations on foreign investment to purchase all of Escorts' remaining equity, transforming the joint venture into a wholly owned subsidiary.

Having gained full control, in early 2005 JCB increased its investment in India, announcing it would build a second factory in Pune that it would use to serve the Indian market. In 2007, in what represented a bold bet on future demand in the Indian market in the face of a global economic slowdown, JCB embarked on a major overhaul and expansion of its original India factory in Ballabgarh. To sell the additional Indian output, JCB rapidly expanded its dealer network, doubling the number of outlets in six years to reach 400 by 2011. The company also localized production for more than 80 percent of the parts used in its best-selling backhoe loader. This was done both to keep costs low and to make sure dealers had immediate access to spare parts. The strategy worked; between 2001 and 2012 JCB's Indian revenues increased tenfold, and the company is now the leading manufacturer of backhoes in the country.

Sources: P. Marsh, "Partnerships Feel the Indian Heat," *Financial Times*, June 22, 2006, p. 11; P. Marsh, "JCB Targets Asia to Spread Production," *Financial Times*, March 16, 2005, p. 26; D. Jones, "Profits Jump at JCB," *Daily Post*, June 20, 2006, p. 21; R. Bentley, "Still Optimistic about Asia," *Asian Business Review*, October 1, 1999, p. 1; "JCB Launches India-Specific Heavy Duty Crane," *The Hindu*, October 18, 2008; P. M. Thomas, "JCB Hits Pay Dirt in India," *Forbes.com*, December 6, 2011; and J. Moulds, "JCB Unearths Record Sales and Profits," *The Guardian*, April 17, 2012.

Case Discussion Questions

1. Why do you think that India was an attractive market for JCB?

2. Historically, JCB entered foreign markets through exports. Why do you think JCB generally favoured exports?

3. In India, JCB decided to enter via a joint venture. What was the articulated rationale for this? In what other ways might the joint venture strategy have benefited JCB?

4. What were the risks associated with the joint venture strategy? How did JCB deal with these risks?

5. What are the benefits to JCB of localizing significant production in India? What are the disadvantages? Do the benefits outweigh the disadvantages?

© Chris Ryan/agefotostock

Chapter 13

Exporting, Importing, and Countertrade

GROWING THROUGH EXPORTS

It is not always appreciated that small firms comprise the majority of Canadian and U.S. exporters. One company that has illustrated the power of exporting for a small business is Sono-Tek Corp, a developer of ultrasonic spray coating technology in Milton, New York. Sono-Tek's primary overseas customers include contract manufacturers for electronic and medical equipment firms. Some $6 million of Sono-Tek's annual revenues now come from exports to customers in Europe, Southeast Asia, and Latin America. Sono-Tek's CEO, Chris Coccio, believes that without exporting the company would be one-third of its current size.

Another New York company, Vision Quest Lighting, has had a similar experience. Vision Quest Lighting, which has around 30 employees, makes decorative lighting for retail chains, including Limited Brands, Ann Taylor, and, until its recent bankruptcy, Abercrombie and Fitch. As these brands expanded their international presence, Vision

Quest Lighting grew with them. According to the company's management, its international exposure helped the company to survive in the recessionary years of 2008–2009 when demand in the United States was very soft. Looking forward, Vision Quest Lighting sees great growth opportunities in China, where it has recently established a factory to produce products for the local market.

Both of these companies have found exporting to be challenging. Sono-Tek's Chris Coccio notes that his biggest worries include recruiting foreign staff that understand the local market, the costs of business travel, problems associated with communicating with far-flung clients, and getting paid. He is not alone in this last worry. According to the Small Business Exporters Association, getting paid can be a major headache. In a recent survey conducted by the Association, 41 percent of respondents indicated that they worried about getting paid. The association urges small exporters to work with banks and to make sure that they get letters of credit from foreign importers before shipping goods or performing services.

At Vision Quest Lighting, management notes that being successfully requires a bilingual agent or foreign employee who understands the business system, lives in country, and can help the foreign company to navigate its way through a culturally challenging environment. There is no substitute, according to the company, for someone with his or her feet on the ground who understands the local business culture. In Vision Quests' case, for example, their business in China did not start to take off until they hired a local Chinese employee.

Sources: R. Colvin, "The Cost of Expanding Overseas," *The Wall Street Journal*, February 26, 2014; John Grossman, "New Path for Trade: Selling in China," *The New York Times*, January 23, 2013; and N. Levy, "LI Lighting Firm Learns the Ropes in China," *Newsday*, October 20, 2013.

LEARNING OBJECTIVES

By the end of this chapter you should be able to:

1. Summarize the opportunities and risks associated with exporting.
2. Explain the different steps companies can take to improve their export performance including the information sources and municipal, provincial, and federal government programs that exist to support Canadian exporters.
3. Demonstrate the basic steps involved in financing exporting.
4. Give examples of how countertrade can be used to facilitate exporting.
5. Explain the implications for business.

Introduction

In the previous chapter, we reviewed exporting from a strategic perspective. We considered exporting as just one of a range of strategic options for profiting from international expansion. This chapter is more concerned with the nuts and bolts of exporting (and importing). We take the choice of strategy as a given and look at how to export. As the opening case makes clear, exporting is not just for large enterprises; many small firms have benefited significantly from the moneymaking opportunities of exporting.

The volume of export activity in the world economy is increasing as exporting has become easier. The gradual decline in trade barriers under the umbrella of GATT and now the WTO (see Chapter 6), along with regional economic agreements such as the European Union and the North American Free Trade Agreement (see Chapter 8) have significantly increased export opportunities. At the same time, modern communication and transportation technologies have alleviated the logistical problems associated with exporting. Modern communication and transportation technologies have alleviated the logistical problems associated with exporting. Firms are increasingly using the Internet, toll-free phone numbers, and international air express services to reduce the costs of exporting. Consequently, it is not unusual to find thriving exporters among small companies.

Nevertheless, exporting remains a challenge for many firms. Smaller enterprises can find the process intimidating. The firm wishing to export must identify foreign market opportunities, avoid a host of unanticipated problems often associated with doing business in a foreign market, familiarize itself with the mechanics of export and import, learn where it can get financing and export credit insurance, and learn how it should deal with foreign exchange risk. The process is made more problematic by currencies that are not freely convertible. As a result, there is the problem of arranging payment for exports to countries with weak currencies. This brings us to the complex topic of countertrade, by which payment for exports is received in goods and services rather than money. In this chapter, we will discuss all these issues with the exception of foreign exchange risk, which was covered in Chapter 9. We open the chapter by considering the promise and pitfalls of exporting.

LO1 The Promise and Pitfalls of Exporting

The great promise of exporting is that large revenue and profit opportunities are to be found in foreign markets for most firms in most industries. This was true for Vision Quest Lighting, which was profiled in the opening case. The international market is normally so much larger than the firm's domestic market that exporting is nearly always a way to increase the revenue and profit base of a company. By expanding the size of the market, exporting can enable a firm to achieve economies of scale, thereby lowering its unit costs. Firms that do not export often lose out on significant opportunities for growth and cost reduction.[1]

ANOTHER PERSPECTIVE

Product Naming May Be Tricky, Even in English

Heublein had a cranberry liqueur that was popular in the United States called Boggs Cranberry Liqueur. For North Americans, this name makes sense because we are aware that cranberries are grown in bogs, so the name communicates an authenticity and connects us to our heritage. When Heublein test-marketed Boggs Cranberry Liqueur in the United Kingdom, it quickly learned something about British slang: *bogs* is an informal term for what Americans call an outhouse or privy—an outdoor toilet. Boggs did not sell well.

Studies have shown that while many large firms tend to be proactive about seeking opportunities for profitable exporting, systematically scanning foreign markets to see where the opportunities lie for leveraging their technology, products, and marketing skills in foreign countries, many medium-size and small firms are very reactive.[2] Typically, such reactive firms do not even consider exporting until their domestic market is saturated and the emergence of excess productive capacity at home forces them to look for growth opportunities in foreign markets. Also, many small- and medium-sized firms tend to wait for the world to come to them, rather than going out into the world to seek opportunities. There is a need for firms to become more proactive about seeking export opportunities. One reason more firms are not proactive is that they are unfamiliar with foreign market opportunities; they simply do not know how big the opportunities actually are or where they might lie. Simple ignorance of the potential opportunities is a huge barrier to exporting.[3] Also, many would-be exporters, particularly smaller firms, are often intimidated by the complexities and mechanics of exporting to countries where business practices, language, culture, legal systems, and currency are very different from the home market.[4]

To make matters worse, many neophyte exporters have run into significant problems when first trying to do business abroad and this has soured them on future exporting ventures. Common pitfalls include poor market analysis, poor understanding of competitive conditions in the foreign market, failure to customize the product to the needs of foreign customers, lack of an effective distribution program, poorly executed promotion in the foreign market, and problems securing financing.[5] Novice exporters tend to underestimate the time and expertise needed to cultivate business in foreign countries.[6] Few realize the amount of management resources that have to be dedicated to this activity. Many foreign customers require face-to-face negotiations on their home turf. An exporter may have to spend months learning about a country's trade regulations, business practices, and more before a deal can be closed.

Exporters often face voluminous paperwork, complex formalities, and many potential delays and errors. According to a UN report on trade and development, a typical international trade transaction may involve 30 parties, 60 original documents, and 360 document copies, all of which have to be checked, transmitted, re-entered into various information systems, processed, and filed. The United Nations has calculated that the time involved in preparing documentation, along with the costs of common errors in paperwork, often amounts to 10 percent of the final value of goods exported.[7]

LO2 Improving Export Performance

Inexperienced exporters have a number of ways to gain information about foreign market opportunities and avoid common pitfalls that tend to discourage and frustrate novice exporters.[8] In this section, we look at information sources that exporters can utilize to increase their knowledge of foreign market opportunities, we consider the pros and cons of using export management companies (EMCs) to assist in the export process, and we review various exporting strategies that can increase the probability of successful exporting. We begin, however, with a look at how several nations try to help domestic firms export.

An International Comparison

One big impediment to exporting is the simple lack of knowledge of the opportunities available. Often there are many markets for a firm's product, but because they are in countries separated from the firm's home base by culture, language, distance, and time, the firm does not know of them. Identifying export opportunities is made even more complex by the fact that more than 192 countries with widely differing cultures compose the world of potential opportunities. Faced with such complexity and diversity, firms sometimes hesitate to seek export opportunities.

The way to overcome ignorance is to collect information. In Germany—one of the world's most successful exporting nations—trade associations, government agencies, and commercial banks gather information, helping small firms identify export opportunities. A similar function is provided by the Japanese Ministry of International Trade and Industry (MITI), which is always on the lookout for export opportunities. In addition, many Japanese firms are affiliated in some way with the ***sogo shosha***, Japan's great trading houses. The *sogo shosha* have offices all over the world, and they proactively and continuously seek export opportunities for their affiliated companies, large and small.[9] German and Japanese firms can draw on the large reservoirs of experience, skills, information, and other resources of their respective export-oriented institutions.

ANOTHER PERSPECTIVE

Autarky: Not in the Vocabulary of Globalization!

The word *autarky* refers to the belief that a country should be self-sufficient and avoid trade with other nations. Despite the recent statements about trade from U.S. President Trump, most economists regard autarky as an idealistic, but impractical, goal. Throughout history, countries have tried to achieve autarky, but soon discovered they could not produce the wide range of goods their population wants and make those goods available at competitive prices. In fact, those countries found themselves worse off economically than nations that engage in international trade. Word to the wise: Unless your country can efficiently produce everything it needs, it needs to trade.

Source: "Economics A-Z," www.economist.com.

Unlike their German and Japanese competitors, many Canadian firms are relatively blind when they seek export opportunities. While they have information than previously, Canadian firms are still more comfortable with the American market than beyond. Both Germany and Japan have long made their living as trading nations, whereas, until recently, Canada had been a part of a relatively self-contained continental economy in which international trade played a minor role. This is changing: both imports and exports now play a much greater role in the Canadian economy than they did 20 years ago. However, Canada has not yet evolved an institutional structure to the degree that exists in Japan and Germany. The Canadian government is addressing this need, and one of the services it offers is the Industry Canada Web site, which offers national and international business information about Canadian government programs and services.

Export Information Sources

Canadian firms are increasingly becoming aware of international business opportunities. There are many different sources of information available through municipal, provincial, and federal governments. At the federal level, Global Affairs Canada helps Canadian tourists and business people abroad, while striving towards a more peaceful and secure world. It also supports the development of trade by providing services to exporters, developing policy, and attracting investment in the Canadian economy.[10]

Several Web-based sources provide information on international trade matters relating to Canada and the world. Industry Canada and Statistics Canada provide extensive Web resources on a plethora of international-trade-related subjects. Some reports and trade data are free, while others require payment of a small document access fee. The Foreign Policy, Trade, and Development Canada Web site (found under Global Affairs Canada at http://www.international.gc.ca/international/index. aspx?lang=eng) provides extensive information, such as market reports, cultural reports, strategies for culture and trade, Infoexport, virtual trade commissioner, and tips for new exporters to border states. (Learn about Nexterra's experience with the federal government in the Management Focus later in this section. Also see the Country Focus on the Business Development Bank of Canada in the next section.)

The Canadian government initiates international trade fairs, seminars, and conferences, at home and abroad, and trade visits in cooperation with various government agencies, including the International Trade Centres (ITCs) located across Canada. In the past the government organized Team Canada trade missions to other countries, and now sponsors Government of Canada Trade Missions. In addition to ITCs, trade commissioners working at Canadian high commissions, consuls general, and embassies around the world have teams of employees working to connect Canadian businesses to host country opportunities.

The Forum for International Trade Training (FITT) is a not-for-profit organization dedicated to providing international business training, resources, and professional certification to individuals and businesses. FITT's international business training

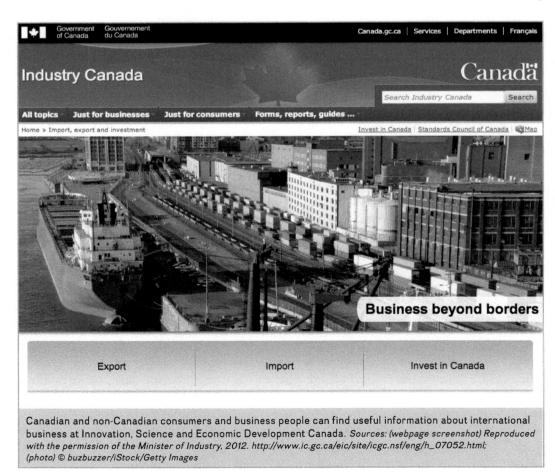

Canadian and non-Canadian consumers and business people can find useful information about international business at Innovation, Science and Economic Development Canada. *Sources: (webpage screenshot) Reproduced with the permission of the Minister of Industry, 2012. http://www.ic.gc.ca/eic/site/icgc.nsf/eng/h_07052.html; (photo) © buzbuzzer/iStock/Getty Images*

solutions have become the standard of excellence for global trade professionals across Canada and around the world. In support of international trade, FITT undertakes the following activities:

- Identifying and promoting essential international trade knowledge and insights about the competency gaps that most commonly impede the success of business, and competency-related promotion

- Developing, delivering, and promoting international trade training and other enabling knowledge, skill, and ability-building products and services

- Responding to specific industries, trade sectors, and disciplines to build proficiencies, including the knowledge, skills, and abilities required to become more competitive in international trade

- Developing proficiency standards for successful international trade, a certification system for trade practitioners, the Certified International Trade Professional (CITP/FIBP) designation, and accreditation for academic providers that meet these standards

This government support also plays out at the provincial and municipal levels. Most provincial governments have trade representation offices, not only in other provinces, but in other countries as well, aimed at attracting business to the home province.

At the municipal levels are boards of trade and local chambers of commerce, all linked to the provincial and Canadian Chamber of Commerce, the voice of Canadian business at the International Chamber of Commerce in Paris, and at World Trade Organization conferences, through the designate cabinet minister. Tied in with international trade norms are Incoterms, first formulated in Paris in 1936 by the International Chamber of Commerce. **Incoterms** are a set of international trading rules that determine the rights and obligations of buyers and sellers in international trade transactions. Without Incoterms, international trade would not be possible.

A number of private organizations are also beginning to provide more assistance to would-be exporters. Commercial banks and major accounting firms are more willing to assist small firms in starting export operations than they were a decade ago. In addition, large multinationals that have been successful in the global arena are typically willing to discuss opportunities overseas with the owners or managers of small firms.[11]

ANOTHER PERSPECTIVE

Is Chinese Exporting the Next Edge for the Country?

With hundreds of television sets stacked high, Changhong Electronics' warehouse in Shunde resembles many other storage depots in southern China, but their destinations reveal an important shift in global trade patterns. While Changhong's smaller sets are headed for Europe, its 50-inch plasma screens, which dominate the warehouse, will be shipped to South Africa. Fast growth in developing countries and sluggish Western economies are prompting these companies to abandon their obsession with the United States and Europe and to try and capitalize on rapidly growing markets in Asia, Africa, and Latin America. The so-called China price—a vastly lower price because of low labour costs and the low cost of capital for large government-owned companies—now applies to industrial goods, not just consumer goods. Experts believe that cheap Chinese exports could provide a boost to investment in the developing world, just as they once did to consumption in the developed world. Can China boost investment in the developing world and also boost its own economy?

Source: R. Jacob, "Chinese Exporters Seek New Markets," *Financial Times*, June 12, 2012.

Utilizing Export Management Companies

One way for first-time exporters to identify the opportunities associated with exporting and to avoid many of the associated pitfalls is to hire an **export management company** (EMC). EMCs are export specialists who act as the export marketing department or international department for their client firms. EMCs normally accept two types of export assignments. In the first case they start exporting operations for a firm with the understanding that the firm will take over operations after they are well established. In another type, start-up services are performed with the understanding that the EMC will have continuing responsibility for selling the firm's products. Many EMCs specialize in serving firms in particular industries and in particular areas of the world. Thus, one EMC may specialize in selling agricultural products in the Asian market, while another may focus on exporting electronics products to Eastern Europe.

In theory, the advantage of EMCs is that they are experienced specialists who can help the neophyte exporter identify opportunities and avoid common pitfalls. A good EMC will have a network of contacts in potential markets, have multilingual employees, have a good knowledge of different business mores, and be fully conversant with the ins and outs of the exporting process and with local business regulations. However, the quality of EMCs varies.[12] While some perform their functions very well, others appear to add little value to the exporting company. Therefore, it is important for an exporter to review a number of EMCs carefully and to check references. One drawback of relying on EMCs is that the company can fail to develop its own exporting capabilities in-house.

Exporting Strategy

In addition to using EMCs, a firm can reduce the risks associated with exporting if it is careful about its choice of exporting strategy. A few guidelines can help firms improve their odds of success. For example, one of the most successful exporting firms in the world, the Minnesota Mining and Manufacturing Co. (3M), has built its export success on three main principles—enter on a small scale to reduce risks, add additional product lines once the exporting operations start to become successful, and hire locals to promote the firm's products. Also see the Country Focus on the Business Development Bank of Canada in the next section.

The probability of exporting successfully can be increased dramatically by taking a handful of simple strategic steps. First, particularly for the novice exporter, it helps to hire an EMC or at least an experienced export consultant to help identify opportunities and navigate through the web of paperwork and regulations so often involved in exporting. Second, it often makes sense to initially focus on one market or a handful of markets. The idea is to learn about what is required to succeed in those markets, before moving on to other markets. The firm that enters many markets at once runs the risk of spreading its limited management resources too thinly. The result of such a "shotgun approach" to exporting may be a failure to become established in any one market. Third, as with 3M, it often makes sense to enter a foreign market on a small scale to reduce the costs of any subsequent failure. Most importantly, entering on a small scale provides the time and opportunity to learn about the foreign country before making significant capital commitments to that market. Fourth, the exporter needs to recognize the time and managerial commitment involved in building export sales and should hire additional personnel to oversee this activity. Fifth, in many countries, it is important to devote a lot of attention to building strong and enduring relationships with local distributors and/or customers. Sixth, as 3M often does, it is important to hire local personnel to help the firm establish itself in a foreign market. Local people are likely to have a much greater sense of how to do business in a given country than a manager from an exporting firm who has previously never set foot in that country. Seventh, several studies have suggested the firm needs to be proactive about seeking export opportunities.[13] Armchair exporting does not work! The world will not normally beat a path to your door.

MANAGEMENT FOCUS

Nexterra Finances Its Export Growth

Nexterra Systems Corp. is a fifteen-year-old firm that is headquartered in Vancouver. The company produces plant-scale, energy-from-waste gasification systems for the production of renewable heat and power. The company's gasification technology delivers lower costs, higher reliability, and lower emissions when compared to other energy systems. It is jointly owned by Tandem Expansion Fund and the Business Development Bank of Canada (BDC). Nexterra has also received funding for Research, Development and Demonstration (RD&D) of over $10 million from Canada's federal government and the British Columbia government to support the company's research and demonstration efforts.

The company has completed seven commercial products in Canada and the United States, and has recently completed its first sale in the United Kingdom. It continues to look for opportunities where biomass waste is high and where this waste would otherwise end up in landfill. The systems convert the waste, cost-effectively and reliably, into higher value renewable energy, fuel, and chemicals.

One of the most challenging hurdles, according to the company's Michael Scott, President and CEO, is bridging the gap from the pilot phase to the demonstration phase. As Scott notes, one of the key requirements is a performance bond, which is very difficult to obtain if your company has never had such a bond before.

That is the role performed by the Export Development Canada (EDC). The EDC facilitated the issuance of a performance bond through one of EDC's surety partners. With this bond in place, the buyer was comfortable with the company's ability to execute its promises, and Nexterra was able to conclude the contract. Says Michael Scott, "EDC was hugely important for us getting that project bonding done."

According to Scott, "EDC has been very actively involved in meeting with potential customers, trying to understand the financing challenges that the projects we're working on may face, and finding creative solutions for some of the other challenges that we, as a Canadian company, faces as we entered the international markets."

Questions

1. If EDC did not exist, what would happen to a company such as Nexterra?
2. What organizations do other countries fund and support, similar to Canada's BDC and the EDC?

Sources: Nexterra Systems Corp. Corporate Profile, http://www.nexterra.ca/files/corporate-profile.php (accessed January 2014); Nexterra Development Partners, http://www.nexterra.ca/files/partners.php; and Export Development Canada, *Corporate Social Responsibility Report 2011*, http://www.edc.ca/EN/About-Us/Corporate-Social-Responsibility/Documents/csr-report-2011.pdf (p. 52).

Finally, it is important for the exporter to keep the option of local production in mind. Once exports reach a sufficient volume to justify cost-efficient local production, the exporting firm should consider establishing production facilities in the foreign market. Such localization helps foster good relations with the foreign country and can lead to greater market acceptance. Exporting is often not an end in itself, but merely a step on the road toward establishment of foreign production (again, 3M provides an example of this philosophy).

LO3 | Export and Import Financing

Mechanisms for financing exports and imports have evolved over the centuries in response to a problem that can be particularly acute in international trade: the lack of trust that exists when one must put faith in a stranger. In this section we examine the

COUNTRY FOCUS

Enhancing Financing Possibilities—The Business Development Bank of Canada

It is not a new idea for businesses and government to work together. For example, the BDC, formed on July 13, 1995, under the Business Development Bank of Canada Act, has a broad and dynamic public interest mandate, particularly focusing on Canadian exporting businesses in the technology sector. It does provide assistance to non-export ventures, but increasingly small businesses are using its services for export-specific purposes.

The BDC was conceived at the end of the World War II era when, in September 1944, the Canadian Parliament proclaimed the Industrial Development Bank of Canada (IDB) Act. Over the next few years, the IDB Act was amended several times, expanding its ability to grant loans to many companies across a variety of industry sectors. By 1964, the bank had 22 cross-Canada branches.

Today the BDC's mandate is to offer financing, venture capital, and consulting services, with a focus on small and medium-sized enterprises. Services are offered in both official languages through 100 business centres across Canada (see https://www.bdc.ca/en/pages/home.aspx)

Its financing and venture capital services include:

- Financing for new equipment
- Financing for commercial real estate
- Money for buying an existing business
- Working capital
- Start-up financing
- Financing for expanding into foreign or domestic markets

Its consulting services include:

- Business planning
- Market research
- Export planning
- Managing human resources
- Selling a business
- Improving efficiency

The functions of the BDC can also be understood by looking at what it does *not* provide, which includes grants, interest-free loans, lines of credit, bank accounts, non-commercial loans (i.e., mortgage loans for houses and personal loans), and loans for businesses such as night clubs, bars, lounges, casinos, and a listing of other restricted businesses.

Questions

1. Given the fact that Canada has a well-developed network of commercial banks across the country, is there still a need for the BDC?
2. Why do you think the BDC focused its efforts on small and medium-sized (SME) enterprises?

Sources: Business Development Bank of Canada (BDC): BDC's history, http://www.bdc.ca/EN/about/overview/history/Pages/default.aspx; BDC: Who we are, http://www.bdc.ca/EN/about/overview/Pages/overview1.aspx; Government of Canada, Canada Business Network, http://www.canadabusiness.ca/eng/; BDC: What we do, http://www.bdc.ca/EN/about/overview/Pages/what_we_do.aspx (accessed January 2014).

financial devices that cope with this problem in the context of international trade: the letter of credit, the draft (or bill of exchange), and the bill of lading. Then we will trace the 14 steps of a typical export–import transaction.

DEBATE THE ISSUE

How Trusting Can You Be?

In this chapter we discuss the fact that firms that are engaged in international trade have to trust someone they may have never seen, who lives in a different country, who speaks a different language, who abides by (or does not abide by) a different legal system, and who could be very difficult to track down if he or she defaults on an obligation. Basically, there is a lot of potential for unknown issues to arise and for complications to happen given the lack of established trust between trading partners. With more than 200 countries in the world, lots of cultural values and beliefs, and many potential avenues to run into complications, how much trust would you place on a relationship that (1) involved an organization from a country like yours (e.g., Swedish people doing business with Danish people) or (2) involved an organization from a country very different from yours (e.g., a Canadian doing business with someone from Turkey)?

Lack of Trust

Firms engaged in international trade have to trust someone they may have never seen, who lives in a different country, who speaks a different language, who abides by (or does not abide by) a different legal system, and who could be very difficult to track down if he or she defaults on an obligation. Consider a Canadian firm exporting to a distributor in France. The Canadian businessman might be concerned that if he ships the products to France before he receives payment for them from the French businesswoman, she might take delivery of the products and not pay him. Conversely, the French importer might worry that if she pays for the products before they are shipped, the Canadian firm might keep the money and never ship the products or might ship defective products. Neither party to the exchange completely trusts the other. This lack of trust is exacerbated by the distance between the two parties—in space, language, and culture—and by the problems of using an underdeveloped international legal system to enforce contractual obligations.

Due to the (quite reasonable) lack of trust between the two parties, each has his or her own preferences as to how they would like the transaction to be configured. To make sure he is paid, the manager of the Canadian firm would prefer the French distributor to pay for the products before he ships them (see Figure 13.1). Alternatively, to ensure she

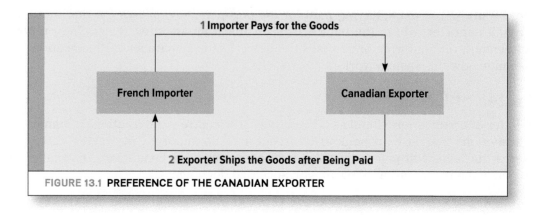

FIGURE 13.1 **PREFERENCE OF THE CANADIAN EXPORTER**

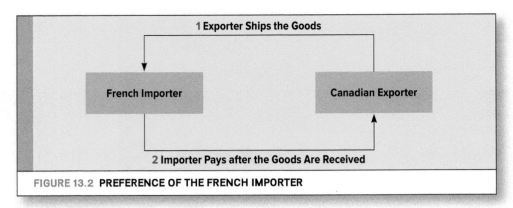

1 Exporter Ships the Goods

French Importer   Canadian Exporter

2 Importer Pays after the Goods Are Received

FIGURE 13.2 **PREFERENCE OF THE FRENCH IMPORTER**

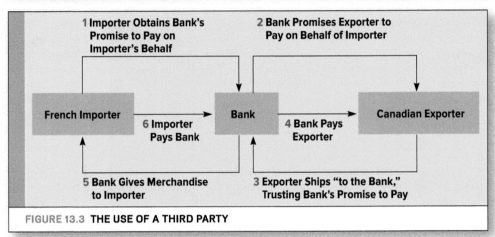

1 Importer Obtains Bank's Promise to Pay on Importer's Behalf   **2 Bank Promises Exporter to Pay on Behalf of Importer**

French Importer   Bank   Canadian Exporter

6 Importer Pays Bank   **4 Bank Pays Exporter**

5 Bank Gives Merchandise to Importer   **3 Exporter Ships "to the Bank," Trusting Bank's Promise to Pay**

FIGURE 13.3 **THE USE OF A THIRD PARTY**

receives the products, the French distributor would prefer not to pay for them until they arrive (see Figure 13.2). Thus, each party has different preferences. Unless there is some way of establishing trust between the parties, the transaction might never take place.

The problem is solved by using a third party trusted by both—normally a reputable bank—to act as an intermediary. EDC is another intermediary that many small- and medium-sized businesses use. What happens can be summarized as follows (see Figure 13.3). First, the French importer obtains the bank's promise to pay on her behalf, knowing the Canadian exporter will trust the bank. This promise is known as a letter of credit. Having seen the letter of credit, the Canadian exporter now ships the products to France. Title to the products is given to the bank in the form of a document called a bill of lading. In return, the Canadian exporter tells the bank to pay for the products, which the bank does. The document for requesting this payment is referred to as a draft. The bank, having paid for the products, now passes the title on to the French importer, whom the bank trusts. At that time or later, depending on their agreement, the importer reimburses the bank. In the remainder of this section, we examine how this system works in more detail.

Letter of Credit

A letter of credit, abbreviated as L/C, stands at the centre of international commercial transactions. Issued by a bank at the request of an importer, the **letter of credit** states the bank will pay a specified sum of money to a beneficiary, normally the exporter, on presentation of particular, specified documents.

Consider again the example of the Canadian exporter and the French importer. The French importer applies to her local bank, say the Bank of Paris, for the issuance of a letter of credit. The Bank of Paris then undertakes a credit check of the importer. If the Bank of Paris is satisfied with her creditworthiness, it will issue a letter of credit. However, the Bank of Paris might require a cash deposit or some other form of collateral from her first. In addition, the Bank of Paris will charge the importer a fee for this service. Typically this amounts to between 0.5 percent and 2 percent of the value of the letter of credit, depending on the importer's creditworthiness and the size of the transaction. (As a rule, the larger the transaction, the lower the percentage.)

Let us assume the Bank of Paris is satisfied with the French importer's creditworthiness and agrees to issue a letter of credit. The letter states that the Bank of Paris will pay the Canadian exporter for the merchandise as long as it is shipped in accordance with specified instructions and conditions. At this point, the letter of credit becomes a financial contract between the Bank of Paris and the Canadian exporter. The Bank of Paris then sends the letter of credit to the Canadian exporter's bank, say the Bank of Montreal. The Bank of Montreal tells the exporter that it has received a letter of credit and that he can ship the merchandise. After the exporter has shipped the merchandise, he draws a draft against the Bank of Paris in accordance with the terms of the letter of credit, attaches the required documents, and presents the draft to his own bank, the Bank of Montreal, for payment. The Bank of Montreal then forwards the letter of credit and associated documents to the Bank of Paris. If all the terms and conditions contained in the letter of credit have been complied with, the Bank of Paris will honour the draft and will send payment to the Bank of Montreal. When the Bank of Montreal receives the funds, it will pay the Canadian exporter.

As for the Bank of Paris, once it has transferred the funds to the Bank of Montreal, it will collect payment from the French importer. Alternatively, the Bank of Paris may allow the importer some time to resell the merchandise before requiring payment.

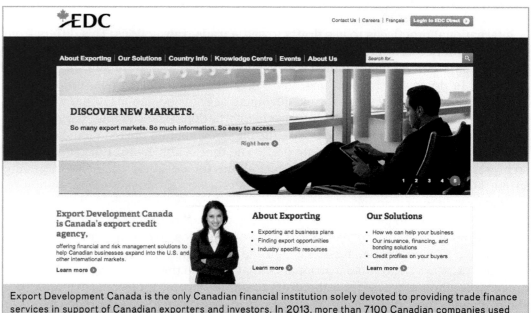

Export Development Canada is the only Canadian financial institution solely devoted to providing trade finance services in support of Canadian exporters and investors. In 2013, more than 7100 Canadian companies used $95 billion ($Cdn) of EDC's financial solutions to undertake business in more than 180 countries. Founded in 1944, EDC is a Crown corporation that operates as a commercial financial institution. © *Export Development Canada. Reproduced with permission.*

This is not unusual, particularly when the importer is a distributor and not the final consumer of the merchandise, since it helps the importer's cash flow. The Bank of Paris will treat such an extension of the payment period as a loan to the importer and will charge an appropriate interest rate.

The great advantage of this system is that both the French importer and the Canadian exporter are likely to trust reputable banks, even if they do not trust each other. Once the Canadian exporter has seen a letter of credit, he knows that he is guaranteed payment and will ship the merchandise. Also, an exporter may find that having a letter of credit will facilitate obtaining pre-export financing. For example, having seen the letter of credit, the Bank of Montreal might be willing to lend the exporter funds to process and prepare the merchandise for shipping to France. This loan may not have to be repaid until the exporter has received his payment for the merchandise. As for the French importer, she does not have to pay for the merchandise until the documents have arrived and unless all conditions stated in the letter of credit have been satisfied. The drawback for the importer is the fee she must pay the Bank of Paris for the letter of credit. In addition, since the letter of credit is a financial liability against her, it may reduce her ability to borrow funds for other purposes.

Draft

A **draft,** sometimes referred to as a **bill of exchange**, is the instrument normally used in international commerce to effect payment. A draft is simply an order written by an exporter instructing an importer, or an importer's agent, to pay a specified amount of money at a specified time. In the example of the Canadian exporter and the French importer, the exporter writes a draft that instructs the Bank of Paris, the French importer's agent, to pay for the merchandise shipped to France. The person or business initiating the draft is known as the maker (in this case, the Canadian exporter). The party to whom the draft is presented is known as the drawee (in this case, the Bank of Paris).

International practice is to use drafts to settle trade transactions. This differs from domestic practice in which a seller usually ships merchandise on an open account, followed by a commercial invoice that specifies the amount due and the terms of payment. In domestic transactions, the buyer can often obtain possession of the merchandise without signing a formal document acknowledging his or her obligation to pay. In contrast, due to the lack of trust in international transactions, payment or a formal promise to pay is required before the buyer can obtain the merchandise.

Drafts fall into two categories, sight drafts and time drafts. A **sight draft** is payable on presentation to the drawee. A **time draft** allows for a delay in payment—normally 30, 60, 90, or 120 days. It is presented to the drawee, who signifies acceptance of it by writing or stamping a notice of acceptance on its face. Once accepted, the time draft becomes a promise to pay by the accepting party. When a time draft is drawn on and accepted by a bank, it is called a banker's acceptance. When it is drawn on and accepted by a business firm, it is called a trade acceptance.

Time drafts are negotiable instruments; that is, once the draft is stamped with an acceptance, the maker can sell the draft to an investor at a discount from its face value. Imagine the agreement between the Canadian exporter and the French importer calls for the exporter to present the Bank of Paris (through the Bank of Montreal) with a time draft requiring payment 120 days after presentation. The Bank of Paris stamps the time draft with an acceptance. Imagine further that the draft is for $100,000.

The exporter can either hold onto the accepted time draft and receive $100,000 in 120 days or he can sell it to an investor, say the Bank of Montreal, for a discount from the face value. If the prevailing discount rate is 7 percent, the exporter could receive $97,700 by selling it immediately (7 percent per annum discount rate for 120 days for $100,000 equals $2300, and $100,000 − $2300 = $97,700). The Bank of Montreal would then collect the full $100,000 from the Bank of Paris in 120 days. The exporter might sell the accepted time draft immediately if he needed the funds to finance merchandise in transit and/or to cover cash flow shortfalls.

Bill of Lading

The third key document for financing international trade is the bill of lading. The **bill of lading** is issued to the exporter by the common carrier transporting the merchandise. It serves three purposes: it is a receipt, a contract, and a document of title. As a receipt, the bill of lading indicates the carrier has received the merchandise described on the face of the document. As a contract, it specifies that the carrier is obligated to provide a transportation service in return for a certain charge. As a document of title, it can be used to obtain payment or a written promise of payment before the merchandise is released to the importer. The bill of lading can also function as collateral against which funds may be advanced to the exporter by its local bank before or during shipment and before final payment by the importer.

A Typical International Trade Transaction

Now that we have reviewed the elements of an international trade transaction, let us see how the process works in a typical case, sticking with the example of the Canadian exporter and the French importer. The typical transaction involves 14 steps (see Figure 13.4).

1. The French importer places an order with the Canadian exporter and asks the Canadian if he would be willing to ship under a letter of credit.

2. The Canadian exporter agrees to ship under a letter of credit and specifies relevant information such as prices and delivery terms.

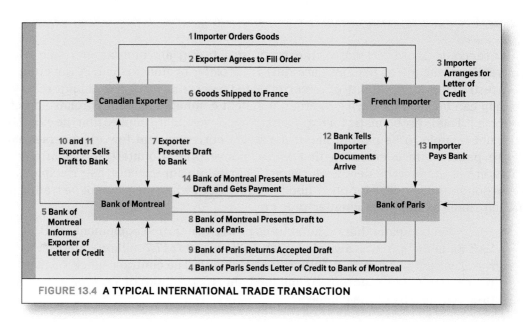

FIGURE 13.4 **A TYPICAL INTERNATIONAL TRADE TRANSACTION**

3. The French importer applies to the Bank of Paris for a letter of credit to be issued in favour of the Canadian exporter for the merchandise the importer wishes to buy.

4. The Bank of Paris issues a letter of credit in the French importer's favour and sends it to the Canadian exporter's bank, the Bank of Montreal.

5. The Bank of Montreal advises the exporter of the opening of a letter of credit in his favour.

6. The Canadian exporter ships the goods to the French importer on a common carrier. An official of the carrier gives the exporter a bill of lading.

7. The Canadian exporter presents a 90-day time draft drawn on the Bank of Paris in accordance with its letter of credit and the bill of lading to the Bank of Montreal. The exporter endorses the bill of lading so title to the goods is transferred to the Bank of Montreal.

8. The Bank of Montreal sends the draft and bill of lading to the Bank of Paris. The Bank of Paris accepts the draft, taking possession of the documents and promising to pay the now-accepted draft in 90 days.

9. The Bank of Paris returns the accepted draft to the Bank of Montreal.

10. The Bank of Montreal tells the Canadian exporter that it has received the accepted bank draft, which is payable in 90 days.

11. The exporter sells the draft to the Bank of Montreal at a discount from its face value and receives the discounted cash value of the draft in return.

12. The Bank of Paris notifies the French importer of the arrival of the documents. She agrees to pay the Bank of Paris in 90 days. The Bank of Paris releases the documents so the importer can take possession of the shipment.

13. In 90 days, the Bank of Paris receives the importer's payment, so it has funds to pay the maturing draft.

14. In 90 days, the holder of the matured acceptance (in this case, the Bank of Montreal) presents it to the Bank of Paris for payment. The Bank of Paris pays.

LO4 Countertrade

Countertrade is an alternative means of structuring an international sale when conventional means of payment are difficult, costly, or nonexistent. A government may restrict the convertibility of its currency to preserve its foreign exchange reserves so they can be used to service international debt commitments and purchase crucial imports.[14] This is problematic for exporters. Nonconvertibility implies that the exporter may not be able to be paid in his or her home currency; and few exporters would desire payment in a currency that is not convertible. Countertrade is often the solution.[15] Countertrade denotes a range of barterlike agreements; its principle is to trade goods and services for other goods and services when they cannot be traded for money. Some examples of countertrade are:

- An Italian company that manufactures power-generating equipment, ABB SAE Sadelmi SpA, was awarded a 720-million baht ($17.7 million) contract by the Electricity Generating Authority of Thailand. The contract specified that the company had to accept 218 million baht ($5.4 million) of Thai farm products as part of the payment.

- Saudi Arabia agreed to buy ten 747 jets from Boeing with payment in crude oil, discounted at 10 percent below posted world oil prices.
- General Electric won a contract for a $150-million electric-generator project in Romania by agreeing to market $150 million of Romanian products in markets to which Romania did not have access.
- The Venezuelan government negotiated a contract with Caterpillar under which Venezuela would trade 350 000 tonnes of iron ore for Caterpillar earthmoving equipment.
- Albania offered such items as spring water, tomato juice, and chrome ore in exchange for a $60-million fertilizer and methanol complex.
- Philip Morris ships cigarettes to Russia, for which it receives chemicals that can be used to make fertilizer. Philip Morris ships the chemicals to China, and in return, China ships glassware to North America for retail sale by Philip Morris.[16]

The Popularity of Countertrade

In the modern era, countertrade arose in the 1960s as a way for the Soviet Union and the Communist states of Eastern Europe, whose currencies were generally nonconvertible, to purchase imports. During the 1980s, the technique grew in popularity among many developing nations that lacked the foreign exchange reserves required to purchase necessary imports. Today, reflecting their own shortages of foreign exchange reserves, many of the successor states to the former Soviet Union and the Eastern European Communist nations are engaging in countertrade to purchase their imports. Estimates of the percentage of world trade covered by some sort of countertrade agreement range from a high of 10 percent by value to a low of 2 percent. There was a notable increase in the volume of countertrade after the Asian financial crisis of 1997. That crisis left many Asian nations with little hard currency to finance international trade. In the tight monetary regime that followed the 1997 crisis, many Asian firms found it difficult to get export credits to finance their own international trade. Consequently, they turned to the only option available—countertrade.

Given the importance of countertrade as a means of financing world trade, prospective exporters will have to engage in this technique from time to time to gain access to international markets. The governments of developing nations sometimes insist on a certain amount of countertrade.[17]

Types of Countertrade

With its roots in the simple trading of goods and services for other goods and services, countertrade has evolved into a diverse set of activities that can be categorized as five distinct types of trading arrangements: barter, counter-purchase, offset, switch trading, and compensation or buyback.[18] Many countertrade deals involve not just one arrangement, but elements of two or more.

BARTER

Barter is the direct exchange of goods and/or services between two parties without a cash transaction. Although barter is the simplest arrangement, it is not common. Its problems are twofold. First, if goods are not exchanged simultaneously, one party ends up financing the other for a period. Second, firms engaged in barter run the risk of having to accept goods they do not want, cannot use, or have difficulty reselling at a reasonable price. For these reasons, barter is viewed as the most restrictive countertrade arrangement. It is primarily used for one-time-only deals in transactions with trading partners who are not creditworthy or trustworthy.

ANOTHER PERSPECTIVE

There's More Than One Type of Countertrade

Countertrades can take many forms, and there are several examples of how it works internationally. For instance in the early part of this decade, the Malaysian government bought 20 diesel electric locomotives from General Electric. Officials of the government said that GE will be paid with palm oil supplied by a plantation company. The company will supply about 200 000 metric tons of palm oil over a period of 30 months. This was GE's first barter deal for palm oil and palm products although its division GE Trading has several other countertrade agreements worldwide. No money changed hands, and no third parties were involved. As another example, in order to save foreign exchange reserves the Philippine government offered some creditors tinned tuna to repay part of a state $4 billion debt. In other examples General Motors Corporation sold $12 million worth of locomotive and diesel engines to Yugoslavia and took cash and $4 million in Yugoslavian cutting tools as payment.

Source: "Types of Counter Trade," *International Marketing*, January 10, 2011, www.citeman.com/13236-types-of-counter-trade.html.

COUNTERPURCHASE

Counterpurchase is a reciprocal buying agreement. It occurs when a firm agrees to purchase a certain amount of materials back from a country to which a sale is made. Suppose a Canadian firm sells some products to China. China pays the Canadian firm in dollars, but in exchange, the Canadian firm agrees to spend some of its proceeds from the sale on textiles produced by China. Thus, although China must draw on its foreign exchange reserves to pay the Canadian firm, it knows it will receive some of those dollars back because of the counterpurchase agreement. In one counterpurchase agreement, Rolls-Royce sold jet parts to Finland. As part of the deal, Rolls-Royce agreed to use some of the proceeds from the sale to purchase Finnish-manufactured TV sets that it would then sell in Great Britain.

OFFSET

Offset is similar to counterpurchase insofar as one party agrees to purchase goods and services with a specified percentage of the proceeds from the original sale. The difference is that this party can fulfill the obligation with any firm in the country to which the sale is being made. From an exporter's perspective, this is more attractive than a straight counterpurchase agreement because it gives the exporter greater flexibility to choose the goods that it wishes to purchase.

SWITCH TRADING

Switch trading refers to the use of a specialized third-party trading house in a countertrade arrangement. When a firm enters a counterpurchase or offset agreement with a country, it often ends up with what are called counterpurchase credits, which can be used to purchase goods from that country. Switch trading occurs when a third-party trading house buys the firm's counterpurchase credits and sells them to another firm that can better use them. For example, a Canadian firm concludes a counterpurchase agreement with Poland for which it receives some number of counterpurchase credits for purchasing Polish goods. The Canadian firm cannot use and does not want any Polish goods, however, so it sells the credits to a third-party trading house at a discount. The trading house finds a firm that can use the credits and sells them at a profit.

In one example of switch trading, Poland and Greece had a counterpurchase agreement that called for Poland to buy the same U.S.-dollar value of goods from Greece that it sold to Greece. However, Poland could not find enough Greek goods that it required, so it ended up with a dollar-denominated counterpurchase balance in Greece that it was unwilling to use. A switch trader bought the right to 250,000 counterpurchase dollars from Poland for $225,000 and sold them to a European grape merchant for $235,000, who used them to purchase sultana grapes from Greece.

BUYBACKS

A **buyback** occurs when a firm builds a plant in a country—or supplies technology, equipment, training, or other services to the country—and agrees to take a certain percentage of the plant's output as partial payment for the contract. For example, Occidental Petroleum negotiated a deal with Russia under which Occidental would build several ammonia plants in Russia and as partial payment receive ammonia over a 20-year period.

The Pros and Cons of Countertrade

Countertrade's main attraction is that it can give a firm a way to finance an export deal when other means are not available. Given the problems that many developing nations have in raising the foreign exchange necessary to pay for imports, countertrade may be the only option available when doing business in these countries. Even when countertrade is not the only option for structuring an export transaction, many countries prefer countertrade to cash deals. Thus, if a firm is unwilling to enter a countertrade agreement, it may lose an export opportunity to a competitor that is willing to make a countertrade agreement.

In addition, a countertrade agreement may be required by the government of a country to which a firm is exporting goods or services. Boeing often has to agree to counterpurchase agreements to capture orders for its commercial jet aircraft. For example, in exchange for gaining an order from Air India, Boeing may be required to purchase certain component parts, such as aircraft doors, from an Indian company. Taking this one step further, Boeing can use its willingness to enter into a counterpurchase agreement as a way of winning orders in the face of intense competition from its global rival, Airbus. Thus, for firms such as Boeing, countertrade can become a strategic marketing weapon.

However, the drawbacks of countertrade agreements are substantial. Other things being equal, firms would normally prefer to be paid in hard currency. Countertrade contracts may involve the exchange of unusable or poor-quality goods that the firm cannot dispose of profitably. For example, a few years ago, one U.S. firm got burned when 50 percent of the television sets it received in a countertrade agreement with Hungary were defective and could not be sold. In addition, even if the goods it receives are of high quality, the firm still needs to dispose of them profitably. To do this, countertrade requires the firm to invest in an in-house trading department dedicated to arranging and managing countertrade deals. This can be expensive and time consuming.

Given these drawbacks, countertrade is most attractive to large, diverse multinational enterprises that can use their worldwide network of contacts to dispose of goods acquired in countertrading. The masters of countertrade are Japan's giant trading firms, the *sogo shosha*, which use their vast networks of affiliated companies to profitably dispose of goods acquired through countertrade agreements. The trading firm of Mitsui & Company, for example, has about 120 affiliated companies in almost every sector of the manufacturing and service industries. If one of Mitsui's affiliates receives goods in a countertrade agreement that it cannot consume, Mitsui & Company will normally be able to find another affiliate that can profitably use them. Firms affiliated with one of Japan's *sogo shosha* often have a competitive advantage in countries where countertrade agreements are preferred.

North American firms that are large, diverse, and have a global reach (e.g., General Electric, Philip Morris, and 3M) have similar profit advantages from countertrade agreements. Indeed, 3M has established its own trading company—3M Global Trading, Inc.—to develop and manage the company's international countertrade programs. Unless there is no alternative, small- and medium-sized exporters should probably try to avoid countertrade deals because they lack the worldwide network of operations that may be required to profitably utilize or dispose of goods acquired through them.[19]

LO5 IMPLICATIONS FOR BUSINESS

As Crown corporations, EDC plays a vital role in providing export advisory and financial services to Canadian exporters. However, real risks remain in any global business dealings. For example, Canadian exporters frequently view developing countries as a source of the highest risk for non-payment on goods received, yet this is not always the case. The highest rate of defaults on commercial transactions for Canadian exporters comes from U.S. firms. The reasons are varied, but can include the fact that certain American importers are aware that, up to a certain dollar amount (for example $70,000), Canadian exporters will not consider litigation due to the cost of retaining an American lawyer and other expenses of following up in a U.S. court of law. In addition, the U.S. bankruptcy laws are more friendly (and quicker) to take advantage of than they are in Canada. Some U.S. business people might also know that the EDC has covered the loss of the Canadian exporter and thus feel a sense of quasi-entitlement to abscond without payment.

There are many warning signs that an exporter can experience in the transaction and post-transaction processes that might indicate that a deal is going to fall apart. For example, a Canadian shirt manufacturer might succeed in exporting its shirts to another country only to discover, after a period, that the importer wishes to change the current contract provisions. This should alert the Canadian exporter that the importer may be experiencing financial difficulties that could manifest in non-payment of shipped items. Extra vigilance and revision of terms of payment would be helpful.

If a company is eager to close a deal, it might consider barter as a business transaction tool. Barter is one of the oldest forms of exchanging one product (or service) with another deemed to be of equal value. During the era of the Soviet Union and in some cases today, where poor countries do not have the disposable hard currency (U.S. dollars) to pay for goods, barter continues to serve as a commercial instrument for buying and selling.

Once a deal is secured, there are still risks to be overcome. Accurate documentation is paramount during the export and import processes. If waybills between the importer and exporter fail to match up, the merchandise could be refused entry into a foreign country. It has happened that a detail, as seemingly insignificant as a missing comma, has scrapped an order. The buyer is not obliged to take delivery of orders where the paperwork does not match up. The foreign buyer could feasibly tell a Canadian exporter that it will accept the product rather than having it returned to Canada, at 10 cents on the dollar. Of course this would jeopardize long-term business relations between the two firms, yet it could, and does, happen.

Tied in with international trade norms are Incoterms, first formulated in Paris in 1936 by the International Chamber of Commerce. Incoterms are a set of international trading rules that determine the rights and obligations of buyers and sellers in international trade transactions. Without Incoterms, international trade would not be possible.

Key Terms

barter

bill of exchange

bill of lading

buyback

counterpurchase

countertrade

draft

export management company

Incoterms

letter of credit

offset

sight draft

sogo shosha

switch trading

time draft

LO Learning Objectives Summary

1. One big impediment to exporting is ignorance of foreign market opportunities. Neophyte exporters often become discouraged or frustrated with the exporting process because they encounter many problems, delays, and pitfalls.

2. The way to overcome ignorance is to gather information. In Canada, Foreign Affairs, Trade, and Development Canada can help firms gather information in the matchmaking process. EMCs can also help identify export opportunities. Many of the pitfalls associated with exporting can be avoided if a company hires an experienced EMC, or export consultant, and if it adopts the appropriate export strategy.

3. Firms engaged in international trade must do business with people they cannot trust and people who may be difficult to track down if they default on an obligation. Due to the lack of trust, each party to an international transaction has a different set of preferences regarding the configuration of the transaction. The problems arising from lack of trust between exporters and importers can be solved by using a third party that is trusted by both, normally a reputable bank. A letter of credit is issued by a bank at the request of an importer. It states that the bank promises to pay a beneficiary, normally the exporter, on presentation of documents specified in the letter. A draft is the instrument normally used in international commerce to effect payment. It is an order written by an exporter instructing an importer, or an importer's agent, to pay a specified amount of money at a specified time. Drafts are either sight drafts or time drafts. Time drafts are negotiable instruments. A bill of lading is issued to the exporter by the common carrier transporting the merchandise. It serves as a receipt, a contract, and a document of title.

4. Countertrade includes a range of barterlike agreements. It is primarily used when a firm exports to a country whose currency is not freely convertible and may lack the foreign exchange reserves required to purchase the imports. The main attraction of countertrade is that it gives a firm a way to finance an export deal when other means are not available. A firm that insists on being paid in hard currency may be at a competitive disadvantage vis-à-vis one that is willing to engage in countertrade. The main disadvantage of countertrade is that the firm may receive unusable or poor-quality goods that cannot be disposed of profitably.

5. Businesses should always be aware of the possibility of default. Accurate documentation is also important to any firm importing or exporting. Barter can be a useful tool in order to close a deal.

Critical Thinking and Discussion Questions

1. A firm based in British Columbia wants to export a shipload of finished lumber to the Philippines. The would-be importer cannot get sufficient credit from domestic sources to pay for the shipment but insists that the finished lumber can quickly be resold in the Philippines for a profit. Outline the steps the exporter should take to effect this export to the Philippines.

2. You are the assistant to the CEO of a small textile firm that manufactures high-quality, premium-priced, stylish clothing. The CEO has decided to see what the opportunities are for exporting and has asked you for advice as to the steps the company should take. What advice would you give the CEO?

3. An alternative to using a letter of credit is export credit insurance. What are the advantages and disadvantages of using export credit insurance rather than a letter of credit for exporting (a) a luxury yacht from California to Canada, and (b) machine tools from New York to Ukraine?

4. How do you explain the popularity of countertrade? Under what scenarios might its popularity increase still further by the year 2027? Under what scenarios might its popularity decline by 2027?

5. How might a company make strategic use of countertrade schemes as a marketing weapon to generate export revenues? What are the risks associated with pursuing such a strategy?

Research Task   globalEDGE™   globaledge.msu.edu

Use the globalEDGE™ site to complete the following exercises:

1. The Internet is rich with resources that provide guidance for companies that wish to expand their markets through exporting. GlobalEDGE provides links to these "tutorial" Web sites. Identify five of these sources and provide a description of the services available for new exporters through each of these sources.

2. Utilize the globalEDGE™ Glossary of International Business Terms to identify the definitions of the following exporting terms: air waybill, certificate of inspection, certificate of product origin, wharfage charge, and export broker.

CLOSING CASE

EMPIRE STEEL AND THE REUSE OF A SIEMENS PLANT

Hamilton has always been a town that was built around the steel industry, though the industry itself has changed dramatically over time. Stelco was founded in Hamilton in 1910, and continued in operation for almost 100 years, until it filed for bankruptcy in 2007 and was eventually purchased by U.S. Steel. The facility has not produced steel since 2010, and is effectively closed as of 2014.

Against this backdrop is the rise of the fifteen-year-old company Empire Steel, which started in Canada as a customer of ArcelorMittal Dofasco in Hamilton. The company's main business is selling flat rolled steel coils to the automotive, construction, and appliance manufacturing sectors in Europe and Africa. But the firm is moving away from simply shipping steel. In 2013, the company moved into 100 000 square feet of space in a former Siemens plant in Hamilton (Siemens left the City in 2011, taking 500 jobs with them). The Siemens facility has the heavy cranes, 65-foot-high ceilings, and access to rail and port facilities that are necessary for this steel company. Empire Steel plans to produce some manufactured steel products at its new facility as well. As the company notes, its areas of expertise include global steel trading, steel distribution and manufacturing, logistics, warehousing and distribution, supply chain management, and procurement.

In Empire's new expanded space its plans for the future are to do more than just buy and sell steel and steel products. It will provide logistics, storage, distribution, rail and container services to on-site clients as well as to distributors and manufacturers of all types. Ultimately, Empire Steel's mandate is to be the low-cost provider in every market that they serve. The fact that they are still in operation in 2017, in a tough industry, is a credit to the firm.

Sources: "Empire Steel is empire-building in Hamilton," *Hamilton Spectator*, May 16, 2013, http://www.thespec.com/news-story/2878027-empire-steel-is-empire-building-in-hamilton; "Rebirth of a Siemens Plant," *Bisnow*, November 14, 2013; and Empire Steel Inc. Web site, http://empiresteel.ca (accessed January 2014).

Case Discussion Questions

1. How can a company in a mature industry like the steel industry position itself for growth?

2. Despite the rise of the Canadians service economy, manufacturing still plays a part in the local economies of many cities across Canada. What can cities and provinces do to attract and retain manufacturing industries?

© Sarunyu L/Shutterstock

Chapter 14

Global Marketing, and Research and Development

OPENING CASE

GLOBAL BRANDING OF AVENGERS AND IRON MAN

In a global brand move, the post-credits to the original Iron Man movie had S.H.I.E.L.D. Director Nick Fury visit Tony Stark's home. Fury told Stark that Iron Man is not "the only superhero in the world," and says that he wants to discuss the "Avenger's Initiative."

The Avengers and Iron Man movie franchises have made billions of dollars for Marvel Studios, a television and motion picture studio that is part of the Walt Disney Company. They have also contributed heavily to making Robert Downey Jr. one of the highest paid actors in Hollywood. Robert Downey Jr. was born in 1965 in the United States. He made his movie debut at the age of 5 when he appeared in his father's movie titled Pound. The "up-and-down-and-up" career of Robert Downey Jr. is also a fascinating global brand story. He is riding high with three incredible multi-sequel franchises—Iron Man, The Avengers, and to a lesser degree Sherlock Holmes. But the focus here is on The Avengers and Iron Man.

Iron Man premiered April 30, 2008, in international markets and a few days later in the United States and Canada. Amazingly, the movie had been in development since 1990 at Universal Pictures, 20th Century Fox, and New Line Cinema. Marvel Studios reacquired the rights to the movie in 2006. The basic plot has playboy, philanthropist, and genius Tony Stark (played by Robert Downey Jr.) as the "superhero." Iron Man 2 was released in 2010 and Iron Man 3 was released in 2013, with plans for additional sequels after more Avengers movies.

The Avengers premiered on April 11, 2012, at the El Capitan Theatre in Hollywood. The film's development began in 2005, is based on the Marvel Comics superhero team with the same name, and was written and directed by Joss Whedon. The Avengers is a superhero team with familiar heroes such as Iron Man, Captain America, Hulk, Thor, Black Widow, Hawkeye, and so on. No one really plays the superhero, although Scarlett Johansson's role as Black Widow was important to the movie franchise; they set the release date back from 2011 to 2012 to accommodate her inclusion. The second installment of the Avengers franchise was released in 2015 (Avengers: Age of Ultron). A third Avengers is planned for a 2018 release.

While the movie character Iron Man is heavily connected to Robert Downey Jr., he also plays an integral part of Tony Stark in The Avengers. In doing so, Robert Downey Jr. has been part of Marvel Studios productions that have brought in more than $1.5 billion (The Avengers) and $1.2 billion (Iron Man 3). Iron Man 1 and Iron Man 2, respectively, made more than $600 million each as well. In total, Robert Downey Jr. has starred in six films that have made more than $500 million each at the box office worldwide.

Clearly, the connection between Tony Stark as Iron Man in the Iron Man franchise and in the Avengers franchise is perhaps not needed for the movie plot in The Avengers or its sequel. Marvel Comics has drawn from more than 100 characters for its Avengers superheroes since 1963, but Iron Man was one of the original ones (along with Ant-Man, the Wasp, Thor, and the Hulk). The global branding success of Tony Stark as played by Robert Downey Jr. across these two brands is also very advantageous for Marvel Studios' global branding.

Marvel Studios was originally known as Marvel Films from 1963 to 1996. It is an American TV and motion picture studio that is a part of Marvel Entertainment, a wholly owned subsidiary of The Walt Disney Company. Given that Marvel Studios is a part of the Walt Disney Empire, it operates jointly with Walt Disney Studios on distribution and marketing of Iron Man and Avengers movies. Other high-profile projects of Marvel Studios have included the X-Men, Spider-Man, and Captain America franchises, with more to come. Anything embedded in the global branding of The Walt Disney Company has tremendous potential, reach, and longevity.

Walter Elias "Walt" Disney was an American business mogul as well as animator, cartoonist, director, philanthropist, producer, screenwriter, and voice actor who lived from 1901 to 1966. An international icon, he started Disney Brothers Cartoon Studio in 1923. Disney has one of the largest and most well-known studios in the world. It also operates numerous related businesses, such as the ABC broadcast TV network, cable TV networks (e.g., Disney Channel, ESPN), publishing, merchandising, theatre divisions, theme parks (e.g., Disney World, Disneyland), and much more. Mickey Mouse is the primary symbol of The Walt Disney Company, and one of the most globally recognized brands ever.

Sources: K. Buchanan and J. Wolk, "How Vulture Ranked Its 2013 Most Valuable Stars List," *Vulture*, October 22, 2013; T. Culpan, "HTC Said to Hire Robert Downey Jr. for $12 Million Ad Campaign," *Bloomberg Businessweek*, June 20, 2013; C. Isidore, "Avengers Set to Rescue Disney and Hollywood," *CNNMoney*, May 7, 2012; "Iron Man 3: Clank Clank Bang Bang," *The Wall Street Journal*, May 2, 2013; http://marvel.com/universe/Iron_Man; and http://marvel.com/universe/Avengers.

LO LEARNING OBJECTIVES

By the end of this chapter you should be able to:

1. Explain why and how it may make sense to vary the attributes of a product among countries.

2. Describe why and how a firm's distribution strategy might vary among countries.

3. Illustrate why and how advertising and promotional strategies might vary among countries.

4. Summarize why and how a firm's pricing strategy might vary among countries.

5. Give examples of how the globalization of the world economy is affecting new-product development within international businesses.

Introduction

This chapter focuses on how marketing and research and development (R&D) can be performed in the international business so that they will reduce the costs of value creation and add value by better serving customer needs. In Chapter 11, we spoke of the tension existing in most international businesses between the needs to reduce costs and at the same time to respond to local conditions, which tends to raise costs. This tension continues to be a persistent theme in this chapter. A global marketing strategy that views the world's consumers as similar in their tastes and preferences is consistent with the mass production of a standardized output. By mass-producing a standardized output, the firm can realize substantial unit cost reductions from experience curve and other scale economies. But ignoring country differences in consumer tastes and preferences can lead to failure. Thus, an international business's marketing function needs to determine when product standardization is appropriate and when it is not, and to adjust the marketing strategy accordingly. Similarly, the firm's R&D function needs to be able to develop globally standardized products when appropriate as well as products customized to local requirements. We consider marketing and R&D within the same chapter because of their close relationship. A critical aspect of the marketing function is identifying gaps in the market so new products can be developed to fill those gaps. Developing new products requires R&D, which links marketing to R&D. New products should be developed with market needs in mind, and only marketing can define those needs for R&D personnel. Also, only marketing can tell R&D whether to produce globally standardized or locally customized products. Academic research has long maintained that a major factor of success for product introductions is the closeness of the relationship between marketing and R&D. The closer the linkage, the greater the success rate.[1]

In some way, the movie industry is becoming more and more standardized around the world, and the influence of the United States, via its strong film-making industry, on world culture is, in fact, making the globe more homogenous in customers' needs and wants (see the opening case). Such homogenization, especially of younger populations across developed and emerging nations, helps marketing professionals sell products and services globally. These days, it is commonplace to see a movie launched worldwide on the same day, whereas in the past movies were typically screened first in the United States and maybe in Canada, and then promoted region by region in the world in the weeks that followed. Interestingly, Iron Man premiered a few days earlier internationally than it did in the United States—such a launch pattern would seldom be seen with large-scale movies in the past. Globalization has increased the pressure on marketing to deliver on product quality and availability in a far-spanning way worldwide, with effective distribution strategies, appropriate communication strategies, and competitive pricing strategies.

We consider marketing and R&D within the same chapter because of their close relationship. A critical aspect of the marketing function is identifying gaps in the market so that the firm can develop new products to fill those gaps. Developing new products requires R&D—thus the linkage between marketing and R&D. A firm should develop new products with market needs in mind, and marketing is best suited to define those needs for R&D personnel given, among many things, its closeness to the market via front-line customer service personnel. Also, marketing personnel are well suited to communicate to R&D personnel whether to produce globally standardized or locally customized products. The reason marketing is so well positioned to communicate with R&D about (1) customer needs and wants and (2) degree of product standardization or customization needed is that the marketing function is responsible for the international marketing research that is conducted by the global company. Overall, our thinking here is in line with long-standing research that maintains that a major contributor to the success of new-product introductions is a close relationship between marketing and R&D.

In this chapter, we begin by reviewing the debate on the globalization of markets. Then we discuss the issue of market segmentation. Next we look at four elements that constitute a firm's **marketing mix**: product attributes, distribution strategy, communication strategy, and pricing strategy. The marketing mix is the set of choices the firm offers to its targeted markets. Many firms vary their marketing mix from country to country depending on differences in national culture, economic development, product standards, and distribution channels. The chapter closes with a look at new-product development in an international business and at the implications of this for the organization of the firm's R&D function.

The Globalization of Markets and Brands

In a now-famous *Harvard Business Review* article, the late Theodore Levitt wrote passionately about the globalization of world markets. Levitt's arguments have become something of a lightning rod in the debate about the extent of globalization. According to Levitt:

> A powerful force drives the world toward a converging commonalty, and that force is technology. It has proletarianized communication, transport, and travel. The result is a new commercial reality—the emergence of global markets for standardized consumer products on a previously unimagined scale of magnitude.

> Gone are accustomed differences in national or regional preferences. . . . The globalization of markets is at hand. With that, the multinational commercial world nears its end, and so does the multinational corporation. The multinational corporation operates in a number of countries and adjusts its products and practices to each—at high relative costs. The global corporation operates with resolute consistency—at low relative cost—as if the entire world were a single entity; it sells the same thing in the same way everywhere.

> Commercially, nothing confirms this as much as the success of McDonald's from the Champs Élysées to the Ginza, of Coca-Cola in Bahrain and Pepsi-Cola in Moscow, and of

rock music, Greek salad, Hollywood movies, Revlon cosmetics, Sony television, and Levi's jeans everywhere.

Ancient differences in national tastes or modes of doing business disappear. The commonalty of preference leads inescapably to the standardization of products, manufacturing, and the institutions of trade and commerce.[2]

This is eloquent and evocative writing, but is Levitt correct? The rise of global media such as MTV and CNN, and the ability of such media to help shape a global culture, would seem to lend weight to Levitt's argument. If Levitt is correct, his argument has major implications for the marketing strategies pursued by international business. However, the current consensus among academics seems to be that Levitt overstates his case.[3] Although Levitt may have a point when it comes to many basic industrial products, such as steel, bulk chemicals, and semiconductor chips, globalization seems to be the exception rather than the rule in many consumer goods markets and industrial markets. Even a firm such as McDonald's, which Levitt holds up as the archetypal example of a consumer products firm that sells a standardized product worldwide, modifies its menu from country to country in light of local consumer preferences.[4]

ANOTHER PERSPECTIVE

Toyota's Ambitious Plan for No. 1 Global Market

Yundong, or Cloud Action, is Toyota China's first-ever strategic plan for its business in China. China is the "most important" market in the world, but the Japanese carmaker has less than 10 percent of the auto market, far behind global rivals such as General Motors and Volkswagen. The auto giant aims to become a company "that is beyond consumers' expectations and creates happiness and fortune for consumers and the regions where it operates" emphasizing local responsiveness to Chinese customers, but still maintaining a global strategy. The Yundong plan combines the company's global strategy and local marketing operation, which will bring advanced technologies to the local market, improve the local management and marketing system, and build "exciting" products "that touch the hearts of Chinese consumers and are beyond their expectations," according to company officials. China is clearly an important market if Toyota is to maintain the overall world leadership in auto sales.

Source: Zhang Zhao, "Toyota's ambitious plan for No 1 global market," *China Daily*, 2012-03-05, www.chinadaily.com.cn/bizchina/2012-03/05/content_14757469.htm.

On the other hand, Levitt is probably correct to assert that modern transportation and communications technologies are facilitating a convergence of certain tastes and preferences among consumers in the more advanced countries of the world, and this has become even more prevalent since he wrote. The movie example in the opening case of this chapter highlights this convergence of tastes. In the long run, such technological forces may lead to the evolution of a global culture. At present, however, the continuing persistence of cultural and economic differences between nations acts as a brake on any trend toward the standardization of consumer tastes and preferences across nations. Indeed, that may never occur. Some writers have argued that the rise of global culture does not mean that consumers share the same tastes and preferences.[5] Rather, people in different nations, often with conflicting viewpoints, are increasingly participating in a shared "global" conversation, drawing upon shared symbols that include global brands from Nike and Dove to Coca-Cola

Shoppers around the world have responded to Quicksilver, a company whose products range from clothing to wet suits. Quicksilver uses similar marketing tactics regardless of where stores are located because the popularity of surfing and winter sports transcends international boundaries. © *Naruto4836/ Dreamstime.com*

and Sony. But the way in which these brands are perceived, promoted, and used still varies from country to country, depending on local differences in tastes and preferences. Furthermore, trade barriers and differences in product and technical standards also constrain a firm's ability to sell a standardized product to a global market using a standardized marketing strategy. We discuss the sources of these differences in subsequent sections when we look at how products must be altered from country to country. In short, Levitt's globally standardized market is some way off in many industries.

Market Segmentation

Market segmentation refers to identifying distinct groups of consumers whose purchasing behaviour differs from others in important ways. Markets can be segmented in numerous ways: by geography, demography (sex, age, income, race, education level, etc.), social-cultural factors (social class, values, religion, lifestyle choices), and psychological factors (personality). Because different segments exhibit different patterns of purchasing behaviour, firms often adjust their marketing mix from segment to segment. Thus, the precise design of a product, the pricing strategy, the distribution channels used, and the choice of communication strategy may all be varied from segment to segment. The goal is to optimize the fit between the purchasing behaviour of consumers in a given segment and the marketing mix, thereby maximizing sales to that segment. Automobile companies, for example, use a different marketing mix to sell cars to different socioeconomic segments. Thus, Toyota uses its Lexus division to sell high-priced luxury cars to high-income consumers, while selling its entry-level models, such as the Toyota Corolla, to lower-income consumers. Similarly, personal computer manufacturers will offer different computer models, embodying different combinations of product attributes and price points, precisely to appeal to consumers from different market segments (e.g., business users and home users).

When managers in an international business consider market segmentation in foreign countries, they need to be cognizant of two main issues: the differences between countries in the structure of market segments and the existence of segments that transcend national borders. The structure of market segments may differ significantly from country to country. An important market segment in a foreign country may have no parallel in the firm's home country, and vice versa. The firm may have to develop a marketing mix to appeal to the unique purchasing behaviour of a segment in a given country. For example, a research project identified a segment of 45-to-55-year-old consumers in China that has few parallels in other countries.[6] This group came of age during China's violent and repressive Cultural Revolution in the

MANAGEMENT FOCUS

Dove's Global "Real Beauty" Campaign

In 2003, Dove was not a beauty brand; it was a bar of soap that was positioned and sold differently in different markets. Unilever, the company that marketed Dove, was a consumer product multinational with global reach, had a strong position in fast-growing developing nations, and had a reputation for customizing products to conditions prevailing in local markets. In India, for example, women often oil their hair before washing it, so Western shampoos that do not remove the oil have not sold well. Unilever reformulated its shampoo for India and was rewarded with market leadership. But sometimes Unilever went too far. It used different formulations for shampoo in Hong Kong and mainland China, for example, even though hair and washing habits were very similar in both markets. Unilever would also often vary the packaging and marketing message in similar products, even for its most commoditized products. The company tended to exaggerate complexity, and by 2003 its financial performance was suffering.

A decade later, Unilever's financial performance has improved, in no small part because it has shifted toward a more global emphasis, and the Dove brand has led the way. The Dove story dates to 2003 when the global brand director, Sylvia Lagnado, who was based in New York, decided to move the positioning of Dove from one based on the product to one of an entire beauty brand. The basic message was that the brand should stand for the real beauty of all women. Dove's mission was to make women feel more beautiful every day by widening the stereotypical definition of beauty and inspiring them to take care of themselves.

But how was this mission to be executed? Following a series of workshops held around the globe that asked brand managers and advertising agency partners to find ways to communicate an inclusive definition of beauty, the Canadian brand manager asked 67 female photographers to submit work that best reflects real beauty. The photographs were not portraits of models, but of women from all walks of life who come in all shapes, sizes, and ages. It led to a coffee table book and travelling exhibition, called the Dove Photo Tour, which garnered a lot of positive press in Canada. Sylvia Lagnado realized that the Canadians were on to something. Around the same time, the German office of Unilever's advertising agency, Ogilvy and Mather Worldwide, came up with a concept for communicating "real beauty" based on photographs showing, instead of skinny models, ordinary women in their underwear. The original German advertisements quickly made their way to the United Kingdom, where a London newspaper article stated the campaign was not advertising; it was politics. Lagnado was not surprised by this. She had commissioned research that revealed only 2 percent of women worldwide considered themselves beautiful, and that half thought their weight was too high.

In 2004, the "Dove Campaign for Real Beauty" was launched globally. This was a radical shift for Unilever and the Dove brand, which until then had left marketing in the hands of local brand managers.

In Canada, the campaign opened with billboard "tick box" advertisements on real women in their underwear that invited people to call a toll-free number and vote on provocative tickers, such as "Fat/Fabulous?" The votes were tallied and displayed in real time on the billboards. This created a huge buzz, and the technique was quickly adopted in other markets, including the United States. As the campaign gained traction and a positive groundswell of media attention occurred (in the United States, for example, the Dove Women were invited to Oprah Winfrey's TV talk show), Unilever soon extended the Dove product line to include skin creams, shampoos, and shower gels. In 2005, the campaign was followed by the launch of the Dove "self-esteem fund," a worldwide campaign to persuade girls and young women to embrace a more positive image of themselves. Unilever also made an online video, loaded onto YouTube, called "Onslaught," which was critical of the beauty industry and ended with the slogan "Talk to your daughter before the beauty industry does." Another video, "Evolution," showed how the face of a girl can be changed, partly through computer graphics, to create an image of beauty. The video ended with the tag line "No wonder our perception of beauty is distorted." Made for very little money, the YouTube videos created a viral buzz around the campaign that helped to transform Dove into one of Unilever's leading brands. By its use of such techniques, the campaign has become a model for how to revitalize and build a new global brand. Today, more than a decade later, the campaign has broadened to include in Canada the "Beauty Bias" campaign and the "My Beauty, My Say" campaigns.

Questions

1. How do companies define their "social mission"? Is it the same throughout the world?
2. What do you think the impact may be of the Dove campaign on Unilever's other products, which include AXE body products, Ponds cremes, and Sunsilk hair products.

Sources: "The Legacy That Got Left on the Shelf," *The Economist,* February 2, 2008, pp. 77–79; R. Rothenberg, "Dove Effort Gives Package-Goods Marketers Lessons for the Future," *Advertising Age,* March 5, 2007, p. 18; J. Neff, "A Real Beauty: Dove's Viral Makes Big Splash for No Cash," *Advertising Age,* 2006, pp. 1–2; K. Mazurkewich, "Dove Story: You Know the Name, and Some of the Story," *Strategy,* January 2007, pp. 37–39; https://www.dove.com/us/en/stories/about-dove/dove-self-esteem-project.html; http://www.dove.com/ca/en/stories/campaigns.html (accessed January 2014); and http://www.dove.com/ca/en/home.html.

late 1960s and early 1970s. The values of this group have been shaped by their experiences during the Cultural Revolution. They tend to be highly sensitive to price and respond negatively to new products and most forms of marketing. The existence of this group implies that firms doing business in China may need to customize their marketing mix to address the unique values and purchasing behaviour of the group. The existence of such a segment constrains the ability of firms to standardize their global marketing strategy.

In contrast, the existence of market segments that transcends national borders clearly enhances the ability of an international business to view the global marketplace as a single entity and pursue a global strategy, selling a standardized product worldwide and using the same basic marketing mix to help position and sell that product in a variety of national markets. For a segment to transcend national borders, consumers in that segment must have some compelling similarities along important dimensions—such as age, values, lifestyle choices—and those similarities must translate into similar purchasing behaviour. Although such segments exist in certain industrial markets, they are rare in consumer markets. However, one emerging global segment that is attracting the attention of international marketers of consumer goods is the so-called global youth segment. Global media are paving the way for a global youth segment. Evidence that such a segment exists comes from a study of the cultural attitudes and purchasing behaviour of more than 6500 teenagers in 26 countries.[7] The findings suggest that teens around the world are increasingly living parallel lives that share many common values. It follows that they are likely to purchase the same kind of consumer goods and for the same reasons. Even here though, marketing specialists argue that some customization in the marketing mix is required.

LO1 | Product Attributes

A product can be viewed as a bundle of attributes.[8] For example, the attributes that make up a car include power, design, quality, performance, fuel consumption, and comfort; the attributes of a hamburger include taste, texture, and size; a hotel's attributes include atmosphere, quality, comfort, and service. Products sell well when their attributes match consumer needs (and when their prices are appropriate). BMW cars sell well to people who have high needs for luxury, quality, and performance, precisely because BMW builds those attributes into its cars. If consumer needs were the same the world over, a firm could simply sell the same product worldwide. However, consumer needs vary from country to country depending on culture and the level of economic development. A firm's ability to sell the same product worldwide is further constrained by countries' differing product standards. In this section, we review each of these issues and discuss how they influence product attributes.

Cultural Differences

We discussed countries' cultural differences in Chapter 3. Countries differ along a whole range of dimensions, including social structure, language, religion, and education. And as alluded to in Chapter 3, these differences have important implications for marketing strategy. For example, "hamburgers" do not sell well in Islamic countries, where the consumption of ham is forbidden by Islamic law. The most important aspect of cultural differences is probably the impact of tradition. Tradition is particularly important in foodstuffs and beverages. For example, reflecting differences in traditional eating habits, the Findus frozen food division of Nestlé, the Swiss food giant, markets fish cakes and fish fingers in Great Britain, but beef bourguignon and coq au vin in France and vitéllo con funghi and braviola in Italy. In addition to its normal range of products, Coca-Cola in Japan markets Georgia, a cold coffee in a can, and Aquarius, a tonic drink, both of which appeal to traditional Japanese tastes.

For historical and idiosyncratic reasons, a range of other cultural differences exist between countries. For example, scent preferences differ from one country to another. S. C. Johnson Wax, a manufacturer of waxes and polishes, encountered resistance to its lemon-scented Pledge furniture polish among older consumers in Japan. Careful market research revealed that the polish smelled similar to a latrine disinfectant used widely in Japan in the 1940s. Sales rose sharply after the scent was adjusted.[9] In another example, Cheetos, the bright orange and cheesy-tasting snack from PepsiCo's Frito-Lay unit, do not have a cheese taste in China. Chinese consumers generally do not like the taste of cheese because it has never been part of traditional cuisine and because many Chinese are lactose-intolerant.[10]

There is some evidence of the trends Levitt talked about. Tastes and preferences are becoming more cosmopolitan. Coffee is gaining ground against tea in Japan and Great Britain, while American-style frozen dinners have become popular in Europe (with some fine-tuning to local tastes). Taking advantage of these trends, Nestlé has found that it can market its instant coffee, spaghetti bolognese, and Lean Cuisine frozen dinners in essentially the same manner in both North America and Western Europe. However, there is no market

Tastes and preferences vary from country to country. To suit its global customers, Coca-Cola has a wide variety of products, such as Georgia, which is sold in Japan.
© *Junkgirl/Dreamstime.com*

for Lean Cuisine dinners in most of the rest of the world, and there may not be for years or decades. Although some cultural convergence has occurred, particularly among the advanced industrial nations of North America and Western Europe, Levitt's global culture is still a long way off.

Economic Development

Just as important as differences in culture are differences in the level of economic development. We discussed the extent of country differences in economic development in Chapter 2. Consumer behaviour is influenced by the level of economic development of a country. Firms based in highly developed countries such as Canada and the United States tend to build a lot of extra performance attributes into their products. These extra attributes are not usually demanded by consumers in less-developed nations, where the preference is for more basic products. Thus, cars sold in less developed nations typically lack many of the features found in the West, such as air-conditioning, power steering, power windows, radios, and CD players. For most consumer durables, product reliability may be a more important attribute in less developed nations, where such a purchase may account for a major proportion of a consumer's income, than it is in advanced nations.

Contrary to Levitt's suggestions, consumers in the most-developed countries are often not willing to sacrifice their preferred attributes for lower prices. Consumers in the most advanced countries often shun globally standardized products that have been developed with the lowest common denominator in mind. They are willing to pay more for products that have additional features and attributes customized to their tastes and preferences. For example, demand for top-of-the-line four-wheel-drive sport utility vehicles—such as Chrysler's Jeep, Ford's Explorer, and Toyota's Land Cruiser—has been largely restricted to the United States. This is due to a combination of factors, including the high income level of U.S. consumers, the country's vast distances, the relatively low cost of gasoline, and the culturally grounded "outdoor" theme of American life.

Product and Technical Standards

Even with the forces that are creating some convergence of consumer tastes and preferences among advanced, industrialized nations, Levitt's vision of global markets may still be a long way off because of national differences in product and technological standards.

Differing government-mandated product standards can rule out mass production and marketing of a standardized product. Differences in technical standards also constrain the globalization of markets. Some of these differences result from idiosyncratic decisions made long ago, rather than from government actions, but their long-term effects are profound. For example, DVD equipment manufactured for sale in the United States will not play DVDs recorded on equipment manufactured for sale in Great Britain, Germany, and France (and vice versa). Different technical standards for television signal frequency emerged in the 1950s that require television and video equipment to be customized to prevailing standards. RCA stumbled in the 1970s when it failed to account for this in its marketing of TVs in Asia. Although several Asian countries adopted the U.S. standard, Singapore, Hong Kong, and Malaysia adopted the British standard. People who bought RCA TVs in those countries could receive a picture but no sound![11]

LO2 | Distribution Strategy

A critical element of a firm's marketing mix is its distribution strategy: the means it chooses for delivering the product to the consumer. The way the product is delivered is determined by the firm's entry strategy, which we discussed in Chapter 12. In this section, we examine a typical distribution system, discuss how its structure varies between countries, and look at how appropriate distribution strategies vary from country to country.

A Typical Distribution System

Figure 14.1 illustrates a typical distribution system consisting of a channel that includes a wholesale distributor and a retailer. If the firm manufactures its product in the particular country, it can sell directly to the consumer, to the retailer, or to the wholesaler. The same options are available to a firm that manufactures outside the country. Plus, this firm may decide to sell to an import agent, which then deals with the wholesale distributor, the retailer, or the consumer. The factors that determine the firm's choice of channel are considered later in this section.

Differences Between Countries

The three main differences between distribution systems are retail concentration, channel length, and channel exclusivity.

RETAIL CONCENTRATION

In some countries, the retail system is very concentrated, but it is fragmented in others. In a **concentrated retail system**, a few retailers supply most of the market. A **fragmented retail system** is one in which there are many retailers, no one of which has a major share of the market. Many of the differences in concentration are rooted in history and tradition. In Canada and the United States, the importance of the

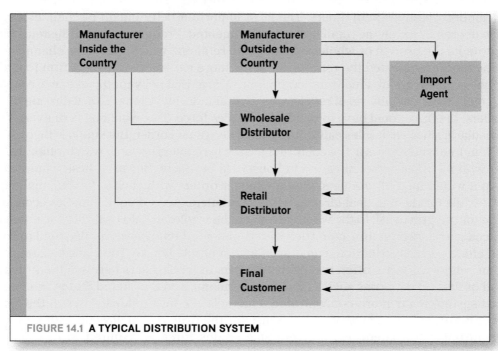

FIGURE 14.1 **A TYPICAL DISTRIBUTION SYSTEM**

automobile and the relative youth of many urban areas have resulted in a retail system centred around large stores or shopping malls to which people can drive. This has facilitated system concentration. Japan's much greater population density together with the large number of urban centres that grew up before the automobile have yielded a more fragmented retail system of many small stores that serve local neighbourhoods and to which people frequently walk. In addition, the Japanese legal system protects small retailers. Small retailers can block the establishment of a large retail outlet by petitioning their local government.

There is a tendency for greater retail concentration in developed countries. Three factors that contribute to this are the increases in car ownership, number of households with refrigerators and freezers, and number of two-income households. All these factors have changed shopping habits and facilitated the growth of large retail establishments sited away from traditional shopping areas. During the last decade there has been a tendency for consolidation in the global retail industry, with companies such as Wal-Mart and Carrefour asserting their positions as global retailers by acquiring retailers in different countries. This has continually increased retail concentration. In contrast, retail systems are very fragmented in many developing countries, which can make for interesting distribution challenges. In India, for example, Unilever has to sell to retailers in 600 000 rural villages, many of which cannot be accessed via paved roads, which means that products can reach their destination only by bullock, bicycle, or cart. In neighbouring Nepal, the terrain is so rugged that even bicycles and carts are not practical, and businesses rely on yak trains and the human back to deliver products to thousands of small retailers.

CHANNEL LENGTH

Channel length refers to the number of intermediaries between the producer (or manufacturer) and the consumer. If the producer sells directly to the consumer, the channel is very short. If the producer sells through an import agent, a wholesaler, and a retailer, a long channel exists. The choice of a short or long channel is in part a strategic decision for the producing firm. However, some countries have longer distribution channels than others. The most important determinant of channel length is the degree to which the retail system is fragmented. Fragmented retail systems tend to promote the growth of wholesalers to serve retailers, which lengthens channels.

The more fragmented the retail system, the more expensive it is for a firm to make contact with each individual retailer. Imagine a firm that sells toothpaste in a country with more than a million small retailers, as in rural India and China. To sell directly to the retailers, the firm would have to build a huge sales force. This would be very expensive, particularly since each sales call would yield a very small order. But suppose there are a few hundred wholesalers in the country that supply retailers not only with toothpaste but also with all other personal care and household products. Because these wholesalers carry a wide range of products, they get bigger orders with each sales call, making it worthwhile for them to deal directly with the retailers. Accordingly, it makes economic sense for the firm to sell to the wholesalers and the wholesalers to deal with the retailers.

Because of such factors, countries with fragmented retail systems also tend to have long channels of distribution, sometimes with multiple layers. The classic example is Japan, where there are often two or three layers of wholesalers between the firm and retail outlets. In countries such as Canada, Germany, and the United States, where the retail system is far more concentrated, channels are much shorter. When the retail sector is very concentrated, it makes sense for the firm to deal directly with retailers, cutting out wholesalers. A relatively small sales force is required to deal with a concentrated retail sector, and the orders generated from each sales call can be large.

Such circumstances tend to prevail in the United States, where large food companies sell directly to supermarkets rather than going through wholesale distributors.

The rapid development of the Internet in recent years has helped to shorten channel length. For example, the Seattle-based outdoor equipment retailer REI sells its products in Japan via a Japanese-language Web site, thereby cutting out the need for a retail presence on the ground in Japan, which obviously shortens the channel length between REI and its customers. However, there are obvious drawbacks with such a strategy. In the case of REI, it is not possible to offer the same level of advice over the Internet as it is in physical retail stores, where salespeople can help customers choose the right gear. So although REI benefits from a short channel in Japan, it may lose significant sales due to the lack of point-of-sale service.

CHANNEL EXCLUSIVITY

An **exclusive distribution channel** is one that is difficult for outsiders to access. For example, new firms often have trouble getting access to shelf space in supermarkets. This occurs because retailers tend to prefer to carry the products of long-established manufacturers of foodstuffs with national reputations rather than gamble on the products of unknown firms. The exclusivity of a distribution system varies between countries. Japan's system is often held up as an example of a very exclusive system. In Japan, relationships between manufacturers, wholesalers, and retailers often go back decades. Many of these relationships are based on the understanding that distributors will not carry the products of competing firms. In return, the distributors are guaranteed an attractive markup by the manufacturer. As many U.S. and European manufacturers have learned, the close ties that result from this arrangement can make access to the Japanese market very difficult.

Choosing a Distribution Strategy

The choice of distribution strategy determines which channel the firm will use to reach potential consumers. Should the firm try to sell directly to the consumer or should it go through retailers? Should it go through a wholesaler? Should it use an import agent? The optimal strategy is determined by the relative costs and benefits of each alternative.

DEBATE THE ISSUE

Is the Google Advertising Model Viable in the Long Term?

Google's share of Internet ads is at about 33 percent of the $117 billion market, making it the undisputed Goliath of online advertising. Google also continues to grow thanks to acquisitions like DoubleClick, YouTube, and even drone company Titan Aerospace. Facebook is solidly in the number 2 spot in Internet ads but is gaining market share (it has about 5 percent of the online ad market). Google is also a heavyweight in mobile ads with about 56 percent of the $16 billion market (Facebook has about 13 percent of this market). Research experts predict that new ad dollars will come from emerging markets such as China, Russia, and Indonesia. Over the next three years, about half of all global ad growth will come from ten developing markets—with Brazil, Russia, India, and China combined accounting for 33 percent. Currently, there are four markets in which Internet ads account for more than 30 percent of total spending: Canada, Norway, Sweden, and the United Kingdom. Basically, the world is shifting its ad spending to the Internet and similar options. With that in mind, where can global companies reach you via advertisements if they wanted to target you? And, do you think the Google advertisement business model is viable as a way to reach customers for the long term?

Source: A. Efrati, "In Online Ads, There's Google—and Then Everybody Else," *The Wall Street Journal*, June 13, 2013.

The relative costs and benefits of each alternative vary from country to country, depending on the three factors we have just discussed: retail concentration, channel length, and channel exclusivity.

Because each intermediary in a channel adds its own markup to the products, there is generally a critical link between channel length, the final selling price, and the firm's profit margin. The longer a channel, the greater is the aggregate markup, and the higher the price that consumers are charged for the final product. To ensure that prices do not get too high due to markups by multiple intermediaries, a firm might be forced to operate with lower profit margins. Thus, if price is an important competitive weapon, and if the firm does not want to see its profit margins squeezed, the firm would prefer to use a shorter channel.

ANOTHER PERSPECTIVE

Spotify and Coca-Cola Form Marketing Partnership

Swedish music-streaming service Spotify gains access to Coca-Cola's global marketing engine, and Coca-Cola can use Spotify tunes in its online marketing. Spotify is hoping that Coke will teach the world to click its play button. The Swedish digital music service on Wednesday announced a broad-ranging marketing deal with Coca-Cola Co. that could help turbocharge the number of people who are exposed to, and ultimately sign up for, Spotify. Although the partnership does not involve any money changing hands, both parties describe it as invaluable to their efforts to market their products. For Spotify, getting access to Coca-Cola's formidable global marketing engine will come in handy as it expands its international footprint. In return, Coca-Cola can now use Spotify's service to instantly add music to its online marketing repertoire. For instance, the drink giant can add songs to its Facebook page via Spotify without having to negotiate licences for each tune. (Spotify already has financial agreements with major record labels to pay royalties for every song that is played on its digital service.)

Source: A. Pham, "Spotify and Coca-Cola Form Marketing Partnership," *Los Angeles Times*, April 18, 2012. Copyright © 2012. Los Angeles Times. Reprinted with permission. http://articles.latimes.com/2012/apr/18/business/la-fi-ct-spotify-coca-cola-20120419

However, the benefits of using a longer channel often outweigh these drawbacks. As we have seen, one benefit of a longer channel is that it cuts selling costs when the retail sector is very fragmented. Thus, it makes sense for an international business to use longer channels in countries where the retail sector is fragmented and shorter channels in countries where the retail sector is concentrated. Another benefit of using a longer channel is market access—the ability to enter an exclusive channel. Import agents may have long-term relationships with wholesalers, retailers, and/or important consumers and thus be better able to win orders and get access to a distribution system. Similarly, wholesalers may have long-standing relationships with retailers and be better able to persuade them to carry the firm's product than the firm itself would.

Import agents are not limited to independent trading houses; any firm with a strong local reputation could serve as well. For example, to break down channel exclusivity and gain greater access to the Japanese market, when Apple Computer originally entered Japan it signed distribution agreements with five large Japanese firms, including business equipment giant Brother Industries, stationery leader Kokuyo, Mitsubishi, Sharp, and Minolta. These firms used their own long-established distribution relationships with consumers, retailers, and wholesalers to push Apple computers through the Japanese distribution system. Today, Apple has supplemented this strategy with its own stores in the country.

If such an arrangement is not possible, the firm might want to consider other, less traditional alternatives to gaining market access. Frustrated by channel exclusivity in Japan, some foreign manufacturers of consumer goods have attempted to sell directly to Japanese consumers using direct mail and catalogues. REI had trouble persuading Japanese wholesalers and retailers to carry its products, so it began a direct-mail campaign and then a Internet-based strategy to enter Japan that is proving very successful.

LO3 | Communication Strategy

Another critical element in the marketing mix is communicating the attributes of the product to prospective customers. A number of communication channels are available to a firm, including direct selling, sales promotion, direct marketing, and advertising. A firm's communication strategy is partly defined by its choice of channel. Some firms rely primarily on direct selling, others on point-of-sale promotions or direct marketing, others on mass advertising; still others use several channels simultaneously to communicate their message to prospective customers. In this section, we will look first at the barriers to international communication. Then we will survey the various factors that determine which communication strategy is most appropriate in a particular country. After that we discuss global advertising.

Barriers to International Communication

International communication occurs whenever a firm uses a marketing message to sell its products in another country. The effectiveness of a firm's international communication can be jeopardized by three potentially critical variables: cultural barriers, source effects, and noise levels.

CULTURAL BARRIERS

Cultural barriers can make it difficult to communicate messages across cultures. We discussed some sources and consequences of cultural differences between nations in Chapter 3 and in the previous section of this chapter. Due to cultural differences, a message that means one thing in one country may mean something quite different in another. In a TV commercial, a Japanese man walked into the bathroom while his wife was bathing. The woman began telling her husband all about her new soap, but the husband, stroking her shoulder, hinted that suds were not on his mind. This ad had been very popular in Europe, but it flopped in Japan because it is considered very bad manners there for a man to intrude on his wife.[12] Benetton, the Italian clothing manufacturer and retailer, is another firm that has run into cultural problems with its advertising. The company launched a worldwide advertising campaign with the theme "United Colours of Benetton" that had won awards in France. One of its ads featured a black woman breast-feeding a white baby, and another one showed a black man and a white man handcuffed together. Benetton was surprised when the ads were attacked by U.S. civil rights groups for promoting white racial domination. Benetton withdrew its ads and fired its advertising agency, Eldorado of France.

The best way for a firm to overcome cultural barriers is to develop cross-cultural literacy (see Chapter 3). In addition, it should use local input, such as a local advertising agency, in developing its marketing message. If the firm uses direct selling rather than advertising to communicate its message, it should develop a local sales force whenever possible. Cultural differences limit a firm's ability to use the same marketing message and selling approach the world over. What works well in one country may be offensive in another.

SOURCE AND COUNTRY OF ORIGIN EFFECTS

Source effects occur when the receiver of the message (the potential consumer in this case) evaluates the message based on the status or image of the sender. Source effects can be damaging for an international business when potential consumers in a target country have a bias against foreign firms. For example, a wave of "Japan bashing" swept the United States in the early 1990s. Worried that U.S. consumers might view its products negatively, Honda responded by creating ads that emphasized the U.S. content of its cars to show how "American" the company had become. Many international businesses try to counter negative source effects by de-emphasizing their foreign origins. When British Petroleum acquired Mobil Oil's extensive network of U.S. gas stations, it changed its name to BP, diverting attention away from the fact that one of the biggest operators of gas stations in the United States is a British firm.

A subset of source effects is referred to as **country of origin effects**. Country of origin effects refers to the extent to which the place of manufacture influences product evaluations. Research suggests that country of origin is often used as a cue when evaluating a product, particularly if the consumer lacks more detailed knowledge of the product. For example, one study found that Japanese consumers tended to rate Japanese products more favourably than U.S. products across multiple dimensions, even when independent analysis showed that they were actually inferior.[13] When a negative country of origin effect exists, an international business may have to work hard to counteract this effect by, for example, using promotional messages that stress the positive performance attributes of the product. Thus, the Korean automobile company Hyundai tried to overcome negative perceptions about the quality of its vehicle in the United States by running advertisements that favourably compare the company's cars to more prestigious brands.

Source effects and country of origin effects are not always negative. French wine, Italian clothes, and German luxury cars benefit from nearly universal positive source effects. In such cases, it may pay a firm to emphasize its foreign origins. In Japan, for example, there is strong demand for high-quality foreign goods, particularly those from Europe. It has become chic to carry a Gucci handbag, sport a Rolex watch, drink expensive French wine, and drive a BMW.

NOISE LEVELS

Noise tends to reduce the probability of effective communication. **Noise** refers to the amount of other messages competing for a potential consumer's attention, and this too varies across countries. In highly developed countries such as Canada and the United States, noise is extremely high. Fewer firms vie for the attention of prospective customers in developing countries, and the noise level is lower.

Push versus Pull Strategies

The main decision with regard to communications strategy is the choice between a push strategy and a pull strategy. A **push strategy** emphasizes personal selling rather than mass media advertising in the promotional mix. Although very effective as a promotional tool, personal selling requires intensive use of a sales force and is relatively costly. A **pull strategy** depends more on mass media advertising to communicate the marketing message to potential consumers.

Although some firms employ only a pull strategy and others only a push strategy, still other firms combine direct selling with mass advertising to maximize communication effectiveness. Factors that determine the relative attractiveness of push and pull strategies include product type relative to consumer sophistication, channel length, and media availability.

PRODUCT TYPE AND CONSUMER SOPHISTICATION

A pull strategy is generally favoured by firms in consumer goods industries that are trying to sell to a large segment of the market. For such firms, mass communication has cost advantages, and direct selling is rarely used. An exception to this rule can be found in poorer nations with low literacy levels, where direct selling may be the only way to reach consumers. A push strategy is favoured by firms that sell industrial products or other complex products. Direct selling allows the firm to educate potential consumers about the features of the product. This may not be necessary in advanced nations where a complex product has been in use for some time, where the product's attributes are well understood, and where consumers are sophisticated. However, customer education may be very important when consumers have less sophistication toward the product, which can be the case in developing nations or in advanced nations when a complex product is being introduced.

CHANNEL LENGTH

The longer the distribution channel, the more intermediaries there are that must be persuaded to carry the product for it to reach the consumer. This can lead to inertia in the channel, which can make entry very difficult. Using direct selling to push a product through many layers of a distribution channel can be very expensive. In such circumstances, a firm may try to pull its product through the channels by using mass advertising to create consumer demand—once demand is created, intermediaries will feel obliged to carry the product.

ANOTHER PERSPECTIVE

The Four Ps

The marketing mix is often referred to as the four Ps. These refer to the main ingredients that a firm uses to define its product. They are:

Price: What price will the item sell at. How is it determined? Will it be the same in all markets?

Product: What are you selling? What are its attributes? Are they the same everywhere that the product is being sold?

Promotion: How will people find out about your product and its unique features?

Place: Where will your product be sold? Where in the world will it be sold? What types of stores will it be sold in?

In Japan, products often pass through two, three, or even four wholesalers before they reach the final retail outlet. This can make it difficult for foreign firms to break into the Japanese market. Not only must the foreigner persuade a Japanese retailer to carry her product, but she may also have to persuade every intermediary in the chain to carry the product. Mass advertising may be one way to break down channel resistance in such circumstances. However, in countries such as India, which has a very long distribution channel to serve its massive rural population, low literacy levels may imply that mass advertising may not work, in which case, the firm may need to fall back on direct selling, or rely on the goodwill of distributors.

MEDIA AVAILABILITY

A pull strategy relies on access to advertising media. In Canada and the United States, a large number of media are available, including print media (newspapers and magazines), broadcasting media (television and radio), and the Internet. For example, the rise of cable television in the United States facilitated extremely focused advertising (e.g., MTV for teens and young adults, ESPN for sports enthusiasts). The same is true of the Internet, given that different sites attract different kinds of users. While this level of media sophistication is found in some other developed countries, it is not universal. Many other advanced nations have far fewer electronic media available for advertising than Canada and the United States. In Scandinavia, for example, no commercial television or radio stations existed in 1987; all electronic media were state owned and carried no commercials, although this has now changed with the advent of satellite television deregulation. In many developing nations, the situation is even more restrictive because mass media of all types are typically more limited. A firm's ability to use a pull strategy is limited in some countries by media availability. In such circumstances, a push strategy is more attractive.

Media availability is limited by law in some cases. Few countries allow advertisements for tobacco and alcohol products on television and radio, though they are usually permitted in print media. When the leading Japanese whiskey distiller, Suntory, entered the U.S. market, it had to do so without television, its preferred medium. The firm spends about $50 million annually on television advertising in Japan. Similarly, while advertising pharmaceutical products directly to consumers is allowed in the United States, it is prohibited in many other advanced nations. In such cases, pharmaceutical firms must rely heavily on advertising and direct-sales efforts focused explicitly at doctors to get their products prescribed.

PUSH OR PULL?

The optimal mix between push and pull strategies depends on product type and consumer sophistication, channel length, and media sophistication. Push strategies tend to be emphasized:

- for industrial products and/or complex new products;
- when distribution channels are short;
- when few print or electronic media are available.

Pull strategies tend to be emphasized:

- for consumer goods;
- when distribution channels are long;
- when sufficient print and electronic media are available to carry the marketing message.

Global Advertising

In recent years, largely inspired by the work of visionaries such as Theodore Levitt, there has been much discussion about the pros and cons of standardizing advertising worldwide.[14] One of the most successful standardized campaigns in history was Philip

Morris's promotion of Marlboro cigarettes. The campaign was instituted in the 1950s, when the brand was repositioned, to assure smokers that the flavour would be unchanged by the addition of a filter. The campaign theme of "Come to where the flavour is. Come to Marlboro country." was a worldwide success. Marlboro built on this when it introduced "the Marlboro man," a rugged cowboy smoking his Marlboro while riding his horse through the great outdoors. This ad proved successful in almost every major market around the world, and it helped propel Marlboro to the top in world market share.

ARGUMENTS FOR STANDARDIZED ADVERTISING

The support for global advertising is threefold. First, it has significant economic advantages. Standardized advertising lowers the costs of value creation by spreading the fixed costs of developing the advertisements over many countries. For example, Levi Strauss paid an advertising agency $550,000 to produce a series of TV commercials. By reusing this series in many countries rather than developing a series for each country, the company enjoyed significant cost savings. Similarly, Coca-Cola's advertising agency, McCann-Erickson, claims to have saved Coca-Cola $90 million over 20 years by using certain elements of its campaigns globally.

Second, there is the concern that creative talent is scarce and so one large effort to develop a campaign will produce better results than 40 or 50 smaller efforts. A third justification for a standardized approach is that many brand names are global (the Avengers and Iron Man franchises being good examples, see the opening case).

With the substantial amount of international travel today and the considerable overlap in media across national borders, many international firms want to project a single brand image to avoid confusion caused by local campaigns. This is particularly important in regions such as Western Europe, where travel across borders is almost as common as travel across state lines in the United States.

ARGUMENTS AGAINST STANDARDIZED ADVERTISING

There are two main arguments against globally standardized advertising. First, as we have seen repeatedly in this chapter and in Chapter 3, cultural differences between nations are such that a message that works in one nation can fail miserably in another. Due to cultural diversity, it is extremely difficult to develop a single advertising theme that is effective worldwide. Messages directed at the culture of a given country may be more effective than global messages.

Second, advertising regulations may block implementation of standardized advertising. For example, Kellogg could not use a television commercial it produced in Great Britain to promote its cornflakes in many other European countries. A reference to the iron and vitamin content of its cornflakes was not permissible in

Many global companies do not use standardized advertising because one message may have different meanings in different countries. For example, Kellogg's tag line "Kellogg's makes their cornflakes the best they have ever been," could not be used in Germany because of a prohibition against competitive claims. © *McGraw-Hill Education/John Thoeming*

the Netherlands, where claims relating to health and medical benefits are outlawed. A child wearing a Kellogg T-shirt had to be edited out of the commercial before it could be used in France, because French law forbids the use of children in product endorsements. The key line, "Kellogg's makes their cornflakes the best they have ever been," was disallowed in Germany because of a prohibition against competitive claims.[15] Similarly, American Express ran afoul of regulatory authorities in Germany when it launched a promotional scheme that had proved very successful in other countries. The scheme advertised the offer of "bonus points" every time American Express cardholders used their cards. According to the advertisements, these "bonus points" could be used toward air travel on three airlines and for hotel accommodations. American Express was charged with breaking Germany's competition law, which prevents an offer of free gifts in connection with the sale of goods, and the firm had to withdraw the advertisements at considerable cost.[16]

DEALING WITH COUNTRY DIFFERENCES

Some firms are experimenting with capturing some benefits of global standardization while recognizing differences in countries' cultural and legal environments. A firm may select some features to include in all its advertising campaigns and localize other features. By doing so, it may be able to save on some costs and build international brand recognition and yet customize its advertisements to different cultures.

Nokia, the Finnish cell phone manufacturer, has tried to do this. Historically, Nokia had used a different advertising campaign in different markets. A few years ago, however, the company launched a global advertising campaign that used the slogan "1001 reasons to have a Nokia imaging phone." Nokia did this to reduce advertising costs and capture some economies of scale. In addition, in an increasingly integrated world the company believes there is value in trying to establish a consistent global brand image. At the same time, Nokia tweaked the advertisements for different cultures. The campaign used actors from the region where the ad ran to reflect the local population, though they said the same lines. Local settings were also modified when showcasing the phones by, for example, using a marketplace when advertising in Italy or a bazaar when advertising in the Middle East.[17] Another example of this process is given in the Management Focus earlier in the chapter, which looks at how Unilever built a global brand for its Dove products, while still tweaking the message to consider local sensibilities.

LO4 | Pricing Strategy

International pricing strategy is an important component of the overall international marketing mix.[18] In this section, we look at three aspects of international pricing strategy. First, we examine the case for pursuing price discrimination, charging different prices for the same product in different countries. Second, we look at what might be called strategic pricing. Third, we review regulatory factors, such as government-mandated price controls and antidumping regulations, which limit a firm's ability to charge the prices it would prefer in a country.

Price Discrimination

Price discrimination exists whenever consumers in different countries are charged different prices for the same product.[19] Price discrimination involves charging whatever the market will bear; in a competitive market prices may have to be lower than in a market where the firm has a monopoly. Price discrimination can help a company maximize its profits. It makes economic sense to charge different prices in different countries.

Two conditions are necessary for profitable price discrimination. First, the firm must be able to keep its national markets separate. If it cannot do this, individuals or businesses may undercut its attempt at price discrimination by engaging in arbitrage. Arbitrage occurs when an individual or business capitalizes on a price differential for a firm's product between two countries by purchasing the product in the country where prices are lower and reselling it in the country where prices are higher. For example, many automobile firms have long practised price discrimination in Europe. A Ford Escort once cost $2000 more in Germany than it did in Belgium. This policy broke down when car dealers bought Escorts in Belgium and drove them to Germany, where they sold them at a profit for slightly less than Ford was selling Escorts in Germany. To protect the market share of its German auto dealers, Ford had to bring its German prices into line with those being charged in Belgium. Ford could not keep these markets separate.

However, Ford still practises price discrimination between Great Britain and Belgium. A Ford car can cost up to $3000 more in Great Britain than in Belgium. In this case, arbitrage has not been able to equalize the price, because right-hand-drive cars are sold in Great Britain and left-hand-drive cars in the rest of Europe. Because there is no market for left-hand-drive cars in Great Britain, Ford has been able to keep the markets separate.

The second necessary condition for profitable price discrimination is different price elasticities of demand in different countries. The **price elasticity of demand** is a measure of the responsiveness of demand for a product to changes in price. Demand is said to be **elastic** when a small change in price produces a large change in demand; it is said to be **inelastic** when a large change in price produces only a small change in demand. Figure 14.2 illustrates elastic and inelastic demand curves. Generally, for reasons that will be explained shortly, a firm can charge a higher price in a country where demand is inelastic.

THE DETERMINANTS OF DEMAND ELASTICITY

The elasticity of demand for a product in a given country is determined by a number of factors, of which income level and competitive conditions are the two most

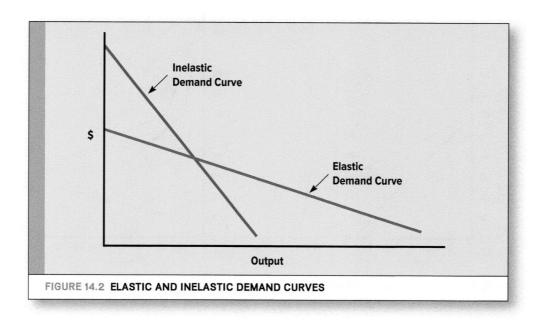

FIGURE 14.2 ELASTIC AND INELASTIC DEMAND CURVES

important. Price elasticity tends to be greater in countries with low income levels. Consumers with limited incomes tend to be very price conscious; they have less to spend, so they look much more closely at price. Thus, price elasticities for products such as television sets are greater in countries such as China, where a television set is still a luxury item, than in Canada and the United States, where it is considered a necessity.

In general, the more competitors there are, the greater consumers' bargaining power will be and the more likely consumers will be to buy from the firm that charges the lowest price. Thus, many competitors cause high elasticity of demand. In such circumstances, if a firm raises its prices above those of its competitors, consumers will switch to the competitors' products. The opposite is true when a firm faces few competitors. When competitors are limited, consumers' bargaining power is weaker and price is less important as a competitive weapon. Thus, a firm may charge a higher price for its product in a country where competition is limited than in a country where competition is intense.

MAXIMIZING PROFIT UNDER PRICE DISCRIMINATION

For those readers with some grasp of economic logic, we can offer a more formal presentation of the above argument. (Readers unfamiliar with basic economic terminology may want to skip this subsection.) Figure 14.3 shows the situation facing a firm that sells the same product in only two countries: Japan and the United States. The Japanese market is very competitive, so the firm faces an elastic demand curve (D_J) and marginal revenue curve (MR_J). The U.S. market is not competitive, so there the firm faces an inelastic demand curve (D_U) and marginal revenue curve (MR_U). Also shown in the figure are the firm's total demand curve (D_{J+U}), total marginal revenue curve (MR_{J+U}), and marginal cost curve (MC). The total demand curve is simply the summation of the demand facing the firm in Japan and the United States, as is the total marginal revenue curve.

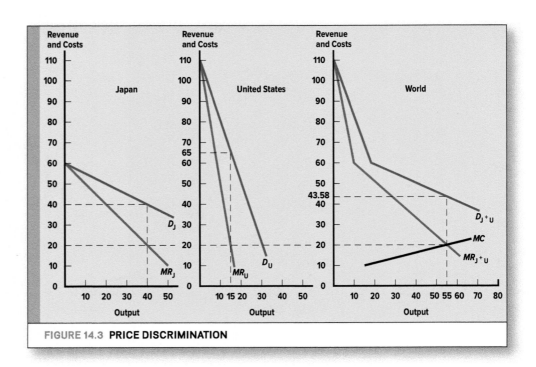

FIGURE 14.3 **PRICE DISCRIMINATION**

To maximize profits, the firm must produce at the output where MR = MC. In Figure 14.3, this implies an output of 55 units. If the firm does not practice price discrimination, it will charge a price of $43.58 to sell an output of 55 units. Thus, without price discrimination, the firm's total revenues are $43.58 × 55 = $2396.90.

That changes when the firm decides to engage in price discrimination. It will still produce 55 units, since that is where MR = MC. However, the firm must now allocate this output between the two countries to take advantage of the difference in demand elasticity. Proper allocation of output between Japan and the United States can be determined graphically by drawing a line through their respective graphs at $20 to indicate that $20 is the marginal cost in each country (see Figure 14.3). To maximize profits, prices are now set in each country at that level where the marginal revenue for that country equals marginal costs. In Japan, this is a price of $40, and the firm sells 40 units. In the United States, the optimal price is $65, and it sells 15 units. Thus, reflecting the different competitive conditions, the price charged in the United States is over 50 percent more than the price charged in Japan. Look at what happens to total revenues. With price discrimination, the firm earns revenues of

$$\$40 \times 40 \text{ units} = \$1600$$

in Japan and

$$\$65 \times 15 \text{ units} = \$975$$

in the United States. By engaging in price discrimination, the firm can earn total revenues of

$$\$1600 + \$975 = \$2575$$

which is $178.10 more than the $2396.90 it earned before. Price discrimination pays!

Strategic Pricing

The concept of **strategic pricing** uses price to gain a competitive advantage over rivals and has three aspects, which we will refer to as predatory pricing, multipoint pricing, and experience curve pricing. Both predatory pricing and experience curve pricing may violate antidumping regulations. After we review predatory and experience curve pricing, we will look at antidumping rules and other regulatory policies.

PREDATORY PRICING

Predatory pricing is the use of price as a competitive weapon to drive weaker competitors out of a national market. Once the competitors have left the market, the firm can raise prices and enjoy high profits. For such a pricing strategy to work, the firm must normally have a profitable position in another national market, which it can use to subsidize aggressive pricing in the market it is trying to monopolize. Many Japanese firms have been accused of pursuing such a policy. The argument runs like this: because the Japanese market is protected from foreign competition by high informal trade barriers, Japanese firms can charge high prices and earn high profits at home. They then use these profits to subsidize aggressive pricing overseas, with the goal of driving competitors out of those markets. Once this has occurred, so it is claimed, the Japanese firms then raise prices. Matsushita (now Panasonic Corporation) was accused of using this strategy to enter the U.S. TV market. As one of the major TV producers in Japan, Matsushita earned high profits at home. It then used these profits to subsidize the losses it made in the United States during its early years there, when it priced low to increase its market penetration. Ultimately, Matsushita became the world's largest manufacturer of TVs.[20]

MULTIPOINT PRICING STRATEGY

Multipoint pricing becomes an issue when two or more international businesses compete against each other in two or more national markets. For example, a historic example of multipoint pricing was the case of Kodak and Fuji Photo because both companies competed against each other in different national markets for film products around the world. **Multipoint pricing** refers to the fact that a firm's pricing strategy in one market may have an impact on its rivals' pricing strategies in another market. Aggressive pricing in one market may elicit a competitive response from a rival in another market. In the case of Kodak and Fuji, Fuji launched an aggressive competitive attack against Kodak in the American company's home market in January 1997, cutting prices on multiple-roll packs of 35mm film by as much as 50 percent.[21] This was at the end of the era of everyone photographing on film and printing every photo. This price cutting resulted in a 28 percent increase in shipments of Fuji colour film during the first six months of 1997, while Kodak's shipments dropped by 11 percent. This attack created a dilemma for Kodak; the company did not want to start price discounting in its largest and most profitable market. Kodak's response was to aggressively cut prices in Fuji's largest market, Japan. This strategic response recognized the interdependence between Kodak and Fuji and the fact that they compete against each other in many different nations. Fuji responded to Kodak's counterattack by pulling back from its aggressive stance in the United States.

The Kodak story illustrates an important aspect of multipoint pricing—aggressive pricing in one market may elicit a response from rivals in another market. The firm needs to consider how its global rivals will respond to changes in its pricing strategy before making those changes. A second aspect of multipoint pricing arises when two or more global companies focus on particular national markets and launch vigorous price wars in those markets in an attempt to gain market dominance. In the Brazil market for disposable diapers, two U.S. companies, Kimberly-Clark Corp. and Procter & Gamble, entered a price war as each struggled to establish dominance in the market.[22] As a result, the cost of disposable diapers fell from $1 per diaper in 1994 to 33 cents per diaper in 1997, while several other competitors, including indigenous Brazilian firms, were driven out of the market. Kimberly-Clark and Procter & Gamble are engaged in a global struggle for market share and dominance, and Brazil is one battleground. Both companies can afford to engage in this behaviour, even though it reduces their profits in Brazil, because they have profitable operations elsewhere in the world that can subsidize these losses.

Pricing decisions around the world need to be centrally monitored. It is tempting to delegate full responsibility for pricing decisions to the managers of various national subsidiaries. However, because pricing strategy in one part of the world can elicit a competitive response in another part, central management needs to at least monitor and approve pricing decisions in a given national market, and local managers need to recognize that their actions can affect competitive conditions in other countries.

COUNTRY FOCUS

Are Canada and the United States always Good Neighbours?

For over two decades, one of the longest trade disputes between Canada and the United States has involved a product that this country has been exporting for over a century: lumber. The dollar amounts around this dispute are large, and both countries took many actions and counter-actions along the way.

The Canadian lumber industry exports over $10 billion per year to the United States. According to some sources, the Canadian lumber industry provides lumber for approximately one-third of the U.S. demand. More specifically, it is softwood lumber, used in the home construction industry, which has been a headline grabber on both sides of the border for decades.

Despite the slowdown in U.S. home construction as a result of the recent global economic slowdown, demand for Canadian softwood lumber will continue. But what happens when demand for a product conflicts with a country's competition policy and results in charges of dumping and predatory pricing? In most provinces Canada's logging companies have historically cut trees from land leased from the Crown (that is, public land). When viewed from south of the border, this practice is seen as a form of Canadian government subsidy. The American government categorizes this "Canadian state intervention" as dumping, or selling the product cheaper in the United States than in Canada, supposedly giving Canadian companies an unfair competitive advantage compared to American lumber companies.

The first actions formalizing this complaint occurred in the early 1980s when the Canadian lumber industry vigorously defended itself against the heavy-hitting U.S. lumber industry lobby group. The initial ruling in that case was that the Canadian lumber industry did not breech standard business practices, and thus, the Americans lost the battle to impose countervailing (antidumping) penalties on the Canadian lumber industry.

Since then the Canadian Lumber Trade Alliance, which is the primary association for the Canadian lumber industry, voiced its trade protests to the Canadian government, which were met with counter complaints from the U.S. Coalition for Fair Lumber Imports (a voice to over 50 percent of the U.S. lumber industry) via the American government. NAFTA and the WTO panels (the NAFTA panel includes three Americans and two Canadians) ruled that although much of Canada's lumber industry is subsidized, the 18 to 27 percent punitive duties imposed on Canadian lumber imports by the U.S. government was too high. The NAFTA and WTO panels also ruled that imposing countervailing duties on Canadian softwood lumber was illegal. Even the United States International Trade Commission (ITC) insisted that Canadian lumber imports were being threatened by the U.S. lumber industry.

The 1996–2001 Bilateral Softwood Lumber Agreement between Canada and the United States appeared to have placated the aggressive U.S. lumber groups. During the course of this agreement, which expired on March 31, 2001, Canadian softwood lumber exporters were largely assured market access to the United States, free of U.S. trade action during the five-year accord. In a sense, Canada agreed to a kind of voluntary export restraint, free of U.S. customs duties, as long as Canadian lumber exports from Crown lands and thus, primarily from British Columbia, Alberta, Ontario, and Quebec, did not exceed 14.7 billion board feet per year. Above that limit, the onus was on the Government of Canada to collect fees that varied according to the 1996–2001 Softwood Lumber Agreement. The agreement seemed to bring about commercial peace and stability.

Interfor's Hammond Cedar Mill in Maple Ridge, B.C., is one of the many Canadian lumber firms affected by the ongoing U.S./Canada softwood lumber agreements. © genkur/Shutterstock

However, problems flared up again upon expiry of the agreement. Somewhere in the twilight zone following the expiry of the lumber agreement, U.S. Customs began to take a public stand on the issue and the United States even required cash deposits on lumber imported from Canada amounting to almost $5 billion.

It was time for another agreement. In 2006, Canada and the United States signed the Softwood Lumber Agreement, which saw the return of the $5 billion in duty deposits and created a stable, if complex, series of export charges and volume restraints. (For details, go to the Global Affairs Canada, Treaty Law Division Web site at http://www.international.gc.ca/ and search for "softwood lumber export controls.")

The agreement had a set term of seven years, and was extended by both governments for an additional two years until October 2015.

Is everything done? Not quite. In mid-2012, an article appeared in the *Globe and Mail* with the title "Softwood-lumber victory unlikely to halt conflict between Canada and U.S." It detailed a favourable ruling to Canada from the London Court of Appeal based on a complaint that British Columbia was subsidizing wood damaged by the pine beetle. And a year later, in 2013, the U.S. Lumber Coalition suggested to the U.S. government that a change in B.C. log exporting policies would have the effect of insulating B.C lumber mills from world market prices for logs, and would thus be in violation of the Softwood Lumber Agreement.

The Softwood Lumber Agreement expired on October 12, 2015. On October 12, 2016, a one-year moratorium on trade since the expiration of the deal ended, so Canadian producers of softwood lumber now have access to the U.S. softwood lumber market.

Will there be a new Agreement? Any renegotiation of NAFTA, led by the Trump administration, will likely include this issue. Meanwhile in early 2017, The U.S. International Trade Commission says Canadian imports of softwood lumber caused harm to U.S. producers, thereby setting the stage for duties to be imposed. Stay tuned to this ever-changing situation.

Questions

1. Who wins when products are dumped into a market? Who loses?
2. With respect to competition policy, how often do monopolies occur? Can you give any examples? Are there any monopolies in the public sector as well as the private sector?

Sources: http://www.international.gc.ca/controls-controles/softwood-bois_oeuvre/index.aspx?lang=eng; http://www.mapleleafweb.com/features/canada-us-softwood-lumber-dispute; http://www.cbc.ca/news2/background/softwood_lumber/; http://www.cbc.ca/news/canada/canada-will-obey-softwood-ruling-harper-1.812248; http://www.newsroom.gov.bc.ca/2012/07/total-victory-for-bc-and-canada-on-softwood-lumber.html; http://www.theglobeandmail.com/report-on-business/industry-news/energy-and-resources/softwood-lumber-victory-unlikely-to-halt-conflict-between-canada-and-us/article4425659/; http://www.randomlengths.com/In-Depth/US-Canada-Lumber-Trade-Dispute/; and http://www.cbc.ca/news/business/canada-us-softwood-1.3925105.

EXPERIENCE CURVE PRICING

We first encountered the experience curve in Chapter 11. As a firm builds its accumulated production volume over time, unit costs fall due to "experience effects." Learning effects and economies of scale underlie the experience curve. Price comes into the picture because aggressive pricing (along with aggressive promotion and advertising) can build accumulated sales volume rapidly and thus move production down the experience curve. Firms further down the experience curve have a cost advantage vis-à-vis firms further up the curve.

Many firms pursuing an experience curve pricing strategy on an international scale price low worldwide in an attempt to build global sales volume as rapidly as possible, even if this means taking large losses initially. Such a firm believes that several years in the future, when it has moved down the experience curve, it will be making substantial profits and have a cost advantage over its less-aggressive competitors.

Regulatory Influences on Prices

The ability to engage in either price discrimination or strategic pricing may be limited by national or international regulations. Most important, a firm's freedom to set its own prices is constrained by antidumping regulations and competition policy.

ANTIDUMPING REGULATIONS

Both predatory pricing and experience curve pricing can run afoul of antidumping regulations. Dumping occurs whenever a firm sells a product for a price that is less than the cost of producing it. Most regulations, however, define dumping more vaguely. For example, a country is allowed to bring antidumping actions against an importer under Article 6 of GATT as long as two criteria are met: sales at "less than fair value" and "material injury to a domestic industry." The problem with this terminology is that it does not indicate what is a fair value. The ambiguity has led some to argue that selling abroad at prices below those in the country of origin, as opposed to below cost, is dumping.

Such logic led the first Bush administration to place a 25 percent duty on imports of Japanese light trucks in 1988. The Japanese manufacturers protested that they were not selling below cost. Admitting that their prices were lower in the United States than in Japan, they argued that this simply reflected the intensely competitive nature of the U.S. market (i.e., different price elasticities). In a similar example, the European Commission found Japanese exporters of dot-matrix printers to be violating dumping regulations. To correct what they saw as dumping, the EU placed a 47 percent import duty on imports of dot-matrix printers from Japan and required that the import duty be passed on to European consumers as a price increase.[23]

Antidumping rules set a floor under export prices and limit firms' ability to pursue strategic pricing. The rather vague terminology used in most antidumping actions suggests that a firm's ability to engage in price discrimination also may be challenged under antidumping legislation.

COMPETITION POLICY

Most industrialized nations have regulations designed to promote competition and to restrict monopoly practices. These regulations can be used to limit the prices a firm can charge in a given country. For example at one time, the Swiss pharmaceutical manufacturer Hoffmann-LaRoche had a monopoly on the supply of Valium and Librium tranquilizers. The company was investigated by the British Monopolies and Mergers Commission, which is responsible for promoting fair competition in Great Britain. The commission found that Hoffmann-LaRoche was overcharging for its tranquilizers and ordered the company to reduce its prices 35 to 40 percent. Hoffmann-LaRoche maintained unsuccessfully that it was merely engaging in price discrimination. Similar actions were later brought against Hoffmann-LaRoche by the German cartel office and by the Dutch and Danish governments.[24]

Configuring the Marketing Mix

A firm might vary aspects of its marketing mix from country to country to take into account local differences in culture, economic conditions, competitive conditions, product and technical standards, distribution systems, government regulations, and the like. Such differences may require variation in product attributes, distribution strategy, communications strategy, and pricing strategy. The cumulative effect of these factors makes it rare for a firm to adopt the same marketing mix worldwide.

For example, financial services is often thought of as an industry where global standardization of the marketing mix is the norm. However, while a financial services company such as American Express may sell the same basic charge card service worldwide, utilize the same basic fee structure for that product, and adopt the same basic global advertising message ("My Life. My Card."), differences in national regulations still mean it has to vary aspects of its communications strategy from country to country (as pointed out earlier, the promotional strategy it had developed in the United States was illegal in Germany). Similarly, while McDonald's is often thought of as the quintessential example of a firm that sells the same basic standardized product worldwide, in reality it varies one important aspect of its marketing mix—its menu—from country to country. McDonald's also varies its distribution strategy. In Canada and the United States, most McDonald's outlets are located in areas that are easily accessible by car, whereas in more densely populated and less automobile-reliant societies of the world, such as Japan and Great Britain, location decisions are driven by the accessibility of a restaurant to pedestrian traffic. Because countries typically still differ along one or more of the dimensions discussed above, some customization of the marketing mix is normal.

However, there are often significant opportunities for standardization along one or more elements of the marketing mix.[25] Firms may find that it is possible and desirable to standardize their global advertising message and/or core product attributes to realize substantial cost economies. They may find it desirable to customize their distribution and pricing strategy to take advantage of local differences. In reality, the "customization versus standardization" debate is not an all or nothing issue; it frequently makes sense to standardize some aspects of the marketing mix and customize others, depending on conditions in various national marketplaces. Decisions about what to customize and what to standardize should be driven by a detailed examination of the costs and benefits of doing so for each element in the marketing mix.

LO5   New-Product Development

Firms that successfully develop and market new products can earn enormous returns. Examples include Du Pont, which has produced a steady stream of successful innovations such as cellophane, nylon, Freon, and Teflon (nonstick pans); Sony, whose successes include the Walkman, the compact disc, the PlayStation, and the Blu-ray high-definition DVD player; Pfizer, the drug company that during the 1990s produced several major new drugs, including Viagra; 3M, which has applied its core competency in tapes and adhesives to developing a wide range of new products; Intel, which has consistently managed to lead in the development of innovative microprocessors to run personal computers; and Apple with its string of hits, including the iPhone, iPad, and Apple Watch.

In today's world, competition is as much about technological innovation as anything else. The pace of technological change has accelerated since the Industrial Revolution in the eighteenth century, and it continues to do so today. The result has been a dramatic shortening of product life cycles. Technological innovation is both creative and destructive.[26] An innovation can make established products obsolete overnight.

But an innovation can also make a host of new products possible. Witness recent changes in the electronics industry. For 40 years before the early 1950s, vacuum tubes were a major component in radios and then in record players and early computers. The advent of transistors destroyed the market for vacuum tubes, but at the same time it created new opportunities connected with transistors. Transistors took up far less space than vacuum tubes, creating a trend toward miniaturization that continues today. The transistor held its position as the major component in the electronics industry for just a decade.

Microprocessors were developed in the 1970s and the market for transistors declined rapidly. The microprocessor created yet another set of new-product opportunities—handheld calculators (which destroyed the market for slide rules), compact disc players (which destroyed the market for analog record players), and personal computers (which destroyed the market for typewriters), to name a few.

This "creative destruction" unleashed by technological change makes it critical that a firm stay on the leading edge of technology lest it lose out to a competitor's innovations. As we explain in the next subsection, this not only creates a need for the firm to invest in research and development, but it also requires the firm to establish R&D activities at those locations where expertise is concentrated. As we shall see, leading-edge technology on its own is not enough to guarantee a firm's survival. The firm must also apply that technology to developing products that satisfy consumer needs, and it must design the product so that it can be manufactured in a cost-effective manner. To do that, the firm needs to build close links between R&D, marketing, and manufacturing. This is difficult enough for the domestic firm, but it is even more problematic for the international business competing in an industry where consumer tastes and preferences differ from country to country. With all this in mind, we move on to examine locating R&D activities and building links between R&D, marketing, and manufacturing.

The Location of R&D

Ideas for new products are stimulated by the interactions of scientific research, demand conditions, and competitive conditions. Other things being equal, the rate of new-product development seems to be greater in countries where:

- more money is spent on basic and applied research and development;
- underlying demand is strong;
- consumers are affluent;
- competition is intense.[27]

Basic and applied research and development discovers new technologies and then commercializes them. Strong demand and affluent consumers create a potential market for new products. Intense competition between firms stimulates innovation as the firms try to beat their competitors and reap potentially enormous first-mover advantages that result from successful innovation.

For most of the post-World War II period, the country that ranked highest on these criteria was the United States. The United States devoted a greater proportion of its gross domestic product (GDP) to R&D than any other country did. Its scientific establishment was the largest and most active in the world. American consumers were the most affluent, the market was large, and competition among U.S. firms was brisk. Due to these factors, the United States was the market where most new products were developed and introduced. Accordingly, it was the best location for R&D activities; it was where the action was.

Over the past 20 years, things have been changing quickly. The U.S. monopoly on new-product development has weakened considerably. Although U.S. firms are still at the leading edge of many new technologies, Asian and European firms are also strong players, with companies such as Sony, Sharp, Samsung, Ericsson, Nokia, and Philips driving product innovation in their respective industries. In addition, both Japan and the European Union are large, affluent markets, and the wealth gap between them and the United States is closing.

As a result, it is often no longer appropriate to consider the United States as the lead market. In video games, for example, Japan is often the lead market, with companies such as Sony and Nintendo introducing their latest video game players in Japan some six months before they introduce them in the United States. In wireless telecommunications, Europe was long considered to be ahead of the United States. Some of the most advanced applications of wireless telecommunications services were pioneered not in the United States but in Finland where, until recently, wireless penetration rates were much higher than in the United States. However, it is often questionable whether any developed nation can be considered the lead market. To succeed in today's high-technology industries, it is often necessary to simultaneously introduce new products in all major industrialized markets. When Intel introduces a new microprocessor, for example, it does not first introduce it in the United States and then roll it out in Europe a year later. It introduces it simultaneously around the world. The same is true of Microsoft with each new version of its Windows operating systems.

Because leading-edge research is now carried out in many locations around the world, the argument for centralizing R&D activity in Canada and the United States is much weaker than it was two decades ago. (It used to be argued that centralized R&D eliminated duplication.) Much leading-edge research is now occurring in Japan and Europe. Dispersing R&D activities to those locations allows a firm to stay close to the centre of leading-edge activity to gather scientific and competitive information and to draw on local scientific resources.[28] This may result in some duplication of R&D activities, but the cost disadvantages of duplication are outweighed by the advantages of dispersion.

For example, to expose themselves to the research and new-product development work being done in Japan, many U.S. firms have set up satellite R&D centres in Japan. U.S. firms that have established R&D facilities in Japan include Corning, Texas Instruments, IBM, Procter & Gamble, Pfizer, Du Pont, Monsanto, and Microsoft.[29] The National Science Foundation (NSF) has documented a sharp increase in the proportion of total R&D spending by U.S. firms that is now done abroad.[30] For example, Bristol-Myers Squibb has 12 facilities in five countries. At the same time, to internationalize their own research and gain access to U.S. talent, many European and Asian firms are investing in U.S.-based research facilities, according to the NSF.

Integrating R&D, Marketing, and Production

Although a firm that is successful at developing new products may earn enormous returns, new-product development has a high failure rate. One study of product development in 16 companies in the chemical, drug, petroleum, and electronics industries suggested that only about 20 percent of R&D projects result in commercially successful products or processes.[31] Another in-depth case study of product development in three companies (one in chemicals and two in drugs) reported that about 60 percent of R&D projects reached technical completion, 30 percent were commercialized, and only

12 percent earned an economic profit that exceeded the company's cost of capital.[32] Similarly, a study by the consulting division of Booz, Allen & Hamilton found that more than one-third of 13 000 consumer and industrial products introduced between 1976 and 1981 failed to meet company-specific financial and strategic performance criteria.[33] A more recent study found that 45 percent of new products did not meet their profitability goals.[34] This evidence suggests that many R&D projects do not result in a commercial product, and that between 33 percent and 60 percent of all new products that do reach the marketplace fail to generate an adequate economic return. Well-publicized product failures include Apple Computer's Newton personal digital assistant, Sony's Betamax format in the video player and recorder market, and Sega's Dreamcast video game console.

The reasons for such high failure rates are varied and include development of a technology for which there is only limited demand, failure to adequately commercialize promising technology, and inability to manufacture a new product cost effectively. Firms can avoid such mistakes by insisting on tight cross-functional coordination and integration between three core functions involved in the development of new products: R&D, marketing, and production.[35] Tight cross-functional integration between R&D, production, and marketing can make sure:

1. Product development projects are driven by customer needs.
2. New products are designed for ease of manufacture.
3. Development costs are kept in check.
4. Time to market is minimized.

Close integration between R&D and marketing is required to ensure that product development projects are driven by the needs of customers. A company's customers can be a primary source of new-product ideas. Identification of customer needs, particularly unmet needs, can set the context within which successful product innovation occurs. As the point of contact with customers, the marketing function of a company can provide valuable information in this regard. Integration of R&D and marketing are crucial if a new product is to be properly commercialized. Without integration of R&D and marketing, a company runs the risk of developing products for which there is little or no demand.

Integration between R&D and production can help a company design products with manufacturing requirements in mind. Designing for manufacturing can lower costs and increase product quality. Integrating R&D and production can also help lower development costs and speed products to market. If a new product is not designed with manufacturing capabilities in mind, it may prove too difficult to build. Then the product will have to be redesigned, and both overall development costs and the time it takes to bring the product to market may increase significantly. Making design changes during product planning could increase overall development costs by 50 percent and add 25 percent to the time it takes to bring the product to market.[36] Many quantum product innovations require new processes to manufacture them, which makes it all the more important to achieve close integration between R&D and production. Minimizing time to market and development costs may require the simultaneous development of new products and new processes.[37]

Cross-Functional Teams

One way to achieve cross-functional integration is to establish product development teams composed of representatives from R&D, marketing, and production. Because these functions may be located in different countries, the team will sometimes have a multinational membership. The objective of a team should be to take a product development project from the initial concept development to market introduction. A number of attributes seem to be important for a product development team to function effectively and meet all its development milestones.[38]

First, the team should be led by a "heavyweight" project manager who has high status within the organization and the authority required to get the financial and human resources the team needs to succeed. The "heavyweight" leader should be dedicated primarily, if not entirely, to the project. The leader should be someone who believes in the project (a champion) and who is skilled at integrating the perspectives of different functions and at helping personnel from different functions and countries work together for a common goal. The leader should also be able to act as an advocate of the team to senior management.

Second, the team should be composed of at least one member from each key function. The team members should have a number of attributes, including an ability to contribute functional expertise, high standing within their function, a willingness to share responsibility for team results, and an ability to put functional and national advocacy aside. It is generally preferable if core team members are 100 percent dedicated to the project for its duration. This assures their focus on the project, not on the ongoing work of their function.

Third, the team members should be physically co-located if possible to create a sense of camaraderie and to facilitate communication. This presents problems if the team members are drawn from facilities in different nations. One solution is to transfer key individuals to one location for the duration of a product development project. Fourth, the team should have a clear plan and clear goals, particularly with regard to critical development milestones and development budgets. The team should have incentives to attain those goals, such as receiving pay bonuses when major development milestones are hit. Fifth, each team needs to develop its own processes for communication and conflict resolution. For example, one product development team at Quantum Corporation, a California-based manufacturer of disk drives for personal computers, instituted a rule that all major decisions would be made and conflicts resolved at meetings that were held every Monday afternoon. This simple rule helped the team meet its development goals. In this case, it was also common for team members to fly in from Japan, where the product was to be manufactured, to the U.S. development centre for the Monday meetings.[39]

IMPLICATIONS FOR BUSINESS

The need to integrate R&D and marketing to adequately commercialize new concepts and designs poses special problems in the international business, since commercialization may require different versions of a new product to be produced for different countries.[40]

For some companies, the integration of R&D, marketing, and production in an international business may require R&D centres in North America, Asia, and Europe that are linked by formal and informal integrating mechanisms with marketing operations in each country in their regions and with the various manufacturing facilities. In addition, the international business may have to establish cross-functional teams whose members are dispersed around the globe. This complex endeavour requires the company to utilize formal and informal integrating mechanisms to knit its far-flung operations together so they can produce new products in an effective and timely manner.

While there is no single best model for allocating product development responsibilities to various centres, one solution adopted by many international businesses involves establishing a global network of R&D centres. Within this model, fundamental research is undertaken at **basic research**

centres around the globe. These centres are normally located in regions or cities where valuable scientific knowledge is being created and where there is a pool of skilled research talent (e.g., Kanata and Waterloo, Ontario, in Canada; Silicon Valley in the United States; Cambridge in England; Kobe in Japan). These centres are the innovation engines of the firm. Their job is to develop the basic technologies that become new products. These technologies are picked up by R&D units attached to global product divisions and are used to generate new products to serve the global marketplace. At this level, emphasis is placed on commercialization of the technology and design for manufacturing. If further customization is needed so the product appeals to the tastes and preferences of consumers in individual markets, such redesign work will be done by an R&D group based in a subsidiary in that country or at a regional centre that customizes products for several countries in the region.

Hewlett-Packard (HP) has several basic research centres located in Palo Alto, California; Bangalore, India; Beijing, China; Bristol, England; Fusionopolis, Singapore; Haifa, Israel; and St. Petersburg, Russia.[41] These labs are the seedbed for technologies that ultimately become new products and businesses. They are the company's innovation engines. The Palo Alto centre, for example, pioneered HP's thermal ink-jet technology. The products are developed by R&D centres associated with HP's global product divisions. Thus, the Consumer Products Group, which has its worldwide headquarters in San Diego, California, designs, develops, and manufactures a range of imaging products using HP-pioneered thermal ink-jet technology. Subsidiaries might then customize the product so that it best matches the needs of important national markets. HP's subsidiary in Singapore, for example, is responsible for the design and production of thermal ink-jet printers for Japan and other Asian markets. This subsidiary takes products originally developed in San Diego and redesigns them for the Asian market. In addition, the Singapore subsidiary has taken the lead from San Diego in the design and development of certain portable thermal ink-jet printers. HP delegated this responsibility to Singapore because this subsidiary has built important competencies in the design and production of thermal ink-jet products, so it has become the best place in the world to undertake this activity.

Microsoft offers a similar example. The company has research sites in Redmond, Washington (its headquarters); Cambridge, England; Beijing, China; Bangalore, India; Silicon Valley, California; Cairo, Egypt; Cambridge, Massachusetts; and Aachen, Germany.[42] Staff members at these research sites work on the fundamental problems that underlie the design of future products. For example, a group at Redmond is working on natural language recognition software, while another works on artificial intelligence. These research centres do not produce new products; rather, they produce the technology that is used to enhance existing products or help produce new products. The products are produced by dedicated product groups (e.g., desktop operating systems, applications). Customization of the products to match the needs of local markets is sometimes carried out at local subsidiaries. Thus, the Chinese subsidiary in Singapore will do some basic customization of programs such as Microsoft Office, adding Chinese characters and customizing the interface.

Key Terms

basic research centres	marketing mix
channel length	multipoint pricing
concentrated retail system	noise
country of origin effects	predatory pricing
elastic demand	price elasticity of demand
exclusive distribution channel	pull strategy
fragmented retail system	push strategy
inelastic demand	source effects
market segmentation	strategic pricing

Learning Objectives Summary

1. Market segmentation refers to the process of identifying distinct groups of consumers whose purchasing behaviour differs from each other in important ways. Managers in an international business need to be aware of two main issues relating to segmentation: the extent to which there are differences between countries in the structure of market segments, and the existence of segments that transcend national borders. A product can be viewed as a bundle of attributes. Product attributes need to be varied from country to country to satisfy different consumer tastes and preferences. Country differences in consumer tastes and preferences are due to differences in culture and economic development. In addition, differences in product and technical standards may require the firm to customize product attributes from country to country.

2. A distribution strategy decision is an attempt to define the optimal channel for delivering a product to the consumer. Significant country differences exist in distribution systems. In some countries, the retail system is concentrated; in others, it is fragmented. In some countries, channel length is short; in others, it is long. Access to distribution channels is difficult to achieve in some countries, and the quality of the channel may be poor.

3. A critical element in the marketing mix is communication strategy, which defines the process the firm will use in communicating the attributes of its product to prospective customers. Barriers to international communication include cultural differences, source effects, and noise levels. A communication strategy is either a push strategy or a pull strategy. A push strategy emphasizes personal selling, and a pull strategy emphasizes mass media advertising. Whether a push strategy or a pull strategy is optimal depends on the type of product, consumer sophistication, channel length, and media availability. A globally standardized advertising campaign, which uses the same marketing message all over the world, has economic advantages, but it fails to account for differences in culture and advertising regulations.

4. Price discrimination exists when consumers in different countries are charged different prices for the same product. Price discrimination can help a firm maximize its profits. For price discrimination to be effective, the national markets must be separate and their price elasticities of demand must differ. Predatory pricing is the use of profit gained in one market to support aggressive pricing in another market to drive competitors out of that market. Multipoint pricing refers to the fact that a firm's pricing strategy in one market may affect rivals' pricing strategies in another market. Aggressive pricing in one market may elicit a competitive response from a rival in another market that is important to the firm. Experience curve pricing is the use of aggressive pricing to build accumulated volume as rapidly as possible to quickly move the firm down the experience curve.

5. New-product development is a high-risk, potentially high-return activity. To build a competency in new-product development, an international business must do two things: disperse R&D activities to those countries where new products are being pioneered, and integrate R&D with marketing and manufacturing. Achieving tight integration among R&D, marketing, and manufacturing requires the use of cross-functional teams.

Critical Thinking and Discussion Questions

1. Imagine you are the marketing manager for a Canadian manufacturer of disposable diapers. Your firm is considering entering the Brazilian market. Your CEO believes the advertising message that has been effective in Canada will suffice in Brazil. Outline some possible objections to this. Your CEO also believes that the pricing decisions in Brazil can be delegated to local managers. Why might she be wrong?

2. "Within 20 years, we will have seen the emergence of enormous global markets for standardized consumer products." Do you agree with this statement? Justify your answer.

3. You are the marketing manager of a food products company that is considering entering the South Korean market. The retail system in South Korea tends to be very fragmented. Also, retailers and wholesalers tend to have long-term ties with South Korean food companies, which makes access to distribution channels difficult. What distribution strategy would you advise the company to pursue? Why?

4. "Price discrimination is indistinguishable from dumping." Discuss the accuracy of this statement.

5. You work for a company that designs and manufactures personal computers. Your company's R&D centre is in North Dakota. The computers are manufactured under contract in Taiwan. Marketing strategy is delegated to the heads of three regional groups: a North American group (based in Chicago), a European group (based in Paris), and an Asian group (based in Singapore). Each regional group develops the marketing approach within its region. In order of importance, the largest markets for your products are North America, Germany, Great Britain, China, and Australia. Your company is experiencing problems in its product development and commercialization process. Products are late to market, the manufacturing quality is poor, costs are higher than projected, and market acceptance of new products is less than hoped for. What might be the source of these problems? How would you fix them?

Research Task   globalEDGE™   globaledge.msu.edu

Use the globalEDGE™ site to complete the following exercises:

1. Locate and retrieve the most current ranking of the global brands. Identify the criteria that are utilized in the ranking. Which country dominates the top 100 global brands list? Prepare a short report identifying the countries that possess global brands and the potential reasons for success.

2. Thorough planning is essential to export success. In this respect, pricing is one of the critical components for successful planning. Considering that your company tries to be price competitive, prepare an executive summary of how to do initial pricing analysis for international markets.

CLOSING CASE

DOMINO'S PIZZA

Domino's Pizza made its name by pioneering home delivery service in the United States. In recent years, however, the growth story has been overseas. With the U.S. fast-food market saturated and consumer demand weak, Domino's is looking to international markets for growth opportunities. The company is no newcomer to international business—it opened its first international store in Canada in 1983. Today the company, headquartered in Windsor, has over 370 locations in all of the Canadian Provinces and Territories. All of the Canadian stores are franchises, which cost between $200,000–$300,000 to open, with a need for an additional $100,000 in unencumbered personal cash. Almost all new store openings are outside of the United States. As of 2014 it has more international stores than it does stores in the United States. The company plans call for opening another 350 to 450 international stores a year for the next few years.

As it expands its international businesses, there are some things that Domino's has kept the same as in the United States, and there are some things that are very different. What is the same is the basic business model of home delivery. This sets it apart from many of its U.S. rivals, who changed their basic offering when they entered foreign markets. For example, when Yum Brands Inc. introduced Pizza Hut into China, it radically altered the format, establishing Pizza Hut Casual Dining, a chain that offers a vast selection of American fare—including ribs, spaghetti, and steak—in a full-service setting. Pizza Hut adopted this format because table service was what the locals were used to, but Domino's isn't interested. "We go in there with a tried-and-true business model of delivery and carry-out pizza that we deploy around the world," states Domino's international president, Richard Allison. "In emerging markets, we've got more tables than you would find in the U.S., but we have no plans to lean toward a casual dining model where the server comes out and takes an order."

On the other hand, there are things that vary from country to country. In the United States, pizza is viewed as casual food, frequently mentioned in the same breath as beer and football. In Japan, it's viewed as more upscale fare. This is reflected in the offering. Japanese pizzas come with toppings that the average American couldn't fathom. Domino's has sold a

$50 pizza in Japan featuring foie gras. Other premium toppings include snow crab, Mangalitsa pork with Bordeaux sauce, and beef stew with fresh mozzarella. Japanese consumers value aesthetics and really care about the look of food, so presentation is key. Patrons expect every slice to have precisely the same amount of toppings, which must be uniformly spaced. Shrimp, for example, are angled with the tails pointing the same way.

Pizza consumption is low in Japan—the average Japanese pizza customer only consumes the product four times a year. To boost consumption, Domino's has been working to create more occasions to enjoy its pizza. For example, on Valentine's Day, its Japanese stores deliver heart-shaped pizzas in pink boxes. Heart-shaped pizzas also appear on Mother's Day.

To promote the offering in Japan, rather than spending money on commercials, Domino's tries to create news, like topics that people talk about. If the topic is fun and hot, Domino's believes that people will talk about it, which ultimately translates into better sales. One promotion in particular received heavy coverage. The chain offered 2.5 million yen (about $31,000) for one hour's work at a Domino's store. In all, about 12 000 people applied for the "job." The lucky winner was a rural housewife who had never eaten pizza. She flew to a small island to deliver pizza to schoolchildren, who were also new to pizza. The event received heavy news coverage—free advertising in other words.

In India, where Domino's has more than 400 stores and has plans for 1000 more, 50 percent of the menu is vegetarian to match the preferences of the large Hindu population. For delivery, Domino's has a fleet of mopeds, which makes sense in large cities like Mumbai where traffic congestion is awful. Because Indians like things spicy, instead of including Parmesan cheese packets, Domino's includes an "Oregano Spice Mix." In general, the toppings have far more spice than in the United States. Although Indians are used to full service in restaurants, Domino's doesn't use servers or bus boys in their stores, even though they typically have a few tables in each store for those who want to eat on premises. Instead, they are educating their customers to clean up after themselves, with in-store trashcans that say "Use Me" in big bold letters.

Domino's today has focused on branding itself with high-quality ingredients, efficiency but at a speed that fosters quality, and a devotion to maintaining a cultural fabric that allows for a strong entrepreneurial mindset among employees and franchisees. The company captures the global marketplace effectively, either as a first-mover or as a strong follower. "For Domino's the development and eventual channelization of industries is important strategically," said Michael Lawton, chief financial officer (CFO) of Domino's. He continued: "It led the company to decide in some foreign markets that the best alternative was to let someone else introduce the pizza category with a sit down concept and then Domino's moved in and captured their part of the industry as delivery and carry-out developed." In other cases, Domino's led the market entry into foreign countries. These decision choices make for great global strategy. Domino's has certainly captured the "taste" of the global marketplace.

Sources: A. Gasparro, "Domino's Sticks to Its Ways Abroad," *The Wall Street Journal*, April 17, 2012, p. B10; A. C. Beattie, "In Japan, Pizza Is Recast as a Meal for Special Occasions," *Advertising Age*, April 2, 2012, p. 16; A. Gasparro, "Domino's Sees Bigger Slice Overseas," *The Wall Street Journal*, February 29, 2012, p. B7; and R. Shah, "How Domino's Pizza Is Taking a Bite Out of India," *Getting More Awesome*, www.gettingmoreawesome.com/2012/02/08/how-dominos-is-taking-a-bite-out-of-india, www.dominos.ca (accessed January 2014).

Case Discussion Questions

1. Do you think it is wise for Domino's to stick to its traditional "home delivery" business model, even when that is not the norm in a country, and when its international rivals have changed their format?

2. What do you think Domino's does from an organizational perspective to make sure that it accommodates local differences in consumer tastes and preferences?

3. How does the marketing mix for Domino's Pizza in Japan differ from that in the United States? How does that in India differ from the U.S. marketing mix?

4. What lessons can we draw from the Domino's case study that might be useful for other international businesses selling consumer goods?

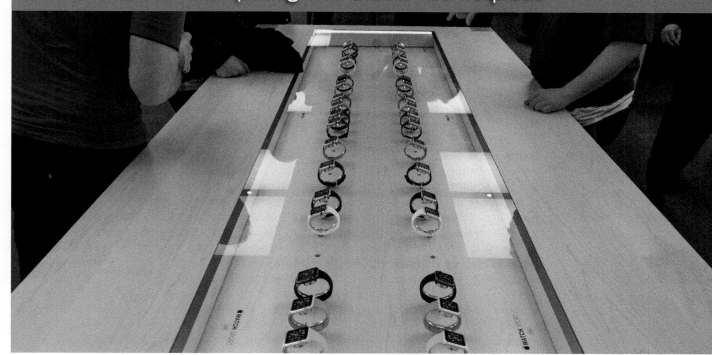

© Yun Wang/Alamy

Chapter 15

Global Production, Outsourcing, and Logistics

OPENING CASE

APPLE: THE BEST SUPPLY CHAIN IN THE WORLD?

For many years, Apple has been recognized as having the best worldwide supply chains in the "Gartner Global Supply Chain Top 25" ranking. Numerous accolades have also been made about Apple's supply chain strategy, operations, and results. For example, Apple's supply chains "best demonstrate leadership in applying demand-driven principles to drive business results." "Apple dominates because it consistently brings both operational and innovation excellence to bear in some of the most competitive markets in the world." Basically, Apple gets a lot of credit in the supply chain profession for being able to ramp up volumes both in hardware and software while also innovatively helping to redefine the consumer electronics market (e.g., iPhone, iPad, Mac, Apple Watch).

Apple is the world's second-largest information technology company by revenue after Samsung and the third-largest mobile phone producer after Samsung and Nokia. In Interbrand's "Best Global Brands" report, Apple is now also the most valuable brand in the world. It overtook Coca-Cola for the number one position after Coca-Cola's 13-year run at the top. Apple has an estimated brand value of more than $98 billion. "Few brands have enabled so many people to do so much so easily, which is why Apple has legions of adoring fans." These "fans" or customers have downloaded apps for Apple's electronic gadgets more than 50 billion times.

The company's general supply chain model follows the path of most large multinational corporation's supply chains. They do research and development to cultivate new technologies and/or to acquire intellectual property needed for future products. They test the product concepts via marketing research, product testing, and total cost analysis. After that, Apple typically does a pre-launch of new products, where global production, sourcing commitments, inventory management, and so on are evaluated. The product launch involves doing demand forecasts, resolving potential backlogs, and ensuring that the products are in the hands of its customers in as fast cycle time as possible. After the launch, monitoring starts with periodic reviews of inventory, demand, life-cycle status, and component cost forecasts.

A number of factors make Apple's global supply chains world leading. First, early on, Apple took steps to manage the total value created in its global supply chains by managing its suppliers and all other providers within the chains. Predetermined expectations of suppliers, exclusivity in supplier arrangements, and volume guarantees ensured a supply chain infrastructure that could support Apple's aggressive market leadership. Apple's relationship building with its network partners is also a strength that has helped with increased scaling of production and resulted in improved quality in the manufacturing processes. Plus, and not to be underestimated, Apple has amassed lots of cash! The available cash funds have partially been used to place high-volume orders, which strengthen supplier relationships, and in other ways maintain global supply chain leadership.

Using its supply chain infrastructure, Apple has managed to solve most of the challenges it has faced. For example, while the global economic downturn in 2008 presented problems for virtually all companies, Apple came through it in great shape. At the time, Steve Jobs said, "We're armed with the strongest product line in our history, the most talented employees and the best customers in our industry . . . Apple just reported one of the best quarters in its history." Other challenges that Apple has faced include obtaining enough quality components for its consumer electronics, potential for supply chain disruptions (natural and people created), dependence on third-party logistics providers, and inventory management issues. In each case, so far, Apple has strategically solved major issues to the satisfaction of the marketplace (the company consistently ranks at the top in "customer satisfaction" in the American Customer Satisfaction Index).

However, everything is not all positive about Apple. The company's reputation has taken a few hits in the years since 2008. For example, Apple was found guilty by a U.S. court of conspiring with publishers to set the price of e-books that were bought using iTunes. The ongoing feud with Samsung regarding various patents keeps lingering year-by-year, and worldwide customers are almost fanatically taking sides for or against Apple. There have also been allegations about the treatment of employees at Foxconn in China (one of the Apple suppliers). Plus, there was a U.S. Senate hearing that investigated Apple's "highly questionable" tax minimization strategies. Now, on the more positive side, Apple has a portfolio of potential blockbuster products, welcomed upgrades, and innovative services in the making that are sure to remind its fans why they favour Apple products.

The challenges attached to these new offerings are sure to test Apple's leadership in both brand value and best global supply chains. To some degree, the future challenges are clear. To stay at the top of its industry, Apple has to succeed in slowing Samsung's momentum and capturing the booming Chinese mobile phone market. As always with Apple, as set in our expectations over the years by Steve Jobs' "one more thing" announcements, Tim Cook and the current Apple leadership team must keep communicating to the market that their vision, innovations, and leadership can drive the idea that Apple's best days are ahead. As one way to do this, Apple is on a hiring binge in Asia, adding hundreds of engineers and supply chain managers to its staff in Shangai and Taipei as it seeks to increase the speed at which it introduces new products. Plus, with Tim Cook as the CEO, Apple has a global production and supply chain management expert at the helm who constantly scrutinizes Apple's supply chains, production operations, and fair labour practices.

Sources: D. Hofman, "The Gartner Supply Chain Top 25," 2013, www.gartner.com/technology/supply-chain/top25.jsp, accessed April 13, 2014; "Interbrand's Best Global Brands 2013," http://interbrand.com/best-brands/best-global-brands/2013/ranking/, accessed April 13, 2014; "Apple Is the World's Most Valuable Brand at $98 Billion," *The Huffington Post*, September 30, 2013; "Apple Reports Fourth Quarter Results," Apple Press Info, October 21, 2008; E. Doe, "Apple Goes on Hiring Binge in Asia to Speed Product Releases," *The Wall Street Journal*, March 3, 2014; American Customer Satisfaction Index, http://theacsi.org; and "Fixing Apple's Supply Chains," *The New York Times*, April 2, 2012.

LO LEARNING OBJECTIVES

By the end of this chapter you should be able to:

1. Explain why production and logistics decisions are of central importance to many multinational businesses.

2. Explain how country differences, production technology, and product features all affect the choice of where to locate production activities.

3. Recognize how the role of foreign subsidiaries in production can be enhanced over time as they accumulate knowledge.

4. Identify the factors that influence a firm's decision of whether to source supplies from within the company or from foreign suppliers.

5. Describe what is required to efficiently coordinate a globally dispersed production system.

Introduction

As trade barriers fall and global markets develop, many firms increasingly confront a set of interrelated issues. First, where in the world should productive activities be located? Should they be concentrated in a single country or should they be dispersed around the globe, matching the type of activity with country differences in factor costs, tariff barriers, political risks, and the like to minimize costs and maximize value added? Second, what should be the long-term strategic role of foreign production sites? Should the firm abandon a foreign site if factor costs change, moving production to another more favourable location, or is there value to maintaining an operation at a given location even if underlying economic conditions change? Third, should the firm own foreign productive activities, or is it better to outsource those activities to independent vendors? Fourth, how should a globally dispersed supply chain be managed, and what is the role of Internet-based information technology in the management of global logistics? Fifth, should the firm manage global logistics itself, or should it outsource the management to enterprises that specialize in this activity?

In this chapter we shall consider all these questions and discuss the various factors that influence decisions in this arena.

The example of Apple's global supply chains discussed in the opening case touches on some of these issues. Like many modern products, different components for Apple's consumer electronics are manufactured in different locations to produce a low-cost product. In choosing which company should make which components, Apple was guided by the need to keep the cost of the component parts low so that it could price aggressively and gain market share from its global rivals, Samsung and Nokia. However, as the case demonstrates, Apple may have miscalculated in some areas and the company's reputation has taken a few hits. As the Apple example illustrates, companies also need to be very careful when deciding to outsource production to foreign suppliers, and they need to think about the total costs of their supply chains, not just basic differentials in production cost.

LO1 Strategy, Production, and Supply Chain Management

In Chapter 11, we introduced the concept of the value chain and discussed a number of value creation activities, including production, marketing, materials management (logistics), R&D, human resources, and information systems. In this chapter, we will focus on two of these activities—production and supply chain management (logistics)—and attempt to clarify how they might be performed internationally to (1) lower the costs of value creation, and (2) add value by better serving customer needs. We will discuss the contributions of information technology, which has become particularly important in the era of the Internet.

We can define production as "the activities involved in creating a product." We use the term *production* to denote both service and manufacturing activities, since one can produce a service or produce a physical product. In this chapter, we focus more on manufacturing than on service activities, so we will use the term *manufacturing* as well as *production*. **Materials management** is the activity that controls the transmission of physical materials through the value chain, from procurement through production and into distribution. Materials management includes **logistics**, which refers to the procurement and physical

Global production and logistics is becoming an increasingly important part of the global value chain. © *Robert Churchill/Getty Images* transmission of material through the supply chain, from suppliers to customers. Manufacturing and materials management are closely linked, since a firm's ability to perform its manufacturing function efficiently depends on a continuous supply of high-quality material inputs, for which materials management is responsible.

The production and supply chain management functions of an international firm have a number of important strategic objectives.[1] One is to lower costs. Dispersing production activities to various locations around the globe where each activity can be performed most efficiently can lower costs. Costs can also be lowered by managing the global supply chain efficiently so as to better match supply and demand. Efficient supply chain management reduces the amount of inventory in the system and increases inventory turnover, which means the firm has to invest less working capital in inventory and is less likely to have excess inventory that cannot be sold and has to be written off.

A second strategic objective shared by production and materials management is to increase product quality by eliminating defective products from both the supply chain and the manufacturing process.[2] The objectives of reducing costs and increasing quality are not independent of each other. As illustrated in Figure 15.1, the firm that improves its quality control will also reduce its costs of value creation. Improved quality control reduces costs in three ways, by:

- increasing productivity because time is not wasted manufacturing poor-quality products that cannot be sold, leading to a direct reduction in unit costs;
- lowering rework and scrap costs;
- lowering warranty costs.

The effect is to lower the costs of value creation by reducing both manufacturing and service costs.

Companies are utilizing **total quality management** (TQM) to boost their product quality. TQM takes as its central focus the need to improve the quality of a company's

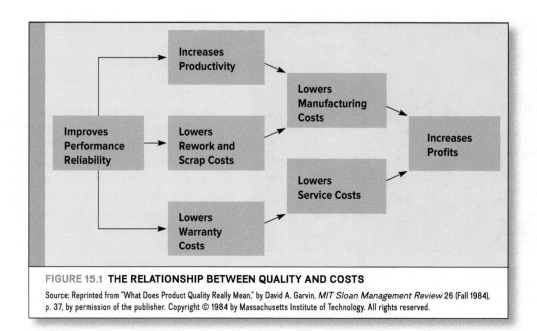

FIGURE 15.1 **THE RELATIONSHIP BETWEEN QUALITY AND COSTS**

Source: Reprinted from "What Does Product Quality Really Mean," by David A. Garvin, *MIT Sloan Management Review* 26 (Fall 1984), p. 37, by permission of the publisher. Copyright © 1984 by Massachusetts Institute of Technology. All rights reserved.

products and services. The TQM philosophy was developed by a number of American consultants such as the late W. Edwards Deming, Joseph Juran, and A. V. Feigenbaum.[3] Deming identified a number of steps that should be part of any TQM program. He argued that management should embrace the philosophy that mistakes, defects, and poor-quality materials are not acceptable and should be eliminated. He suggested that the quality of supervision should be improved by allowing more time for supervisors to work with employees and by providing them with the tools they need to do the job. Deming recommended that management should create an environment in which employees will not fear reporting problems or recommending improvements. He believed that work standards should be defined not only as numbers or quotas, but also should include some notion of quality to promote the production of defect-free output. He argued that management has the responsibility to train employees in new skills to keep pace with changes in the workplace. In addition, he believed that achieving better quality requires the commitment of everyone in the company.

Six Sigma, the modern successor to TQM, is a statistically based philosophy that aims to reduce defects, boost productivity, eliminate waste, and cut costs throughout a company. Six Sigma programs have been adopted by several major corporations, such as Motorola, General Electric, and Allied Signal. Sigma comes from the Greek letter that statisticians use to represent a standard deviation from a mean; the higher the number of "sigmas," the smaller the number of errors. At six sigma, a production process would be 99.99966 percent accurate, creating just 3.4 defects per million units. While it is almost impossible for a company to achieve such perfection, Six Sigma quality is a goal that several strive toward. Increasingly, companies are adopting Six Sigma programs to try to boost their product quality and productivity.[4]

The growth of international standards has also focused greater attention on the importance of product quality. In Europe, for example, the European Union requires that the quality of a firm's manufacturing processes and products be certified under a quality standard known as **ISO 9000** before the firm is allowed access to the EU marketplace. Although the ISO 9000 certification process has proved to be a somewhat bureaucratic and costly process for many firms, it does focus management attention on the need to improve the quality of products and processes.[5]

General Electric is one of the major corporations that have embraced Six Sigma. Its commitment to quality is evident in all its industries, from retail to insurance to aviation. © Jonathan Weiss/Dreamstime.com

In addition to the objectives of lowering costs and improving quality, two other objectives have particular importance in international businesses. First, production and materials management must be able to accommodate demands for local responsiveness. As we saw in Chapter 11, demands for local responsiveness arise from national differences in consumer tastes and preferences, infrastructure, distribution channels, and host-government demands. Demands for local responsiveness create pressures to decentralize manufacturing activities to the major national or regional markets in which the firm does business or to implement flexible manufacturing processes that enable the firm to customize the product coming out of a factory according to the market in which it is to be sold.

Second, manufacturing and materials management must be able to respond quickly to shifts in customer demand. In recent years, time-based competition has grown more important.[6] When consumer demand is prone to large and unpredictable shifts, the firm that can adapt most quickly to these shifts will gain an advantage. As we shall see, both manufacturing and materials management play critical roles here.

LO2 | Where to Produce

An essential decision facing an international firm is where to locate its manufacturing activities to achieve the goals of minimizing costs and improving product quality. For the firm contemplating international production, a number of factors must be considered. These factors can be grouped under three broad headings: country factors, technological factors, and product factors.[7]

Country Factors

We reviewed country-specific factors in some detail earlier in the book and we will not dwell on them here. Political economy, culture, and relative factor costs differ from country to country. In Chapter 5, we saw that due to differences in factor costs, certain countries have a comparative advantage for producing certain products. In Chapters 2 and 3, we saw how differences in political economy and national culture influence the benefits, costs, and risks of doing business in a country. Other things being equal, a firm should locate its various manufacturing activities where the economic, political, and cultural conditions, including relative factor costs, are conducive to the performance of those activities. In Chapter 11, we referred to the benefits derived from such a strategy as location economies. We argued that one result of the strategy is the creation of a global web of value creation activities.

Also important in some industries is the presence of global concentrations of activities at certain locations. In Chapter 7, we discussed the role of location externalities in influencing foreign direct investment decisions. Externalities include the presence of an appropriately skilled labour pool and supporting industries.[8] Such externalities can play an important role in deciding where to locate manufacturing activities. For example, because of a cluster of semiconductor manufacturing plants in Taiwan, a pool of labour with experience in the semiconductor business has developed. In addition, the plants have attracted a number of supporting industries, such as the manufacturers of semiconductor capital equipment and silicon, which have established facilities in Taiwan to be near their customers. This implies that there are real benefits to locating in Taiwan, as opposed to another location that lacks such externalities. Other things being equal, the externalities make Taiwan an attractive location for semiconductor manufacturing facilities.

Philips in China

The Dutch consumer electronics, lighting, semiconductor, and medical equipment conglomerate Philips Electronics NV has been operating factories in China since 1985, when the country first opened its markets to foreign investors. When Philips initially entered China, it had dreams of Chinese consumers snapping up its products by the millions. However, the company soon found out that the reason it liked China—low wage rates—also meant that few Chinese workers could afford to buy its products. So Philips hit on a new strategy: Keep the factories in China, but export most of the goods to developed nations.

The initial attractions of China to Philips included low wage rates, an educated workforce, a robust Chinese economy, a stable exchange rate that is linked to the U.S. dollar through a managed float, a rapidly expanding industrial base that includes many other Western and Chinese companies that Philips uses as suppliers, and easier access to world markets given China's entry into the WTO in 2001. By the early 2000s, Philips employed some 30 000 people in China either directly or indirectly at joint ventures. Philips exported nearly two-thirds of the $7 billion in products that its Chinese factories were producing. At this point, 25 percent of everything that Philips made worldwide came from China.

As time passed, Philips started to give its Chinese factories a greater role in product development. In the TV business, for example, basic development used to occur in Holland but was moved to Singapore in the early 1990s. In the early 2000s, Philips transferred TV development work to a new R&D center in Suzhou near Shanghai. Similarly, basic product development work on LCD screens for cell phones was shifted to Shanghai. In 2011, in a testament to just how important China had become to Philips, the company moved the global headquarters of its domestic appliances business from Amsterdam to Shanghai. By this point, China was far more than just an export base. Demand in China had accelerated rapidly, and the country was now the second-largest market for Philips.

Some worry that Philips and companies pursuing a similar strategy might be overdoing it. Too much dependence on China could be dangerous if political, economic, or other problems disrupt production and the company's ability to supply global markets. Some observers believe that it might be better if the manufacturing facilities of companies were more geographically diverse as a hedge against problems in China. These fears have taken on added importance recently as labour costs have accelerated in China due to labour shortages. According to estimates, labour costs have been growing by 20 percent per year since the 2000s. On the other hand, there is a silver lining to this cloud: Chinese consumption of many of the products that Philips makes there is now rising rapidly.

Questions

1. Other than rising labour costs, what are some other risks of having facilities in China?
2. Using the risks you identified above, how can these risks be mitigated?

Source: B. Einhorn, "Philips' Expanding Asia Connections," *Businessweek Online*, November 27, 2003; K. Leggett and P. Wonacott, "The World's Factory: A Surge in Exports from China Jolts the Global Industry," *The Wall Street Journal*, October 10, 2002, p. A1; J. Blau, "Philips Tears Down Eindhoven R&D Fence," *Research Technology Management* 50, no. 6 (2007), pp. 9–11; and L. Baijia, "Philips Elevates China's Market Status," *China Daily*, May 26, 2011.

Of course, other things are not equal. Differences in relative factor costs, political economy, culture, and location externalities are important, but other factors also loom large. Formal and informal trade barriers obviously influence location decisions (see Chapter 6), as do transportation costs and rules and regulations regarding foreign direct investment (see Chapter 7). For example, although relative factor costs may make a country look attractive as a location for performing a manufacturing activity,

ANOTHER PERSPECTIVE

Careers in Supply Chain Management

With increased outsourcing, and overseas production sites and customers, supply chain management is a growing field. The Council of Supply Chain Management Professionals (CSCMP), a professional association with more than 8500 members worldwide, says the industry offers a promising outlook. What's more, potential employers are everywhere—manufacturers and distributors; government agencies; consulting firms; the transport industry; universities and colleges; service firms such as banks, hospitals, and hotels; and third-party logistics providers. For more information about the organization and careers in this field, visit the CSCMP Web site at www.cscmp.org.

regulations prohibiting foreign direct investment may eliminate this option. Similarly, a consideration of factor costs might suggest that a firm should source production of a certain component from a particular country, but trade barriers could make this uneconomical.

Another country factor is expected future movements in its exchange rate (see Chapters 9 and 10). Adverse changes in exchange rates can quickly alter a country's attractiveness as a manufacturing base. Currency appreciation can transform a low-cost location into a high-cost location. Many Japanese corporations have had to grapple with this problem since the 1990s. The relatively low value of the yen on foreign exchange markets between 1950 and 1980 helped strengthen Japan's position as a low-cost location for manufacturing. Between 1980 and the mid-1990s, however, the yen's steady appreciation against the dollar increased the dollar cost of products exported from Japan, making Japan less attractive as a manufacturing location. In response, many Japanese firms moved their manufacturing offshore to lower-cost locations in East Asia. The impact of the strong Canadian dollar on the selection of manufacturing locations, at least in comparison to the U.S. dollar, remains to be seen.

Technological Factors

The technology we are concerned with in this subsection is manufacturing technology—the technology that performs specific manufacturing activities. The type of technology a firm uses in its manufacturing can be pivotal in location decisions. For example, because of technological constraints, in some cases it is necessary to perform certain manufacturing activities in only one location and serve the world market from there. In other cases, the technology may make it feasible to perform an activity in multiple locations. Three characteristics of a manufacturing technology are of interest here: the level of fixed costs, the minimum efficient scale, and the flexibility of the technology.

FIXED COSTS

As we noted in Chapter 11, in some cases the fixed costs of setting up a manufacturing plant are so high that a firm must serve the world market from a single location or from a very few locations. For example, it now costs more than $1 billion to set up a state-of-the-art plant to manufacture semiconductor chips. Given this, serving the world market from a single plant sited at a single (optimal) location makes sense. Conversely, a relatively low level of fixed costs can make it economical to perform a

In 2009, Ford Motor Company renovated its Louisville truck plant allowing for flexible manufacturing. What other industries could benefit from flexible manufacturing? © *Vladimir Salman/Dreamstime.com*

particular activity in several locations at once. This allows the firm to better accommodate demands for local responsiveness. Manufacturing in multiple locations may also help the firm avoid becoming too dependent on one location. Being too dependent on one location is particularly risky in a world of floating exchange rates. Many firms disperse their manufacturing plants to different locations as a "real hedge" against potentially adverse moves in currencies.

MINIMUM EFFICIENT SCALE

The concept of economies of scale tells us that as plant output expands, unit costs decrease. The reasons include the greater utilization of capital equipment and the productivity gains that come with specialization of employees within the plant.[9] However, beyond a certain level of output, few additional scale economies are available. Thus, the "unit cost curve" declines with output until a certain output level is reached, at which point further increases in output realize little reduction in unit costs. The level of output at which most plant-level scale economies are exhausted is referred to as the minimum efficient scale of output. This is the scale of output a plant must operate at to realize all major plant-level scale economies (see Figure 15.2).

The implications of this concept are as follows: The larger the minimum efficient scale of a plant, the greater the argument for centralizing production in a single location or a limited number of locations. Alternatively, when the minimum efficient scale of production is relatively low, it may be economical to manufacture a product at several locations. As in the case of low fixed costs, the advantages are allowing the firm to accommodate demands for local responsiveness or to hedge against currency risk by manufacturing the same product in several locations.

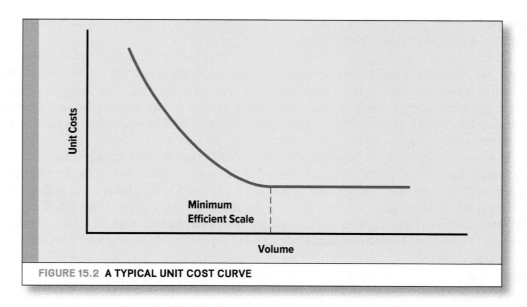

FIGURE 15.2 **A TYPICAL UNIT COST CURVE**

FLEXIBLE MANUFACTURING AND MASS CUSTOMIZATION

Central to the concept of economies of scale is the idea that the best way to achieve high efficiency, and hence low unit costs, is through the mass production of a standardized output. The trade-off implicit in this idea is between unit costs and product variety. Producing greater product variety from a factory implies shorter production runs, which in turn implies an inability to realize economies of scale. That is, wide product variety makes it difficult for a company to increase its production efficiency and thus reduce its unit costs. According to this logic, the way to increase efficiency and drive down unit costs is to limit product variety and produce a standardized product in large volumes.

This view of production efficiency has been challenged by the rise of flexible manufacturing technologies. The term **flexible manufacturing technology**—or *lean production*, as it is often called—covers a range of manufacturing technologies designed to (1) reduce setup times for complex equipment; (2) increase the utilization of individual machines through better scheduling; and (3) improve quality control at all stages of the manufacturing process.[10] Flexible manufacturing technologies allow the company to produce a wider variety of end products at a unit cost that at one time could be achieved only through the mass production of a standardized output. Research suggests the adoption of flexible manufacturing technologies may actually increase efficiency and lower unit costs relative to what can be achieved by the mass production of a standardized output, while at the same time enabling the company to customize its product offering to a much greater extent than was once thought possible. The term **mass customization** has been coined to describe the ability of companies to use flexible manufacturing technology to reconcile two goals that were once thought to be incompatible—low cost and product customization.[11]

Flexible manufacturing technologies vary in their sophistication and complexity. One of the most famous examples of a flexible manufacturing technology, Toyota's production system, is relatively unsophisticated, but it has been credited with making Toyota the most efficient auto company in the world. Toyota's flexible manufacturing system was developed by one of the company's engineers, Ohno Taiichi. After working at Toyota for five years and visiting Ford's U.S. plants, Ohno became convinced that the mass production philosophy for making cars was flawed. He saw numerous problems with the mass production system.

First, long production runs created massive inventories that had to be stored in large warehouses. This was expensive, both because of the cost of warehousing and because inventories tied up capital in unproductive uses. Second, if the initial machine settings were wrong, long production runs resulted in the production of a large number of defects (i.e., waste). Third, the mass production system was unable to accommodate consumer preferences for product diversity.

In response, Ohno looked for ways to make shorter production runs economical. He developed a number of techniques designed to reduce setup times for production equipment (a major source of fixed costs). By using a system of levers and pulleys, he reduced the time required to change dies on stamping equipment from a full day in 1950 to 3 minutes by 1971. This made small production runs economical, which allowed Toyota to respond better to consumer demands for product diversity. Small production runs also eliminated the need to hold large inventories, thereby reducing warehousing costs. Furthermore, small product runs and the lack of inventory meant that defective parts were produced in small numbers and entered the assembly process immediately. This reduced waste and helped trace defects back to their source to fix the problem. In sum, Ohno's innovations enabled Toyota to produce a more diverse product range at a lower unit cost than was possible with conventional mass production.[12]

Flexible machine cells are another common flexible manufacturing technology. A **flexible machine cell** is a grouping of various types of machinery, a common materials handler, and a centralized cell controller (computer). Each cell normally contains four to six machines capable of performing a variety of operations. The typical cell is dedicated to the production of a family of parts or products. The settings on machines are computer controlled, which allows each cell to switch quickly between the production of different parts or products. Improved capacity utilization and reductions in work-in-progress inventory (that is, stockpiles of partly finished products) as well as reductions in waste are major efficiency benefits of flexible machine cells. Improved capacity utilization arises from the reduction in setup times and from the computer-controlled coordination of production flow between machines, which eliminates bottlenecks. The tight coordination between machines also reduces work-in-progress inventory. Reductions in waste are due to the ability of computer-controlled machinery to identify ways to transform inputs into outputs while producing a minimum of unusable waste material. While freestanding machines might be in use 50 percent of the time, the same machines when grouped into a cell can be used more than 80 percent of the time and produce the same end product with half the waste. This increases efficiency and results in lower costs.

The efficiency benefits of installing flexible manufacturing technology can be dramatic. Avcorp Industries Inc., a public company based in Delta, British Columbia, is a supplier to the high technology and aerospace industries. Their products are flight structures, wing and fuselage components, flight control surfaces, and navigation and landing light lenses. In 1998, Avcorp worked with Dassault Aviation to engineer customized automated robotics. The automated assembly cell used in this robotic system performed coordinated movements for fastening operations, as well as independent movements for drilling and sealing for operational flexibility. This operation is unique to Avcorp; the design enables the robotic cells to work on more than one type of assembly, while traditional robotic cells are confined to only one application. Avcorp's robotic assembly time is estimated to be from 50 to 67 percent less than manual assembly time. Lowering the assembly time results in decreases in costs for the aero-structures supplier and the aircraft operator.[13] Similarly, Lexmark, a producer of computer printers, has also converted 80 percent of its 2700-employee factory in Lexington, Kentucky, to flexible manufacturing cells, and it too has seen productivity increase by about 25 percent.[14] Besides improving efficiency and lowering costs, flexible manufacturing technologies also enable companies to customize products to the unique demands of small consumer groups—at a cost that at one time could be achieved only by mass producing a standardized output. Thus, the technologies help a company achieve mass customization, which increases its customer responsiveness. Most important for an international business, flexible manufacturing technologies can help the firm customize products for different national markets. The importance of this advantage cannot be overstated. When flexible manufacturing technologies are available, a firm can manufacture products customized to various national markets at a single factory sited at the optimal location. And it can do this without absorbing a significant cost penalty. Thus, companies no longer need to establish manufacturing facilities in each major national market to provide products that satisfy specific consumer tastes and preferences, part of the rationale for a multidomestic strategy (Chapter 11).

SUMMARY

A number of technological factors support the economic arguments for concentrating manufacturing facilities in a few choice locations or even in a single location. Other things being equal, when fixed costs are substantial, the minimum efficient scale of production is high, and/or flexible manufacturing technologies are available, the arguments for concentrating production at a few choice locations are strong. This is true even when substantial differences in consumer tastes and preferences exist between national markets, since flexible manufacturing technologies allow the firm to customize products to national differences at a single facility. Alternatively, when fixed costs are low, the minimum efficient scale of production is low, and flexible manufacturing technologies are not available, the arguments for concentrating production at one or a few locations are not as compelling. In such cases, it may make more sense to manufacture in each major market in which the firm is active if this helps the firm better respond to local demands. This holds only if the increased local responsiveness more than offsets the cost disadvantages of not concentrating manufacturing. With the advent of flexible manufacturing technologies and mass customization, such a strategy is becoming less attractive. In sum, technological factors are making it feasible, and necessary, for firms to concentrate manufacturing facilities at optimal locations. Trade barriers and transportation costs are major brakes on this trend.

Product Factors

Two product features affect location decisions. The first is the product's *value-to-weight ratio* because of its influence on transportation costs. Many electronic components and pharmaceuticals have high value-to-weight ratios; they are expensive and they do not weigh very much. Thus, even if they are shipped halfway around the world, their transportation costs account for a very small percentage of total costs. Given this, there is great pressure to manufacture these products in the optimal location and to serve the world market from there. The opposite holds for products with low value-to-weight ratios. Refined sugar, certain bulk chemicals, paint, and

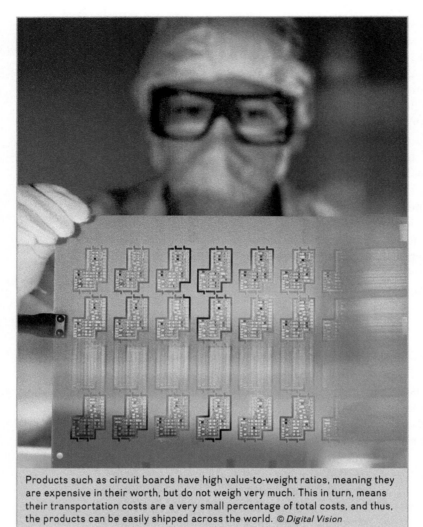

Products such as circuit boards have high value-to-weight ratios, meaning they are expensive in their worth, but do not weigh very much. This in turn, means their transportation costs are a very small percentage of total costs, and thus, the products can be easily shipped across the world. © *Digital Vision*

petroleum products all have low value-to-weight ratios; they are relatively inexpensive products that weigh a lot. Accordingly, when they are shipped long distances, transportation costs account for a large percentage of total costs. Thus there is great pressure to manufacture these products in multiple locations close to major markets to reduce transportation costs.

The other product feature that can influence location decisions is whether the product serves *universal needs*, needs that are the same all over the world. Examples include many industrial products (e.g., industrial electronics, steel, bulk chemicals) and modern consumer products (e.g., handheld calculators and personal computers). Since there are few national differences in consumer taste and preference for such products, the need for local responsiveness is reduced. This increases the attractiveness of concentrating manufacturing at an optimal location.

Locating Production Facilities

There are two basic strategies for locating production facilities: concentrating them in a centralized location and serving the world market from there, or decentralizing them in various regional or national locations that are close to major markets. The appropriate strategic choice is determined by the various country, technological, and product factors we have discussed in this section and are summarized in Table 15.1. As can be seen, concentration of production makes the most sense when:

- differences between countries in factor costs, political economy, and culture have a substantial impact on the costs of manufacturing in various countries;
- trade barriers are low;
- externalities arising from the concentration of like enterprises favour certain locations;
- important exchange rates are expected to remain relatively stable;
- the production technology has high fixed costs, a high minimum efficient scale, or a flexible manufacturing technology exists;

TABLE 15.1 Location Strategy and Manufacturing	Concentrated Production Favoured	Decentralized Production Favoured
Country Factors		
Differences in political economy	Substantial	Few
Differences in culture	Substantial	Few
Differences in factor costs	Substantial	Few
Substantial trade barriers	Low	High
Location externalities	Important in industry	Not important in industry
Exchange rates	Stable	Volatile
Technological Factors		
Fixed costs	High	Low
Minimum efficient scale	High	Low
Flexible manufacturing technology	Available	Not available
Product Factors		
Value-to-weight ratio	High	Low
Serves universal needs	Yes	No

- the product's value-to-weight ratio is high; and
- the product serves universal needs.

Alternatively, decentralization of manufacturing is appropriate when:

- differences between countries in factor costs, political economy, and culture do not have a substantial impact on the costs of manufacturing in various countries;
- trade barriers are high;
- location externalities are not important;
- volatility in important exchange rates is expected;
- the production technology has low fixed costs, low minimum efficient scale, and flexible manufacturing technology is not available;
- the product's value-to-weight ratio is low; and
- the product does not serve universal needs (that is, significant differences in consumer tastes and preferences exist between nations).

ANOTHER PERSPECTIVE

Ethics with Outsourcing

As Nike has learned through its outsourced operations, the world citizen tends to see the ethical standards followed in production as a responsibility of the company. Imagine the challenge of monitoring such operations, many of which tend to be rural. As soon as you land at the regional airport for an on-site visit, the rural production site managers know you are there. They have time to pull together the face they know you want to see, the standards you included in your outsourcing contract. A long-term relationship with the supplier, insistence on acceptable production standards and human resource policies, including wage requirements, and the involvement of the supplier's local employees on workers councils are some ways to maintain knowledge of the actual standards in the production facility.

In practice, location decisions are seldom clear-cut. For example, it is not unusual for differences in factor costs, technological factors, and product factors to point toward concentrated manufacturing while a combination of trade barriers and volatile exchange rates points toward decentralized manufacturing. For example, this seems to be the case in the world automobile industry. Although the availability of flexible manufacturing and cars' relatively high value-to-weight ratios suggest concentrated manufacturing, the combination of formal and informal trade barriers, and the uncertainties of the world's current floating exchange rate regime (see Chapter 10) have inhibited firms' ability to pursue this strategy. For these reasons, several automobile companies have established "top-to-bottom" manufacturing operations in three major regional markets: Asia, North America, and Western Europe.

The Hidden Costs of Foreign Locations

There may be some "hidden costs" to basing production in a foreign location. Numerous anecdotes suggest that high employee turnover, shoddy workmanship, poor product quality, and low productivity are significant issues in some outsourcing locations.[15] Microsoft, for example, established a major facility in Hyderabad, India, for four very good reasons: (1) the wage rate of software programmers in India is one-third of that in the United States; (2) India has an excellent higher education system that graduates a lot of computer science majors every year; (3) there was already a high concentration of information technology companies and workers in Hyderabad; and (4) many of Microsoft's highly skilled Indian employees, after spending years in the United States, wanted to return home, and Microsoft saw the Hyderabad facility as a way of holding on to this valuable human capital.

However, the company has found that the turnover rate among its Indian employees is higher than in the United States. Demand for software programmers in India is high, and many employees are prone to switch jobs to get better pay. Although Microsoft has tried to limit turnover by offering good benefits and long-term incentive pay, such as stock grants to high performers who stay with the company, many of the Indians who were hired locally apparently place little value on long-term incentives and prefer higher current pay. High employee turnover, of course, has a negative impact on productivity. One Microsoft manager in India noted that 40 percent of his core team had left within the past 12 months, making it very difficult to stay on track with development projects.[16]

Microsoft is not alone in experiencing this problem. The manager of an electronics company that outsourced the manufacture of wireless headsets to China noted that after four years of frustrations with late deliveries and poor quality, his company decided to move production *back* to the United States. In his words: "On the face of it, labour costs seemed so much lower in China that the decision to move production there was a very easy one. In retrospect, I wish we had looked much closer at productivity and workmanship. We have actually lost market share because of this decision."[17] The lesson here is that it is important to look beyond pay rates and make judgments about employee productivity before deciding whether to outsource activities to foreign locations.

LO3 The Strategic Role of a Foreign Production Site

Whatever the rationale behind establishing a foreign manufacturing facility, the strategic role of foreign factories can evolve over time.[18] Initially, many foreign factories are established where labour costs are low. Their strategic role typically is to produce labour-intensive products at as low a cost as possible. For example, beginning in the 1970s, many North American firms in the computer and telecommunication equipment businesses established factories across Southeast Asia to manufacture electronic components, such as circuit boards and semiconductors, at the lowest possible cost. They located their factories in countries such as Malaysia, Thailand, and Singapore precisely because each of these countries offered an attractive combination of low labour costs, adequate infrastructure, and a favourable tax and trade regime. Initially, the components produced by these factories were designed elsewhere and the final product would be assembled elsewhere. Over time, however, the strategic role of some factories has expanded; they have become important centres for the design and final assembly of products for the global marketplace. An example is Hewlett-Packard's operation in Singapore. Originally established as a low-cost location for the production of circuit boards, the facility has become the centre for the design and final assembly of portable ink-jet printers for the global marketplace.

Such upward migration in the strategic role of foreign factories arises because many foreign factories upgrade their own capabilities.[19] This improvement comes from two sources. First, pressure from the head office to improve a factory's cost structure and/or customize a product to the demands of consumers in a particular nation can start a chain of events that ultimately leads to development of additional capabilities at that factory. For example, to meet head-office mandated directions to drive down costs, engineers at HP's Singapore factory argued that they needed to redesign products so they could be manufactured at a lower cost. This led to the establishment of a design centre in Singapore. As this design centre proved its worth, HP executives realized the importance of co-locating design and manufacturing operations. They increasingly transferred more design responsibilities to the Singapore factory. In addition, the Singapore factory ultimately became the centre for the design of products tailored to the needs of the Asian market. This too made good strategic sense because it meant products were being designed by engineers who were close to the Asian market and probably had a good understanding of the needs of that market, as opposed to engineers located in the United States.

A second source of improvement in the capabilities of a foreign factory can be the increasing abundance of advanced factors of production in the nation in which the factory is located. Many nations that were considered economic backwaters a generation ago have been experiencing rapid economic development during the 1980s and 1990s. Their communication and transportation infrastructures and the education level of the population have improved. While these countries once lacked the advanced infrastructure required to support sophisticated design, development, and manufacturing operations, this is often no longer the case. This has made it much easier for factories based in these nations to take on a greater strategic role.

Because of such developments, many international businesses are moving away from a system in which their foreign factories were viewed as nothing more than low-cost manufacturing facilities and toward one where foreign factories are viewed as globally dispersed centres of excellence. In this new model, foreign factories take the lead role for the design and manufacture of products to serve important national or regional markets or even the global market. The development of such dispersed centres of excellence is consistent with the concept of a transnational strategy, which we introduced in Chapter 11. A major aspect of a transnational strategy is a belief in global learning—the idea that valuable knowledge does not reside just in a firm's domestic operations; it may also be found in its foreign subsidiaries. Foreign factories that upgrade their capabilities over time are creating valuable knowledge that might benefit the whole corporation. Managers of international businesses need to remember

MANAGEMENT FOCUS

GE Moves Manufacturing from China to the United States

For decades, General Electric has been at the forefront of the move to shift production offshore from high-cost locations inside the United States to cheaper locations, such as China. But there are now some signs that the relentless flow of production offshore may be slowing down and, in some cases, starting to reverse. There are several reasons for this. Wage rates in China and some other developing nations have been rising fast, closing the differential between costs in the United States and overseas. In dollar terms, wage rates in China were some five times higher in 2012 than they were in 2000, and they are still rising fast. Labour productivity has also increased significantly in the United States, further closing the gap in labour costs. Meanwhile, high oil prices have raised the cost of shipping products across oceans, while the abundance of cheap natural gas in the United States is helping to lower production costs. If this were not enough, there are signs that there are benefits to having product design and manufacturing co-located, and in some cases, this is driving a shift in production back to the United States.

A case in point is GE's GeoSpring water heater. This was originally designed in the United States and manufactured in China. The finished product was then shipped back across the ocean for sale in the United States. In 2010, given the macro trends in labour productivity and energy prices, GE decided to see what would happen if it brought some of its appliance products back to the United States. The GeoSpring was one of its first attempts at this. GE established a team of engineers and production workers at its appliance plant in Louisville, Kentucky, to see what they could do with the GeoSpring. The team quickly concluded that the GeoSpring was not easy to manufacture due to poor design. They redesigned the product for ease of assembly, eliminating one out of every five parts and cutting material costs by 25 percent. As a result, GE cut the time required to assemble the product from 10 hours in China to 2 hours in Louisville.

The end result: Material costs went down, labour requirement went down, and product quality went up. Indeed, the cost savings were so big that GE was able to reduce the price of the GeoSpring 20 percent below that of the Chinese-manufactured product and still maintain a decent profit margin. Time to market also improved greatly. It used to take five weeks to get a GeoSpring from China into a U.S. retail store—now GE can do that in a matter of days, which improves inventory management.

Having learned from experiences like this, GE is now planning to ramp up production of other appliance products at Louisville. It has recently doubled the workforce there to 3700, and has also hired 500 new designers and engineers to redesign many of its products for ease of manufacture. A few years ago, less than half of the revenues of the appliance business came from products made in the United States. GE now plans to have 75 percent of the revenue of the appliance business to come from American-made products.

Questions

1. Do you see this as the beginning of a trend, or is GE's experience unique?
2. What types of firms can you predict may eventually move back to North America?

Sources: Charles Fishman, "The Insourcing Boom," *The Atlantic*, December 2012; and J. R. Immelt, "Sparking an American Manufacturing Renewal," *Harvard Business Review*, March 2012.

that foreign factories can improve their capabilities over time, and this can be of immense strategic benefit to the firm. Rather than viewing foreign factories simply as sweatshops where unskilled labour churns out low-cost goods, managers need to view them as potential centres of excellence and to encourage and foster attempts by local managers to upgrade the capabilities of their factories and, thereby, enhance their strategic standing within the corporation.

DEBATE THE ISSUE

Do You Expect a Trend in Bringing Jobs Back from Overseas?

The United States may be on the verge of bringing back manufacturing jobs from China. Outsourcing manufacturing to China is not as cheap as it used to be. Many companies, especially in the auto and furniture industries, moved plants overseas once China opened its doors to free trade and foreign investment in the last few decades. Labour was cheaper for American companies—less than $1 per hour by some estimates at the time. Today, labour costs in China have risen dramatically, and shipping and fuel costs have skyrocketed. As China's economy has expanded and as China has built new factories all across the country, the demand for workers has risen. As a result, wages are up as new companies compete to hire the best workers. Experts note the fears that U.S. manufacturing is in decline are overstated and that the United States is still a manufacturing giant. However, both China and the United States each account for about 20 percent global manufacturing value added. The U.S. share of about 20 percent of global manufacturing value added "has declined only slightly over the past three decades," according to the Boston Consulting Group. With these estimates in mind, do you expect more and more outsourced jobs to be "insourced" in the future? Will the Donald Trump administration have anything to do with this?

Source: "Made in America: Trend against outsourcing brings jobs back from China," *NBC News*, January 14, 2012, http://rockcenter.nbcnews.com/_news/2012/01/14/10156162-made-in-america-trend-against-outsourcing-brings-jobs-back-from-china?chromedomain=usnews.

LO4 | Outsourcing Production: Make-or-Buy Decisions

International businesses frequently face **sourcing decisions**, decisions about whether they should make or buy the component parts that go into their final product. Should the firm vertically integrate to manufacture its own component parts, or should it outsource them, buying them from independent suppliers? Make-or-buy decisions are important factors in many firms' manufacturing strategies. In the automobile industry, for example, the typical car contains more than 10 000 components, so automobile firms constantly face make-or-buy decisions. Ford of Europe, for example, produces only about 45 percent of the value of a car in its own plants. The remaining 55 percent, mainly accounted for by component parts, comes from independent suppliers. In the athletic shoe industry, the make-or-buy issue has been taken to an extreme with companies such as Nike and Reebok having no involvement in manufacturing; all production has been outsourced, primarily to manufacturers based in low-wage countries.

Make-or-buy decisions pose plenty of problems for purely domestic businesses but even more problems for international businesses. These decisions in the international arena are complicated by the volatility of countries' political economies, exchange rate movements, changes in relative factor costs, and the like. In this section, we examine the arguments for making components and for buying them, and we consider the trade-offs involved in these decisions. Then we discuss strategic alliances as an alternative to manufacturing component parts within the company.

The Advantages of Make

The arguments that support making component parts in-house—vertical integration—are fivefold. Vertical integration may be associated with lowering costs, facilitating investments in highly specialized assets, protecting proprietary product technology, accumulating dynamic capabilities, and facilitating the scheduling of adjacent processes.

LOWER COSTS

It may pay a firm to continue manufacturing a product or component in-house if the firm is more efficient at that production activity than any other enterprise. Boeing, for example, has looked closely at its make-or-buy decisions with regard to commercial jet aircraft. It decided to outsource the production of some component parts but keep the production of aircraft wings in-house. Boeing's rationale was that it has a core competence in the production of wings, and it is more efficient at this activity than any other comparable enterprise in the world. Therefore, it makes little sense for Boeing to outsource this particular activity.

FACILITATE SPECIALIZED INVESTMENTS

We first encountered the concept of specialized assets in Chapter 7 when we looked at the eclectic paradigm theory. A variation of that concept explains why firms might want to make their own components rather than buy them.[20] When one firm must invest in specialized assets to supply another, mutual dependency is created. In such circumstances, each party fears the other will abuse the relationship by seeking more favourable terms.

For example, imagine Ford of Europe has developed a high-performance, high-quality, and uniquely designed fuel-injection system. The fuel-injection system's increased fuel efficiency will help sell Ford cars. Ford must decide whether to make the system in-house or to contract out the manufacturing to an independent supplier. Manufacturing these uniquely designed systems requires investments in equipment that can be used only for this purpose; it cannot be used to make fuel-injection systems for any other auto firm. Thus, investment in this equipment constitutes an investment in specialized assets.

Let us first examine this situation from the perspective of an independent supplier who has been asked by Ford to make this investment. The supplier might reason that once it has made the investment, it will become dependent on Ford for business since Ford is the only possible customer for the output of this equipment. The supplier perceives this as putting Ford in a strong bargaining position and worries that once the specialized investment has been made, Ford might use this to squeeze down prices for the fuel-injection systems. Given this risk, the supplier declines to make the investment in specialized equipment.

Now take the position of Ford. Ford might reason that if it contracts out production of these systems to an independent supplier, it might become too dependent on that supplier for a vital input. Because specialized equipment is required to produce the fuel-injection systems, Ford cannot easily switch its orders to other suppliers who lack that equipment. (It would face high switching costs.) Ford perceives this as increasing the bargaining power of the supplier and worries that the supplier might use its bargaining strength to demand higher prices.

Thus, the mutual dependency that outsourcing would create makes Ford nervous and scares away potential suppliers. Neither party completely trusts the other to play fair. Consequently, Ford might reason that the only safe way to get the new fuel-injection systems is to manufacture them itself. It may be unable to persuade any independent supplier to manufacture them. Thus, Ford decides to make rather than buy.

In general, we can predict that when substantial investments in specialized assets are required to manufacture a component, the firm will prefer to make the component internally rather than contract it out to a supplier. A growing amount of empirical evidence supports this prediction.[21]

PROTECT PROPRIETARY PRODUCT TECHNOLOGY

Proprietary product technology is technology unique to a firm. If it enables the firm to produce a product containing superior features, proprietary technology can give the firm a competitive advantage. The firm would not want this technology to fall into the hands of competitors. If the firm contracts out the manufacture of components containing proprietary technology, it runs the risk that those suppliers will expropriate the technology for their own use or that they will sell it to the firm's competitors. Thus, to maintain control over its technology, the firm might prefer to make such component parts in-house. Boeing has decided to outsource a number of important components that go toward the production of an aircraft, and has explicitly decided not to outsource the manufacture of wings and cockpits because it believes that doing so would give away key technology to potential competitors.

ACCUMULATE DYNAMIC CAPABILITIES

Competitive advantage is not a static concept. The capability to effectively and efficiently produce goods and services is one that evolves over time. Firms can learn through their experience how to lower costs, design better products, increase product reliability, and so on. Their capabilities (skills), in other words, are dynamic; they are learned through experience (the term **dynamic capabilities** is used to describe skills that become more valuable over time through learning).[22] Also, the experience learned producing one kind of product might create a capability that is then useful for producing another kind of product.

For example, in the late 1990s under the leadership of CEO Steve Jobs, Apple developed some very valuable design capabilities. Under Jobs' direction, Apple hired talented industrial designers and gave them a *major* say in product development. Originally, these designers worked on Apple's line of desktop and laptop computers. They produced computers that were differentiated by superior design elegance from those produced by its rivals. Through this process, over time the design team built up considerable capabilities in industrial design as applied to computing devices for consumers. Subsequently, Apple has been able to leverage these capabilities to produce a range of elegantly designed products that have been very successful, including the iPod, iPhone, and iPad.

Now imagine if in an effort to save costs, instead of hiring its own designers, Apple had outsourced design to an independent design firm (such firms do exist). If it had done so, Apple may never have acquired the capabilities that subsequently enabled it to design products like the iPhone and iPad. Instead, those capabilities would have resided in the design firm. Put differently, Apple would have missed out on the opportunity to establish a competitive advantage based on a capability in industrial design.

ANOTHER PERSPECTIVE

Japanese Supply Chain Management

Many Japanese manufacturers are vertically integrated to the point where they own their own shipping fleets. As the volume of their exports increased, Japanese auto manufacturers, for example, decided to buy their own ships. What are the benefits of such a move? What costs might it have?

The Apple example points to one of the problems with outsourcing. Firms that outsource activities to gain a short-term cost advantage may miss out on the opportunity to subsequently build important capabilities in that activity. Critics claim that the rush by American firms to outsource activities to low-cost foreign suppliers during the 1990s and 2000s has had just this effect.[23] Although each decision may have seemed reasonable in isolation when it was taken, the cumulative effect of outsourcing may be to pass up on the opportunity to develop capabilities in that activity—capabilities that might subsequently lead to a competitive advantage. When Amazon was deciding who should make the display screen for the Kindle, for example, it contracted the work to a Taiwanese firm. But, considering that the online retailer is branching out into consumer electronics with Kindle products, including the tablet and Fire Phone, the outsourcing decision has become less obvious.

The key point here is that firms should be very careful about what they outsource. They should not outsource activities for a short-term cost saving if those activities are potentially important for the long-term competitive advantage of the enterprise.

IMPROVE SCHEDULING

The weakest argument for vertical integration is that production cost savings result from it because it makes planning, coordination, and scheduling of adjacent processes easier.[24] This is particularly important in firms with just-in-time inventory systems (which we discuss later in the chapter). In the 1920s, for example, Ford profited from tight coordination and scheduling made possible by backward vertical integration into steel foundries, iron ore shipping, and mining. Deliveries at Ford's foundries on the Great Lakes were coordinated so well that ore was turned into engine blocks within 24 hours. This substantially reduced Ford's production costs by eliminating the need to hold excessive ore inventories.

For international businesses that source worldwide, scheduling problems can be exacerbated by the time and distance between the firm and its suppliers. This is true whether the firms use their own subunits as suppliers or use independent suppliers. Ownership is not the issue here. Companies such as Samsung, LG, TCL, and Hisense can succeed with tight scheduling and efficient production through vertical integration. Thus, although this argument for vertical integration is often made, it is not compelling. See the Country Focus earlier in this chapter.

The Advantages of Buy

The advantages of buying component parts from independent suppliers are that it gives the firm greater flexibility, it can help drive down the firm's cost structure, and it may help the firm capture orders from international customers.

STRATEGIC FLEXIBILITY

The great advantage of buying component parts from independent suppliers is that the firm can maintain its flexibility, switching orders between suppliers as circumstances dictate. This is particularly important internationally, where changes in exchange rates and trade barriers can alter the attractiveness of supply sources. One year Hong Kong might be the lowest-cost source for a particular component, and the next year, Mexico may be. Many firms source the same parts from suppliers based in two different countries, primarily as a hedge against adverse movements in factor costs, exchange rates, and the like.

Sourcing component parts from independent suppliers can also be advantageous when the optimal location for manufacturing a product is beset by political risks. Under such circumstances, foreign direct investment to establish a component manufacturing operation in that country would expose the firm to political risks. The firm can avoid many of these risks by buying from an independent supplier in that country, thereby maintaining the flexibility to switch sourcing to another country if a war, revolution, or other political change alters that country's attractiveness as a supply source.

However, maintaining strategic flexibility has its downside. If a supplier perceives the firm will change suppliers in response to changes in exchange rates, trade barriers, or general political circumstances, that supplier might not be willing to make specialized investments in plant and equipment that would ultimately benefit the firm.

LOWER COSTS

Although vertical integration is often undertaken to lower costs, it may have the opposite effect. When this is the case, outsourcing may lower the firm's cost structure. Vertical integration into the manufacture of component parts increases an organization's scope, and the resulting increase in organizational complexity can raise a firm's cost structure for three reasons.

First, the greater the number of subunits in an organization, the greater are the problems of coordinating and controlling those units. Coordinating and controlling subunits require top management to process large amounts of information about subunit activities. The greater the number of subunits, the more information top management must process and the harder it is to do well. Theoretically, when the firm becomes involved in too many activities, headquarters management will be unable to effectively control all of them, and the resulting inefficiencies will more than offset any advantages derived from vertical integration.[25] This can be particularly serious in an international business, where the problem of controlling subunits is exacerbated by distance and differences in time, language, and culture.

Second, the firm that vertically integrates into component part manufacture may find that because its internal suppliers have a captive customer in the firm, they lack an incentive to reduce costs. The fact that they do not have to compete for orders with other suppliers may result in high operating costs. The managers of the supply operation may be tempted to pass on cost increases to other parts of the firm in the form of higher transfer prices, rather than looking for ways to reduce those costs.

Third, vertically integrated firms have to determine appropriate prices for goods transferred to subunits within the firm. This is a challenge in any firm, but it is even more complex in international businesses. Different tax regimes, exchange rate movements, and headquarters' ignorance about local conditions all increase the complexity of transfer pricing decisions. This complexity enhances internal suppliers' ability to manipulate transfer prices to their advantage, passing cost increases downstream rather than looking for ways to reduce costs.

The firm that buys its components from independent suppliers can avoid all these problems and the associated costs. The firm that sources from independent suppliers has fewer subunits to control. The incentive problems that occur with internal suppliers do not arise when independent suppliers are used. Independent suppliers know they must continue to be efficient if they are to win business from the firm. Also, because independent suppliers' prices are set by market forces, the transfer pricing problem does not exist. In sum, the bureaucratic inefficiencies and resulting costs that can arise when firms vertically integrate backward and manufacture their own components are avoided by buying component parts from independent suppliers.

OFFSETS

Another reason for outsourcing some manufacturing to independent suppliers based in other countries is that it may help the firm capture more orders from that country.

For example, before Air India places a large order with Boeing, the Indian government might ask Boeing to push some subcontracting work toward Indian manufacturers. This kind of quid pro quo is not unusual in international business, and it affects far more than just the aerospace industry. Representatives of the U.S. government have repeatedly urged Japanese automobile companies to purchase more component parts from U.S. suppliers to partially offset the large volume of automobile exports from Japan to the United States.

Trade-Offs

Trade-offs are involved in make-or-buy decisions. The benefits of manufacturing components in-house seem to be greatest when highly specialized assets are involved, when vertical integration is necessary for protecting proprietary technology, or when the firm is simply more efficient than external suppliers at performing a particular activity. When these conditions are not present, the risk of strategic inflexibility and organizational problems suggest it may be better to contract out component part manufacturing to independent suppliers. Since issues of strategic flexibility and organizational control loom even larger for international businesses than purely domestic ones, an international business should be particularly wary of vertical integration into component part manufacture. In addition, some outsourcing in the form of offsets may help a firm gain larger orders in the future.

Strategic Alliances with Suppliers

Several international businesses have tried to reap some benefits of vertical integration without the associated organizational problems by entering strategic alliances with essential suppliers. For example, there was an alliance between Kodak and Canon, under which Canon built photocopiers for sale by Kodak; an alliance between Microsoft and Flextronics, under which Flextronics built the Xbox for Microsoft; and an alliance between Boeing and several Japanese companies to build its jet aircraft, including the 787. By these alliances, Kodak, Microsoft, and Boeing committed themselves to long-term relationships with these suppliers, which have encouraged the suppliers to undertake specialized investments. Strategic alliances build trust between the firm and its suppliers. Trust is built when a firm makes a credible commitment to continue purchasing from a supplier on reasonable terms. For example, the firm may invest money in a supplier—perhaps by taking a minority shareholding—to signal its intention to build a productive, mutually beneficial long-term relationship.

ANOTHER PERSPECTIVE

Logistics in the Service Sector: Global Account Management

Like manufacturers, professional service firms have also been learning how to better manage their delivery on a global basis. For example, some global accounting firms are dealing with other global firms in a new way, using one supplier for all their accounting-related needs around the world. The traditional approach involved the development of market-specific relationships, so the same multinational client would have many individual accounting relationships, one in each major market for each company division. Under a global account management approach, one relationship has a global span—and one contract. Such logistics allow for more effective relationship management, a better sense of what the client needs, more product extension opportunities, and better pricing and economies.

In general, the increased utilization of just-in-time inventory systems (JIT), computer-aided design (CAD), and computer-aided manufacturing (CAM) over the past 15 years seems to have increased pressures for firms to establish long-term relationships with their suppliers. JIT, CAD, and CAM systems all rely on close links between firms and their suppliers supported by substantial specialized investment in equipment and information systems hardware. To get a supplier to agree to adopt such systems, a firm must make a credible commitment to an enduring relationship with the supplier—it must build trust with the supplier. It can do this within the framework of a strategic alliance.

Alliances are not all good. Like formal vertical integration, a firm that enters long-term alliances may limit its strategic flexibility by the commitments it makes to its alliance partners. As we saw in Chapter 11, when we considered alliances between competitors, a firm that allies itself with another firm risks giving away key technological know-how to a potential competitor.

LO5 | IMPLICATIONS FOR BUSINESS

The implications for international businesses of the material discussed in this chapter fall into four main areas: coordination through materials management, just-in-time systems, the importance of information technology, and the coordination in global supply chains

COORDINATING A GLOBAL PRODUCTION SYSTEM

Materials management, which encompasses logistics, embraces the activities necessary to get materials from suppliers to a manufacturing facility, through the manufacturing process, and out through a distribution system to the end user.[26] The twin objectives of materials management are to achieve this at the lowest possible cost and in a way that best serves customer needs, thereby lowering the costs of value creation and helping the firm establish a competitive advantage through superior customer service. The potential for reducing costs through more efficient materials management is enormous. For the typical manufacturing enterprise, material costs account for between 50 and 70 percent of revenues, depending on the industry. Even a small reduction in these costs can have a substantial impact on profitability. According to one estimate, for a firm with revenues of $1 million, a return on investment rate of 5 percent, and materials costs that are 50 percent of sales revenues, a $15,000 increase in total profits could be achieved either by increasing sales revenues 30 percent or by reducing materials costs by 3 percent.[27] In a saturated market, it would be much easier to reduce materials costs by 3 percent than to increase sales revenues by 30 percent.

THE POWER OF JUST-IN-TIME

Pioneered by Japanese firms during the 1950s and '60s, just-in-time inventory systems now play a major role in most manufacturing firms. The basic philosophy behind **just-in-time (JIT) inventory systems** is to economize on inventory holding costs by having materials arrive at a manufacturing plant just in time to enter the production process and not before. The major cost saving comes from speeding up inventory turnover. This reduces inventory holding costs, such as warehousing and storage costs. It also means the company is less likely to have excess unsold inventory that it has to write off against earnings or price low to sell. In addition to the cost benefits, JIT systems can also help firms improve product quality. Under a JIT system, parts enter the manufacturing process immediately; they are not warehoused. This allows defective inputs to be spotted right away. The problem can then be traced to the supply source and fixed before more defective parts are produced. Under a more traditional system, warehousing parts for months before they are used allows many defective parts to be produced before a problem is recognized.

The drawback of a JIT system is that it leaves a firm without a buffer stock of inventory. Although buffer stocks are expensive to store, they can tide a firm over shortages brought about by disruption among suppliers (such as a labour dispute). Buffer stocks can also help a firm respond quickly to increases in demand. However, there are ways around these limitations. To reduce the risks associated with depending on one supplier for an important input, some firms source these inputs from several suppliers.

THE ROLE OF INFORMATION TECHNOLOGY AND THE INTERNET

Web-based information systems play a crucial role in modern materials management. By tracking component parts as they make their way across the globe toward an assembly plant, information systems enable a firm to optimize its production scheduling according to when components are expected to arrive. By locating component parts in the supply chain precisely, good information systems allow the firm to accelerate production when needed by pulling key components out of the regular supply chain and having them flown to the manufacturing plant.

Firms increasingly use electronic data interchange (EDI) to coordinate the flow of materials into manufacturing, through manufacturing, and out to customers. EDI systems require computer links between a firm, its suppliers, and its shippers. These electronic links are then used to place orders with suppliers, to register parts leaving a supplier, to track them as they travel toward a manufacturing plant, and to register their arrival. Suppliers typically use an EDI link to send invoices to the purchasing firm. One consequence of an EDI system is that suppliers, shippers, and the purchasing firm can communicate with each other with no time delay, which increases the flexibility and responsiveness of the whole supply system. A second consequence is that much of the paperwork between suppliers, shippers, and the purchasing firm is eliminated. Good EDI systems can help a firm decentralize materials management decisions to the plant level by giving corporate-level managers the information they need for coordinating and controlling decentralized materials management groups.

Before the emergence of the Internet as a major communication medium, firms and their suppliers normally had to purchase expensive proprietary software solutions to implement EDI systems. The ubiquity of the Internet and the availability of Web-based applications have made most of these proprietary solutions obsolete. Less-expensive, Web-based systems that are much easier to install and manage now dominate the market for supply chain management software. These Web-based systems are rapidly transforming the management of globally dispersed supply chains, allowing even small firms to achieve a much better balance between supply and demand, thereby reducing the inventory in their systems and reaping the associated economic benefits. With increasing numbers of firms adopting these systems, those that do not may find themselves at a significant competitive disadvantage.

COORDINATION IN GLOBAL SUPPLY CHAINS

Consider how to turn an aircraft, and think in terms of coordination and leverage points. That is, aircraft are typically steered using an integrated system of ailerons on the wings and the rudder at the tail of the aircraft. In comparison to the aircraft, the ailerons and the rudder seem very small. However, leverage allows the coordinated effort of the ailerons and the rudder to turn the aircraft. In other words, putting the right combination of a little leverage on the right places together with a coordinated effort leads to incredible maneuvering ability for the plane. Global supply chains are the same. Integration and coordination are critically important. Global supply chain coordination refers to shared decision-making opportunities and operational collaboration of key global supply chain activities.

Shared decision making—such as joint consideration of replenishment, inventory holding costs, collaborative planning, costs of different processes, frequency of orders, batch size, and product development—creates a more integrated, coherent, efficient, and effective global supply chain. This includes shared decision making by supply chain members both inside an organization (e.g., logistics, purchasing, operations, and marketing channels employees) and across organizations (e.g., raw materials producers, transportation companies, manufacturers, wholesalers, retailers). Shared decision making is not joint decision making; it is decision making involving joint considerations. Shared decision making helps in resolving potential conflicts among global supply chain members and fosters a culture of coordination and integration. In most supply chains, certain parties are more influential, and shared decision making, at a minimum, should include the critically important chain members.

To achieve operational integration and collaboration within a global supply chain, six operational objectives should be addressed: responsiveness, variance reduction, inventory reduction, shipment consolidation, quality, and life-cycle support. Responsiveness refers to a global firm's ability to satisfy customers' requirements across global supply chain functions in a timely manner. Variance reduction refers to integrating a control system across global supply chain functions to eliminate global supply chain disruptions. Inventory reduction refers to integrating an inventory system, controlling asset commitment, and turning velocity across global supply chain functions. Shipment consolidation refers to using various programs to combine small shipments and provide timely, consolidated movement. This includes multiunit coordination across global supply chain functions. Quality refers to integrating a system so that it achieves zero defects throughout global supply chains. Finally, life-cycle support refers to integrating the activities of reverse logistics, recycling, after-market service, product recall, and product disposal across global supply chain functions.

Key Terms

dynamic capabilities

flexible machine cell

flexible manufacturing technology

ISO 9000

just-in-time (JIT) inventory system

logistics

mass customization

materials management

Six Sigma

sourcing decisions

total quality management

LO Learning Objectives Summary

1. Efficient production and logistics functions can improve an international business's competitive position by lowering the costs of value creation and by performing value creation activities in such ways that customer service is enhanced and value added is maximized. The choice of an optimal production location must consider country factors, technological factors, and product factors.

2. Country factors include the influence of factor costs, political economy, and national culture on production costs, along with the presence of location externalities. Technological factors include the fixed costs of setting up production facilities, the minimum efficient scale of production, and the availability of flexible manufacturing technologies that allow for mass customization. Product factors include the value-to-weight ratio of the product and whether the product serves universal needs. Location strategies either concentrate or decentralize manufacturing. The choice should be made in light of country, technological, and product factors. All location decisions involve trade-offs.

3. Foreign factories can improve their capabilities over time, and this can be of immense strategic benefit to the firm. Managers need to view foreign factories as potential centres of excellence and to encourage and foster attempts by local managers to upgrade factory capabilities.

4. An essential issue in many international businesses is determining which component parts should be manufactured in-house and which should be outsourced to independent suppliers. Making components in-house facilitates investments in specialized assets and helps the firm protect its proprietary technology. It may also improve scheduling between adjacent stages in the value chain. In-house production also makes sense if the firm is an efficient, low-cost producer of a technology. Buying components from independent suppliers facilitates strategic flexibility and helps the firm avoid the organizational problems associated with extensive vertical integration. Outsourcing might also be employed as part of an "offset" policy, which is designed to win more orders for the firm from a country by pushing some subcontracting work to that country. Several firms have tried to attain the benefits of vertical integration and avoid its associated organizational problems by entering into long-term strategic alliances with essential suppliers. Although alliances with suppliers can give a firm the benefits of vertical integration without dispensing entirely with the benefits of a market relationship, alliances have drawbacks. The firm that enters a strategic alliance may find its strategic flexibility limited by commitments to alliance partners.

5. Logistics encompasses all the activities that move materials to a production facility, through the production process, and out through a distribution system to the end user. The logistics function is

complicated in an international business by distance, time, exchange rates, custom barriers, and other things. Just-in-time systems generate major cost savings from reducing warehousing and inventory holding costs and from reducing the need to write off excess inventory. In addition, JIT systems help the firm spot defective parts and remove them from the manufacturing process quickly, thereby improving product quality. Information technology, particularly Internet-based EDI, plays a major role in materials management. EDI facilitates the tracking of inputs, allows the firm to optimize its production schedule, lets the firm and its suppliers communicate in real time, and eliminates the flow of paperwork between a firm and its suppliers.

Critical Thinking and Discussion Questions

1. An electronics firm is considering how best to supply the world market for microprocessors used in consumer and industrial electronic products. A manufacturing plant costs about $500 million to construct and requires a highly skilled workforce. The total value of the world market for this product over the next ten years is estimated to be between $10 billion and $15 billion. The tariffs prevailing in this industry are currently low. Should the firm adopt a concentrated or decentralized manufacturing strategy? What kind of location(s) should the firm favour for its plant(s)?

2. A chemical firm is considering how best to supply the world market for sulfuric acid. A manufacturing plant costs approximately $20 million to construct and requires a moderately skilled workforce. The total value of the world market for this product over the next ten years is estimated to be between $20 billion and $30 billion. The tariffs prevailing in this industry are moderate. Should the firm favour concentrated manufacturing or decentralized manufacturing? What kind of location(s) should the firm seek for its plant(s)?

3. A firm must decide whether to make a component part in-house or to contract it out to an independent supplier. Manufacturing the part requires a nonrecoverable investment in specialized assets. The most efficient suppliers are located in countries with currencies that many foreign exchange analysts expect to appreciate substantially over the next decade. What are the pros and cons of (a) manufacturing the component in-house and (b) outsourcing manufacturing to an independent supplier? Which option would you recommend and why?

4. Explain how an efficient materials management function can help an international business compete more effectively in the global marketplace. Use examples.

Research Task   globalEDGE™   globaledge.msu.edu

Use the globalEDGE™ site to complete the following exercises:

1. The U.S. Department of Labor's Bureau of International Labor Affairs publishes a *Chartbook of International Labor Comparisons*. Locate the latest edition of this report and identify the hourly compensation costs for manufacturing workers in the United States, Japan, Korea, Taiwan, Germany, and the United Kingdom.

2. *Industry Week* magazine ranks the world's largest manufacturing companies by sales revenue. Identify the largest Chinese manufacturing companies as provided in the most recent ranking, paying special attention to the industries in which these companies operate.

CLOSING CASE

H&M'S GLOBAL SUPPLY CHAIN

David Beckham, Beyoncé, Gisele Bündchen, Georgia May Jagger, Miranda Kerr, Madonna, Vanessa Paradis, Katy Perry, Lana Del Rey, Rihanna, and so many more. Yes, it sounds like a list of celebrities and they are. But these celebrities represent just a partial list of well-known people around the world who have worked with H&M. But, let's move on from the "name dropping" to Hennes & Mauritz, or H&M as it is more commonly known. H&M is a Swedish multinational retail-clothing giant known for its fashion clothing for women, men, teenagers, and children. H&M has effectively used superstar celebrities like David Beckham, Beyoncé, and Gisele Bündchen for years to carry their advertising message worldwide. Behind the scenes, H&M's global supply chains are equally well orchestrated and are as high powered as its advertising campaigns.

H&M Hennes & Mauritz AB is now the full name of the company (it started simply as "Hennes" in 1947 in a small Swedish town called Västerås). The idea for the company emerged when, in 1946, Erling Persson, the company's founder, came up with the idea of offering fashionable clothing at relatively low prices while he was on a business trip to the United States. At that time, Erling Persson decided to focus on women's clothing only, and "Hennes," which means "her" or "hers" in Swedish, was started. A couple of decades later, in 1968, Hennes acquired the building and inventory of hunting equipment retailer Mauritz Widforss. A supply of men's clothing was also a part of the inventory. This resulted in menswear being included in the company's collection—and gave birth to Hennes & Mauritz (H&M). H&M now has some 3200 stores in 54 countries and approximately 116 000 employees. It is the second-largest clothing retailer in the world after Spain-based Inditex (parent company of ZARA) and ahead of U.S.-based GAP Inc.

H&M Hennes & Mauritz AB comprises six different brands, although the H&M brand is the most recognizable worldwide. The other brands are COS, Monki, Weekday, Cheap Monday, and & Other Stories. H&M designs sustainable fashion for all people at relatively modest prices and sells its products in 54 countries and online in an additional 10 markets. COS explores the concept of style over fashion and sells its products in stores and online in 38 countries. Monki is promoted as a fashion experience and is offered in 30 markets in stores and online. Weekday is a jeans-focused fashion destination with sales in 25 markets. Cheap Monday combines "influences from street fashion and subculture with a catwalk vibe" and is offered in some 20 markets. The last brand, called "& Other Stories," was launched in 2013 and focuses on personal expression and styling, with availability in 17 markets. The collection of these brands, driven by the H&M collection and its footprint in 64 countries, presents a unique global supply chain challenge for the company.

The collections of clothing are created by a team of 160 in-house designers and 100 pattern makers. The design and pattern team is large and diverse, representing different age groups and nationalities. H&M Hennes & Mauritz AB's (H&M from now on) design process is about "striking the right balance between fashion, quality and the best price . . . and it always involves sustainability awareness." H&M does not own its own factories but instead works with around 900 independent suppliers to implement the team's designs into reality. These independent suppliers are mostly located in Europe and Asia. They manufacture all of H&M's products, and they also generally source fabrics and other components needed to create the fashion statements we have come to know from the H&M brands. Some 80 people in the H&M organization are dedicated to constantly audit the working conditions at the factories of suppliers, including safety and quality testing, and ensuring that chemicals requirements are met.

Within the global supply chain infrastructure, one key aspect of H&M is the ordering of each product. Specifically, ordering each product at the optimal moment is an important part of H&M achieving the right balance among price, cycle time, and quality. To realize the effectiveness needed to ultimately sell fashion-oriented clothing at affordable prices, H&M works closely with long-term partners and invests significant resources into the sustainability of the work needed in its supply chains. In these areas, H&M strives to promote lasting improvements in working conditions and environmental impact throughout the footprint that it makes worldwide. Through its 900 suppliers, the company is connected to some 1900 factories and about 1.6 million workers.

Sources: H&M Web site, http://hm.com, accessed April 12, 2014; L. Siegle, "Is H&M The New Home of Ethical Fashion?" *The Observer*, April 7, 2012; G. Petro, "The Future of Fashion Retailing—The H&M Approach," *Forbes*, November 5, 2012; K. Stock, "H&M's New Store Blitz Moves Faster Than Its Digital Expansion," *Bloomberg Businessweek*, March 17, 2014; and M. Kerppola, R. Moody, L. Zheng, and A. Liu, "H&M's Global Supply Chain Management Sustainability: Factories and Fast Fashion," *GlobaLens*, a division of the William Davidson Institute at the University of Michigan, February 8, 2014.

Case Discussion Questions

1. Does it surprise you that the second-largest clothing retailer is only selling in stores in 54 countries plus an additional 10 countries online? Why do you think it is not covering more of the world's countries?

2. H&M does not own any of the factories that produce its clothes. Instead, it relies on some 1900 factories and 900 suppliers to create what its team designed. These factories and suppliers are mostly in Europe and Asia. How can H&M ensure that its customers receive the quality expected in the clothing?

3. H&M stresses sustainability in its promotional campaigns. How can it ensure that the working conditions are appropriate for the 1.6 million people that serve in its supplier network? Is it even H&M's role to ensure that the working conditions and environmental impact are great in every market it engages in?

4. If you worked for H&M, what would you suggest that it focus on to become even larger than it is now? Should it have its own factories? Should it expand to more than the 64 countries (54 with stores and 10 online) that it is in now? Should it control more of the global supply chains?

Chapter 16

Global Human Resource Management

DIVERSITY MATTERS

One of the most pressing issues in human resources management globally is the issue of diversity. The concept of diversity is to ensure that all people have access to opportunities in a fair and balanced way. It can include, but is not limited to, addressing diversity based on gender, race, sexual orientation, religion, or disability. Not only are companies being questioned more on their policies, but corporate shareholders are more frequently demanding policies that encourage fair and equitable employment. This has become a lightning rod in particular for development of the female workforce. While women have made significant strides in the corporate world and bringing attention to pay equity issues, there remains a road block in terms of opportunities for promotion and leadership roles.

The "Gender Gap" is a term used to explain the differences in pay and opportunity that women experience in the workforce. Analysis compares both full-time and part-time annual earnings and/or hourly rates, and is expressed as a percentage of male earnings. Data from numerous reports suggests that women in Canada still earn substantially less than their male counterparts. This is not merely a Canadian issue, but a global one. The OECD regularly publishes updates to wage disparity between the sexes. Out of 34 countries in the OECD, Canada had the 7th highest gender wage gap in 2014. The average man in Canada's workforce makes 19 percent more than the average Canadian woman, while the OECD average is 17 percent. This suggests that there is room for improvement, not only in Canada but in other economies that are Canada's peers.

The pay gap is perniciously and stubbornly unchanging. While some factors are of a woman's choosing, such as wanting flexible or part-time work to accommodate family responsibilities, this may also be of necessity, as better jobs may not be available. Men are more likely to be in full-time employment, and get promoted faster and more frequently than women. Furthermore, traditional "women's work" is valued less compared to traditional "men's work," which highlights the systemic bias against females. Women have also discovered that, despite being the majority of university graduates (62 percent), they still earn less than men at the start of their careers. In 2008, female university graduates earned about $62,800 annually, while men earned $91,800. More recently, the "millennial" generation, those born between 1980 and 1994, have improved the gap but still face impediments to growing their careers and getting promoted. About 23 percent of millennial women believe their gender has held them back in their careers.

While many will dismiss these statistics, it is clearly apparent that women are generally in more junior positions, have more limited promotion opportunities, and, therefore, earn less than men. This can have an impact on social programs, as it means that more women are trapped in lower wage jobs, may be less able to save for major purchases, which impacts economic growth, and may be saving less for retirement, even though women live longer. (It is estimated that nearly twice as many senior women live in poverty than men.) Therefore, improving the economic power of women would actually be of benefit to society overall.

While the path to equal pay is the most pressing issue in the diversity question, getting women into positions of power is also a challenge. Globally, only about 20 percent of corporate board positions are held by women. Recent analysis of publicly-listed firms have painted a troubling picture of the trend for women trying to enter senior level positions, as well as gaining access to board positions, where decisions are made on the direction of organizations. Large organizations such as MSCI and Bloomberg have conducted significant global surveys identifying geographic trends and challenges in diversity.

This is of concern, not only because it does not suggest that the best candidates are necessarily getting those positions, but also because it can lead to a potential liability on the part of a company if decisions are made that are not in the best interests of shareholders or owners. As well, if discrimination can be proved, it can lead to increased legal costs, impacting earnings and potentially damaging a company's brand.

"One bright light in this issue is that female-led companies—however rare—actually tend to outperform male-led companies in terms of profitability and shareholder return," says Arlene Tober, Consultant in gender issues. "This can only bode well for increasing representation of women in the most senior levels of corporations, as firms look to add value in an increasingly demanding global economy."

Bloomberg has reported industry-specific research on gender-related corporate performance. One of their studies clearly shows the need to address inequality: "One gender-focused strategy investing in S&P 500 companies with the most women in board, management and workforce roles has outperformed the benchmark by 141 percent over the past 10 years. Shares of women-led companies outperformed the S&P 500 Index by 7 percent, improving on their prior 12-month advantage by 3 percent. These and similar outcomes are driving a growing focus on diverse leadership—and the kind of data investors can use to build parallel investment strategies."

In short, investors are getting "short-changed" by the lack of diversity, and should demand more results-oriented strategies from companies. HR managers will need to be cognizant of these results and ensure accountability in their firms, especially if they are expected to add to the bottom line.

Ms. Tober continued, "Take stock of women's roles in the organization, including regular feedback on opportunities for development, promotions, mentoring. Do regular reviews of pay equity to ensure fairness and motivation for women. It would be a shame if women left a company—taking their knowledge, experience and capabilities—because they felt they weren't being valued in the same way as their male counterparts. When women leave a company, these resources, which can impact the success of a firm, go with them."

While it can be challenging to determine the effectiveness of a diversity policy, making the effort to do so will improve human resources management and ensure that quality employees or candidates will have opportunities, regardless of gender, race, or other diversifiers. This will encourage HR to become more aligned to the success of the organization, as it will help make better hires, encourage longevity in employees (instead of seeing higher turnover rates and dissatisfaction in the workplace), and, perhaps, help increase revenue, as all employees will be more motivated to participate in the success of the firm.

Sources: Interview and information from Arlene Tober, January and February 2017; Organisation for Economic Co-operation and Development (OECD), Gender wage gap, http://www.oecd.org/gender/data/genderwagegap.htm; "Ready for change: Harness the potential of your female workforce—Women in Work Index: Canadian insights," PwC Canada, http://www.pwc.com/ca/en/services/consulting/people-change/women-in-work-canadian-insights.html; Canadian Women's Foundation; Dahlia Bazzaz, "Millennial Women Face Familiar Obstacles at Work," *The Wall Street Journal*, September 27, 2016, https://www.wsj.com/articles/millennial-women-face-familiar-obstacles-at-work-1474963261; "Did you know senior women are twice as likely to live in poverty as men?" March 3, 2015, Canadian Labour Congress, http://canadianlabour.ca/issues-research/did-you-know-senior-women-are-twice-likely-live-poverty-men; Vignesh R S and Constantin Cosereanu, "A Gender-Focused Strategy Beat the S&P 500 by 141 Percent," *Bloomberg Markets*, June 16, 2016, https://www.bloomberg.com/news/articles/2016-06-16/a-gender-focused-strategy-beat-the-s-p-500-by-141-percent.

LO | LEARNING OBJECTIVES

By the end of this chapter you should be able to:

1. Summarize the strategic role of human resource management in the international business.

2. Identify the pros and cons of different approaches to staffing policy in international business.

3. Recognize how management development and training programs can increase the value of human capital in the international business firm.

4. Explain how and why performance appraisal systems might vary across nations.

5. Understand how and why compensation systems might vary across nations.

6. Understand how organized labour can influence strategic choices in international business firms.

Introduction

Continuing our survey of specific functions within an international business, this chapter examines international human resource management (HRM). **Human resource management** refers to the activities an organization carries out to use its human resources effectively.[1] These activities include determining the firm's human resource strategy, staffing, performance evaluation, management development, compensation, and labour relations. None of these activities is performed in a vacuum; all are related to the strategy of the firm because, as we will see, HRM has an important strategic component.[2] Through its influence on the character, development, quality, and productivity of the firm's human resources, the HRM function can help the firm achieve its primary strategic goals of reducing the costs of value creation and adding value by better serving customer needs.

The strategic role of HRM is complex enough in a purely domestic firm, but it is more complex in an international business, where staffing, management development, performance evaluation, and compensation activities are complicated by profound differences between countries in labour markets, culture, legal systems, and economic systems (see Chapters 2 and 3). For example,

- compensation practices may vary from country to country depending on prevailing management customs;
- labour laws may prohibit union organization in one country and mandate it in another;
- equal employment legislation may be strongly pursued in one country and not in another.

If it is to build a cadre of managers capable of managing a multinational enterprise, the HRM function must deal with a host of issues. It must decide how to staff key management posts in the company, how to develop managers so that they are familiar with the nuances of doing business in different countries, and how to compensate people in different nations. HRM must also deal with issues specifically related to expatriate managers. (An **expatriate manager** is a citizen of one country who is working abroad in one of the firm's other locations.) It must decide whom to send on expatriate postings, be clear about why they are doing it, compensate expatriates appropriately, and make sure that they are adequately debriefed and reoriented once they return home.

It is clear that keeping employees happy and motivated goes beyond just issues of total compensation (salary and bonuses + benefits). For many employees, especially those who are more highly educated, geographic location coupled with giving employees a sense of purpose and an understanding of their worth to an organization may be just as important as compensation.

In this chapter, we will look closely at the role of HRM in an international business. We begin by briefly discussing the strategic role of HRM. Then we turn our attention to four major tasks of the HRM function: staffing policy, management training and development, performance appraisal, and compensation policy. We will point out the strategic implications of each of these tasks. The chapter closes with a look at the challenges faced by foreign service employees (FSE) working internationally.

LO1 | The Strategic Role of International HRM

A large and expanding body of academic research suggests that a strong fit between human resource practices and strategy is required for high profitability. You will recall from Chapter 13 that superior performance requires not only the right strategy, but the strategy must also be supported by the right organizational architecture. Strategy is implemented through organization and people are the linchpin of a firm's organizational architecture. For a firm to outperform its rivals in the global marketplace, it must have the right people in the right postings. Those people must be trained appropriately so that they have the skill sets required to perform their jobs effectively and so that they behave in a manner that is congruent with the desired culture of the firm. Their compensation packages must create incentives for them to take actions that are consistent with the strategy of the firm, and the performance appraisal system the firm uses must measure the behavior that the firm wants to encourage.

The HRM function, through its staffing, training, compensation, and performance appraisal activities, has a critical impact upon the people, culture, incentive, and control system elements of the firm's organization architecture (performance appraisal systems are part of the control systems in an enterprise). Thus, HRM professionals have a critically important strategic role. It is incumbent upon them to shape these elements of a firm's organization architecture in a manner that is consistent with the strategy of the enterprise, so that the firm can effectively implement its strategy.

In short, superior HRM can be a sustained source of high productivity and competitive advantage in the global economy. At the same time, research suggests that many international businesses have room for improving the effectiveness of their HRM function. In one study of competitiveness among 326 large multinationals, the authors found that human resource management was one of the weakest capabilities in most firms, suggesting that improving the effectiveness of international HRM practices might have substantial performance benefits.[3]

In Chapter 11 we examined four strategies pursued by international businesses—the multidomestic, the international, the global, and the transnational strategies. Multidomestic firms try to create value by emphasizing local responsiveness; international firms, by transferring core competencies overseas; global firms, by realizing experience curve and location economies; and transnational firms, by doing all these things simultaneously.

In this chapter, we will see that success also requires HRM policies to be congruent with the firm's strategy. For example, a transnational strategy imposes very different requirements for staffing, management development, and compensation practices than a multidomestic strategy does.

LO2 | Staffing Policy

Staffing policy is concerned with the selection of employees for particular jobs. At one level this involves selecting individuals who have the skills required to do particular jobs. At another level staffing policy can be a tool for developing and promoting corporate culture.[4] By **corporate culture**, we mean the organization's norms and value systems. A strong corporate culture can help a firm pursue its strategy. General

Electric, for example, is not just concerned with hiring people who have the skills required for performing particular jobs; it wants to hire individuals whose behavioural styles, beliefs, and value systems are consistent with those of GE. This is true whether a Canadian, an Italian, a German, or an Australian is being hired and whether the hiring is for a Canadian operation or a foreign operation. The belief is that if employees are predisposed toward the organization's norms and value systems by their personality type, the firm will be able to attain higher performance.

Types of Staffing Policy

Research has identified three types of staffing policies in international businesses: the ethnocentric approach, the polycentric approach, and the geocentric approach.[5] We will review each policy and link it to the strategy pursued by the firm. The most attractive staffing policy is probably the geocentric approach, although there are several impediments to adopting it.

THE ETHNOCENTRIC APPROACH

An **ethnocentric staffing policy** is one in which all key management positions are filled by parent-country nationals. This practice was very widespread at one time. Firms such as Procter & Gamble, Philips, and Matsushita originally followed it. In the Dutch firm, Philips, for example, all important positions in most foreign subsidiaries were at one time held by Dutch nationals who were referred to by their non-Dutch colleagues as the Dutch Mafia. In many Japanese and South Korean firms today, such as Toyota, Matsushita, and Samsung, key positions in international operations are still often held by home-country nationals. According to the Japanese Overseas Enterprise Association, in 1996 only 29 percent of foreign subsidiaries of Japanese companies had presidents who were not Japanese. In contrast, 66 percent of the Japanese subsidiaries of foreign companies had Japanese presidents.[6]

Firms pursue an ethnocentric staffing policy for three reasons. First, the firm may believe the host country lacks qualified individuals to fill senior management positions. This argument is heard most often when the firm has operations in less-developed countries. Second, the firm may see an ethnocentric staffing policy as the best way to maintain a unified corporate culture. Many Japanese firms, for example, prefer their foreign operations to be headed by expatriate Japanese managers because these managers will have been socialized into the firm's culture while employed in Japan.[7]

Third, if the firm is trying to create value by transferring core competencies to a foreign operation, as firms pursuing an international strategy are, it may believe that the best way to do this is to transfer parent-country nationals who have knowledge of that competency to the foreign operation. Imagine what might occur if a firm tried to transfer a core competency in marketing to a foreign subsidiary without supporting the transfer with a corresponding transfer of home-country marketing management personnel.

Despite this rationale for pursuing an ethnocentric staffing policy, the policy is now on the wane in most international businesses for two reasons. First, an ethnocentric staffing policy limits advancement opportunities for host-country nationals. This can lead to resentment, lower productivity, and increased turnover among that group.

Second, an ethnocentric policy can lead to "cultural myopia," the firm's failure to understand host-country cultural differences that require different approaches to marketing and management. The adaptation of expatriate managers can take a long time, during which they may make major mistakes. For example, expatriate managers may fail to appreciate how product attributes, distribution strategy, communications strategy, and pricing strategy should be adapted to host-country conditions. The result may be costly blunders. They may also make decisions that are ethically suspect simply because they do not understand the culture in which they are managing.[8] In one highly publicized case in the United States, Mitsubishi Motors was sued by the Federal Equal Employment Opportunity Commission for tolerating extensive and systematic sexual harassment in a plant in Illinois. The plant's top

At Caterpillar, expatriate managers and their families receive culture and language training, as well as relocation assistance, before relocating to one of Caterpillar's global facilities. © *Arne9001/Dreamstime.com*

management, all Japanese expatriates, denied the charges. The Japanese managers may have failed to realize that behaviour that would be viewed as acceptable in Japan was not acceptable in the United States.[9]

Although one might cite corporate goodwill as a motivating force for ethical and equitable workplace hiring practices, there are also laws that in effect mandate good corporate citizenship. In Canada, for example, the Employment Equity Act was passed in 1995 and mandates equality in the workplace. Section 2 outlines the purpose of the Act:

> 2. The purpose of this Act is to achieve equality in the workplace so that no person shall be denied employment opportunities or benefits for reasons unrelated to ability and, in the fulfillment of that goal, to correct the conditions of disadvantage in employment experienced by women, aboriginal peoples, persons with disabilities and members of visible minorities by giving effect to the principle that employment equity means more than treating persons in the same way but also requires special measures and the accommodation of differences.[10]

Companies have to be compliant with these laws within Canada or they can be subject to a graded scale of monetary fines, depending on the size of the company.

THE POLYCENTRIC APPROACH

A **polycentric staffing policy** requires host-country nationals to be recruited to manage subsidiaries, while parent-country nationals occupy key positions at corporate headquarters. In many respects a polycentric approach is a response to the shortcomings of an ethnocentric approach. One advantage of adopting a polycentric approach is that the firm is less likely to suffer from cultural myopia. Host-country managers are unlikely to make the mistakes arising from cultural misunderstandings to which expatriate managers are vulnerable. A second advantage is that a polycentric approach may be less expensive to implement, reducing the costs of value creation. Expatriate managers can be very expensive to maintain.

A polycentric approach also has its drawbacks. Host-country nationals have limited opportunities to gain experience outside their own country and thus cannot progress beyond senior positions in their own subsidiary. As in the case of an ethnocentric policy, this may cause resentment. Perhaps the major drawback with a polycentric approach, however, is the gap that can form between host-country managers and parent-country managers. Language barriers, national loyalties, and a range of cultural differences may isolate the corporate headquarters staff from the various foreign subsidiaries. The lack of management transfers from home to host countries, and vice versa, can exacerbate this isolation and lead to a lack of integration between corporate headquarters and foreign subsidiaries.

THE GEOCENTRIC APPROACH

A **geocentric staffing policy** seeks the best people for key jobs throughout the organization, regardless of nationality. Air Canada, with offices around the world and flights to 200 destinations on six continents,[11] is a good example of a company that has adopted a geocentric staffing policy. There are a number of advantages to this policy. First, it enables the firm to make the best use of its human resources. Second, and perhaps more important, a geocentric policy enables the firm to build a cadre of international executives who feel at home working in a number of cultures. Creation of such a cadre may be a critical first step toward building a strong unifying corporate culture and an informal management network, both of which are required for global and transnational strategies.[12] Firms pursuing a geocentric staffing policy may be better able to create value from the pursuit of experience curve and location economies and from the multidirectional transfer of core competencies than firms pursuing other staffing policies. In addition, the multinational composition of the management team that results from geocentric staffing tends to reduce cultural myopia and to enhance local responsiveness. Thus, a geocentric staffing policy seems the most attractive.

ANOTHER PERSPECTIVE

What Can HR Do to Create Policies on Diversity?

According to Arlene Tober, who you read about in the opening case, there are many policies an HR department can implement:

- The first step is awareness: develop a diversity policy; compare ratios of women at executive and board levels within the same industry to determine if a proactive approach is needed to improve diversity

- Encourage mentoring and opportunities to interact with senior management

- Raise awareness of potential biases

- Hold senior management accountable for diversity, including a part of their pay structure; senior executives need to ensure there are no reprisals if HR leaders ask for change

- Develop a "career path" for employees to plan their progression to more senior roles

- Companies in STEM industries (Science, Technology, Engineering, Mathematics) can provide career fairs, networking opportunities, internships, and other policies to support women entering these higher-paying fields

- Ensure the corporate environment allows women or minorities to speak up on their career aspirations

- Ensure transparency and ongoing communication with staff so that they understand the opportunities available to them

A number of problems limit the firm's ability to pursue a geocentric policy. Many countries want foreign subsidiaries to employ their citizens. To achieve this goal, they use immigration laws to require the employment of host-country nationals if they are available in adequate numbers and have the necessary skills. Most countries (including Canada) require firms to provide extensive documentation if they wish to hire a foreign national instead of a local national. This documentation can be time consuming, expensive, and, at times, futile. A geocentric staffing policy also can be very expensive to implement. Increased training and relocation costs are involved in transferring managers from country to country. The company may also need a compensation structure with a standardized international base pay level higher than national levels in many countries. In addition, the higher pay enjoyed by managers placed on an international "fast track" may be a source of resentment within a firm.

SUMMARY

The advantages and disadvantages of the three approaches to staffing policy are summarized in Table 16.1. Broadly speaking, an ethnocentric approach is compatible with an international strategy, a polycentric approach is compatible with a multidomestic strategy, and a geocentric approach is compatible with both global and transnational strategies. (See Chapter 11 for details of the strategies.)

While the staffing policies described here are well known and widely used among both practitioners and scholars of international businesses, recently some critics have claimed that the typology is too simplistic and that it obscures the internal differentiation of management practices within international businesses. The critics claim that within some international businesses, staffing policies vary significantly from national subsidiary to national subsidiary; while some are managed on an ethnocentric basis, others are managed in a polycentric or geocentric manner.[13] Other critics note that the staffing policy adopted by a firm is primarily driven by its geographic scope as opposed to its strategic orientation. Firms that have a very broad geographic scope are the most likely to have a geocentric mindset.[14] Thus by this argument, Air Canada, with its wide network of offices and destination countries, is more likely to have a geocentric mindset than a firm that is involved in only three countries.

TABLE 16.1	Comparison of Staffing Approaches		
Staffing Approach	**Strategic Appropriateness**	**Advantages**	**Disadvantages**
Ethnocentric	International	Overcomes lack of qualified managers in host nation Unified culture Helps transfer core competencies	Produces resentment in host country Can lead to cultural myopia
Polycentric	Multidomestic	Alleviates cultural myopia Inexpensive to implement	Limits career mobility Isolates headquarters from foreign subsidiaries
Geocentric	Global and Transnational	Uses human resources efficiently Helps build strong culture and informal management network	National immigration policies may limit implementation Expensive

Expatriate Managers

Two of the three staffing policies we have discussed—the ethnocentric and the geocentric—rely on extensive use of expatriate managers. As defined earlier, expatriates are citizens of one country who are working in another country. Sometimes the term *inpatriates* is used to identify a subset of expatriates who are citizens of a foreign country working in the home country of their multinational employer.[15] Thus, a citizen of Japan who moves to Canada to work at Air Canada would be classified as an inpatriate. With an ethnocentric policy, the expatriates are all home-country nationals who are transferred abroad. With a geocentric approach, the expatriates need not be home-country nationals; the firm does not base transfer decisions on nationality.

A prominent issue in the international staffing literature is **expatriate failure**—the premature return of an expatriate manager to his or her home country.[16] Here we briefly review the evidence on expatriate failure before discussing a number of ways to minimize the expatriate failure rate.

EXPATRIATE FAILURE RATES

Expatriate failure represents a failure of the firm's selection policies to identify individuals who will not thrive abroad. The costs of expatriate failure are high. One estimate is that the average cost per failure to the parent firm can be as high as three times the expatriate's annual domestic salary plus the cost of relocation (which is affected by currency exchange rates and location of assignment).[17] Research suggests that between 16 and 40 percent of all American employees sent abroad to developed nations return from their assignments early, and almost 70 percent of employees sent to developing nations return home early.[18] Although detailed data are not available for other nationalities, one suspects that high expatriate failure is a universal problem. Estimates of the costs of each failure run between $250,000 and $1 million.[19] In addition, approximately 30 to 50 percent of American expatriates, whose average annual compensation package runs to $250,000, stay at their international assignments but are considered ineffective or marginally effective by their firms.[20] In a seminal study,

R. L. Tung surveyed a number of U.S., European, and Japanese multinationals.[21] Her results suggested that 76 percent of U.S. multinationals experienced expatriate failure rates of 10 percent or more, and 7 percent experienced a failure rate of more than 20 percent. Tung's work also suggests that U.S.-based multinationals experience a much higher expatriate failure rate than either European or Japanese multinationals.

Tung asked her sample of multinational managers to indicate reasons for expatriate failure. For U.S. multinationals, the reasons, in order of importance, were:

1. Inability of spouse to adjust.
2. Manager's inability to adjust.
3. Other family problems.
4. Manager's personal or emotional maturity.
5. Inability to cope with larger overseas responsibilities.

Managers of European firms gave only one reason consistently to explain expatriate failure: the inability of the manager's spouse to adjust to a new environment. For the Japanese firms, the reasons for failure were:

1. Inability to cope with larger overseas responsibilities.
2. Difficulties with new environment.
3. Personal or emotional problems.
4. Lack of technical competence.
5. Inability of spouse to adjust.

The most striking difference between these lists is that "inability of spouse to adjust" was the top reason for expatriate failure among U.S. and European multinationals but only the number-five reason among Japanese multinationals. Tung comments that this difference is not surprising given the role and status to which Japanese society traditionally relegates the wife and the fact that most of the Japanese expatriate managers in the study were men.

Since Tung's study, a number of other studies have consistently confirmed that the inability of a spouse to adjust, the inability of the manager to adjust, or other family problems remain major reasons for continuing high levels of expatriate failure. One study by International Orientation Resources, an HRM consulting firm, found that 60 percent of expatriate failures occur due to these three reasons.[22] Another study found that the most common reason for assignment failure is lack of partner (spouse) satisfaction, which was listed by 27 percent of respondents.[23] The inability of expatriate managers to adjust to foreign postings seems to be caused by a lack of cultural skills on the part of the manager being transferred. According to one HRM management consulting firm, this is because the expatriate selection process at many firms is fundamentally flawed. "Expatriate assignments rarely fail because the person cannot accommodate to the technical demands of the job. Typically, the expatriate selections are made by line managers based on technical competence. They fail because of family and personal issues and lack of cultural skills that haven't been part of the selection process."[24]

The failure of spouses to adjust to a foreign posting seems to be related to a number of factors. Often spouses find themselves in a foreign country without the familiar network of family and friends. Language differences make it difficult for them to make new friends. While this may not be a problem for the manager, who can make friends at work, it can be difficult for the spouse who might feel trapped at home. The problem is often exacerbated by immigration regulations prohibiting the spouse from taking employment. With the rise of two-career families in many developed nations, this has become a much more important issue. One recent survey found that 69 percent of expatriates are married, with spouses accompanying them 77 percent of the time. Of those spouses, 49 percent were employed before an assignment and only 11 percent were employed during an assignment.[25] Recent research suggests that a main reason managers now turn down international assignments is concern over the impact such an assignment might have on their spouse's career.[26]

ANOTHER PERSPECTIVE

The World's Friendliest Countries

An HSBC survey ranked (surprisingly) Spain, Kuwait, the UK, Italy, and Ireland as the most challenging (ranked) locations for expats, overall. In the same HSBC survey. China, Germany, Singapore and the Cayman Islands topped the list. Australia ranked fifth place and Canada, sixth place.

Source: HSBC Bank International Limited, Expat Explorer survey, http://www.expatexplorer.hsbc.com/#/countries.

EXPATRIATE SELECTION

One way to reduce expatriate failure rates is by improving selection procedures to screen out inappropriate candidates. In a review of the research on this issue, Mendenhall and Oddou state that a major problem in many firms is that HRM managers tend to equate domestic performance with overseas performance potential.[27] Domestic performance and overseas performance potential are not the same thing. An executive who performs well in a domestic setting may not be able to adapt to managing in a different cultural setting. From their review of the research, Mendenhall and Oddou identified four dimensions that seem to predict success in a foreign posting: self-orientation, others-orientation, perceptual ability, and cultural toughness.

1. *Self-orientation.* The attributes of this dimension strengthen the expatriate's self-esteem, self-confidence, and mental well-being. Expatriates with high self-esteem, self-confidence, and mental well-being were more likely to succeed in foreign postings. Mendenhall and Oddou concluded that such individuals were able to adapt their interests in food, sport, and music; had interests outside of work that could be pursued (e.g., hobbies); and were technically competent.

2. *Others-orientation.* The attributes of this dimension enhance the expatriate's ability to interact effectively with host-country nationals. The more effectively the expatriate interacts with host-country nationals, the more likely he or she is to succeed. Two factors seem to be particularly important here: relationship development and willingness to communicate. Relationship development refers to the ability to develop long-lasting friendships with host-country nationals. Willingness to communicate refers to the expatriate's willingness to use the host-country language. Although language fluency helps, an expatriate need not be fluent to show willingness to communicate. Making the effort to use the language is what is important. Such gestures tend to be rewarded with greater cooperation by host-country nationals.

3. *Perceptual ability.* This is the ability to understand why people of other countries behave the way they do; that is, the ability to empathize. This

dimension seems critical for managing host-country nationals. Expatriate managers who lack this ability tend to treat foreign nationals as if they were home-country nationals. As a result, they may experience significant management problems and considerable frustration. As one expatriate executive from Hewlett-Packard observed, "It took me six months to accept the fact that my staff meetings would start 30 minutes late, and that it would bother no one but me." According to Mendenhall and Oddou, well-adjusted expatriates tend to be nonjudgmental and none-valuative in interpreting the behaviour of host-country nationals and willing to be flexible in their management style, adjusting it as cultural conditions warrant.

4. *Cultural toughness.* This dimension refers to the fact that how well an expatriate adjusts to a particular posting tends to be related to the country of assignment. Some countries are much tougher postings than others because their cultures are more unfamiliar and uncomfortable. For example, many North Americans find postings in non-Western cultures, such as India, Southeast Asia, and the Middle East, to be tougher.[28] The reasons are many, including poor health care and housing standards, inhospitable climate, lack of Western entertainment, and language difficulties. Also, many cultures are extremely male dominated and may be particularly difficult postings for female Western managers.

Mendenhall and Oddou note that standard psychological tests can be used to assess the first three of these dimensions, whereas a comparison of cultures can give managers a feeling for the fourth dimension. They contend that these four dimensions, in addition to domestic performance, should be considered when selecting a manager for foreign posting. However, current practice does not conform to Mendenhall and Oddou's recommendations. Tung's research, for example, showed that only 5 percent of the firms in her sample used formal procedures and psychological tests to assess the personality traits and relational abilities of potential expatriates.[29] Research by International Orientation Resources suggests that when selecting employees for foreign assignments, only 10 percent of the 50 Fortune 500 firms they surveyed tested for important psychological traits such as cultural sensitivity, interpersonal skills, adaptability, and flexibility. Instead, 90 percent of the time employees were selected on the basis of their technical expertise, not their cross-cultural fluency.[30]

Mendenhall and Oddou do not address the problem of expatriate failure due to a spouse's inability to adjust. According to a number of other researchers, a review of the family situation should be part of the expatriate selection process.[31] A survey by Windam International, another international HRM management consulting firm, found that spouses were included in preselection interviews for foreign postings only 21 percent of the time, and that only half of them receive any cross-cultural training. The rise of dual-career families has added an additional and difficult dimension to this long-standing problem.[32] Increasingly, spouses wonder why they should have to sacrifice their own career to further that of their partner.[33]

LO3 Training and Management Development

Selection is just the first step in matching a manager with a job. The next step is training the manager to do the specific job. For example, an intensive training program might be used to give expatriate managers the skills required for success in a foreign posting. Management development is a much broader concept. It is intended to develop the manager's skills over his or her career with the firm. Thus, as part of a management development program, a manager might be sent on several foreign postings over a number of years to build her cross-cultural sensitivity and experience. At the same time, along with other managers in the firm, she might attend management education programs at regular intervals. The thinking behind job transfers is that broad international experience will enhance the management and leadership skills of executives. Research suggests this may be the case.[34]

Historically, most international businesses have been more concerned with training than with management development. Plus, they tended to focus their training efforts on preparing home-country nationals for foreign postings. Recently, however, the shift toward greater global competition and the rise of transnational firms have changed this. It is increasingly common for firms to provide general management development programs in addition to training for particular posts. In many international businesses, the explicit purpose of these management development programs is strategic. Management development is seen as a tool to help the firm achieve its strategic goals.

With this distinction between training and management development in mind, we first examine the types of training managers receive for foreign postings. Then we discuss the connection between management development and strategy in the international business.

Training for Expatriate Managers

Earlier in the chapter we saw that the two most common reasons for expatriate failure were the inability of a manager's spouse to adjust to a foreign environment and the manager's own inability to adjust to a foreign environment. Training can help both the manager and spouse cope with these problems. Cultural training, language training, and practical training all seem to reduce expatriate failure.[35] Despite the usefulness of these kinds of training, evidence suggests that many managers receive no training before they are sent on foreign postings. One study found that only about 30 percent of managers sent on one- to five-year expatriate assignments received training before their departure.[36]

CULTURAL TRAINING

Cultural training seeks to foster an appreciation for the host country's culture. The belief is that understanding a host country's culture will help the manager empathize with the culture, which will enhance her effectiveness in dealing with host-country nationals. It has been suggested that expatriates should receive training in the host country's culture, history, politics, economy, religion, and social and business practices.[37] If possible, it is also advisable to arrange for a familiarization trip to the host country before the formal transfer, as this seems to ease culture shock. Given the problems related to spouse adaptation, it is important that the spouse, and perhaps the whole family, be included in cultural training programs.

LANGUAGE TRAINING

English is the language of world business; it is quite possible to conduct business all over the world using only English. For example, at ABB Group, a Swiss electrical equipment giant, the company's top 13 managers hold frequent meetings in different countries. Because they share no common first language, they speak only English, a foreign tongue to all but one.[38] Despite the prevalence of English, however, an exclusive reliance on English diminishes an expatriate manager's ability to interact with host-country nationals. As noted earlier, a willingness to communicate in the language of the host country, even if the expatriate is far from fluent, can help build rapport with local employees and improve the manager's effectiveness. Despite this, J. C. Baker's study of 74 executives of U.S. multinationals found that only 23 believed knowledge of foreign languages was necessary for conducting business abroad.[39] Those firms that did offer foreign language training for expatriates believed it improved their employees' effectiveness and enabled them to relate more easily to a foreign culture, which fostered a better image of the firm in the host country.

PRACTICAL TRAINING

Practical training is aimed at helping the expatriate manager and family ease themselves into day-to-day life in the host country. The sooner a routine is established, the better are the prospects that the expatriate and her family will adapt successfully. One critical need is for a support network of friends for the expatriate. Where an expatriate community exists, firms often devote considerable effort to ensuring the new expatriate family is quickly integrated into that group. The expatriate community can be a useful source of support and information and can be invaluable in helping the family adapt to a foreign culture.

Lenovo decided that English was to be the official language of the company, even though it is a Chinese enterprise. © Achy0701/Dreamstime.com

Repatriation of Expatriates

A largely overlooked but critically important issue in the training and development of expatriate managers is to prepare them for re-entry into their home-country organization.[40] Repatriation should be seen as the final link in an integrated, circular process that connects good selection and cross-cultural training of expatriate managers with completion of their term abroad and reintegration into their national organization. However, instead of having employees come home to share their knowledge and encourage other high-performing managers to take the same international career track, expatriates too often face a different scenario.[41]

Often when they return home after a stint abroad—where they have typically been autonomous, well-compensated, and celebrated as a big fish in a little pond—they face an organization that does not know what they have done for the last few years, does not know how to use their new knowledge, and does not particularly care. In the worst cases, re-entering employees have to scrounge for jobs, or firms will create standby positions that do not use the expatriate's skills and capabilities and fail to make the most of the business investment the firm has made in that individual.

Research illustrates the extent of this problem. According to one study of repatriated employees, 60 to 70 percent did not know what their position would be when they returned home. Also, 60 percent said their organizations were vague about repatriation, about their new roles, and about their future career progression within the company, while 77 percent of those surveyed took jobs at a lower level in their home organization than in their international assignments.[42] It is small wonder then that 15 percent of returning expatriates leave their firms within a year of arriving home, while 40 percent leave within three years.[43]

COUNTRY FOCUS

Countries Want to Hold on to Their Jobs

Canadians and others in the developed world do not like to see jobs that could be given to their own citizens disappear to other countries. From China to India, developing countries are enticing companies from developed countries like Canada and the United States to take advantage of their cheap and skilled labour forces in areas from call centre operators to computer and pharmaceutical industry experts. English linguists and culturalists are busy at work teaching the "right English" and colloquialisms to call centre employees in developing countries around the world, but the rumblings of discontent are heard frequently in home markets. In Canada, labour unions decry the loss of jobs to foreigners and pin the blame for outsourcing and Canadian plant closures on lower-cost foreign competitors. And in the United States, President Donald Trump was able to tap into the feelings of many Americans that their jobs were being lost to other countries, and in particular China.

A recent controversy shows that the replacement of Canadian workers will almost always generate headlines. A few years ago the Royal Bank terminated 45 employees in its technical operations centres. One former bank employee made the allegation that the Royal Bank was bringing in workers from India to replace the fired high-tech workers. This was supposedly done under Canada's temporary foreign worker program, which is a program meant to fill jobs for which no Canadians are available. The Royal Bank denied that it hired foreign workers, and the outsourcing company, iGate, said that it complies with all Canadian laws. iGate supplies employees to companies all around the world, including General Electric, Honda Europe, and HP. This particular story faded from the headlines as quickly as it emerged.

In reality, low-paid jobs in other countries have been in existence for a long time, since well before the WTO agreements and NAFTA. The fact of cheap labour alone, although attractive, is not conclusively enough for a company to uproot and head to a new destination. According to some, high taxes, overbearing labour legislation, and unrealistically restrictive environmental regulations are the real culprits of job loss and, if given the choice, many Canadian companies will take flight to other business climates.

Oftentimes, the road to curbing job losses and making businesses less motivated to seek greener pastures abroad might not lie in the reduction of personal income taxes, but instead in the further reduction of corporate taxes. Jobs leave the country because of competitiveness issues, and one take on resolving this is through lower corporate taxes. Historically speaking, lower corporate taxes pave the way for more research and development, but the issue of jobs going to foreigners does not stop there.

The notion of foreigners "taking away" jobs from one country can quickly become highly emotional. This issue will not disappear anytime soon. As the world increasingly becomes one marketplace, perhaps it might be best to expect the job markets to follow suit.

Questions

1. Should a country "hold onto its jobs"? How can it do this in a rapidly changing and increasingly global world?
2. What else, besides labour costs, influences a company to move or change locations?

Source: Dana Flavelle, "Outsourcing firm iGate says it will create Canadian jobs," *The Toronto Star*, April 11, 2013.

The key to solving this problem is good human resource planning. Just as the HRM function needs to develop good selection and training programs for its expatriates, it also needs to develop good programs for reintegrating expatriates back into work life within their home-country organization, for preparing them for changes in their physical and professional landscape, and for utilizing the knowledge they acquired while abroad. See the accompanying Country Focus that looks at the home job market and the issue of outsourcing.

Management Development and Strategy

Management development programs are designed to increase the overall skill levels of managers through a mix of ongoing management education and rotations of managers through a number of jobs within the firm to give them varied experiences. They are attempts to improve the overall productivity and quality of the firm's management resources.

International businesses are increasingly using management development as a strategic tool. This is particularly true in firms pursuing a transnational strategy, as increasing numbers are. Such firms need a strong unifying corporate culture and informal management networks to assist in coordination and control. In addition, transnational firm managers need to be able to detect pressures for local responsiveness, and that requires them to understand the culture of a host country.

Management development programs help build a unifying corporate culture by socializing new managers into the norms and value systems of the firm. In-house company training programs and intense interaction during off-site training can foster esprit de corps—shared experiences, informal networks, perhaps a company language or jargon—as well as develop technical competencies. These training events often include songs, picnics, and sporting events that promote feelings of togetherness. These rites of integration may include "initiation rites" wherein personal culture is stripped, company uniforms are donned (e.g., T-shirts bearing the company logo), and humiliation is inflicted (e.g., a pie in the face). All these activities aim to strengthen a manager's identification with the company.[44]

Bringing managers together in one location for extended periods and rotating them through different jobs in several countries help the firm build an informal management network. Such a network can then be used as a conduit for exchanging valuable performance-enhancing knowledge within the organization.[45] Consider the Swedish telecommunications company Ericsson. Inter-unit cooperation is extremely important at Ericsson, particularly for transferring know-how and core competencies from the parent to foreign subsidiaries, from foreign subsidiaries to the parent, and between foreign subsidiaries. To facilitate cooperation, Ericsson transfers large numbers of people back and forth between headquarters and subsidiaries. Ericsson sends a team of 50 to 100 engineers and managers from one unit to another for a year or two. This establishes a network of interpersonal contacts. This policy is effective for both solidifying a common culture in the company and coordinating the company's globally dispersed operations.[46]

LO4 Performance Appraisal

A particularly thorny issue in many international businesses is how best to evaluate its expatriate managers' performance.[47] In this section, we look at this issue and consider some guidelines for appraising expatriate performance.

Performance Appraisal Problems

Unintentional bias makes it difficult to evaluate the performance of expatriate managers objectively. In most cases, two groups evaluate the performance of expatriate managers—host-nation managers and home-office managers—and both are subject to bias. The host-nation managers may be biased by their own cultural frame of reference and expectations. For example, Oddou and Mendenhall report the case of a U.S. manager who introduced participative decision making while working in an Indian subsidiary.[48] The manager subsequently received a negative evaluation from host-country managers because the strong social stratification in India means managers are seen as experts who should not have to ask subordinates for help. The local employees apparently viewed the U.S. manager's attempt at participatory management as an indication that he was incompetent and did not know his job.

Home-country managers' appraisals may be biased by distance and by their own lack of experience working abroad. Home-office managers are often not aware of what is going on in a foreign operation. Accordingly, they tend to rely on hard data in evaluating an expatriate's performance, such as the subunit's productivity, profitability, or market share. Such criteria may reflect factors outside the expatriate manager's control (e.g., adverse changes in exchange rates, economic downturns). Also, hard data do not take into account many less-visible "soft" variables that are also important, such as an expatriate's ability to develop cross-cultural awareness and to work productively with local managers.

Due to such biases, many expatriate managers believe that headquarters management evaluates them unfairly and does not fully appreciate the value of their skills and experience. This could be one reason many expatriates believe a foreign posting does not benefit their careers. In one study of personnel managers in U.S. multinationals, 56 percent of the managers surveyed stated that a foreign assignment is either detrimental or immaterial to one's career.[49]

Guidelines for Performance Appraisal

Several things can reduce bias in the performance appraisal process.[50] First, most expatriates appear to believe more weight should be given to an on-site manager's appraisal than to an off-site manager's appraisal. Due to proximity, an on-site manager is more likely to evaluate the soft variables that are important aspects of an expatriate's performance. The evaluation may be especially valid when the on-site manager is of the same nationality as the expatriate, since cultural bias should be alleviated. In practice, home-office managers often write performance evaluations after receiving input from on-site managers. When this is the case, most experts recommend that a former expatriate who served in the same location should be involved in the appraisal to help reduce bias. Finally, when the policy is for foreign on-site managers to write performance evaluations, home-office managers should be consulted before an on-site manager completes a formal termination evaluation. This gives the home-office manager the opportunity to balance what could be a very hostile evaluation based on a cultural misunderstanding.

LO5 Compensation

Two issues are raised in every discussion of compensation practices in an international business. One is how compensation should be adjusted to reflect national differences in economic circumstances and compensation practices. The other issue is how expatriate managers should be paid.

National Differences in Compensation

Few facts are as private than someone's salary. Human resource firms that collect salary information undertake massive surveys that are anonymous, and add in the results that come from their own work in helping companies set appropriate salaries for their employees. Quite naturally, these same firms do not make their results public, as they charge their clients significant fees in order to help them set their own compensation.

One company that provides such services is Mercer Consulting. Go to www.mercer.com and search for the most recent Global Compensation Planning Report. This massive and expensive work covers nearly 125 countries and shows 15-year trends in compensation. Towers Watson, another global HR firm, offers its own survey, found at www.willistowerswatson.com (search for "executive compensation survey").

ANOTHER PERSPECTIVE

Rewarding the Performance of a Global Team

Imagine that you are leading a global team composed of members from each of your company's seven operating regions: Asia, Southeast Asia, North America, South America, Europe, Eastern Europe and Russia, the Middle East and Africa. The team meets quarterly and communicates daily via computer and phone. How will you motivate and reward team performance on such a culturally diverse team? Team members from cultures that value the group before the individual may be motivated by group-level rewards and benefits, whereas team members from more individualist cultures, such as those found in North America, may well be motivated by individual-level rewards. In Japan, which values the group highly, a trip for salespeople who achieve the team's target for individual members may not motivate nearly as well as a reward for the entire group if the group goal is reached. North American managers who assume that they can motivate anyone with money incentives have learned the hard way that this is not always the case. In some cultures, people work for the greater good first, and then for the individual. How would you motivate your team?

The data below is the latest data that is freely made public by the Hay Group, another global HR Consulting firm. Note that substantial differences exist in the total remuneration for the "average" level employee. Not shown are the differences for executive compensation which, while higher than the numbers for "average" compensation, show a similar wide variation between countries.

These differences in compensation raise a perplexing question for an international business: Should the firm pay employees in different countries according to the prevailing standards in each country, or should it equalize pay on a global basis? The problem does not arise in firms pursuing ethnocentric or polycentric staffing policies. In ethnocentric firms, the issue can be reduced to that of how much home-country expatriates should be paid (which we will consider later). As for polycentric firms, the lack of managers' mobility among national operations implies that pay can and should be kept country-specific. There would seem to be no point in paying employees in Great Britain the same as Canadian executives if they never work side by side.

However, this problem is very real in firms with geocentric staffing policies. A geocentric staffing policy is consistent with a transnational strategy. One aspect of this policy is the need for a cadre of international managers that may include many different nationalities. Should all members of such a cadre be paid the same salary and the same incentive pay? For a Canadian-based firm, this would mean raising the compensation of foreign nationals to Canadian levels, which could be very expensive. If the firm does not equalize pay, it could cause considerable resentment among foreign nationals who are members of the international cadre and work with Canadian nationals. If a firm is serious about building an international cadre, it may have to pay its international managers the same basic salary irrespective of their country of origin or assignment.

Rank	Country	Reward Package (US$)
	TABLE 16.2 Highest and Lowest Compensation Packages (2011). Reprinted with permission of Hay Group, Inc.		
1	Switzerland	104,100
2	Norway	90,300
3	Japan	85,000
4	Germany	79,700
5	Belgium	75,000
54	Ukraine	11,400
55	Bulgaria	11,400
56	Indonesia	10,100
57	Vietnam	10,000
58	India	8900

Source: The Korn Ferry Intellectual Property entitled *2011 Global Total Remuneration Report*, p. 5. Copyright © 2016, Korn Ferry Hay Group, Inc. All Rights Reserved.

Expatriate Pay

The most common approach to expatriate pay is the balance sheet approach. This approach equalizes purchasing power across countries so employees can enjoy the same living standard in their foreign posting that they enjoyed at home. In addition, the approach provides financial incentives to offset qualitative differences between assignment locations.[51] Figure 16.1 shows a typical balance

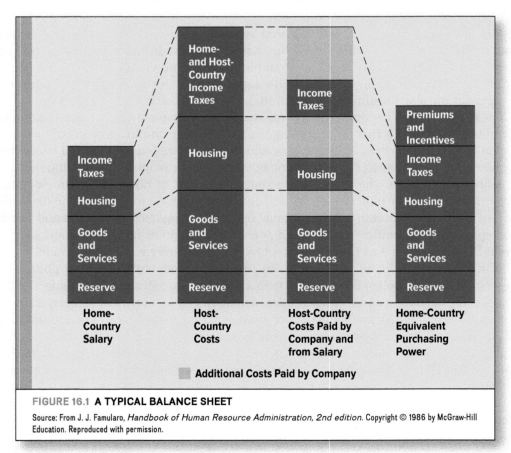

Additional Costs Paid by Company

FIGURE 16.1 A TYPICAL BALANCE SHEET

Source: From J. J. Famularo, *Handbook of Human Resource Administration, 2nd edition.* Copyright © 1986 by McGraw-Hill Education. Reproduced with permission.

MANAGEMENT FOCUS

Customer Experience and Employee Engagement at the Bank of Montreal

One of the latest trends in those companies that serve large customer bases (which are not just retail operations, but in this example include banks as well) is to focus on what the customer experiences when they interact with the business. Are the fully satisfied? Are all of their needs met? All these go to building a relationship with the customers.

As Kelly Harper, Director of Customer Experience Learning at BMO Bank of Montreal explains, "We believe engaged employees will deliver great customer experiences, great customer experiences draw loyalty, loyalty is important to us because we know that loyal customers buy more, stay longer, refer family and friends—and that drives growth."

This is no easy task for BMO, which employs about 50 000 people. The company began with a two-stage process: asking employees what experience they believed they delivered to the customer, then asking customers what was their experience, and how was it important to them.

BMO focused on several aspects:

- All of the company's employees were part of the "customer experience journey," not just those who interacted with customers on a daily basis. For those working far away from the ultimate customer, the company had employees write down how many steps were between them and the customer, in order to show that they were closer to the consumer than they might have believed. According to Harper, "When you think of the customer experience, it's everything within the organization, not just the service side."

- Measurement of the process is key, as is making sure that the right things are measured. For example, call centres are frequently measured by how many calls can be handled in a certain time-frame. This may not be the right way to measure the experience that the customer is receiving.

- These changes are more than just simple slogans. They involve reengineering the company and thus require broad support, including buy-in from senior management.

- HR plays a key role in this process. Building a customer-experience-driven company begins with hiring the right people, orienting them and educating them to the process, and rewarding them throughout.

None of this can happen overnight. It will be interesting to track how the program rolls out, as well as its impact on the bank and its revenues and earnings.

Questions

1. Can focusing on the customer's experience become a competitive difference for BMO?
2. What types of companies would benefit the most from becoming customer-experience driven?

Sources: A. Silliker, "Truly Putting the Customer First," *Canadian HR Reporter*, Fall 2013; and B. Kofman, "Organizational Effectiveness," *Canadian HR Reporter*, Fall 2013.

sheet. Note that home-country outlays for the employee are designated as income taxes, housing expenses, expenditures for goods and services (food, clothing, entertainment, etc.), and reserves (savings, pension contributions, etc.). The balance sheet approach attempts to provide expatriates with the same standard of living in their host countries as they enjoy at home plus a financial inducement (i.e., premium, incentive) for accepting an overseas assignment.

The components of the typical expatriate compensation package are a base salary, a foreign service premium, allowances of various types, tax differentials, and benefits. We shall briefly review each of these components.[52] An expatriate's total compensation package may amount to three times what he or she would cost the firm in a home-country posting. Because of the high cost of expatriates, many firms have reduced their use of them in recent years. However, a firm's ability to reduce its use of expatriates may be limited, particularly if it is pursuing an ethnocentric or geocentric staffing policy.

ANOTHER PERSPECTIVE

Expat Resources on the Web

Not so many years ago, business professionals whose companies sent them overseas to work had few outside resources to help them become acclimated to their new status as expatriates. Today, however, a wealth of information is available online.

A simple keyword search for "expatriate" on a search engine yields an almost endless supply of links: newspapers and magazines published exclusively for expats; Internet sites catering to expatriates in specific regions or countries; general information sites offering insiders' guides to different countries and their finance, culture, and health-care systems; not to mention blogs and other forums. The expatriate boom has even fuelled an industry offering a broad array of services for expats, from mail forwarding to tax preparation to health and life insurance.

BASE SALARY

An expatriate's base salary is normally in the same range as the base salary for a similar position in the home country. The base salary is normally paid in either the home-country currency or in the local currency.

FOREIGN SERVICE PREMIUM

A foreign service premium is extra pay the expatriate receives for working outside his or her country of origin. It is offered as an inducement to accept foreign postings. It compensates the expatriate for having to live in an unfamiliar country isolated from family and friends, having to deal with a new culture and language, and having to adapt to new work habits and practices. Many firms pay foreign service premiums as a percentage of base salary ranging from 10 to 30 percent after tax with 16 percent being the average premium.[53]

ALLOWANCES

Four types of allowances are often included in an expatriate's compensation package: hardship allowances, housing allowances, cost-of-living allowances, and education allowances. A hardship allowance is paid when the expatriate is being sent to a difficult location, usually defined as one where such basic amenities as health care, schools, and retail stores are grossly deficient by the standards of the expatriate's home country. A housing allowance is normally given to ensure that the expatriate can afford the same quality of housing in the foreign country as at home. In locations where housing is very expensive (e.g., London, Tokyo), this allowance can be substantial—as much as 10 to 30 percent of the expatriate's total compensation package. A cost-of-living allowance ensures that the expatriate will enjoy the same standard of living in the foreign posting as at home. An education allowance ensures that an expatriate's children receive adequate schooling (by home-country standards). Host-country public schools are sometimes not suitable for an expatriate's children, in which case they must attend a private school.

TAXATION

Unless a host country has a reciprocal tax treaty with the expatriate's home country, the expatriate may have to pay income tax to both the home- and host-country governments. When a reciprocal tax treaty is not in force, the firm typically pays the expatriate's income tax in the host country. In addition, firms normally make up the difference when a higher income tax rate in a host country reduces an expatriate's take-home pay.

BENEFITS

Many firms also ensure that their expatriates receive the same level of medical and pension benefits abroad that they received at home. This can be very costly for the firm, since many benefits that are tax deductible for the firm in the home country (e.g., medical and pension benefits) may not be deductible out of the country.

LO6 IMPLICATIONS FOR BUSINESS

The HRM function of an international business is typically responsible for international labour relations. From a strategic perspective, the key issue in international labour relations is the degree to which organized labour can limit the choices of an international business. A firm's ability to integrate and consolidate its global operations to realize experience curve and location economies can be limited by organized labour, constraining the pursuit of a transnational or global strategy. C. Prahalad and Y. Doz cite the example of General Motors, which bought peace with labour unions by agreeing not to integrate and consolidate operations in the most efficient manner.[54] In the early 1980s, General Motors made substantial investments in Germany—matching its new investments in Austria and Spain—at the demand of the German metalworkers' unions.

One task of the HRM function is to foster harmony and minimize conflict between the firm and organized labour. With this in mind, this section is divided into three parts. First, we review organized labour's concerns about multinational enterprises. Second, we look at how organized labour has tried to deal with these concerns. And third, we look at how international businesses manage their labour relations to minimize labour disputes.

THE CONCERNS OF ORGANIZED LABOUR

Labour unions generally try to get better pay, greater job security, and better working conditions for their members through collective bargaining with management. Unions' bargaining power is derived largely from their ability to threaten to disrupt production, either by a strike or some other form of work protest (e.g., refusing to work overtime). This threat is credible, however, only insofar as management has no alternative but to employ union labour.

A principal concern of domestic unions about multinational firms is that the company can counter its bargaining power with the power to move production to another country. Ford, for example, very clearly threatened British unions with a plan to move manufacturing to continental Europe unless British workers abandoned work rules that limited productivity, showed restraint in negotiating for wage increases, and curtailed strikes and other work disruptions.[55]

Another concern of organized labour is that an international business will keep highly skilled tasks in its home country and farm out only low-skilled tasks to foreign plants. Such a practice makes it relatively easy for an international business to switch production from one location to another as economic conditions warrant. Consequently, the bargaining power of organized labour is once more reduced.

A final union concern arises when an international business attempts to import employment practices and contractual agreements from its home country. When these practices are alien to the host country, organized labour fears the change will reduce its influence and power. This concern has surfaced in response to Japanese multinationals that have been trying to export their style of labour relations to other countries. For example, much to the annoyance of the United Auto Workers (UAW), most Japanese auto plants in the United States are not unionized. As a result, union influence in the auto industry is declining.

THE STRATEGY OF ORGANIZED LABOUR

Organized labour has responded to the increased bargaining power of multinational corporations by taking three actions: (1) trying to establish international labour organizations; (2) lobbying for national legislation to restrict multinationals; and (3) trying to achieve international regulations on multinationals through such organizations as the United Nations. These efforts have not been very successful.

In the 1960s, organized labour began to establish international trade secretariats (ITSs) to provide worldwide links for national unions in particular industries. The long-term goal was to be able to bargain transnationally with multinational firms. However, the ITSs have had virtually no real success. Although national unions may want to cooperate, they also compete with each other to attract investment from international businesses, and hence jobs for their members. For example, in attempting to gain new jobs for their members, national unions in the auto industry often court auto firms that are seeking locations for new plants. One reason Nissan chose to build its European production facilities in Great Britain rather than Spain was that the British unions agreed to greater concessions than the Spanish unions did. As a result of such competition between national unions, cooperation is difficult to establish.

A further impediment to cooperation has been the wide variation in union structure. Trade unions developed independently in each country. As a result, the structure and ideology of unions tend to vary significantly from country to country, as does the nature of collective bargaining. For example, in Great Britain, France, and Italy many unions are controlled by left-wing socialists, who view collective bargaining through the lens of "class conflict." In contrast, most union leaders in Germany, the Netherlands, Scandinavia, and Switzerland are far more moderate politically. The ideological gap between union leaders in different countries has made cooperation difficult.

Divergent ideologies are reflected in radically different views about the role of a union in society and the stance unions should take toward multinationals.

Organized labour has also met with only limited success in its efforts to get national and international bodies to regulate multinationals. Such international organizations as the International Labour Organization (ILO) and the Organisation for Economic Co-operation and Development (OECD) have adopted codes of conduct for multinational firms to follow in labour relations. However, these guidelines are not as far-reaching as many unions would like. Many researchers report that such guidelines are of only limited effectiveness.[56]

The International Labour Organization was set up to promote social justice and internationally recognize human and labour rights. © Zoonar GmbH/Alamy

APPROACHES TO LABOUR RELATIONS

International businesses differ markedly in their approaches to international labour relations. The main difference is the degree to which labour relations activities are centralized or decentralized. Historically, most international businesses have decentralized international labour relations activities to their foreign subsidiaries because labour laws, union power, and the nature of collective bargaining varied so much from country to country. It made sense to decentralize the labour relations function to local managers. The belief was that there was no way central management could effectively handle the complexity of simultaneously managing labour relations in a number of different environments.

Although this logic still holds, there is now a trend toward greater centralized control. This trend reflects international firms' attempts to rationalize their global operations. The general rise in competitive pressure in industry after industry has made it more important for firms to control their costs. Since labour costs account for such a large percentage of total costs, many firms are now using the threat to move production to another country in their negotiations with unions to change work rules and limit wage increases (as Ford did in Europe). Because such a move would involve major new investments and plant closures, this bargaining tactic requires the input of headquarters management. Thus, the level of centralized input into labour relations is increasing.

In addition, the realization is growing that the way work is organized within a plant can be a major source of competitive advantage. Much of the competitive advantage of Japanese automakers, for example, has been attributed to the use of self-managing teams, job rotation, cross-training, and the like in their Japanese plants.[57] To replicate their domestic performance in foreign plants, the Japanese firms have tried to replicate their work practices there. This often brings them into direct conflict with traditional work practices in those countries, as sanctioned by the local labour unions, so the Japanese firms have often made their foreign investments contingent on the local union accepting a radical change in work practices. To achieve this, the headquarters of many Japanese firms bargain directly with local unions to get union agreement to changes in work rules before committing to an investment. For example, before Nissan decided to invest in northern England, it got a commitment from British unions to agree to a change in traditional work practices. By its very nature, pursuing such a strategy requires centralized control over the labour relations function.

Key Terms

corporate culture	geocentric staffing policy
ethnocentric staffing policy	human resource management
expatriate failure	polycentric staffing policy
expatriate manager	staffing policy

LO Learning Objectives Summary

1. Firm success requires HRM policies to be congruent with the firm's strategy and with its formal and informal structure and controls.

2. Staffing policy is concerned with selecting employees who have the skills required to perform particular jobs. Staffing policy can be a tool for developing and promoting a corporate culture. An ethnocentric approach to staffing policy fills all key management positions in an international business with parent-country nationals. The policy is congruent with an international strategy. A drawback is that ethnocentric staffing can result in cultural myopia. A polycentric staffing policy uses host-country nationals to manage foreign subsidiaries and parent-country nationals for the key positions at corporate headquarters. This approach can minimize the dangers of cultural myopia, but it can create a gap between home- and host-country operations. The policy is best suited to a localization strategy. A geocentric staffing policy seeks the best people for key jobs throughout the organization, regardless of their nationality. This approach is consistent with building a strong unifying culture and informal management network, and is well suited to both global standardization and transnational strategies. Immigration policies of national governments may limit a firm's ability to pursue this policy. A prominent issue in the international staffing literature is expatriate failure, defined as the premature return of an expatriate manager to his or her home country. Expatriate failure can be reduced by selection procedures that screen out inappropriate candidates. The most successful expatriates seem to be those who have high self-esteem and self-confidence, can get along well with others, are willing to attempt to communicate in a foreign language, and can empathize with people of other cultures. Training can lower the probability of expatriate failure.

3. Management development programs attempt to increase the overall skill levels of managers through a mix of ongoing management education and rotation of managers through different jobs within the firm to give them varied experiences. Management development is often used as a strategic tool to build a strong unifying culture and informal management network, both of which support transnational and global standardization strategies.

4. It can be difficult to evaluate the performance of expatriate managers objectively because of unintentional bias. A firm can take a number of steps to reduce this bias.

5. Country differences in compensation practices raise a difficult question for an international business: Should the firm pay executives in different countries according to the standards in each country or equalize pay on a global basis? The most common approach to expatriate pay is the balance sheet approach. This approach aims to equalize purchasing power so employees can enjoy the same living standard in their foreign posting that they had at home.

6. A key issue in international labour relations is the degree to which organized labour can limit the choices available to an international business. A firm's ability to pursue a transnational or global standardization strategy can be significantly constrained by the actions of labour unions. A principal concern of organized labour is that the multinational can counter union bargaining power with threats to move production to another country. Organized labour has tried to counter the bargaining power of multinationals by forming international labour organizations. In general, these efforts have not been effective.

Critical Thinking and Discussion Questions

1. What are the main advantages and disadvantages of the ethnocentric, polycentric, and geocentric approaches to staffing policy? When is each approach appropriate?

2. Research suggests that many expatriate employees encounter problems that limit both their effectiveness in a foreign posting and their contribution to the company when they return home. What are the main causes and consequences of these problems, and how might a firm reduce the occurrence of such problems?

3. What is the link between an international business's strategy and its HRM policies, particularly with regard to the use of expatriate employees and their pay scale?

4. In what ways can organized labour constrain the strategic choices of an international business? How can an international business limit these constraints?

Research Task   globalEDGE™   globaledge.msu.edu

Use the globalEDGE™ site to complete the following exercises:

1. According to Expatistan (www.expatistan.com /cost-of-living/index) there are many international cities more expensive to live than Toronto, which ranked 51st. Vancouver comes in at number 59 with Calgary on its heels in 77th place. Ottawa at 89th, Edmonton is 96th, Halifax 90th, Victoria 99th, Winnipeg ranks as the 118th, and Montreal 126th most expensive city in the world! Can you think of

any advantages and disadvantages of living in Toronto instead of in Winnipeg?

2. You work in the human resources department at the headquarters of a multinational corporation. Your company is about to send several Canadian managers overseas as expatriates. Utilize resources available on the globalEDGE Web site regarding expatriate life to compile a short checklist of concerns and steps for your company to go through before sending its managers overseas.

CLOSING CASE

LEARNING FROM THE ORIGINAL EXPATRIATES

According to Ambassador Fernando López-Fabregat, Director General for International Economic Affairs, Uruguayan Ministry of Foreign Affairs, and former Consul General of Uruguay in Toronto, we can learn a lot from what he calls foreign service employees (FSEs), people working for governments but based internationally and for international agencies, who were the first expatriates to appear in the international arena. The most successful employees have a tolerance for ambiguity, sophisticated interpersonal relations and communication skills, high cultural empathy, and are open-minded. These skills are always crucial for any employee but in the case of FSEs are essential to balance the national interests of their country with the desires of their host country. They must be highly flexible, as it is not unusual for the FSE to deal today with an issue (for example trade promotion) and tomorrow with a very different one (for instance cultural affairs).

One of the adjustments in organizational culture that FSEs have to make is the shift from working in a large government department at home to a smaller group located in the host country. When in the head office at home, the FSE will work in an organization with, perhaps, thousands of other employees that give them adequate back up services. But, suddenly, when posted overseas they begin to work in an organization (such as an embassy, consulate, etc.) that is very similar to a small- or medium-sized company.

There is continuing debate about whether FSEs have to be generalists or specialists. According to López-Fabregat, the correct answer is that they have to be both. They can be specialists on certain areas (for example political analysis, marketing) but particularly when abroad, to really understand the surrounding social, political, economic environment they have to be generalists, duly prepared to work in a team, to coordinate efforts with other services, agencies, or private companies, and, finally, to give their authorities at home the very useful broad picture of the situation in the host country.

Source: Interview with Fernando López-Fabregat in Toronto, 2015.

Case Discussion Questions

1. What are some of the skills that can make an expatriate manager successful? Give an example of each of the traits and how they would be found in a foreign environment.

2. Give an example of when an FSE would have to apply generalist knowledge.

3. How would an expatriate manager adjust the shift from working in a large organization to a small one in a foreign environment?

Sustainability in Practice

INTERFACE: AN ENVIRONMENTALLY SUSTAINABLE COMMITMENT TO BUSINESS AND MATERIAL MANAGEMENT

The following case study describes a company's efforts to be both profitable and environmentally sustainable.

Interface, Inc. is the world's largest manufacturer of carpet tiles and upholstery fabrics for commercial interiors. But Interface's core vision is not about carpet or fabrics per se; it is about becoming a leading example of a sustainable and restorative enterprise. Interface notes on its Web site (www.interfaceglobal.com) that its goal is to "be the first company that, by its deeds, shows the entire world what sustainability is in all its dimensions: People, process, product, place and profits—and in doing so, become restorative through the power of influence."

That is a substantial challenge for a company that grew through more than 50 acquisitions, has sales offices in 110 countries, and relies on a supply chain heavily dependent on petrochemicals.

Founder and Chairman Ray Anderson presented this challenge to the organization in 1994. "After 21 years of unwittingly plundering the Earth, I read Paul Hawken's book *The*

Ecology of Commerce (Harper 1993). . . . It convinced me on the spot, not only as a plunderer of Earth, but also as part of an industrial system that is destroying Earth's biosphere, the source and nurturer of all life. . . . I was struck to the core by Hawken's central point, that only business and industry, the major culprit, is also large enough, powerful enough, pervasive enough, wealthy enough, to lead humankind away from the abyss toward which we are plunging. It was an epiphanal experience for me, a 'spear in the chest.' . . . I myself became a recovering plunderer. At Interface we call this new direction, climbing Mount Sustainability, the point at its peak symbolically representing zero environmental 'footprint'— our definition of sustainability for ourselves, to reach a state in which our petro-intensive company (energy and materials) takes nothing from the Earth that is not naturally and rapidly renewable, and does no harm to the biosphere: zero footprint."

As a result, Interface has undergone considerable transformation in its effort to reorient the entire organization. Throughout Interface, all employees were trained in the principles of systems thinking. They were required to examine the impact of their work and how they could work more sustainably in their business area. Training was necessary, according to Anderson, because traditional education "continues to teach economics students to trust the 'invisible hand' of the market, when the invisible hand is clearly blind to the externalities. . . . The truth is, we have an essentially illiterate populace when it comes to the environment." The feedback on this training has been very positive and a great deal of progress has been made as a result. However, there were three areas where Interface could have improved the process.

The first is always establishing a positive environment for inspired employees, fresh from their training courses, to return to. The company found that employees became passionate as their understanding of sustainability grew, and they needed an outlet for action. Although there were many areas of good supportive management across the business, there were also too many areas where local managers were not prepared well enough to facilitate motivated employees wanting to make a difference.

Second, people engage in different ways with sustainability issues, and learning programs need to provide the space to explore these differences. Programs need to be flexible enough to go into detail on a hot issue such as climate change, while the next question may well be about equity of resource use. To keep people motivated, programs need to maintain this flexibility.

Third, follow-up was not quick enough; it takes much more than two days for people to really understand sustainability. Sustainability issues need to be revisited again and again, as employees begin to understand how it impacts their daily lives. It is a big commitment to revisit these issues on an ongoing basis, but the company recognized that it was vital for employees to continually buy in.

The company is also upfront about the challenges yet to be overcome. The greatest is to replace petrochemically derived fibres with recycled fibres. Achieving a zero footprint and building and sustaining an engaged culture at the company are also goals for the year 2020.

Sources: Interface, Inc. information was adapted by Dr. Debra Rowe and is used with permission. Quotes from Ray Anderson are from the chairman's speech at the National Council for Science and the Environment's 2003 conference. The full text of the speech is available at www.ncseglobal.org; and www.interfaceglobal.com (accessed January 2014).

Glossary

absolute advantage Ability of a country to produce a good more efficiently than any other country at producing it.

accommodative stance In taking this stance, a company exceeds its customers' expectations.

ad valorem tariff Tariff levied as a proportion of the value of an imported good.

administrative trade policies Bureaucratic rules adopted by governments used to restrict imports or boost exports.

Andean Pact A 1969 agreement among Bolivia, Chile, Ecuador, Colombia, and Peru to establish a customs union.

antidumping policies Policies designed to punish foreign firms that engage in dumping and thus protect domestic producers from unfair foreign competition.

arbitrage The purchase of securities in one market for immediate resale in another to profit from a price discrepancy.

Association of Southeast Asian Nations (ASEAN) An attempt to establish a free trade area among Brunei, Cambodia, Indonesia, Laos, Malaysia, Myanmar, the Philippines, Singapore, Thailand, and Vietnam.

balance-of-payments accounts National accounts that track both payments to and receipts from foreigners.

banking crisis A loss of confidence in the banking system that leads to a run on banks as individuals and companies withdraw their deposits.

barter The direct exchange of goods or services between two parties without a cash transaction.

basic research centres Sites for fundamental research located in regions where valuable scientific knowledge is being created; where teams develop the basic technologies that become new products.

bill of exchange Order written by an exporter instructing an importer, or an importer's agent, to pay a specified amount of money at a specified time; also called a draft.

bill of lading Document issued to an exporter by a common carrier transporting merchandise. It serves as a receipt, a contract, and a document of title.

Bill S-21 Otherwise known as the Corruption of Foreign Officials Act that received Royal Assent on December 10, 1998. It is Canadian legislation that makes the bribery, or other business corruption "tool" of a foreign official by a Canadian business person, a criminal offence.

business ethics Accepted principles of right or wrong governing the conduct of business people.

buyback When a firm builds a plant in a country and agrees to take a certain percentage of the plant's output as partial payment of the contract.

capital flight Residents convert domestic currency into a foreign currency.

Caribbean Single Market and Economy (CSME) Unites six CARICOM members in agreeing to lower trade barriers and harmonize macroeconomic and monetary policies.

CARICOM An association of English-speaking Caribbean states that are attempting to establish a customs union.

caste system System of social stratification in which social position is determined by the family into which a person is born, and change in that position is usually not possible during an individual's lifetime.

Central America Free Trade Agreement (CAFTA) The agreement of the member states of the Central American Common Market joined by the Dominican Republic to trade freely with the United States.

Central American Common Market A trade pact among Costa Rica, El Salvador, Guatemala, Honduras, and Nicaragua, which began in the early 1960s but collapsed in 1969 due to war.

central bank The generic name given to a country's primary monetary authority. It usually has the responsibility for issuing currency, administering monetary policy, holding member banks' deposits, and facilitating the nation's banking industry.

channel length Number of intermediaries that a product has to go through before it reaches the final consumer.

civil law System of law based on a very detailed set of written laws and codes.

class consciousness Tendency for individuals to perceive themselves in terms of their class background.

class system System of social stratification in which social status is determined by the family into which a person is born and by subsequent socioeconomic achievements. Mobility between classes is possible.

code of ethics A business's formal statement of ethical priorities.

collectivism Political system that emphasizes collective goals as opposed to individual goals.

command economy Economic system where the allocation of resources, including determination of what goods and services should be produced, and in what quantity, is planned by the government.

common law System of law based on tradition, precedent, and custom. When law courts interpret common law, they do so with regard to these characteristics.

common market A group of countries committed to (1) removing all barriers to the free flow of goods, services, and factors of production between each other; (2) pursuing a common external trade policy; and (3) allowing factors of production to move freely among members.

communist totalitarianism Version of collectivism advocating that socialism can only be achieved through a totalitarian dictatorship.

communists Those who believe socialism can be achieved only through revolution and totalitarian dictatorship.

comparative advantage Theory that a country should specialize in producing goods and services it can produce most efficiently even if this means buying goods from other countries that it could produce more efficiently itself. A country is said to have a comparative advantage in the production of such goods and services.

concentrated retail system A few retailers supply most of the market.

Confucian dynamism Theory that Confucian teachings affect attitudes toward time, persistence, ordering by status, protection of face, respect for tradition, and reciprocation of gifts and favours.

constant returns to specialization Costs stay the same as specialization increases.

contract Document that specifies the conditions under which an exchange is to occur and details the rights and obligations of the parties involved.

contract law Body of law that governs contract creation and enforcement.

Convention on Combating Bribery of Foreign Public Officials in International Business Transactions The convention obliges member states to make the bribery of foreign public officials a criminal offence.

copyrights Exclusive legal rights of authors, composers, playwrights, artists, and publishers to publish and dispose of their work as they see fit.

core competence Firm skills that competitors cannot easily match or imitate.

corporate culture Organization's norms and value systems.

corporate social responsibility The idea that managers of enterprises should consider the social consequences of economic actions when making business decisions.

counterpurchase Reciprocal buying agreement.

countertrade Trade of goods and services for other goods and services.

countervailing duties Antidumping duties.

country of origin effects Extent to which the place of manufacture influences product evaluations.

cross-licensing agreement Arrangement in which a company licenses valuable intangible property to a foreign partner and receives a licence for the partner's valuable knowledge; reduces risk of licensing.

cultural relativism The belief that ethics are culturally determined and that firms should adopt the ethics of the cultures in which they operate.

currency board Means of controlling a country's currency by holding reserves of a foreign currency equal at a fixed exchange rate to at least 100 percent of the domestic currency issued.

currency crisis Occurs when a speculative attack on the exchange value of a currency results in a sharp depreciation in the value of the currency or forces authorities to expend large volumes of international currency reserves and sharply increase interest rates to defend the prevailing exchange rate.

currency speculation Involves short-term movement of funds from one currency to another in hopes of profiting from shifts in exchange rates.

currency swap Simultaneous purchase and sale of a given amount of foreign exchange for two different value dates.

current account In the balance of payments, records transactions involving the export or import of goods and services.

customs union A group of countries committed to (1) removing all barriers to the free flow of goods and services between each other, and (2) the pursuit of a common external trade policy.

D'Amato Act Act passed in 1996, similar to the Helms–Burton Act, aimed at Libya and Iran.

defensive stance Companies taking this stance deny responsibility for the cause of concern.

democracy Political system in which government is by the people, exercised either directly or through elected representatives.

deregulation Removal of government restrictions concerning the conduct of business.

dirty-float system A system under which a country's currency is nominally allowed to float freely against other currencies, but in which the government will intervene, buying and selling currency, if it believes that the currency has deviated too far from its fair value.

draft Order written by an exporter instructing an importer, or an importer's agent, to pay a specified amount of money at a specified time; also called a bill of exchange.

dumping Selling goods in a foreign market for less than their cost of production or below their "fair" market value.

dynamic capabilities Key skills (capabilities) of a corporation that evolve and become more valuable over time.

eclectic paradigm Argument that combining location-specific assets or resource endowments and the firm's own unique assets often requires FDI; it requires the firm to establish production facilities where those foreign assets or resource endowments are located.

economic risk Likelihood that events, including economic mismanagement, will cause drastic changes in a country's business environment that adversely affect the profit and other goals of a particular business enterprise.

economic union A group of countries committed to (1) the removal of all barriers to the free flow of goods, services, and factors of production between each other; (2) the adoption of a common currency; (3) the harmonization of tax rates; and (4) the pursuit of a common external trade policy.

economies of scale Cost advantages associated with large-scale production.

economies of scope Cost advantages associated with using specialized competencies across different product lines or businesses.

efficient market A market where prices reflect all available information.

elastic demand When a small change in price produces a large change in demand.

ethical dilemma A situation in which there is no ethically acceptable solution.

ethical strategy A course of action that does not violate a company's business ethics.

ethical systems Cultural beliefs about what is proper behaviour and conduct.

ethnocentric behaviour Behaviour that is based on the belief in the superiority of one's own ethnic group or culture; often shows disregard or contempt for the culture of other countries.

ethnocentric staffing policy Staffing approach within the MNE in which all key management positions are filled by parent-country nationals.

European Free Trade Association (EFTA) A free trade association including Norway, Iceland, Liechtenstein, and Switzerland.

exchange rate The rate at which one currency is converted into another.

exclusive distribution channel Distribution channel that outsiders find difficult to access.

expatriate failure Premature return of an expatriate manager to the home country.

expatriate manager A national of one country appointed to a management position in another country.

experience curve Systematic production cost reductions that occur over the life of a product.

export management company Export specialists who act as an export marketing department for client firms.

exporting Sale of products produced in one country to residents of another country.

external stakeholders Individuals or groups who have some claim on a firm, such as customers, suppliers, and unions.

externalities Knowledge spillovers.

externally convertible currency Non-residents can convert their holdings of domestic currency into foreign currency, but the ability of residents to convert the currency is limited in some way.

first-mover advantages Advantages accruing to the first to enter a market.

first-mover disadvantages Drawbacks associated with entering a foreign market before other international businesses.

fixed exchange rates A system under which the exchange rate for converting one currency into another is fixed.

flexible machine cell Adjustable manufacturing technology in which a grouping of various machine types, a common materials handler, and a centralized cell controller produce a family of products.

flexible manufacturing technology Manufacturing technologies designed to improve job scheduling, reduce setup time, and improve quality control.

floating exchange rates A system under which the exchange rate for converting one currency into another is continuously adjusted depending on the laws of supply and demand.

flow of foreign direct investment (FDI) The amount of foreign direct investment undertaken over a given time period (normally one year).

folkways Routine conventions of everyday life.

Foreign Corrupt Practices Act U.S. law regulating behaviour regarding the conduct of international business in the taking of bribes and other unethical actions.

foreign debt crisis Situation in which a country cannot service its foreign debt obligations, whether private-sector or government debt.

foreign direct investment (FDI) Direct investment in business operations in a foreign country. The acquisition or construction of physical capital by a firm from one (source) country in another (host) country.

foreign exchange market A market for converting the currency of one country into that of another country.

foreign exchange risk The risk that changes in exchange rates will hurt the profitability of a business deal.

forward exchange When two parties agree to exchange currency and execute a deal at some specific date in the future.

forward exchange rates The exchange rates governing forward exchange transactions.

fragmented retail system Many retailers, with no single one having a major share of the market.

franchising A specialized form of licensing in which the franchiser sells intangible property to the franchisee and insists on rules to conduct the business.

free trade Absence of barriers to the free flow of goods and services between countries.

free trade area A group of countries committed to removing all barriers to the free flow of goods and services between each other, but pursuing independent external trade policies.

freely convertible currency A country's currency is freely convertible when the government of that country allows both residents and nonresidents to purchase unlimited amounts of foreign currency with the domestic currency.

fundamental analysis Draws on economic theory to construct sophisticated econometric models for predicting exchange rate movements.

General Agreement on Tariffs and Trade (GATT) International treaty that committed signatories to lowering barriers to the free flow of goods across national borders and led to the World Trade Organization (WTO).

geocentric staffing policy Staffing policy where the best people are sought for key jobs throughout an MNE, regardless of nationality.

global learning The flow of skills and product offerings from foreign subsidiary to home country and from foreign subsidiary to foreign subsidiary.

global web When different stages of value chain are dispersed to those locations around the globe where value added is maximized or where costs of value creation are minimized.

globalization Trend away from distinct national economic units and toward one huge global market.

globalization of markets Moving away from an economic system in which national markets are distinct entities, isolated by trade barriers and barriers of distance, time, and culture, and toward a system in which national markets are merging into one global market.

globalization of production Trend by individual firms to disperse parts of their productive processes to different locations around the globe to take advantage of differences in cost and quality of factors of production.

gold standard The practice of pegging currencies to gold and guaranteeing convertibility.

greenfield investment Establishing a new operation in a foreign country.

gross national income (GNI) Total income of all citizens of a county, including the income from factors of production used abroad. Since 2001, the World Bank has used this measure of economic activity instead of the previously used GNP.

group Association of two or more individuals who have a shared sense of identity and who interact with each other in structured ways on the basis of a common set of expectations about each other's behaviour.

Helms–Burton Act Act passed in 1996 that allowed Americans to sue foreign firms that use Cuban property confiscated from them after the 1959 revolution.

Human Development Index (HDI) Attempt by the United Nations to assess the impact of a number of factors on the quality of human life in a country.

human resource management Activities an organization conducts to use its human resources effectively.

import quota Direct restriction on the quantity of a good that can be imported into a country.

Incoterms Set of international trading rules that determine the rights and obligations of buyers and sellers in international trade transactions.

individualism Emphasis on the importance of guaranteeing individual freedom and self-expression.

individualism versus collectivism Theory focusing on the relationship between the individual and his or her fellows. In individualistic societies, the ties between individuals are loose and individual achievement is highly valued. In societies where collectivism is emphasized, ties between individuals are tight, people are born into collectives, such as extended families, and everyone is supposed to look after the interests of his or her collective.

inefficient market A market in which prices do not reflect all available information.

inelastic demand When a large change in price produces only a small change in demand.

inflows of FDI Flow of foreign direct investment into a country.

innovation Development of new products, processes, organizations, management practices, and strategies.

internal stakeholders People who work for or who own the business such as employees, directors, and shareholders.

internalization theory A theory that seeks to explain why firms often prefer foreign direct investment over licensing as a strategy for entering foreign markets.

international business Any firm that engages in international trade or investment.

International Fisher Effect For any two countries, the spot exchange rate should change in an equal amount but in the opposite direction to the difference in nominal interest rates between countries.

International Monetary Fund (IMF) International institution set up to maintain order in the international monetary system.

international monetary system Institutional arrangements countries adopt to govern exchange rates.

international trade Occurs when a firm exports goods or services to consumers in another country.

ISO 9000 Certification process that requires certain quality standards that must be met.

joint venture A cooperative undertaking between two or more firms.

just distribution A distribution that is considered fair and equitable.

just-in-time (JIT) inventory system Manufacturing strategy in which parts are produced or delivered only as needed.

karoshi Japanese term meaning to die from overwork.

late-mover disadvantages Handicap experienced by being a late entrant in a market.

law of one price In competitive markets free of transportation costs and barriers to trade, identical products sold in different countries must sell for the same price when their price is expressed in the same currency.

learning effects Cost savings from learning by doing.

legal risk Likelihood that a trading partner will opportunistically break a contract or expropriate intellectual property rights.

legal system System of rules that regulates behaviour and the processes by which the laws of a country are enforced and through which redress of grievances is obtained.

letter of credit Issued by a bank, a document indicating that the bank will make payments under specific circumstances.

licensing Occurs when a firm (the licensor) licenses the right to produce its product, use its production processes, or use its brand name or trademark to another firm (the licensee). In return for giving the licensee these rights, the licensor collects a royalty fee on every unit the licensee sells.

licensing agreement Arrangement in which a licensor grants the rights to intangible property to the licensee for a specified period and receives a royalty fee in return.

local content requirement Demand that some specific fraction of a good be produced domestically.

location economies Cost advantages from performing a value creation activity at the optimal location for that activity.

location-specific advantages Advantages that arise from using resource endowments or assets that are tied to a particular foreign location and that a firm finds valuable to combine with its own unique assets (such as the firm's technological, marketing, or management know-how).

logistics Procurement and physical transmission of material through the supply chain, from suppliers to customers.

long-term versus short-term orientation Theory that deals with virtue regardless of truth; values associated with long-term orientation are thrift and perseverance; values associated with short-term orientation are respect for tradition, fulfilling social obligations, and protecting one's "face."

Maastricht treaty Treaty agreed to in 1991, but not ratified until January 1, 1994, that committed the 12 member-states of the European Community to adopt a common currency.

maquilladoras NAFTA-related Mexican work zones of cheap labour that are commonly found along the Texas–Mexican borders.

market economy Economic system wherein the interaction of supply and demand determines the quantity in which goods and services are produced.

market imperfections Aspects of a market that make transactions less efficient than they could be or that endanger the strategic advantages held by a company.

market segmentation Identifying groups of consumers whose purchasing behaviour differs from others in important ways.

marketing mix Choices about product attributes, distribution strategy, communication strategy, and pricing strategy that a firm offers its targeted markets.

masculinity versus femininity Theory of the relationship between gender and work roles. In masculine cultures, sex roles are sharply differentiated and traditional "masculine values," such as achievement and the effective exercise of power, determine cultural ideals. In feminine cultures, sex roles are less sharply distinguished, and little differentiation is made between men and women in the same job.

mass customization Ability of a company to use flexible manufacturing technology to achieve both low cost per unit and product customization.

materials management Activity that controls the transmission of physical materials through the value chain, from procurement through production and into distribution.

mercantilism Economic philosophy advocating that countries should simultaneously encourage exports and discourage imports.

mixed economy Economic system wherein certain sectors are left to private ownership and free market mechanisms, while others have significant government ownership and government planning.

Moore's Law The power of microprocessor technology doubles and its costs of production fall by half every 18 months.

moral hazard Arises when people behave recklessly because they know they will be saved if things go wrong.

mores Norms seen as central to the functioning of a society and to its social life.

Multilateral Agreement on Investment (MAI) An agreement that would make it illegal for signatory states to discriminate against foreign investors; would have liberalized rules governing FDI between OECD states.

multinational enterprise (MNE) A firm that owns business operations in more than one country.

multipoint competition Arises when two or more enterprises encounter each other in different regional markets, national markets, or industries.

multipoint pricing Occurs when a pricing strategy in one market may have an impact on a rival's pricing strategy in another market.

naive immoralist Asserts that if a manager of a multinational sees that firms from other nations are not following ethical norms in a host nation, that manager should not either.

noise Amount of other messages competing for a potential consumer's attention.

nonconvertible currency A currency is not convertible when both residents and nonresidents are prohibited from converting their holdings of that currency into another currency.

norms Social rules and guidelines that prescribe appropriate behaviour in particular situations.

obstructionist stance Companies taking this stance create barriers that make it difficult for customers to address their concerns.

offset Buying agreement similar to counterpurchase, but the exporter can then fulfill the agreement with any firm in the country to which the sale is being made.

oligopoly An industry composed of a limited number of large firms.

optimal currency area A group of countries where similarities among the economic structures of countries make it feasible to adopt a single currency.

Organisation for Economic Co-operation and Development (OECD) A Paris-based intergovernmental organization of "wealthy" nations whose purpose is to provide its 35 member-states with a forum in which governments can compare their experiences, discuss the problems they share, and seek solutions that can then be applied within their own national contexts.

organization culture The values and norms shared among an organization's employees.

outflows of FDI Flow of foreign direct investment out of a country.

Paris Convention for the Protection of Industrial Property International agreement to protect intellectual property; signed by 187 countries.

patent Grants the inventor of a new product or process exclusive rights to the manufacture, use, or sale of that invention.

pegged exchange rate Currency value is fixed relative to a reference currency.

pioneering costs The price an early entrant bears that later entrants avoid, such as the time and effort in learning the rules, failure due to ignorance, and the liability of being a foreigner.

political economy Political, economic, and legal systems of a country.

political risk Likelihood that political forces will cause drastic changes in a country's business environment that adversely affect the profit and other goals of a particular business enterprise.

political system System of government in a nation.

political union A central political apparatus that coordinates economic, social, and foreign policy.

polycentric staffing policy Staffing policy in an MNE in which host-country nationals are recruited to manage subsidiaries in their own country, while parent-country nationals occupy key positions at corporate headquarters.

positive-sum game Situation in which all countries can benefit even if some benefit more than others.

power distance Theory of how a society deals with the fact that people are unequal in physical and intellectual capabilities. High power distance cultures are found in countries that let inequalities grow over time into inequalities of power and wealth. Low power distance cultures are found in societies that try to play down such inequalities as much as possible.

predatory pricing Reducing prices below fair market value as a competitive weapon to drive weaker competitors out of the market ("fair" being cost plus some reasonable profit margin).

price elasticity of demand Measure of how responsive demand for a product is to changes in price.

private action Theft, piracy, blackmail, and the like by private individuals or groups.

privatization Sale of state-owned enterprises to private investors.

proactive stance In taking this stance, companies respond to issues as soon as they arise and inform their customers of how they will be proceeding.

product liability Involves holding a firm and its officers responsible when a product causes injury, death, or damage.

product safety laws Laws that set certain safety standards to which a product must adhere.

profit Difference between total revenues and total costs.

profitability A ratio or rate of return concept.

property rights Bundle of legal rights over the use to which a resource is put and over the use made of any income that may be derived from the resource.

public action Extortion of income or resources from property holders by public officials, such as politicians and government bureaucrats.

pull strategy Market strategy emphasizing mass media advertising as opposed to personal selling.

purchasing power parity (PPP) Adjustment in gross domestic product per capita to reflect differences in the cost of living.

push strategy Marketing strategy emphasizing personal selling rather than mass media advertising.

regional economic integration Agreements among countries in a geographic region to reduce and ultimately remove tariff and nontariff barriers to the free flow of goods, services, and factors of production between each other.

relatively efficient markets One in which few impediments to international trade and investment exist.

religion System of shared beliefs and rituals concerned with the realm of the sacred.

representative democracy Political system in which citizens periodically elect individuals to represent them in government.

right-wing totalitarianism Political system in which political power is monopolized by a party, group, or individual that generally permits individual economic freedom but restricts individual political freedom, including free speech, often on the grounds that it would lead to the rise of communism.

righteous moralist Claims that a multinational's home-country standards of ethics are the appropriate ones to follow in foreign countries.

rights theories A twentieth century theory that human beings have fundamental rights and privileges that transcend national boundaries and cultures.

sight draft Bill of exchange payable on presentation to the drawee.

Six Sigma Statistically based methodology for improving product quality.

social democrats Those committed to achieving socialism by democratic means.

social mobility Extent to which individuals can move out of the social stratum into which they are born.

social strata Hierarchical social categories often based on family background, occupation, and income.

society Group of people who share a common set of values and norms.

sogo shosha Large, vertically integrated Japanese trading houses whose affiliates offer a wide range of products and materials. The size and breadth of the organizations allow them to generate captive supply and demand and to provide risk management, financial, and export services to their affiliates.

source effects When the receiver of the message evaluates the message based on the status or image of the sender.

sourcing decisions Whether a firm should make or buy component parts.

specific tariff Tariff levied as a fixed charge for each unit of good imported.

spot exchange rate The exchange rate at which a foreign exchange dealer will convert one currency into another that particular day.

staffing policy Strategy concerned with selecting employees for particular jobs.

stakeholders The individuals or groups who have an interest, stake, or claim in the actions and overall performance of a company.

stock of foreign direct investment The total accumulated value of foreign-owned assets at a given time.

strategic alliances Cooperative agreements between two or more firms.

strategic commitment A decision that has a long-term impact and is difficult to reverse, such as entering a foreign market on a large scale.

strategic pricing Pricing aimed at giving a company a competitive advantage over its rivals.

strategy Actions managers take to attain the firm's goals.

subsidy Government financial assistance to a domestic producer.

switch trading Using of a specialized third-party trading house in a countertrade arrangement.

tariff Tax levied on imports.

technical analysis Uses price and volume data to determine past trends, which are expected to continue into the future.

theocratic law System of law based on religious teachings.

theocratic totalitarianism Political system in which political power is monopolized by a party, group, or individual that governs according to religious principles.

time draft Promise to pay by the accepting party at some future date.

timing of entry Entry is early when a firm enters a foreign market before other foreign firms and late when a firm enters after other international businesses have established themselves.

total quality management Management philosophy that takes as its central focus the need to improve the quality of a company's products and services.

totalitarianism Form of government in which one person or political party exercises absolute control over all spheres of human life and opposing political parties are prohibited.

trade creation Trade created due to regional economic integration; occurs when high-cost domestic producers are replaced by low-cost foreign producers in a free trade area.

trade diversion Trade diverted due to regional economic integration; occurs when low-cost foreign suppliers outside a free trade area are replaced by higher-cost foreign suppliers in a free trade area.

trademarks Designs and names, often officially registered, by which merchants or manufacturers designate and differentiate their products.

transnational strategy Plan to exploit experience-based cost and location economies, transfer core competencies with the firm, and pay attention to local responsiveness.

tribal totalitarianism Political system in which a party, group, or individual that represents the interests of a particular tribe (ethnic group) monopolizes political power.

turnkey project A venture in which a firm agrees to set up an operating plant for a foreign client and hand over the "key" when the plant is fully operational.

uncertainty avoidance Extent to which cultures socialize members to accept ambiguous situations and to tolerate uncertainty.

United Nations International organization made up of representatives from 193 countries. It is headquartered in New York City and was formed in 1945 to promote peace, security, and cooperation.

United Nations Convention on Contracts for the International Sale of Goods (CISG) Set of rules governing certain aspects of the making and performance of commercial contracts between sellers and buyers who have their places of business in different nations.

Universal Declaration of Human Rights A United Nations document that lays down the basic principles of human rights that should be adhered to.

universal needs Needs that are the same all over the world, such as steel, bulk chemicals, and industrial electronics.

value creation Activities performed that increase the value of goods or services to consumers.

values Abstract ideas about what a society believes to be good, right, and desirable.

voluntary export restraint (VER) Quota on trade imposed from the exporting country's side instead of the importer's; usually imposed at the request of the importing country's government.

wholly owned subsidiary A subsidiary in which the firm owns 100 percent of the stock.

World Bank International institution set up to promote general economic development in the world's poorer nations.

World Trade Organization (WTO) Organization that succeeded the General Agreement on Tariffs and Trade (GATT) as a result of the successful completion of the Uruguay Round of GATT negotiations.

zero-sum game Situation in which an economic gain by one country results in a economic loss by another.

Endnotes

CHAPTER 1

1. Hibernia at www.hibernia.ca/about. html.
2. See G. McLeod, "Forex Market Size: A Traders Advantage," *Daily FX*, January 23, 2014, https://www.dailyfx. com/forex/education/trading_tips/ daily_trading_lesson/2014/01/24/ FX_Market_Size.html.
3. T. L. Friedman, *The World Is Flat* (New York: Farrar, Straus and Giroux, 2005).
4. Ibid.
5. T. Levitt, "The Globalization of Markets," *Harvard Business Review*, May–June 1983, pp. 92–102.
6. See F. T. Knickerbocker, *Oligopolistic Reaction and Multinational Enterprise* (Boston: Harvard Business School Press, 1973), and R. E. Caves, "Japanese Investment in the US: Lessons for the Economic Analysis of Foreign Investment," *The World Economy* 16 (1993), pp. 279–300.
7. Bombardier, "Bombardier Delivers First CS300 Aircraft to airBaltic," Press Release, November 28, 2016, http://news.commercialaircraft. bombardier.com/wp-content/ uploads/2016/11/20161128_First-CS300-Delivery-to-airBaltic_EN.pdf.
8. Honeywell, "Honeywell Agrees to Acquire Matrikon Inc." Press Release May 13, 2010, http:// www51.honeywell.com/honeywell/ news-events/press-releases-details/ 05.13.10HoneywellAcquiresMatrikon. html.
9. United Nations, The UN in Brief, http://www.un.org/esa/about_esa. html.
10. J. A. Frankel, "Globalization of the Economy," National Bureau of Economic Research, working paper No. 7858, 2000.
11. J. Bhagwati, *Protectionism* (Cambridge, MA: MIT Press, 1989).
12. F. Williams, "Trade Round Like This May Never Be Seen Again," *Financial Times*, April 15, 1994, p. 8.
13. W. Vieth, "Major Concessions Lead to Success for WTO Talks," *Los Angeles Times*, November 14, 2001, p. A1; and "Seeds Sown for Future Growth," *The Economist*, November 17, 2001, pp. 65–66.

14. Vieth, "Major Concessions Lead to Success."
15. World Trade Organization, *International Trade Trends and Statistics*, 2000 (Geneva: WTO, 2001).
16. World Trade Organization, "Trade Growth to Ease in 2011 Despite 2010 Record Surge," Press Release, April 7, 2011; World Trade Organization, "Trade to Remain Subdued in 2013 after Sluggish Growth in 2012 as European Economies Continue to Struggle," Press Release, April 10, 2013; and https://www.wto.org/ english/news_e/pres17_e/pr791_e.htm.
17. World Trade Organization, *International Trade Statistics, 2011*. (Geneva: WTO, 2011); and United Nations, *World Investment Report, 2008*, http://unctad.org/en/ pages/PublicationArchive. aspx?publicationid=732.
18. United Nations, *World Investment Report, 2011*, http://unctad.org/en/ pages/PublicationWebflyer. aspx?publicationid=84.
19. Moore's Law is named after Intel founder Gordon Moore, http:// news.bbc.co.uk/1/hi/technology/ 4446285.stm.
20. Frankel, "Globalization of the Economy."
21. J. G. Fernald and V. Greenfield, "The Fall and Rise of the Global Economy," *Chicago Fed Letters*, April 2001, pp. 1–4.
22. Statista, "U.S. retail e-commerce sales from 2010 to 2018 (in billion U.S. dollars)," 2014, http://www. statista.com/statistics/272391/us-retail-e-commerce-sales-forecast/.
23. For a counterpoint, see "Geography and the Net: Putting It in Its Place," *The Economist*, August 11, 2001, pp. 18–20.
24. Ibid.
25. "War of the Worlds," *The Economist: A Survey of the Global Economy*, October 1, 1994, pp. 3–4.
26. Ibid.
27. World Trade Organization (WTO), Tariff Profile, Canada, http:// stat.wto.org/TariffProfile/ WSDBTariffPFView.aspx? Language=E&Country=CA.
28. International Road Dynamics, http:// www.irdinc.com/pages/company. html, accessed June 9, 2017.

29. http://www.iceculture.com/gallery? t=220 accessed June 5, 2017.
30. United Nations Conference on Trade and Development (UNCTAD), *World Investment Report 2015: Reforming International Investment Governance*, http://unctad.org/en/ PublicationsLibrary/wir2015_en.pdf, Table 1.1, p. 2.
31. See, for example, Ravi Batra, *The Myth of Free Trade* (New York: Touchstone Books, 1993); William Greider, *One World, Ready or Not: The Manic Logic of Global Capitalism* (New York: Simon and Schuster, 1997); and D. Radrik, *Has Globalization Gone Too Far?* (Washington, DC: Institution for International Economics, 1997).
32. See http://www1.gildan.com/ corporate/downloads/annual_ report_2009_en.pdf.
33. "Safe meets sexy: Gildan spices up image with American Apparel bid," *Montreal Gazette*, November 29, 2016, http://montrealgazette.com/ business/local-business/safe-meets-sexy-gildan-spices-up-image-with-american-apparel-bid, May 3, 2017.
34. D. L. Bartlett and J. B. Steele, "America: Who Stole the Dream," *Philadelphia Inquirer*, September 9, 1996.
35. For example, see Paul Krugman, *Pop Internationalism* (Cambridge, MA: MIT Press, 1996).
36. For example, see B. Milanovic and L. Squire, "Does Tariff Liberalization Increase Wage Inequality?" National Bureau of Economic Research, working paper no. 11046, January 2005; and B. Milanovic, "Can We Discern the Effect of Globalization on Income Distribution?" *World Bank Economic Review* 19 (2005), pp. 21-44. Also see the summary in F. Jaumotte and I. Tytell, "The Globalization of Labor," *Finance & Development* 44, no. 2 (2007) http://www.imf.org/external/pubs/ft/ fandd/2007/06/picture.htm.
37. See Jaumotte and Tytell, "The Globalization of Labor."
38. The 2010 data are from an unpublished OECD study cited in S. Moffett, "Income Inequality Increases," *The Wall Street Journal*, May 3, 2011.

39. M. Forster and M. Pearson, "Income Distribution and Poverty in the OECD Area," *OECD Economic Studies* 34 (2002); Moffett, "Income Inequality Increases"; and OECD, "Growing Income Inequality in OECD Countries," *OECD Forum*, May 2, 2011.

40. See Jaumotte and Tytell, "The Globalization of Labor."

41. See Paul Krugman, *Pop Internationalism*, (Cambridge, MA: The MIT Press, 1996); and D. Belman and T. M. Lee, "International Trade and the Performance of U.S. Labor Markets," in *U.S. Trade Policy and Global Growth*, ed. R. A. Blecker (New York: Economic Policy Institute, 1996).

42. Freeman, "Labor Market Imbalances."

43. E. Goldsmith, "Global Trade and the Environment," in *The Case Against the Global Economy: and for a Turn Toward the Local*, ed. J. Mander, E. Goldsmith (San Francisco: Sierra Club Books, 1997).

44. P. Choate, *Jobs at Risk: Vulnerable U.S. Industries and Jobs under NAFTA* (Washington, DC: Manufacturing Policy Project, 1993).

45. Ibid.

46. B. Lomborg, *The Skeptical Environmentalist* (Cambridge: Cambridge University Press, 2001).

47. H. Nordstrom and S. Vaughan, *Trade and the Environment*, World Trade Organization Special Studies No.4 (Geneva: WTO, 1999).

48. Environment and Climate Change Canada, Greenhouse Gas Emissions, http://www.ec.gc.ca/indicateurs-indicators/default.asp?lang=en&n=FBF8455E-1, accessed June 9, 2017.

49. Environment Canada, National Greenhouse Gas Emissions, http://www.ec.gc.ca/indicateurs-indicators/default.asp?lang=en&n=FBF8455E-1. (August 8, 2010).

50. OECD, *Key Environmental Indicators*, 2004, p. 18.

51. For an exhaustive review of the empirical literature, see B. R. Copeland and M. Scott Taylor, "Trade, Growth and the Environment," *Journal of Economic Literature*, March 2004, pp. 7–77.

52. G. M. Grossman and A. B. Krueger, "Economic Growth and the Environment," *Quarterly Journal of Economics* 110 (1995), pp. 353–78.

53. Krugman, *Pop Internationalism*.

54. R. Kuttner, "Managed Trade and Economic Sovereignty," in *U.S. Trade Policy and Global Growth*, ed. R. A. Blecker (New York: Economic Policy Institute, 1996).

55. L. Pritchett, "Divergence, Big Time," *Journal of Economic Perspectives*, 11, No. 3 (Summer 1997), pp. 3–18.

56. Ibid.

57. See D. Ben-David, H. Nordstrom, and L. A. Winters, *Trade, Income Disparity and Poverty*, World Trade Organization Special Studies No.5 (Geneva: WTO, 1999).

58. William Easterly, "Debt Relief," *Foreign Policy*, November/December 2001, pp. 20–26.

59. J. Sachs, "Sachs on Development: Helping the World's Poorest," *The Economist*, August 14, 1999, pp. 17–20.

60. Easterly, "Debt Relief."

61. WTO, Understanding the WTO, at https://www.wto.org/english/thewto_e/whatis_e/tif_e/understanding_e.pdf, p. 10.

62. World Trade Organization, Regional Trade Agreements, https://www.wto.org/english/tratop_e/region_e/region_e.htm.

CHAPTER 2

1. Although as we shall see, there is not a strict one-to-one correspondence between political systems and economic systems. See A. O. Hirschman, "The On-and-Off Again Connection between Political and Economic Progress," *American Economic Review* 84, No. 2 (1994), pp. 343–48.

2. For a discussion of the roots of collectivism and individualism, see H. W. Spiegel, *The Growth of Economic Thought* (Durham, NC: Duke University Press, 1991). An easily accessible discussion of collectivism and individualism can be found in M. Friedman and R. Friedman, *Free to Choose* (London: Penguin Books, 1980).

3. For a classic summary of the tenets of Marxism, see A. Giddens, *Capitalism and Modern Social Theory* (Cambridge: Cambridge University Press, 1971).

4. J. S. Mill, *On Liberty* (London: Longman's, 1865), p. 6.

5. A. Smith, *The Wealth of Nations*, Vol. I (London: Penguin Books), p. 325.

6. R. Wesson, *Modern Government—Democracy and Authoritarianism*, 2nd ed. (Englewood Cliffs, NJ: Prentice Hall, 1990).

7. For a detailed but accessible elaboration of this argument, see Friedman and Friedman, *Free to Choose*. Also see P. M. Romer, "The Origins of Endogenous Growth," *Journal of Economic Perspectives* 8, No. 1 (1994), pp. 2–32.

8. T. W. Lippman, *Understanding Islam* (New York: Meridian Books, 1995).

9. J. Sturcke, "Sharia Law in Canada, Almost," *The Guardian*, February 8, 2008, https://www.theguardian.com/news/blog/2008/feb/08/sharialawincanadaalmost.

10. "Islam's Interest," *The Economist*, January 18, 1992, pp. 33–34.

11. International Court of Arbitration, https://iccwbo.org/about-us/who-we-are/.

12. D. North, *Institutions, Institutional Change, and Economic Performance* (Cambridge: Cambridge University Press, 1991).

13. P. Klebnikov, "Russia's Robber Barons," *Forbes*, November 21, 1994, pp. 74–84; C. Mellow, "Russia: Making Cash from Chaos," *Fortune*, April 17, 1995, pp. 145–51; and "Mr. Tatum Checks Out," *The Economist*, November 9, 1996, p. 78.

14. K. van Wolferen, *The Enigma of Japanese Power* (New York: Vintage Books, 1990), pp. 100–5.

15. P. Bardhan, "Corruption and Development: A Review of the Issues," *Journal of Economic Literature*, September 1997, pp. 1320–46.

16. K. M. Murphy, A. Shleifer, and R. Vishny, "Why Is Rent Seeking So Costly to Growth?" *American Economic Review* 83, No. 2 (1993), pp. 409–14.

17. "Ornge overspending slammed by Ontario auditor general," CBC News, March 21, 2012, http://www.cbc.ca/news/canada/toronto/ornge-overspending-slammed-by-ontario-auditor-general-1.1150507.

18. J. Coolidge and S. R. Ackerman, "High Level Rent Seeking and Corruption in African Regimes," World Bank policy research working paper # 1780, June 1997; and Murphy, Shleifer, and Vishny, "Why Is Rent Seeking So Costly to Growth?"

19. Department of Justice Canada at http://publications.gc.ca/collections/Collection/J2-161-1999E.pdf, p. 5.

20. Ibid, p. 11.

21. For an interesting discussion of strategies for dealing with the low cost of copying and distributing digital information, see the chapter on rights management in C. Shapiro and H. R. Varian, *Information Rules* (Boston: Harvard Business School Press, 1999).

22. Douglass North has argued that the correct specification of intellectual property rights is one factor that lowers the cost of doing business and, thereby, stimulates economic growth and development. See North, *Institutions, Institutional Change, and Economic Performance*, (Cambridge: Cambridge University Press, 1990).

23. For more on WIPO, go to www.wipo.int/treaties/en/text.jsp?file_id=288514.

24. International Federation of the Phonographic Industry, *The Commercial Music Industry Global Piracy Report, 2005*, www.ifpi.org.

25. Business Software Alliance, "Eight Annual BSA and IDC Global Software Piracy Study," May 2011, www.bsa.org.

26. "Trade Tripwires," *The Economist*, August 27, 1994, p. 61.

27. World Bank at https://datahelpdesk.worldbank.org/knowledgebase/articles/378832-the-world-bank-atlas-method-detailed-methodology.

28. World Bank at http://databank.worldbank.org/data/download/GNIPC.pdf; also, based on interviews with Alexander Fry, Partner, KPMG Montevideo, and Rodrigo F. Ribeiro, CFA, Director Advisory Services KPMG, Montevideo.

29. P. Sinha and N. Singh, "The Economy's Black Hole," *The Times of India*, March 22, 2010. EU estimates for 2012 can be found at http://europa.eu/rapid/press-release_MEMO-12-492_en.htm.

30. A. Sen, *Development as Freedom* (New York: Alfred A. Knopf, 1999).

31. G. M. Grossman and E. Helpman, "Endogenous Innovation in the Theory of Growth," *Journal of Economic Perspectives* 8, No. 1 (1994), pp. 23–44, and P. M. Romer, "The Origins of Endogenous Growth," *Journal of Economic Perspectives* 8, No. 1 (1994), pp. 3–22.

32. F. A. Hayek, *The Fatal Conceit: Errors of Socialism* (Chicago: University of Chicago Press, 1989).

33. J. Gwartney, R. Lawson, and W. Block, *Economic Freedom of the World: 1975–1995*. (London: Institute of Economic Affairs, 1996).

34. North, *Institutions, Institutional Change, and Economic Performance*. See also Murphy, Shleifer, and Vishny, "Why Is Rent Seeking So Costly to Growth?" See also K. E. Maskus, *Intellectual Property Rights in the Global Economy* (Institute for International Economics, 2000).

35. H. de Soto, *The Other Path*, (New York: Harper & Row, 1989).

36. Hirschman, "The On-and-Off Again Connection between Political and Economic Progress," and A. Przeworski and F. Limongi, "Political Regimes and Economic Growth," *Journal of Economic Perspectives* 7, No. 3 (1993), pp. 51–59.

37. As an example, see "Why Voting Is Good for You," *The Economist*, August 27, 1994, pp. 15–17.

38. Ibid.

39. For details of this argument, see M. Olson, "Dictatorship, Democracy, and Development," *American Political Science Review*, September 1993.

40. For example, see J. Diamond's Pulitzer prize-winning book, *Guns, Germs, and Steel* (New York: W. W. Norton, 1997). Also see J. Sachs, "Nature, Nurture and Growth," *The Economist*, June 14, 1997, pp. 19–22.

41. Sachs, "Nature, Nurture and Growth."

42. Ibid.

43. "What Can the Rest of the World Learn from the Classrooms of Asia?" *The Economist*, September 21, 1996, p. 24.

44. J. Fagerberg, "Technology and International Differences in Growth Rates," *Journal of Economic Literature* 32 (September 1994), pp. 1147–75.

45. Freedom House, "Democracy's Century," Freedom in the World 2000. https://freedomhouse.org/report/freedom-world/freedom-world-2000.

46. F. Fukuyama, "The End of History," *The National Interest* 16 (Summer 1989), p. 18.

47. S. P. Huntington, *The Clash of Civilizations and the Remaking of World Order* (New York: Simon & Schuster, 1996).

48. Ibid., p. 116.

49. S. Fisher, R. Sahay, and C. A. Vegh, "Stabilization and the Growth in Transition Economies: The Early Experience," *Journal of Economic Perspectives* 10 (Spring 1996), pp. 45–66.

50. J. C. Brada, "Privatization Is Transition—Is It?" *Journal of Economic Perspectives*, Spring 1996, pp. 67–86.

51. See S. Zahra et al., "Privatization and Entrepreneurial Transformation," *Academy of Management Review* 3, No. 25 (2000), pp. 509–24.

52. Fischer, Sahay, and Vegh, "Stabilization and Growth in Transition Economies."

53. J. Nellis, "Time to Rethink Privatization in Transition Economies?" *Finance and Development* 36, No. 2 (1999), pp. 16–19.

54. M. S. Borish and M. Noel, "Private Sector Development in the Visegrad Countries," World Bank, March 1997.

55. See S. Fisher and R. Sahay, "The Transition Economies after Ten Years," IMF working paper 00/30 (Washington: International Monetary Fund, 2000).

56. International Monetary Fund, *World Economic Outlook: Focus on Transition Economies* (Geneva: IMF, October 2000).

57. "Lessons of Transition," *The Economist*, June 29, 1996, p. 81.

58. For a discussion of first-mover advantages, see M. Lieberman and D. Montgomery, "First-Mover Advantages," *Strategic Management Journal* 9 (Summer Special Issue, 1988), pp. 41–58.

59. S. H. Robock, "Political Risk: Identification and Assessment," *Columbia Journal of World Business*, July/August 1971, pp. 6–20.

60. S. L. Myers, "Report Says Business Interests Overshadow Rights," *New York Times*, December 5, 1996, p. A8.

61. J. Mort, "Sweated Shopping," *The Guardian*, September 8, 1997, p. 11.

62. B. Pranab, "Corruption and Development," *Journal of Economic Literature* 36 (September 1997), pp. 1320–46.

63. A. Shleifer and R. W. Vishny, "Corruption," *Quarterly Journal of Economics*, No. 108 (1993), pp. 599–617.

64. P. Mauro, "Corruption and Growth," *Quarterly Journal of Economics*, No. 110 (1995), pp. 681–712.

CHAPTER 3

1. M. Y. Brannen, "When Micky Loses Face: Recontextualization, Semantic Fit, and the Semiotics of Foreignness," *Academy of Management Review*, 2004, pp. 593–616.

2. See R. Dore, *Taking Japan Seriously* (Stanford, CA: Stanford University Press, 1987).

3. Office for National Statistics, "Pay once again the main cause of working days lost to labour disputes," July 4, 2013, http://www.ons.gov.uk/ons/rel/bus-register/labour-disputes/annual-article-2012/sty-labour-disputes.html; Employment and Social Development Canada, Work Stoppages by Jurisdiction and Year, All Jurisdictions, https://www.canada.ca/en/employment-social-development/services/collective-bargaining-data/work-stoppages/work-stoppages-year-jurisdiction.html.

4. E. B. Tylor, *Primitive Culture* (London: Murray, 1871).

5. G. Hofstede, *Culture's Consequences: International Differences in Work-Related Values* (Beverly Hills, CA: Sage Publications, 1984), p. 21.

6. J. Z. Namenwirth and R. B. Weber, *Dynamics of Culture* (Boston: Allen & Unwin, 1987), p. 8.

7. R. Mead, *International Management: Cross Cultural Dimensions* (Oxford: Blackwell Business, 1994), p. 7.

8. "Iraq: Down But Not Out," *The Economist*, April 8, 1995, pp. 21–23.

9. S. P. Huntington, *The Clash of Civilizations* (New York, Simon & Schuster, 1996).

10. M. Thompson, R. Ellis, and A. Wildavsky, *Cultural Theory* (Boulder, CO: Westview Press, 1990).

11. M. Douglas, "Cultural Bias," in *Active Voice* (London: Routledge, 1982), pp. 183–254.

12. M. L. Dertouzos, R. K. Lester, and R. M. Solow, *Made in America* (Cambridge, MA: MIT Press, 1989).

13. C. Nakane, *Japanese Society* (Berkeley, CA: University of California Press, 1970).

14. Ibid.

15. For details, see M. Aoki, *Information, Incentives, and Bargaining in the Japanese Economy* (Cambridge: Cambridge University Press, 1988), and Dertouzos, Lester, and Solow, *Made in America*.

16. For an excellent historical treatment of the evolution of the English class system, see E. P. Thompson, *The Making of the English Working Class* (London: Vintage Books, 1966). See also R. Miliband, *The State in Capitalist Society* (New York: Basic Books, 1969), especially

Chapter 2. For more recent studies of class in British societies, see S. Brook, *Class: Knowing Your Place in Modern Britain* (London: Victor Gollancz, 1997); A. Adonis and S. Pollard, *A Class Act: The Myth of Britain's Classless Society* (London: 1997); and J. Gerteis and M. Savage, "The Salience of Class in Britain and America: A Comparative Analysis," *British Journal of Sociology*, June 1998.

17. N. Goodman, *An Introduction to Sociology* (New York: Harper Collins, 1991).

18. M. Weber, *The Protestant Ethic and the Spirit of Capitalism* (New York: Scribner's Sons, 1958, original 1904–1905). For an excellent review of Weber's work, see A. Giddens, *Capitalism and Modern Social Theory* (Cambridge: Cambridge University Press, 1971).

19. Weber, *The Protestant Ethic and the Spirit of Capitalism*, p. 35.

20. A. S. Thomas and S. L. Mueller, "The Case for Comparative Entrepreneurship," *Journal of International Business Studies* 31, No. 2 (2000), pp. 287–302, and S. A. Shane, "Why Do Some Societies Invent More Than Others?" *Journal of Business Venturing* 7 (1992), pp. 29–46.

21. See S. M. Abbasi, K. W. Hollman, and J. H. Murrey, "Islamic Economics: Foundations and Practices," *International Journal of Social Economics* 16, No. 5 (1990), pp. 5–17, and R. H. Dekmejian, *Islam in Revolution: Fundamentalism in the Arab World* (Syracuse: Syracuse University Press, 1995).

22. T. W. Lippman, *Understanding Islam* (New York: Meridian Books, 1995).

23. Dekmejian, *Islam in Revolution*.

24. M. K. Nydell, *Understanding Arabs* (Yarmouth, ME: Intercultural Press, 1987).

25. Lippman, *Understanding Islam*.

26. The material in this section is based largely on Abbasi, Hollman, and Murrey, "Islamic Economics."

27. "Islam's Interest," *The Economist*, January 18, 1992, pp. 33–34.

28. For details of Weber's work and views, see Giddens, *Capitalism and Modern Social Theory*.

29. See, for example, the views expressed in "A Survey of India: The Tiger Steps Out," *The Economist*, January 21, 1995.

30. See R. Dore, *Taking Japan Seriously* (Stanford, CA: Stanford

University Press, 1987), and C. W. L. Hill, "Transaction Cost Economizing as a Source of Comparative Advantage: The Case of Japan," *Organization Science* 6 (1995).

31. See Aoki, *Information, Incentives, and Bargaining in the Japanese Economy*, and J. P. Womack, D. T. Jones, and D. Roos, *The Machine That Changed the World* (New York: Rawson Associates, 1990).

32. For examples of this line of thinking, see the work by Mike Peng and his associates: M. W. Peng and P. S. Heath, "The Growth of the Firm in Planned Economies in Transition," *Academy of Management Review* 21 (1996), pp. 492–528; M. W. Peng, *Business Strategies in Transition Economies* (Thousand Oaks, CA: Sage, 2000); and M. W. Peng and Y. Luo, "Managerial Ties and Firm Performance in a Transition Economy," *Academy of Management Journal*, June 2000, pp. 486–501.

33. This hypothesis dates back to two anthropologists, Edward Sapir and Benjamin Lee Whorf. See E. Sapir, "The Status of Linguistics as a Science," *Language* 5 (1929), pp. 207–14, and B. L. Whorf, *Language, Thought, and Reality* (Cambridge, MA: MIT Press, 1956).

34. In fact, the tendency has been documented empirically. See A. Annett, "Social Fractionalization, Political Instability, and the Size of Government," IMF Staff Papers 48 (2001), pp. 561–92.

35. "Most Widely Spoken Languages in the World," www.infoplease.com/ipa/A0775272.html.

36. D. A. Ricks, *Big Business Blunders: Mistakes in Multinational Marketing* (Homewood, IL: Dow Jones-Irwin, 1983).

37. M. E. Porter, *The Competitive Advantage of Nations* (New York: Free Press, 1990).

38. Ibid., pp. 395–97.

39. G. Hofstede, "The Cultural Relativity of Organizational Practices and Theories," *Journal of International Business Studies*, Fall 1983, pp. 75–89.

40. For a more detailed critique, see R. Mead, *International Management: Cross-Cultural Dimensions* (Oxford: Blackwell, 1994), pp. 73–75.

41. For example, see W. J. Bigoness and G. L. Blakely, "A Cross-National Study of Managerial Values," *Journal of International Business*

Studies, December 1996, p. 739; D. H. Ralston, D. H. Holt, R. H. Terpstra, and Y. Kai-Cheng, "The Impact of National Culture and Economic Ideology on Managerial Work Values," *Journal of International Business Studies* 28, No. 1 (1997), pp. 177–208; and P. B. Smith, M. F. Peterson, and Z. Ming Wang, "The Manager as a Mediator of Alternative Meanings," *Journal of International Business Studies* 27, No. 1 (1996), pp. 115–37.

42. G. Hofstede and M. H. Bond, "The Confucius Connection," *Organizational Dynamics* 16, No. 4 (1988), pp. 5–12.

43. R. S. Yeh and J. J. Lawrence, "Individualism and Confucian Dynamism," *Journal of International Business Studies* 26, No. 3 (1995), pp. 655–66.

44. Mead, *International Management: Cross-Cultural Dimensions,* Chap. 17.

45. "Free, Young, and Japanese," *The Economist,* December 21, 1991.

46. Namenwirth and Weber, *Dynamics of Culture.*

47. G. Hofstede, "National Cultures in Four Dimensions," *International Studies of Management and Organization* 13, No. 1, pp. 46–74.

48. Ibid.

49. See Aoki, *Information, Incentives, and Bargaining in the Japanese Economy;* Dertouzos, Lester, and Solow, *Made in America;* and Porter, *The Competitive Advantage of Nations,* pp. 395–97.

50. For empirical work supporting such a view, see Annett, "Social Fractionalization, Political Instability, and the Size of Government."

51. J. Goodwin and D. Goodwin, "Ethical Judgments Across Cultures," *Journal of Business Ethics* 18, No. 3 (February 1999), pp. 267–81.

52. T. Donaldson, "Values in Tension: Ethics Away from Home," *Harvard Business Review,* September–October 1996.

53. R. T. DeGeorge, "Ethics in International Business—A Contradiction in Terms?" *Business Credit,* September 2000, pp. 50–52.

54. S. Lovett, L. C. Simmons, and R. Kali, "Guanxi versus the Market: Ethics and Efficiency," *Journal of International Business Studies* 30, No. 2 (1999), pp. 231–48.

55. Donaldson, "Values in Tension: Ethics Away from Home." See also, R. J. Barnet and J. Cavanagh, *Global Dreams: Imperial Corporations and the New World Order* (New York: Touchstone Books, 1994), p. 33.

CHAPTER 4

1. Details can be found at http://www.oecd.org/document/20/0,3343,en_2649_34859_2017813_1_1_1_1,00.html.

2. OECD, Bribery in International Business, http://www.oecd.org/daf/anti-bribery/countryreportsontheimplementationoftheoecdanti-briberyconvention.htm.

3. OECD, Convention on Combating Bribery of Foreign Public Officials in International Business Transactions, http://www.oecd.org/daf/anti-bribery/ConvCombatBribery_ENG.pdf.

4. A. Shleifer and R. W. Vishny, "Corruption," *Quarterly Journal of Economics,* No. 108 (1993), pp. 599–617, and I. Ehrlich and F. Lui, "Bureaucratic Corruption and Endogenous Economic Growth," *Journal of Political Economy* 107 (December 1999), pp. 270–92.

5. M. Patriquin, "Quebec: The most corrupt province," *Maclean's,* September 24, 2010, http://www2.macleans.ca/2010/09/24/the-most-corrupt-province/.

6. See http://www.newstatesman.com/world/2016/11/did-fake-news-facebook-swing-us-election.

7. See https://www.thestar.com/news/world/2016/04/04/how-offshore-tax-havens-are-costing-canada-billions-of-dollars-a-year.html.

8. K. Leong, "Is Your Company Using Employee Data Ethically?" *Harvard Business Review,* March 13, 2017, https://hbr.org/2017/03/is-your-company-using-employee-data-ethically.

9. The Editorial Board, "The University of California Does Itself a Disservice by Outsourcing Jobs," *The Highlander,* January 16, 2017, https://highlandernews.org/27026/university-california-disservice-outsourcing-jobs/. See also M. Hiltzik, "How the University of California Exploited a Visa Loophole to Move Tech Jobs to India," *LA Times,* January 6, 2017, http://www.latimes.com/business/hiltzik/la-fi-hiltzik-uc-visas-20170108-story.html.

10. "Sri Lankan court issues notice on controversial glove maker and government agencies over water pollution charges," Colombo Page, November 27, 2013, http://www.colombopage.com/archive_13B/Nov27_1385571228JR.php.

11. D. Oakley, "Truckers protest pollution regulations at Port of Oakland," *San Jose Mercury News,* November 27, 2013 http://www.mercurynews.com/breaking-news/ci_24611551/truckers-protest-rising-costs-at-port-oakland.

12. P. Singer, *One World: The Ethics of Globalization* (New Haven, CT: Yale University Press, 2002).

13. K. Auletta, "The Pirate," The New Yorker, November 13, 1995, http://www.newyorker.com/magazine/1995/11/13/the-pirate.

14. Details can be found at BP's Web site, http://www.bp.com.

15. This is known as the "when in Rome perspective." T. Donaldson, "Values in Tension: Ethics Away from Home," *Harvard Business Review,* September 1996.

16. R. T. DeGeorge, *Competing with Integrity in International Business* (Oxford: Oxford University Press, 1993).

17. Donaldson, "Values in Tension: Ethics Away from Home."

18. S. W. Gellerman, "Why Good Managers Make Bad Ethical Choices," in *Ethics in Practice: Managing the Moral Corporation,* ed. K. R. Andrews (Cambridge, MA: Harvard Business School Press, 1989).

19. D. Messick and M. H. Bazerman, "Ethical Leadership and the Psychology of Decision Making," *Sloan Management Review* 37 (Winter 1996), pp. 9–20.

20. R. Bryce, *Pipe Dreams: Greed, Ego and the Death of Enron* (New York: Public Affairs, 2002).

21. "TD Bank under Pressure over Sales Tactics Claims," *Financial Times,* March 2017, https://www.ft.com/content/75c0d240-05e6-11e7-ace0-1ce02ef0def9.

22. M. Friedman, "Social Responsibility of Business Is to Increase Profits," *The New York Times Magazine,* September 13, 1970. Reprinted in T. L. Beauchamp and N. E. Bowie, *Ethical Theory and Business,* 7th ed. (Prentice Hall, 2001).

23. Ibid., p. 55.

24. For example, see Donaldson, "Values in Tension: Ethics Away from Home." See also N. Bowie, "Relativism and the Moral Obligations of Multination Corporations," in T. L. Beauchamp and N. E. Bowie, *Ethical Theory and Business.*

25. For example, see DeGeorge, *Competing with Integrity in International Business*.

26. "Fostering Transparency and Anti-Corruption," Sustainability, BP, http://www.bp.com/en/global/corporate/sustainability/value-to-society/fostering-transparency.html/.

27. This example is often repeated in the literature on international business ethics. It was first outlined by A. Kelly in "Case Study-Italian Style Mores," printed in T. Donaldson and P. Werhane, *Ethical Issues in Business* (Englewood Cliffs, NJ: Prentice Hall, 1979).

28. T. Donaldson, *The Ethics of International Business* (Oxford: Oxford University Press. 1989).

29. The Universal Declaration of Human Rights. Found at http://www.un.org/en/universal-declaration-human-rights/index.html.

30. Donaldson, *The Ethics of International Business*.

31. See Chapter 10 in Beauchamp and Bowie, *Ethical Theory and Business*.

32. J. Rawls, *A Theory of Justice*, rev. ed. (Cambridge, MA: Belknap Press, 1999).

33. For example, see R. E. Freeman and D. Gilbert, *Corporate Strategy and the Search for Ethics* (Englewood Cliffs, NJ: Prentice Hall, 1988); T. Jones, *Journal of Management Review* 16 (1991), pp. 366–95; and J. R. Rest, *Moral Development: Advances in Research and Theory* (New York: Praeger, 1986).

34. Ibid.

35. See E. Freeman, *Strategic Management: A Stakeholder Approach* (Boston: Pitman Press, 1984); C. W. L. Hill and T. M. Jones, "Stakeholder-Agency Theory," *Journal of Management Studies* 29 (1992), pp. 131–54; and J. G. March and H. A. Simon, *Organizations* (New York: Wiley, 1958).

36. Hill and Jones, "Stakeholder-Agency Theory," and March and Simon, *Organizations*.

37. DeGeorge, *Competing with Integrity in International Business*.

38. C. Grant, "Whistle Blowers: Saints of Secular Culture," *Journal of Business Ethics*, September 2002, pp. 391–400.

39. Unilever Code of Business Principles and Code Policies, https://www.unilever.com/Images/4394-cobp-code-policies-booklet-external.v12_tcm244-480369_en.pdf, accessed June 12, 2017.

40. S. A. Waddock and S. B. Graves, "The Corporate Social Performance–Financial Performance Link," *Strategic Management Journal* 8 (1997), pp. 303–19.

CHAPTER 5

1. H. W. Spiegel, *The Growth of Economic Thought* (Durham, NC: Duke University Press, 1991).

2. G. deJonquieres, "Mercantilists Are Treading on Thin Ice," *Financial Times*, July 3, 1994, p. 16.

3. J. Hagelstam, "Mercantilism Still Influences Practical Trade Policy at the End of the Twentieth Century," *Journal of World Trade*, 1991, pp. 95–105.

4. S. Hollander, *The Economics of David Ricardo* (Toronto: The University of Toronto Press, 1979).

5. D. Ricardo, *The Principles of Political Economy and Taxation* (Homewood, IL: Irwin, 1967, first published in 1817).

6. For example, R. Dornbusch, S. Fischer, and P. Samuelson, "Comparative Advantage: Trade and Payments in a Ricardian Model with a Continuum of Goods," *American Economic Review* 67 (December 1977), pp. 823–39.

7. B. Balassa, "An Empirical Demonstration of Classic Comparative Cost Theory," *Review of Economics and Statistics*, 1963, pp. 231–38.

8. See P. R. Krugman, "Is Free Trade Passé?" *Journal of Economic Perspectives* 1 (Fall 1987), pp. 131–44.

9. P. Samuelson, "The Gains from International Trade Once Again," *Economic Journal* 72 (1962), pp. 820–29.

10. S. Lohr, "An Elder Challenges Outsourcing's Orthodoxy," *The New York Times*, September 9, 2004, p. C1.

11. P. Samuelson, "Where Ricardo and Mill Rebut and Confirm Arguments of Mainstream Economist Supporting Globalization," *Journal of Economic Perspectives* 18, No. 3 (Summer 2004), p. 143.

12. A. Dixit and G. Grossman, "Samuelson Says Nothing About Trade Policy," mimeo, Princeton University, 2004.

13. J. Bhagwati, A. Panagariya, and T. N. Sirinivasan, "The Muddles over Outsourcing," *Journal of Economic Perspectives* 18, No. 4 (Fall 2004), pp. 93–114.

14. J. D. Sachs and A. Warner, "Economic Reform and the Process of Global Integration," *Brookings Papers on Economic Activity*, 1995, pp. 1–96.

15. Ibid., pp. 35–36.

16. R. Wacziak and K. Welch, "Trade Liberalization and Growth: New Evidence," *World Bank Economic Review* 22, 2 (June 2008), pp. 187–231.

17. T. Singh, "Does International Trade Cause Economic Growth?" *The World Economy* 33, no. 11 (November 2010), pp. 1517–64.

18. J. A. Frankel and D. Romer, "Does Trade Cause Growth?" *American Economic Review* 89, No. 3 (June 1999), pp. 379–99.

19. A recent skeptical review of the empirical work on the relationship between trade and growth questions these results. See F. Rodriguez and D. Rodrik, "Trade Policy and Economic Growth: A Skeptics Guide to the Cross-National Evidence," *National Bureau of Economic Research, Working Paper Series* No. 7081, April 1999. Even these authors, however, cannot find any evidence that trade hurts economic growth or income levels.

20. B. Ohlin, *Interregional and International Trade* (Cambridge: Harvard University Press, 1933). For a summary, see R. W. Jones and J. P. Neary, "The Positive Theory of International Trade," in *Handbook of International Economics*, ed. R. W. Jones and P. B. Kenen (Amsterdam: North Holland, 1984).

21. W. Leontief, "Domestic Production and Foreign Trade: The American Capital Position Re-Examined," *Proceedings of the American Philosophical Society* 97 (1953), pp. 331–49.

22. R. M. Stern and K. Maskus, "Determinants of the Structure of U.S. Foreign Trade," *Journal of International Economics* 11 (1981), pp. 207–44.

23. See H. P. Bowen, E. E. Leamer, and L. Sveikayskas, "Multicountry, Multifactor Tests of the Factor Abundance Theory," *American Economic Review* 77 (1987), pp. 791–809.

24. D. Trefler, "The Case of the Missing Trade and Other Mysteries," *American Economic Review* 85 (December 1995), pp. 1029–46.

25. D. R. Davis and D. E. Weinstein, "An Account of Global Factor Trade," *American Economic Review*, December 2001, pp. 1423–52.

26. R. Vernon, "International Investments and International Trade in the Product Life Cycle," *Quarterly Journal of Economics*, May 1966,

pp. 190–207, and R. Vernon and L. T. Wells, *The Economic Environment of International Business*, 4th ed. (Englewood Cliffs, NJ: Prentice Hall, 1986).

27. For a good summary of this literature, see E. Helpman and P. Krugman, *Market Structure and Foreign Trade: Increasing Returns, Imperfect Competition, and the International Economy* (Boston: MIT Press, 1985). Also see P. Krugman, "Does the New Trade Theory Require a New Trade Policy?" *World Economy* 15, No. 4 (1992), pp. 423-41.

28. J. R. Tybout, "Plant and Firm Level Evidence on New Trade Theories," *National Bureau of Economic Research Working Paper Series*, working paper no. 8418, August 2001. Paper available at www.nber.org; S. Deraniyagala and B. Fine, "New Trade Theory versus Old Trade Policy: A Continuing Enigma," *Cambridge Journal of Economics* 25 (November 2001), pp. 809–25.

29. A. D. Chandler, *Scale and Scope* (New York: Free Press, 1990).

30. Krugman, "Does the New Trade Theory Require a New Trade Policy?"

31. M. E. Porter, *The Competitive Advantage of Nations* (New York: Free Press, 1990). For a good review of this book, see R. M. Grant, "Porter's Competitive Advantage of Nations: An Assessment," *Strategic Management Journal* 12 (1991), pp. 535–48.

32. B. Kogut, ed., *Country Competitiveness: Technology and the Organizing of Work* (New York: Oxford University Press, 1993).

33. Porter, *The Competitive Advantage of Nations*, p. 121.

34. M. B. Lieberman and D. B. Montgomery, "First-Mover Advantages," *Strategic Management Journal* 9 (Summer 1988), pp. 41–58.

CHAPTER 6

1. For a detailed welfare analysis of the effect of a tariff, see P. R. Krugman and M. Obstfeld, *International Economics: Theory and Policy* (New York: HarperCollins, 2000), Ch.8.

2. Y. Sazanami, S. Urata, and H. Kawai, *Measuring the Costs of Protection in Japan* (Washington, DC: Institute for International Economics, 1994).

3. J. Bhagwati, *Protectionism* (Cambridge, MA: MIT Press, 1988); and "Costs of Protection," *Journal of Commerce*, September 25, 1991, p. 8A.

4. "From the Sublime to the Subsidy," *The Economist*, February 24, 1990, p. 71.

5. The study was undertaken by Kym Anderson of the University of Adelaide. "A Not So Perfect Market," *The Economist: Survey of Agriculture and Technology*, March 25, 2000, pp. 8–10.

6. R. W. Crandall, *Regulating the Automobile* (Washington, DC: Brookings Institute, 1986).

7. Quoted in Krugman and Obstfeld, *International Economics*.

8. G. Hufbauer and K. A. Elliott, *Measuring the Costs of Protectionism in the United States* (Washington, DC: Institute for International Economics, 1993).

9. A. Tanzer, "The Great Quota Hustle," *Forbes*, March 6, 2000, pp. 119–25.

10. J. Steinman, "Expiration of Textile Quota Act Takes Toll on U.S. Manufacturers," *Inc.com*, January 13, 2005, http://www.inc.com/news/articles/200501/textiles.html.

11. A. Goldstein, "Sematech Members Facing Dues Increase; 30% Jump to Make Up for Loss of Federal Funding," *Dallas Morning News*, July 27, 1996, p. 2F.

12. C. Dobby, "Ottawa rejects Manitoba Telecom's sale of Allstream, citing national security," *Financial Post*, October 7, 2013.

13. N. Dunne and R. Waters, "US Waves a Big Stick at Chinese Pirates," *Financial Times*, January 6, 1995, p. 4.

14. Health Canada, Consumer Product Safety, Is Your Child Safe? Children's Products, 2012, https://www.canada.ca/en/health-canada/services/consumer-product-safety/reports-publications/consumer-education/your-child-safe/is-your-child-safe.html#a42.

15. "Fisher-Price recalls millions of products," CBC News, September 30, 2010, http://www.cbc.ca/news/fisher-price-recalls-millions-of-products-1.887235.

16. A. Manasan, "GMO fears do not 'translate to the average consumer,'" CBC News, April 11, 2013, http://www.cbc.ca/news/canada/gmo-fears-do-not-translate-to-the-average-consumer-1.1362542.

17. Environmental Assessment Report 2, 3.9 Genetically Modified Organisms, p. 2 https://www.eea.europa.eu/publications/92-9157-202-0.

18. P. S. Jordan, "Country Sanctions and the International Business Community," *American Society of International Law Proceedings of the Annual Meeting* 20 No. 9 (1997), pp. 333–42.

19. "Brazil's Auto Industry Struggles to Boost Global Competitiveness," *Journal of Commerce*, October 10, 1991, p. 6A.

20. For reviews, see J. A. Brander, "Rationales for Strategic Trade and Industrial Policy," in *Strategic Trade Policy and the New International Economics*, ed. P. R. Krugman (Cambridge, MA: MIT Press, 1986); P. R. Krugman, "Is Free Trade Passé?" *Journal of Economic Perspectives* 1 (1987), pp. 131–44; and P. R. Krugman, "Does the New Trade Theory Require a New Trade Policy?" *World Economy* 15, No. 4 (1992), pp. 423–41.

21. "Airbus and Boeing: The Jumbo War," *The Economist*, June 15, 1991, pp. 65–66.

22. For details see Krugman, "Is Free Trade Passé?" and Brander, "Rationales for Strategic Trade and Industrial Policy."

23. Krugman, "Is Free Trade Passé?"

24. This dilemma is a variant of the famous prisoner's dilemma, which has become a classic metaphor for the difficulty of achieving cooperation between self-interested and mutually suspicious entities. For a good general introduction, see A. Dixit and B. Nalebuff, *Thinking Strategically: The Competitive Edge in Business, Politics, and Everyday Life* (New York: W. W. Norton & Co., 1991).

25. Note that the Smoot-Hawley tariff did not cause the Great Depression. However, the beggar-thy-neighbour trade policies that it ushered in certainly made things worse. See Bhagwati, *Protectionism*.

26. Ibid.

27. See https://www.wto.org/english/res_e/booksp_e/anrep_e/anrep16_chap6_e.pdf.

28. F. Williams, "Telecoms: World Pact Set to Slash Costs of Calls," *Financial Times*, February 17, 1997.

29. G. De Jonquieres, "Happy End to a Cliff Hanger," *Financial Times*, December 15, 1997, p. 15.

30. Data at www.wto.org/english/tratop_e/adp_e/adp_e.htm. See also

https://www.wto.org/english/
tratop_e/adp_e/AD_
InitiationsBySector.pdf.

31. Data at www.wto.org/english/
tratop_e/adp_e/adp_e.htm.
32. Ibid.
33. K. Anderson, W. Martin, and D. van
der Mensbrugghe, "Distortions to
World Trade: Impacts on
Agricultural Markets and Farm
Incomes," *Review of Agricultural
Economics* 28, No. 2, pp. 168–94.
34. World Trade Organization, *Annual
Report 2002.* (Geneva: WTO,
2002).
35. S. C. Bradford, P. L. E. Grieco, and
G. C. Hufbauer, "The Payoff to
America from Global Integration," in
*The United States and the World
Economy: Foreign Policy for the
Next Decade*, C. F. Bergsten, ed.
(Washington, DC: Institute for
International Economics, 2005).
36. World Bank, *Global Economic
Prospects 2005.* (Washington, DC:
World Bank, 2005).
37. "Doha Development Agenda," *OECD
Observer*, September 2006, pp. 64–67.
38. Simon Lester, "Is the Doha Round
Over? The WTO's Negotiating
Agenda for 2016 and Beyond," CATO
Institute, February 11, 2016, at
https://www.cato.org/publications/
free-trade-bulletin/doha-round-over-
wtos-negotiating-agenda-2016-
beyond, accessed June 6 2017.
39. W. Vieth, "Major Concessions Lead
to Success for WTO Talks," *Los
Angeles Times*, November 14, 2001,
p. A1; and "Seeds Sown for Future
Growth," *The Economist*, November
17, 2001, pp. 65–66.
40. "The WTO under Fire—The Doha
Round," *The Economist*, September
20, 2003, pp. 30–32.
41. For more information, see https://
insidetrade.com/daily-news/
us-other-wto-members-dispute-
meaning-ministerial-declaration-
language-doha.
42. See http://www.bbc.com/news/
business-35145377.

CHAPTER 7

1. United Nations, *World Investment
Report*, 2000 (New York and Geneva:
United Nations, 2001).
2. World Trade Organization,
*International Trade Statistics,
2011.* (Geneva: WTO, 2011); and
United Nations, *World Investment
Report*, 2011 (New York and Geneva:
United Nations, 2011).
3. United Nations, *World Investment
Report, 2011.*

4. M. Caruso-Cabrera, "Chinese
Investment in US May Break Record
in 2013," CNBC, January 2, 2013.
5. See D. J. Ravenscraft and F. M.
Scherer, *Mergers, Selloffs and
Economic Efficiency* (Washington,
DC: The Brookings Institution,
1987).
6. *Compete to Win*, Government of
Canada, June 2008, http://www.ic.
gc.ca/eic/site/cprp-gepmc.nsf/vwapj/
Compete_to_Win.pdf/$FILE/
Compete_to_Win.pdf.
7. For example, see S. H. Hymer, *The
International Operations of
National Firms: A Study of Direct
Foreign Investment* (Cambridge,
MA: MIT Press, 1976); A. M. Rugman,
*Inside the Multinationals: The
Economics of Internal Markets*
(New York: Columbia University
Press, 1981); D. J. Teece,
"Multinational Enterprise, Internal
Governance, and Industrial
Organization," *American Economic
Review* 75 (May 1983), pp. 233–38;
C. W. L. Hill and W. C. Kim,
"Searching for a Dynamic Theory of
the Multinational Enterprise: A
Transaction Cost Model," *Strategic
Management Journal* 9 (special
issue, 1988), pp. 93–104; A. Verbeke,
"The Evolutionary View of the MNE
and the Future of Internalization
Theory," *Journal of International
Business Studies* 34 (2003),
pp. 498–501; and J. H. Dunning,
"Some Antecedents of Internalization
Theory," *Journal of International
Business Studies* 34 (2003),
pp. 108–28.
8. J. P. Womack, D. T. Jones, and
D. Roos, *The Machine That
Changed the World* (New York:
Rawson Associates, 1990).
9. The argument is most often
associated with F. T. Knickerbocker,
*Oligopolistic Reaction and
Multinational Enterprise* (Boston:
Harvard Business School Press, 1973).
10. R. E. Caves, *Multinational
Enterprise and Economic Analysis*
(Cambridge: Cambridge University
Press, 1982).
11. See R. E. Caves, "Japanese
Investment in the U.S.: Lessons for
the Economic Analysis of Foreign
Investment" *The World Economy* 16
(1993), pp. 279–300; B. Kogut and S.
J. Chang, "Technological
Capabilities and Japanese Direct
Investment in the United States,"
Review of Economics and Statistics
73 (1991), pp. 401–43; and J. Anand
and B. Kogut, "Technological

Capabilities of Countries, Firm
Rivalry, and Foreign Direct
Investment," *Journal of
International Business Studies*,
Third Quarter 1997, pp. 445–65.
12. H. Haveman and L. Nonnemaker,
"Competition in Multiple
Geographical Markets,"
Administrative Science Quarterly
45 (2000), pp. 232–67; and L.
Fuentelsaz and J. Gomez,
"Multipoint Competition, Strategic
Similarity and Entry into
Geographic Markets," *Strategic
Management Journal* 27 (2006),
pp. 447–57.
13. For the use of Vernon's theory to
explain Japanese direct investment
in the United States and Europe,
see S. Thomsen, "Japanese Direct
Investment in the European
Community," *The World Economy* 16
(1993), pp. 301–15.
14. J. H. Dunning, *Explaining
International Production* (London:
Unwin Hyman, 1988).
15. P. Krugman, "Increasing Returns
and Economic Geography," *Journal
of Political Economy* 99, No. 3
(1991), pp. 483–99.
16. J. H. Dunning and R. Narula,
"Transpacific Foreign Direct
Investment and the Investment
Development Path," *South Carolina
Essays in International Business*,
No. 10 (May 1995), CIBER:
University of South Carolina.
17. W. Shan and J. Song, "Foreign Direct
Investment and the Sourcing of
Technological Advantage: Evidence
from the Biotechnology Industry,"
*Journal of International Business
Studies*, Second Quarter 1997,
pp. 267–84.
18. For elaboration, see S. Hood and
S. Young, *The Economics of the
Multinational Enterprise*
(London: Longman, 1979) and
P. M. Sweezy and H. Magdoff, *The
Dynamics of U.S. Capitalism*
(New York: Monthly Review Press,
1972).
19. "Canada's international investment
position," *The Daily*, http://www.
statcan.gc.ca/tables-tableaux/
sum-som/l01/cst01/econ08-eng.htm;
"Frequently Asked Questions—
Amendments to the Competition
Act," Government of Canada
Competition Bureau, April 29, 2011,
http://www.competitionbureau.gc.
ca/eic/site/cb-bc.nsf/eng/03046.html
20. CRTC at www.crtc.gc.caleng/NEWS/
SPEECHES/2002/s021212.htm;
Department of Justice, "Direction to

the CRTC (Ineligibility of Non-Canadians)," http://laws-lois.justice.gc.ca/eng/regulations/SOR-97-192/page-1.html#h-1

21. P. M. Romer, "The Origins of Endogenous Growth," *Journal of Economic Perspectives* 8, No. 1 (1994), pp. 3–22.

22. A. Jack, "French Go into Overdrive to Win Investors," *Financial Times*, December 10, 1997, p. 6.

23. "Foreign Friends," *The Economist*, January 8, 2000, pp. 71–72.

24. G. Hunya and K. Kalotay, *Privatization and Foreign Direct Investment in Eastern and Central Europe* (Geneva: UNCTAD, 2001).

25. P. R. Krugman and M. Obstfeld, *International Economics: Theory and Policy* (New York: Harper Collins, 1994), chap. 9. See also, P. Krugman, *The Age of Diminished Expectations* (Cambridge, MA: MIT Press, 1990).

26. United Nations, *World Investment Report, 2002.* (New York and Geneva: United Nations, 2002).

27. R. B. Reich, *The Work of Nations: Preparing Ourselves for the 21st Century* (New York: Alfred A. Knopf, 1991).

28. For a review, see J. H. Dunning, "Re-evaluating the Benefits of Foreign Direct Investment," *Transnational Corporations* 3, No. 1 (February 1994), p. 23–51.

29. This idea has been articulated, although not quite in this form, by C. A. Bartlett and S. Ghoshal, *Managing Across Borders: The Transnational Solution* (Boston: Harvard Business School Press, 1989).

30. C. Johnston, "Political Risk Insurance," in *Assessing Corporate Political Risk*, ed. D. M. Raddock (Totowa, NJ: Rowan & Littlefield, 1986).

31. "Geographic Distribution of International Stores," *Toys R Us Inc. 10-K*, January 28, 2017, https://www.toysrusinc.com/investors/financial-reports/report-detail/financial-document-detail?id=11525623&vid=aHR0cDovL2FwaS50ZW5rd2l6YXJkLmNvbS9maWxpbmcueG1sP2lwYWdlPTExNTI1NjIzJkRTRVE9MSZTRVE9JlNRREVTQz1TRUNUSU9OX0VOVElSRSZzdWJzaWQ9NTc%3D, p. 9.

32. M. Tolchin and S. Tolchin, *Buying into America: How Foreign Money Is Changing the Face of Our Nation* (New York: Times Books, 1988).

33. J. Behrman and R. E. Grosse, *International Business and Government: Issues and Institutions* (Columbia: University of South Carolina Press, 1990).

34. G. DeJonquiers and S. Kuper, "Push to Keep Alive Effort to Draft Global Investment Rules," *Financial Times*, April 29, 1988, p. 5.

35. See Caves, *Multinational Enterprise and Economic Analysis.*

36. For a good general introduction to negotiation strategy, see M. H. Bazerman, *Negotiating Rationally* (New York: Free Press, 1999), A. Dixit and B. Nalebuff, *Thinking Strategically: The Competitive Edge in Business, Politics, and Everyday Life* (New York: W. W. Norton, 1991), and H. Raiffa, *The Art and Science of Negotiation* (Cambridge, MA: Harvard University Press, 1982).

CHAPTER 8

1. Information taken from World Trade Organization Web site and current as of May 31, 2017, https://www.wto.org/english/tratop_e/region_e/regfac_e.htm.

2. H. Smith, "France to Oppose Turkish EU Entry," *The Guardian*, April 8, 2004, https://www.theguardian.com/world/2004/apr/08/turkey.eu.

3. The Andean Pact has been through a number of changes since its inception. The latest version was established in 1991. See "Free-Trade Free for All," *The Economist*, January 4, 1991, p. 63.

4. D. Swann, *The Economics of the Common Market*, 6th ed. (London: Penguin Books, 1990).

5. See J. Bhagwati, "Regionalism and Multilateralism: An Overview," Columbia University discussion paper 603, Department of Economics, Columbia University, New York; A. de la Torre and M. Kelly, "Regional Trade Arrangements," occasional paper 93, Washington, DC: International Monetary Fund, March 1992; and J. Bhagwati, "Fast Track to Nowhere," *The Economist*, October 18, 1997, pp. 21–24.

6. N. Colchester and D. Buchan, *Europower: The Essential Guide to Europe's Economic Transformation in 1992.* (London: The Economist Books, 1990); and Swann, *The Economics of the Common Market.*

7. E. J. Morgan, "A Decade of EC Merger Control," *International Journal of Economics and Business*, November 2001, pp. 451–73.

8. "One Europe, One Economy," *The Economist*, November 30, 1991, pp. 53–54; and "Market Failure: A Survey of Business in Europe," *The Economist*, June 8, 1991, pp. 6–10.

9. A. Riley, "The Single Market Ten Years On," *European Policy Analyst*, December 2002, pp. 65–72.

10. See C. Wyploze, "EMU: Why and How It Might Happen," *Journal of Economic Perspectives* 11 (1997), pp. 3–22; and M. Feldstein, "The Political Economy of the European Economic and Monetary Union," *Journal of Economic Perspectives* 11 (1997), pp. 23–42.

11. Ibid.

12. "One Europe, One Economy," *The Economist*; and Feldstein, "The Political Economy of the European Economic and Monetary Union."

13. "Time for Europhoria?" *The Economist*, January 4, 2003, p. 58.

14. "Euro Still the World's Second Reserve Currency," *The Economic Times*, July 22, 2011.

15. Details regarding conditions of membership and the progression of enlargement negotiations can be found at http://europa.eu/european-union/topics/enlargement_en.

16. "What Is NAFTA?" *Financial Times*, November 17,1993, p. 6; and S. Garland, "Sweet Victory," *Business Week*, November 29, 1993, pp. 30–31.

17. "NAFTA: The Showdown," *The Economist*, November 13, 1993, pp. 23–36.

18. N. C. Lustog, "NAFTA: Setting the Record Straight," *The World Economy*, 1997, pp. 605–14; and G. C. Hufbauer and J. J. Schott, *NAFTA Revisited: Achievements and Challenges* (Washington, DC: Institute for International Economics, 2005).

19. W. Thorbecke and C. Eigen-Zucchi, "Did NAFTA Cause a Giant Sucking Sound?" *Journal of Labor Research*, Fall 2002, pp. 647–58; G. Gagne, "North American Free Trade, Canada, and U.S. Trade Remedies: An Assessment after Ten Years," *The World Economy*, 2000, pp. 77–91; Hufbauer and Schott, *NAFTA Revisited: Achievements and Challenges*; and J. Romalis, "NAFTA's and Custfa's Impact on International Trade," *Review of Economics and Statistics* 98, no. 3 (2007), pp. 416–35.

20. All trade figures from U.S. Department of Commerce Trade Stat Express Web site at http://tse.export.gov/.

21. J. Cavanagh et al., "Happy Ever NAFTA?" *Foreign Policy,* September–October 2002, pp. 58–65.

22. "Mexico's Drug War: Number of Dead Passes 30,000," *The BBC,* December 16, 2010. See also J. Bender, "Mexico's Drug War is Taking Worse Turn," *Business Insider,* May 14, 2015, http://www.businessinsider.com/mexicos-drug-war-is-taking-worse-turn-2015-5.

23. "The Business of the American Hemisphere," *The Economist,* August 24, 1991, pp. 37–38.

24. "NAFTA Is Not Alone," *The Economist,* June 18, 1994, pp. 47–48.

25. "Murky Mercosur," *The Economist,* July 26, 1997, pp. 66–67.

26. See M. Philips, "South American Trade Pact Under Fire," *Wall Street Journal,* October 23, 1996, p. A2; A. J. Yeats, *Does Mercosur's Trade Performance Justify Concerns about the Global Welfare-Reducing Effects of Free Trade Arrangements? Yes!* (Washington, DC: World Bank, 1996); and D. M. Leipziger et al., "Mercosur: Integration and Industrial Policy," *The World Economy,* 1997, pp. 585–604.

27. "Another Blow to Mercosur," *The Economist,* March 31, 2001, pp. 33–34.

28. "Lula Lays Out Mercosur Rescue Mission," *Latin America Newsletters,* February 4, 2003, p. 7.

29. J. McGregor, "Canada Restarts Free Negotiations with South America's Mercosur Trading Bloc," *CBC News,* April 28, 2017, http://www.cbc.ca/news/politics/mercosur-free-trade-talks-canada-1.4090441.

30. "CARICOM Single Market Begins," *EIU Views,* February 3, 2006.

31. M. Esterl, "Free Trade Area of the Americas Stalls," *The Economist,* January 19, 2005, p. 1.

32. M. Moffett and J. D. McKinnon, "Failed Summit Casts Shadow on Global Trade Talks," *The Wall Street Journal,* November 7, 2005, p. A1.

33. "Every Man for Himself: Trade in Asia," *The Economist,* November 2, 2002, pp. 43–44.

34. L. Gooch, "Asian Free-Trade Zone Raises Hopes," *The New York Times,* January 1, 2010, p. B3.

35. "Aimless in Seattle," *The Economist,* November 13, 1993, pp. 35–36.

36. G. de Jonquieres, "APEC Grapples with Market Turmoil," *Financial Times,* November 21, 1997, p. 6; and G. Baker, "Clinton Team Wins Most of the APEC Tricks," *Financial Times,* November 27, 1997, p. 5.

37. M. Turner, "Trio Revives East African Union," *Financial Times,* January 16, 2001, p. 4.

38. "World Economic Survey," *The Economist,* September 19, 1992, p. 17.

39. 3M Canada, "The 3M Canada Story," at http://solutions.3mcanada.ca/wps/portal/3M/en_CA/about-3M/information/more-info/history/local/.

40. Ibid.

41. P. Davis, "A European Campaign: Local Companies Rush for a Share of EC Market While Barriers Are Down," *Minneapolis–St. Paul City Business,* January 8, 1990, p. 1.

42. "The Business of Europe," *The Economist,* December 7, 1991, pp. 63–64.

43. E. G. Friberg, "1992: Moves Europeans Are Making," *Harvard Business Review,* May–June 1989, pp. 85–89.

CHAPTER 9

1. For a good general introduction to the foreign exchange market, see R. Weisweiller, *How the Foreign Exchange Market Works* (New York: New York Institute of Finance, 1990). A detailed description of the economics of foreign exchange markets can be found in P. R. Krugman and M. Obstfeld, *International Economics: Theory and Policy* (New York: Harper-Collins, 1994).

2. Forex Blog, Archive for the 'Canadian Dollar' Category, http://www.forexblog.org/category/canadian-dollar.

3. C. Fournier, "Canadian Currency Climbs as Stocks Rally, Potash Receives Takeover Offer," Bloomberg.com, August 17, 2010, http://www.bloomberg.com/news/2010-08-17/canadian-dollar-appreciates-as-stocks-advance-crude-trades-above-76.html; http://www.theglobeandmail.com/report-on-business/top-business-stories/economist-slams-bank-of-canada-over-loonies-rise/article1804203/, accessed November 18, 2010; Scotiabank Group, "Global Forecast Update," May 3, 2011, http://www.scotiacapital.com/English/bns_econ/forecast.pdf.

4. XE.com at www.xe.com.

5. CLS Group Holdings AG, "CLS Market Report," May 3, 2017, https://www.cls-group.com/CLS%20Information/CLS_Market_Report_Apr_2017.pdf, accessed June 21, 2017; and A. Nag and J. McGeever, "Foreign Exchange, the World's Biggest Market, is Shrinking," Reuters, https://www.cls-group.com/CLS%20Information/CLS_Market_Report_Apr_2017.pdf, accessed June 21, 2017.

6. For a comprehensive review, see M. Taylor, "The Economics of Exchange Rates," *Journal of Economic Literature* 33 (1995), pp. 13–47.

7. Krugman and Obstfeld, *International Economics.*

8. M. Friedman, *Studies in the Quantity Theory of Money* (Chicago: University of Chicago Press, 1956). For an accessible explanation, see M. Friedman and R. Friedman, *Free to Choose* (London: Penguin Books, 1979), chap. 9.

9. J.-A. Morales, "Inflation Stabilization in Bolivia," in *Inflation Stabilization: The Experience of Israel, Argentina, Brazil, Bolivia, and Mexico,* ed. M. Bruno et al. (Cambridge, MA: MIT Press, 1988), and The Economist, *World Book of Vital Statistics* (New York: Random House, 1990).

10. For reviews and recent articles, see L. H. Officer, "The Purchasing Power Parity Theory of Exchange Rates: A Review Article," International Monetary Fund staff papers, March 1976, pp. 1–60; Taylor, "The Economics of Exchange Rates"; H. J. Edison, J. E. Gagnon, and W. R. Melick, "Understanding the Empirical Literature on Purchasing Power Parity," *Journal of International Money and Finance* 16 (February 1997), pp. 1–18; J. R. Edison, "Multi-Country Evidence on the Behavior of Purchasing Power Parity under the Current Float," *Journal of International Money and Finance* 16 (February 1997), pp. 19–36; and K. Rogoff, "The Purchasing Power Parity Puzzle," *Journal of Economic Literature* 34 (1996), pp. 647–68.

11. M. Obstfeld and K. Rogoff, "The Six Major Puzzles in International Economics," National Bureau of Economic Research working paper 7777, July 2000.

12. Ibid.

13. See M. Devereux and C. Engel, "Monetary Policy in the Open Economy Revisited: Price Setting and Exchange Rate Flexibility," National Bureau of Economic Research working paper 7665, April 2000. Also P. Krugman, "Pricing to Market When the Exchange Rate

Changes," in *Real Financial Economics*, ed. S. Arndt and J. Richardson (Cambridge, MA: MIT Press).

14. Applied Materials Web site, http://www.appliedmaterials.com/about/company.

15. S. Sharf, "The World's Largest Tech Companies 2016: Apple Bests Samsung, Microsoft and Alphabet," *Forbes*, May 26, 2016, https://www.forbes.com/sites/samanthasharf/2016/05/26/the-worlds-largest-tech-companies-2016-apple-bests-samsung-microsoft-and-alphabet/#51c2a631b661, accessed June 21, 2017.

16. For a summary of the evidence, see the survey by Taylor, "The Economics of Exchange Rates."

17. R. E. Cumby and M. Obstfeld, "A Note on Exchange Rate Expectations and Nominal Interest Differentials: A Test of the Fisher Hypothesis," *Journal of Finance*, June 1981, pp. 697–703.

18. Taylor, "The Economics of Exchange Rates."

19. See H. L. Allen and M. P. Taylor, "Charts, Noise, and Fundamentals in the Foreign Exchange Market," *Economic Journal* 100 (1990), pp. 49–59, and T. Ito, "Foreign Exchange Rate Expectations: Micro Survey Data," *American Economic Review* 80 (1990), pp. 434–49.

20. For example, see E. Fama, "Forward Rates as Predictors of Future Spot Rates," *Journal of Financial Economics*, October 1976, pp. 361–77.

21. R. M. Levich, "The Efficiency of Markets for Foreign Exchange," in *International Finance*, ed. G. D. Gay and R. W. Kold (Richmond, VA: Robert F. Dane, Inc., 1983).

22. J. Williamson, *The Exchange Rate System* (Washington, DC: Institute for International Economics, 1983).

23. R. M. Levich, "Currency Forecasters Lose Their Way," *Euromoney*, August 1983, p. 140.

24. Rogoff, "The Purchasing Power Parity Puzzle."

25. C. Engel and J. D. Hamilton, "Long Swings in the Dollar: Are They in the Data and Do Markets Know It?" *American Economic Review*, September 1990, pp. 689–713.

26. J. R. Carter and J. Gagne, "The Do's and Don'ts of International Countertrade," *Sloan Management Review*, Spring 1988, pp. 31–37.

27. For details on how various firms manage their foreign exchange exposure, see the articles contained in the special foreign exchange issue of *Business International Money Report*, December 18, 1989, pp. 401–12.

28. Ibid.

29. S. Arterian, "How Black & Decker Defines Exposure," *Business International Money Report*, December 18, 1989, pp. 404, 405, 409.

CHAPTER 10

1. The argument goes back to 18th century philosopher David Hume. See D. Hume, "On the Balance of Trade," reprinted in *The Gold Standard in Theory and in History*, ed. B. Eichengreen (London: Methuen, 1985).

2. J. Powell, *A History of the Canadian Dollar*, (Ottawa: Bank of Canada, 2005) p. 14.

3. Report of the Royal Commission on Banking and Currency in Canada, (Macmillan Report), 1933, p. 22.

4. Ibid., p.18.

5. Ibid., p. 23.

6. Ibid., p. 25.

7. R. Solomon, *The International Monetary System, 1945–1981*. (New York: Harper & Row, 1982).

8. International Monetary Fund, *World Economic Outlook, 1998*. (Washington, DC: IMF, May 1998).

9. For a feel for the issues contained in this debate, see P. Krugman, *Has the Adjustment Process Worked?* (Washington, DC: Institute for International Economics, 1991); "Time to Tether Currencies," *The Economist*, January 6, 1990, pp. 15–16; P. R. Krugman and M. Obstfeld, *International Economics: Theory and Policy* (New York: Harper Collins, 1994); J. Shelton, *Money Meltdown* (New York: Free Press, 1994); and S. Edwards, "Exchange Rates and the Political Economy of Macroeconomic Discipline," *American Economic Review* 86, No. 2 (May 1996), pp. 159–63.

10. The argument is made by several prominent economists, particularly Stanford's Robert McKinnon. See R. McKinnon, "An International Standard for Monetary Stabilization," *Policy Analyses in International Economics* 8 (1984). The details of this argument are beyond the scope of this book. For a relatively accessible exposition, see P. Krugman, *The Age of Diminished Expectations* (Cambridge, MA: MIT Press, 1990).

11. A. R. Ghosh and A. M. Gulde, "Does the Exchange Rate Regime Matter for Inflation and Growth?" *Economic Issues*, No. 2, (1997).

12. "The ABC of Currency Boards," *The Economist*, November 1, 1997, p. 80.

13. International Monetary Fund, *World Economic Outlook*, 1998.

14. Ibid.

15. T. S. Shorrock, "Korea Starts Overhaul; IMF Aid Hits $60 Billion," *Journal of Commerce*, December 8, 1997, p. 3A.

16. See J. Sachs, "Economic Transition and Exchange Rate Regime," *American Economic Review* 86, No. 92 (May 1996), pp. 147–52; and J. Sachs, "Power unto Itself," *Financial Times*, December 11, 1997, p. 11.

17. Sachs, "Power unto Itself."

18. Martin Wolf, "Same Old IMF Medicine," *Financial Times*, December 9, 1997, p. 12.

19. Sachs, "Power unto Itself."

20. "New Fund, Old Fundamentals," *The Economist*, May 2, 2009, p. 78.

21. P. Gumbel and B. Coleman, "Daimler Warns of Severe 95 Loss Due to Strong Mark," *New York Times*, June 29, 1995, pp. 1, 10; and M. Wolf, "Daimler-Benz Announces Major Losses," *Financial Times*, June 29, 1995, p. 1.

CHAPTER 11

1. The concept of consumer surplus is an important one in economics. For a more detailed exposition, see D. Besanko, D. Dranove, and M. Shanley, *Economics of Strategy* (New York: John Wiley & Sons, 1996).

2. However, P = V only in the special case where the company has a perfect monopoly, and where it can charge each customer a unique price that reflects the value of the product to that customer (i.e., where perfect price discrimination is possible). More generally, except in the limiting case of perfect price discrimination, even a monopolist will see most consumers capture some of the value of a product in the form of a consumer surplus.

3. This point is central to the work of M. Porter, *Competitive Advantage* (New York: Free Press, 1985). See also chap. 4 in P. Ghemawat, *Commitment: The Dynamic of Strategy* (New York: Free Press, 1991).

4. M. E. Porter, *Competitive Strategy* (New York: Free Press, 1980).

5. M. E. Porter, "What Is Strategy?" *Harvard Business Review*, On-point Enhanced Edition article, February 1, 2000.

6. Porter, *Competitive Advantage*.

7. Japan-Guide.com, http://www.japan-guide.com/e/e644.html, accessed December 18, 2010; "Exports of Goods on a Balance-of-Payments Basis, by Product," Statistics Canada, http://www.statcan.gc.ca/tables-tableaux/sum-som/l01/cst01/gblec04-eng.htm, accessed May 29, 2017; D. Workman, "United States Top 10 Exports," World's Top Experts Web site, http://www.worldstopexports.com/united-states-top-10-exports/, and accessed June 21, 2017; D. Workman, "United States Top 10 Imports," World's Top Experts Web site, http://www.worldstopexports.com/united-states-top-10-imports/, accessed June 21, 2017; "U.S. Relations with Switzerland," U.S. Department of State, December 7, 2010, http://www.state.gov/r/pa/ei/bgn/3431.htm; "U.S. Relations with the Republic of Korea," U.S. Department of State, December 10, 2010, http://www.state.gov/r/pa/ei/bgn/2800.htm

8. G. Hall and S. Howell, "The Experience Curve from an Economist's Perspective," *Strategic Management Journal* 6 (1985), pp. 197–212.

9. A. A. Alchain, "Reliability of Progress Curves in Airframe Production," *Econometrica* 31 (1963), pp. 693–97.

10. Hall and Howell, "The Experience Curve from an Economist's Perspective."

11. For a full discussion of the source of scale economies, see D. Besanko, D. Dranove, and M. Shanley, *Economics of Strategy* (New York: Wiley & Sons, 1996).

12. This estimate was provided by the Pharmaceutical Manufacturers Association.

13. "Matsushita Electrical Industrial in 1987," in *Transnational Management*, eds. C. A. Bartlett and S. Ghoshal (Homewood, IL: Richard D. Irwin, 1992).

14. This concept has been popularized by G. Hamel and C. K. Prahalad, *Competing for the Future* (Boston: Harvard Business School Press, 1994). The concept is grounded in the resource-based view of the firm.

For a summary, see J. B. Barney, "Firm Resources and Sustained Competitive Advantage," *Journal of Management* 17 (1991), pp. 99–120, and K. R. Conner, "A Historical Comparison of Resource-Based Theory and Five Schools of Thought within Industrial Organization Economics: Do We Have a New Theory of the Firm?" *Journal of Management* 17 (1991), pp. 121–54.

15. See J. Birkinshaw and N. Hood, "Multinational Subsidiary Evolution: Capability and Charter Change in Foreign Owned Subsidiary Companies," *Academy of Management Review* 23 (October 1998), pp. 773–95; A. K. Gupta and V. J. Govindarajan, "Knowledge Flows within Multinational Corporations," *Strategic Management Journal* 21 (2000), pp. 473–96; V. J. Govindarajan and A. K. Gupta, *The Quest for Global Dominance* (San Francisco: Jossey Bass, 2001); T. S. Frost, J. M. Birkinshaw, and P. C. Ensign, "Centers of Excellence in Multinational Corporations," *Strategic Management Journal* 23 (2002), pp. 997–1018; and U. Andersson, M. Forsgren, and U. Holm, "The Strategic Impact of External Networks," *Strategic Management Journal* 23 (2002), pp. 979–96.

16. McDonald's Europe Virtual Press Office, Restaurant Interior, http://www.mcdpressoffice.eu/photography/cat02/.

17. S. Leung, "Armchairs, TVs and Espresso: Is It McDonald's?" *The Wall Street Journal*, August 30, 2002, pp. A1, A6.

18. J. E. Garten, "Wal-Mart Gives Globalization a Bad Name," *BusinessWeek*, March 8, 2004, p. 24.

19. C. K. Prahalad and Y. L. Doz, *The Multinational Mission: Balancing Local Demands and Global Vision* (New York: Free Press, 1987). Prahalad and Doz actually talk about local responsiveness rather than local customization.

20. T. Levitt, "The Globalization of Markets," *Harvard Business Review*, May–June 1983, pp. 92–102.

21. C. A. Bartlett and S. Ghoshal, *Managing Across Borders* (Boston: Harvard Business School Press, 1989).

22. Bombardier Web site, http://www.bombardier.com/en/corporate/about-us.

23. C. J. Chipello, "Local Presence Is Key to European Deals," *Wall Street Journal*, June 30, 1998, p. A15.

24. This section is based on Bartlett and Ghoshal, *Managing Across Borders*.

25. "Good Business," McCain Web site, http://www.mccain.com/good-business/responsible-business, accessed June 21, 2017; "About Us," McCain Web site, http://www.mccain.com/about-us, accessed June 21, 2017; "McCain Potato Products," McCain UK Web site, http://www.mccain.co.uk/our-food/, accessed June 21, 2017.

26. Bartlett and Ghoshal, *Managing Across Borders*.

27. An empirical study seems to confirm this hypothesis. See J. Birkinshaw, N. Hood, and S. Jonsson, "Building Firm-Specific Advantages in Multinational Corporations: The Role of Subsidiary Initiative," *Strategic Management Journal* 19 (1998), pp. 221–41.

28. See P. Marsh and S. Wagstyle, "The Hungry Caterpillar," *Financial Times*, December 2, 1997, p. 22; and T. Hout, M. E. Porter, and E. Rudden, "How Global Firms Win Out," *Harvard Business Review*, September–October 1982, pp. 98–108.

29. G. de Jonquieres, "Unilever Adopts a Clean Sheet Approach," *Financial Times*, October 21, 1991, p. 13.

30. See K. Ohmae, "The Global Logic of Strategic Alliances," *Harvard Business Review*, March–April 1989, pp. 143–54; G. Hamel, Y. L. Doz, and C. K. Prahalad, "Collaborate with Your Competitors and Win!" *Harvard Business Review*, January–February 1989, pp. 133–39; W. Burgers, C. W. L. Hill, and W. C. Kim, "Alliances in the Global Auto Industry," *Strategic Management Journal* 14 (1993), pp. 419–32; and P. Kale, H. Singh, and H. Perlmutter, "Learning and Protection of Proprietary Assets in Strategic Alliances: Building Relational Capital," *Strategic Management Journal* 21 (2000), pp. 217–37.

31. L. T. Chang, "China Eases Foreign Film Rules," *The Wall Street Journal*, October 15, 2004, p. B2.

32. B. L. Simonin, "Transfer of Marketing Know-How in International Strategic Alliances," *Journal of International Business Studies*, 1999, pp. 463–91; and J. W. Spencer, "Firms' Knowledge Sharing Strategies in the Global Innovation System," *Strategic Management Journal* 24 (2003), pp. 217–33.

33. C. Souza, "Microsoft Teams with MIPS, Toshiba," *EBN*, February 10, 2003, p. 4.

34. Kale, Singh, Perlmutter, "Learning and Protection of Proprietary Assets."

35. R. B. Reich and E. D. Mankin, "Joint Ventures with Japan Give Away Our Future," *Harvard Business Review,* March–April 1986, pp. 78–90.

36. J. Bleeke and D. Ernst, "The Way to Win in Cross-Border Alliances," *Harvard Business Review,* November–December 1991, pp. 127–35.

37. W. Roehl and J. F. Truitt, "Stormy Open Marriages Are Better," *Columbia Journal of World Business,* Summer 1987, pp. 87–95.

38. K. McQuade and B. Gomes-Casseres, "Xerox and Fuji Xerox," HBC Case: Harvard Business School, http://hbr.org/product/xerox-and-fuji-xerox/an/391156-PDF-ENG?Ntt-Krista1McQuade.

39. See T. Khanna, R. Gulati, and N. Nohria, "The Dynamics of Learning Alliances: Competition, Cooperation, and Relative Scope," *Strategic Management Journal* 19 (1998), pp. 193–210; and Kale, Singh, and Perlmutter, "Learning and Protection of Proprietary Assets."

40. Kale, Singh, and Perlmutter, "Learning and Protection of Proprietary Assets."

41. Hamel, Doz, and Prahalad, "Collaborate with Your Competitors and Win!"; and Khanna, Gulati, and Nohria, "The Dynamics of Learning Alliances."

42. B. Wysocki, "Cross-Border Alliances Become Favorite Way to Crack New Markets," *Wall Street Journal,* March 4, 1990, p. A1.

43. Hamel, Doz, and Prahalad, "Collaborate with Your Competitors and Win!" p. 138.

CHAPTER 12

1. For interesting empirical studies that deal with the issues of timing and resource commitments, see T. Isobe, S. Makino, and D. B. Montgomery, "Resource Commitment, Entry Timing, and Market Performance of Foreign Direct Investments in Emerging Economies," *Academy of Management Journal* 43, No. 3, (2000), pp. 468–84, and Y. Pan and P. S. K. Chi, "Financial Performance and Survival of Multinational Corporations in China," *Strategic Management Journal* 20, No. 4, (1999), pp. 359–74.

2. This can be reconceptualized as the resource base of the entrant, relative to indigenous competitors. For work that focuses on this issue, see W. C. Bogenr, H. Thomas, and J. McGee, "A Longitudinal Study of the Competitive Positions and Entry Paths of European Firms in the U.S. Pharmaceutical Market," *Strategic Management Journal* 17 (1996), pp. 85–107; D. Collis, "A Resource-Based Analysis of Global Competition," *Strategic Management Journal* 12 (1991), pp. 49–68; and S. Tallman, "Strategic Management Models and Resource-Based Strategies among MNEs in a Host Market," *Strategic Management Journal* 12 (1991), pp. 69–82.

3. For a discussion of first-mover advantages, see M. Lieberman and D. Montgomery, "First-Mover Advantages," *Strategic Management Journal* 9 (Summer Special Issue, 1988), pp. 41–58.

4. J. M. Shaver, W. Mitchell, and B. Yeung, "The Effect of Own Firm and Other Firm Experience on Foreign Direct Investment Survival in the United States, 1987–92," *Strategic Management Journal* 18 (1997), pp. 811–24.

5. S. Zaheer and E. Mosakowski, "The Dynamics of the Liability of Foreignness: A Global Study of Survival in the Financial Services Industry," *Strategic Management Journal* 18 (1997), pp. 439–64.

6. Shaver, Mitchell, and Yeung, "The Effect of Own Firm and Other Firm Experience on Foreign Direct Investment Survival in the United States."

7. P. Ghemawat, *Commitment: The Dynamics of Strategy* (New York: Free Press, 1991).

8. Isobe, Makino, and Montgomery, "Resource Commitment, Entry Timing, and Market Performance of Foreign Direct Investments in Emerging Economies"; and Pan and Chi, "Financial Performance and Survival of Multinational Corporations in China."

9. C. Bartlett and S. Ghoshal, "Going Global: Lessons from Late Movers," *Harvard Business Review,* March–April 2000, pp. 132–45.

10. This section draws on several studies, including C. W. L. Hill, P. Hwang, and W. C. Kim, "An Eclectic Theory of the Choice of International Entry Mode," *Strategic Management Journal* 11 (1990), pp. 117–28; C. W. L. Hill and W. C. Kim, "Searching for a Dynamic Theory of the Multinational Enterprise: A Transaction Cost Model," *Strategic Management Journal* 9 (Special Issue on Strategy Content, 1988), pp. 93–104; E. Anderson and H. Gatignon, "Modes of Foreign Entry: A Transaction Cost Analysis and Propositions," *Journal of International Business Studies* 17 (1986), pp. 1–26; F. R. Root, *Entry Strategies for International Markets* (Lexington, MA: D. C. Heath, 1980); A. Madhok, "Cost, Value and Foreign Market Entry: The Transaction and the Firm," *Strategic Management Journal* 18 (1997), pp. 39–61; K. D. Brouthers and L. B. Brouthers, "Acquisition or Greenfield Start-up?" *Strategic Management Journal* 21, No. 1 (2000), pp. 89–97.

11. For a general discussion of licensing, see F. J. Contractor, "The Role of Licensing in International Strategy," *Columbia Journal of World Business,* Winter 1982, pp. 73–83.

12. Fuji Xerox at http://www.fujixerox.com/eng/.

13. See E. Terazono and C. Lorenz, "An Angry Young Warrior," *Financial Times,* September 19, 1994, p. 11; and K. McQuade and B. Gomes-Casseres, "Xerox and Fuji-Xerox," Harvard Business School Case No. 9-391-156.

14. O. E. Williamson, *The Economic Institutions of Capitalism* (New York: Free Press, 1985).

15. J. H. Dunning and M. McQueen, "The Eclectic Theory of International Production: A Case Study of the International Hotel Industry," *Managerial and Decision Economics* 2 (1981), pp. 197–210.

16. A. E. Serwer, "McDonald's Conquers the World," *Fortune,* October 17, 1994, pp. 103–16.

17. For an excellent review of the basic theoretical literature of joint ventures, see B. Kogut, "Joint Ventures: Theoretical and Empirical Perspectives," *Strategic Management Journal* 9 (1988), pp. 319–32. More recent studies include T. Chi, "Option to Acquire or Divest a Joint Venture," *Strategic Management Journal* 21, No. 6 (2000), pp. 665–88; H. Merchant and D. Schendel, "How Do International Joint Ventures Create Shareholder Value?" *Strategic Management Journal* 21, No. 7 (2000), pp. 723–37; and H. K. Steensma and M. A. Lyles, "Explaining IJV Survival in a Transitional Economy through

Social Exchange and Knowledge Based Perspectives," *Strategic Management Journal* 21, No. 8 (2000), pp. 831–51.

18. D. G. Bradley, "Managing against Expropriation," *Harvard Business Review*, July–August 1977, pp. 78–90.

19. Speech given by Tony Kobayashi at the University of Washington Business School, October 1992.

20. A. C. Inkpen and P. W. Beamish, "Knowledge, Bargaining Power, and the Instability of International Joint Ventures," *Academy of Management Review* 22 (1997), pp. 177–202; and S. H. Park and G. R. Ungson, "The Effect of National Culture, Organizational Complementarity, and Economic Motivation on Joint Venture Dissolution," *Academy of Management Journal* 40 (1997), pp. 279–307.

21. Inkpen and Beamish, "Knowledge, Bargaining Power, and the Instability of International Joint Ventures."

22. See Brouthers and Brouthers, "Acquisition or Greenfield Start-up?"; and J. F. Hennart and Y. R. Park, "Greenfield Versus Acquisition: The Strategy of Japanese Investors in the United States," *Management Science*, 1993, pp. 1054–70.

23. This section draws on Hill, Hwang, and Kim, "An Eclectic Theory of the Choice of International Entry Mode."

24. C. W. L. Hill, "Strategies for Exploiting Technological Innovations: When and When Not to License," *Organization Science* 3 (1992), pp. 428–41.

25. Ibid.

26. For evidence on acquisitions and performance, see R. E. Caves, "Mergers, Takeovers, and Economic Efficiency," *International Journal of Industrial Organization* 7 (1989), pp. 151–74; M. C. Jensen and R. S. Ruback, "The Market for Corporate Control: The Scientific Evidence," *Journal of Financial Economics* 11 (1983), pp. 5–50; R. Roll, "Empirical Evidence on Takeover Activity and Shareholder Wealth," in *Knights, Raiders and Targets*, ed. J. C. Coffee, L. Lowenstein, and S. Rose (Oxford: Oxford University Press, 1989); A. Schleifer and R. W. Vishny, "Takeovers in the 60s and 80s: Evidence and Implications," *Strategic Management Journal* 12 (Winter 1991 Special Issue),

pp. 51–60; T. H. Brush, "Predicted Changes in Operational Synergy and Post-Acquisition Performance of Acquired Businesses," *Strategic Management Journal* 17 (1996), pp. 1–24; and A. Seth, K. P. Song, and R. R. Pettit, "Value Creation and Destruction in Cross-Border Acquisitions," *Strategic Management Journal* 23 (October 2002), pp. 921–40.

27. J. Warner, J. Templeman, and R. Horn, "The Case against Mergers," *BusinessWeek*, October 30, 1995, pp. 122–34.

28. "Few Takeovers Pay Off for Big Buyers," *Investor's Business Daily*, May 25, 2001, p. 1.

29. S. A. Christofferson, R. S. McNish, and D. L. Sias, "Where Mergers Go Wrong," *The McKinsey Quarterly* 2 (2004), pp. 92–110.

30. D. J. Ravenscraft and F. M. Scherer, *Mergers, Selloffs, and Economic Efficiency* (Washington, DC: Brookings Institution, 1987).

31. See P. Ghemawat and F. Ghadar, "The Dubious Logic of Global Mega-Mergers," *Harvard Business Review*, July–August 2000, pp. 65–72.

32. R. Roll, "The Hubris Hypothesis of Corporate Takeovers," *Journal of Business* 59 (1986), pp. 197–216.

33. "Marital Problems," *The Economist*, October 14, 2000; C. Isadore, "Daimler pays to dump Chrysler," CNN.com, May 14, 2007, http://money.cnn.com/2007/05/14/news/companies/chrysler_sale/index.htm.

34. See J. P. Walsh, "Top Management Turnover Following Mergers and Acquisitions," *Strategic Management Journal* 9 (1988), pp. 173–83.

35. B. Vlasic and B. A. Stertz, *Taken for a Ride: How Daimler-Benz Drove off with Chrysler* (New York: Harper Collins, 2000).

36. See A. A. Cannella and D. C. Hambrick, "Executive Departure and Acquisition Performance," *Strategic Management Journal* 14 (1993), pp. 137–52.

37. P. Haspeslagh and D. Jemison, *Managing Acquisitions* (New York: Free Press, 1991).

38. Ibid.

39. McCain Foods Limited, PotatoPro.com, http://www.potatopro.com/lists/companies/dispform.aspx?ID=1; McCain at http://www.foodnavigator-asia.com/Business/McCain-Foods-doubles-capacity-at-China-plant; K. McArthur, "McCain Set To Build Fry Plant in China in

August," *The Globe and Mail*, July 24, 2004, p. B3, www.globetechnology.com/servlet/ArticleNews/TPStory/LAC/20040624/RMCCAIN24/TPTechInvestor.

CHAPTER 13

1. R. A. Pope, "Why Small Firms Export: Another Look," *Journal of Small Business Management* 40 (2002), pp. 17–26.

2. S. T. Cavusgil, "Global Dimensions of Marketing," in *Marketing*, ed. P. E. Murphy and B. M. Enis (Glenview, IL: Scott, Foresman, 1985), pp. 577–99.

3. W. Pavord and R. Bogart, "The Dynamics of the Decision to Export," *Akron Business and Economic Review*, 1975, pp. 6–11.

4. W. J. Burpitt and D. A. Rondinelli, "Small Firms' Motivations for Exporting: To Earn and Learn?" *Journal of Small Business Management*, October 2000, pp. 1–14.

5. A. O. Ogbuehi and T. A. Longfellow, "Perceptions of U.S. Manufacturing Companies Concerning Exporting," *Journal of Small Business Management*, October 1994, pp. 37–59.

6. R. W. Haigh, "Thinking of Exporting?" *Columbia Journal of World Business* 29 (December 1994), pp. 66–86.

7. F. Williams, "The Quest for More Efficient Commerce," *Financial Times*, October 13, 1994, p. 7.

8. See Burpitt and Rondinelli, "Small Firms' Motivations for Exporting," and C. S. Katsikeas, L. C. Leonidou, and N. A. Morgan, "Firm Level Export Performance Assessment," *Academy of Marketing Science* 28 (2000), pp. 493–511.

9. M. Y. Yoshino and T. B. Lifson, *The Invisible Link* (Cambridge, MA: MIT Press, 1986).

10. Department of Foreign Affairs and International Trade Canada at http://www.international.gc.ca/commerce/index.aspx?lang=eng.

11. L. W. Tuller, *Going Global* (Homewood, IL: Business One-Irwin, 1991).

12. Haigh, "Thinking of Exporting?"

13. J. Francis and C. Collins-Dodd, "The Impact of Firms' Export Orientation on the Export Performance of High-Tech Small and Medium Sized Enterprises," *Journal of International Marketing* 8, No. 3 (2000), pp. 84–103.

14. *Exchange Agreements and Exchange Restrictions* (Washington,

DC: International Monetary Fund, 1989).

15. It's also sometimes argued that countertrade is a way of reducing the risks inherent in a traditional money-for-goods transaction, particularly with entities from emerging economies. See C. J. Choi, S. H. Lee, and J. B. Kim, "A Note of Countertrade: Contractual Uncertainty and Transactional Governance in Emerging Economies," *Journal of International Business Studies* 30, No. 1 (1999), pp. 189–202.

16. J. R. Carter and J. Gagne, "The Do's and Don'ts of International Countertrade," *Sloan Management Review,* Spring 1988, pp. 31–37, and W. Maneerungsee, "Countertrade: Farm Goods Swapped for Italian Electricity," *Bangkok Post,* July 23, 1998.

17. Carter and Gagne, "The Do's and Don'ts of International Countertrade."

18. For details, see Carter and Gagne, "Do's and Don'ts of International Countertrade"; J. F. Hennart, "Some Empirical Dimensions of Countertrade," *Journal of International Business Studies,* 1990, pp. 240–60; and West, "Countertrade."

19. D. J. Lecraw, "The Management of Countertrade: Factors Influencing Success," *Journal of International Business Studies,* Spring 1989, pp. 41–59.

CHAPTER 14

1. See R. W. Ruekert and O. C. Walker, "Interactions between Marketing and R&D Departments in Implementing Different Business-Level Strategies," *Strategic Management Journal* 8 (1987), pp. 233–48, and K. B. Clark and S. C. Wheelwright, *Managing New Product and Process Development* (New York: Free Press), 1993.

2. T. Levitt, "The Globalization of Markets," *Harvard Business Review,* May–June 1983, pp. 92–102. Reprinted by permission of *Harvard Business Review,* an excerpt from "The Globalization of Markets," by Theodore Levitt, May–June 1983. Copyright © 1983 by the President and Fellows of Harvard College. All rights reserved.

3. For example, see S. P. Douglas and Y. Wind, "The Myth of Globalization," *Columbia Journal of World Business,* Winter 1987, pp. 19–29; and C. A. Bartlett and S. Ghoshal,

Managing Across Borders: The Transnational Solution (Boston: Harvard Business School Press, 1989).

4. "Slow Food," *The Economist,* February 3, 1990, p. 64.

5. D. B. Holt, J. A. Quelch, and E. L. Taylor, "How Global Brands Compete," *Harvard Business Review,* September 2004.

6. J. T. Landry, "Emerging Markets: Are Chinese Consumers Coming of Age?" *Harvard Business Review,* May–June 1998, pp. 17–20.

7. C. Miller, "Teens Seen as the First Truly Global Consumers," *Marketing News,* March 27, 1995, p. 9.

8. This approach was originally developed in K. Lancaster, "A New Approach to Demand Theory," *Journal of Political Economy* 74 (1965), pp. 132–57.

9. V. R. Alden, "Who Says You Can't Crack Japanese Markets?" *Harvard Business Review,* January–February 1987, pp. 52–56.

10. T. Parker-Pope, "Custom Made," *Wall Street Journal,* September 26, 1996, p. 22.

11. "RCA's New Vista: The Bottom Line," *BusinessWeek,* July 4, 1987, p. 44.

12. "After Early Stumbles P&G Is Making Inroads Overseas," *Wall Street Journal,* February 6, 1989, p. B1.

13. Z. Gurhan-Cvanli and D. Maheswaran, "Cultural Variation in Country of Origin Effects," *Journal of Marketing Research,* August 2000, pp. 309–17.

14. See M. Laroche, V. H. Kirpalani, F. Pons, and L. Zhou, "A Model of Advertising Standardization in Multinational Corporations," *Journal of International Business Studies,* 32 (2001), pp. 249–66, and D. A. Aaker and E. Joachimsthaler, "The Lure of Global Branding," *Harvard Business Review,* November–December 1999, pp. 137–44.

15. "Advertising in a Single Market," *The Economist,* March 24, 1990, p. 64.

16. D. Waller, "Charged up over Competition Law," *Financial Times,* June 23, 1994, p. 14.

17. R. G. Matthews and D. Pringle, "Nokia Bets One Global Message Will Ring True in Many Markets," *The Wall Street Journal,* September 27, 2004, p. B6.

18. R. J. Dolan and H. Simon, *Power Pricing* (New York: Free Press, 1999).

19. B. Stottinger, "Strategic Export Pricing: A Long Winding Road," *Journal of International Marketing* 9, (2001), pp. 40–63.

20. These allegations were made on a PBS *Frontline* documentary telecast in the United States in May 1992.

21. G. Smith and B. Wolverton, "A Dark Moment for Kodak," *Business Week,* August 4, 1997, pp. 30–31.

22. R. Narisette and J. Friedland, "Disposable Income: Diaper Wars of P&G and Kimberly-Clark Now Heat up in Brazil," *Wall Street Journal,* June 4, 1997, p. A1.

23. "Printers Reflect Pattern of Trade Rows," *Financial Times,* December 20, 1988, p. 3.

24. J. F. Pickering, *Industrial Structure and Market Conduct* (London: Martin Robertson, 1974).

25. S. P. Douglas, C. Samuel Craig, and E. J. Nijissen. "Integrating Branding Strategy across Markets," *Journal of International Marketing* 9, no 2, (2001), pp. 97–114.

26. The phrase was first used by economist Joseph Schumpeter in *Capitalism, Socialism, and Democracy* (New York: Harper Brothers, 1942).

27. See D. C. Mowery and N. Rosenberg, *Technology and the Pursuit of Economic Growth* (Cambridge, UK: Cambridge University Press, 1989), and M. E. Porter, *The Competitive Advantage of Nations* (New York: The Free Press, 1990).

28. W. Kuemmerle, "Building Effective R&D Capabilities Abroad," *Harvard Business Review,* March–April 1997, pp. 61–70.

29. "When the Corporate Lab Goes to Japan," *The New York Times,* April 28, 1991, sec. 3, p. 1.

30. D. Shapley, "Globalization Prompts Exodus," *Financial Times,* March 17, 1994, p. 10.

31. E. Mansfield, "How Economists See R&D," *Harvard Business Review,* November–December, 1981, pp. 98–106.

32. Ibid.

33. Booz, Allen, & Hamilton, "New Products Management for the 1980s," privately published research report, 1982.

34. A. L. Page, "PDMA's New Product Development Practices Survey: Performance and Best Practices," PDMA 15th Annual International Conference, Boston, October 16, 1991.

35. K. B. Clark and S. C. Wheelwright, *Managing New Product and Process Development* (New York: Free Press, 1993), and M. A. Shilling and C. W. L. Hill, "Managing the New Product Development Process," *Academy of Management Executive* 12, No. 3 (1998), pp. 67–81.

36. O. Port, "Moving Past the Assembly Line," *BusinessWeek* Special Issue: Reinventing America, 1992, pp. 177–80.

37. K. B. Clark and T. Fujimoto, "The Power of Product Integrity," *Harvard Business Review,* November–December 1990, pp. 107–18; Clark and Wheelwright, *Managing New Product and Process Development*; S. L. Brown and K. M. Eisenhardt, "Product Development: Past Research, Present Findings, and Future Directions," *Academy of Management Review* 20 (1995), pp. 348–78; and G. Stalk and T. M. Hout, *Competing Against Time* (New York: Free Press, 1990).

38. Shilling and Hill, "Managing the New Product Development Process."

39. C. Christensen, "Quantum Corporation-Business and Product Teams," Harvard Business School Case # 9-692-023.

40. R. Nobel and J. Birkinshaw, "Innovation in Multinational Corporations: Control and Communication Patterns in International R&D Operations," *Strategic Management Journal* 19 (1998), pp. 479–96.

41. See the HP Labs Web site for more details, http://www.hpl.hp.com/about/sites.html.

42. Find out more at the Microsoft Web site, http://research.microsoft.com/en-us/.

CHAPTER 15

1. B. C. Arntzen, G. G. Brown, T. P. Harrison, and L. L. Trafton, "Global Supply Chain Management at Digital Equipment Corporation," *Interfaces* 25 (1995), pp. 69–93.

2. D. A. Garvin, "What Does Product Quality Really Mean," *Sloan Management Review* 26 (Fall 1984), pp. 25–44.

3. For general background information, see "How to Build Quality," *The Economist,* September 23, 1989, pp. 91–92; A. Gabor, *The Man Who Discovered Quality* (New York: Penguin, 1990); and P. B. Crosby, *Quality Is Free* (New York: Mentor, 1980).

4. G. T. Lucier and S. Seshadri, "GE Takes Six Sigma beyond the Bottom Line," *Strategic Finance,* May 2001, pp. 40–46; and U. D. Kumar et al., "On the Optimal Selection of Process Alternatives in a Six Sigma Implementation," *International Journal of Production Economics* 111, No. 2 (2008), pp. 456–70.

5. M. Saunders, "U.S. Firms Doing Business in Europe Have Options in Registering for ISO 9000 Quality Standards," *Business America,* June 14, 1993, p. 7.

6. G. Stalk and T. M. Hout, *Competing Against Time* (New York: Free Press, 1990).

7. M. A. Cohen and H. L. Lee, "Resource Deployment Analysis of Global Manufacturing and Distribution Networks," *Journal of Manufacturing and Operations Management* 2 (1989), pp. 81–104.

8. P. Krugman, "Increasing Returns and Economic Geography," *Journal of Political Economy* 99, No. 3 (1991), pp. 483–99, and J. M. Shaver and F. Flyer, "Agglomeration Economies, Firm Heterogeneity, and Foreign Direct Investment in the United States," *Strategic Management Journal* 21 (2000), pp. 1175–93.

9. For a review of the technical arguments, see D. A. Hay and D. J. Morris, *Industrial Economics: Theory and Evidence* (Oxford: Oxford University Press, 1979). See also C. W. L. Hill and G. R. Jones, *Strategic Management: An Integrated Approach* (Boston: Houghton Mifflin, 1995).

10. See P. Nemetz and L. Fry, "Flexible Manufacturing Organizations: Implications for Strategy Formulation," *Academy of Management Review* 13 (1988), pp. 627–38; N. Greenwood, *Implementing Flexible Manufacturing Systems* (New York: Halstead Press, 1986); J. P. Womack, D. T. Jones, and D. Roos, *The Machine That Changed the World* (New York: Rawson Associates, 1990); and R. Parthasarthy and S. P. Seith, "The Impact of Flexible Automation on Business Strategy and Organizational Structure," *Academy of Management Review* 17 (1992), pp. 86–111.

11. B. J. Pine, *Mass Customization: The New Frontier in Business Competition* (Boston: Harvard Business School Press, 1993); S. Kotha, "Mass Customization: Implementing the Emerging Paradigm for Competitive Advantage," *Strategic Management Journal* 16 (1995), pp. 21–42; and J. H. Gilmore and B. J. Pine II, "The Four Faces of Mass Customization," *Harvard Business Review,* January–February 1997, pp. 91–101.

12. M. A. Cusumano, *The Japanese Automobile Industry* (Cambridge, MA: Harvard University Press, 1989); T. Ohno, *Toyota Production System* (Cambridge, MA: Productivity Press, 1990); and Womack, Jones, and Roos, *The Machine That Changed the World.*

13. See the company profile, "Avcorp Industries Inc.," on the Directories of Canadian Companies found on the Research and Business Intelligence page of the Government of Canada Web site, http://www.ic.gc.ca/app/ccc/srch/nvgt.do?lang=eng&prtl=1&estblmntNo=123456165234&profile=cmpltPrfl&profileId=2056&app=sold.

14. "The Celling Out of America," *The Economist,* December 17, 1994, pp. 63–64.

15. "The Boomerang Effect," *The Economist,* April 21, 2012.

16. This anecdote was told to the author by a Microsoft manager while the author was visiting Microsoft facilities in Hyderabad, India.

17. Interview by author. The manager was a former executive-MBA student of the author.

18. K. Ferdows, "Making the Most of Foreign Factories," *Harvard Business Review,* March–April 1997, pp. 73–88.

19. This argument represents a simple extension of the dynamic capabilities research stream in the strategic management literature. See D. J. Teece, G. Pisano, and A. Shuen, "Dynamic Capabilities and Strategic Management," *Strategic Management Journal* 18 (1997), pp. 509–33.

20. The material in this section is based primarily on the transaction cost literature of vertical integration; for example, O. E. Williamson, *The Economic Institutions of Capitalism* (New York: The Free Press, 1985).

21. For a review of the evidence, see Williamson, *The Economic Institutions of Capitalism.*

22. Teece, Pisano, and Shuen, "Dynamic Capabilities and Strategic Management."

23. G. P. Pisano and W. C. Shih, "Restoring American Competitiveness," *Harvard Business Review*, July–August 2009, pp. 114–26.

24. A. D. Chandler, *The Visible Hand* (Cambridge, MA: Harvard University Press, 1977).

25. For a review of these arguments, see C. W. L. Hill and R. E. Hoskisson, "Strategy and Structure in the Multiproduct Firm," *Academy of Management Review* 12 (1987), pp. 331–41.

26. See R. Narasimhan and J. R. Carter, "Organization, Communication and Coordination of International Sourcing," *International Marketing Review* 7 (1990), pp. 6–20, and Arntzen, Brown, Harrison, and Trafton, "Global Supply Chain Management at Digital Equipment Corporation."

27. H. F. Busch, "Integrated Materials Management," *IJPD & MM* 18 (1990), pp. 28–39.

CHAPTER 16

1. P. J. Dowling and R. S. Schuler, *International Dimensions of Human Resource Management* (Boston: PSW-Kent, 1990).

2. J. Millman, M. A. von Glinow, and M. Nathan, "Organizational Life Cycles and Strategic International Human Resource Management in Multinational Companies," *Academy of Management Review* 16 (1991), pp. 318–39.

3. R. Colman, "HR Management Lags behind at World Class Firms," *CMA Management*, July–August 2002, p. 9.

4. E. H. Schein, *Organizational Culture and Leadership* (San Francisco: Jossey-Bass, 1985).

5. H. V. Perlmutter, "The Tortuous Evolution of the Multinational Corporation," *Columbia Journal of World Business* 4 (1969), pp. 9–18; D. A. Heenan and H. V. Perlmutter, *Multinational Organizational Development* (Reading, MA: Addison-Wesley, 1979); and D. A. Ondrack, "International Human Resources Management in European and North American Firms," *International Studies of Management and Organization* 15 (1985), pp. 6–32.

6. V. Reitman and M. Schuman, "Men's Club: Japanese and Korean Companies Rarely Look Outside for People to Run Their Overseas Operations," *Wall Street Journal*, September 26, 1996, p. 17.

7. S. Beechler and J. Z. Yang, "The Transfer of Japanese Style Management to American Subsidiaries," *Journal of International Business Studies* 25 (1994), pp. 467–91.

8. M. Banai and L. M. Sama, "Ethical Dilemma in MNCs' International Staffing Policies," *Journal of Business Ethics*, June 2000, pp. 221–35.

9. Reitman and Schuman, "Men's Club: Japanese and Korean Companies Rarely Look Outside for People to Run Their Overseas Operations."

10. Employment Equity Act at http://laws-lois.justice.gc.ca/PDF/E-5.401.pdf.

11. See "About Air Canada" at Air Canada Web site, http://www.aircanada.com/en/about/index.html.

12. S. J. Kobrin, "Geocentric Mindset and Multinational Strategy," *Journal of International Business Studies* 25 (1994), pp. 493–511.

13. P. M. Rosenzweig and N. Nohria, "Influences on Human Resource Management Practices in Multinational Corporations," *Journal of International Business Studies* 25 (1994), pp. 229–51.

14. Kobrin, "Geocentric Mindset and Multinational Strategy."

15. M. Harvey and H. Fung, "Inpatriate Managers: The Need for Realistic Relocation Reviews," *International Journal of Management* 17 (2000), pp. 151–59.

16. S. Black, M. Mendenhall, and G. Oddou, "Towards a Comprehensive Model of International Adjustment," *Academy of Management Review* 16 (1991), pp. 291–317, and J. Shay and T. J. Bruce, "Expatriate Managers," *Cornell Hotel & Restaurant Administration Quarterly*, February 1997, p. 30–40.

17. M. G. Harvey, "The Multinational Corporation's Expatriate Problem: An Application of Murphy's Law," *Business Horizons* 26 (1983), pp. 71–78.

18. Shay and Bruce, "Expatriate Managers." See also J. S. Black and H. Gregersen, "The Right Way to Manage Expatriates," *Harvard Business Review*, March–April 1999, pp. 52–63.

19. S. Caudron, "Training Ensures Overseas Success," *Personnel Journal*, December 1991, p. 27.

20. Black, Mendenhall, and Oddou, "Towards a Comprehensive Model of International Adjustment."

21. R. L. Tung, "Selection and Training Procedures of U.S., European, and Japanese Multinationals," *California Management Review* 25 (1982), pp. 57–71.

22. C. M. Solomon, "Success Abroad Depends upon More than Job Skills," *Personnel Journal*, April 1994, pp. 51–58.

23. C. M. Solomon, "Unhappy Trails," *Workforce*, August 2000, pp. 36–41.

24. Solomon, "Success Abroad Depends upon More than Job Skills."

25. Solomon, "Unhappy Trails."

26. M. Harvey, "Addressing the Dual Career Expatriation Dilemma," *Human Resource Planning* 19, No. 4 (1996), pp. 18–32; S. Blackhurst and S. Cummins, "Expatriates and the Continuing Dual Career Challenge," *International HR Journal*, Fall 2005, http://www.permitsfoundation.com/docs/Dual-Career.pdf.

27. M. Mendenhall and G. Oddou, "The Dimensions of Expatriate Acculturation: A Review," *Academy of Management Review* 10 (1985), pp. 39–47.

28. I. Torbiorin, *Living Abroad: Personal Adjustment and Personnel Policy in the Overseas Setting* (New York: John Wiley & Sons, 1982).

29. R. L. Tung, "Selection and Training of Personnel for Overseas Assignments," *Columbia Journal of World Business* 16 (1981), pp. 68–78.

30. Solomon, "Success Abroad Depends upon More than Job Skills."

31. S. Ronen, "Training and International Assignee," in *Training and Career Development*, ed. I. Goldstein (San Francisco: Jossey-Bass, 1985); and Tung, "Selection and Training of Personnel for Overseas Assignments."

32. Solomon, "Success Abroad Depends upon More than Job Skills."

33. Harvey, "Addressing the Dual Career Expatriation Dilemma"; and J. W. Hunt, "The Perils of Foreign Postings for Two," *Financial Times*, May 6, 1998, p. 22.

34. C. M. Daily, S. T. Certo, and D. R. Dalton, "International Experience in the Executive Suite: A Path to Prosperity?" *Strategic Management Journal* 21 (2000), pp. 515–23.

35. Dowling and Schuler, *International Dimensions of Human Resource Management*.

36. Ibid.

37. G. Baliga and J. C. Baker, "Multinational Corporate Policies for Expatriate Managers: Selection, Training, and Evaluation," *Advanced*

Management Journal, Autumn 1985, pp. 31–38.

38. C. Rapoport, "A Tough Swede Invades the U.S.," *Fortune,* June 20, 1992, pp. 67–70.

39. J. C. Baker, "Foreign Language and Departure Training in U.S. Multinational Firms," *Personnel Administrator,* July 1984, pp. 68–70.

40. A 1997 study by the Conference Board looked at this in depth. For a summary, see L. Grant, "That Overseas Job Could Derail Your Career," *Fortune,* April 14, 1997, p. 166. Also see J. S. Black and H. Gregersen, "The Right Way to Manage Expatriates," *Harvard Business Review,* March–April 1999, pp. 52–63.

41. J. S. Black and M. E. Mendenhall, *Global Assignments: Successfully Expatriating and Repatriating International Managers* (San Francisco: Jossey-Bass, 1992).

42. Ibid.

43. Figures from the Conference Board study. For a summary, see Grant, "That Overseas Job Could Derail Your Career."

44. S. C. Schneider, "National v. Corporate Culture: Implications for Human Resource Management," *Human Resource Management* 27 (Summer 1988), pp. 231–46.

45. I. M. Manve and W. B. Stevenson, "Nationality, Cultural Distance and Expatriate Status," *Journal of International Business Studies* 32 (2001), pp. 285–303.

46. C. A. Bartlett and S. Ghoshal, *Managing Across Borders: The Transnational Solution* (Boston: Harvard Business School Press, 1989).

47. See G. Oddou and M. Mendenhall, "Expatriate Performance Appraisal: Problems and Solutions," in *International Human Resource Management,* ed. M. Mendenhall and G. Oddou (Boston: PWS-Kent, 1991); Dowling and Schuler, *International Dimensions;* R. S. Schuler and G. W. Florkowski, "International Human Resource Management," in *Handbook for International Management Research,* ed. B. J. Punnett and O. Shenkar (Oxford: Blackwell, 1996); and K. Roth and S. O'Donnell, "Foreign Subsidiary Compensation Strategy: An Agency Theory Perspective," *Academy of Management Journal* 39, No. 3 (1996), pp. 678–703.

48. Oddou and Mendenhall, "Expatriate Performance Appraisal: Problems and Solutions."

49. "Expatriates Often See Little Benefit to Careers in Foreign Stints, Indifference at Home," *Wall Street Journal,* December 11, 1989, p. B1.

50. Oddou and Mendenhall, "Expatriate Performance Appraisal: Problems and Solutions"; and Schuler and Florkowski, "International Human Resource Management."

51. C. Reynolds, "Compensation of Overseas Personnel," in *Handbook of Human Resource Administration,* ed. J. J. Famularo (New York: McGraw-Hill, 1986).

52. M. Helms, "International Executive Compensation Practices," in *International Human Resource Management,* ed. M. Mendenhall and G. Oddou (Boston: PWS-Kent, 1991).

53. G. W. Latta, "Expatriate Incentives," *HR Focus* 75, No. 3 (March 1998), p. S3.

54. C. K. Prahalad and Y. L. Doz, *The Multinational Mission* (New York: The Free Press, 1987).

55. Ibid.

56. Schuler and Florkowski, "International Human Resource Management."

57. See J. P. Womack, D. T. Jones, and D. Roos, *The Machine that Changed the World* (New York: Rawson Associates, 1990).

Index